TOURISM
Principles, Practices, Philosophies

TOURISM
Principles, Practices, Philosophies

SEVENTH EDITION

Robert W. McIntosh
Emeritus, Michigan State University

Charles R. Goeldner
University of Colorado

J. R. Brent Ritchie
University of Calgary

John Wiley & Sons, Inc.
New York · Chichester · Brisbane · Toronto · Singapore

Part-Opening Photo Credits

Part One: Courtesy Arab Information Center **Part Two:** Courtesy British Tourist Authority **Part Three:** Courtesy Australian Tourist Commission **Part Four:** Courtesy Government of Quebec, Tourist Branch **Part Five:** Courtesy United Nations **Part Six:** Courtesy Rhodesia Ministry of Information

This text is printed on acid-free paper.

This publication is designed to provide accurate and authoritative information in regard to the subject matter covered. It is sold with the understanding that the publisher is not engaged in rendering legal, accounting, or other professional services. If legal advice or other expert assistance is required, the services of a competent professional person should be sought.

Library of Congress Cataloging-in-Publication Data:

McIntosh, Robert Woodrow, 1917–
    Tourism : principles, practices, philosophies.—7th ed. / Robert
  W. McIntosh, Charles R. Goeldner, J. R. Brent Ritchie.
      p.   cm.
    Includes index.
    ISBN 0-471-01557-1 (acid-free)
    1. Tourist trade. I. Goeldner, Charles R. II. Ritchie, J. R.
  Brent. III. Title.
  G155.A1M386   1995
  338.4′791—dc20   94-26244

Printed in the United States of America

10 9 8 7 6 5 4 3 2

Preface

Tourism can be defined as the science, art, and business of attracting and transporting visitors, accommodating them, and graciously catering to their needs and wants. (See additional definitions in Chapter 1.)

All progressive countries throughout the world are interested in tourism. Political and industrial leaders almost universally have recognized the economic advantages of tourism. However, what these countries have done to make tourism a viable, growing segment of their economy diverges widely—from virtually nothing to creating superbly organized, highly productive tourism plants. While the economic benefits of tourism have long been recognized, today attention is being directed to its social impact, which can be positive or negative, depending on how tourism is planned and managed.

This book explores major concepts in tourism, what makes tourism possible, and how tourism can become an important factor in the wealth of any nation. It is written in broad, global terms, setting forth principles, practices, and philosophies of tourism that have been found to be advantageous. Some of the topics included are introductory principles, study approaches, the importance of tourism, tourism history, careers in tourism, the organization of tourism, components of tourism, travel motivations, elements of tourism demand and supply, economics, planning and development principles, tourism and the environment, sustainable tourism, research, marketing, and some concepts for the future.

It is our intention that this book be used as a textbook for college and university courses in tourism. However, the book also provides useful information and guidance for chambers of commerce, tourism promotion and development organizations, tourist accommodations and other businesses, transport and carrier firms, oil companies, and any other organization that is interested or involved in the movement of persons from their homes to vacation or business destinations.

As this seventh edition goes to press, we celebrate the thousands of students who have already begun their education in travel and tourism with previous editions of this book. We also acknowledge their participation by their letters to us or our publisher. Our goal has been to maintain the book's comprehensiveness and to keep it up to date in a rapidly changing industry. Many readers have responded positively to the readings at the ends of chapters. Therefore, we have retained those that were still pertinent and have added some new ones.

We are grateful for the help of all of the educators who have contributed to this edition through their constructive comments. We especially wish to thank Philip L. Pearce, Department of Tourism, James Cook University, Townsville, Queensland, Australia, for his contribution of Chapter 9, "Pleasure Travel Motivation."

Robert W. McIntosh
Charles R. Goeldner
J. R. Brent Ritchie

Contents

TOURISM
Principles, Practices, Philosophies

TOURISM OVERVIEW

Tourism in Perspective

LEARNING OBJECTIVES

- Appreciate how important this industry is to the economy of the world and of many countries.
- Understand what tourism is and its many definitions.
- Examine the various approaches to studying tourism and determine which is of greatest interest to you.
- Know the benefits and costs of tourism.

THE STUDY OF TOURISM

Human beings are innately curious concerning the world in which we live. We yearn to know what other places look like—what the people, their culture, the animals and plant life, and landforms may be elsewhere. Today, higher levels of education and the influence of television and other communication media have combined to create in us a much greater awareness of our entire world. We are now in a global economy and our industries must be globally competitive. We must think globally. Material prosperity in many developed countries, with accompanying higher standards of living, has made travel attainable for hundreds of millions of us. Although travel can be undertaken for many reasons, the most common are pleasure, business, and study. In this book we explore the multiplicity of social and economic phenomena that bring about and are created by this vast worldwide industry.

The subject of travel is exciting and fascinating. Humanlike beings have been moving from place to place for about 1 million years. Our early ancestors, *Homo erectus,* originated in eastern and southern Africa. But remains of these same forms of early humankind have also been found in China and Java (Indonesia). It has been estimated that migrations of this type took about 15,000 years, but this is a brief span of time in the long history of humanity. Various theories have been proposed regarding the motivation for such amazing journeys. Foremost is that these wanderings were in search of food and to escape from danger. Another theory is that people observed the migrations of birds and wanted to know where the birds came from and where they were going. Recently, in the most dramatic discovery of its kind ever made, the preserved body of a man dubbed the "iceman," who died 5,000 years ago, was found in the ice in mountainous northern Italy. Some of the scientists studying his body and accoutrements have concluded that he was returning to his home in what is now Switzerland from a journey to the south of what is now Italy.

Since the times of the wanderings of ancient peoples, we have been traveling in ever-widening patterns about the earth. From the days of such early explorers as Marco

> Travel and tourism is the world's largest industry. In 1994 it accounted for some:
>
> - $3.4 trillion in gross national product—6 percent of the world total
> - 204 million jobs—1 in every 9 workers
> - 10.7 percent of global capital investment
> - 11 percent of worldwide consumer spending
> - 11.7 percent of indirect corporate taxes

Source: WTTC Report, 1993.

Polo, Ibn Battuta, Christopher Columbus, Ferdinand Magellan, and James Cook to the present, there has been a steady growth in travel. In the twentieth century, the invention of the automobile and all-weather roads has brought about unprecedented growth. Following World War II, the invention of the jet airplane, especially the wide-bodied type, and the establishment of global air routes have made possible rapid travel for many millions. Thus national and international travel by air has experienced explosive growth. Luxurious cruise ships, comfortable motor coaches, streamlined passenger trains, and fine hotels, resorts, and motels have provided pleasant transportation and accommodations.

ECONOMIC IMPORTANCE

Today, the authoritative World Travel and Tourism Council (WTTC) has declared that tourism is the world's largest industry, surpassing autos, steel, electronics, and agriculture. In 1994 this global industry's gross output of goods and services reached $3.4 trillion (U.S.). During the same year, $655 billion in taxes were paid in corporate, personal, and other forms. The WTTC also estimated that tourism created employment for 204 million men and women—1 in 9 workers worldwide. Their estimates expect 1994 tourism jobs will account for $1.7 trillion or 10.3 percent of employee wages and salaries globally. Tourism also accounts for 11 percent of consumer spending. During 1991 the tourism industry invested $613 billion in new capital. This represents 11.2 percent of worldwide capital investment.

The economic figures cited show that tourism has grown to be an activity of worldwide importance and significance. For a number of countries, tourism is the largest commodity in international trade. In many others it ranks among the top three industries. Tourism has grown rapidly to become a major social and economic force in the world.

As tourism has grown, it has moved from being the province of the rich to accessibility to the masses, involving millions of people. The World Tourism Organization (WTO) attempts to document tourism's growth in an annual publication entitled *Tourism Compendium.* The 1993 edition estimates that some 475.5 million international tourist arrivals were recorded in 1992, up from the 455.6 peak recorded in 1990. The series shows strong growth from 1950 (see Table 1.1).

While not yet finalized, WTO is estimating 500 million arrivals in 1993. According

**Table 1.1   International Tourist Arrivals:
1950, 1960, 1970, and 1980–1993**

Year	Arrivals[a] (millions)	Percent of Growth
1950	25.3	—
1960	69.3	173.9
1970	165.8	139.2
1980	287.8	73.6
1981	289.9	0.7
1982	289.2	− 0.2
1983	292.7	1.2
1984	320.1	9.4
1985	329.6	3.0
1986	340.8	3.4
1987	366.8	7.6
1988	393.9	7.4
1989	427.9	8.6
1990	455.6	6.5
1991	455.1 (r)	− 0.1
1992	475.6 (p)	4.5

[a](r), Revised figures; (p), preliminary.
Source: World Tourism Organization.

to WTO forecasts, the number of international arrivals is expected to reach 661 million by the year 2000 and 937 million by the year 2010.

The *WTTC Report* examines travel and tourism in 24 countries belonging to the Organization for Economic Cooperation and Development (OECD) that account for about 75 percent ($2.550 trillion) of the world's tourism industry gross output in 1994. Of these countries the United States led the list with $820.1 billion, almost 25 percent of the world total. Japan and Germany were second and third, grossing $435.4 billion (12.79 percent) and $263.9 billion (7.75 percent), respectively. France, United Kingdom, Italy, and Spain exceeded $100 billion, with France recording $196.4 billion, United Kingdom $177.7 billion, Italy $161.4 billion, and Spain $102.0 billion. See Figure 1.1.

STATISTICAL DATA AVAILABILITY

One of the problems in collecting and reporting statistical data for a book is the data lag. As this book was being revised, 1992 data and some 1993 data were just becoming available. Unfortunately, data lags are increasing rather than decreasing. This disturbing reality is especially upsetting when one considers that travel is a dynamic and changing industry. The data in this book provide a perspective on the size and importance of the industry and its sectors. Users are encouraged to access the sources provided to update the information and determine if trends are continuing or changing.

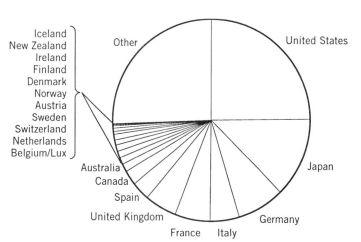

1994 Travel & Tourism Gross Output
(Share of World Total)

Figure 1.1 1994 Travel and Tourism Gross Output (Share of World Total) (*Source: WTTC Report*, 1993)

In the United States, tourism is ranked as the third largest retail industry behind food and auto sales. In employment it is second to health services. Although tourism is often thought of as leisure travel, it also encompasses business and convention travel, meetings, seminars, recreation and student travel (if less than a year) and transportation services and accommodations. According to the U.S. Travel Data Center travel and tourism generate about $397 billion in domestic spending in the United States, including expenditures by foreign travelers here in 1993. During the past 10 years, tourism employment has grown by 56.3 percent and now totals over 6 million direct jobs. This is more than twice the job rate increase for the economy as a whole. Every job in tourism generates three more jobs in businesses supplying goods and services to the industry and in government service promoting and servicing tourism, such as customs inspectors. Furthermore, this business creates more tax dollars proportionate to its size than does any other industry. So, indeed, this is a dynamic and most valuable growth enterprise.

Directly or indirectly, tourism is part of the fabric of most of the world's industries, including transportation, retailing, advertising, sports, sporting goods and equipment, clothing, the food industry, and health care. Tourism also plays a part in most communication media, particularly in the travel sections of newspapers. There are many print and visual media of direct interest to tourism suppliers and students of this subject, in addition to those engaged in marketing tourism, especially those of interest to airlines, cruise lines, motorcoach and rail lines, tour companies, travel agencies, auto rental companies, accommodations, attractions including theme parks, and tourism educational organizations.

Politicians at all levels are typically very concerned with tourism. They look increasingly at tourism as a tool for economic development. In development, they have

TOURISM: WHAT IT MEANS TO THE U.S. ECONOMY

- In 1992 spending on travel services in the United States reached approximately $361.8 billion. Of this total, domestic travel spending represented 85 percent and international visitor spending, 15 percent (excluding international fare payments to U.S. carriers).
- Tourism in the United States in 1993 generated an estimated $397 billion in expenditures.
- In 1993 travel spending in the United States averaged over $1.08 billion per day, $45 million per hour, $688,394 per minute, or $11,773 per second.
- Travel and tourism in 1993 was once again the nation's leading export, generating $75 billion in expenditures from 46 million international visitors, while the 45 million Americans traveling abroad only spent $53 billion, creating a $22 billion surplus as international visitors spent more money here than Americans spent abroad.
- Tourism accounts for 6 percent of the nation's gross national product. The travel and tourism industry is the third largest retail industry in terms of business receipts, following only automotive dealers and food stores.
- Nearly 6 million Americans were employed directly in the travel industry in 1992, making this industry the second largest employer in the country, following only health services. Travel industry employment has grown 56.3 percent in the past 10 years—over twice the growth rate for all U.S. industries.
- Travel spending by international visitors ($75 billion in 1993) supported nearly 1.4 million U.S. jobs. Each $53,000 in new travel receipts supports 1 new job.
- Travel-generated payroll is estimated at over $99.2 billion in 1992 (latest data)—four times that of the nation's steel and motor vehicle manufacturing industries combined. Tourism provides more than 650,000 executive level positions.
- The travel industry provides a disproportionate number of jobs for the traditionally disadvantaged: African-Americans (11.5 percent of total 1989 travel industry employment, compared to 10.2 percent nationwide), Hispanic-Americans (10.5 percent versus 7.3 percent nationwide), and women (51.5 percent versus 45.2 percent of total U.S. employment).
- Federal, state, and local tax revenues generated from travel expenditures were an estimated $51.6 billion in 1992—13 cents of each travel dollar spent.

Source: U.S. Travel and Tourism Administration, U.S. Travel Data Center, and the Travel Industry Association of America.

enacted laws requiring land use plans with subsequent zoning and building codes to control location, number, and manner of construction of tourist facilities. Parks and recreation programs are enjoyed by tourists as well as local residents. Many governments impose taxes of which all or part are paid directly or indirectly by tourists and their suppliers. The power of tourism politically is sometimes manifested in unusual ways. An example was the threat of a travel boycott of Alaska by environmental groups protesting the state's planned aerial shooting of 300 wolves. The plan was canceled.

Travel and tourism can double in size by 2005.

- Forecasts by the WEFA suggest that travel and tourism will continue to expand faster than the economy as a whole and faster than comparable industries. Independent forecasts support the growth trends.
- By 2005 travel and tourism is expected to account for:

  Over twice as much output, at $7.9 trillion
  Over 40 percent more jobs to total 348 million employees
  More than 2.4 times the investment, at $1.7 trillion
  2.3 times the consumer spending, at $4.6 trillion

- This growth depends on enlightened government policy to liberalize markets, improve infrastructure, reduce bureaucratic regulation, eliminate barriers to travel, and diminish taxes.

Source: WTTC Report. 1993.

Many industry analysts project a doubling of tourism by the year 2005, with constructive government policies. We believe such policies will indeed be forthcoming if tourism leaders will convey their message effectively. It is in all our interests to achieve this growth, provided that it is accomplished in an intelligent, planned, and thoughtful manner by developers and the public alike. There is an unequivocable responsibility to review the social and environmental factors vigilantly in order to preserve and enhance those qualities that give any destination its special appeal and character. These comprise its culture, natural resources, host population, and the spirit of the place. We hope that you will strive to assist in the achievement of these ultimate worthy goals.

WHAT IS TOURISM?

When we think of tourism, we think primarily of people who are visiting a particular place for sightseeing, visiting friends and relatives, taking a vacation, and having a good time. They may spend their leisure time engaging in various sports, sunbathing, talking, singing, taking rides, touring, reading, or simply enjoying the environment. If we consider the subject further, we may include in our definition of tourism people who are participating in a convention, a business conference, or some other kind of business or professional activity, as well as those who are taking a study tour under an expert guide or doing some kind of scientific research or study.

These visitors use all forms of transportation, from hiking in a wilderness park to flying in a jet to an exciting city. Transportation can include taking a chairlift up a Colorado mountainside or standing at the rail of a cruise ship looking across the blue Caribbean. Whether people travel by one of these means or by car, motorcoach, camper, train, taxi, motorbike, or bicycle, they are taking a trip and thus are engaging in tourism. That is what this book is all about—why people travel (and why some don't) and the socioeconomic effects that their presence and expenditures have on a society.

Any attempt to define tourism and to describe its scope fully must consider the various groups that participate in and are affected by this industry. Their perspectives are vital to the development of a comprehensive definition. Four different perspectives of tourism can be identified:

1. *The tourist.* The tourist seeks various psychic and physical experiences and satisfactions. The nature of these will largely determine the destinations chosen and the activities enjoyed.
2. *The businesses providing tourist goods and services.* Businesspeople see tourism as an opportunity to make a profit by supplying the goods and services that the tourist market demands.
3. *The government of the host community or area.* Politicians view tourism as a wealth factor in the economy of their jurisdictions. Their perspective is related to the incomes their citizens can earn from this business. Politicians also consider the foreign exchange receipts from international tourism as well as the tax receipts collected from tourist expenditures, either directly or indirectly.
4. *The host community.* Local people usually see tourism as a cultural and employment factor. Of importance to this group, for example, is the effect of the interaction between large numbers of international visitors and residents. This effect may be beneficial or harmful, or both.

Airport ticket counter personnel provide pleasant and efficient service for departing air travelers, making vacation or business travel an enjoyable experience. (Photo courtesy of USAir)

Thus, *tourism* may be defined as *the sum of the phenomena and relationships arising from the interaction of tourists, business suppliers, host governments, and host communities in the process of attracting and hosting these tourists and other visitors.* (See the Glossary for definitions of *tourist* and *excursionist.*)

Tourism is a composite of activities, services, and industries that delivers a travel experience: transportation, accommodations, eating and drinking establishments, shops, entertainment, activity facilities, and other hospitality services available for individuals or groups that are traveling away from home. It encompasses all providers of visitor and visitor-related services. Tourism is the entire world industry of travel, hotels, transportation, and all other components, including promotion, that serves the needs and wants of travelers. Finally, tourism is the sum total of tourist expenditures within the borders of a nation or a political subdivision or a transportation-centered economic area of contiguous states or nations. This economic concept also considers the income multiplier of these tourist expenditures (discussed in Chapter 14).

One has only to consider the multidimensional aspects of tourism and its interactions with other activities to understand why it is difficult to come up with a meaningful definition that will be universally accepted. Each of the many definitions that have arisen is aimed at fitting a special situation and solving an immediate problem, and the lack of uniform definitions has hampered study of tourism as a discipline. Development of a field depends on (1) uniform definitions, (2) description, (3) analysis, (4) prediction, and (5) control.

Modern tourism is a discipline that has only recently attracted the attention of scholars from many fields. The majority of studies have been conducted for special purposes and have used narrow operational definitions to suit particular needs of researchers or government officials; these studies have not encompassed a systems approach. Consequently, many definitions of "tourism" and "the tourist" are based on distance traveled, the length of time spent, and the purpose of the trip. This makes it difficult to gather statistical information that scholars can use to develop a database, describe the tourism phenomenon, and do analyses.

The problem is not trivial. It has been tackled by a number of august bodies over the years, including the League of Nations, the United Nations, the World Tourism Organization (WTO), the Organization for Economic Cooperation and Development (OECD), the National Tourism Resources Review Commission, and the U.S. Senate's National Tourism Policy Study.

The following review of various definitions illustrates the problems of arriving at a consensus. We examine the concept of the movement of people and the terminology and definitions applied by the World Tourism Organization and those of the United States, Canada, the United Kingdom, and Australia. Later, a comprehensive classification of travelers is provided that endeavors to reflect a consensus of current thought and practice.

World Tourism Organization

The International Conference on Travel and Tourism Statistics convened by the World Tourism Organization (WTO) in Ottawa, Canada, in 1991 reviewed, updated, and expanded on the work of earlier international groups. The Ottawa Conference made some fundamental recommendations on definitions of *tourism, travelers,* and *tourists.* The United Nations Statistical Commission adopted WTO's recommendations on tourism statistics on March 4, 1993.

TOURISM   WTO has taken the concept of *tourism* beyond a stereotypical image of "holiday-making." The officially accepted definition is: "Tourism comprises the activities of persons traveling to and staying in places outside their usual environment for not more than one consecutive year for leisure, business and other purposes." The term *usual environment* is intended to exclude trips within the area of usual residence and frequent and regular trips between the domicile and the workplace and other community trips of a routine character.

1. *International tourism*:
   a. *Inbound tourism:* visits to a country by nonresidents
   b. *Outbound tourism:* visits by residents of a country to another country
2. *Internal tourism:* visits by residents of a country to their own country
3. *Domestic tourism:* internal tourism plus inbound tourism (the tourism market of accommodation facilities and attractions within a country)
4. *National tourism:* Internal tourism plus outbound tourism (the resident tourism market for travel agents and airlines)

TRAVELER TERMINOLOGY FOR INTERNATIONAL TOURISM   Underlying the foregoing conceptualization of tourism is the overall concept of *traveler,* defined as "any person on a trip between two or more countries or between two or more localities within his/her country of usual residence." All types of travelers engaged in tourism are described as *visitors,* a term that constitutes the basic concept of the entire system of tourism statistics. Visitors are persons who travel to a country other than the one in which they generally reside for a period not exceeding 12 months, whose main purpose is other than the exercise of an activity remunerated from within the place visited. Visitors are subdivided into two categories:

1. *Same-day visitors:* visitors who do not spend the night in a collective or private accommodation in the country visited: for example, a cruise ship passenger spending four hours in a port.
2. *Tourists:* visitors who stay in the country visited for at least one night: for example, a visitor on a two-week vacation.

There are many purposes for a visit, notably pleasure, business, and other purposes, such as family reasons, health, and transit.

United States

The Western Council for Travel Research in 1963 employed the term *visitor* and defined a *visit* as occurring every time a visitor entered an area under study. The definition of *tourist* used by the National Tourism Resources Review Commission in 1973 was: "A tourist is one who travels away from home for a distance of at least 50 miles (one way) for business, pleasure, personal affairs, or any other purpose except to commute to work, whether he stays overnight or returns the same day."

The *National Travel Survey* of the U.S. Travel Data Center in 1994 reports on all round-trips with a one-way route mileage of 100 miles or more, and since 1984 on all trips involving one or more nights away from home, regardless of distance. Trips are included regardless of purpose, excluding only crews, students, military personnel on active duty, and commuters.

Canada

In a series of quarterly household sample surveys known as the Canadian Travel Survey which began in 1978, trips qualifying for inclusion are similar to those covered in the *National Travel Survey* in the United States. The main difference is that in the Canadian survey, the lower limit for the one-way distance is 50 miles (80 kilometers) rather than 100 miles. The 50-mile figure was a compromise to satisfy concerns regarding the accuracy of recall for shorter trips and the possibility of the inclusion of trips completed entirely within the boundaries of a large metropolitan area such as Toronto.

The determination of which length of trip to include in surveys of domestic travel has varied according to the purpose of the survey methodology employed. Whereas there is general agreement that commuting journeys and one-way trips should be excluded, qualifying distances vary. The province of Ontario favors 25 miles.

In Canada's international travel surveys the primary groups of travelers identified are nonresident travelers, resident travelers, and other travelers. Both nonresident and resident travelers include both same-day and business travelers. Commuters are included and are not distinguished from other same-day business travelers. Other travelers consist of immigrants, former residents, military personnel, and crews.

United Kingdom

The National Tourist Boards of England, Scotland, and Northern Ireland sponsor a continuous survey of internal tourism, the United Kingdom Tourism Survey (UKTS). It measures all trips away from home lasting one night or more, taken by residents for holidays, visits to friends and relatives (nonholiday), or for business, conferences, and most other purposes. In its findings the UKTS distinguishes between short (1 to 3 nights)- and long (4+ nights)-duration holiday trips.

The International Passenger Survey collects information on both overseas visitors to the United Kingdom and travel abroad by U.K. residents. It distinguishes five different types of visits: holiday independent, holiday inclusive, business, visits to friends and relatives, and miscellaneous.

Australia

The Australian Bureau of Industry Economics in 1979 placed length of stay and distance traveled constraints in its definition of *tourist* as follows: "A person visiting a location at least 40 km from his usual place of residence, for a period of at least 24 hours and not exceeding twelve months."

In supporting the use of the WTO definitions, the Australian Bureau of Statistics notes that the term "'usual environment' is somewhat vague." It states that "visits to tourist attractions by local residents should not be included" and that visits to second homes should be included only "where they are clearly for temporary recreational purposes."

Serving pleasure travelers on shipboard is a pleasant assignment. (Photo courtesy of the Royal Cruise Line)

Comprehensive Classification of Travelers

The main types of travelers are indicated in Figure 1.2. Shown is the fundamental distinction between residents and visitors and the interest of travel and tourism practitioners in the characteristics of nontravelers as well as travelers. It also reflects the apparent consensus that business and same-day travel both fall within the scope of travel and tourism.

Placed to one side are some other types of travelers generally regarded as being outside the area of interest, although included in some travel surveys. Foremost among these exclusions are commuters, who seem to fall outside the area of interest to all in the travel and tourism community. Other travelers generally excluded from studies on travel and tourism are those who undertake trips within the community, which for convenience are described arbitrarily as trips involving less than a specific one-way distance, such as 100 miles. These "other travelers" have been focused on in the Nationwide Personal Transportation Surveys of 1969, 1977, 1983, and 1990 conducted by the U.S. Department of Transportation. The broad class of travelers categorized as migrants, both international and domestic, is also commonly excluded from tourism or travel research. They are excluded on the grounds that their movement is not temporary,

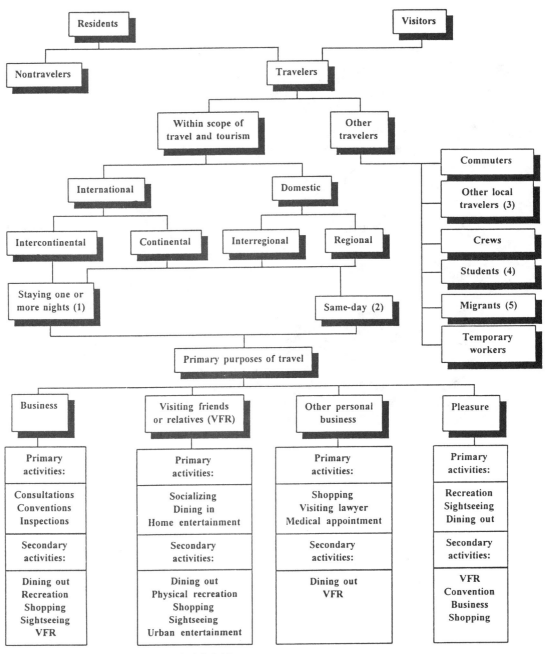

(1) *Tourists* in international technical definitions.
(2) *Excursionists* in international technical definitions.
(3) Travelers whose trips are shorter than those that qualify for travel and tourism; e.g., under 50 miles (80 km) from home.
(4) Students traveling between home and school only—other travel of students is within scope of travel and tourism.
(5) All persons moving to a new place of residence including all one-way travelers, such as emigrants, immigrants, refugees, domestic migrants, and nomads.

Figure 1.2   Classification of Travelers

although they use the same facilities as other travelers, albeit in one direction, and frequently require temporary accommodation on reaching their destination. The real significance of migration to travel and tourism, however, is not in the one-way trip in itself, but in the long-run implications of a transplanted demand for travel and the creation of new travel destinations for separated friends and relatives.

Other groups of travelers are commonly excluded from travel and tourism studies because their travel is not affected by travel promotion, although they tend to compete for the same types of facilities and services. Students and temporary workers traveling purely for reasons of education or temporary employment are two leading examples. Another frequently excluded group consists of crews, although they can be regarded as special subsets of tourists and excursionists.

Of those travelers directly within the scope of travel and tourism, basic distinctions are made among those whose trips are completed within one day. An additional meaningful division may also be made between those international travelers whose travel is between continents and those whose international travel is confined to countries within the same continent. In the case of the United States, the distinction is between trips to or from the neighboring countries of Canada and Mexico or elsewhere in the Americas and trips made to or from countries in Europe or on other continents.

The same type of distinction may be made between interregional and regional domestic travel. In the United States there are eight travel regions. Travel between them would be regarded as interregional and within them as regional. In Canada, five major regions may be identified: Atlantic, central, prairies, west, and north. In practice, travel studies in Canada tend to show interprovincial data because of the large size of some provinces and the research and planning needs of each provincial department of tourism.

The purposes of travel identified in Figure 1.2 go beyond those traditionally accepted because of the growing evidence that "visits to friends and relatives" (VFR) is a basic travel motivation and a distinctive factor in marketing, accounting for a major proportion of travel. In any event, "primary purpose" is an arbitrary concept because many journeys are undertaken for a combination of reasons, such as "business and vacation" as recognized in the U.S. National Travel Survey conducted by the U.S. Travel Data Center.

Travel, Tourism, and Recreation

For the purposes of this book, the terms *travel* and *tourism* will be synonymous. Tourism may also be defined as people taking trips away from home, and it embraces the entire range of transportation, lodging, food service, and other activities relating to and serving the traveler. Consequently, a *tourist* is someone who travels away from home. The term *tourist industry* is used to describe the economic sectors (transportation, lodging, etc.) supplying the tourist, who is the consumer of the industry's products. The term *visitor*, which is common in international travel, will be synonymous with *tourist*. These definitions of *tourism, travel,* and *tourist* admittedly are very broad, but they permit the development of additional subcategories to define market segments, such as *out-of-state visitors, recreationists, conventioneers, the sports-minded,* and others. The definitions are also in keeping with those used by the *National Tourism Policy Study*, which construed the three terms *travel, tourism,* and *recreation* as follows:

The definition of a trip typically requires travel 100 miles away from home. Many trips are taken on the Blue Ridge Parkway, America's most popular scenic parkway. It is a unique mountaintop drive designed solely for vacation travel. Approximately 250 miles of the parkway are in North Carolina. (Photo by William Russ, courtesy of the North Carolina Travel and Tourism Division)

1. *Travel:* the action and activities of people taking trips to a place or places outside their home communities for any purpose except daily commuting to and from work.
2. *Tourism:* a term that is synonymous with *travel.*
3. *Recreation:* the action and activities of people engaging in constructive and personally pleasurable use of leisure time. Recreation may include passive or active participation in individual or group sports, cultural functions, natural and human history appreciation, nonformal education, pleasure travel, sightseeing, and entertainment.[1]

[1]*National Tourism Policy Study Final Report* (Washington, D.C.: U.S. Government Printing Office, 1978), p. 5.

BASIC APPROACHES TO THE STUDY OF TOURISM

Tourism commonly is approached through a variety of methods. However, there is little or no agreement on how the study of tourism should be undertaken. The following are several methods that have been used.

Institutional Approach

The institutional approach to the study of tourism considers the various intermediaries and institutions that perform tourism activities. It emphasizes institutions such as the travel agency. This approach requires an investigation of the organization, operating methods, problems, costs, and economic place of travel agents who act on behalf of the customer, purchasing services from airlines, rental car companies, hotels, and so on. An advantage of this approach is that the U.S. Census Bureau conducts a survey every five years on selected services that includes travel agents and lodging places, thus providing a database for further study.

Product Approach

The product approach involves the study of various tourism products and how they are produced, marketed, and consumed. For example, one might study an airline seat—how it is created, the people who are engaged in buying and selling it, how it is financed, how it is advertised, and so on. Repeating this procedure for rental cars, hotel rooms, meals, and other tourist services gives a full picture of the field. Unfortunately, the product approach tends to be too time consuming; it does not allow the student to grasp the fundamentals of tourism quickly.

Historical Approach

The historical approach is not widely used. It involves an analysis of tourism activities and institutions from an evolutionary angle. It searches for the cause of innovations, their growth or decline, and shifts in interest. Because mass tourism is a fairly recent phenomenon, this approach has limited usefulness.

Managerial Approach

The managerial approach is firm oriented (microeconomic), focusing on the management activities necessary to operate a tourist enterprise, such as planning, research, pricing, advertising, control, and the like. It is a popular approach, using insights gleaned from other approaches and disciplines. Although a major focus of this book is managerial, readers will recognize that other perspectives are also being used. Regardless of which approach is used to study tourism, it is important to know the managerial approach. Products change, institutions change, society changes; this means that managerial objectives and procedures must be geared to change to meet shifts in the tourism

Down-river white-water rafting is an exciting and memorable vacation experience. (Photo courtesy of the West Virginia Department of Commerce)

environment. The *Journal of Travel Research* and *Tourism Management*, leading journals in the field, both feature this approach.

Economic Approach

Because of its importance to both domestic and world economies, tourism has been examined closely by economists, who focus on supply, demand, balance of payments, foreign exchange, employment, expenditures, development, multipliers, and other economic factors. This approach is useful in providing a framework for analyzing tourism and its contributions to a country's economy and economic development. The disadvantage of the economic approach is that whereas tourism is an important economic phenomenon, it has noneconomic impacts as well. The economic approach does not usually pay adequate attention to the environmental, cultural, psychological, sociological, and anthropological approaches.

Sociological Approach

Tourism tends to be a social activity. Consequently, it has attracted the attention of sociologists, who have studied the tourism behavior of individuals and groups of people and the impact of tourism on society. This approach examines social classes, habits, and customs of both hosts and guests. The sociology of leisure is a relatively undeveloped

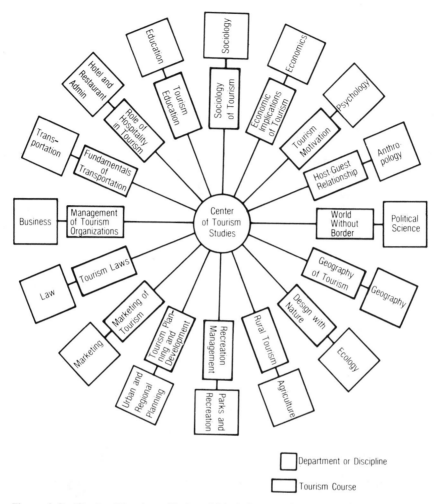

Figure 1.3 Study of Tourism: Choice of Discipline and Approach (*Source:* Jafar Jafari, University of Wisconsin–Stout)

field, but it shows promise of progressing rapidly and becoming more widely used. As tourism continues to make a massive impact on society, it will be studied more and more from a social point of view.

A prime reference in this area is *The Tourist, A New Theory of the Leisure Class,* by Dean MacCannell (Schocken Books, New York, 1976). Erik Cohen, of the Hebrew University of Jerusalem, has made many contributions in this area (see Chapter 11). Roy Buck of Pennsylvania State University has also been a leader in this area, producing a number of studies of the Amish sect and tourism.

Geographical Approach

Geography is a wide-ranging discipline, so it is natural that geographers should be interested in tourism and its spatial aspects. The geographer specializes in the study of location, environment, climate, landscape, and economic aspects. The geographer's approach to tourism sheds light on the location of tourist areas, the movements of people created by tourism locales, the changes that tourism brings to the landscape in the form of tourism facilities, dispersion of tourism development, physical planning, and economic, social, and cultural problems. Since tourism touches geography at so many points, geographers have investigated the area more thoroughly than have scholars in many other disciplines. Because the geographers' approach is so encompassing—dealing with land use, economic aspects, demographic impacts, and cultural problems—a study of their contributions is highly recommended. Recreational geography is a common course title used by geographers studying this specialty. Because tourism, leisure, and recreation are so closely related, it is necessary to search for literature under all these titles to discover the contributions of various fields. Geographers were instrumental in starting both the *Journal of Leisure Research* and *Leisure Sciences*, which should be read regularly by all serious students of tourism.

Interdisciplinary Approaches

Tourism embraces virtually all aspects of our society. We even have cultural tourism, which calls for an anthropological approach. Because people behave in different ways and travel for different reasons, it is necessary to use a psychological approach to determine the best way to promote and market tourism products. Since tourists cross

Lindbergh's Spirit of St. Louis, the Wright Brothers' engine-powered biplane, and the Apollo 11 command module represent a small portion of the Air and Space Museum's enormous collection of flying machinery. Over 7.5 million tourists visit the museum annually, making it the most frequented site in Washington, D.C. (Photo courtesy of the Washington, D.C., Convention and Visitors Association)

borders and require passports and visas from government offices, and since most countries have government-operated tourism development departments, we find that political institutions are involved and are calling for a political science approach. Any industry that becomes an economic giant affecting the lives of many people attracts the attention of legislative bodies (along with that of the sociologists, geographers, economists, and anthropologists), which create the laws, regulations, and legal environment in which the tourist industry must operate; so we also have a legal approach. The great importance of transportation suggests passenger transportation as another approach. The fact simply is that tourism is so vast, so complex, and so multifaceted that it is necessary to have a number of approaches to studying the field, each geared to a somewhat different task or objective. Figure 1.3 illustrates the interdisciplinary nature of tourism studies and their reciprocity and mutuality. *The Annals of Tourism Research,* an interdisciplinary social sciences journal, is another publication that should be on the serious tourism student's reading list.

The Systems Approach

What is really needed to study tourism is a systems approach. A system is a set of interrelated groups coordinated to form a unified whole and organized to accomplish a set of goals. It integrates the other approaches into a comprehensive method dealing with both micro and macro issues. It can examine the tourist firm's competitive environment, its market, its results, its linkages with other institutions, the consumer, and the interaction of the firm with the consumer. In addition, a system can take a macro viewpoint and examine the entire tourism system of a country, state, or area and how it operates within and relates to other systems, such as legal, political, economic, and social systems.

TOURIST SUPPLIERS AND ACTIVITIES

The tourist industry can be described as shown in Figure 1.4. Accommodations include all forms of lodging, even camping and caravanning, and all types of food and beverage services. Shopping encompasses any form of retail purchase, such as souvenirs, arts and crafts, clothing, groceries, and others. Activities comprise services such as entertainment, sports, sightseeing, local tours, cultural events, festivals, and gambling. Transportation includes all forms by land, air, or water.

The entire tourism industry rests on a base of natural resources, which must be wholesome and attractive, preferably possessing unusual natural beauty and appeal to vacationers. These natural resources must be adequate in dimension to avoid crowding, and they should be free from such hazards as pollution, dangerous or poisonous plants, animals, or insects. Similarly, development of tourism should be on sites free from natural disasters, such as floods, droughts, landslides, or earthquakes.

Strictly speaking, tourism is typically not defined as an industry. Even though there is no Standard Industrial Classification (SIC) code for tourism, it is a major economic activity. There is a market for—a demand for—travel, lodging, food, shops, entertainment, and other tourism services. This demand has created the need for tour operators,

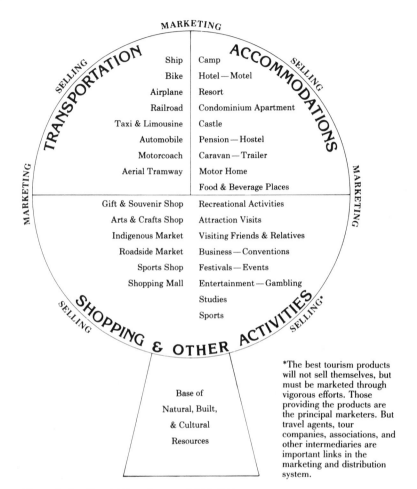

Figure 1.4   Tourist Suppliers and Activities

travel agents, airlines, cruise ships, buses, accommodations, food and beverage facilities, and other goods and services that supply tourist needs. This economic activity *is* the tourist industry, or more properly, simply *tourism*.

Tourism is a fragmented industry with many parts and varied activities. As a young industry, it has not yet achieved the cohesiveness necessary for all components to work together for the common good. Each segment makes its own contributions to the total tourism picture, yet the segments are interrelated and depend on each other. For example, the success of a Colorado ski resort depends on transportation to bring skiers to the slopes, housing to accommodate them, restaurants to feed them, and other services (medical facilities, après-ski lounges, and retail shops) to take care of their needs. Most of the enterprises affiliated with skiing are small. They have a variety of operating policies and although they are operated as independent businesses, they do in fact depend on each other and serve as small parts of the total picture. This dependence calls for cooperative effort and similar policies; however, the fact that the businesses often compete with each other for the consumer's dollar makes cooperation difficult. Many of them are fiercely independent, dominated by their own self-interest. As tourism grows and matures, the industry will become more united and speak with a single voice on major issues. Firms will become larger, and the weak links in tourism's chain of services will be eliminated. Thus the future of tourism promises to be bright, dynamic, and exciting.

BENEFITS AND COSTS OF TOURISM

Tourism brings both economic and noneconomic benefits and costs to host communities. Some of the considerable economic impact and benefits were described in the preceding section. There are additional areas of benefit that have not received much research attention. These relate to the benefits occurring to the traveler, such as the contribution of pleasure travel to rest and relaxation, the educational benefit, the understanding of other people and cultures, and the physical and mental well-being of the traveler.

There is no question that tourism delivers benefits, but tourism is not perfect. Even advocates for tourism such as your authors (we have been accused of being cheerleaders for tourism) acknowledge that tourism is not an unqualified blessing. There are costs and benefits, and they do not accrue equally. Many of the social costs incurred are difficult or impossible to measure. Books such as *The Golden Hordes, Tourism: Blessing or Blight,* and *The Holiday Makers* (see the Selected References) point out some of the unpleasant aspects of tourism.

Improperly planned and developed tourism can create problems. The demands of tourism may come into conflict with the needs and wishes of local residents. Thoughtless development, inappropriate development, overdevelopment, or unfinished development can easily damage the environment.

Tourism has been blamed for polluting beaches; raising the price of labor, land, goods, and so on; spoiling the countryside; contaminating the values of native people; crowding; congestion; noise; litter; crime; loss of privacy; creating social tensions; environmental deterioration; lack of control over a destination's future; and low-paid seasonal employment. These problems are common to many forms of development and in many cases represent dissatisfaction with change for the status quo or overdevelopment. They emphasize the need for a coordinated overall economic development plan of which tourism will be one part.

We must accept that tourism is neither a blessing nor a blight, neither poison nor panacea. Tourism can bring great benefits but it can also bring social problems. The world has experience in how to increase the benefits of tourism, and at least some experience in how to lessen social problems. What has to be done is to balance the benefits and costs to come up with the best cost/benefit result.

Tourism students and executives must have a clear understanding of both the positive and negative impacts of tourism on the quality of life of a nation, a province or state, or a community. What are the positive aspects? The negative aspects? We need a balance sheet.

First we look at the plus side of the ledger.

- Provides employment opportunities, both skilled and unskilled, because it is a labor-intensive industry
- Generates a supply of needed foreign exchange
- Increases incomes
- Creates increased gross national product
- Can be built on existing infrastructure
- Develops an infrastructure that will also help stimulate local commerce and industry
- Can be developed with local products and resources
- Helps to diversify the economy
- Tends to be one of the most compatible economic development activities available to an area, complementing other economic activities
- Spreads development
- Has a high multiplier impact
- Increases governmental revenues
- Broadens educational and cultural horizons and improves feelings of self-worth
- Improves the quality of life related to a higher level of income and improved standards of living
- Reinforces preservation of heritage and tradition
- Justifies environmental protection and improvement
- Visitor interest in local culture provides employment for artists, musicians, and other performing artists, enhancing the cultural heritage
- Provides tourist and recreational facilities that may be used by a local population
- Breaks down language barriers, sociocultural barriers, class barriers, racial barriers, political barriers, and religious barriers
- Creates a favorable worldwide image for a destination
- Promotes a global community
- Promotes international understanding and peace

On the minus side of the ledger we find a number of problems that can be created by tourism, especially by its overdevelopment.

- Develops excess demand for resources
- Creates the difficulties of seasonality
- Causes inflation
- Can result in unbalanced economic development
- Creates social problems
- Degrades the natural physical environment and creates pollution
- Degrades the cultural environment
- Increases the incidence of crime, prostitution, and gambling
- Increases vulnerability to economic and political changes
- Threatens family structure
- Commercializes culture, religion, and the arts
- Creates misunderstanding
- Creates conflicts in the host society
- Contributes to disease, economic fluctuation, and transportation problems

Like all change, tourism exacts a price. However, it is here, it is huge, and it needs to be planned and managed. The challenge is to get the right balance, which is to have the benefits outweigh the costs and take steps to lessen the unfavorable impacts that are a part of change. Tourism development must be a part of overall economic development and done in a manner that is sustainable.

THE AGE OF TRAVEL

We close the chapter with a message that was delivered by David J. Humpreys, national chairman of the Travel Industry Association of America (TIA), in May 1991 at its international meeting in Denver. Mr. Humpreys provides a vision that we should all think about. Excerpts from his opening remarks deal with "The Age of Travel."

> I want to take the opportunity to leave us with a thought we should keep with us as we help our industry march along on its determined path to become the largest in this nation and in this world. We should contemplate and think aloud about the special role and responsibility of being the most significant economic force in our global society. Because all of history—especially recent history—has an economic signature to it: The Agricultural Age; The Industrial Age; The Post Industrial Age; The Age of the Automobile; The Electronic Age; and The Computer Age. Some are, or have been, separate and distinct. Some have overlapped. But all have signified and continue to signify. All have left with us their special language, idiomatic expression, dress, and their culture.
>
> The Agricultural Age left us in the United States with a nine-month school year, land-grant state colleges that first focused on agricultural training, research and development, and with an almost singular form-related meaning to the English word, "commodity."
>
> The Industrial Age here left us with row housing, clustered urban areas with the factory as community hub, lunch buckets, mass production, and the assembly line.
>
> The Computer Age has provided our language with new verbs such as "to access," "to network," "to download," and all of them are already in use outside of the medium that spawned them. So it has been, so it is, and so it shall be with The Age of Travel.
>
> As delegates and as messengers, we have an obligation that goes along with our commercial obligations as business, and professional people. And that is to think ahead. To have vision. To look forward to that time and that age that will be known as The Age of Travel.
>
> How will our global society grow and change when the economic, cultural and sociological impact of travel and tourism is fully felt?
>
> And when we achieve our full presence in the political economy of the world, will we use our position widely and responsibly?
>
> As business people and educators we will have to face this and other challenges in the next century. As delegates and messengers, we should start to think about these challenges now.

SUMMARY

In this chapter we have examined the subject of tourism. The rapid growth in the movement of people, both domestically and internationally, has brought about an industry of vast proportions and diversity. Also, it is universal—found in all countries of the world, but in greatly varied qualities and proportions.

The economic importance and future prospects are also worthy of careful study. These considerations lead to the ways in which the study of tourism can be undertaken. There are a number of basic approaches to the study of tourism, and in this book we include all of them in the various chapters. By the time you complete the book you will know a great deal about the social and economic implications of tourism, and you will have developed a keen interest in our world and the fascinating panorama of places, peoples, cultures, beauty, and learning that travel provides in such abundance.

Key Concepts

accommodations
Age of Travel
basic aspects of tourism
benefits of tourism
business or convention travel
costs of tourism
cultural resources
domestic tourism
economic contributions
excursionist
expenditure patterns
foreign tourism
host community
host community government
importance of tourism
inbound tourism
internal tourism
international tourism

marketing and selling
national tourism
natural resources
outbound tourism
recreation
same-day visitors
shopping
study approaches to tourism
suppliers
tourism definitions
the tourist
tourist activities
tourist attractions
tourist businesses
transportation
trip
visitor

For Review and Discussion

1. Identify and describe the four perspectives contained in the definition of tourism, in terms of your home community.
2. Why do bodies such as the United States need specific tourism definitions? Why does a state or country need them? A county? A city?
3. What approach to tourism study does this course take? Which approach interests you most?
4. Have travel patterns changed a great deal in the past 20 years? What elements have not changed?
5. How important are tourist attractions?
6. Why are geographers, sociologists, anthropologists, and economists interested in tourism?
7. What will the tourism industry be like in the year 2000?
8. What are the benefits of tourism?
9. What are some negative aspects of tourism?
10. Why is tourism so popular?
11. Identify the principal factors creating The Age of Travel.

Case Problems

1. Suppose that you are a high school economics teacher. You plan to visit your principal's office and convince her that tourism should be included as part of one of your courses. What arguments would you use?

2. You are the minister of tourism of Jamaica, an island country. Identify the instructions you would issue to your statistics department concerning collecting data on tourist arrivals.

Selected References

Boniface, Brian, G., and Christopher Cooper. *The Geography of Travel and Tourism.* London: Heinemann, 1987.

Burkart, A. J., and S. William Medlik. *Tourism: Past, Present, and Future.* London: Heinemann, 1981.

Cook, Suzanne, and William Evans. *A Portrait of Travel Industry Employment in the U.S. Economy.* Washington D.C.: TIA Foundation, 1994.

Crossley, John C., and Lynn M. Jamieson. *Introduction to Commercial and Entrepreneurial Recreation.* Champaign, Ill.: Sagamore Publishing, 1988.

Feder, Anthony, J. "Are Leisure, Recreation, and Tourism Interrelated?" *Annals of Tourism Research,* Vol. 14, No. 3 (1987), pp. 311–313.

Frechtling, Douglas C. *Annotated Bibliography on Health and Tourism Issues.* Washington D.C.: Pan American Health Organization, 1992.

Fridgen, Joseph D. *Dimensions of Tourism.* East Lansing, Mich.: Educational Institute of the American Hotel and Motel Association, 1991.

Gee, Chuck, James Makens, and Dexter Choy. *The Travel Industry.* New York: Van Nostrand Reinhold, 1989.

Goeldner, C. R., and Karen Dicke. *Bibliography of Tourism and Travel Research Studies, Reports and Articles.* 9 Vols. Boulder, Colo.: Business Research Division, University of Colorado, 1980.

Goeldner, C. R., and Karen Duea. *Travel Trends in the United States and Canada.* Boulder, Colo.: Business Research Division, University of Colorado, 1984. Published in Cooperation with the Travel and Tourism Research Association.

Gunn, Clare A. *Tourism Planning.* New York: Taylor & Francis, 1994.

Hawkins, Donald E., and J. R. Brent Ritchie. *World Travel and Tourism Review: Indicators, Trends, and Forecasts.* Tucson, Ariz.: CAB International, Vol. 1, 1991, Vol. 2, 1992, Vol. 3, 1993.

Holloway, J. Christopher. *The Business of Tourism.* London: Macdonald and Evans, 1983.

Howell, David W. *Passport: An Introduction to the Travel and Tourism Industry.* Cincinnati, Ohio: South-Western Publishing Company, 1993.

Hudman, Lloyd E., and Donald E. Hawkins. *Tourism in Contemporary Society.* Englewood Cliffs, N.J.: Prentice Hall, 1989.

Hunt, John, and Donlynne Layne. "Evaluation of Travel and Tourism Terminology and Definitions." *Journal of Travel Research,* Vol. 29, No. 4 (Spring 1991), pp. 7–11.

Jafari, Jafar. "Anatomy of the Travel Industry." *Cornell Hotel and Restaurant Administration Quarterly,* Vol. 24, No. 1 (May 1983), pp. 71–77.

Jansen-Verbeke, Myriam, and Adri Dietvorst. "Leisure, Recreation, Tourism: A Geographic View on Integration." *Annals of Tourism Research,* Vol. 14, No. 3 (1987), pp. 361–375.

Khan, Mahmood, Michael Olsen, and Turgut Var. *VNR's Encyclopedia of Hospitality and Tourism.* New York: Van Nostrand Reinhold, 1993.

Krippendorf, Jost. *The Holiday Makers.* London: Heinemann, 1987.

Lavery, Patrick, and Carlton S. Van Doren. *Travel and Tourism: A North-American–European Perspective.* Huntingdon, England: Elm Publications, 1990.

Leighfield, M. A., ed. *Leisure, Recreation, and Tourism Abstracts.* Wallingford, Oxon, England: CAB International, quarterly.

Leiper, Neil. "The Framework of Tourism: Towards a Definition of Tourism, Tourist and the Tourism Industry." *Annals of Tourism Research,* Vol. 6, No. 4 (October–December 1979), pp. 390–407.

Medlik, S. *Managing Tourism.* Oxford, England: Butterworth–Heinemann, 1991.

Metekla, Charles J. *The Dictionary of Tourism.* Wheaton, Ill.: Merton House Travel and Tourism, 1986.

Mill, Robert Christie, and Alastair M. Morrison. *The Tourism System.* Englewood Cliffs, N.J.: Prentice Hall, 1992.

Morley, Clive L. "What Is Tourism? Definitions, Concepts and Characteristics." *Journal of Tourism Studies,* Vol. 1, No. 1 (May 1990).

National Tourism Resources Review Commission. *Destination USA.* Vol. 1, *Summary Report.* Washington, D.C.: NTRRC, June 1973.

Pearce, Douglas. *Tourism Today: A Geographical Analysis.* New York: Wiley, 1988.

Powers, Tom. *Introduction to Management in the Hospitality Industry.* New York: Wiley, 1992.

Sebo, Roberto L. *The Traveler's World-Destination Geography.* Cincinnati, Ohio: South-Western Publishing Company, 1990.

Smith, Stephen L. J., "Defining Tourism: A Supply-Side View." *Annals of Tourism Research,* Vol. 15, No. 2 (1988), pp. 179–190.

Smith, Valene L., and William R. Eadington. *Tourism Alternatives: Potentials and Problems in the Development of Tourism.* Philadelphia: University of Pennsylvania Press, 1992.

Starr, Nona, *Viewpoint: An Introduction to Travel, Tourism and Hospitality.* Boston: Houghton Mifflin, 1993.

The President's Commission on Americans Outdoors: A Literature Review. Washington, D.C.: U.S. Government Printing Office, 1986.

Timmons, Veronica. *Travel and Tourism: Focus Canada.* Vancouver, British Columbia, Canada: Timmons and Associates, 1991.

Travel Trade Publications. *Travel Trade 50, 1929–1979 Golden Anniversary Edition.* New York: Travel Trade, 1979.

Travel Trade Publications. *Travel Trade: Our 60th Anniversary Edition.* New York: Travel Trade, 1989.

Turner, Louis, and John Ash. *The Golden Hordes.* London: Constable, 1975.

University of Colorado Research Division, *Tourism's Top Twenty.* Boulder, Colo.: University of Colorado, 1992. Published in cooperation with the U.S. Travel Data Center.

Van Doren, Carlton S., and Sam A. Lollar. "The Consequences of Forty Years of Tourism Growth." *Annals of Tourism Research,* Vol. 12, No. 3 (1985), pp. 467–489.

Waters, Somerset R. "The U.S. Travel Industry: Where We're Going." *Cornell Hotel and Restaurant Administration Quarterly,* Vol. 30, No. 4 (February 1990), pp. 26–33.

Waters, Somerset R. *Travel Industry World Yearbook: The Big Picture–1992.* New York: Child & Waters, 1993 (annual).

Weiler, Betty, and Colin Michael Hall. *Special Interest Tourism.* New York: Wiley, 1992.

Witt, Stephen F., and Luiz Moutinho. *Tourism Marketing and Management Handbook.* London: Prentice Hall, 1994.

World Tourism Organization. *Definitions Concerning Tourism Statistics.* Madrid: WTO, 1983.

World Tourism Organization. *Yearbook of Tourism Statistics,* Volumes I and II. Madrid: WTO, 1992.

World Travel Organization. *Tourism Compendium.* Madrid: WTO, 1993.

World Travel and Tourism Council. *The WTTC Report.* Brussels: WTTC, 1993.

Young, George. *Tourism: Blessing or Blight?* Baltimore: Penguin Books, 1973.

CHAPTER 2

Tourism Through the Ages

LEARNING OBJECTIVES

- Recognize the antiquity of human travel over vast distances on both sea and land.
- Understand how these journeys have evolved from trips that were difficult and often dangerous, to mass travel for millions today.
- Learn the names of some of the great travelers in history who wrote astonishing accounts of exotic places they had visited.
- Discover the many similarities in travel motivations, economic conditions, political situations, attractions, and tourist facilities during the period of the Roman Empire and today.

INTRODUCTION

> We travel long roads and cross the water to see what we disregard when it is under our eyes. This is either because nature has so arranged things that we go after what is far off and remain indifferent to what is nearby, or because any desire loses its intensity by being easily satisfied, or because we postpone whatever we can see whenever we want, feeling sure we will often get around to it. Whatever the reason, there are numbers of things in this city of ours and its environs which we have not even heard of, much less seen; yet, if they were in Greece or Egypt or Asia . . . we would have heard all about them, read all about them, looked over all there was to see.   The younger Pliny, second century C.E.[1]

Twentieth-century travelers, tiredly pulling their carry-on bags from the overhead bin and waiting to walk down the jetway to a foreign destination, may think their experience is uniquely modern. But they are the latest in a long line of travelers reaching back to antiquity. From earliest times "all modes of carriage, from animal to the sonic jet, and accommodations from the meanest hovel to the five-star luxury hotel, have given a livelihood to countless legions."[2] Like today's travelers, these travelers did not do it alone. "Guiding, counseling, and harboring the traveler is among the world's earliest vocations."[3]

Typically, modern travelers enlist a travel agent to make plane reservations, book some hotels, and make recommendations for special tours upon arrival in Athens or Madrid. Despite specialized help, they typically arrive feeling dirty and tired, complain

---

[1]Lionel Casson, *Travel in the Ancient World* (London: George Allen & Unwin, 1974), p. 253. *A note on style:* B.C.E. (Before the Common Era) and C.E. (Common Era), used by some authors and often used in scholarly literature, are the alternative designations corresponding to B.C. and A.D.
[2]Eric Friedheim, *Travel Agents: From Caravans and Clippers to the Concorde.* (New York: Travel Agent Magazine Books, 1992), pp. 27–28.
[3]Ibid., p. 5.

about the crowded flight, and hope to clear customs without waiting in a long line. A middle-aged couple ruefully recall that the travel agent was not able to book a hotel that she could recommend. (An automobile festival or a visit by the Pope had filled major hotels, and there was little choice.) Also, the local bank was out of pesatas or zylotis or won—or whatever the name of the destination country's currency. So the couple have to exchange money before getting a cab to that unpromising hotel and are sure that the driver won't speak English, will spot them as greenhorns, and will drive them all over—with the meter running on and on.

EARLY BEGINNINGS

The invention of money by the Sumerians (Babylonians) and the development of trade beginning about 4000 B.C.E. mark the beginning of the modern era of travel. Not only were the Sumerians first to grasp the idea of money and use it in business transactions but also to invent cuneiform writing and the wheel, so they should be credited as the founders of the travel business. People could now pay for transportation and accommodations with money or by barter.

Five thousand years ago, cruises were organized and conducted from Egypt. Probably the first journey ever made for purposes of peace and tourism was made by Queen Hatshepsut to the lands of Punt (believed to be on the east coast of Africa) in 1480 B.C.E. Descriptions of this tour have been recorded on the walls of the Temple of Deit El Bahari at Luxor. These texts and bas reliefs are among the world's rarest artworks and are universally admired for their wondrous beauty and artistic qualities. The Colossi of Memnon at Thebes have on their pedestals the names of Greek tourists of the fifth century B.C.E.

Beginning in 2700 B.C.E. the pharaohs began to take advantage of the abundance of good building stone in the Nile valley to build their elaborate burial tombs. They included the step pyramid of Djoser, the Sphinx, the three great pyramids at Gizeh, and the pyramid complex at Abusir.[4] These great outdoor wonders began attracting large numbers as early as the New Kingdom from 1600 to 1200 B.C.E. "Each monument was a hallowed spot, so the visitors always spent some moments in prayer, yet their prime motivation was curiosity or disinterested enjoyment, not religion."

They left evidence of their visit in inscriptions such as the following: "Hadnakhte, scribe of the treasury, came to make an excursion and amuse himself on the west of Memphis together with his brother, Panakhti, scribe of the Vizier."[5] Like tourists through the ages, they felt the need to leave evidence of their visit. Some hastily painted their names; others scratched their names in the soft stone with a sharp point. The latter method was so common that the technical term we give to such scribblings is *graffiti*, Italian for "scratching."

A second recognizable tourist trait was the urge to acquire souvenirs. Harkhuf, an envoy of the pharoh to the Sudan, brought home a pygmy trained in native dances to

[4]Casson, *Travel in the Ancient World*, p. 32.
[5]Ibid., p. 32.

The world-famous temple complex of Abu Simbel near the Aswan High Dam in Egypt is a major historical tourist attraction. (Photo courtesy of the Boeing Company)

present his ruler! Early Egyptians also purchased bargains or specialties abroad for their friends and relatives. In 1800 B.C.E. young Uzalum received this request: "I have never before written to you for something precious I wanted. But if you want to be like a father to me, get me a fine string full of beads, to be worn around the head."[6]

Herodotus reported: "The Egyptians meet to celebrate festivals not once a year but a number of times. The biggest and most popular is at Bubastis . . ., the next at Busiris . . ., the third at Said . . ., the fourth at Heliopolis . . ., the fifth at Buto . . ., the six at Papremis. . . . They go there on the river, men and women together, a big crowd of each in each boat. As they sail, some of the women keep clicking castanets and some of the men playing on the pipes, and the rest, both men and women, sing and beat time with their hands. . . . And when they arrive at Bubastis, they celebrate the occasion with great sacrifices, and more wine is consumed at this one festival than during the whole rest of the year."[7]

When this holiday throng arrived at its sites there were no commercial facilities offering food and lodging. Like modern attendees at a Grateful Dead concert, they had to sleep in the open and feed themselves as best they could.[8] In contrast, government officials such as Harkhuf, the provider of the dancing pygmy, enjoyed the comforts of temples and government depots in their travels.

[6]Ibid., p. 34.
[7]Ibid., p. 31.
[8]Ibid., p. 35.

Early Roads

The wheel led to the development of a heavy wagon that could be drawn by teams of oxen or onagers, a type of wild ass. "A walker or animal needs only a track,"[9] but a vehicle needs a road. There were not many routes that could take wheeled traffic. A king of Ur bragged that he went from Nippur to Ur, a distance of some 100 miles, and back in a day. This boast, sometime around 2050 B.C.E., implies the existence of a carriage road.[10] Even the best of the highways, however, were minimal. Paving was almost nonexistent until the time of the Hittites, who paved a mile and a third of road between their capital and a nearby sanctuary to carry heavily loaded wagons on festal days. Even then their war chariots, light horse-drawn carts invented for war, rolled over the countryside on dirt roads. Also, bridges were rare in a land that experienced frequent flooding. A hymn tells of King Shulgi exulting, " 'I enlarged the footpaths, straightened the highways of the land.' . . . but not every Mesopotamian monarch was a Shulgi, and there must have been long periods with nobody to 'straighten' the roads."[11]

Roads were better on the island of Crete, where the Minoans flourished from 2000 to 1500 B.C.E. and on the Greek peninsula of the Myceneans, who flourished from 1600 to 1200 B.C.E.[12] A two-lane road, $13\frac{1}{2}$ feet wide, ran from the coast of Crete to the capital at Cnossus. In Greece roads were usually one-lane, although some were as much as $11\frac{1}{2}$ feet wide, making two-way traffic possible. Bridges and culverts kept them passable.

Who traveled? Mainly three groups: the military, government officials, and caravans. The warlike Assyrians, like the Romans after them, realized that roads were basic to moving their war chariots efficiently. As their empire expanded from the Mediterranean in the west to the Persian Gulf in the east, they [the Assyrians] improved roads, largely for military use.

The Epic of Gilgamesh (ca. 2000 B.C.E) recounts the travels of a Sumerian king who is given directions by a deity. By only a slight stretch of the imagination, Gilgamesh's deity might be regarded as the first travel guide! This adds a fourth reason to credit the Sumerians with the beginnings of the travel industry.

The history of roads is thus related to the centralizing of populations in powerful cities. Alexander the Great found well-developed roads in India in 326 B.C.E. In Persia (now Iran) all the cities and provinces were connected by roads to the capital, Susa. These roads were built between 500 and 400 B.C.E. One of these roads was 1500 miles long.

The Romans started building roads in about 150 B.C.E. These were quite elaborate in construction. The roadway was surveyed using a cross-staff hung with plumb bobs. Soldiers and laborers dug the roadbed, then stones and concrete were evenly placed. Paving stones were then laid on top and the highway edged with curbstones and contoured to a sloping crown to shed the rain. Some of these roads are still in use.

By the time of emperor Trajan (ruled from C.E. 98 to 117), the Roman roads comprised a network of some 50,000 miles. They girdled the Roman Empire, extending from near Scotland and Germany in the north to the south well within Egypt and along the

---

[9]Ibid., p. 25.
[10]Ibid., p. 25.
[11]Ibid., p. 27.
[12]Ibid., p. 27.

southern shores of the Mediterranean Sea. To the east, roads extended to the Persian Gulf in what is now Iraq and Kuwait.

The Romans could travel as much as 100 miles a day using relays of horses furnished from rest posts 5 to 6 miles apart. Romans also journeyed to see famous temples in the Mediterranean area, particularly the pyramids and monuments of Egypt. Greece and Asia Minor were popular destinations, offering the Olympic Games, medicinal baths and seaside resorts, theatrical productions, festivals, athletic competitions, and other forms of amusement and entertainment. The Roman combination of empire, roads, the need for overseeing the empire, wealth, leisure, tourist attractions, and the desire for travel created a demand for accommodations and other tourist services that came into being as an early form of tourism.

Roman tourists went about sightseeing much as we do today. They used guidebooks, employed guides, left graffiti everywhere, and bought souvenirs. The examples are diverse and often amusing. A Greek named Pausanias wrote a *Guidebook of Greece*, which is the only guidebook to survive from ancient times. Written between C.E. 160 and 180 (during the reigns of emperors Hadrian, Antoninus Pius, and Marcus Aurelius), it "marks a milestone in the history of tourism. He [Pausanias] is the direct ancestor of the equally sober and unimaginative, painstakingly comprehensive and scrupulously accurate Karl Baedeker."[13]

The Classical World

The lands of the Mediterranean Sea (2000 B.C.E. to C.E. 500) produced a remarkable evolution in travel. In the cradle of Western civilization, travel for trade, commerce, religious purposes, festivals, medical treatment, or education developed at an early date. There are numerous references to caravans and traders in the Old Testament.

Beginning in 776 B.C.E., citizens of the city states came together every four years to honor Zeus through athletic competition. Eventually, four of these national festivals emerged: the Olympic Games, Pythian Games, Isthmian Games, and Nemean Games. Each festival included sacrifice and prayer to a single god. They honored the deity by offering up a superlative athletic or artistic performance.

Thus "the festivals furnished in one unique package the spectrum of attractions that have drawn tourists in all times and places: the feeling of being part of a great event and of enjoying a special experience; a gay festive mood punctuated by exalted religious moments; elaborate pageantry; the excitement of contests between performers of the highest calibre—and, on top of all this, a chance to wander among famous buildings and works of art. Imagine the modern Olympics taking place at Easter in Rome, with the religious services held at St. Peter's. . . ."[14]

Greek inns provided little more than a night's shelter. A guest who wanted to wash had to carry his own towel down the street to the nearest public bath. Once there, he took off his clothes in a dressing room and put his clothes in someone's care, lest they be stolen while he bathed. "The bath itself . . . was a big basin over which he leaned while an attendant sloshed water over him."[15]

[13]Ibid., p. 299.
[14]Ibid., pp. 76–77.
[15]Ibid., p. 89.

Everyday folk could also be found wending their way to the sanctuaries of the healing gods, especially Asclepius. Such places were usually located in a beautiful setting that included pure air and water (often with mineral springs). The sanctuary at Epidaurus also included facilities for rest and diversion, including the temple with admired sculptures, colonnades for shaded walks, a stadium for athletic events, and the second-largest theater in Greece. The Greeks recognized rest and diversion as important elements in treatment of the sick.

People also traveled to seek advice of the oracles, especially those at Dodona and Delphi. Statesmen, generals, and other powerful figures sought advice before taking an important action. Socrates' disciple inquired about his master's wisdom at the temple of Delphi.[16]

While visitors to festivals, businessmen, the sick, and advice seekers comprised the bulk of travelers in the fifth and fourth centuries B.C.E., there was also another small category, the tourist. Greece's "Father of History," Herodotus, would undoubtedly have qualified for the top category of frequent traveler miles if such awards had been given. In addition to traveling all over Greece and the Aegean Islands, he sailed to Cyrene in north Africa; explored southern Italy and Sicily, and sailed from Ephesus on the west coast of Asia Minor to Sardis. He got as far east as Babylon by sailing to Syria, then striking east to the Euphrates and following a caravan track for weeks. There he looked upon the ancient city of Babylon:

> square in shape, with each side 14 miles long, a total of 56 miles. Babylon is not only of enormous size; it has a splendour such as no other city of all we have seen. . . . The city wall is $85\frac{1}{2}$ feet wide and 3342 high. . . . Its circuit is pierced by one hundred entrances, with gates, jambs, and lintels of bronze. . . . The town is full of three- and four-storey houses and is cut through with streets that are absolutely straight, not only the main ones but also the sidestreets going down to the river.[17]

His figures are inflated, probably because he got them from his guides. He loved doing the sights and, like most modern tourists, was dependent on guides for information. A Greek entering Asia minor would encounter strange tongues and Oriental ways. It would not be until Alexander conquered the Persian empire that the Greek ways would spread into the ancient east.

Herodotus writes of many Greeks going to Egypt: "some, as might be expected, for business, some to serve in the army, but also some just to see the country itself." Possibly Herodotus's travel combined business and pleasure, as did that of Solon, who led Athens through a crisis, then took a trip abroad. Athens developed into a tourist attraction from the second half of the fifth century on, as people went to see the Parthenon and other new buildings atop the Acropolis.

Today's traveler who gets into trouble in a foreign city usually turns to his country's consul. The ancient Greek turned to his *proxenos* (Gr. *pro*, before or for, and *xenos*, foreigner). The primary duty of the *proxenos* was to aid and assist in all ways possible any of his compatriots who turned up in the place of his residence, particularly those who had come in some official capacity.[18] His more mundane duties might include extending hospitality, obtaining theater tickets, or extending a loan for someone who

---

[16]Ibid., pp. 84–85.
[17]Ibid., p. 99.
[18]Ibid., p. 93.

had run short of funds while visiting. More complex duties included negotiating ransom for relatives of someone taken as a prisoner of war. The heirs of someone who died in the city might ask the *proxenos* to wind up essential financial matters there.[19]

As the fourth century B.C.E. came to a close in Greece, people traveled despite its discomfort and dangers. Traveling by sea, they worried about storms and pirates; by land, about bad roads, dismal inns, and highwaymen. Only the wealthy described by Homer could escape the worst pitfalls.

Those who traveled for business, healing, or entertainment at festivals represented the majority. A small minority traveled for the sheer love of it—like Herodotus, the world's first great travel writer.

The museum, born in the ancient Near East, came of age with the Greeks. Sanctuaries such as Apollo's at Delphi and that of Zeus at Olympia gradually accumulated valuable objects donated as thank-you offerings for services rendered or bribes for acts the supplicant hoped would be rendered. Herodotus describes six gold mixing bowls dedicated by Gyges of Lydia and weighing some 1730 pounds and a gold lion from Crosesus weighing 375 pounds. While Herodotus singled these out because of their cost, others were notable for their aesthetic qualities. The Greeks had few precious metals, but hewed the plentiful marble with consummate skill. The temple of Hera exemplifies the scope and quality of sculpture acquired from the seventh through the third centuries B.C.E. "All over the Greek world through generous gifts of statues and paintings from the hopeful or the satisfied, temples became art galleries as well as houses of worship— exactly as Europe's cathedrals and churches were destined to become. . . . And they drew visitors the same way that art-laden churches do today to see the treasures and only incidentally, to say a prayer."[20]

In Asia Minor, beginning with the installation of a democratic government in Ephesus by Alexander the Great in 334 B.C., some 700,000 tourists would crowd in Ephesus (in what is now Turkey) in a single season to be entertained by the acrobats, animal acts, jugglers, magicians, and prostitutes who filled the streets. Ephesus also became an important trading center and, under Alexander, was one of the most important cities in the ancient world.

Early Ships

The Phoenicians were master shipwrights, building tubby wooden craft with a single square sail. By 800 B.C.E. they had built a network of trading posts around the Mediterranean emanating from their own thriving cities along the coast in what is now Lebanon. Acting as middlemen for their neighbors, they purveyed raw materials and also finished goods, such as linen and papyrus from Egypt, ivory and gold from Nubia, grain and copper from Sardinia, olive oil and wine from Sicily, cedar timbers from their homeland, and perfume and spices from the East. Presumably, they also occasionally carried a few passengers. They were the first creators of a maritime empire.

The Greeks followed the Phoenicians in becoming great sea traders. Improved ships accelerated a flourishing Mediterranean trade. Merchant ships also carried paying passengers (although Noah with his ark probably deserves credit for being the first

[19]Ibid., pp. 240–241.
[20]Ibid., pp. 240–241.

cruise operator, even though his passengers were primarily animals). Unlike Noah's passengers, those sailing on Greek ships had to bring their own servants, food, and wine. Widely varying accommodations aboard, stormy seas, and pirate attacks were worrisome realities.

Oceanians

Among early voyages, those in Oceania were amazing. Small dugout canoes not over 40 feet in length were used for voyages from Southeast Asia southward and eastward through what is now called Micronesia across the Pacific to the Marquesas Islands, the Tuamotu Archipelago, and the Society Islands. About C.E. 500, Polynesians from the Society Islands traveled to Hawaii, a distance of over 2000 miles. Navigation was accomplished by observing the position of the sun and stars, ocean swells, clouds, and bird flights. Considering the problems of fresh water and food supplies, such sea travel was astonishing. Later, navigation by the early explorers was facilitated by using a sandglass to measure time, a "log" line trailed behind the ship to measure distance, and a compass to gauge direction.

Europeans

The collapse of the Roman Empire in the fourth and fifth centuries spelled disaster for pleasure travel and tourism in Europe. During the Dark Ages (from the fall of the Western Roman Empire, C.E. 476, to the beginning of the modern era, C.E. 1450), only the most adventurous persons would travel. A trip during this period in history was dangerous; no one associated travel with pleasure. The most notable exception to this in Europe during the period was the Crusades.

By the end of the Dark Ages, large numbers of pilgrims were traveling to such popular shrines as Canterbury in England (immortalized in Chaucer's *Canterbury Tales*) and St. James of Compostella. Fewer made the long, expensive, and often dangerous journey to the Holy Land. Beginning in 1388, King Richard II required pilgrims to carry permits, the forerunner of the modern passport. Despite hardship and dangers, they went by the thousands to pay reverence to hallowed sites, to atone for sins, or to fulfill promises they had made while ill.

A fourteenth-century travelers' guide gave pilgrims detailed directions about the regions through which they would pass and the types of inns they would encounter along the often inhospitable routes. Innkeeping had nearly disappeared except for local taverns and a few inns scattered throughout Europe. They typically were filthy, vermin-infested warrens. In Germany and other areas, guests commonly had to share beds. At the other end of the spectrum lay an inn of quality, such as the one described in Mandeville's guide. He quotes the mistress of the inn: "Jenette lyghte the candell, and lede them ther above in the solere (upper room), and bere them hoot watre for to wasshe their feet, and covere them with uysshons." Inns in Spain and Italy provided a bed for each guest.

Travelers of any social distinction were, however, generally entertained in castles or private houses. Church monasteries or hospices offered accommodations for the majority. They offered services well beyond bed and board. They could provide a doctor and furnish medicines, replace worn garments, provide guides to show a visitor around the sights, or even grant a loan of money. They also offered opportunities for meditation and prayer.

The most famous stopover was the French Alpine hospice of the Great Saint Bernard, established in 962. (The Saint Bernard dogs that were sent to find and rescue travelers have been made famous by ads showing a little flask of wine appended to the dogs' collars.) St. Catherine's Monastery at the foot of Mt. Sinai still flourishes. Those who could afford to pay were expected to leave a generous donation.

Eventually, providing hospitality services for increasing numbers became burdensome to the religious houses. They could not turn the poor away, since Christian charity was an important element in the Church's mission; nor could they turn away the nobles, who made generous financial contributions. But they could, and increasingly did, refer the middle classes to taverns, inns, and wine shops. The church thus played an important role in the development of the hospitality industry during this period.

The Grand Tour

The "Grand Tour" of the seventeenth and eighteenth centuries was made by diplomats, businesspeople, and scholars who traveled to Europe, mainly to the cities of France and Italy. It became fashionable for scholars to study in Paris, Rome, Florence, and other cultural centers. While making the Grand Tour began as an educational experience, it has been criticized as eventually degenerating into the simple pursuit of pleasure. The following description from *A Geography of Tourism* describes the Grand Tour.

One of the interesting aspects of the Grand Tour was its conventional and regular form. As early as 1678 John Gailhard, in his *Compleat Gentlemen,* had prescribed a three-year tour as customary. A generally accepted itinerary was also laid down which involved a long stay in France, especially in Paris, almost a year in Italy visiting Genoa, Milan, Florence, Rome, and Venice, and then a return by way of Germany and the Low Countries via Switzerland. Of course, there were variations to this itinerary but this was the most popular route: it was generally believed that "there was little more to be seen in the rest of the civil world after Italy, France, and the Low Countries, but plain and prodigious barbarism."[21]

The term *Grand Tour* persists today, and the trip to Europe—the Continent—can be traced back to the early Grand Tour. Today's concept is far different, however, the tour is more likely to be three weeks, not three years.

Americans

The vast continent of North America, principally in what is now Florida and in the Southwest, was originally explored by the Spanish in the sixteenth century. Remarkably long journeys were made, often under severe conditions. The Spanish used horses, which were unknown to the American Indians until that time. In the East, Cape Cod was discovered by Gosnold in 1602 and the Plymouth Colony was established in 1620.

Early travel was on foot or on horseback, but travel by small boat or canoe provided access to the interior of the country. Generally, travel was from east to west. As roads

[21]H. Robinson, *A Geography of Tourism* (London: Macdonald and Evans, 1976), p. 13.

Reenactment of pioneers crossing the Kansas River near Topeka provides historical insight for visitors. (Photo courtesy of the Kansas Department of Commerce and Housing, Division of Travel and Tourism)

were built, stagecoach travel became widespread, and "ordinaries" (small hotels) came into common use. Among the most remarkable journeys were those by covered wagon to the West across the Great Plains. This movement followed the Civil War (1861–1865). Construction of railroads across the country (the first transcontinental link was at Promontory, Utah, in 1869) popularized rail travel. The Wells, Fargo Company organized the American Express Company in 1850. This pioneer company issued the first traveler's checks in 1891 and began other travel services, later becoming travel agents and arranging tours. Today, American Express is known throughout the world for its traveler's checks, credit cards, and various travel and financial services.

One of the most significant events in America's travel history is the amount of travel done by service men and women during World War II. Over 12 million Americans served in the armed forces from 1941 to 1945. Most were assigned to duty at places far removed from their homes, such as the European and Pacific theaters of war. Extensive domestic travel was commonplace, introducing the military traveler to different and often exotic places and bringing a broader perspective of what the North American continent and foreign countries had to offer visitors. Travel thus became a part of their experience. Following the war, a large increase in travel occurred when gasoline rationing was removed and automobiles were again being manufactured. Air, rail, and bus travel also expanded.

EARLY (AND LATER) TOURIST ATTRACTIONS

Sightseeing has always been a major activity of tourists; this has been true since ancient times. Most of us have heard of the seven wonders of the ancient world, but few could win a trivia contest by naming them:

1. The Great Pyramids of Egypt, including the Sphinx
2. The Hanging Gardens of Babylon, sometimes including the Walls of Babylon and the Palace, in what is now Iraq
3. The Tomb of Mausolus at Halicarnassus, in what is now Turkey
4. The Statue of Zeus at Olympia in Greece
5. The Collosus of Rhodes in the Harbor at Rhodes, an island belonging to Greece
6. The Great Lighthouse (Pharos) in Alexandria, Egypt
7. The Temple Artemis (also called the Temple of Diana) at Ephesus, at the time part of Greece, now in Turkey

The Great Pyramids of Egypt are the sole remaining wonder.

Just as tourists in ancient times traveled to see these wonders, modern tourists travel to see such natural wonders as the Grand Canyon, Yosemite National Park, Yellowstone, Niagara Falls, the oceans, the Great Lakes, and human-built wonders such as great cities, museums, dams, and monuments.

Spas, Baths, Seaside Resorts

Another interesting aspect in the history of tourism was the development of spas, after their original use by the Romans, which took place in Britain and on the continent. In

The Great Pyramids of Egypt are the sole remaining wonder of the seven wonders of the ancient world. (Photo courtesy of the Boeing Company)

the eighteenth century, spas became very fashionable among members of high society, not only for their curative aspects but also for the social events, games, dancing, and gambling that they offered. The spa at Bath, England, was one such successful health and social resort.

Sea bathing also became popular, and some believed that saltwater treatment was more beneficial than that at the inland spas. Well known in Britain were Brighton, Margate, Ramsgate, Worthing, Hastings, Weymouth, Blackpool, and Scarborough. By 1861 these successful seaside resorts indicated that there was a pent-up demand for vacation travel. Most visitors did not stay overnight but made one-day excursions to the seaside. Patronage of the hotels at these resorts was still limited to those with considerable means.

Tourism thus owes a debt to medical practitioners who advocated the medicinal value of mineral waters and sent their patients to places where mineral springs were known to exist. Later, physicians also recommended sea bathing for its therapeutic value. While spas and seaside resorts were first visited for reasons of health, they soon became centers of entertainment, recreation, and gambling, attracting the rich and fashionable with or without ailments. This era of tourism illustrates that it is usually a combination of factors rather than one element that spells the success or failure of an enterprise. Today, one finds that hot springs, although they are not high on travelers' priority lists, are still tourist attractions. Examples in the United States are Hot Springs, Arkansas; French Lick, Indiana; and Glenwood Springs, Colorado. The sea, particularly in the Sunbelt, continues to have a powerful attraction and is one of the leading forces in tourism development, which is evident by the number of travelers to Hawaii, Florida, the Caribbean, and Mexico.

EARLY ECONOMIC REFERENCES

As tourists traveled to see pyramids, visit seaside resorts, and attend festivals and athletic events, they needed food and lodging, and they spent money for these services. Traders did the same. Then as now, the economic impact of these expenditures was difficult to measure, as evidenced by the following quotation from Thomas Mun, who in 1620 wrote in *England's Treasure by Foreign Trade:* "There are yet some other petty things which seem to have a reference to this balance of which the said officers of His Majesty's Customs can take no notice to bring them into the account; as mainly, the expenses of the travelers."[22]

THE FIRST TRAVEL AGENTS

In 1822, Robert Smart of Bristol, England, announced himself as the first steamship agent. He began booking passengers on steamers to various Bristol Channel ports and to Dublin, Ireland.

[22]George Young, *Tourism: Blessing or Blight?* (Middlesex, England: Pelican Books, 1973), p. 1.

Visiting Christiana Campbell's Tavern in restored Colonial Williamsburg, Virginia, provides a most interesting look at what such early taverns were like. Many political issues of the day were debated here. Meals are served daily to visitors. (Photo courtesy of the Virginia Division of Tourism)

In 1841, Thomas Cook began running a special excursion train from Leicester to Loughborough (in England), a trip of 12 miles. On July 5 of that year, Cook's train carried 570 passengers at a round-trip price of 1 shilling per passenger. This is believed to be the first publicly advertised excursion train. Thus Cook can rightfully be recognized as the first rail excursion agent; his pioneering efforts were eventually copied widely in all parts of the world. Cook's company grew rapidly, providing escorted tours to the Continent and later to the United States and around the world. The company continues to be one of the world's largest travel organizations.

The first specialist in individual inclusive travel (the basic function of travel agents) was probably Thomas Bennett (1814–1898), an Englishman who served as secretary to the British consul-general in Oslo, Norway. In this position, Bennett frequently arranged individual scenic tours in Norway for visiting British notables. Finally, in 1850 he set up a business as a "trip organizer" and provided individual tourists with itineraries, carriages, provisions, and a "traveling kit." He routinely made advance arrangements for horses and hotel rooms for his clients.

HISTORIC TRANSPORTATION

Another element in the tourism equation is transportation. The early tourists traveled on foot, on beasts of burden, by boat, and on wheeled vehicles.

Stagecoach Travel

Coaches were invented in Hungary in the fifteenth century and provided regular service there on prescribed routes. By the nineteenth century, stagecoach travel had become quite popular, especially in Great Britain. The development of the famous English tavern was brought about by the need for overnight lodging by stagecoach passengers.

Water Travel

Market boats picked up passengers as well as goods on ship canals in England as early as 1772. The Duke of Bridgewater began such service between Manchester and London Bridge (near Warrington). Each boat had a coffee room from which refreshments were sold by the captain's wife. By 1815 steamboats were plying the Clyde, the Avon, and the Thames. A poster in 1833 announced steamboat excursion trips from London. By 1841 steamship excursions on the Thames were so well established that a publisher was bringing out a weekly *Steamboat Excursion Guide*.

Rail Travel

Railways were first built in England in 1825 and carried passengers beginning in 1830. The newly completed railway between Liverpool and Manchester featured special provisions for passengers. The railroad's directors did not expect much passenger

Older-style rail travel is available in Connecticut so that tourists can experience this memorable mode of transportation. (Photo courtesy of the Connecticut Department of Economic Development)

business, but time proved them wrong. The typical charge of only 1 penny per mile created a sizable demand for rail travel—much to the delight of the rail companies. As these fares were much lower than stagecoach fares, rail travel became widely accepted even for those with low incomes.

Early rail travel in Britain was not without its detractors, however. Writers in the most powerful organs of public opinion of that day seemed to consider the new form of rail locomotion a device of Satan. When a rail line was proposed from London to Woolrich to carry passengers at a speed of 18 miles per hour, one aghast contributor to the *Quarterly Review* wrote, "We should as soon expect the people of Woolrich to be fired off upon one of Congreve's ricochet rockets as trust themselves to the mercy of such a machine going at such a rate." Another writer deemed the railroads for passenger transportation as "visionary schemes unworthy of notice." Between 1826 and 1840 the first railroads were built in the United States.

Automobile and Motorcoach Travel

Automobiles entered the travel scene in the United States when Henry Ford introduced his famous Model T in 1908. The relatively cheap "tin lizzie" revolutionized travel in the country, creating a demand for better roads. By 1920 a road network became available, leading to the automobile's current dominance of the travel industry. Today, the automobile accounts for about 84 percent of intercity miles traveled and is the mode of travel for approximately 80 percent of all trips. The auto traveler brought about the early tourist courts in the 1920s and 1930s, which have evolved into the motels and motor hotels of today. Motorcoaches also came into use soon after the popularization of the automobile and remain a major mode of transportation.

Automobiles dominate travel today, but visiting the William F. Harrah Automobile Museum in Reno, Nevada, provides an appreciation of the old days, when cars were not quite so comfortable. (Photo courtesy of the Reno News Bureau)

Full-scale reproductions of the Wright Brothers' 1902 glider and 1903 flying machine are located in the visitors center at the Wright Brothers National Memorial at Kill Devil Hills, North Carolina. The world's first powered aircraft flight took place here on December 17, 1903. (Photo courtesy of the North Carolina Travel and Tourism Division; photo by Clay Nolen)

Air Travel

Nearly 16 years after the airplane's first flight at Kitty Hawk, North Carolina, in 1903, regularly scheduled air service began in Germany. This was a Berlin–Leipzig–Weimar route, and the carrier later became known as Deutsche Lufthansa. Today, Lufthansa is a major international airline. The first transatlantic passenger was Charles A. Levine, who flew with Clarence Chamberlin nonstop from New York to Germany. The plane made a forced landing 118 miles from Berlin, their destination, which they reached on June 7, 1927. This was shortly after Charles Lindbergh's historic solo flight from New York to Paris.

The first U.S. airline, Varney Airlines, was launched in 1926 and provided scheduled airmail service. However, this airline was formed only 11 days before Western Airlines, which began service on April 17, 1926. Varney Airlines later merged with three other lines to form United Airlines. On April 1, 1987, Western merged with Delta Airlines. At first, only one passenger was carried in addition to the mail, if the weight limitations permitted. The first international mail route was flown by Pan American Airways from Key West, Florida, to Havana, Cuba, on October 28, 1927. Pan Am flew the first passengers on the same route on January 16, 1928. The trip took 1 hour 10 minutes, and the fare was $50 each way.

The Buffalo Bill Historical Center in Cody, Wyoming, is a fine example of capturing historically significant events in an attractive setting. (Photo courtesy of the Wyoming Travel Commission)

The various U.S. airlines gradually expanded their services to more cities and international destinations. During World War II their equipment and most staff were devoted to war service. Development of the DC-3 and the Boeing 314A transoceanic Clipper in the early 1940s established paying passenger traffic and brought about much wider acceptance of air travel. The jet engine, invented in England by Frank Whittle, was used on such military planes as the B-52. The first American commerical jet was the Boeing 707. The first U.S. transcontinental jet flight was operated by American Airlines on January 25, 1959, from Los Angeles to New York City, and the jumbo jet era began in January 1970 when Pan American World Airways flew 352 passengers from New York to London using the new Boeing 747 equipment.

Because of its speed, comfort, and safety, air travel is the leading mode of public transportation today, as measured in revenue passenger miles (one fare-paying passenger transported one mile).

ACCOMMODATIONS

The earliest guest rooms were parts of private dwellings, and travelers were hosted almost like members of the family. In the Middle East and in the Orient, caravansaries and inns go back into antiquity. In more modern times, first the stagecoach, and then railroads, steamships, the automobile, motorcoach, and airplane, expanded the need for adequate accommodations. The railroad brought the downtown city hotel, the automobile and motorcoach the motel, and the airplane the boom in accommodations within or near airports. Housing, feeding, and entertaining travelers is one of the world's most important industries.

CHRONOLOGIES OF TRAVEL

Herein are two chronologies of travel: (1) a chronology of ancient migrations, early explorers, and great travelers, and (2) a chronology of travel arrangers of their business and their suppliers. The selected travelers and explorers not only made remarkably long and arduous journeys to little known (and often mistaken) places, but also wrote vivid descriptions or had scribes write for them. Sometimes their hardships were unbelievably difficult, often dangerous, and occasionally fatal.

The comfortable and pleasant (even inspiring, sometimes) traveling facilities of today are truly a tribute to the development of modern technology, design, and engineering.

Chronology of Ancient Migrations, Early Explorers, and Great Travelers

1 million years ago	*Homo erectus* originates in eastern and southern Africa; make extensive migrations north to the Middle East and to Asia.
350,000 years ago	Early *Homo sapiens* evolves from *H. erectus;* dwell in Africa, Europe, and Asia.
50,000–30,000 years ago	Anatomically modern man, *H. sapiens,* evolves and expands into Australia from southeastern Asia and into northeastern Asia.
15,000 years ago	Upper Palaeolithic people cross into northern latitudes of the New World from northeast Asia on a land bridge.

B.C.E.

4000	Sumerians (Mesopotamia–Babylonia) invent money, cuneiform writing, and the wheel; also, the concept of a tour guide.
2000–332	Phoenicians begin maritime trading and navigating over the entire Mediterranean Sea area. They may possibly have sailed as far as the British Isles and probably along the coast of western Africa and to the Azores.
1501–1481	Queen Hatshepsut makes the journey from Egypt to the lands of Punt—believed to an area along the eastern coast of Africa.
336–323	Alexander the Great leads his army from Greece into Asia, crossing the Indu Kush mountains (Afghanistan–Kashmir area), and to the Indus River.

C.E.

500	Polynesians from the Society Islands sail to Hawaii, a distance of over 2000 miles.
800–1100	Vikings establish trade and explore Iceland, Greenland, and the coast of North America.
1271–1295	Marco Polo, a Venetian merchant, travels to Persia, Tibet, Gobi desert, Burma, Siam, Java, Sumatra, India, Ceylon, the Siberian arctic, and other places.
1325–1354	Ibn Battuta, the "Marco Polo of Islam," a Moroccan, makes six pilgrimages to Mecca; also visits India, China, Spain, and Timbuctoo in Africa.
1492–1502	Christopher Columbus explores the New World, including the Bahamas, Cuba, Jamaica, Central America, and the northern coast of South America.
1497	John Cabot, an Italian navigator, sailing from Bristol, England, discovers North America at a point now known as Nova Scotia.
1513	Vasco Núñez de Balboa, a Spanish explorer, discovers the Pacific Ocean.
1519	Ferdinand Magellan sails west from Spain to circumnavigate the globe. He was killed in the Philippines, but some of his crew completed the circumnavigation.
1540–1541	Francisco Vasquez de Coronado, a Spanish explorer, seeks gold, silver, and precious jewels (without success) in what is now Arizona, New Mexico, Texas, Oklahoma, and other areas of the American Southwest.
1602	Bartholomew Gosnold, English explorer and colonizer, navigates the eastern coast of the (now) United States from Maine to Narragansett Bay; discovers and names Cape Cod. In 1606 his ship carried some of the first settlers to Virginia.
1768–1780	James Cook, an English naval officer, explores the northeastern coast of North America, and in the Pacific discovers New Caledonia, New Zealand, Australia, and Hawaii. He was killed in Hawaii.
1784–1808	Alexander Mackenzie, a Scot, made the first overland exploration across North America north of Mexico; discovers the river now named for him which flows into the Arctic Ocean and the Fraser River, which discharges into the Pacific.
1804–1806	Meriwether Lewis and William Clark, Americans, lead an expedition that opened the American West, discovering the Columbia River and traveling to the Pacific coast.
1860–1863	John H. Speke, an Englishman, discovers the source of the Nile River to be the Victorian Nile flowing out of Ripon Falls, issuing from the north shore of Lake Victoria.

1925–1934	William Beebe, American underwater explorer and inventor, develops the "bathysphere" and dives to 3034 feet offshore Bermuda.
1951–1955	Elizabeth Marshall Thomas, an American, explores the Kalahari desert in central Africa.
1969	Neil Armstrong, Edwin Aldrin, Jr., and Michael Collins, American astronauts, make pioneer journey to the moon in the *Saturn V* space vehicle. First Armstrong and then Aldrin step out of the lunar module onto the moon's surface. Collins continues to pilot the command and service module, which later joins with the lunar module for their return to earth.

Chronology of Travel Arrangers, Their Businesses, Facilities, Equipment, and Suppliers

B.C.E.

2000	Caravansaries (inns) established in the Near East and the Orient in ancient times. Located on caravan routes, they provided overnight rest needs for travelers and traders and for their donkeys and camels. These people traveled in groups for mutual assistance and defense.
776	Greeks begin travels to the Olympic Games. Subsequently, the games were held every four years.

C.E.

500–1450	During Europe's Middle Ages, a royal party in unfamiliar territory sends out a "harbinger" to scout the best route, find accommodations and food, then return to the group as a guide.
1605	The hackney coach introduced in London.
1801	Richard Trevithick, in England, perfects a steam locomotive capable of pulling heavy railcars.
1815	John L. McAdam and Thomas Telford, Britishers, invent all-weather roads, subsequently with a bituminous top.
1822	Robert Smart of Bristol, England, starts booking passengers on steamships sailing to Ireland.
1826–1840	Railroads begin service in the United States, first hauling minerals such as coal and later, passengers.
1829	The Tremont House opens in Boston, the first "modern" hotel.
1830	First passengers carried by rail in England.
1838	Stendhal, the pseudonym of Henri-Marie Boyle of France, authors *Les Mémoires d'un touriste*, believed to be the first disseminated printed use of the French word *tourist*.
1841	Thomas Cook organizes a special excursion train carrying

	570 passengers from Leicester to Loughborough, England, a trip of 12 miles.
1850	Thomas Bennett, secretary to the British consul general in Oslo, Norway, sets up a "trip organizer" business as a sideline. He provides individual pleasure travel itineraries and other services.
1873	American Express Company created by joining the original American Express Company formed in 1850 with the Wells, Fargo Company, founded in 1852.
1902	The American Automobile Association (AAA) founded in Chicago.
1903	Wilbur and Orville Wright make the first successful gasoline-powered airplane flight at Kitty Hawk, North Carolina.
1908	Henry Ford introduces the famous Model T automobile.
1918	Deutsche Lufthansa provides the first scheduled air passenger service from Berlin to Leipzig and Weimer.
1920	U.S. road system begins great improvement.
1926	Varney Airlines and Western Airlines become the first airlines in the United States.
1927	Charles A. Lindbergh flies solo from New York to Paris nonstop.
1927	Charles A. Levine becomes the first transatlantic passenger, flying from New York to within 118 miles of Berlin, his destination, because of a forced landing.
1927	Pan American Airways flies first international commercial mail flight from Key West, Florida to Havana, Cuba.
1928	Pan Am flies first passenger flight on the same route.
1931	American Society of Steamship Agents founded in New York.
1936	Air Transport Association (ATA) formed in Chicago.
1939	Frank Whittle, an Englishman, develops the first jet engine capable of powering a full-sized airplane.
1944	The American Society of Travel Agents (ASTA) founded from the American Society of Steamship Agents.
1951	Founding of Pacific Asia Travel Association (PATA) in Honolulu, Hawaii.
1952	The U.S. Congress creates the National System of Interstate Highways.
1954	Great Britain produces the Comet, the first passenger jet plane.
1958	Boeing Commercial Airplane Company produces the B-707, first commercial jet plane built in the United States.
1959	American Airlines flies the first transcontinental B-707 flight from Los Angeles to New York.

1961	The U.S. Congress creates the U.S. Travel Service, now the U.S. Travel and Tourism Administration (USTTA).
1964	American Airlines inaugurates the SABRE computerized reservation system (CRS).
1970	Pan American World Airways flies the first Boeing 747 "jumbo jet" plane with 352 passengers from New York to London.
1978	British Airways and Air France begin passenger service on the supersonic Concorde airplane.
1994	The "age of travel," wherein the most complex trip can be planned and arranged by a single phone call from the traveler; might involve numerous airlines, a cruise ship, sightseeing tours, a local rental car, other ground services, and entertainment—all reserved by amazing computerized reservation systems worldwide—the entire trip, except for incidentals, paid for by a single credit card.
1994	The "Chunnel" undersea railway opens, providing rail travel under the English Channel between England and France.

SUMMARY

Early explorers, traders, and shippers laid the groundwork upon which our modern age of travel is based. Human needs to arrange trips and facilitate movements have not changed over the ages. Building roads, vehicles, and ships and providing overnight rest accommodations go back into antiquity. The brave explorers who went into the unknown made available to their contemporaries knowledge of what the world was really like.

Over the centuries, inventions such as the sandglass to measure time, the "log" line to measure distance, and the compass to gauge direction made possible successful sea exploration. The roads of early Persia and those of the Roman Empire were used for exploration, for military purposes, for transporting tribute, and for pleasure trips and recreation.

Subsequent inventions of better roads, stagecoaches, passenger railroads, passenger ships, automobiles, motorcoaches, and airplanes created an ever speedier and more pleasant means of travel. Hotels and inns became more commodious and comfortable, with the added convenience of location, services, and appointments.

However, the conditions for an ever-expanding tourism market are little different now from Roman times. Tourism will flourish if prospective travelers are convinced that they will be safe and comfortable and well rewarded by their trip. When the Roman Empire declined, tourism declined. The wealthy class was reduced, roads deteriorated, and the countryside was plagued by bandits and scoundrels. Today, wars, unrest, and terrorism are similarly detrimental to tourism. Peace, prosperity, effective marketing, and reasonable travel costs remain the essential ingredients needed for the universal growth of travel.

Key Concepts

accommodations
air travel
American Express
Americans
attractions
automotive travel
classical world
early beginnings
early roads
early ships
Egyptians
Europeans
Grand Tour
Greeks

Middle Ages
Oceanians
Olympic Games
Pan American Airways
Phoenicians
rail travel
Romans
stagecoaches
Sumerians
Thomas Bennett
Thomas Cook
travel agents
water travel

For Review and Discussion

1. Of what value is learning the fundamentals of tourism's long history?
2. Do today's travelers have motivations and concerns similar to those of travelers who lived during the Classical Era?
3. What were the principal travel impulses of such early sea explorers as Columbus, Cabot, Balboa, Magellan, and Gosnold?
4. Give some examples of how guides operated in early tourism. Why were they so important? Are their functions the same today? Their ethics? (When discussing, include tour escorts.)
5. Describe the parallels that exist between tourism in Roman times and those of today.
6. Why have the Olympic Games survived since 776 B.C.E.?
7. In the 1990s how consequential for the international traveler is an ability in foreign languages?
8. Can one's money be converted to that of any other country?
9. Are museums, cathedrals, and art galleries really important to most visitors? Provide some outstanding examples.
10. How significant were religious motivations in early travel? Do these still exist? Examples?
11. Early religious houses such as churches and monasteries often accommodated travelers. Give reasons for this.
12. What, if any, were the impacts of Marco Polo's writings on the growth of travel by Europeans during the Renaissance (fourteenth through sixteenth centuries)?
13. Specifically, why did travel by rail supersede that by stagecoach?
14. Are medical and health travel motivations still important?
15. Describe ancient tourist attractions. How significant are they now?
16. Why has air travel become the primary mode for middle- and long-distance trips?
17. Who was the first travel agent, and what services did he provide? The first rail passenger agent? Tour operator? Steamship agent?

18. How have computerized reservations systems (CRSs) aided travel agencies and the traveler?
19. What will travel be like 20 years from now?

Selected References

Belasco, Warren James. *Americans on the Road: From Autocamp to Motel, 1920–1945.* Cambridge, Mass: MIT Press, 1979.

Burkut, A. J., and S. Medlik. *Historical Development of Tourism.* Aix-en-Province, France: Centre des Hautes Études Touristiques, 1990.

Casson, Lionel. *Travel in the Ancient World.* London: George Allen & Unwin, 1974.

Fagan, Brian M. *The Great Journey: The Peopling of Ancient America.* New York: Thames and Hudson, 1987.

Friedhiem, Eric. *Travel Agents: From Caravans and Clippers to the Concorde.* New York: Travel Agent Magazine Books, 1992.

Gee, Chuck Y., and Matt Lurie, eds. *The Story of the Pacific Asia Travel Association.* San Francisco: Pacific Asia Travel Association, 1993.

Jakle, John A. *The Tourist: Travel in the Twentieth Century North America.* Lincoln, Nebr.: University of Nebraska Press, 1985.

Lerner, Judith. "Traveling When the World Was Flat." *The Travel Agent Magazine* (March 8, 1982), pp. 26–29.

Lewin, Roger. *In the Age of Mankind: A Smithsonian Book of Human Evolution.* Washington, D.C.: Smithsonian Books, 1988.

McIntosh, Robert W. "Early Tourism Education in the United States." *Journal of Tourism Studies,* Vol. 3, No. 1 (May 1992), pp. 2–7.

National Geographic. *Into the Unknown: The Story of Exploration.* Washington, D.C.: The National Geographic Society, 1987.

National Geographic. *Peoples and Places of the Past: The National Geographic Illustrated Cultural Atlas of the Ancient World.* Washington, D.C.: National Geographic Society, 1983.

Rae, W. Fraser. *The Business of Travel: Fifty Years' Record of Progress.* London: Thomas Cook & Son, 1891.

Rinschede, Gisbert. "Form of Religious Tourism." *Annals of Tourism Research,* Vol. 19, No. 1 (1992), pp. 57–67.

Robinson, H. A. *A Geography of Tourism.* London: Macdonald and Evans, 1976.

Rugoff, Milton. *The Great Travelers.* New York: Simon and Schuster, 1960.

Towner, John. "Approaches to Tourism History." *Annals of Tourism Research,* Vol. 15, No. 1 (1988), pp. 47–62.

Towner, John. "The Grand Tour: A Key Phase in the History of Tourism." *Annals of Tourism Research,* Vol. 12, No. 3 (1985), pp. 297–333.

Towner, John. "The Grand Tour: Sources and a Methodology for an Historical Study of Tourism." *Tourism Management,* Vol. 5, No. 3 (September 1984), pp. 215–222.

Towner, John, and Geoffrey Wall. "History and Tourism." *Annals of Tourism Research,* Vol. 18, No. 1 (1991), pp. 71–84.

Van Doren, Carlton S. "Pan Am's Legacy to World Tourism." *Journal of Travel Research,* Vol. 32, No. 1 (Summer 1993), pp. 3–12.

Career Opportunities

- Evaluate future job opportunities in the tourism field.
- Learn about the careers available.
- Discover which careers might match your interests and abilities.
- Know additional sources of information on careers.

INTRODUCTION

Every student eventually must leave the college or university campus and seek a career-oriented job. This is a difficult decision-making time, often filled with doubt as to what goals or ambitions should be pursued. Coming face to face with the problem of getting a first major career-oriented job is a challenging task. You are marketing a product—yourself—and you will have to do a good job of communicating to convince a prospective employer that you have the abilities needed and that you will be an asset to the firm.

EMPLOYMENT FORECASTS

Generally, occupations in which current participants have the most education are projected to have the most rapid growth rates. Service-producing industries will account for much of the projected growth. These industries will expand (1986 to 2000) by more than 10 million jobs. In 1986, service industries accounted for about 23 percent of all nonfarm wage-paying and salaried jobs. In 2000, they will account for somewhat over 27 percent. More than 32 million payroll jobs will be in the services division in the year 2000—an awesome growth. Business services will be important contributors as they continue to produce new services that greatly add to their overall demand and employment growth.[1] Table 3.1 provides employment projections for various tourism-related industries.

JOB REQUIREMENTS

Are you suited to work in the tourism field? Do you like working with people? Would you be genuinely concerned for a customer's comfort, needs, and well-being even if the

[1]U.S. Department of Labor, *Projections 2000* (Washington, D. C.: U.S. Government Printing Office, 1988).

Table 3.1   Tourism Employment Forecasts to Year 2000

	Employment (thousands)					Annual Rate of Change (percent)	
			Projected, 2000				
Industry	1979	1986	Low	Moderate	High	Employment	Output
Transportation	3021	3041	3315	3500	3568	1.0	2.4
Local passenger	263	282	300	308	315	.6	1.3
Air transportation	438	570	690	721	725	1.7	3.7
Arrangement of passenger transportation	—	158	217	227	230	2.6	5.9
Miscellaneous transportation services	—	126	153	164	172	1.9	3.0
Eating and drinking places	4513	5879	8084	8365	8501	2.6	1.9
Miscellaneous shopping stores	569	746	1038	1085	1103	2.7	—
Hotels and other lodging places	1060	1401	1848	1971	2061	2.5	1.9
Advertising	146	202	284	302	310	2.9	3.5
Research, management, and consulting services	—	788	1186	1301	1394	3.6	4.3
Automotive rentals without drivers	120	161	210	233	241	2.7	2.6
Amusement and recreation services	712	915	1143	1204	1235	2.0	4.6
Business and professional associations	118	135	144	159	165	1.2	2.2

Source: U.S. Department of Labor, *Projections 2000* (Washington, D.C.: U.S. Government Printing Office, 1988).

customer might be rude and obnoxious? If you can answer in the affirmative, you can find a place in this industry. You have to like to do things for other people and work helpfully with them. If not, this is not the industry for you. Courtesy comes easily when customers are pleasant and gracious. But a great deal of self-discipline is required to serve every type of person—especially demanding and undecisive ones. In tourism, the customer might often change his or her mind. This requires patience and an unfailing cheerful personality.

You must also ask if you have the physical stamina required to carry out many of the jobs available. It is difficult to work long hours on your feet or working in a hot, humid, or cold environment. You might be involved in the pressure of a crush of people, such as at an airline ticket counter. A travel agency counselor must have keen vision, excellent hearing, and well-endowed nerves. Try to evaluate your physical attributes and skills to determine if you can perform.

To enhance your chances of getting a job and deciding if you would like it, visit several types of tourist-related organizations. Watch the activities being performed. Talk to managers, supervisors, and employees. Try to obtain an internship. Work experience means a great deal. Once you have had that, these skills can be utilized in a wide variety of tourism enterprises in any number of locations.

CAREER POSSIBILITIES

Tourism today is one of the world's largest industries. It is made up of many segments, the principal ones being transportation, accommodations, food service, shopping, travel arrangement, and activities for tourists, such as history, culture, adventure, sports, recreation, entertainment, and other similar activities. The businesses that provide these services require knowledgeable business managers.

Familiarity with tourism, recreation, business, and leisure equips one to pursue a career in a number of tourism-related fields. Even during times of severe economic downturn, tourism has performed well. Tourism skills are critically needed, and there are many opportunities available in a multitude of fields.

Because tourism is diverse, complex, and each sector has many job opportunities and career paths, it is virtually impossible to list and describe all the jobs one might consider in this large field. However, as a student interested in tourism, you could examine the following areas, many of which are discussed in more detail in Chapters 5 to 8.

AIRLINES   The airlines are a major travel industry employer, offering a host of jobs at many levels, ranging from entry level to top management. Illustrative jobs are reservation agents, flight attendants, pilots, flight engineers, aircraft mechanics, maintenance staff, baggage handlers, airline food service jobs, sales representatives, sales jobs, computer specialists, training staff, office jobs, clerical positions, ticket agents, and research jobs. Since airlines have to meet safety and other requirements, opportunities also exist with the Federal Aviation Administration (FAA). The FAA hires air traffic controllers and various other specialists. Airports also use a wide range of personnel from parking attendants to managers. Other air-related jobs are available with associations such as the Air Transport Association.

Becoming an airline pilot requires extensive training, education, and experience. It is one of the highest paid professions in tourism. (Photo courtesy of USAir)

Professional chefs find much satisfaction in creating tasty, nutritious, and almost irresistible buffet food items. (Photo courtesy of the Royal Cruise Line)

BUS COMPANIES   Bus companies require management personnel, ticket agents, sales representatives, tour representatives, hostesses, information clerks, clerical positions, bus drivers, personnel people, and training employees.

CRUISE COMPANIES   The cruise industry is the fastest-growing segment of the tourism industry today. Job opportunities include those for sales representatives, clerical workers, market researchers, and recreation directors. Because of its similarity in operations, the cruise industry has many of the same jobs as the lodging industry.

RAILROADS   Passenger rail service is currently dominated by Amtrak, which hires passenger service representatives, sales representatives, reservation clerks and other types of clerks, conductors, engineers, firefighters, and station agents.

RENTAL CAR COMPANIES   With increased pleasure air travel and the growth of fly/drive programs, rental car companies are becoming an even more important segment of the travel industry. This sector of tourism employs reservation agents, rental sales agents, clerks of various kinds, service agents, mechanics, and district and regional managers.

HOTELS, MOTELS, AND RESORTS   The range of jobs in hotels and motels is extremely broad. The following list is representative: general manager, resident manager,

Being courteous and thoughtful are essential qualities for anyone employed in the car rental business. (Photo courtesy of Hertz Corporation)

comptroller, accountants, management trainees, director of sales, director of convention sales, director of personnel, director of research, mail clerks, room clerks, reservation clerks, front office manager, housekeepers, superintendent of service, bellhops, lobby porters, doormen, maids, chefs, cooks, kitchen helpers, storeroom employees, dishwashers, waiters, bartenders, apprentice waiters, heating and air conditioning personnel, maintenance workers, engineers, electricians, plumbers, carpenters, painters, and laundry workers.

Resorts tend to have the same jobs as those mentioned for hotels and motels; however, larger resorts will have greater job opportunities and require more assistants in all areas. Resorts also have a number of additional job opportunities in the areas of social events, entertainment, and recreation, such as for tennis and golf pros. At ski resorts there will be ski instructors, members of a safety patrol, and so on. The American Hotel and Motel Association estimates that the lodging industry employs approximately 1.64 million people, and by the year 2000, lodging industry labor demands will increase 25 percent.

TRAVEL AGENCIES   Travel agencies range from very small to very large businesses. The smaller businesses are very much like any other small business. Very few people carry out all the business operations, and jobs include secretarial, travel counseling, and managerial activities. In large offices job opportunities are more varied and include commercial account specialists, domestic travel counselors, international travel counselors, research directors, and advertising managers. Trainee group sales consultants, accountants, file clerks, sales personnel, tour planners, tour guides, reservationists, group coordinators, trainees, operations employees, administrative assistants, advertising specialists, and computer specialists are other possibilities.

TOUR COMPANIES   Tour companies offer employment opportunities in such positions as tour manager or escort, tour coordinator, tour planner, publicist, reservations

Employment as a skilled mechanic or technician requires a natural aptitude for such work, coupled with a foundation of comprehensive training and experience. (Photo courtesy of United Airlines)

specialist, accountant, sales representative, group tour specialist, incentive tour coordinator, costing specialist, hotel coordinator, office supervisor, and managerial positions. Often, a graduate will begin employment as a management trainee, working in all the departments of the company before a permanent assignment is made.

FOOD SERVICE   Many job opportunities are available in the rapidly growing food service industry, such as head waiters, captains, waiters, waitresses, bus persons, chefs, cooks, bartenders, restaurant managers, assistant managers, personnel directors, dieticians, menu planners, cashiers, food service supervisors, purchasing agents, butchers, beverage workers, hostesses, kitchen helpers, and dishwashers.

TOURISM EDUCATION   As tourism continues to grow, the need for training and education grows. In recent years many colleges and universities have added travel and tourism programs, existing programs have expanded, vocational schools have launched programs, trade associations have introduced education and certification programs, and private firms have opened travel schools. There are job opportunities for administrators, teachers, professors, researchers, and support staff.

Knowledge, interest, drive, and enthusiasm can take someone to an executive position in tourism. Here Sandra Fulton, head of the Tennessee Tourism Development Department discusses a promotional booklet with one of her associates. (Photo courtesy of Tennessee Tourist Development)

TOURISM RESEARCH   Tourism research consists of the collection and analysis of data from both primary and secondary sources. The tourism researcher plans market studies, consumer surveys, and the implementation of research projects. Research jobs are available in tourism with airlines, cruise lines, management consulting firms, state travel offices, and so on.

TRAVEL JOURNALISM   There are a number of opportunities available in travel writing as editors, staff writers, and freelance writers. Most major travel firms have a need for public relations people who write and edit, disseminate information, develop communication vehicles, obtain publicity, arrange special events, do public speaking, plan public relations campaigns, and so on. A travel photographer could find employment either in public relations or travel writing.

RECREATION AND LEISURE   Jobs in recreation and leisure are enormous. Some examples are activity director, aquatics specialist, ski instructor, park ranger, naturalist, museum guide, handicapped program planner, forester, camping director, concert promoter, lifeguards, tennis and golf instructors, coaches for various athletic teams, and drama directors. Many recreation workers teach handicrafts. Resorts, parks, and recreation departments often employ recreation directors who hire specialists to work with senior citizens or youth groups, to serve as camp counselors, or to teach such skills as boating and sailing. Management, supervisory, and administrative positions are also available.

ATTRACTIONS   Attractions such as amusement parks and theme parks are a major source of tourism employment. Such large organizations as Disney World, Disneyland, Six Flags, Worlds of Fun, and Sea World provide job opportunities ranging from top management jobs to clerical and maintenance jobs.

TOURIST OFFICES AND INFORMATION CENTERS   Numerous jobs are available in tourist offices and information centers. Many chambers of commerce function as information centers and hire employees to provide this information. Many states operate welcome centers. Job titles found in state tourism offices are: director, assistant director, deputy director, travel representative, economic development specialist, assistant director for travel promotion, statistical analyst, public information officer, assistant director for public relations, marketing coordinator, communications specialist, travel editor, media liaison, media specialist, photographer, administrative assistant, information specialist, media coordinator, manager of travel literature, writer, chief of news and information, marketing coordinator, market analyst, research analyst, economist, reference coordinator, secretary, package tour coordinator, and information clerk.

CONVENTION AND VISITORS BUREAUS   As more and more cities enter the convention and visitor industry, employment opportunities in this segment grow. Many cities are devoting public funds to build convention centers to compete in this growing market. Convention and visitors bureaus require managers, assistant managers, research directors, information specialists, marketing managers, public relations staff, sales personnel, secretaries, and clerks.

MEETING PLANNERS   A growing profession is meeting planning. Many associa-

Not everyone aspires to a job as a reptile expert. But in this unusual occupation, absorbing enlightenment is provided for the many visitors at Busch Gardens in Tampa, Florida. (Photo courtesy of Busch Gardens)

Gambling or gaming intrigues many players at hotels, resorts, and on shipboard. It is a growing attraction in many areas and provides employment opportunities. (Photo courtesy of Merv Griffin's Resorts, Atlantic City, New Jersey)

tions and corporations are hiring people whose job responsibilities are to arrange, plan, and conduct meetings.

GAMING   One of the fastest-growing sectors is gaming. Today, one is hard-pressed to find a state where gambling is not allowed or a gaming proposal is in front of the state legislature. From riverboats to Indian reservations to land-based casinos, new destinations are being created. Casinos provide job opportunities ranging from managers to marketers to mechanics to clerical and maintenance jobs.

OTHER OPPORTUNITIES   A fairly comprehensive list of career opportunities has been presented. Others that do not fit the general categories listed are club management, corporate travel departments, hotel representative companies, in-flight and trade magazines, and trade and professional associations.

CAREER PATHS IN TOURISM

In addition to considering one of the foregoing kinds of positions within a particular segment of the tourism sector, it is also useful to examine the various career paths that might be pursued. Because the tourism industry is so large and so diverse, it offers a broad range of challenging positions. While each of these positions offers its own unique opportunities and demands, people will find that the experience gained from working

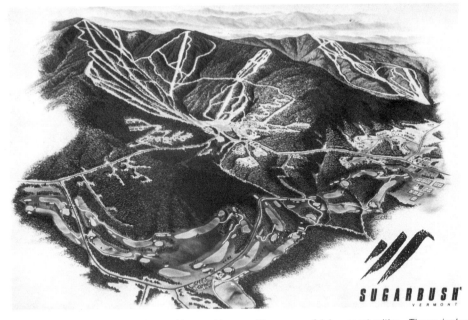

A major resort complex such as this provides a wide range of job opportunities. These include maintenance, lift operators, food and beverage service, accommodations, ski, golf and tennis professionals and instructors, department heads, supervisors, and management. (Photo courtesy of the Vermont Department of Travel and Tourism)

in a range of jobs in different subsectors of tourism can strengthen their understanding of the industry as a whole. Depending on one's career objectives, this broader understanding of tourism can be especially valuable when applying for certain types of positions. Examples include those in destination management organizations and national or provincial/state tourism offices.

To offer employees opportunities for growth and development, educators and personnel managers attempt continually to develop the concept of *career paths* in tourism. A schematic model illustrating the concept is shown in Figure 3.1. The fundamental premise of this general model is that people can pursue a variety of reasonably well-defined alternative routes, first through the educational system and subsequently, through the industry itself. Based on the training and experience gained, combined with high-quality performance, a person can pursue a career path starting at different levels, with the ultimate goal of achieving the position of senior executive. While not everyone will have the ability or will necessarily want to pass through all levels of the model, it does provide defined career paths for those who are interested. It also indicates what combination of training and experience is normally required to achieve various positions.

Although clearly an oversimplification, the career path model demonstrates that people may take a variety of routes in pursuing their careers at different levels within and across the various subsectors of tourism. The specific positions that will appeal to different people will, of course, vary according to their particular educational back-

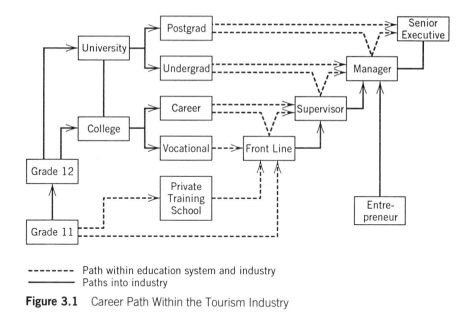

-------- Path within education system and industry
———————— Paths into industry

Figure 3.1   Career Path Within the Tourism Industry

ground and their occupational skills. The chosen career path will also reflect a person's values and interests. Just how the chosen occupation might reflect individual values and interest is shown in Figure 3.2. As indicated, front-line staff (entry level and operations) must like dealing with people and possess a strong interest in providing them with high-quality service. Supervisors, managers, and entrepreneurs must possess additional values and interests which enable them to face the challenges of change as they attempt to meet the needs of a demanding and ever-shifting marketplace.

Other Sources of Career Information

Most of the career opportunities available in the travel field have been listed. It is hoped that this overview will provide you with a guide and point out that industries are so large that they are worthy of much further study by themselves. In considering career opportunities, it is important to gather information before you invest a great deal of time looking for a job. The following are good references:

Milne, Robert Scott. *Opportunities in Travel Careers.* Lincolnwood, Ill.: National Textbook Company, 1985.
Stevens, Laurence. *Your Career in Travel and Tourism.* Albany, N. Y.: Delmar Publishers, 1988.
Whitzky, Herbert K. *Your Career in Hotels and Motels.* New York: Dodd Mead, 1971.
Rubin, Karen. *Flying High in Travel, A Complete Guide to Careers in the Travel Industry.* New York: John Wiley & Sons, 1992.

These books discuss tourism jobs. One book on how to get a job is particularly recommended:

Bolles, Richard. *What Color Is Your Parachute?* Berkeley, Calif.: Ten Speed Press, 1993.

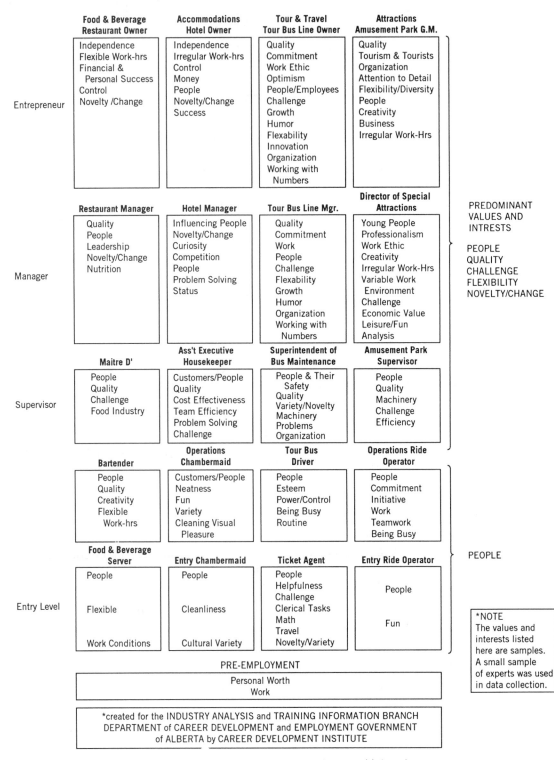

	Food & Beverage Restaurant Owner	Accommodations Hotel Owner	Tour & Travel Tour Bus Line Owner	Attractions Amusement Park G.M.	

Entrepreneur	Independence
	Flexible Work-hrs
	Financial &
	  Personal Success
	Control
	Novelty /Change
		Independence
		Irregular Work-hrs
		Control
		Money
		People
		Novelty/Change
		Success
			Quality
			Commitment
			Work Ethic
			Optimism
			People/Employees
			Challenge
			Growth
			Humor
			Flexability
			Innovation
			Organization
			Working with
			  Numbers
				Quality
				Tourism & Tourists
				Organization
				Attention to Detail
				Flexibility/Diversity
				People
				Creativity
				Business
				Irregular Work-Hrs
					PREDOMINANT
					VALUES AND
					INTRESTS
					
					PEOPLE
					QUALITY
					CHALLENGE
					FLEXIBILITY
					NOVELTY/CHANGE

	Restaurant Manager	Hotel Manager	Tour Bus Line Mgr.	Director of Special Attractions	

Manager	Quality
	People
	Leadership
	Novelty/Change
	Nutrition
		Influencing People
		Novelty/Change
		Curiosity
		Competition
		People
		Problem Solving
		Status
			Quality
			Commitment
			Work
			People
			Challenge
			Flexability
			Growth
			Humor
			Organization
			Working with
			  Numbers
				Young People
				Professionalism
				Work Ethic
				Creativity
				Irregular Work-Hrs
				Variable Work
				  Environment
				Challenge
				Economic Value
				Leisure/Fun
				Analysis	

	Maitre D'	Ass't Executive Housekeeper	Superintendent of Bus Maintenance	Amusement Park Supervisor	
Supervisor	People Quality Challenge Food Industry	Customers/People Quality Cost Effectiveness Team Efficiency Problem Solving Challenge	People & Their Safety Quality Variety/Novelty Machinery Problems Organization	People Quality Machinery Challenge Efficiency	
	Bartender	Operations Chambermaid	Tour Bus Driver	Operations Ride Operator	

	People
	Quality
	Creativity
	Flexible
	  Work-hrs
		Customers/People
		Neatness
		Fun
		Variety
		Cleaning Visual
		  Pleasure
			People
			Esteem
			Power/Control
			Being Busy
			Routine
				People
				Commitment
				Initiative
				Work
				Teamwork
				Being Busy	

	Food & Beverage Server	Entry Chambermaid	Ticket Agent	Entry Ride Operator	PEOPLE
Entry Level	People Flexible Work Conditions	People Cleanliness Cultural Variety	People Helpfulness Challenge Clerical Tasks Math Travel Novelty/Variety	People Fun	*NOTE The values and interests listed here are samples. A small sample of experts was used in data collection.

PRE-EMPLOYMENT

Personal Worth
Work

*created for the INDUSTRY ANALYSIS and TRAINING INFORMATION BRANCH
DEPARTMENT of CAREER DEVELOPMENT and EMPLOYMENT GOVERNMENT
of ALBERTA by CAREER DEVELOPMENT INSTITUTE

Figure 3.2   Career Paths in Tourism, Sample Occupations, Values, and Interests

The information provided in this section should be an important starting point for you. However, it is really just the tip of the iceberg. It is up to you to explore the subject further and to gain additional information. You not only need to learn about careers in tourism and travel-related fields, but also about the task of marketing yourself—how to work up résumés and how to conduct yourself during interviews. General books on getting a job will help you in this task.

SUMMARY

A career in tourism offers many exciting and challenging employment opportunities. As indicated in Chapter 1, tourism is the largest industry in the world today. In the United States over the past decade, travel industry employment has grown at a rate more than twice the growth rate for all U.S. industries. This growth is expected to continue. The labor-intensive tourism industry has a need for motivated people of all ages and backgrounds. Those who prepare themselves, maintain high energy, have a talent for working with people, and have a dedication to high-quality service will find themselves climbing the career ladder to success.

Key Concepts

airlines	railroads
accommodations	recreation
attractions	rental car companies
bus companies	tour companies
career path	tourism education
convention and visitors bureaus	tourism job requirements
cruise lines	tourism research
employment forecasts	tourist offices and information centers
food service	travel agencies
meeting planning	travel journalism

For Review and Discussion

1. What is the growth potential for tourism jobs?
2. As a career in tourism, what position appeals to you at present?
3. What preparation will be needed for that position?
4. What are its probable rewards?
5. Identify the position's advancement opportunities.
6. Are your writing and speaking skills good enough to land a job?
7. What criteria would you use to choose a company for an interview?
8. How important is salary in your job choice?
9. Evaluate the job satisfaction in your chosen career.
10. What will tourism be like in the year 2000? What position might you visualize yourself to be in by that date?

Case Problems

1. Donnell C. is graduating from a four-year travel and tourism curriculum. She has had several job offers. What type of organization would afford her the broadest range of experiences? How important is her beginning salary?
2. Jim B. is a successful local travel agency manager. He is visited one day by a very bright high school senior who is most interested in becoming a travel agent. What educational preparation advice would you offer?

Selected References

American Society of Travel Agents. Future Travel Professionals Club brochure. Alexandria, Va.: ASTA, no date.

Antil, Frederick H. "Career Planning in the Hospitality Industry." *The Cornell Hotel and Restaurant Administration Quarterly*, Vol. 25, No. 1 (May 1984), pp. 46–52.

Antil, Frederick H. "Learning Hospitality Management Through a Rigorous Work–Study Experience." *Hospitality and Tourism Educator*, Vol. 1, No. 2 (Summer/Fall 1988), pp. 24–29.

Career Press Inc. *Travel & Hospitality Career Directory.* Hawthorne, N.J.: Career Press, 1989.

Charles, Kwame R. "Career Influences, Expectations, and Perceptions of Caribbean Hospitality and Tourism Studies: A Third World Perspective." *Hospitality and Tourism Educator*, Vol. 4, No. 3 (May 1992), pp. 9–14.

Cook, Suzanne and William Evans. *A Portrait of Travel Industry Employment in the U.S. Economy.* Washington D.C.: TIA Foundation, 1994.

Crafts, Peter C. "Career Development Programs: How to Recruit and Retain Growing People in a Shrinking Market." *Hospitality and Tourism Educator*, Vol. 1, No. 2 (Summer/Fall 1988), pp. 30–33.

Day, W., and A. Williams. "Preparing for Your Field Experience aka Co-op, Practicum or Internship." *Hosteur*, Vol. 2, No. 1 (Spring 1992), pp. 10–11.

Educational Institute. *Hotel/Motel Careers.* East Lansing, Mich.: Educational Institute, no date.

English Tourist Board. *The Handbook of Tourism and Leisure.* London: Hobsons Publishing, 1988.

Gagnon, Patricia, and Karen Silva. *Travel Career Development.* Homewood, Ill.: Irwin Mirror Press, 1992.

McCleary, K., and Pam Weaver. "Expectations of Hospitality Students Regarding Entry Level Positions in the Hospitality Industry." *Hospitality Education and Research Journal*, Vol. 12, No. 2 (1988), pp. 163–174.

National Recreation and Parks Association. *Careers in Parks, Recreation and Leisure Services.* Alexandria, Va.: NRPA, no date.

Rubin, Karen. *Flying High in Travel: A Complete Guide to Careers in the Travel Industry.* New York: Wiley, 1992.

Starr, Nona. *Viewpoint: An Introduction to Travel, Tourism and Hospitality.* Boston: Houghton Mifflin, 1993.

Stevens, L. *Your Career in Travel, Tourism and Hospitality.* Albany, N.Y.: Delmar Publishers, 1988.

Timmons, Veronica. *Career Exploration in Tourism: A Guide to Finding and Getting a Job in the Tourism Industry.* Vancouver, British Columbia, Canada: Timmons and Associates, 1991.

Tourism Canada. *Career Guide to the Tourism & Hospitality/Recreation Industry.* Ottawa: Tourism Canada, 1986.

U.S. Department of Commerce. *U.S. Industrial Outlook 1993.* Washington, D.C.: U.S. Government Printing Office, 1993.

U.S. Department of Labor. *Occupational Outlook Handbook.* Washington D.C.: U.S. Government Printing Office, 1993.

World Travel and Tourism Council. *Education for Careers in European Travel and Tourism.* Brussels: WTTC, 1991.

World Travel and Tourism Council. *The WTTC Report: Travel and Tourism in the World Economy.* Brussels: WTTC, 1992.

Zedlitz, Robert H. *Getting a Job in the Travel Industry.* Cincinnati, Ohio: South-Western Publishing Company, 1990.

PART TWO

HOW TOURISM IS ORGANIZED

CHAPTER 4

World, National, Regional, and Other Organizations

LEARNING OBJECTIVES

- Understand the magnitude of world tourism in terms of the vast numbers of organizations that serve the needs of their diverse memberships.
- Recognize the variety of types and functions of tourism organizations.
- Know why states support official offices of tourism.
- Learn how national, regional, and trade organizations are structured and operated.

The complex organization of tourism involves literally hundreds of thousands of units. Tourism organizations can be reviewed (1) geographically with the following breakdowns: international, regional within world, national, regional within nation, state or provincial, regional within state or province, and local categories; (2) by ownership, such as government, quasi-government, or private; (3) by function or type of activity, such as regulators, suppliers, marketers, developers, consultants, researchers, educators, publishers, professional associations, trade organizations, and consumer organizations; (4) by industry, such as transportation (air, bus, rail, auto, cruise), travel agents, tour wholesalers, lodging, attractions, and recreation; and (5) by motive, profit or nonprofit.

The purpose of Chapters 4 through 8 is to discuss the major types of tourist organizations and how they interrelate and operate, focusing on *illustrative examples*. The discussion begins with official international tourism groups in this chapter and ends with the private organizations and firms that make up the tourism industry covered in Chapters 5, 6, 7, and 8. Additional important supplemental areas that facilitate the tourism process, such as education, publishing, and marketing and publicity, are also included in Chapter 8.

INTERNATIONAL ORGANIZATIONS

World Tourism Organization

The World Tourism Organization (WTO) is the most widely recognized organization in tourism today. Located in Madrid, Spain, it is the only organization that represents all national and official tourist interests. Private commercial interests are allied members. The WTO is an official consultative organization to the United Nations, particularly to ECOSOC (the Economic and Social Council of the UN), and has the following objectives:

1. To accelerate and enlarge the contribution of tourism (international and domestic) to peace, understanding, health, and prosperity throughout the world
2. To facilitate, in travel, people's access to education and culture
3. To raise standards of living in the less developed areas of the world by helping to provide facilities for foreign tourism and the promotion of tourist traffic to these areas
4. To improve the conditions of country dwellers and so to contribute to an expanding world economy
5. To act as an international agency of coordination and cooperation to spread tourism
6. To provide a service to members valuable to them in their national operations in the field of tourism
7. To provide a point for meeting and coordination of all tourist interests of member countries concerning both the national tourist organizations and professional sectors and organizations representing the interests of the travelers
8. To establish permanent liaison and consultation with the various sectors of tourist operators
9. To do all this in the most efficient way

Generally, WTO concentrates on the informed promotion of tourism, spreading an appreciation of tourism and its advantages and dangers and recommending positive measures like the creation of new facilities. The organization attempts to harmonize tourist policies among nations through formulating and applying principles of international tourism. As mentioned, WTO is instrumental in the representation of tourism in the United Nations and acts as the central authoritative voice for world tourism and the tourist, complementing the central authority and position of the national tourist organizations. Additionally, WTO concludes multilateral international instruments and supports their implementation, as well as the implementation of the appropriate existing instruments, and fosters settlement of international technical tourism disagreements.

Other activities of WTO include helping developing countries and organizing and stimulating cooperation among all countries in technical matters affecting tourism. This is done through standardization of equipment, terms, phraseology, and signs as an aid to easier travel and comprehension for foreign visitors. WTO also acts as an international clearinghouse for information and encourages the application of new knowledge to tourism development and marketing. One important contribution of WTO is research, which includes studying the features of international tourism and devising methods of measurement, forecasting, development, and marketing that would be of use to national tourist organizations in their own activities. Research activities lead to improvement in the comparability of statistics. WTO carries out a regular survey of world tourism, appraising and measuring both progress and obstacles to further progress. WTO attempts to facilitate world travel through elimination or reduction of governmental measures for international travel as well as standardization of requirements for passports, visas, police registration, frontier formalities, and so forth. WTO also provides technical help to developing countries, primarily through the United Nations.

World Travel and Tourism Council

This council is a global coalition of chief executive officers from all sectors of the industry. These include transportation, accommodation, catering, recreational, cultural, and travel service activities. Offices are located in Brussels, Belgium (headquarters); Canada; the United Kingdom; and New York. The mission of WTTC is threefold: (1) to convince governments of the enormous contribution of travel and tourism to national and world economic development and to ensure that policies appropriately reflect this fact, (2) to promote the expansion of travel and tourism markets in harmony with the environment, and (3) to eliminate barriers to growth of the industry.

The WTTC report, *Travel and Tourism in the World Economy,* is their primary vehicle used to convey the message that this is the world's largest industry, that it has been growing faster than most other industries, that it will continue to grow strongly, and that it can create jobs and increase gross domestic product (GDP). WTTC plans to continue publishing this report and enhance its methodology. The organization's goal is to convince governments to adopt policies that reflect the preeminent role of travel and tourism in world and national economic development, such as elevating the industry to cabinet rank.

WTTC plans to continue its support for aviation liberalization: the expansion of bilateral and multilateral decontrol, privatization, and airline ownership deregulation. Governments would retain their safety, security, and competition oversight functions.

The environment is the core of travel and tourism and a critical political issue. WTTC shares the global concern for environmental protection. It took a number of steps in 1992 to strengthen its work in this area. In 1992, also, guidelines for travel and tourism companies were formally adopted by the WTTC, focusing on audits, impact assessment, and management commitment. In 1991, WTTC established the World Travel and Tourism Environment Research Center at Oxford in the United Kingdom. The center has put into place a comprehensive database of industry action, government policy, and best practice approaches on the environment.

Bureaucratic barriers to travel, such as exit and entry procedures, irritate consumers and lower the quality of the travel experience. WTTC urges visa-free travel consistent with security requirements while challenging all forms of exit barriers.

International Air Transport Association

The International Air Transport Association (IATA) is the global organization for virtually all the international air carriers. The principal function of IATA is to facilitate the movement of persons and goods from any point on the world air network to any other by any combination of routes. This can be accomplished by a single ticket bought at a single price in one currency and valid everywhere for the same amount and quality of service. The same principles apply to the movement of freight and mail.

Resolutions of the traffic conferences of IATA standardize not only tickets but waybills, baggage checks, and other similar documents. These resolutions coordinate and unify handling and accounting procedures to permit rapid interline bookings and connections. They also create and maintain a stable pattern of international fares and rates. In effect, they permit the linking of many individual international airline routes into a single public service system.

Setting rates is the most significant part of IATA work. The need for agreement on rates among the IATA airlines is both practical and political—the fares and rates of international airlines are controlled by the governments of the individual countries that are served. Each country is absolute in its own airspace, and each country can bar or admit whom it pleases and set what conditions it likes.

IATA traffic conferences are held after governments have decided bilaterally on the exchange of rights and after each government decides individually what air carriers are going to serve its area. The IATA traffic conferences are, in effect, an important adjunct to government. Also, the rules that IATA formulate must be approved by the governments involved.

To be a member of IATA and the conferences, an airline must hold a certificate for scheduled air carriage from a government eligible for membership in the International Civil Aviation Organization (ICAO), a specialized agency of the United Nations. IATA's travel agency accreditation services are conducted by its Passenger Network Services (PNS) Corporation. There are three IATA traffic conferences: Western Hemisphere; Europe, Africa, and the Middle East; Asia and Australia.

International Civil Aviation Organization

ICAO is an organization of some 80 governments joined to promote civil aviation on a worldwide scale. This organization, established in 1944, has the following specific objectives:

1. To ensure the safe and orderly growth of international civil aviation throughout the world
2. To encourage the arts of aircraft design and operation for peaceful purposes
3. To encourage the development of airways, airports, and air navigation facilities for international civil aviation
4. To meet the needs of the people of the world for safe, regular, efficient, economical air transport
5. To encourage economic means to prevent unreasonable competition
6. To ensure that the rights of contracting countries are fully respected and that every contracting country has a fair opportunity to operate international airlines
7. To avoid discrimination between contracting countries
8. To promote safety on flight in international air navigation
9. To promote generally the development of all aspects of international civil aeronautics

DEVELOPMENTAL ORGANIZATIONS (INTERNATIONAL AND NATIONAL)

Financing is always a major problem in tourism development. Large financial organizations are willing to make developmental loans. Examples include the International

Bank for Reconstruction and Development, also known as the World Bank (U.S.), International Finance Corporation (U.S.), the OPEC Fund for International Development (Austria), African Development Bank (Côte d'Ivoire), East African Development Bank (Uganda), Inter-American Development Bank (U.S.), Caribbean Development Bank (Barbados), Asian Development Bank (Philippines), European Investment Bank (Luxembourg), European Development Fund (Belgium), European Bank for Reconstruction and Development (U.K.), Islamic Development Bank (Saudi Arabia), and the Arab Fund for Economic and Social Development (Kuwait). Examples of national organizations are FONATUR (Mexico) and EMBRATUR (Brazil). Further sources include governments of countries that want additional hotel development or other supply components and are willing to make low-interest loans or grants or offer other financial inducements for such types of development.

REGIONAL INTERNATIONAL ORGANIZATIONS

Organization for Economic Cooperation and Development

The Organization for Economic Cooperation and Development (OECD) was set up under a convention, signed in Paris on December 14, 1960, that provides that the OECD shall promote policies designed to (1) achieve the highest sustainable economic growth and employment and a rising standard of living in member countries while maintaining financial stability, and thus to contribute to the development of the world economy; (2) contribute to sound economic expansion in member as well as nonmember countries in the process of economic development; and (3) contribute to the expansion of world trade on a multilateral, nondiscriminatory basis in accordance with international obligations.

Members of OECD are Australia, Austria, Belgium, Canada, Denmark, Finland, France, Germany, Greece, Iceland, Ireland, Italy, Japan, Luxembourg, the Netherlands, New Zealand, Norway, Portugal, Spain, Sweden, Switzerland, Turkey, the United Kingdom, and the United States. OECD's Tourism Committee fosters development of tourism in member countries by studying the tourism problems confronting the governments and sectors of the economy in view of the large development of transit traffic in recent years, and by making recommendations based on its findings. The Tourism Committee actively seeks standard definitions and methods for compiling tourism statistics and issues an annual report entitled *Tourism Policy and International Tourism in OECD Member Countries.*

Pacific Asia Travel Association

The Pacific Asia Travel Association (PATA) represents 34 countries in the Pacific and Asia that have united to achieve a common goal—excellence in travel and tourism growth in this vast region. Its work has been to promote tourism through programs of research, development, education, and marketing. PATA has gained a reputation for outstanding accomplishment among similar world organizations. For this reason a more detailed look at this association's organization and activities is presented as a reading at the end of this chapter.

NATIONAL ORGANIZATIONS

United States Travel and Tourism Administration

The United States Travel and Tourism Administration (USTTA) serves as the nation's official government tourist office charged with developing tourism policy, promoting inbound tourism from abroad and stimulating travel within the United States. An agency of the Department of Commerce, USTTA seeks to develop tourism travel within the United States in an effort to spark economic growth and stability, improve international competitiveness, and expand international exchange earnings.

Established by the International Travel Act of 1961 as the United States Travel Service, the agency was given its present name under the National Tourism Policy Act of 1981. Eleven years later, on September 30, 1992, Congress passed the Tourism Policy and Export Promotion Act, which further amended the agency's mission.

The agency coordinates and negotiates international tourism policy, conducts statistical and market research, and directs a dynamic program of tourism trade development. USTTA's programs are designed to support U.S. states, cities, regions, and private industry, with special emphasis on small businesses, cultural and ethnic communities, and rural areas.

The agency's activities can range from making arrangements for members of the Japanese press to visit Yosemite National Park to negotiating with top officials from the Commonwealth of Independent States (the former Soviet Union) to increase two-way tourism, from organizing trade shows for travel agents to promoting U.S. tour packages to visitors from Brazil. USTTA also conducts training and marketing seminars to help business professionals in culturally diverse communities throughout this country develop tourism as well as to provide technical guidance to rural and urban community leaders looking to tourism as a basis for economic growth.

Supported by a 15-member industry-based Travel and Tourism Advisory Board and a coordinating interagency Tourism Policy Council, the agency directs its operations from headquarters in Washington, D.C. The agency also maintains offices in the 10 international markets that have the greatest potential for sending visitors to the United States from abroad.

The organization structure of USTTA is shown in Figure 4.1. A reading at the end of the chapter provides more information on USTTA.

Tourism Canada

Tourism Canada, the Canadian agency responsible for maintaining the orderly growth of tourism in Canada, has one of the most comprehensive tourism programs in the world and serves as a model that many other nations strive to equal. For this reason a detailed look at the scope, structure, and operations of Tourism Canada is presented as a reading at the end of the chapter.

Federal Aviation Administration

Numerous responsibilities for efficient and safe air travel are assigned to the Federal Aviation Administration (FAA). This U.S. government organization in the Department

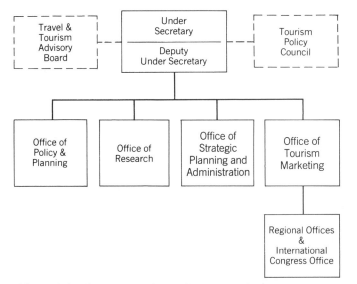

Figure 4.1   Organization Chart of the United States Travel and Tourism Administration

of Transportation formulates regulations and supervises or controls various aspects of airline and airport operations. Examples of these functions are air traffic control, air safety, flight standards, aviation engineering, airport administration districts, airways facilities, and certification of new aircraft. The FAA also examines and licenses pilots and flight engineers. The FAA is illustrative of governmental regulating bodies.

The U.S. Federal Aviation Administration certifies new jet aircraft as well as providing air traffic control, air safety, and other vital aviation regulations and services. (Photo courtesy of USAir)

Department of Transportation

The Department of Transportation has the federal authority to protect air travelers and to police industry practices. It has responsibility for in-flight smoking rules, charters, denied boarding compensation, baggage liability, handicapped traveler rules, passenger notices, computer reservations bias, and antitrust authority.

Other Government Agencies

Numerous other government agencies play an active role in tourism. The department of State issues passports, the Customs Service monitors international travel, Statistics Canada and the U.S. Bureau of Census compile travel statistics and data, the Interstate Commerce Commission regulates bus transportation, the National Maritime Commission deals with ships, the National Park Service and the Forest Service provide and administer many scenic attractions and facilities, the Bureau of Land Management is involved in several tourism initiatives, such as Back Country Byways, Adventures in the Past, and Watchable Wildlife, the Bureau of Reclamation administers over 300 recreation areas in 17 western states, and the Federal Highway Administration is involved in the National Scenic Byways program, with the objective of increasing tourism while preserving the environment. Others are the National Trust for Historic Preservation, National Marine Sanctuary Program, Tennessee Valley Authority, Army Corps of Engineers, Fish and Wildlife Service, and the Immigration and Naturalization Service.

Travel Industry Association of America

The Travel Industry Association of America (TIA) is the leading private organization that promotes tourism in the United States, and it serves as the voice for the diverse segments of the industry. Originally incorporated in 1941, TIA has grown from a small association of travel officials into a national nonprofit organization with a membership that now represents all components of the travel industry: airlines, attractions, hotels and motels, travel agents, tour operators and brokers, convention and visitors bureaus, state government travel offices, area and regional tourism organizations, food service establishments, intercity bus and rail lines, cruise lines, and other components of what is known today as the travel industry.

TIA has always worked to benefit the travel industry as a whole by coordinating private industry efforts toward common goals and encouraging and promoting travel within and to the United States. In recent years, the association has increasingly supported research and has become more involved with government policies that affect tourism. TIA's objectives are to (1) promote and facilitate travel to and within the United States, (2) bring cohesion to the travel industry and to increase its recognition by seeking and presenting unified positions of its components on matters of common concern; (3) promote a wider understanding of travel as a major U.S. industry that contributes substantially to the economic well being of the nation; (4) develop and implement programs beneficial to the travel supplier and consumer, which no single organization would be expected to carry out on its own; (5) encourage reciprocal travel between nations and oppose any restrictions on such travel; and (6) initiate and to cooperate with federal entities in developing and implementing programs, policies, and legislation that are responsive to the needs of the industry, and to intervene in those federal issues and initiatives that would directly affect the facilitation and promotion of travel to and within the United States.

TIA has also taken a leadership role in organizing industry councils to provide a unified voice for segments of the industry that enables them to address legislative issues of mutual concern, carry out educational programs unique to their industry components, and offer guidance in the development of TIA policies and programs. Each of the councils is described briefly.

The National Council of State Travel Directors (NCSTD) is the nationally recognized coordinating body of state and territorial government travel directors. The council provides a forum for its members to exchange ideas and information on issues common to state/territorial offices. It is through the NCSTD that newly appointed travel directors gain a thorough orientation of the industry and its importance to the U.S. economy. The council also affords state travel directors the opportunity to participate in educational programs offering, among others, information on destination travel promotion, marketing, communications, and press and public relations.

The National Council of Area and Regional Travel Organizations (CARTO) was formed in 1976 in response to those destination promotion organizations representing a specific area or region of the United States. This grass-roots group stands ready to respond to legislative calls to action and is involved in providing its members with educational, communications, and marketing vehicles by which they may better themselves and therefore strengthen their voice in the industry. CARTO members are (1) area or regional travel promotion organizations at the county or district level, (2) organizations that service areas larger than a city, (3) multicounty agencies or associations within a state, and (4) statewide or multistate organizations whose concern is the promotion of travel. CARTOGRAM, a quarterly communiqué, supplies CARTO members with current information relating specifically to area and regional travel promotion organizations and provides a vehicle for sharing the planning, development, and production of projects undertaken by individual CARTO members, marketing tips, and other items of interest to all CARTO members.

The National Council of Travel Attractions (NCTA) was organized in 1976 to unify the travel attractions, arts, and cultural institutions component within the association. This unification gives the NCTA the strength and resources necessary to assist its members by improving communications, providing marketing tools specifically geared to this segment, and assuring adequate representation to all levels of government. A quarterly newsletter keeps NCTA members abreast of council activities, relays TIA information pertinent to attractions, arts, and cultural institutions members, and provides research and marketing information specifically produced for them. Membership is representative of historic, cultural, scientific, entertainment, natural, and human-made attractions, as well as attraction-related service organizations.

The National Council of Urban Tourism Organizations (NCUTO) was formed in 1976 by TIA in conjunction with the International Association of Convention and Visitors Bureaus (IACVB) to ensure representation of cities in domestic tourism development. The council fulfills two very important functions for its urban destination promotion organization members. The council works to ensure that national policies and legislation reflect the significance of cities as integral components of the national tourism product, and it monitors trends and developments in the travel industry that affect U.S. urban destinations. Working closely with the Travel and Tourism Government Affairs Council, NCUTO members remain actively prepared to testify before House and Senate groups on legislative issues affecting the travel industry. Membership includes convention and visitors bureaus and chambers of commerce.

To further reflect its leadership role in the U.S. travel industry, TIA created and provides major support for the Travel and Tourism Government Affairs Council and the U.S. Travel Data Center. The Travel and Tourism Government Affairs Council was established on March 17, 1982, as an affiliate of the Travel Industry Association of America, to represent a unified industry viewpoint on legislative and regulatory issues of common concern in Washington, D.C. Other responsibilities of the council include representing the industry on goverment issues that have potentially broad impacts on the industry and maintaining contact with Congress and other federal entities to develop programs and policies that respond to government initiatives affecting the industry. The council also provides a range of professional services, such as research and statistical resources.

The council's membership is made up of a coalition of major national tourism and recreation organizations, including representatives from the sectors of transportation, accommodations, food services, travel agents, tour sales, and attractions. Literally thousands of travel industry companies are represented on the council through their membership in national travel industry organizations.

The U.S. Travel Data Center, the research affiliate of TIA, is the national nonprofit center for travel and tourism research. TIA established the center in 1972 for the purpose of "advancing the common interests of the travel industry and the public it serves by encouraging, sponsoring, and conducting statistical, economic, and scientific research concerning travel, the travel industry, and travel-related industries; by gathering, analyzing, publishing and disseminating the results of such research, and by cooperating with all federal, state, and other government agencies, and all organizations with similar purposes in pursuit of its objectives." Today, the U.S. Travel Data Center devotes its resources to measuring the economic impact of travel and monitoring changes in travel markets. The center has become the recognized source of current data used by business and government to develop tourism policies and marketing strategies.

REGIONAL ORGANIZATIONS

Regional tourism organizations have the goal of attracting tourists to their specific geographic region. There are several types of regional associations, such as multicountry, multistate, and multicounty. Examples range from PATA, which covers the Pacific region of the world, to groups such as Travel South, USA, which promotes travel in the southern states, to the West Michigan Tourist Association, which promotes only a region in Michigan—the northwestern section. Another multistate organization is Foremost West, which promotes tourism in Colorado, Utah, Arizona, New Mexico, Nevada, and Wyoming. Pennsylvania probably has more regional tourism organizations within its boundaries than any other state—59 tourist promotion agencies represent Pennsylvania's 67 counties.

STATE AND CITY ORGANIZATIONS

State

Traditionally, states have promoted tourism as a tool for economic development. In most states, a tourism office has been established by statute and charged with the orderly growth and development of the travel and tourism industry in the state. These offices conduct programs of information, advertising, publicity, and research relating to the recreational, scenic, historic, highway, and tourist attractions in the state at large.

Except for Colorado, each of the 50 states has an official government agency responsible for travel development and promotion. Four states—Alaska, Hawaii, South Carolina, and Texas—have two entities devoting funds and resources to tourism development. In Hawaii, responsibility for travel development rests primarily with a privately operated nonprofit organization, the Hawaii Visitors Bureau, that receives money from the state. The services performed and programs administered by the Hawaii Visitors Bureau are similar to those of the official state travel offices; thus all states are supporting tourism activity. The majority of states house their tourism offices in a Department of Economic Development (or Commerce).

Any review of state travel offices must start with the U.S. Travel Data Center's annual *Survey of State Travel Offices*. The report covering the fiscal year 1993–1994 published in December 1993 shows that the average U.S. state travel office had a budget of $7.6 million, a domestic advertising budget of $2.5 million, an international advertising budget of $438,000, and a staff of 36 people. The average term of the director was 3.7 years. Forty-three states operated approximately 372 state welcome centers, 47 states reported having one or more 800 numbers for travel information inquiries, 34 states

Auto tourists are provided with timely travel information and free phone reservation services at a state highway welcome station. (Photo courtesy of the Michigan Department of Transportation)

State governments have enacted many laws and regulations affecting their tourism. Examples are organizations for promotion, transportation, food products, restaurant inspection, licensing charter boats, and many others. (Photo courtesy of the Montana Travel Promotion Division)

reported using fax machines for fulfillment or information purposes, 25 states reported using voice mail for fulfillment or information purposes, 44 states directed their advertising to stimulate inquires, 47 states published a travel-related newsletter, 6 states operated out-of-state information centers within the United States, and 27 states operated many international tourist information centers. A list of official state travel offices is provided in Appendix A.

City

Most major cities have also recognized the importance of tourism and have established convention and visitors bureaus. In many smaller communities, the chambers of commerce perform this function. Larger cities now own the central convention facilities. A great deal of promotion and sales effort is then devoted to backing these facilities.

CONVENTION AND VISITORS BUREAUS   A convention and visitors bureau is a not-for-profit umbrella organization that represents a city or urban area in the solicitation and

The Jacob K. Javits Convention Center is a splendid facility in New York City. (Photo courtesy of the New York Division of Tourism)

servicing of all types of travelers to that city or area, whether they visit for business, pleasure, or both. It is the single entity that brings together the interests of city government, trade and civic associations, and individual "travel suppliers"—hotels, motels, restaurants, attractions, local transportation—in building outside visitor traffic to the area.

Urban tourism is an increasingly important source of income and employment in most metropolitan areas—and therefore warrants a coordinated and concerted effort to make it grow. This growth is best nurtured by the role a convention and visitors bureau can play in continually improving the scope and caliber of services the city provides to corporate and association meeting planners, to individual business travelers, and to leisure travelers.

The bureau is the city's liaison between potential visitors to the area and the businesses that will host them when they come. It acts as an information clearing-house, convention management consultant, and promotional agency for the city and often as a catalyst for urban development and renewal.

Typical services offered to meeting planners include orientation to the city, liaison between suppliers and meeting planners, and meeting management. The meetings and conventions market is huge. *Meetings and Conventions* magazine conducts a biannual survey of this market and reports that their readers planned over 1 million meetings in 1991, spent $35 billion, and generated more than 81 million attendees.[1]

INTERNATIONAL ASSOCIATION OF CONVENTION AND VISITORS BUREAUS   Most of the city convention and visitors bureaus belong to the International Association of

---

[1]Market Probe International, Inc., *The Meetings Market, 1992* (Secaucus, N.J.: Reed Travel Group, March 1992), p. 3.

Convention and Visitors Bureaus (IACVB), P.O. Box 758, Champaign, Illinois 61820. This group was founded in 1914 as the International Association of Convention Bureaus to promote sound professional practices in the solicitation and servicing of meetings and conventions. In 1974, the words "and Visitors" were added to IACB's name to reflect most bureaus' increasing involvement in the promotion of tourism. Since its inception, the association has taken a strong position of leadership in the travel industry. The organization has over 320 members in 25 countries. IACVB provides its members with numerous opportunities for professional dialogue and exchange of industry data on convention-holding organizations.

IACVB's convention data exchange is the most complete available on the association meetings market. It is an invaluable aid to the member bureau in maximizing its ability to serve convention holding organizations effectively and efficiently. Members receive regular reports from IACVB on future convention bookings in all member cities. Professional members also receive detailed postconvention reports on all meetings within the sphere of their marketing influence.

To encourage exchange between its members, IACVB holds an annual convention, organizes annual educational seminars leading to certificates in sales or bureau operations, organizes topical workshops and seminars, makes regular studies of convention industry trends, maintains a consulting service, and provides its members with government and industry liaison.

SUMMARY

The World Tourism Organization represents governmental tourist interests and aids in the world tourism development. Individual countries, states, and provinces have their own tourist promotion and development organizations that work to promote tourism in their area and coordinate tourism promotion with other groups. Most governments play a regulatory as well as developmental role in tourism through such agencies as civil aeronautics boards, federal aviation administrations, customs offices, passport bureaus, and so on. Government agencies typically compile research statistics and gather data. Governments also operate tourist enterprises such as airlines, national parks, and sometimes hotels and campgrounds.

About the Readings

There are three readings in this chapter. The first two deal with national tourism organizations: USTTA and Tourism Canada. The third covers PATA.

USTTA was established following the passage of the National Tourism Policy Act and replaced the United States Travel Service. This reading examines the role and position of USTTA in promoting tourism.

One of the world's best national tourism organizations is Tourism Canada. Although it operates on a large scale, its basic functions and structure become a model for any country aspiring to improve tourism. Note the breadth of concern of this organization and how its functions aid all facets of Canada's tourism.

Similarly recognized is the Pacific Asia Travel Association. This is a regional association within the world group. It is unique in having a worldwide network of PATA chapters. It is also respected for its outstanding conferences and travel marts that are highly successful and valuable for the attendees.

READING 4.1

United States Travel and Tourism Administration (USTTA)

OFFICE OF THE UNDER SECRETARY FOR TRAVEL AND TOURISM

USTTA is headed by the Under Secretary of Commerce for Travel and Tourism who reports directly to the Secretary of Commerce. The Under Secretary is responsible for the overall policies and direction of USTTA. The Under Secretary serves as Vice Chairman and Chairman pro tem of the Tourism Policy Council and is an ex-officio member of the Travel and Tourism Advisory Board. The Deputy Under Secretary oversees administration and management of the agency as directed by the Under Secretary. The Office of the Under Secretary also carries out USTTA's congressional and intergovernmental affairs and public affairs activities. The agency is divided into four offices: Tourism Marketing, Policy and Planning, Research, and Strategic Planning and Administration.

OFFICE OF TOURISM MARKETING

The Office of Tourism Marketing develops and implements USTTA's tourism trade development programs. The office helps city, state, regional and industry organizations and companies sell their tourism and tourism-related products and services in international markets which have the greatest potential for inbound tourism. Individuals and organizations are encouraged to participate in the wide range of cooperative promotional activities organized by USTTA. This office also administers the International Tourism Trade Development Financial Assistance Program and the Disaster Relief Financial Assistance Program.

USTTA conducts cooperative programs to stimulate inbound tourism, increase the export competitiveness of U.S. travel companies and strengthen the international trade position of the United States. USTTA's ongoing marketing activities are designed to:

- Educate and encourage U.S. public and private sector travel industry organizations and companies to enter markets abroad;
- Aid these organizations and companies to enter markets abroad;
- Coordinate marketing projects and programs with U.S. and international tourism interests;
- Stimulate consumer demand for travel to the U.S.;
- Provide U.S. travel information to prospective travelers and the travel trade;
- Encourage international travel agents, tour operators and wholesalers to sell the U.S. as a destination; and,
- Promote international attendance at U.S. congresses, conferences, conventions, workshops and seminars.

OFFICE OF POLICY AND PLANNING

The Office of Policy and Planning (OPP) develops and establishes broad policy initiatives to encourage travel to and within the United States in order to foster economic stability and growth of the U.S. travel industry. OPP identifies and addresses bilateral and multilateral issues which may create travel barriers affecting the nation's travel account.

The Office's staff supports the interagency Tourism Policy Council and subcommittees reporting to the Council. This Council can consult and coordinate tourism-related policies with other Federal agencies but has no jurisdiction over state, local or private sector policies.

The OPP works with other governmental policy offices, intergovernmental organizations and the travel trade. Its main activities are to:

- Develop domestic and international policies;
- Participate in bilateral and multilateral negotiations with other national governments to reduce or eliminate obstacles to international trade in tourism;
- Represent global U.S. trade in tourism policy interests, with particular emphasis on negotiating greater access for U.S. tourism companies;
- Designate a delegate for the Department of Commerce in U.S./Canada civic aviation negotiations;
- Serve as the directorate of U.S. World's Fairs and Expositions for the Bureau of International Expositions (BIE);
- Initiate the development of rural, cultural and environmental policy in tourism; and
- Extend information and awareness on tourism to educators and trainers.

OFFICE OF RESEARCH

The Office of Research tracks tourism for the agency as well as the industry. It is the chief source of international travel statistics in the United States. On an annual basis, the office responds to more than 8,000 external requests for research information, reports and technical assistance. The activities of the Research Office include:

- Gathering, analyzing and publishing international travel research results;
- Providing statistics to define the size and characteristics of existing and emerging markets;
- Assessing changes in demand and international market potential; and
- Guiding the development of marketing efforts and evaluating their effectiveness.

The following is a sample of Office of Research programs, surveys and reports:

In-Flight Survey of International Air Travelers

This program, conducted monthly on flights leaving the U.S., surveys international air passengers traveling to and from the United States. Over the course of a year, the survey reaches both U.S. citizens and non-resident visitors flying on over 60 different airlines. This program allows USTTA to profile the demographic and travel characteristics (including spending patterns) of international visitors to the U.S. as well as Americans traveling overseas.

International Visitor Arrival Statistics

The "Summary and Analysis of International Travel to the United States" is a report generated from an Immigration and Naturalization Service (INS) form which all overseas travelers entering this country must complete. The form gives USTTA and the industry the information necessary to track changes in international travel patterns to the U.S. The report compiles information on monthly arrivals by visitors for 90 countries.

U.S. International Air Travel Statistics

The Department of Transportation processes the data collected through another INS form. This data base logs origin and destination information for arriving and departing flights on U.S. international air travel by flag of carrier, port of entry, and international vs. U.S. citizens. This is the only source of information collected on the number of U.S. citizens traveling overseas.

Impact of International Travel on State Economies

Using information from the In-Flight Survey and other statistical data bases, USTTA is able to provide annual data on how much international visitors spend at the national, regional and state levels. This effort also provides data on jobs, payroll and taxes generated from international visitor expenditures.

OFFICE OF STRATEGIC PLANNING AND ADMINISTRATION

The Office of Strategic Planning and Administration (OSPA) advises USTTA offices on all administrative matters. It coordinates the planning for and preparation of all budget submissions required by the agency. The Office prepares operating and program budgets for USTTA units, and monitors the funds to ensure effective use is made of them and that established ceiling limits are not exceeded. The Office coordinates and processes all requests for training and personnel actions and all requirements for contracting and procurement requirements. OSPA is responsible for the development and implementation of information resources management and technology initiatives, and for providing technical support to facilitate the proper installation, use, and maintenance of hardware and software. OSPA is also responsible for coordinating the input and preparation of USTTA's strategic plan of operation.

CONTACTS

U.S. Travel and Tourism Administration
U.S. Department of Commerce, Washington, D.C. 20230

Office of the Under Secretary
Telephone: (202) 482-0136

Office of Tourism Marketing
Telephone: (202) 482-4752 Fax: (202) 482-2887

Office of Policy and Planning
Telephone: (202) 482-5211 Fax: (202) 482-2887

Office of Research
Telephone: (202) 482-4028 Fax: (202) 482-2887

Office of Strategic Planning and Administrtion
Telephone: (202) 482-3811 Fax: (202) 482-2887

READING 4.2

Tourism Canada

Tourism Canada supports and promotes the international competitiveness and excellence of the Canadian tourism industry. Tourism Canada focuses on the international marketplace, working with industry and with provinces and territories in cooperative activity to create satisfied customers. Tourism Canada provides leadership to the Canadian tourism industry through its advocacy activities, business services and international marketing.

POLICY AND PLANNING DIRECTORATE

The Policy and Planning Directorate [Figure 4.2], through its policy development and assessment activities, influences the direction and content of federal programs in support of the competitiveness of the Canadian tourism industry. The directorate supports meetings of federal, provincial and territorial Ministers and Deputy Ministers responsible for Tourism.

The 1990 Federal Tourism Policy identified key areas of policy focus: promoting a tax and regulatory system which supports tourism competitiveness, upgrading service through human resource development, increasing access to and within Canada through better transportation links, maintaining Canada's reputation for preserving an unspoiled environment, and improving industry prospects for securing financing. Within its advocacy role, the directorate conducts major industry consultations to identify issues of concern to industry and to establish the strategic framework within which action can be pursued by the federal government, tourism enterprises and national associations.

The directorate promotes and protects Canada's tourism interests internationally through membership in the World Tourism Organization, the OECD Tourism Committee, the Asia Pacific Economic Cooperation forum, and other organizations. It develops Canadian positions on the removal of impediments to tourism services and to the free movement of international tourists through the GATT and other trade agreements.

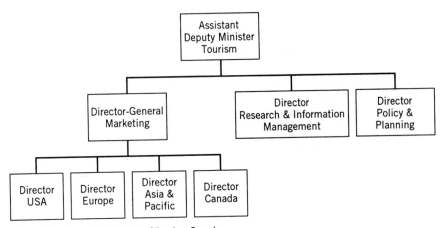

Figure 4.2 Organization Chart of Tourism Canada

RESEARCH AND INFORMATION MANAGEMENT DIRECTORATE

This directorate provides data, information and technical advice to facilitate decision-making by Tourism Canada, its partners and the tourism industry. The directorate concentrates technical expertise related to the collection, storage, retrieval, analysis and dissemination of data and information.

The directorate carries out a program of demand-driven research on Canada's tourism products, Canada's domestic and international markets, and issues facing the industry. Among the directorate's business services are surveys, economic analyses, intelligence-gathering, customer segmentation, advertising evaluations, conferences, provision of a documentation/reference centre and information publications. The directorate is also an international advocate for statistical standards relating to the scope of the tourism industry and to the credibility of tourism statistics.

The directorate also manages the information resources and technology of Tourism Canada, including the Tourism Canada local area network (LAN).

MARKETING BRANCH

The four marketing directorates—Canada, U.S.A., Europe and Asia/Pacific—provide information to the Canadian industry on export markets and on product opportunities.

The Canada Directorate delivers business services to help improve the Canadian tourism industry's international competitiveness. Its activities include: competitiveness assessments, the Business Opportunities Sourcing System database for tourism (BOSS-Tourism), studies and seminars, and sponsorship of Rendez-Vous Canada, the international travel marketplace held annually in Canada. The Canada Directorate also monitors and gathers intelligence on the Canadian outbound market.

The U.S.A., Europe and Asia/Pacific directorates deliver international marketing program activities targeting specific high-yield customer segments with the objective of increasing revenue to Canada. Programs benefit the Canadian tourism industry by:

- Establishing a single national image and message;
- Developing and expanding markets beyond natural growth levels; and
- Coordinating provincial, territorial and private sector initiatives to compete with other international destinations and avoid losing market share and export revenues.

The international marketing program provides multi-year strategic and operational plans for market and product development. Activities also include: advertising, public relations and promotions, travel trade development, direct marketing, management of coordination mechanisms (i.e., the Tourism Marketing Council, country program committees, Marketplaces Committee), leading the Canadian presence at major travel marketplaces in all international markets (i.e., World Travel Market, Kanata), and the negotiation and delivery of strategic alliances and marketing agreements.

RECENT KEY TOURISM CANADA ACCOMPLISHMENTS

- Managed the tourism sector consultations on Prosperity and developed the Government's response to the tourism industry's recommendations on improving Canada's international competitiveness as a tourism destination;
- Influenced the direction of Canadian government policies and programs for the benefit of

the tourism industry. Obtained adjustments to the administration of the Goods and Services Tax, transportation policies, customs processing, and wildlife and parks policy;

- Influenced the direction of international tourism policy in the areas of sustainable development and international tourism statistics, specifically:

   Developed a challenge statement for the tourism sector for the Globe '92 Environmental Conference and Trade Fair, developed a case-book of international industry/government best-practices to promote sustainable tourism, and proposed international indicators for sustainable tourism;

   Prepared new definitions of the tourism industry which will be adopted by the United Nations Statistical Commission;

- Signed a new five-year research agreement with the U.S. Travel and Tourism Administration to cost-share overseas travel market research of common interest;
- Supported Statistics Canada's core tourism data bases—the International and Canadian Travel Surveys—in partnership with provincial and territorial governments;
- Through the Tourism Industry Standards and Certification Commitee, developed over 40 occupational standards for the tourism industry. The tourism industry is now considering expanding this forum to create a National Tourism Human Resource Council which will develop national strategies for human resources development in the tourism industry;
- Signed multi-year international marketing partnership accords with the private sector tourism industry, including: a four-year cost-shared $8.1 million accord with Canadian Airlines International, a three-year $3.5 million accord with Saga Holidays, a five-year cost-shared $22 million accord with Air Canada, and a three-year cost-shared $2.8 million accord with Holland America Westours;
- Developed a $3 million Canadian Outbound advertising campaign after a pilot market analysis study of import-replacement;
- Facilitated the creation of a Federal/Provincial/Territorial Council of Tourism Ministers which will give expression to a Ministerial commitment to forge a renewed partnership in support of the industry's efforts to improve international competitiveness;
- Developed, tested and implemented a new computerized appointment scheduling system for Rendez-Vous Canada;
- Launched a new generation of federal/provincial/territorial agreements, providing $235 million for tourism initiatives over a five-year period. These include the Canada-Atlantic Provinces Cooperation Agreement on International Tourism Marketing, the first agreement to include a private sector representative on its Management Committee and to create a regional approach to tourism marketing through involvement of more than one province or territory; and,
- To help tourism businesses improve their international competitiveness:

   Developed and delivered a series of industry seminars on: better identifying and targeting emerging markets, serving and satisfying customers, marketing, and increasing knowledge of Tourism Canada objectives in support of the tourism industry;

   Produced publications that provide in-depth market and industry analyses, such as "Canadian Tourism Facts," "Industry Performance Report";

   Enhanced industry culture through the transfer of scientific and technical capabilities, i.e., Canadian Tourism Research Institute market forecasts, Tourism Canada's Labour Force analysis, and developed, with Statistics Canada, a Tourism Satellite Account within Canada's system of National Accounts.

READING 4.3

Pacific Asia Travel Association

Founded in Hawaii in 1951 to develop, promote, and facilitate travel to and among the destination areas in and bordering the Pacific Ocean, the Pacific Asia Travel Association (PATA) brings together governments, airline and steamship companies, hoteliers, tour operators, travel agents, and a wide range of other tourism-related organizations.

Members exchange ideas, seek solutions to problems, and participate in shaping the future of travel in Asia and the Pacific Area. Membership totals over 2,000 organizations worldwide. Since its founding, the Association has become an important source of accurate, up-to-date information for its members in the fields of marketing, development, research, education, and other travel-related activities. PATA's activities and long-range plans are examined and adjusted each year at the Association's Annual Conference.

COMMITTEES

Standing committees on management, marketing, development, education and research carry out the Association's ongoing program. PATA publishes a variety of textbooks, reports, studies, publicity materials, directories, and periodicals. The principal periodical is *PATA Travel News (PTN)*, a monthly journal with three regional editions and a combined circulation of about 58,000 copies. The main objective of PTN is to promote travel to and within the Pacific-Asia region. Eighty percent of the editorial content is feature material based on research and photographs obtained by the editors in the field.

PATA'S marketing efforts are directed to influencing more individuals to travel to and within the Pacific area. The committee also strives to improve marketing skills at the point of sale and in destination areas.

Development activities are geared to improving and advancing facilities and services in new destinations, increasing the handling capacity of existing destinations, and preserving their heritage and quality.

In research, PATA concentrates on the operation of an annual travel research conference, the publication of an annual Pacific Asia statistical report, and the conduct of cooperative research studies.

PATA CONFERENCES AND MARTS

Two of the more visible activities are the PATA Annual Conference and the PATA Travel Mart. The Conference, held in a member country each year, brings together up to 2,000 people who join in discussions of the current needs and problems of Pacific tourism and participate in the Association's annual business meeting. Sessions of the Conference offer selected themes to assist members in gaining a better working knowledge of tourism. The PATA Travel Marts bring to a single location the buyers and sellers of travel who meet to negotiate contracts for future business. An example would be a tour operator who meets with travel agents in countries which might supply travelers to participate in that company's tour offerings. Specifically, a tour operator in Australia would meet with travel agents from the United States who might be sending clients to Australia or a tour operator in the United States who is operating tours to Australia would be meeting with a ground operator (such as a local tour company) from Australia, who would supply a local tour for this tour group when it arrived in Sydney.

The work of the official PATA organization is greatly augmented by an international network of PATA Chapters. They comprise over 16,000 individual members worldwide. Chapter members meet regularly to learn about the various PATA destinations through educational presentations and out-of-country familiarization trips.

The PATA Secretariat is located in San Francisco, California. Division offices are located in Singapore to serve the Asia Region, in Sydney to serve the Pacific Region, in San Francisco for the Americas Division, and in Monaco for Europe.

Key Concepts

chambers of commerce
convention and visitors bureaus
Department of Transportation
Federal Aviation Administration
International Air Transport Association
International Association of Convention
  and Visitors Bureaus
multicountry
multicounty
multistate
Organization for Economic Cooperation
  and Development

Pacific Asia Travel Association
regulators
state tourism offices
Tourism Canada
Travel Industry Association of America
U.S. Travel and Tourism
  Administration
World Bank
World Tourism Organization
World Travel and Tourism Council

For Review and Discussion

1. If you were minister of tourism for American Samoa, what types of assistance might you request from WTO?
2. Referring to question 1, what aid would probably be forthcoming from the Pacific Asia Travel Association?
3. Tourism is the largest export industry in American Samoa. How might its minister of tourism's office be organized?
4. Do you feel that education should be one of the principal functions of any tourism organization? Why or why not?
5. If you were the president of a large international development bank such as FONATUR, what interest would you have in the World Travel and Tourism Council (WTTC)?
6. Speaking philosophically, why should a *national* government transportation department have any authority to regulate or control passenger fares or cargo rates?
7. Referring to question 6, should a *private* international organization such as the International Air Transport Association (IATA) have any authority to govern passenger airfares? If so, why?
8. Explain how the OECD, headquartered in Paris, could help develop tourism in its European member countries.

9. What main points would you expound if you were supporting next year's USTAA's budget on the floor of the U.S. House of Representatives?

10. Is there any need for a private national organization such as the Travel Industry Association of America (TIA)?

11. A state senator strongly opposes the budget for tourism promotion. "Let the hotels and transportation companies promote our state," he exclaims, "we need this money for better schools." As a member of the senate's tourism committee, what would your rebuttal be?

12. If you are a Canadian citizen, how do you feel about your tax dollars being spent on research jointly with the USTTA?

13. Is there a relationship between the work of the U.S. Travel and Tourism Administration and the U.S. trade deficit?

14. In what ways does a city's convention and visitors bureau function? How is this organization usually financed?

15. As the manager of a fine resort lodge, what arguments would you use with your board of directors to obtain financial support for your local and regional tourism promotion organization?

16. If you, as manager of a motor hotel, had joined a tourist association and placed an ad in their publication, how would you ascertain if such investments were paying off?

17. What attributes of Tourism Canada make it an outstanding national tourism organization?

Case Problems

1. A quite popular tourist state has fallen on hard times. The state government can no longer provide adequate funds for their state park system. The governor has proposed a "group maintainance" policy for the parks. This means that all the parks in a given part of the state would be managed on a "group" basis. Eliminated would be all of the individual local park managers. Several million people visit these parks each year—an important part of the state's tourism. What might be some feasible solutions to this unfortunate situation?

2. Two city council members are having an argument. A proposed budget item for tourist promotion for the coming fiscal year is being considered. One member endorses this item enthusiastically. The other states: "We don't benefit much for tourists' spending here because of the high leakage. I won't vote for this item; let's forget it." You are attending this meeting as a representative of the C&VB. How would you respond? If you felt that your declarations were not very convincing, what research should be conducted immediately to strengthen your pro-tourism position?

Selected References

Gartner, William C. "State Level Research: Typology and Direction." *Visions in Leisure and Business*, Vol. 10, No. 1 (Spring 1991), pp. 50–62.

Gartell, Richard B. *Destination Marketing for Convention and Visitor Bureaus.* Dubuque, Iowa: Kendall/Hunt, 1988.

Hawes, Douglas K., David T. Taylor, and Gary D. Hampe. "Destination Marketing by States." *Journal of Travel Research*, Vol. 30, No. 1 (Summer 1991), pp. 11–17.

National Tourism Policy Study: Ascertainment Phase. Washington, D.C.: U.S. Government Printing Office, 1977.

National Tourism Policy Study: Final Report. Washington, D.C.: U.S. Government Printing Office, 1978.

Organization for Economic Cooperation and Development. *Tourism Policy and International Tourism in OECD Member Countries.* Paris: OECD, 1992.

Owen, Charles. "Building a Relationship Between Government and Tourism." *Tourism Management*, Vol. 13, No. 4 (December 1992), pp. 358–362.

Pritchard, Garth. "Tourism Promotion Pays Off for the States." *Cornell Hotel and Restaurant Administration Quarterly*, Vol. 23, No. 1 (August 1982), pp. 48–57.

Ronkainen, Ilkka A., and Richard J. Farano. "United States Travel and Tourism Policy." *Journal of Travel Research*, Vol. 25, No. 4 (Spring 1987), pp. 2–8.

Sims, Steven L. "Educational Needs and Opportunities for Personnel in Convention and Visitor Bureaus." *Visions in Leisure and Business*, Vol. 9, No. 3 (Fall 1990), pp. 27–32.

U.S. Travel Data Center. *Survey of State Travel Offices: 1992–1993.* Washington, D.C.: The Center, 1993.

CHAPTER 5

Passenger Transportation

LEARNING OBJECTIVES

- Comprehend the importance of transportation in tourism.
- Understand the airline industry and its role in travel.
- Examine the domination of the automobile in travel.
- Learn about the role of rail and motorcoach travel.
- Study the cruise industry.

INTRODUCTION

Since the beginning of time, people have been traveling by various modes—from on foot to riding in a supersonic aircraft. Tourism and transportation are inexorably linked. As world tourism increases, additional demands will be placed on the transportation sectors (see Figure 5.1). Looking at the position occupied by the various modes of passenger transportation, one finds that air travel dominates long-distance and middle-distance tourism. The private automobile dominates for shorter trips and is the most popular means of travel for most domestic journeys. The auto is also very important in regional and international tourism. Rail travel now plays a more limited role than in the past. However, this mode could increase its market share, especially in Europe. The development of high-speed trains and the opening of the Channel Tunnel will increase rail traffic. Motorcoach transportation reaches many communities that are not served by any other public mode, but quantitatively, motorcoaches account for a very small percentage of vehicle miles. Cruises are becoming more popular and are the fastest-growing segment of tourism. However, this segment is still small quantitatively.

An increase in traffic due to world tourism growth puts pressure on transportation facilities which can have adverse effects. Situations in the world vary widely within regions, countries, states, and provinces. Also, variations exist between such areas. Even so, the problems seem to be the same all over the world. Those needing urgent attention of policymakers are as follows:

1. *Congestion.* Serious congestion affects most passenger transportation modes, particularly on roads and at airports during peak periods. In major cities there is the danger of reaching gridlock. Congestion means delays that are a serious waste of time and energy.
2. *Safety and security.* Ensuring safety and security in transportation is a basic requirement for tourism.
3. *Environment.* An increase in traffic may harm the environment if an area does not have the carrying capacity for additional tourists. Transportation planning must take

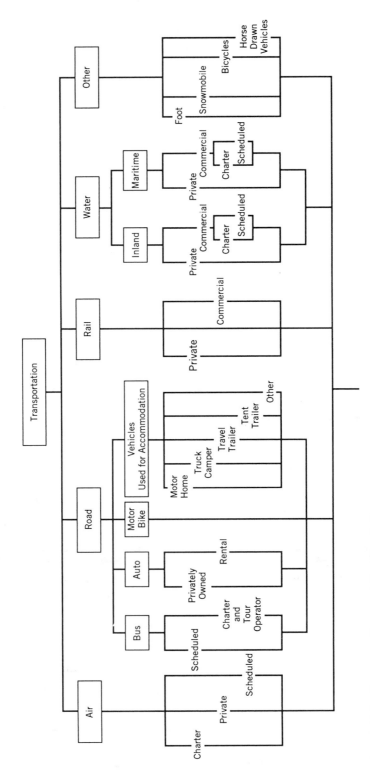

Figure 5.1 Passenger Transportation Structure

economic, social, cultural, and natural resources costs into account when designing expanded facilities.

4. *Seasonality.* Seasonal patterns of travel demand create overcrowding at certain times. Conversely, low occupancies and load factors will occur at other periods. At peak travel periods the problems of congestion, security, and the environment become much more severe.

All of these problems are challenges facing transportation planners. They have had and will continue to have an unfavorable impact on the perception that tourists have of their vacation experiences. Transportation problems have the potential of creating an unfavorable image of a tourist destination. As the modes of transportation are reviewed in this chapter, think about how they can be developed and integrated to serve the tourist in the best possible manner.

THE AIRLINE INDUSTRY

In the span of 50 years the airline industry has grown from infant to giant. The world's airline industry now carries over 1 billion passengers per year. In 1993 the U.S. airline industry launched over 19,800 flights a day, employed more than 537,000 people, carried 1.3 million people each day, and recorded $84 billion in revenues. Unfortunately, these impressive numbers have not resulted in impressive financial results. Over the four-year period 1990–1993 U.S. air carriers lost more than $12.8 billion. The nation's economy and the tourism industry need a healthy air transportation system. Without airline passengers, rental cars go unrented, hotel beds go unsold, and attractions go unvisited.

A typical late-model jet aircraft can carry hundreds of passengers in a minimum of time. Air travel is the most comfortable mode for mid- to long-distance trips. (Photo courtesy of Southwest Airlines)

The airlines have revolutionized travel, and the range and speed of jet travel has greatly expanded what tourists or business travelers could once accomplish with the equivalent time and funds at their disposal. Today, for example, it is possible to fly around the globe in less time than it takes to drive across the United States. The system is also incredibly efficient: you need only make one call to an airline or a travel agent and purchase a ticket to your desired destination; then all you have to do is go to the airport and check your bags through to the final destination. The logistics that make it happen are complex, but the system works well. For example, American Airlines serves over 1100 domestic pairs of points on its system, not including its connections with domestic airlines and worldwide airlines. Other airlines have similar structures and combine to make a total system that blankets the country.

Although the major advantage of air travel is speed, which results in more time for other activities, there are negative aspects for those who wish to travel by air. These include some people's fear of flying and lack of geographic accessibility—many communities in the country are not served by air transportation. An additional problem is the length of time spent getting to and from the airport. Frequently, this time exceeds that spent en route.

The $84 billion air transportation industry in the United States is dominated by a small number of large firms; the major carriers—America West, American, Continental, Delta, Northwest, Southwest, TWA, United, and US Air—all record over $1 billion in revenue annually. Those air carriers recording annual revenues of $100 million to $1 billion include Air Wisconsin, Alaska, Aloha, American Trans Air, Atlantic Southeast, Business Express, DHL Airways, Emery, Evergreen, Hawaiian, Horizon Air, Markair, Midwest Express, Southern Air, Sun Country, Tower, U.S. Air Shuttle, Westair, and World. There are about 127 regional airlines employing nearly 40,000. The top 10 airlines by revenue passenger miles are shown in Table 5.1. Despite the domination by the large carriers, there are a number of smaller firms in the market.

One of the best sources of data on the airline industry is an annual report entitled *Air Transport*, published by the Air Transport Association of America, 1301 Pennsylvania Avenue N.W., Washington, D.C. 20004. Another useful source of information on the

Table 5.1   Top Ten Airlines by Revenue Passenger Miles

Airline	Revenue Passenger Miles (thousands)
1 United	100,990,652
2 American	97,061,729
3 Delta	82,862,795
4 Northwest	58,032,588
5 Continental	39,858,526
6 USAir	35,220,452
7 Trans World	22,664,443
8 Southwest	16,715,742
9 America West	11,188,293
10 Alaska	5,447,426

Source: Air Transport Association, 1994.

airline industry is the Federal Aviation Administration. Consumer protection is the responsibility of the Department of Transportation.

With deregulation, the airline industry has undergone a dramatic change. However, because transportation by definition is an essential ingredient in travel and tourism, the future of the airline industry continues to remain linked to the performance of the entire tourism industry.

Although some additional changes will occur in the airline industry, there will be a slowing and finally an end to airline consolidation. There will be global affiliations. The popular frequent-flyer programs are expected to become more restrictive.

A 1993 survey of air travelers by the Gallup organization revealed that a record 77 percent of the entire adult population in the United States, had flown. One out of every three U.S. citizens flew during the past year. The survey found that 52 percent of airline trips during 1993 were for pleasure or other personal reasons, and 48 percent were for business.

Safety

U.S. air carriers providing scheduled service have an enviable safety record. Table 5.2 shows accident statistics and indicates that being in the air is one of the safest places you can be.

Growth

World and U.S. air transportation is expected to grow at a steady rate in the future. The stronger the world economy, the greater will be the rate of growth. An example of how the FAA expects U.S. carriers to grow is shown in Table 5.3, where forecasts are given to the year 2005.

Table 5.2   Safety: U.S. Air Carriers, Scheduled Service

	Departures (millions)	Fatal Accidents	Fatalities	Fatal Accidents per 100,000 Departures
1983	5.0	4	15	0.079
1984	5.4	1	4	0.018
1985	5.8	4	197	0.069
1986	6.4	2	5	0.016[a]
1987	6.6	4	231	0.046[a]
1988	6.7	3	285	0.030[a]
1989	6.6	8	131	0.012
1990	6.9	6	39	0.087
1991	6.8	4	62	0.059
1992	7.1	4	33	0.057
1993	7.2	1	1	0.014

[a]Sabotage-caused accidents are included in accidents and fatalities but not in the accident rates.
Source: National Transportation Safety Board and the Air Transport Association.

Table 5.3   FAA Aviation Forecasts: Commercial Air Carriers, 1994–2005

Year	Passengers (millions)	RPMs (billions)	Jet Aircraft	Departures (millions)
1994	490.4	499.8	4,363	6.4
1995	512.1	525.6	4,396	6.5
1996	533.8	552.1	4,519	6.6
1997	557.6	581.1	4,722	6.7
1998	580.6	609.5	4,876	6.9
1999	603.7	638.6	4,981	7.0
2000	626.3	667.2	5,069	7.2
2001	649.2	695.8	5,253	7.3
2002	672.2	725.0	5,447	7.5
2003	695.4	755.0	5,644	7.6
2004	718.6	785.5	5,858	7.8
2005	742.2	817.0	6,063	7.9

Source: Air Transport Association.

Taxes

A concern of the travel industry is the taxes being levied. Taxes result in higher prices, which dampen demand. The air sector has been hit particularly hard with new taxes. Table 5.4 shows the magnitude of these taxes.

The airline industry is supported by three major organizations. IATA and ICAO have already been discussed under international organizations; they are two key associations controlling air travel. The major U.S. organization is the Air Transport Association of America, or ATA.

Air Transport Association of America

In 1936, fourteen fledgling airlines met in Chicago to form the Air Transport Association (ATA) "to do all things tending to promote the betterment of airline business, and in general, to do everything in its power to best serve the interest and welfare of the members of this association and the public at large."

Table 5.4   Air Taxes: Fees Levied on the Flying Public

Tax	Amount	Average Annual Cost to Travelers
Ticket tax	10%	$4.376 billion
International departure tax	$6	217 million
Customs fee	$5	150 million
Immigration fee	$5	183 million
Agriculture fee	$2	70 million
Passenger facility charge	$3[a]	1.2 billion

Source: Air Transport Association.
[a]$3/airport, up to a maximum $12/roundtrip.

Today, from its headquarters in Washington, D.C., the ATA represents virtually all of the scheduled airlines in the United States, plus two associate member carriers in Canada, with responsibilities ranging from the continual improvement of safety to planning for the industry's role in national defense.

ATA is the meeting place where the airlines cooperate in noncompetitive areas to improve airline service, safety, and efficiency. The mission of the ATA is to support and assist its member carriers by promoting aviation safety, advocating industry positions, conducting designated industry-wide programs, and assuring public understanding.

Thus, while the carriers are intensely competitive among themselves and with other forms of transportation in their individual promotion of airline service for the traveling and shipping public, they are equally intense in their mutual cooperation on matters of industry-wide importance, such as safety, technological progress, and passenger service improvement.

The focus of ATA activities is to:

- Work effectively with the Federal Aviation Administration and other federal agencies on a broad range of matters affecting safety and operations
- Represent the industry before Congress and before agencies and regulatory bodies of federal, state, and local governments
- Conduct selected industrywide programs that can be carried out more efficiently on a common-industry basis

The following are examples of industrywide programs that meet important common needs of the ATA membership: Airline Scheduling Committees at high-density airports; Airline Clearing House; Airline Inventory Redistribution System (AIRS); Universal Air Travel Plan; and Scheduled Airline Traffic Offices, Overseas (SATOOS). Many of these programs serve both ATA member and nonmember airlines.

The ATA headquarters is located at 1301 Pennsylvania Avenue NW., Washington, D.C. 20004.

THE RAIL INDUSTRY

Rail passenger transportation, once the major mode of travel in the United States, reached its peak volume in 1920. Major railroads have wished to rid themselves of the passenger business, and today the survival of service (other than commuter service) depends largely on Amtrak. In Canada the situation has been similar and future rail travel depends on VIA Rail.

Outside North America, where passenger rail service is less limited, rail transportation assumes a more important role. Ultramodern railway systems with high-speed trains operate in many countries, handling passenger traffic in an economical and efficient manner and providing an alternative to air travel. France and Japan are well known for their high-speed trains. The Community of European Railways, which is made up of the national railways of the European Community members plus Austria and Switzerland, are planning a European high-speed network that could cut rail travel times in half. This development is likely to make rail travel much more competitive with air transportation.

Rail travel is preferred by many, because passengers are able to see the countryside and because of rail's impressive safety record. (Photo courtesy of Amtrak)

Amtrak

Amtrak is the marketing name for the National Railroad Passenger Corporation, an operating railroad corporation, the controlling stock of which is owned by the U.S. government through the U.S. Department of Transportation. Amtrak's business is providing rail passenger transportation in the major intercity markets of the United States. The National Railroad Passenger Corporation was established by the Rail Passenger Service Act of 1970.

Although it receives financial support from the federal government, Amtrak is not a government agency. It is a corporation structured and managed like other large businesses in the United States and competes with all other modes in the transportation marketplace.

Serving 45 states and 500 destinations, Amtrak carried more than 21.3 million intercity passengers 6.1 billion miles in 1992. In addition, Amtrak carried 20.3 million commuters on trains operated under contract. Amtrak employs 24,000 men and women. Approximately 22,000 of its employees are represented by 14 different labor organizations.

Amtrak was intended as an experiment to identify the importance of rail passenger service to a balanced national transportation system. A key for continued support of Amtrak in the mid-1970s was the dramatic impact of the oil embargo and recognition of the need for alternative forms of transportation.

- Total passengers miles have grown to 6.1 billion, up 27 percent since 1981 and *greater* than the passenger miles generated by all passenger railroads in 1970, prior to Amtrak's creation.

- In various transportation corridors, Amtrak is the dominant public carrier. Between Washington and New York, Amtrak is the largest carrier, with 43 percent of the combined air/rail passenger market. Substitution of Amtrak's Washington–New York service with airplanes would require an addition of 37 flights each day. Ridership on the Northeast Corridor exceeds 11 million passengers; ridership between Los Angeles and San Diego is now nearly 2 million passengers annually. Other key corridors: New York–Boston; Chicago–Milwaukee; Chicago–St. Louis; Chicago–Detroit; Portland–Seattle.
- Amtrak also operates for commuter agencies in Virginia, Maryland, Connecticut, Los Angeles, and San Francisco commuter service under contract. Commuter ridership now totals more than Amtrak's intercity ridership.

Amtrak has been providing national rail passenger service at less and less cost to the federal government. Congress grew increasingly alarmed at the high cost of operating the Amtrak system during the 1970s. By 1981, operating grants had reached nearly $700 million and total support (including amounts for capital investment) for Amtrak has reached $900 million. Since, then, under the leadership of Graham Claytor, Amtrak has succeeded in providing enhanced service at reduced federal cost.

Amtrak is now covering 79 percent of its operating costs with self-generated revenue, up from just 48 percent in 1981. By contrast, Canada's VIA Rail covers only 30 percent of its own costs.

One of Amtrak's major problems is that of raising capital to expand its passenger car fleet, because Amtrak has only limited capacity and pales in comparison to rail systems in other countries. Despite this limitation, Amtrak is planning for the future.

Amtrak has embarked on an ambitious high-speed rail improvement program to reduce the travel time between New York and Boston to under three hours. The project marks the first new high-speed rail initiative in this country since the Northeast Corridor Improvement Project, initiated in 1976.

Amtrak is testing the Swedish X2000 high-speed train on the Northeast Corridor to determine customer response to various levels of service and comfort. Designs for a new generation of high-speed passenger equipment will be developed, followed by procurement of some 26 new train sets for use on the fully electrified Northeast Corridor.

A less-than-three-hour schedule between New York and Boston is projected to generate as many as 3 million new passengers and correspondingly, to reduce highway and airport congestion in the densely populated Northeast. The project is a pilot for the incremental high-speed improvement of other rail corridors across the nation on existing railroads.

In addition to high-speed rail improvements, Amtrak is also preparing its long-distance trains for the future. Early in fiscal year 1993, Amtrak placed its first order for 50 Viewliner sleeping cars, which will replace a portion of the 40-year-old Heritage cars used on eastern long-distance routes. Nearly 300 Viewliners ultimately will be ordered for use on most of Amtrak's eastern overnight trains, providing significant additional capacity as well as a new look for the next century. In addition, with delivery of Amtrak's 140 new bilevel Superliner cars, plans are under way for conversion of *Auto Train*, the *Capitol Limited,* and the *City of New Orleans* from the aging Heritage Fleet to these state-of-the-art cars.

Because Amtrak is subsidized, suppliers of the other modes of transportation (especialy bus) feel that Amtrak is attracting its customers with taxpayer assistance. However, even with the controversy, Congress is likely to see that Amtrak remains in business for the foreseeable future.

THE MOTORCOACH INDUSTRY

The fares and routes of the intercity bus industry were closely regulated by the Interstate Commerce Commission (ICC) until 1982, when deregulation eliminated many of the most restrictive regulations while maintaining a regulatory framework for the industry.

In 1987 two very significant events took place in the intercity bus industry. First, Greyhound Lines, Inc., was sold by the Greyhound Corporation in Phoenix, Arizona, to a Dallas firm whose primary business was leasing intercity buses to other bus carriers. Second, this "new" Greyhound Lines bought Trailways Lines, Inc.

Consequently, the intercity route passenger bus market is highly concentrated, with Greyhound the only company with a national network. Greyhound has experienced turbulent times, which included a strike, downsizing, and Chapter 11 bankruptcy. Greyhound is a different company than it was a few years ago in 1989. For example, they now operate a fleet that is about 35 percent smaller than 1989, and regular route miles have been reduced by over 30 percent. In addition, they have virtually moved out of the charter bus business. In 1989 they operated about 45 million charter bus miles, while in 1992 they operated about 1 million. They are now a leaner and profitable company. Greyhound handled approximately 15.1 million passengers, who generated about 5.9 billion passenger miles in 1992. They produced a load factor of 58 percent.

Intercity bus passengers are largely lower-income nonbusiness travelers who are very price sensitive. Intercity bus service has shrunk to a minor transportation alterna-

The motorcoach industry is the most pervasive form of intercity public transportation in the United States. Motorcoaches serve more than 15,000 communities and provide both scheduled and charter service. (Photo courtesy of the National Tour Association)

tive because of increased automobile ownership availability and aggressive airline pricing. Bus travel is characterized by more ridership to and from rural areas and small towns than either the air or rail modes. Greyhound's average trip length is 387 miles, while the average trip on other bus carriers is estimated at 130 miles. A domestic airline trip averages 793 miles. The bus industry has lower average ticket revenues than those of other modes. Greyhound's average ticket price in 1992 was $35.95.

Greyhound has developed a bus passenger reservation system, so for the first time in history customers have the ability to reserve seats on Greyhound. The new system will serve as a powerful marketing tool.

Although Greyhound attracts the attention, the intercity bus industry is not a one-company industry but a small-business industry with a great deal of flexibility. There are approximately 110 regional carriers providing regular route passenger bus service. In 1992 there were 4603 intercity passenger carriers with active ICC authority. The overwhelming number of these were charter and tour bus companies. Many bus companies focus primarily or exclusively on charter, tour, or commuter operations and have found a niche in the market where they can prosper. There is substitutability in some aspects of bus service. Buses used in charter and tour services can be switched to regular route service, if needed.

Bus industry advocates believe that this form of transportation is particularly well suited to certain needs of tourism, especially one-way trips of 150 miles or less. The increase in foreign visitors, who frequently are bus travelers, has benefited the industry. However, one of the problems that bus companies have faced over the years is the public's perception and attitude toward bus travel; that is, bus travel has had a largely negative image. Moreover, buses are perceived as being slow and uncomfortable, even though their fares are inexpensive and they allow the passenger to see the countryside. In response, the bus industry has done a great deal to upgrade its product, putting in rest rooms, heating and air-conditioning controls, reclining seats, and tinted glass windows and building modern terminals.

Bus Organizations

The American Bus Association (ABA) is the national organization of the intercity bus industry and serves as the prime source of industry statistics. ABA members are bus operating companies, other travel industry participants, and others associated with providing bus transportation. Bus operating companies include carriers throughout the United States and Canada. Collectively, these carriers provide more than 90 percent of all intercity bus travel in the United States and Canada. The travel industry category includes hotel/motel chains and properties, food service organizations, attractions and theme parks, and local, state, regional, and federal promotion organizations interested in working with bus companies to expand tourism in North America. Total membership is 3000.

The United Bus Owners of America (UBOA) serves intercity bus owners. With a membership of 1000 UBOA members own all types of bus companies, ranging from the smallest to the largest. Bus manufacturers and other industry suppliers are also members. Major programs of the association are safety, insurance, credit, computer services, resident agent services, meetings, lobbying, and communications.

In 1984 the National Tour Association (NTA) and UBOA announced a joint agreement between the two trade associations for the exchange of certain membership benefits because the relationship between bus companies and tour operators are many, the most fundamental being the use of the motorcoach by both parties for tour and charter business. Many tour operators have become bus owners, and bus owners have opened tour and charter departments. UBOA members benefit from the tour expertise of NTA members, and NTA tour operator members gain valuable insights into the bus industry.

THE AUTOMOBILE

Most of the travel in the world takes place in the automobile. In the United States the U.S. Travel Data Center, in its 1993 *Travel Market Report,* using full-year results from the National Travel Survey reports that 75 percent of the person-trips are made by auto (includes truck and RV) compared to 21 percent by air, 2 percent by bus, and 1 percent by train. Affordability, flexibility, and convenience make auto travel the most popular mode of transportation all over the world. Since passenger car registrations continue to increase worldwide, motor vehicles will continue to be the dominant mode of transportation for decades to come.

All studies show the automobile's dominance, whether the study is from the Air Transport Association, the Highway Administration, the Census Bureau, or the *National Travel Survey* of the U.S. Travel Data Center. There is no doubt that the great bulk of intercity transportation of passengers is by automobile. Data also indicate that this has been constant for several decades. The energy crisis made some inroads into auto travel, causing some shifts to common carriers, but these inroads have been small. However, because of the great dominance of the automobile in travel, only a small shift in automobile travel to the common carriers can result in enormous increases in the carriers' business.

The interstate highway system significantly encouraged vacation travel and especially encouraged long-distance travel. It made automobile travel much faster and more comfortable. A major concern of tourism groups today is the maintenance of the highway network. There is growing evidence that the highway system is in need of substantial repair to prevent it from suffering further deterioration. A poor road system costs the individual driver, the bus operator, and other users additional funds in terms of increased fuel use and vehicle maintenance, and the knowledge that a highway is in poor condition may cause the traveler to select another destination to avoid the problem.

On the whole, people's attitudes are very favorable toward travel by automobile. The key feature of the automobile is immediate accessibility and convenience. The automobile owner can leave from his or her own doorstep at any hour of the day or night and travel by a chosen route to a chosen destination. When two or more persons travel by automobile, the per person cost of travel is more favorable than it is with the other transportation modes. Air is the primary competitor to the automobile when it comes to travel, especially for long trips. The advantages of air travel—the quality of service, speed, and comfort—must be weighed by travelers against the automobile's advantages of price and accessibility.

Recreation Vehicles

The recreation vehicle (RV) segment deserves special mention, as according to the Recreation Vehicle Industry Association (RVIA), over 25 million people use RVs in the

United States. While the RV market has had its ups and downs because of events such as the energy crisis, the recession, and the Gulf War, the market for recreation vehicles is very much alive and its long-term prospects are positive. Overall, the RV industry employs about 32,000 production workers, with payrolls of over $660 million and retail sales of between $7 and $8 billion a year. When examining who buys RVs, one finds that the typical RV buyer is a 49-year-old married homeowner.

Highways and Scenic Byways

Automobile travel in the United States will receive a boost from the Highways and Scenic Byways program. The Intermodal Surface Transportation Efficiency Act of 1991 established the Scenic Byways Program, which provides $80 million over six years for carrying out eligible programs on designated scenic byways. According to the Federal Highway Administration, the United States has 4 million miles of roads and approximately 51,500 have been designated or are potential scenic byways. All 50 states have existing scenic byways, with an average of nine routes per state.

Rental Cars

An important aspect of automobile travel is the rental car industry, whose growth has been paralleling or exceeding the growth in air travel. While there is no question about the rental car business having heavy use by businesses, it also has substantial vacation use and frequent combination trip use.

According to Somerset Waters in his *Travel Industry Yearbook,* the rental car industry grosses around $14 billion. There are an estimated 5000 car rental companies in the United States operating at 26,000 locations. The top 12 companies (see Table 5.5) offer cars at about 7000 locations in the United States. The other locations are typically car dealers and service stations.

Table 5.5   U.S. Rental Car Companies Ranked by Number of Cars[a]

	Worldwide Locations	Number of Vehicles
Hertz	5,500	400,000
Avis	4,800	400,000
National	4,600	276,229
Budget	3,477	250,000
Alamo	118	127,000
Enterprise	1,087	110,000
Dollar	855	97,839
American International	970	81,000
Thrifty	650	45,000
General	60	18,000
Payless	187	7,500
Advantage	60	5,000

[a]Some figures are estimates.
Source: Corporate Travel.

Rental car companies provide essential ground transportation services. These very often complement air travel. Rental cars are found at or near larger airports all over the world. (Photo courtesy of the Hertz Corporation)

A survey conducted by the U.S. Travel Data Center found that 17 percent of the U.S. adult population, or approximately 32 million people, use a rental car over a 12-month period. The typical renter is a male, aged 35 to 44, a resident of the western United States, with a family income of $40,000.

Major companies in the rental car business are Hertz, Avis, National, and Budget, which dominate the airport locations and claim the majority of the market—about 80 percent. The big four are being challenged by a host of small companies, including Alamo, Dollar, Thrifty, American International, and others.

Many of the auto rental systems are international and have services in virtually every tourist destination area in the world. These companies arrange for the purchase, lease, or rental of automobiles domestically and abroad. Companies representative of this type of organization are Americar Rental Systems; Auto-Europe, Inc.; Europcar; Hertz International, Ltd.; The Kemwell Group, Inc.; InterRent; and Open Road International, Inc.

Taxi and Limousine Service

Taxi and limousine companies play an exceedingly important part in tourism. Local transportation companies perform vital services for airlines in servicing departing and arriving passengers as well as providing similar services for bus, rail, and shipping lines. Businesspersons and tourists alike would have a difficult time getting from place to place if these services were not available. Inclines and aerial trams serve as a form of taxi service and are of a special interest to visitors in scenic tourist destination areas as a form of recreation and sightseeing.

The International Taxicab and Livery Association (TLA) in Kensington, Maryland, is the major taxicab association. It was formed in 1966 by a merger of the National

Airports are primary locations for car rental companies. Vans commonly carry rental car customers from airport doors to the rental car site. (Photo courtesy of National Car Rental)

Association of Taxicab Owners, the Cab Research Bureau, and the American Taxicab Association. ITA has 700 members who are fleet taxicab owners operating 60,000 vehicles. The association sponsors an annual convention and trade show, is involved with political action, and publishes *Taxi and Livery Management*, quarterly.

The National Limousine Association is located in Washington, D.C. The association was founded in 1985, has 800 members, is made up of limousine owners and operators, and limousine manufacturers and suppliers to the industry. It seeks to promote and advance industry professionalism, the common interests of members, and the use of limousines. It monitors legislation, sponsors seminars of safety, regulatory issues, and management; compiles statistics, and offers insurance plans.

Oil Companies

Oil companies the world over have a very important stake in automobile tourism and thus are organized in many ways to serve the wants and needs of travelers. In the United States, many of the major oil companies publish road maps as a touring service. Some companies have organized motor clubs, such as the American Oil Motor Club, which provides travel information and routing services for its members, among other services. An example of special travel services is the *Mobil Travel Guide*, which has seven regional editions and lists over 20,000 hotels, motels, and restaurants. These accommodations are rated from one to five stars in quality and indicate the prices of typical meals and accommodations to suit every budget. Each *Guide* also contains a variety of special sightseeing tours with easy-to-follow maps.

Automobile Clubs and Organizations

The American Automobile Association (AAA) is the world's largest single membership travel group, with a membership of over 34 million in the United States and Canada. This organization promotes travel in several different forms among its members, including auto travel as a primary form of transportation. It also operates worldwide travel services similar to those provided by a travel agency or tour company. The AAA Travel Department also provides travel services for nonmembers and is thus competitive with other tour companies and retail travel agencies. This additional service gives the club a certain glamour and status in the community, and nonmembers who are brought into the club office through the travel service become prospects for new members in the automobile club.

The AAA provides insurance protection to motorists through its various state and city affiliate organizations (such as the Automobile Club of Michigan), publishes travel maps and *Tour Books,* and has a national touring board as well as a national touring bureau staff. The principal function of the *Tour Books* is to describe the history, attractions, points of interest, and accommodations in hotels, resorts, motels, and restaurants that have been inspected and approved by AAA field representatives. All accommodations listed have been selected on the basis of a satisfactory report submitted by the AAA field representative.

An organization of wider geographic membership is the World Touring and Automobile Organization, with headquarters in London, England. Other organizations of a similar nature are the International Road Federation of Washington, D.C.; the Pan American Highway Congress, Washington, D.C.; Inter-American Federation of Automobile Clubs, Buenos Aires; and the International Automobile Federation, with headquarters at Paris.

THE CRUISE INDUSTRY

Cruising is currently the fastest-growing segment of the travel industry. It is experiencing a surge of growth in both passengers and ship and passenger capacity. Cruise lines are expanding their fleets, adding new amenities and new ports of call.

Within the last 10 years, the demand for cruising has tripled. In 1970, an estimated 500,000 people took cruises; in 1991 over 4 million people cruised. From 1980 to 1990 the cruise industry has grown at a compounded 9.8 percent rate. The cruise industry has tripled in size every 10 years for the last two decades.

Although ships have been a means of transportation since early times, the cruise industry is young. Its purpose is really to provide a resort experience rather than point-to-point transportation. Since 1970 an estimated 40 million passengers have taken a deep-water cruise of three or more days. About 50 percent of the total passengers have been generated in the past five years.

The cruise industry's performance and satisfaction are the pacesetter for the rest of

CLIA MEMBER LINES

Admiral Cruises	Norwegian Cruise Lines
American Hawaii Cruises	Ocean Cruise Lines
Carnival Cruise Lines	Oceanic Cruises
Chandris Cruises	Paquet French Cruises
Club Med	Premier Cruise Lines
Commodore Cruise Line	Princess Cruises
Costa Cruises	Regency Cruises
Crown Cruise Line	Renaissance Cruises
Crystal Cruises	Royal Caribbean Cruise Line
Cunard Line	Royal Cruise Line
Delta Queen Steamboat Co.	Royal Viking Line
Diamond Cruise	Seabourn Cruise Line
Dolphin Cruise Line	Seawind Cruise Line
Dolphin Hellas Cruises	Seven Seas Cruise Line
Epirotiki Lines	Sun Line Cruises
Holland America Lines	Windstar Cruises
Majesty Cruise Line	World Explorer Cruises

the travel industry. No other vacation category can touch a cruise for product satisfaction and repeat business. Of those who have cruised in the last five years, the average number of cruises per person is 2.4 or one cruise every two years.

Growth has affected not only passenger and ship capacity, but the ports of embarkation as well. In the last 20 years, cruise traffic in Miami has more than doubled, with 24 ships sailing regularly from the city's modern port facilities. Other ports experiencing substantial growth include Port Canaveral, Tampa, New Orleans, Palm Beach, Port Everglades, San Diego, Los Angeles, San Juan, and Vancouver.

Future growth of the cruise industry is expected. New ships are coming on line and the market potential is large. During the next five years Cruise Lines International Association (CLIA) estimates that cruises will be a $50 billion industry. By the year 2000, they project that 10 million passengers a year will cruise. Taking a cruise is a dream of nearly 60 percent of all adults, with the highest interest being exhibited by "baby boomers." One of the obstacles to stronger growth is the fact that only 5 to 6 percent of the U.S. population has ever taken a cruise; consequently, there is not enough awareness of cruising when vacation alternatives are being weighed. Another obstacle is that inaccurate price perceptions exist. Many perceive cruising as being more expensive than it really is.

Trends in the cruise industry show that the average length of a cruise has dropped dramatically as three- and five-day cruises increase in popularity. The demographics of the cruise market has also been changing—shifting rapidly from a predominately older population to one that is younger, married, and includes families vacationing with children.

Cruise capacity will continue to increase. Based on CLIA information, 36 ships are

Steamboat travel is not only a novelty for most passengers but also provides beautiful scenery, shore excursions, good food, and entertainment. (Photo courtesy of the Delta Queen Steamboat Company)

contracted for, scheduled to be refurbished, or will be added to the North American fleet by 1995. The Caribbean continues to be the leading destination for capacity placement. Other leading markets are western Mexico, Alaska, the Mediterranean, Trans-Panama Canal, Europe, Bermuda, and Hawaii.

While CLIA members (see the box) represent 97 percent of the North American cruise market and 90 percent of the ships, the world cruise fleet is supplemented by freighter cruises, river cruises, yachts, ferries, and charters. There are about 80 freighters that provide accommodations for a limited number of passengers, such as 6 to 12. Freighter cruises tend to last a long time, go to unknown parts, have schedules that can change rapidly, and be moderately priced. They appeal to the more adventurous traveler. River cruises are popular in the United States on the Mississippi River on the *Delta Queen* and *Mississippi Queen,* in Egypt on the Nile, in Brazil on the Amazon, and in Europe on the Danube and Rhine, just to mention a few. Riverboat gambling is a recent addition on the Mississippi. Barge and canal trips are also popular in many places.

Cruise Lines International Association

Cruise Lines International Association (CLIA) is a marketing and promotional trade organization comprised of 34 of the major cruise lines serving North America, representing over 129 ships (see the box). CLIA was formed in 1975 out of a need for the cruise industry to develop a vehicle to promote the general concept of cruising. CLIA exists to educate, train, promote, and explain the value, desirability, and profitability of the cruise product.

When, in mid-1984, the Federal Maritime Commission consolidated other industry organizations into CLIA, it became the sole marketing organization of the cruise industry. CLIA represents almost 97 percent of the cruise industry, and more than 20,000 travel agents are affiliated with CLIA and display the CLIA seal, which identifies them as authorities on cruise vacations. The CLIA headquarters is located at 500 Fifth Avenue, Suite 1407, New York, N.Y. 10110.

SUMMARY

Transportation services and facilities are an integral component of tourism. In fact, the success of practically all forms of travel depends on adequate transportation. Travel by air dominates long- and middle-distance travel in the United States. But private automobiles carry the bulk (about 80 percent) of all travelers on short trips. Autos are also very important on long and international trips. Rental cars are popular, as they supplement air travel. Rail travel in the United States has declined substantially since the 1950s but is still important in commuting and longer-haul traffic. Motorcoach transportation is available at far more places than either air or rail, but it constitutes a rather small percentage of total vehicle miles. Vacationing on cruise ships has become the fastest-growing segment of the U.S. travel industry. Passenger numbers have increased sixfold in the past 20 years. New and refurbished cruise ships are appearing regularly.

Associations and groups of passenger carriers are important to their well-being and growth. Some of the most important are Air Transport Association of America, Amtrak, VIA Rail, American Bus Association, United Bus Owners of America, American Automobile Association (affiliated with the Canadian Automobile Association), World Touring and Automobile Association, Recreation Vehicle Industry Association, International Taxicab and Livery Association, National Limousine Association, and the Cruise Lines International Association.

Increases in almost all forms of tourism automatically boost passenger traffic, sometimes creating problems. Congestion can be especially bad on streets and roads and at airport terminals. Safety and security are basic requirements, and successful tourism depends on these factors. The environment will be affected by any form of transportation. Careful planning and increased awareness and preventative measures are needed to minimize such undesirable effects.

Long-term projections show increases in the demand for transportation. However, severe financial losses in the U.S. airline industry during recent years is cause for concern. A healthy airline industry is essential for long-term success. Increased taxes on this industry are having an adverse effect. Hopefully, these can be mitigated in time. Rail travel will probably increase in Europe and in other areas where high-speed trains are coming into use.

Key Concepts

airline industry	Amtrak
Air Transport Association	associations and groups
American Automobile Association	automobile
American Bus Association	cruise lines

highways and scenic byways program
Interstate Commerce Commission
motorcoaches
National Tour Asssociation
oil companies
"open skies" agreements
rail travel

recreational vehicles
rental cars
safety and security
taxes
taxi and limousine service
transportation (importance of)
United Bus Owners of America

For Review and Discussion

1. Explain why air travel now dominates long- and middle-distance travel.
2. What were the main reasons that rail passenger transportation declined in the United States after 1950?
3. Identify the social and economic factors that would bring about a resurgence in motorcoach travel.
4. Describe the principal appeals of cruising.
5. Why is the cruise market expected to continue its extraordinary growth pattern?
6. What might be at least a partial solution to the problem of automobile congestion at major airports?
7. Similarly, make clear your ideas for alleviating flight arrival and departure congestion.
8. If you knew in advance that you would have a long drive through heavy traffic to reach the airport, a wait in line for 20 minutes at the airline departure desk, and that your plane would be remaining on the runway for 30 minutes before taking off, would you still make the pleasure trip?
9. Evaluate the importance of safety and security in all forms of travel. What is the safest mode of passenger transportation?
10. Taking each mode of transportation, what specifically can be done to minimize damage to the environment?
11. If you were vice-president for marketing of an airline, what programs would you undertake to even out peaks and valleys in demand?

Case Problems

1. The Rotary Club program chairman has asked you to give a talk on the advantages of cruises. He has also hinted that the club might be interested in taking a group cruise with their wives and children. What would you include in your talk?
2. Air transportation is truly a global industry. However, future growth in world demand is being impeded by many nations which have enacted various air regulations and restrictive laws. A beginning toward a "new world order" of global competition and interconnectedness has appeared. The first "open skies" agreement has now been established between the United States and the Netherlands. This agreement, dubbed "Open Skies I," signals the beginning of what could become global. The agreement abolishes all legal and diplomatical environments as well as all other trade barriers that impede airline efficiency. It also encourages competition.

The Open Skies I accord completely deregulates air services between the two countries. Should such pacts become a reality on a much wider scale, how would this affect demand for travel on the world's 140 airlines? Explain and give several examples.

Selected References

Air Transportation Association of America. *Air Transport 1993: The Annual Report of the U.S. Scheduled Airline Industry.* Washington, D.C.: ATA, 1994.

Air Transportation Association of America. *Air Travel Survey: 1990.* Washington, D.C.: ATA, 1990.

Air Transportation Association of America. *FAA Aviation Forecasts: Fiscal Years 1990–2001.* Springfield, Va.: National Technical Information Service, 1990.

Center for Transportation Information. *U.S. International Air Travel Statistics.* Cambridge, Mass.: CTI, monthly, quarterly, annual.

Christopher, John. *Airline Deregulation in Canada.* Springfield, Va.: National Technical Information Service, 1989.

Cunningham, Lawrence F., and Kenneth Thompson. "The Intercity Bus Tour Market: A Comparison Between Inquirers and Purchasers." *Journal of Travel Research,* Vol. 25, No. 2 (Fall 1986), pp. 8–12.

Dean, Christopher J. "Travel by Excursion Coach in the United Kingdom." *Journal of Travel Research,* Vol. 31, No. 4 (Spring 1993), pp. 59–65.

Dennis, Nigel. "The North American Air Travel Market." *Travel and Tourism Analyst,* No. 1 (1991), pp. 5–22.

Fockler, Shirley. "The U.S. Domestic Airline Industry." *Travel and Tourism Analyst,* No. 3 (1991), pp. 5–21.

Fujii, Edwin, Eric Im, and James Mak. "Airport Expansion, Direct Flights, and Consumers Choice of Travel Destinations: The Case of Hawaii's Neighbor Islands." *Journal of Travel Research,* Vol. 30, No. 3 (Winter 1992), pp. 38–43.

Hall, J. Anthony, and Ron Braithwaite. "Caribbean Cruise Tourism: A Business of Transnational Partnerships." *Tourism Management,* Vol. 11, No. 4 (December 1990), pp. 339–347.

Hanlon, J. P. "Hub Operations and Airline Competition." *Tourism Management,* Vol. 10, No. 2 (June 1989), pp. 111–124.

Hanlon, J. P. "Regional Air Services and Airline Competition." *Tourism Management,* Vol. 13, No. 2 (June 1992), pp. 181–195.

Heraty, Margaret J. "Tourism Transport: Implications for Developing Countries." *Tourism Management,* Vol. 10, No. 4 (December 1989), pp. 288–292.

Hunt, Jill. "Airlines in Asia." *Travel and Tourism Analyst,* No. 5 (1985), pp. 5–25.

Lowing, Graham. "The European Coach/Bus Holiday Market." *Travel and Tourism Analyst,* No. 6 (1990), pp. 5–16.

National Technical Information Service. *Airport System Capacity: Strategic Choice.* Springfield, Va.: NTIS, 1990.

National Technical Information Service. *Secretary's Task Force on Competition in the U.S. Domestic Airline Industry: Industry and Route Structures,* Volumes I and II. Springfield, Va.: NTIS, 1990.

National Technical Information Service. *Secretary's Task Force on Competition in the U.S. Domestic Airline Industry: International Air Service.* Springfield, Va.: NTIS, 1990.

Pisarski, Alan. *Nationwide Personal Transportation Survey: Travel Behavior Issues in the 90's.* Washington, D.C.: U.S. Department of Transportation, 1992.

Teye, Victor B. "Land Transportation and Tourism in Bermuda." *Tourism Management,* Vol. 13, No. 4 (December 1992), pp. 395–405.

Yunis, Eugenio. "Airlines in South America." *Travel and Tourism Analyst,* No. 3 (1990), pp. 5–18.

CHAPTER **6**

Hospitality and Related Services

LEARNING OBJECTIVES

- Study the lodging industry, its ancient origins, its associations, names of leading companies, and its vital role in the economy.
- Appreciate the immensity of the restaurant–food service industry.
- Learn the current trends in resorts and timesharing mode of operation.
- Discover why meetings and conventions, as well as meeting planners, are so important to tourism.

INTRODUCTION

As noted in Chapter 2, providing overnight accommodations for travelers goes back into antiquity—it is the world's oldest commercial business. Guest rooms were first parts of private dwellings. Then came caravansaries and guest quarters provided in monasteries. Today, lodging and food service activities are enormous in economic importance. Many lodging places provide meeting rooms, convention facilities and services, restaurants, bars, entertainment, gift shops, gaming, health clubs, and other activities and facilities. In this chapter we examine this industry as well as the even-larger food service business, meetings and conventions, and related services.

THE LODGING INDUSTRY

The World Tourism Organization (WTO) states that the world hotel room inventory grows by about 3.8 percent a year. In 1990 there were 12.1 million rooms worldwide. Occupancy rates vary, but average about 66 percent overall. Such places as Thailand, Hawaii, the Caribbean area, and the city of Las Vegas are noted for higher occupancy rates. During the 1980s there was a great deal of overbuilding, especially in North America. Rooms supply outstripped demand. This resulted in low occupancy and low room rates. Currently, in most tourist destinations the creation of new lodging facilities has slowed or stopped, making a better balance. After difficult years in the early 1990s, the remainder of the decade is expected to be profitable.

In Eastern Europe and the former Soviet Union there is now a considerable rush to

The Hong Kong Hilton serves as an example of international hotel development. (Photo courtesy of Hilton International)

build new hotel accommodations to serve an anticipated growing demand. Another trend has been the purchasing of U.S. hotel properties by foreign investors, due to the low value of the dollar. Many fine properties have been acquired at bargain prices.

Hotel accommodations are heavily concentrated in Europe and North America, constituting 75 percent of the world's supply. Europe has 46 percent of these—about 5 million rooms. The United States has slightly over 3 million, East Asia and the Pacific somewhat over 1 million. The following organizations provide data on hotel and motel businesses:

Organization	*Name of Publication*
Smith Travel Research, Gallitin, Tenn.	*Lodging Outlook*
PKF Consulting, San Francisco	*Trends in the Hotel Industry*
Arthur Anderson Real Estate Services Group, Los Angeles	*The Host Report*
American Hotel and Motel Association, Washington, D.C.	*Hotel Operating Statistics*
U.S. Bureau of the Census, Washington, D.C.	*Census of Service Industries*

According to Smith Travel Research, in 1992 the U.S. lodging industry (which includes hotels, motels, suites, and resort properties) generated $66.1 billion in sales, provided jobs for 1.52 million full- and part-time employees, paid over $20 billion in wages and salaries, and generated $6 billion in federal taxes. Revenue is expected to go to $73.7 billion in 1994, exclusive of casino revenue and continue growing for the remainder of the decade.

The lodging industry has practiced market segmentation in recent years. Many of the big chains offer products at almost every price level: full-service luxury hotels, luxury all-suite hotels, resort hotels, moderately priced full-service hotels, moderately priced all-suites, moderately priced limited service, and economy or budget motels (see the box).

Hotels and motels are classified in a variety of ways. One of the most common is by location, such as resort, city center, airport, suburban, or highway. There are a number of very large companies in the lodging industry, and many of the major chains are growing rapidly. *Hotels*, published by Cahners Publishing Company, 1350 East Touhy Avenue, Des Plaines, Illinois 60018, compiles an annual listing of the world's 200 largest corporate hotel chains. The July 1993 issue lists Hospitality Franchise Systems, Parsippany, New Jersey, as the world's largest lodging chain, with 354,997 rooms and 3413 hotels. Their brands include Ramada Hotels, Howard Johnson, HoJo Inns, Days Inns, and Super 8. Hospitality Franchise Systems (HFS) acquired Super 8 in 1993 and that acquisition catapulted HFS past Holiday Inn Worldwide, which had been the world's top hotel chain since *Hotels* first began ranking the chains in 1971. Holiday Inn is in second place, with 328,679 rooms and 1692 hotels. See Table 6.1 for the ranking of the top 25 corporate hotel chains.

Trends

The trend in the lodging industry has been away from independently owned and operated properties toward chain and franchise affiliations. There are also referral groups or voluntary membership associations. Both independents and chains have found it profitable to join together to market their properties.

The trend toward consolidation and acquisition will continue in the 1990s because

GLOSSARY

- **Average Daily Rate per Occupied Room** Total guest room revenue for a given period divided by the total number of occupied rooms during the same period (excluding public rooms).
- **Average Daily Room Rate per Guest** Total guest room revenue for a given period divided by the total number of guests accommodated for the same time period.
- **Percentage of Occupancy** The percentage of available rooms occupied for a given period. It is computed by dividing the number of rooms occupied for a period by the number of rooms available for the same period.
- **Income before Other Fixed Charges** Income after management fees, property taxes, and insurance does not include deductions for depreciation, rent, interest, amortization, and income taxes. Comparisons beyond income after property taxes and insurance are virtually meaningless due to wide variances in ownership, depreciation methods, financing bases, applicable income taxes, etc.
- **Full-Service Hotel** A hotel which provides a wide variety of facilities and amenities, including food and beverage outlets, meeting rooms, and recreational activities.
- **Limited-Service Hotel** A hotel which provides only some of the facilities and amenities of a full-service property. This category includes properties commonly referred to as motels or motor hotels.
- **Resort Hotel** A hotel, usually in a suburban or isolated rural location, with special recreational facilities to attract the pleasure-seeking guests.
- **Suite Hotel** A hotel in which all rooms have "separate," but not necessarily physically divided, "sleeping and living areas."
- **Convention Hotel** A hotel which provides facilities and services geared to meet the needs of large group and association meetings and trade shows. Typically, these hotels have in excess of 400 guest rooms and contain substantial amounts of function and banquet space flexibly designed for use by large meeting groups. They often work in concert with other convention hotels and convention centers to provide facilities for citywide conventions and trade shows.

chains have the potential for improvement in productivity and the advantages that accrue to large size. Chains can most effectively use training programs, employee selection programs, major equipment such as computers, and research. They can experiment with different layouts, prices, advertising, equipment, and so on, and what works well in one property can be employed chainwide. One reason for the popularity of the referral groups is that members who are independent operators achieve the marketing benefits of chains without chain membership.

Franchising is also well known in the lodging industry and has made a rapid penetration into the marketplace. However, franchising generates mixed reports. Many managements believe that it is difficult to control the franchisees and maintain the quality that the chain advertises and the standards that are supposed to be met. Thus many chains are buying back franchises to ensure that management maintains the

Suite-type accommodations have been a growing trend in hotels. They provide additional living space and other facilities for guests, comfort and enjoyment. (Photo courtesy of the Disneyland Hotel)

quality level desired. In other cases, firms are moving ahead rapidly with franchising because they can conserve cash and expand more rapidly by franchising. In addition, the franchisee, having invested his or her own capital, has great motivation to succeed.

Franchisees have the advantage that they receive the knowledge, advice, and assistance of a proven operator. Franchising also spreads the costs of promotion, advertising, and reservation systems over all outlets, making the unit cost much lower. If the franchisor has an excellent reputation and image, the franchisee benefits greatly. Most of the companies with franchise operations also operate company-owned units. Industry predictions are that as the industry grows and matures, there will be less franchising, which will give the chains more control over their properties and operations so that they can maintain the desired quality control. Increased competitiveness and improved properties will necessitate having the ability to make these improvements.

A trend in the lodging industry appears to be that more large properties will be operated under management contracts. Investors, such as insurance companies, frequently purchase hotel properties and turn them over to chains or independents to manage, a process that has advantages to both parties. The owner has the financial resources and the manager has the reputation and experience to manage the property profitably. Other trends are the increased use of central reservation systems, emphasis on service, and the use of yield management techniques.

Table 6.1   Top 25 Hotel Chains

Rank 1992 (1991)	Corporate Chain Headquarters	Rooms 1992 (1991)	Hotels 1992 (1991)
1	Hospitality Franchise Systems	354,997	3,413
(2)	Parsippany, N.J.	(288,990)	(2,298)
2	Holiday Inn Worldwide	328,679	1,692
(1)	Atlanta, Ga.	(327,059)	(1,645)
3	Best Western International	273,804	3,351
(3)	Phoenix, Ariz.	(266,123)	(3,310)
4	Accor	238,990	2,098
(5)	Evry, France	(212,500)	(1,875)
5	Choice Hotels International Inc.	230,430	2,502
(4)	Silver Spring, Md.	(214,411)	(2,295)
6	Marriott Corp.	166,919	750
(6)	Washington, D.C.	160,968	(698)
7	ITT Sheraton Corp.	132,361	426
(7)	Boston	(131,348)	(423)
8	Hilton Hotels Corp.	94,653	242
(8)	Beverly Hills, Calif.	(94,452)	(257)
9	Forte Plc	79,309	871
(9)	London	(76,330)	(853)
10	Hyatt Hotels/Hyatt International	77,579	164
(10)	Chicago	(74,801)	(159)
11	Carlson/Radisson/Colony	76,069	336
(11)	Minneapolis, Minn..	69,104	(315)
12	Promus Cos.	75,558	459
(12)	Memphis, Tenn.	(68,664)	(423)
13	Club Méditerranée SA	63,067	261
(13)	Paris	(66,269)	(269)
14	Hilton International	52,979	160
(15)	Watford Herts, England	(50,799)	(151)
15	Sol Group	40,163	156
(16)	Palma de Mallorca, Spain	(40,150)	(150)
16	Inter-Continental Hotels	39,000	104
(17)	London	(37,052)	(95)
17	Westin Hotels & Resorts	38,029	75
(19)	Seattle, Wash.	(35,613)	(67)
18	New World/Ramada International	36,520	133
(18)	Hong Kong	(36,655)	(127)
19	Canadian Pacific Hotels	27,970	86
(20)	Toronto	(28,100)	(88)
20	Société du Louvre	27,427	398
(24)	Paris	(22,429)	(324)
21	La Quinta Motor Inns Inc.	25,925	209
(22)	San Antonio, Texas	(26,699)	(209)
22	Red Roof Inns	23,443	210
(23)	Hilliard, Ohio	(23,443)	(210)
23	Tokyo Hotel Group	22,671	102
(27)	Tokyo	(20,661)	(76)
24	Hospitality International Inc.	22,425	345
(21)	Tucker, Ga.	(27,300)	(350)
25	Husa Hotels Group	21,500	98
(26)	Barcelona	(21,300)	(105)

[a]Rankings are based on total rooms open as of Dec. 31, 1992. *Hotels* estimate.
Source: *Hotels,* July 1993, p. 44.

Remodeling outstanding older hotel properties has become an important trend. The Ritz-Carlton Huntington Hotel, Pasadena, California, has been redone and beautifully restored. (Photo courtesy of Wimberly, Allison, Tong and Goo, Architects, Honolulu, Hawaii)

Bed and Breakfasts

A discussion of the lodging industry would not be complete without mentioning the burgeoning bed and breakfast (B and B) segment. It is made up of over 12,000 privately owned homes, inns, and reservation services. It is one of the fastest-growing segments of the accommodations industry in the nation. B and Bs provide both luxury and economy accommodations in many areas where major hotel and motel chains do not build. This brings tourism dollars into communities often neglected by most tourists.

B and Bs provide the best possible avenue for travelers of all ages and from all locations to experience firsthand the lifestyles in areas of the country previously unknown to guests. The B and B host can become an area's best ambassador. For many single and retired people, B and Bs provide additional income. In many cases around the nation, the institution of a B and B has saved a historic property that might otherwise have been destroyed.

B and B reservation services inspect and approve B and B homes and inns, maintain ongoing quality control, and provide one-stop shopping for the traveler. They can provide the traveler with a chain of recourse in case of a problem. Reservation services are privately owned corporations, partnerships, or single proprietorships, each representing from 35 to 100 host homes and inns.

Resorts and Timesharing

The United States leads in the resort market with 44 percent of the world's resorts (1329) and half of its timeshare units (60,380). These data are from American Resort Development Association's report prepared by Ragatz Associates' *Annual Report of the World-*

Wide Resort Timesharing Industry. Timeshare resorts are located in 75 countries, and timeshare owners reside in 157 countries. The United States has 53.2 percent (1,257,525) owners "owning in the country" and 59.7 percent (1,410,973) of the "owners residing in the country." Thus 1,257,525 households in the world *own* timeshare intervals in the United States and 1,410,973 households *residing* in the United States own timeshare intervals throughout the world. The second most dominant area for timeshare is Europe, with 21.5 percent of the timeshare units.

According to Ragatz Associates, to place the size of the worldwide resort timesharing industry in proper perspective, one needs to recognize that (1) about 3050 timeshare resorts exist, (2) about 2,400,000 households now own a timeshare interval, and (3) about 440,000 timeshare intervals were sold in 1991. Gross sales were $3.7 billion.

Lodging Organizations

There are a large number of accommodations organizations: international, regional, state, and local. Of these, the American Hotel and Motel Association (AH&MA) is the largest and most prominent in the United States. AH&MA is a federation of hotel and motel associations located in the 50 states, the District of Columbia, Puerto Rico, and the U.S. Virgin Islands and speaks as the trade association for the U.S. lodging industry. Founded in Chicago in 1910, AH&MA now represents 1.3 million transient rooms comprising more than 8900 individual hotels, motels, and resorts. This is essentially 53.4 percent of the total rooms inventory in the United States, accounting for 82.6 percent of total revenues generated by the industry. AH&MA works for favorable amendments to existing laws and coordinates, with almost 100 related groups for maximum industry support and impact. In the past year, for example, AH&MA has spoken out on fire safety regulations, lodging industry labor shortages, liquor liability, and state taxation on advertising.

Internationally, organizations representing accommodations include the European Motel Federation in the Netherlands; the International Hotel Association, in Paris, France; the International Organization of Hotel and Restaurant Associations, in Zurich, Switzerland; and the Caribbean Hotel Association, in Santurce, Puerto Rico. For hostels, there is the International Youth Hostel Federation in Welwyn Garden City, England; and for camping, the International Federation of Camping and Caravanning of Brussels, Belgium.

These organizations provide information and educational services to members, help to avoid unfair legislation and encourage favorable legislation among governmental bodies, and promote the use and development of their facilities and services by the traveling public.

Bed & Breakfast Reservation Services World-Wide (B&BRSWW) was formed in 1985 to promote the use of B and Bs and reservation services (RSOs), educate the traveling public about B and Bs and RSOs, and set standards of excellence in accommodations and services provided by member RSOs and their hosts. Its members include B and Bs from around the world. The association is currently developing a code of ethics for member services and host homes and inns. They have also recently developed an innovative program whereby host homes will be inspected and certified annually through the association.

THE FOOD SERVICE INDUSTRY

Early Food Services

Like the lodging industry, the food service industry is a very old business. Such service came out of the early inns and monasteries. In cities, small restaurants began serving simple dishes such as soups and breads. One such restaurant, *le restaurant divin*—the divine restorative—opened in Paris in 1765. (Like *tourist, restaurant* is a French word.) The famous English taverns provided foods, drink, and lodging.

In the United States the early ordinaries, taverns, and inns typically provided food and lodging. Good examples of these can be found in Colonial Williamsburg, Virginia. Politics and other concerns of the day were often discussed in such taverns.

With the development of stagecoaches, taverns began providing food and lodging along the early roads and in small communities. Some believe that these roadside taverns were really the beginnings of the American hotel industry. As cities grew, so did eating establishments. Some names of historic restaurants in the 1820s in New York City were Niblo's Garden, the San Souci, and Delmonico's.

French service was often used in these early restaurants. In French service, some kinds of entrées are prepared by the dining room captain right at the guests' table,

Elegant food service complements the guest rooms in many popular hotels. Dining in different types of theme restaurants holds particular appeal for tourists, as exemplified by this Italian gourmet restaurant. (Photo courtesy Merv Griffin's Resorts, Atlantic City, New Jersey)

An unusual waiter indeed! This unique dining experience is offered during the summer, holidays, and weekends year 'round. (Photo courtesy of the Disneyland Hotel)

sometimes using heat from a small burner, then serving from larger dishes onto the guest's plate. The kinds and amounts of each food item are chosen individually. By contrast, in Russian service the entire plate, with predetermined portions, is served to each guest.

Menus can be of two types, à la carte and table d'hôte. The à la carte menu consists of a complete list of all the food items being offered on that day. The patron then chooses items desired. In table d'hôte, a combination of items is chosen.

Eating and drinking places are big business. Although much of this activity is local, eating and drinking are favorite pastimes of travelers, and the food service industry would face difficult times without the tourist market. In 1993, the National Restaurant Association projected that food industry sales for that year would total $267 billion, 3.9 percent above the $257 billion recorded in 1992. The industry currently employs more than 9 million people. By the year 2000, eating and drinking places are expected to employ 2.5 million more people, generating the largest number of new jobs in any industry. Nearly two-thirds of all those in food service occupations are women, and one-fourth are teenagers. The food service industry employs more minority managers than any other retail industry.

Travelers contribute about $84 billion to food service sales each year, whether for a coffee shop breakfast, a dinner on an airline, a sandwich from a bus station vending machine, or a 10-course dinner on a cruise ship. Travelers, including foreign visitors,

At the Rio Hotel's carnival buffet the patrons are serenaded by the chef while they partake of international cuisine. (Photo courtesy of the Las Vegas News Bureau)

spend more money on food than anything else except transportation, and travelers account for about one-third of the total sales in the food service industry.

The food service industry consists of restaurants, travel food service, and vending and contract institutional food service. Local restaurants are made up of establishments that include fast-food units, coffee shops, specialty restaurants, family restaurants, cafeterias, and full-service restaurants with carefully orchestrated "atmosphere." Travel food service consists of food operations in hotels and motels, roadside service to automobile travelers, and all food service on airplanes, trains, and ships. Institutional food service in companies, hospitals, nursing homes, and so on, is not considered part of the tourism industry.

Over the past two decades, the food and beverage business has grown at a phenomenal rate. This has been especially true for the fast-food segment, with the franchising portion in the fast-food segment becoming the dominant growth sector. This remarkable increase has been gained at the expense of other food service operators and supermarkets. Franchisees control approximately three-fourths of the fast-food outlets, whose hamburgers, chickens, steaks, and pizzas dominate the fast-food business.

Fast-food chains have enjoyed great success in part because they limit their menus, which gives them greater purchasing power, less waste, and more portion control, and, of importance to the consumer, lower operating costs. They are leaders in labor productivity in the restaurant industry. Most fast-food operations use disposable paper and plastic; the expense for these materials is more than offset by the savings resulting from not providing regular service and from not employing the personnel required to wash the dinner service. Fast-food operations also enjoy the advantages of specialization; they have become specialists in menu items, job simplification, and operating systems. Franchising has been used extensively in both the restaurant field and the lodging field as a means of achieving rapid growth. Using the franchisee's capital, the entrepreneur can get much more rapid penetration of the marketplace.

As noted earlier, franchise units account for approximately three-fourths of the growing fast-food portion of the industry. Advantages of franchising accrue to both sides. The franchisee gets the start-up help, advice from experienced management, buying power, advertising, and low unit costs from spreading fixed costs over large numbers of units. The franchisor has the advantage of a lower capital investment, rapid growth, and royalty income. The fast-food franchise operators have a great deal of concentration in their segment of the industry. The seven largest account for almost half of the fast-food units and almost half of the sales. Franchise firms are household words: McDonald's, Kentucky Fried Chicken, A&W Root Beer, Wendy's, Dairy Queen, Tastee Freeze, Burger King, Pizza Hut, Arby's, and Shakey's.

According to the International Franchising Association, in 1991 there were over 101,000 franchised restaurants in the United States with sales of $85.5 billion, 10 percent more than in 1990. Over 3 million persons are employed. In foreign countries there are over 12,000 U.S.-franchised restaurants. Leading countries are Canada, Japan, the United Kingdom, Australia, the Caribbean area, and Mexico.

Although the fast-food segment is the most rapidly growing segment, the high-quality segment of the restaurant industry must not be overlooked. Much of this business is based on customers seeking a special or different experience in dining out. This demand has been most effectively satisfied by local entrepreneurs who emphasize special menus, varying atmospheres, and high-quality food and service. New concepts or trends include ethnic restaurants, especially those with an oriental or Mexican flavor; increased demand for health foods, fish, local produce, and regional dishes; and variety in portion sizes.

Restaurant Organizations

The National Restaurant Association (NRA), a full-service trade association with about 20,000 members, is the most important trade association in the food service field. Membership is diverse, running the gamut from the New Jersey prison system to Club 21 and including white tablecloth and fast-food members, institutional feeders, and vending machine operators.

The goals and objectives of NRA are channeled in three directions: (1) political action, (2) information, and (3) promotion. Through their Political Action and Political Education Committees, NRA promotes the political and legislative concerns of the industry and combats any potentially harmful attempts by government to regulate the operational aspects of the industry. Their Educational Foundation contributes to the current and future training and educational/informational needs of the food service industry.

NRA works to position the industry and its services before the public in a favorable light. The association regularly publishes surveys and reports on a variety of topics, ranging from employee management to consumer attitudes toward smoking in restaurants. Through its library's information service, NRA responds to thousands of requests for information. NRA is located at 1200 Seventeenth Street N.W., Washington, D.C. 20036.

MEETING PLANNERS

Because of the growth in the meeting and conventions area, it is an area of interest to students of tourism. With the growth of more corporate and association meetings, there is a need for more meeting planners, meeting consultants, and suppliers of goods and services to meeting planners. Professional meeting planners are involved with such tasks as negotiating hotel contracts, negotiating with airlines, writing contracts, planning educational meetings and seminars, developing incentive meetings, negotiating with foreign countries and hotels for incentive travel, budgeting, promotion, public relations, and planning special events and postmeeting tours. Meeting planners are found in corporations, special-interest associations, educational institutions, trade shows, and government.

The most prominent organization serving this group is Meeting Planners International (MPI). This organization, founded in 1972, numbers 5900 members and has the goal of improving meeting methods. The Society of Company Meeting Planners (SCMP) also serves this area. Company and corporate meeting planners and hotel convention service managers have united to promote continuing education and high standards among members. Another organization is the Society of Government Meeting Planners (SGMP), which is made up of individuals involved in planning government meetings on a full- or part-time basis. The association provides education in basic and advanced areas of meeting planning and facilitates professional contact with other government meeting planners.

MEETINGS AND CONVENTIONS

Every two years *Meetings and Convention Magazine* publishes a meetings market report. Their latest report, entitled *The Meetings Market 1992*, contains 1991 data and again documents the huge size of the meetings market as reported by their subscribers. They report that subscribers planned over 1 million meetings in the past year that were attended by 81 million people. Subscribers' organizations spent $35 billion divided among corporate meetings ($8.7 billion), association meetings ($15.3 billion), and major conventions ($11 billion). Expenditures for the total U.S. meetings market are estimated at $38.7 billion.

A study entitled *The Economic Impact of Conventions, Expositions, Meetings and Incentive Travel*, released in May 1993 using 1991 data, estimated that the industry was worth $75.6 billion. The study was conducted by Deloitte & Touche for the Convention Liaison Council (CLC). The study estimates $16.5 billion of meetings spending is on air travel and $22.6 billion is on hotels. The differing results in these two studies illustrate the need for common definitions so that accurate and comparable measurements can be made. Whichever impact figure you choose, the meetings sector is large, important, and growing.

There will probably be an oversupply of convention meeting facilities in the United States as the number of convention centers continues to grow. There are 42 U.S. cities building new convention centers or expanding their existing centers. Even though the United States leads the world in conventions, in terms of both number of attendees and the amount of exhibit and meeting space, the growth in facilities is outpacing demand. There are more than 330 convention centers in the United States, 50 percent more than in 1980.

SUMMARY

Lodging and food services are major essential supply components of tourism. These services go back into antiquity. World hotel room inventory is growing about 3.8 percent yearly. Room occupancy averages about 66 percent. But such data varies considerably. The 1980s saw considerable overbuilding, especially in North America. However, for the remainder of the 1990s, forecasters see a return to more profitability.

About 75 percent of the world's lodging establishments are located in Europe and North America. Four private and one governmental organization publish statistics on the U.S. lodging industry. The typical hotel receives over 64 percent of its revenue from room rentals, about 28 percent from food and beverage sales, and the remainder from other sources. For expenditures, personnel costs are 30.1 percent, operating expense 23.7 percent, and other costs plus profits, 46.2 percent. There is a trend toward more franchising, chain or system ownership, and growth in bed and breakfast lodging.

Resort and timesharing arrangements are also increasing worldwide. The United States dominates this market, with 44 percent of the properties out of a world total of 3050 resorts. About 2.4 million households worldwide own timeshare intervals, and gross sales totaled about $3.7 billion. The American Hotel and Motel Association is the leading trade association in the United States, but many others are active in North America and elsewhere. Eating and drinking places are big business. In the United States this industry grossed $262 billion in 1992, employed over 8 million persons, and is expected to add 2.5 million more people by the year 2000. The National Restaurant Association is the industry's most important trade association.

Meetings and conventions constitute a major incentive for business travel. Expenditure on these stimulates all segments of tourism. In the United States there will probably be an oversupply of convention centers within a few years, as 42 cities are currently building new centers or expanding existing ones.

The profession of meeting planner is an important and growing one. Those attending meetings and conventions expect a rewarding experience. Thus expert planning is critical to the success of such events. Meeting planners provide all arrangements necessary for a successful meeting, from transportation services to special events. They are particularly adept at negotiating elements needed for the meeting. Some corporations, associations, government agencies, and others have created their own meeting planning department, with their own employees handling this important function.

Key Concepts

American Hotel and Motel Association
bed and breakfast
classification of hotels and motels
fast-food companies
food service industry

largest corporate hotel chain companies
lodging industry
lodging statistics
meeting planners
meetings and conventions

National Restaurant Association
oldest commercial business

timesharing resorts
trends in lodging industry

For Review and Discussion

1. Why are the world's lodging businesses growing at the remarkable rate of 3.8 percent per year?
2. Identify the reasons why Las Vegas has a high hotel occupancy.
3. Explain the current trend in the United States for slow or no expansion in the construction of new lodging places.
4. How successful do you think future tourism will be in the countries of Eastern Europe and the former Soviet Union?
5. What reasons have brought about the concentration of lodging businesses in Europe and North America?
6. Why have chain and brand identification hotels and motels continued to expand worldwide versus independent properties?
7. Define franchising. What are the trends and benefits of such groupings? Give examples.
8. List services provided to its members by the American Hotel and Motel Association. Are state hotel and motel associations affiliated?
9. Similarly, what services do members obtain from the National Restaurant Association?
10. Are profit percentages on sales higher in fast-food places than in table service types? If so, why?
11. Explain timesharing. Describe its advantages over owning one's own resort property.
12. What characteristics of lifestyles of contemporary American and Canadian citizens are responsible for the growing attendance at meetings and conventions?
13. Would you be interested in a career as a professional meeting planner? If so, where would you find out more about this field?

Case Problems

1. You are the food and beverage manager of a resort hotel located in an interesting historical destination similar to Colonial Williamsburg, Virginia. Recently, you decided that all the guest servers in the dining room should wear authentic costumes typical of those when the area was at its peak as an early trading center. Some of the staff object to this plan, saying that it is a silly idea and besides, the costumes look like they might be uncomfortable. What would your reaction be?
2. Angelo V. and his son Leonard are co-owners of a fine-quality 150-seat table service restaurant. Leonard has been gradually acquiring more authority and responsibility for management. However, recently he and his father have had some sharp disagreements relating to becoming members of their state's restaurant association and the National Restaurant Association. Angelo feels that membership would be a waste of money. If you were Leonard, what would your arguments in favor be?

Selected References

Angelo, Rocco M., and Andrew N. Vladimir. *Hospitality Today: An Introduction.* East Lansing, Mich.: Educational Institute of the American Hotel and Motel Association, 1991.

Arthur Anderson Real Estate Services Group. *The Host Report: Hotel Operating Statistics.* Los Angeles: Arthur Anderson, 1992.

Astroff, Milton T., and James R. Abbey. *Convention Sales and Services.* Cranbury, N.J.: Waterbury Press, 1991.

Brotherton, Bob, and Sean Mooney. "Yield Management: Progress and Prospects." *International Journal of Hospitality Management,* Vol. 11, No. 1 (1992), pp. 23–32.

Fenich, George. "Convention Center Development: Pros, Cons and Unanswered Questions." *International Journal of Hospitality Management,* Vol. 11, No. 3 (August 1992), pp. 183–196.

Gilbert, David, and Andrew Lockwood. "Budget Hotels: The USA, France and UK Compared." *Travel and Tourism Analyst,* No. 3 (1990), pp. 19–36.

Hall, Stephen. *Ethics in Hospitality Management.* East Lansing, Mich.: Educational Institute of the American Hotel and Motel Association, 1992.

Hiemstra, Stephen J., and Joseph A. Ismail. "Analysis of Room Taxes Levied on the Lodging Industry." *Journal of Travel Research,* Vol. 31, No. 1 (Summer 1992), pp. 42–49.

Hiemstra, Stephen J., and Joseph A. Ismail. "Incidence of the Impacts of Room Taxes on the Lodging Industry." *Journal of Travel Research,* Vol. 31, No. 4 (Spring 1993), pp. 22–26.

Hoyle, Leonard H., David C. Dorf, and Thomas J. A. Jones. *Managing Conventions and Group Business.* East Lansing, Mich.: Educational Institute of the American Hotel and Motel Association, 1989.

Jedrziewski, David R. *The Complete Guide for the Meeting Planner.* Cincinnati, Ohio: 1991.

Kavanaugh, Raphael, and Jack D. Ninemeier. *Supervision in the Hospitality Industry.* East Lansing, Mich.: Educational Institute of the American Hotel and Motel Association, 1991.

Kaven, William H. "Japan's Hotel Industry: An Overview." *Cornell Hotel and Restaurant Administration Quarterly,* Vol. 33, No. 2 (April 1992), pp. 26–32.

Lattin, Gerald W. *The Lodging and Food Service Industry,* 3rd edition. East Lansing, Mich.: Educational Institute of the American Hotel and Motel Association, 1993.

Marvin, Bill. *Restaurant Basics: Why Guests Don't Come Back . . . and What You Can Do About It.* New York: Wiley, 1992.

Mill, Robert. *Managing for Productivity in the Hospitality Industry.* New York: Van Nostrand Reinhold, 1989.

Miller, James J., Cynthia S. McCahon, and Judy L. Miller. "Foodservice Forecasting Using Simple Mathematical Models." *Hospitality Research Journal,* Vol. 15, No. 1 (1991), pp. 43–58.

National Restaurant Association. "1993 Food Industry Forecast." *Restaurants USA,* Vol. 12, No. 11 (December 1992), pp. 13–36.

Nixon, Judith M. *The Hotel and Restaurant Industries: An Information Sourcebook.* Phoenix, Ariz.: Oryx Press, 1988.

Reed Travel Group. *The Meeting Market.* Secaucus, N.J.: Reed, 1992.

Salmen, John. *Accommodating All Guests: The Americans with Disabilities Act and the Lodging Industry.* Washington, D.C.: American Hotel and Motel Association, 1992.

Steadman, Charles E., and Michael L. Kasavana. *Managing Front Office Operations.* East Lansing, Mich.: Educational Institute of the American Hotel and Motel Association, 1988.

Talbot, Randy. *Meeting Management.* McLean, Va.: EPM Publishing, 1990.

Turner, Richard. *Who's Who in the Lodging Industry.* Washington, D.C.: American Hotel and Motel Association, 1992.

Warnick, Rodney B., and Lawrence R. Klar, Jr. "The Bed and Breakfast and Small Inn Industry of the Commonwealth of Massachusetts." *Journal of Travel Research,* Vol. 29, No. 3 (Winter 1991), pp. 17–25.

Woods, Robert H. *Managing Hospitality Human Resources.* East Lansing, Mich.: Educational Institute of the American Hotel and Motel Association, 1992.

CHAPTER 7

Organizations in the Distribution Process

LEARNING OBJECTIVES

- Become familiar with tourism distribution system organizations and their functions.
- Understand the role of travel agents and their dominance in the distribution system.
- Examine the role of the tour wholesaler.
- Recognize that a combination of all channels of distribution can be used by travel suppliers.

HOW DO CHANNEL ORGANIZATIONS WORK?

The tourism channel of distribution is an operating structure, system, or linkage of various combinations of organizations through which a producer of travel products describes, sells, or confirms travel arrangements to the buyer. For example, it would be impractical for a cruise line trying to market cruises to have a sales office in every market city of 5000 or more people. The most efficient method is to market through over 30,000 retail travel agencies in the United States and pay them a commission for every cruise sold. The cruises could also be sold through such intermediaries as tour wholesalers (who would include a cruise in a package vacation), through corporate travel offices, or by an association such as an automobile club and others. Thus the cruise line uses a combination of distribution channel organizations to sell cruises.

Tourism distribution channels are similar to those of other basic industries such as agriculture or manufacturing (see Figure 7.1). Their products flow to the ultimate consumer through wholesalers, distributors, and middlemen. While there are similarities with other industries, the tourism distribution system is unique. Tourism produces mainly services that are intangible. There is no physical product that can be held in inventory and flows from one sales intermediary to another. Instead, the "product," for example, is a hotel room that is available on a certain day, which is very temporal. If the room is not sold, the revenue is lost forever.

TRAVEL AGENTS

Travel, whether for business or pleasure, requires arrangements. The traveler usually faces a variety of choices regarding transportation, accommodations, and if the trip is

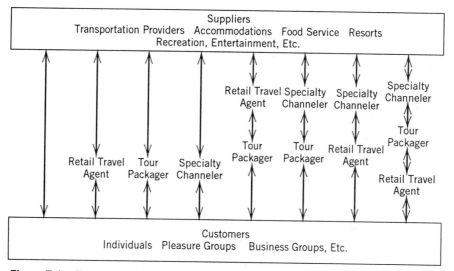

Figure 7.1   Tourism Distribution Channels

for pleasure, destinations, attractions, and activities. The traveler may gather information on prices, value, schedules, characteristics of the destination, and available activities directly, investing a considerable amount of time and possibly money on long-distance telephone calls to complete the trip arrangements. Alternatively, the traveler may use the services of a travel agency, obtaining all these arrangements at no cost.

What Is a Travel Agent?

A travel agency is a middleman—a business or person selling the travel industry's individual parts or a combination of the parts to the consumer. In marketing terms a travel agent is an agent middleman, acting on behalf of the client, making arrangements with suppliers of travel—airlines, hotels, tour operators—and receiving a commission from the suppliers.

In legal terms, a travel agency is an agent of the principal: specifically, transportation companies. The agency operates as a legally appointed agent, representing the principal in a certain geographic area. The agency functions as a broker, bringing buyer and seller together, for the other suppliers, such as hotels, car rentals, ground operators, and tour companies.

A travel agent is thus an expert, knowledgeable in schedules, routing, lodging, currency, prices, regulations, destinations, and all other aspects of travel and travel opportunities. In short, the travel agent is a specialist and counselor.

The *Travel Weekly* studies conducted by Louis Harris and Associates define the travel agent as follows:

> A travel agent, besides selling prepared package tours, also prepares individual itineraries. He arranges for hotels, motels, accommodation at resorts, meals, sightseeing, transfers of passengers and luggage between terminals and hotels; furthermore, he can provide the traveler with a host of other information (for example, on rates,

Automation is a necessary ingredient in travel agency operations. Agency staff receive instruction from an airline representative. (Photo courtesy of United Airlines)

quality and so on) which would normally be hard to get. The travel agent is paid for his services through commissions. For example, if a travel agent writes up an air ticket or makes a reservation in a hotel for a client, he gets paid by the carrier or the hotel in the form of a commission. In short, the travel agent saves the customer both time and money.

Thanks to the reports sponsored by *Travel Weekly* magazine and conducted by Louis Harris and Associates, excellent data are available on the travel agency business. Started in 1970, these studies, conducted every two years, are regarded as the benchmark research in the retail travel industry. The latest *Travel Weekly—Louis Harris Study* was published in August 1994 and represents the twelfth in a series of studies on the character and volume of the U.S. travel agency market. Even though it has slowed, the growth of the travel agency business has been remarkable.

The Dimension of the Travel Agency Business

The *Travel Weekly* survey reported that at the end of 1993 there were 32,466 agency locations in the United States, 1 percent over 1991, and about 4.8 times the 6700 agencies

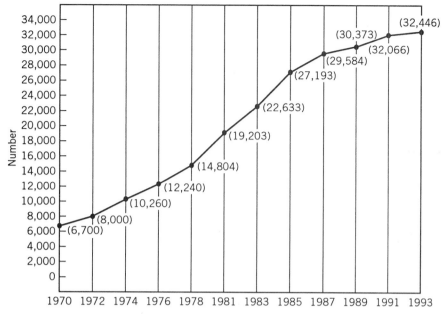

Figure 7.2 Total U.S. Travel Agencies (Source: *Travel Weekly,* copyright © 1994, Reed Travel Group)

reported in 1970 (see Figure 7.2).[1] Since airline deregulation took effect in 1978, the number of agency locations in the United States has more than doubled, from 14,804 to 32,466. The average agency has 5.5 full-time employees, down from 6.3 in 1989.

The *Travel Weekly* study found that the median salary for travel agents with three to five years of experience, working full time on straight salary, was $19,491 in 1993. Median salaries for agency employees with other levels of experience were: less than one year, $12,990; one to three years, $16,481; five to ten years, $22,122, and more than ten years, $24,645.

Just as the number of travel agencies has increased, so has the dollar volume. The annual estimated dollar volume for agencies reached $93.5 billion in 1993, an increase of 9 percent over the $85.9 billion reported in 1991 (see Figure 7.3). Today 13 percent of the agencies reach $5 million or more; 25 percent, $2 to 5 million; 33 percent, reach $1 to 2 million; and 29 percent, less than $1 million. The average revenue per agency is $2.9 million.

Despite many predictions that the independent travel agent would disappear, the species is alive and well, as today's industry is dominated by single-office enterprises. Among the locations in the *Travel Weekly* study, 70 percent are single-office firms, 17 percent are branch offices, and 12 percent are head offices.

Computerized reservations systems have become the rule, as 96 percent of all travel agency locations are now automated. This compares with 90 percent in 1985, 86 percent in 1983, and 69 percent in 1981. Over half (51 percent) of the agencies were located in central cities, 40 percent in suburban areas, and 9 percent in towns and rural areas.

[1]Louis Harris and Associates, *Travel Weekly,* 1994 U.S. Travel Agency Market Survey, Reed Travel Group, August 1994.

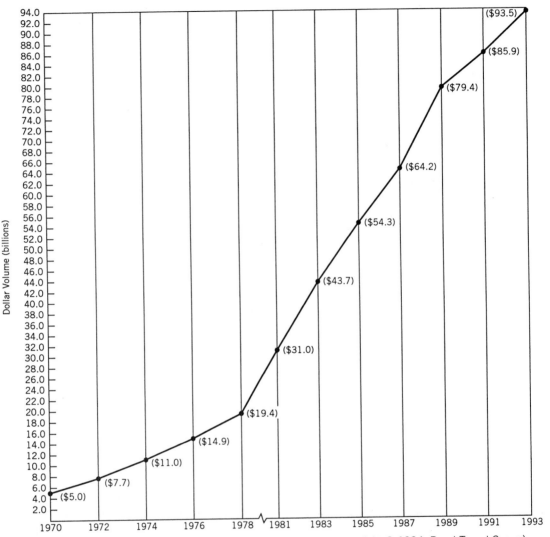

Figure 7.3   Agency Annual Dollar Volume (*Source: Travel Weekly*, copyright © 1994, Reed Travel Group)

Types of Travel Arrangements Made

As would be expected, the most common type of travel arrangement made is for air transportation. In 1993, 60 percent of total dollar volume was for air travel. Cruise sales accounted for 15 percent down from 16 percent in 1991. Much smaller proportions of the total dollar volume are attributable to lodging, car rentals, rail, and miscellaneous arrangements; these activities accounted for 25 percent of total agency dollar volume (see Figure 7.4).

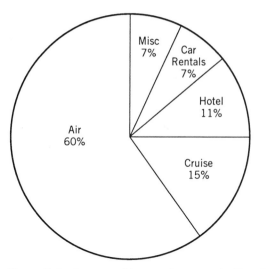

Figure 7.4   Sources of Agency Revenues by Travel Sector (*Source: Travel Weekly,* copyright © 1994, Reed Travel Group)

Travel Agency Organizations

The American Society of Travel Agents (ASTA) is the largest (over 22,000 members) and most influential trade association of travel and tourism professionals worldwide. Established in 1931, ASTA continues to serve the best interests of the travel industry and the traveling public. ASTA's purpose is:

- To promote and encourage travel among people of all nations
- To promote the image and encourage the use of professional travel agents worldwide
- To promote and represent the views and interests of travel agents to all levels of government and industry
- To promote professional and ethical conduct in the travel agency industry worldwide
- To serve as an information resource for the travel industry worldwide
- To promote consumer protection and safety for the traveler
- To sponsor and conduct educational programs for travel agents on subjects related to the travel industry
- To engage in any lawful activity the members of the association shall deem fit and appropriate for the promotion of their common welfare

To be an active ASTA member, a travel agency must be currently accredited with the Airlines Reporting Corporation (ARC), the International Airlines Travel Agent Network (IATAN), National Tour Association (NTA), Cruise Lines International Association (CLIA), or Amtrak. All ASTA members agree to comply with the Society's Principles of Professional Conduct and Ethics.

ASTA is managed by a board of directors elected by travel agency members. Although travel agencies, through an official firm representative, are the voting members, other categories of membership include individual associate, allied (includes most of the world's major travel suppliers), tour operator, travel school, Canadian, and international. The association has 30 U.S. chapters and 35 international chapters, each with its own elected officers and appointed committees. All officers of ASTA are working travel agents. They are elected every two years by the society's active members. Day-to-day activities are administered by a staff of more than 90 professionals located at ASTA's world headquarters in the Washington, D.C., metropolitan area, and a regional office in San Diego, California.

ASTA provides a wide range of services to its members and the travel industry, including educational seminars, the annual World Travel Congress and Trade Show, a consumer affairs program, publication of a monthly magazine *(ASTA Agency Management)* and a weekly newsletter *(ASTA Notes)*, research and statistics programs, and a scholarship foundation.

A smaller organization of travel agents is the Association of Retail Travel Agents (ARTA). The purpose of this organization is similar to that of ASTA, but ARTA does not supply the range of services provided to the members of ASTA. For specialized travel agencies that sell only cruises, there is the National Association of Cruise Only Agencies (NACOA). This group provides promotional and management assistance to its members. On a global scale, travel agent organizations include the International Federation of Travel Agencies, the Universal Federation of Travel Agents Association, and the World Association of Travel Agents.

Particularly in the British Commonwealth and in the United States, there are travel agents' organizations whose purpose is to raise business and professional competency and to award certification. In the United States, the Institute of Certified Travel Agents provides an educational and certification program leading to the designation CTC (Certified Travel Counselor). To become a CTC one must take five courses: The Travel Professional: Selling in a Competitive Service Environment, Communications for the Travel Professional, Travel Industry in the '90s and Beyond, Challenges in Leadership and Management, and Issues in Agency Management. In addition, the institute has developed destination specialist courses, which cover destinations such as North America, The Caribbean, Western Europe, and the South Pacific.

The candidate needs five years of experience in the industry, two of which can be with a carrier or other tourism organization and three years with a travel agency. Similar programs are operated in the British Commonwealth by the Institute of Travel Agents in cooperation with the Association of British Travel Agents. The institute awards the designation M.T.A.I., indicating that the recipient has fulfilled the academic requirements by passing examinations leading to the certification.

Trends

There is a growing trend among independently owned travel agencies to become affiliated with cooperatives, consortia, franchisors, or joint marketing organizations. Such groups exist for the purpose of helping their agency members to build profits and increase staff productivity. Specifically, they provide such aids as an 800-number telephone consultation, educational programs, frequent traveler programs, client newsletters, and arranging preferred suppliers and discount services, such as a preferred rate hotel program. Well-known names of such groups include GEM, GIANTS, UNIGLOBE, and VALU Travel Marketing.

THE TOUR WHOLESALER

The tour wholesaler[2] (also called tour operator) puts together a tour and all its components and sells the tour through his or her own company, through retail outlets, and/or through approved retail travel agencies. Wholesalers can offer vacation packages to the traveling public at prices lower than an individual traveler can arrange because wholesalers can buy services such as transportation, hotel rooms, sightseeing services, airport transfers, and meals in large quantities at discounted prices.

Tour wholesaling became an important segment of the U.S. travel industry after World War II. It has expanded substantially since the 1960s, largely because air carriers wanted to fill the increasing numbers of aircraft seats. The tour wholesale business consists primarily of planning, preparing, and marketing a vacation tour, including making reservations and consolidating transportation and ground services into a tour assembled for a departure date to a specific destination. Tours are then sold to the public through retail outlets such as travel agents and airline ticket offices.

The independent tour operator has grown dramatically over the past decade and now numbers over 2000. A large portion of the business is concentrated in the hands of a small number of large operators.

Independent tour wholesalers provide significant revenue to transportation and ground service suppliers. They also provide the retailer and the public with a wide selection of tours to a large number of destinations at varying costs, for varying durations, and in various seasons. Furthermore, they supply advance notice and increased assurance of future passenger volumes to suppliers.

The independent tour wholesaler's business is characterized by relative ease of entry, high velocity of cash flow, low return on sales, and the potential for high return on equity because the investment necessary to start such a business is small.

Tour wholesaling businesses are usually one of four kinds: (1) the independent tour wholesaler, (2) the airline working in close cooperation with a tour wholesaling business, (3) the retail travel agent who packages tours for its clients, and (4) the operator of motor coach tours. These four entities, along with incentive travel companies and travel clubs, comprise the industry.

Figure 7.5 illustrates the position of the tour wholesaler in the basic structure of the travel industry. The public or the consumer is the driving force and can purchase travel services from a retail travel agent or directly from the suppliers of travel services: the airlines, hotels, and other providers of destination services. The tour wholesaler's role is that of consolidating the services of airlines and other carriers with the ground services needed into one package, which can be sold through travel agents to the consuming public.

In 1993, the direct impact of the group tour industry in North America was estimated to be $8.7 billion in U.S. dollars. That $8.7 billion figure included an estimate of all expenditures by tour operators, both directly related to the tours they operate and for other transportation expenses, as well as the expenditures made by tour travelers while traveling.

Most of the impact was in the United States, with $7.5 billion in estimated direct

[2]Touche Ross, *Tour Wholesaler Industry Study* (New York: Touche Ross, 1975), pp. 1–24.

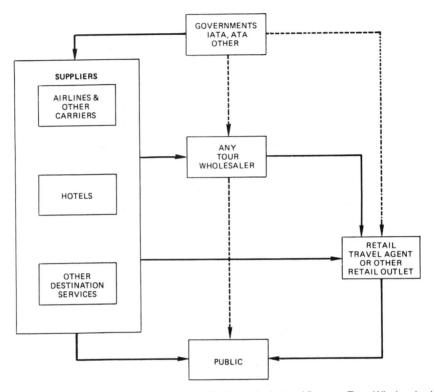

Figure 7.5   Basic Structure of the U.S. Travel Industry (*Source: Tour Wholesaler Industry Study*, Touche, Ross & Co.)

impact in 1993. The impact of the tour industry in Canada was $1.6 billion ($1.2 billion in U.S. dollars).

The typical group tour of 40 passengers produces approximately $5,495 in sales for each overnight stay in an average-sized North American city.

Tour Wholesaler Organizations

The National Tour Association (NTA) founded in 1951 is the primary group tour industry association in North America. Its membership includes group tour operators, who package and sell group tours in the United States, Canada, and Mexico, and suppliers, whose businesses include hotels, attractions, restaurants, bus companies, airlines, passenger vessels, sightseeing companies, destination marketing organizations, and other travel and tourism entities.

The association provides marketing assistance, educational programs, governmental representation and communications for its membership, and annually produces the NTA Convention and Tour and Travel Exchange. This event is one of the largest travel industry gatherings held in North America, offering members the opportunity to conduct intensive business sessions and attend education seminars that increase professionalism in the industry. The association also produces the Spring Tour and Travel

A large resort hotel typically has a major portion of its rooms sold through retail travel agencies. Tour companies using the hotel in their tours are another important distribution organization, as are specialty channelers. (Photo courtesy of Hyatt Hotels Corporation)

Exchange, which provides members with a second opportunity each year to conduct business and participate in educational programs.

The National Tour Association requires its members to adhere to a strict code of ethics that assures proper business activity, between individual members for the ultimate good of the traveling public. The association acts as the primary advocate for consumers of the group tour product in North America and works to promote consumer awareness of that vacation alternative.

The U.S. Tour Operators Association (USTOA) also represents tour operators. The goals of USTOA are to ensure consumer protection and education; to inform the travel industry, government agencies, and the public about tour operators' activities and objectives; to maintain a high level of professionalism within the industry; and to facilitate travel on a worldwide basis. USTOA's members must subscribe to the organization's strict code of ethics. Members are required to represent all information pertaining to tours, to maintain a high level of professionalism, and to state clearly all costs and facilities in advertising and promotional materials.

Most tour operators and wholesalers belong to the American Society of Travel Agents. Many also belong to the various promotional groups such as PATA (Pacific Asia Travel Association), ACTO (Association of Caribbean Tour Operators), and TIA (Travel Industry Association of America).

Local or short tours are conducted by sightseeing companies, and many of them are organized into American Sightseeing International and Grayline. These organizations aid sightseeing companies by providing local sightseeing services and competent personnel. Many sightseeing tour companies are also affiliated with the organizations already mentioned.

SPECIALTY CHANNELERS

Specialty intermediaries include such organizations as incentive travel firms, business meeting and convention planners, corporate travel offices, association executives, hotel representatives, travel consultants, and supplier sales offices. While specialty intermediaries are a small force in distribution compared to travel agencies, they have considerable power to influence when, where, and how people travel. Such groups can represent either buyers or sellers, receiving either a commission or a salary from their employer. Specialty intermediaries are experts in their particular aspect of travel. As tourism becomes more specialized, these types of channelers will become increasingly important.

Incentive Travel Firms

Incentive travel has been enjoying significant growth because travel rewards are one of the most powerful motivators for increased employee performance. Companies can reward distributors, customers, and their employees. There are about 500 travel incentive planning firms in the United States selling their professional services of designing, promoting, and accomplishing incentive travels programs for buyers. They have a national trade association, the Society of Incentive Travel Executives (SITE). E.F. MacDonald and Maritz are leading companies.

Corporate Travel Departments

Just as many corporations have chosen to set up their own meeting planning departments, many also have travel sections. Growth in this area took place when the airline industry was deregulated in the late 1970s. Such in-house offices try to contain travel and entertainment costs by getting the best prices on travel. They typically provide the same services as those of travel agencies serving the corporate market.

Hotel Sales Representative Firms

Companies specialize in representing hotels, motels, resorts, and destination areas. This type of firm provides an alternative to hiring its own sales force and is an economical way to be represented in foreign markets. These firms are also active in the convention and meetings field.

Automated Distribution

Using telephone lines, the Satellite Ticket Printer (STP) enables a travel agency to print tickets electronically in an office of a corporation that the agency serves—thus eliminating the cost of delivering tickets. If this corporation wishes to use a particular agency's expertise, they can do so, regardless of the distance involved. Also, the corporation's travel expenses can be summarized into one periodic account—a beneficial arrangement. Automated ticketing machines (ATMs) are owned by airlines and located in major airports for passenger convenience. The customer inserts a credit card into the machine, which provides flight information, makes a reservation, and prints a ticket and boarding pass.

CHOOSING CHANNELS

Any marketing officer must decide on which combination of distribution channels would be most productive. One of his or her most important tasks is to research and identify distribution possibilities. Then the particular travel product can be integrated into the distributor's operation. Some channels are very evident, such as travel agencies. However, depending on the individual product, additional distributors, such as tour companies, specialty channelers, incentive travel firms, corporate travel departments, hotel sales reps, and associations, can be very sales-effective. Often, associations have huge numbers of members, which make them particularly good avenues for increasing sales.

SUMMARY

Tourism channels of distribution are organizational links in a travel product producer's system of describing, selling, and confirming travel arrangements to the buyer. Such channels are needed because it is impractical for any supplier to own sales outlets in every market city. It is much more feasible and productive to distribute the product, for example, through 30,000 retail travel agencies. A commission is paid for each sale made. There are specialty channelers of many kinds.

These channels are similar to those used in other industries. But tourism products are intangible. They cannot be stored and sold another time. An airplane seat, if not occupied for a trip, is revenue lost forever.

Key Concepts

American Society of Travel Agents	hotel sales representatives
automated distribution	incentive travel firms
channel organizations	intermediaries
choosing channels	National Tour Association
consortia	retail travel agencies
consumers	specialty channelers
cooperatives	tour wholesalers
corporate travel departments	U.S. Tour Operators Association
distribution channels	
domination of travel agencies	
franchise organizations	

For Review and Discussion

1. As a producer of travel products, why not just sell your services directly to the consumer? Think of the money you would save!

2. For what reasons do retail travel agencies dominate tourism distribution channels? What accounts for their remarkable growth in numbers?

3. Give some examples of marketing aids that a supplier might provide to your travel agency.

4. Some counselors are not really good salespersons. As manager of your agency, what skill-building program would you inaugurate if needed?

5. You are marketing director for a cruise line operating truly luxurious ships. These have superb service and cuisine. How would you proceed to identify the most promising distributors?

6. Air travel sales constitute the bulk of a travel agency's business. But auto travel makes up 80 percent of the intercity U.S. market. How could agencies increase their auto travel–related business?

7. As the president of a newly formed tour company, you must now decide if your tours are to be marketed through retail travel agencies or whether you should try to sell them directly to the consumer. Identify the advantages and disadvantages of each alternative. Would it be wise to do both? Discuss.

8. Why should an independently owned and operated travel agency become affiliated with one of the consortia, cooperatives, or franchise groups?

9. Could there be a difference in the functioning of a tour wholesaler and a tour operator? Explain.

10. List the advantages of a tour company becoming a member of USTOA.

11. Similarly, what advantages does a travel agency derive from its membership in ASTA?

12. A fairly large manufacturer of specialty electric products is located in your city. What steps would you take to sell this company on an incentive travel plan?

13. List the names of several prominent hotel rep firms. Explain how they function in behalf of an independently owned resort hotel. Would a Holiday Inn use such a firm? Why or why not?

Case Problems

1. Joan S. and her husband are planning a vacation to a destination about which they know very little. They have seen an exciting ad for this area in a travel magazine. They write, and receive a group of fascinating brochures describing all the attractions, accommodations, shops, climate, and other allures. In the same magazine they saw an ad for an airline that serves this destination, including an 800 telephone number for reservations. Why should they seek the help of a travel agency?

2. A professor recently walked into a travel agency—his first visit there—and asked for a specific cruise brochure. The travel agent rose from her desk, found the promotional piece requested, and handed it to him. The professor thanked her and then asked, "How is the travel business these days?" She replied, "Business and corporate are OK but vacation travel is way off. Very few people are traveling now." She then sat down, looked into her CRS screen and said, "Have a nice day." Can you believe such a scenario? What *should* the conversation have been?

3. A prominent national columnist recently advised his readers that they should bypass their local travel agencies and obtain their air tickets and arrange their cruise

vacations directly from these suppliers. This recommendation was intended to save the public money because, he explained, air and ship lines pay commissions to travel agencies whenever a sale is made. What's wrong with such advice?

4. An international tour company partnership is owned by Bill and Jane W. Bill is a rather deliberate, cautious type; Jane tends to be more aggressive and promotional in her day-to-day business relationships. The company's volume of business has declined somewhat during the past two years. Considering this problem, they recently had an extended discussion as to possible steps that might increase tour sales. Jane finally proposed that they should contact some of the largest travel agency cooperatives. These are also known as coops, consortia, franchisors, joint marketing organizations, stockholder licensee groups, and individual and corporate-owned chains. Jane thought that perhaps if their company could become a so-called "preferred supplier" to one or several of these groups, they would then increase their business considerably. Almost all of their tours are sold through retail travel agencies. Bill listened to this suggestion and then said: "I doubt that this idea would do us any good. The coop movement is not well established and a lot of agencies are not members at all." Who's right? Why? Explain your position.

Selected References

American Express. *Survey of Group Business Travel Management: 1991–1992*. Norcross, Ga.: American Express, 1992.

Duvall, Patricia W., Ray M. Haynes, and Lawrence J. Truitt. "Evaluating Small Travel Agency Productivity." *Journal of Travel Research*, Vol. 31, No. 3 (Winter 1993), pp. 10–13.

Elton, M. A. "U.K. Tour Operations and Retail Travel Agents: ABTA and the Public Interest." *Tourism Management*, Vol, 5, No. 3 (September 1984), pp. 223–228.

Gilbert, D. C., and P. Houghton. "An Exploratory Investigation of Format, Design, and Use of UK Tour Operators' Brochures." *Journal of Travel Research*, Vol. 30, No. 2 (Fall 1991), pp. 20–25.

Hoyle, Leonard, David C. Dorf, and Thomas J. Jones. *Managing Conventions and Group Business*. East Lansing, Mich.: Educational Institute of the American Hotel and Motel Association, 1989.

King, Brian. "Tour Operators and the Air Inclusive Tour Industry in Australia." *Travel and Tourism Analyst*, No. 3 (1991), pp. 66–87.

National Tour Foundation. *Group Travel Report*. Lexington, Ky.: NTF, 1990.

National Tour Foundation. *Predicting NTA Tour Operator Performance*. Lexington, Ky.: NTF, 1990.

Quiroga, Isabel. "Characteristics of Package Tours in Europe." *Annals of Tourism Research*, Vol. 17, No. 2 (1990), pp. 185–207.

Reed Travel Group. *1994 Travel Weekly U.S. Travel Agency Market Survey*. Secaucus, N.J.: Reed, 1994.

Runzheimer and Company. *1990–91 Survey and Analysis of Business Travel Policies and Costs*. Northbrook, Ill.: Runzheimer, 1991.

Sloan, Jim. "Latest Developments in Aviation CRSs." *Travel and Tourism Analyst*, No. 4 (1990), pp. 5–15.

Thompson, Douglas, and Jon Schulberg. *The Complete Guide to Travel Agency Video*. San Francisco: Dendrobium Books, 1988.

Thompson-Smith, Jeanie M. *Travel Agency Guide to Business Travel*. Albany, N.Y.: Delmar Publishers, 1988.

Watson, Graham. "The Incentive Travel Market in Europe." *Travel and Tourism Analyst*, No. 3 (1990), pp. 65–78.

Attractions, Recreation, Entertainment, and Other

LEARNING OBJECTIVES

- Examine the attractions industry.
- Look at the role of theme parks.
- Understand the gaming industry.
- Describe public and commercial recreation facilities.
- Recognize shopping as a travel attraction.

INTRODUCTION

There are so many things for tourists to do and choices to make that it is sometimes difficult to decide which activities one would like to participate in. Figure 8.1 from the USTTA in-flight survey gives a good sampling of the many activity choices available to tourists.

Even though this is an extensive list, there are many others, such as festivals, events, zoos, aquariums, state parks, county parks, city facilities, and other attractions too numerous to list.

ATTRACTIONS

Natural and developed attractions are the "mainspring" that drives many people to travel. The great national parks of the United States and other countries, such as those in Canada, India, Australia, and Japan, are examples. National forests in the United States attract millions of recreationists. State parks exist in many areas that have tourist appeal. The same is so for botanical, zoological, mountain, and seaside parks. Thus these natural wonders lure travelers to enjoy the natural beauty, recreation, and inspiration that they provide.

Human-built attractions such as historical sites and prehistory and archeological sites such as the ancient monuments of Egypt, Greece, Israel, Turkey, Indonesia, India, Mexico, and Peru also have appeal for those inspired to learn more about contemporary and long-vanished civilizations.

Great modern cities with their cultural treasures of many sorts provide powerful attractions to millions of visitors each year. Sightseeing tours are provided in most cities, giving easy access to the city's attractions. Theaters, museums, special buildings, cultural events, festivals, shopping, and dining are some of the appeals.

☐ Water sports/Sunbathing	☐ Shopping	☐ Snow skiing
☐ Concert/Play/Musical	☐ Attend sports event	☐ Golf/Tennis
☐ Art gallery/Museum	☐ Hunting/Fishing	☐ Camping/Hiking
☐ Sightseeing in cities	☐ Dining in restaurants	☐ Touring the countryside
☐ Commercial guided tours	☐ Amusement/Theme parks	☐ Visit National Parks
☐ Nightclubs/Dancing	☐ Visit historical places	☐ Cruises of 1 night or longer
☐ Ranch vacations	☐ Visiting casinos/Gambling	☐ Visit American Indian Communities

Figure 8.1   USTTA In-Flight Survey of Activity Choices

The Attractions Industry

The attractions industry consists of fixed-location amusement parks and attractions in the United States and 40 other countries. They are primarily private businesses, although there are a number of publicly operated facilities. Amusement parks and attractions in the United States generate approximately $5.5 billion in annual revenues. Over 275,000 people are employed seasonally by the industry in the United States, and over 260 million people visited amusement parks and attractions (including water parks, miniature golf courses, and family entertainment centers) according to the International Association of Amusement Parks and Attractions.

The attractions industry is dominated by Disneyland and Disney World, which have been two of the most successful attractions ever developed. However, while theme parks are a major tourist attraction, there are more than 10,000 natural scenic, historical, cultural, and entertainment attractions that appeal to travelers. Attractions include not only theme parks, but the entertainment park, amusement park, animal park, museum, scenic railway, historic village, preserved mansion, scenic cruise, natural wonder, restaurant, music festival, industry exhibit, cave, theater, historic farm, scenic overlook, resort complex, historic site, botanical garden, arboretum, plantation, hall of fame, water show, zoo, sports complex, cultural center, state park, national park, county park, outdoor theater, native American reservation, and transportation exhibit.

Theme Parks

The theme park business has enjoyed spectacular expansion since the opening of Disneyland in 1955 in Anaheim, California. The opening of Disneyland changed the local amusement park business considerably because it expanded the concept of amusement parks from simply rides and carnival barkers to include shows, shops, and restaurants in theme settings with immaculate cleanliness, promising adventure, history, science fiction, or fantasy.

The success of Disneyland brought Disney World, the largest and grandest theme park in the world, with its Magic Kingdom as the focal point of the resort complex. Disney World attracts over 30.2 million visitors annually (see Table 8.1) and is far more than a theme park. It has a 7500-acre conservation project for the preservation of fauna and wildlife of the everglades; an experimental prototype community of tomorrow (EPCOT); the Disney World Showcase, where several nations feature exhibits of their country's attractions and culture; Disney–MGM Studios; and Pleasure Island.

Disneyland characters greet visitors to this famous theme park. Such attractions are important generators of nearby and longer-distance travel. (Photo courtesy of the Walt Disney Company)

As would be expected, the success of the Disney theme parks brought imitators and large corporations to the business. In addition to those listed in Table 8.1, other prominent theme parks are Sea World in San Antonio, Texas; Great America, Santa Clara, California; Opryland, Nashville, Tennessee; Canada's Wonderland, Toronto, Ontario; and Busch Gardens, Williamsburg, Virginia.

The nation's major theme parks appear to be concentrated in Florida and California. Disney has projects in both states, and the Orlando, Florida, area probably has the single largest number of theme parks and attractions in any single location. This concentration is likely to continue, as new attractions or expansions are still taking place in the area.

Industry representatives predict that an area to watch for the future is the development of theme parks in conjunction with shopping malls. The activity at the West Edmonton, Canada mall complex and the Mall of America in Minnesota has encouraged this prediction.

Table 8.1 Top U.S. Theme Park Admissions[a]

	1991	1992
Walt Disney World,[b] Lake Buena Vista, Fla.	28.0	30.2
Disneyland, Anaheim, Calif.	11.6	11.6
Universal Studios Florida, Orlando	5.9	6.7
Universal Studios Hollywood, Universal City, Calif.	4.6	4.8
Sea World of Florida, Orlando	3.4	4.1
Sea World of California, San Diego	3.3	4.0
Knott's Berry Farm, Buena Park, Calif.	4.0	3.9
Paramount's Kings Island, Kings Island, Ohio	2.8	3.3
Six Flags Magic Mountain, Valencia, Calif.	3.2	3.2
Six Flags Great America, Gurnee, Ill.	2.6	3.2
Cedar Point, Sandusky, Ohio	3.1	3.0
Six Flags Great Adventure, Jackson, N.J.	2.9	3.1
Busch Gardens Tampa, Tampa, Fla.	2.9	3.1
Six Flags Over Texas, Arlington, Texas	2.7	3.0
Santa Cruz Beach Boardwalk, Santa Cruz, Calif.	3.0	3.0

[a]In millions.
[b]Includes Magic Kingdom, EPCOT Center, and Disney MGM Studios Theme park.
Source: Travel and Meetings Digest, June 1993.

International Association of Amusement Parks and Attractions

The goals and objectives of the International Association of Amusement Parks and Attractions (IAAPA) include increasing education and instituting training seminars, both regionally and overseas. The association plans to establish an International Institute for amusement industry management. It has also targeted its efforts toward coordinating safety regulations and standards among various countries. IAAPA has scheduled an increase in activities beneficial to members outside the United States.

The long-term goal of the association is to continue as the sole international parks association by increasing the participation of international members, conducting a major trade show and seminar for the industry each year, and raising the standards of management and service in the industry.

GAMING

Gambling, or the gaming industry, has become a major force in the tourism industry. The gaming industry has grown from a narrow Nevada base with limited acceptance in the financial and public sector to a recognized growth industry. While gaming has always been a popular form of recreation, it has also been controversial.

There is no question that gaming generates travel. Nevada has been the leader in gambling, which has made tourism the leading industry in the state. Las Vegas is considered the casino capital of the world. It is interesting to note the differences in the types of tourists and their modes of transportation when comparing Las Vegas and Atlantic City. Las Vegas attracts destination visitors from long distances who fly or drive, while Atlantic City is located in a densely populated area and attracts nearby

Arriving at Six Flags Great America Theme park in Gurnee, Illinois, guests first see this 10-story-tall Columbia carousel, a two-level landmark attraction. (Photo courtesy of Six Flags Great America)

(within 150 miles) residents. Atlantic City has successfully promoted short-duration motorcoach tours to increase its numbers.

Gaming is available in many parts of the world, as well as on cruise ships. Well-known areas for casino gambling include Monaco, the Caribbean, London, Nice, Macau, and Rio de Janeiro. In the United States, gaming is being introduced to Native American reservations to create economic development. Over the last decade, reservation gaming has grown to a $6 billion enterprise. There are about 150 reservations with gaming operations in 24 states.

As new casinos go up in Atlantic City, New Orleans, Colorado, the Mississippi River, South Dakota, Indian reservations, and in the Bahamas, one sees the impact of gaming on tourism and the local economy. Given the current growth in gaming, it is safe to predict that it will continue to play a role in tourism and economic development.

RECREATION

Recreation is a diverse industry, representing over $280 billion in expenditures each year. The industry generates millions of jobs in the manufacturing, sales, and service sectors. Nearly 50 percent of Americans describe themselves as "outdoor people." They enjoy a wide variety of activities to keep fit, to add excitement to their lives, to have fun with family and friends, to pursue solitary activities, and to experience nature firsthand.

The draw of recreation opportunities throughout the United States is one factor in

Animals hold great interest for both children and adults. Close-up encounters are the usual pattern at Theater of the Sea located in the Florida Keys. (Photo courtesy of GAT Marketing)

the rise of domestic travel, as well as in the increase in international visits to the United States. Outdoor adventure travel is gaining in popularity, and travel professionals have better access to information on recreational travel options. People are seeking higher-quality services and amenities.

Illustrative of the range of businesses within the recreation industry are recreation vehicle (RV) manufacturers and dealers, boat manufacturers and dealers, full-line recreation product manufacturers, park concessioners, campground owners, resorts, enthusiast groups, snowmobile manufacturers, recreation publications, motorcoach operators, bicycling interests, and others.

Companies manufacturing recreation products tend to be large. For example, the manufacturing of new RVs is an $8 billion per year industry. According to the Recreation Vehicle Dealers Association, another $6.5 billion is generated through the used and rental RV markets and the sales of after-market parts, accessories, and services.

The Recreation Vehicle Industry Association (RVIA), located in Reston, Virginia, is a primary source of shipment statistics, market research, and technical data. The association also supplies campground directories, publications covering RV maintenance, trip preparation, and safety issues.

In contrast to the large companies involved in manufacturing RVs, boats, pools, mountain bikes, skis, and so on, the private service sector is made up primarily of small businesses, ranging from campgrounds to marinas to wilderness guides. There is also the public sector, providing services through the National Park Service, Forest Service, and state and local agencies.

Gambling or gaming as a recreational pursuit is becoming more popular, especially in the United States. It is often enjoyed along with night club shows and sports activities. (Photo courtesy of the Reno News Bureau)

Parks

Both private and government enterprises operate various kinds of parks, including amusement parks. National parks are often very important parts of a nation's or state's tourism. In some countries (e.g., Africa), national parks are their primary attractions. Typical are Kenya, Rwanda, Uganda, Tanzania, Botswana, and South Africa.

National and State Parks

U.S. National Parks recorded 273.1 million visits in 1993. The National Park System consists of 367 parks, recreation areas, preserves, battlefields, historic sites, lakeshores, monuments, memorials, seashores, parkways, and rivers. In the United States many individual states operate park systems, some of the most outstanding being New York, California, Tennessee, Oregon, Indiana, Kentucky, Florida, and Michigan.

The National Association of State Park Directors reported that attendance at state

Sleeping Bear Dunes National Lakeshore, Michigan, is representative of the spectacular natural wonders that the National Park Service administers and preserves for the enjoyment of visitors. (Photo courtesy of the Michigan Travel Commission)

parks rose 1 percent in 1991, to 734 million visits. Approximately 11 million acres are contained in 5,256 state parks. Parks are also operated by other units of government, such as county or park districts like the Huron–Clinton Metropolitan Authority of the greater Detroit area in southeastern Michigan. This system has six parks within easy access of residents of the Detroit metropolitan area. Counties, townships, and cities also operate parks and often campgrounds as parts of parks.

National Forests

Visitors spent 288 million recreation visitor-days (12 visit-hours by one or more persons) and generated $46.5 million in recreation receipts in 1992, according to the U.S. Forest Service. Part of the Department of Agriculture, the U.S. Forest Service maintains 191 million acres in the National Forest System, with 156 national forests and 20 grasslands in 42 states and Puerto Rico. Especially popular activities are hiking, camping, hunting, fishing, canoeing, and skiing.

Other Recreational Lands

The *Bureau of Land Management* (BLM) oversees more than 270 million of acres of land. In 1992, approximately 76 million people visited BLM lands. BLM issued 94,376 camping and day-use permits in 1991, a 21 percent increase over 1990, generating $1.8 million in user fees. The *Corps of Engineers* manages nearly 12 million acres of land and water in 43 states with approximately 440 recreation areas. Approximately 414 million visitors spent $9 billion during 1992. The *U.S. Fish & Wildlife Service* manages over 91 million acres of fish and wildlife habitats, 340 of which provide recreation opportunities. *The Bureau of Indian Affairs* manages 56 million acres held in trust for Native Americans. Of the 278 reservations in the lower 48 states, 140 contain only tribally owned land. Of the 8.5 million acres administered by the Bureau of Reclamation, 4.7 million acres of land and 1.8 million surface acres of water are available for recreation.

Summer and Winter Sports

In 1991, over 66 million Americans age 7 years and older went swimming, 54 million went biking, 47 million fished, and 25 million played golf, according to the National Sporting Goods Association. Expenditures on boating products totaled $11 billion in 1991. New boat sales sunk to 439,000 in 1991, an 18 percent decrease from 1990, according to the National Marine Manufacturers Association. Skier visits increased 6 percent from the 1991–1992 season to reach 54 million. Skiing is a $7 billion industry in the United States, with $1.5 billion spent at ski areas and $5.5 billion on products and related items, according to the National Ski Areas Association. During 1992–1993, 84,000 snowmobiles with a retail value of $391 million were sold, according to the International Snowmobile Association. Snowmobile sales increased by 2.4 percent during the 1992–1993 season.

Commercial Campgrounds

Approximately 84 million visitor nights were spent in commercial camps in 1992, up 3.7 percent from 1991, according to the National Association of RV Parks & Campgrounds. Commercial campground revenue totaled approximately $3.2 billion in 1992 and camps employed 38,000 people full-time.

Historic Sites

Historic sites have always been popular attractions for both domestic and international travelers. Latest estimates for 1991 indicate that 30 percent of all U.S. households visited historic sites, districts, or buildings while traveling, according to the National Endowment for the Arts. According to the U.S. Travel and Tourism Administration's in-flight survey, 25 percent of all overseas travelers visited an art gallery or museum and another 32 percent visited historic sites during 1991. The National Park Service maintains an estimated 59,634 historic sites, as noted in the National Register of Historic Sites. Approximately 14 percent are historic districts, and about 861,000 are historic properties located within the sites.

Zoos, "Jungles," and Aquariums

The menageries and aviaries of China, Egypt, and Rome were famous in ancient times. Today, zoological parks and aquariums continue to be popular attractions. A recent development in the United States has been the creation of indoor rainforests. Notable are the Lied Jungle in the Henry Doorly Zoo in Omaha, Nebraska and the Rainforest within the Cleveland, Ohio Metropolitan Zoo. The Lied Jungle is the world's largest indoor rainforest, its $15 million cost financed by the Lied Foundation. It recreates rainforests as found in Asia, Africa, and South America. The "jungle" occupies 1.5 acres under one roof. It contains 2000 species of tropical plants and 517 animal species, and attracts over 1.3 million visitors annually. This has become the biggest tourist attraction in Nebraska. The Cleveland Rainforest has also become very successful.

ENTERTAINMENT

Another powerful tourism magnet is entertainment. Live entertainment is often the main attraction for a vacation trip. The deadheads following the Grateful Dead concert tour are a prime example. Another are people traveling to Nashville, Tennessee to hear country and western music at the Grand Ol' Opry. Branson, Missouri has put itself on the map as a music entertainment center and is now challenging Nashville. One of the centerpieces of the famous "I Love New York" advertising campaign was

Hotel theaters and night clubs feature spectacular production shows along the "Strip" in Las Vegas, Nevada. (Photo courtesy of the Las Vegas News Bureau)

The world-famous Hollywood Bowl, the summer home of the Los Angeles Philharmonic, hosts a variety of top musical acts. A favorite spot for picnics, the landmark outdoor amphitheater dates back to the 1920s and also houses a museum of bowl history. (Photo courtesy of the Los Angeles Convention and Visitors Bureau/Donna Carroll)

going to a Broadway play or musical. A theater tour to London is a powerful vacation lure. Large numbers of performing arts tours are offered.

The U.S. Travel Data Center estimates that entertainment travel accounts for 326 million person trips per year or one-fourth of all travel in America. The Institute of Outdoor Drama reports that there are 70 outdoor dramas in the United States, providing 4500 summer jobs and recording $30 million in revenue each year. According to the League of American Theaters and Producers, attendance at professional theaters, symphony, opera, and dance performances totaled 86.3 million in 1991, generating $6.5 billion in revenue.

FESTIVALS AND EVENTS

Among the fastest-growing segments of tourism are these types of celebrations. Countries and cities compete vigorously for megaevents such as the Olympics, World Cup, and World Fairs. Such events produce sizable economic and tourism benefits. For example, World Youth Day, along with the Pope's visit to Denver, Colorado in 1993, drew an estimated 280,000 visitors. Even small communities can stage such events. Many local festivals originally designed to entertain local residents have grown to attract visitors from many miles away. Donald Getz, University of Calgary, has written a book, *Festivals, Special Events and Tourism*. He states that festivals and events appeal to a very broad audience. However, elements of these or specific themes can be effectively targeted to desired tourist market segments. Festivals and events also have the ability to spread tourism geographically and seasonally. Special events allow a region or community to celebrate its uniqueness, promote itself, develop local pride, and enhance its economic well-being. The International Festivals Association estimates that every year there are between 50,000 and 60,000 half-day to one-day events and 5000 or more festivals of two days or longer.

SHOPPING

Shopping is an important part of any tourist's activities. To make shopping as convenient as possible, many hotels provide shops featuring gift items, particularly local handicrafts and artwork. In the shopping areas of each community that caters successfully to tourists are found high-quality gift and souvenir shops featuring items of particular interest to visitors. The chain hotel and motel companies have also organized gift shops as part of their operations. Host International maintains a system of gift and

Shopping delights visitors and is an important tourism activity. (Photo courtesy of the Cayman Islands News Bureau)

merchandise shops in most of the areas in which it has established airport dining rooms, cocktail lounges, snack bars, coffee shops, and in-flight food services. These gift and merchandise shops are an important part of the business operations. In addition, gift shops are provided along the toll roads, where Host International provides dining rooms, coffee shops, and snack bars.

Gift and souvenir shops and the companies operating them are commonly members of the local chambers of commerce, convention and visitors bureaus, and regional or local tourism promotional organizations. Shopping is not only an integral part of any vacation trip but can be the reason for going. The factory outlet store located in a destination resort setting has proven to be a successful and rapidly growing phenomenon. The Mall of America in Bloomington, Minnesota, is the largest mall in the United States. It is proving to be a real tourist attraction. Excursion motorcoach tours in Minnesota and nearby states now feature packages with Mall of America as their destination. This mall is particularly attractive to children as it features LEGO's gigantic space station, dinosaurs, a medieval castle, and other intricate creations. They can also enjoy Knott's Camp Snoopy and plenty of rides. There are 14 theaters in the Upper East Side entertainment district, plus a comedy club, sports bars, and a variety of nightclubs. While shopping at the West Edmonton Mall in Alberta, Canada, one can view sharks from a submarine, live a Roman fantasy, or soak in a bubble-filled spa near a volcano. This mall is the largest in the world. It even contains a full-scale replica of Columbus's ship *Santa Maria*, roulette wheels, the Ice Palace, and, of course, hundreds of stores, plus some theme parks.

EDUCATION

Suppliers of the tourism product look to educational organizations as sources of talent for their industries. These include secondary schools, vocational schools, junior or community colleges, four-year colleges and universities, and trade association schools and institutes. Most high schools, which are known by various terms in different countries, offer curricula and subjects of value to travel firms. Examples are native and foreign languages, geography, history, writing, use of computers, secretarial skills, bookkeeping, and food preparation. Many vocational schools produce entry-level employees for travel agencies, tour companies, airlines, accommodations, food service, and others, and junior and community colleges offer education and training in various skills applicable to the travel industry.

Trade associations and professional societies are also active in education. Examples of these are the educational programs and home study courses of the American Society of Travel Agents, the Institute of Certified Travel Agents, the Educational Institute of the American Hotel and Motel Association, the National Institute for the Foodservice Industry, and, in Britain, the Institute of Travel and Tourism. Most public carriers, especially the airlines, provide rigorous training and educational programs for their employees, as well as for those working for travel agencies and tour companies. The International Labour Organization (a U.N. affiliate in Geneva, Switzerland) has conducted numerous types of training programs in tourism-related vocations. Similarly, the World Tourism Organization conducts a correspondence course for those in official tourism departments.

Four-year colleges and universities provide instruction in similar skills and management education. In keeping with the diversity of the industry, courses are offered in schools of business and hotel and restaurant administration, colleges of natural resources, commercial recreation departments, sociology departments, and anthropology departments. A number of schools are offering graduate programs in travel and tourism. In addition to courses and educational programs, universities and colleges conduct a great deal of research, which is available to the industry.

The Council on Hotel, Restaurant and Institutional Education (CHRIE) reports that there are 835 schools offering bachelor degrees, 30 master degrees, and 10 offering doctorate degrees in the field of travel and tourism. The publication, *A Guide to Programs in Hospitality and Tourism,* provides a description of tourism programs and is available from CHRIE or John Wiley & Sons.

Finally, land-grant schools provide services through the Cooperative Extension Service, which operates in all 50 states. Educational services are available to managers of hotels, motels, restaurants, resorts, clubs, marinas, small service businesses, and similar enterprises from some state organizations. Short courses and conferences are sometimes held for managers of these businesses to make them more efficient and productive. These educational services are provided by the land-grant colleges and universities and the Cooperative Extension Service, which is supported in part by the U.S. Department of Agriculture.

Educational Organizations

The Travel and Tourism Research Association has over 150 educational members. In addition, educators' sessions are held at the annual conference. The National Park and Recreation Association has a section called the Society of Park and Recreation Educators (SPRE). This group works on appropriate curriculum and features programs on education and research. Hotel and restaurant educators formed the Council on Hotel, Restaurant, and Institutional Education (CHRIE), which fosters improved teaching methods and aids in curriculum development for all educational levels, from high school through four-year colleges and universities. The Society of Travel and Tourism Educators holds an annual conference and publishes a newsletter. The Society strives to improve tourism teaching. Finally, there is the International Academy for the Study of Tourism, which seeks to improve tourism education and research.

PUBLISHING

Producers of printed news, feature articles, advertising, and publicity constitute a very important type of business within tourism. Because the field is so fast changing, such news and feature articles must be read in order to keep up to date but also for current information needed for intelligent counseling and management.

Another vital group of publishers includes those who produce reference manuals, tariffs, guides, atlases, timetables, and operational handbooks. Without these, no travel organization could function. Counselors and others who contact travelers must be informed as to the nomenclature of their particular part of the business. They must also know rules and regulations, methods of operation, schedules, transit times, accommodations, equipment and service, tariffs, rates, commissions, and other, such as details of any travel destination. The list of these is long and varies for each country. No single publication could possibly cover the needed information for any particular branch of the industry. References can be grouped as follows:

1. Independently published references for the travel industry, such as the *Official Airline Guide, Hotel and Travel Index, AH & MA Red Book,* the *ABC World Airways Guide,* and the *Official Steamship Guide*
2. Publications of the national tourism organizations
3. Hotel chain or hotel representatives references
4. Guides published mainly for the public but used in the travel industry, such as Michelin, Fodor, Rand McNally, and Frommer
5. Specialized guides such as *Castle Hotels of Europe*

Trade papers and magazines are published in most countries and carry current information (some are published twice weekly) to the travel industry. Examples are *Travel Weekly, Travel Agent, Travel Trade, Tour and Travel News, Canadian Travel News,* and *British Travel News.* A more complete list and a better grasp of all the periodicals, studies, and research bulletins can be obtained by examining Appendix B.

MARKETING AND PUBLICITY ORGANIZATIONS

Travel marketing consultants provide valuable assistance to any organization needing specialized sales services. A travel marketing consultant organization will provide assistance in planning a publicity and sales campaign, selecting markets, selecting media, providing market research, discovering new markets, and overall conducting of a sales and marketing program.

Most state-level tourism promotion programs are conducted through established advertising agencies. To conduct this program successfully, these agencies must do market analysis of the travel industry, and many of these agencies have developed an expertise in this field. The names of the advertising agencies serving the various state tourism organizations can be obtained by writing to the state organization. A list of the state tourism organizations appears in Appendix A or can be obtained from the Travel Industry Association of America, 1100 New York Avenue, N.W., Washington, D.C. 20005.

MISCELLANEOUS SERVICES

Many other organizations provide essential services to tourism. Examples are hospitals and medical services, police services, sanitary trash pickup and disposal services, laundry services, construction services, retail stores such as department stores, drugstores, clothing stores, newspapers (including tourist newspapers and special travel editions), travel writers, and magazines.

SUMMARY

The businesses and organizations that provide attractions, recreation, entertainment, shopping, and others comprise major parts of tourism. For example, just trips for entertainment constitute about one-fourth of all travel in the United States. There are many activities engaged in by tourists—a wealth of opportunities.

Theme parks such as Disneyland and Universal Studios also attract millions each year. Most of these are showing a steady rise in patronage. Gaming or gambling is also a growing industry. It has now been legalized in states other than Nevada and New Jersey, and attendance continues to rise. Parks come in all sizes and types. They serve both local and visitor recreational needs. National parks are of particular interest to both domestic and international visitors. National forests are very popular. Zoos, "jungles," and aquariums, usually located in parks, attract locals as well as millions of tourists. A new development is the recreation of tropical rainforests within zoological parks. Outstanding examples are the Lied Jungle in Omaha, Nebraska, and the Rainforest in Cleveland, Ohio.

Shopping continues to be a major attraction. Spectacular new malls such as the Mall of America in Minnesota and the West Edmonton Mall in Alberta, Canada, have become tourist destinations. They contain an amazing variety of recreational facilities as well as hundreds of shops. Festivals and events are attractions of great and growing importance. Megaevents such as the Olympics are sought-after awards to a city. Local festivals typically attract a wider audience once they become better publicized.

Key Concepts

activities

aquariums

entertainment

events

festivals

gaming or gambling

International Association of Amusement
   Parks and Attractions

"jungles" (rainforests)

Mall of America

National Association of State Park
   Directors

national forests

National Park Service

parks

recreation

Recreational Vehicle Industry Association

shopping

theme parks

West Edmonton Mall

zoological parks

For Review and Discussion

1. Give some of the main reasons that attractions and entertainment places are enjoying growing popularity.
2. How important are these factors as pleasure travel motivators?
3. If you were planning a destination-type resort, how much attention would you give to its recreation and entertainment features?
4. Why have theme parks changed the amusement park business so drastically?
5. Identify the principal appeals of theme parks. Explain their growth trends.
6. What are the directions being taken in the U.S. gambling industry?
7. Is the ownership of recreational vehicles a passing fad?
8. Where are the most famous national parks located? (Select various countries.)

9. Explain why recreated tropical rainforest "jungles" in zoos have become so popular.

10. Should the spectacular new shopping malls include a director of tourism?

11. Suppose that your firm was considering building a new theater or attraction in Branson, Missouri. Where would you seek information and data? What kinds of these would be needed?

12. List the advantages to local people who sponsor a festival that subsequently becomes attractive to a wider market.

13. Evaluate the national forests as recreational resources.

Case Problem

Most of the states in the United States are experiencing budget crunches. A number of legislatures are considering legalizing gaming (gambling). Some states have already done so. As a state representative, you have decided to introduce legislation legalizing gaming, to bolster your state's budget. What would be your arguments supporting this bill? What opposition would you expect?

Selected References

Cammerman, James M., and Ronald Bordessa. *Wonderland Through the Looking Glass.* Ontario: Belsten, 1981.

Center for Survey and Marketing Research. *Attractions: The Heart of the Travel Product.* Kenosha, Wis.: CSMR, 1992.

Deebow, Suzanne M. "Gone Gamblin." *Meeting News* (September 1993), pp. 37–45.

Dombrink, John, and William N. Thompson. *The Last Resort: Success and Failure in Campaigns for Casinos.* Reno, Nev.: University of Nevada Press, 1990.

Eadington, William R., and Judy A. Cornelius. *Gambling Behavior and Problem Gambling.* Reno, Nev.: University of Nevada Press, 1991.

Eadington, William R., and Judy A. Cornelius. *Gambling and Commercial Gaming.* Reno, Nev.: University of Nevada Press, 1991.

Eadington, William R., and Judy A. Cornelius. *Gambling and Public Policy: International Perspectives.* Reno, Nev.: University of Nevada Press, 1991.

Getz, Donald. *Festivals, Special Events, and Tourism.* New York: Van Nostrand Reinhold, 1991.

International Association of Amusement Parks and Attractions. "1992 Amusement Industry Abstract." *Funworld*, Vol. 9, No. 2 (1993), pp. 33–64.

Janiskee, Robert L. "Resort Camping in America." *Annals of Tourism Research*, Vol. 17, No. 3 (1990), pp. 385–407.

Janson-Verbeke, Myriam. "Leisure Shopping: A Magic Concept for the Tourism Industry?" *Tourism Management*, Vol. 12, No. 1 (March 1991), pp. 9–14.

Leiper, Neil. "Tourist Attraction Systems." *Annals of Tourism Research*, Vol. 17, No. 3 (1990), pp. 367–384.

Littlejohn, Margaret, and Gary Machlis. *A Diversity of Visitors: A Report on Visitors to the National Park System.* Lexington, Ky.: National Tour Foundation, 1990.

Mancini, Marc. *Conducting Tours: A Practical Guide.* Cincinnati, Ohio: South-Western Publishing Company, 1990.

McClung, Gordon W. "Theme Park Selection." *Tourism Management*, Vol. 12, No. 2 (June 1991), pp. 132–140.

McClung, Gordon W., et al. *Feasibility of an Amusement/Theme Park in the State of West Virginia.* Morgantown, W.Va.: West Virginia University, 1988.

Milman, Ady. "The Role of Theme Parks as a Leisure Activity for Local Communities." *Journal of Travel Research*, Vol. 29, No. 3 (Winter 1990), pp. 11–16.

National Park Service. *National Park Service Statistical Abstract 1993.* Denver: National Park Service Statistical Office, 1994.

Nolan, Mary Lee, and Sidney Nolan. "Religious Sites as Tourism Attractions in Europe." *Annals of Tourism Research,* Vol. 19, No. 1 (1992), pp. 68–78.

Pearce, Philip L. "Analyzing Tourist Attractions." *The Journal of Tourism Studies,* Vol. 2, No. 1 (May 1991), pp. 46–55.

Robinett, John W. "An Analysis of the U.S. Theme Park Industry." *Funworld,* Vol. 6, No. 1 (1990), pp. 4–8.

Toepper, Lorin K. "Assessing Historic Sites as Tourism Attractions: Implications for Public Policy." *Visions in Leisure and Business,* Vol. 10, No. 1 (Spring 1991), pp. 26–43.

U.S. Bureau of the Census. *Statistical Abstract of the United States: 1993,* Washington, D.C.: U.S. Government Printing Office, 1993.

PART THREE

UNDERSTANDING TRAVEL BEHAVIOR

Pleasure Travel Motivation[1]

LEARNING OBJECTIVES

- Defining a manageable research question on why tourists travel.
- Appreciate the range of ideas on travel motivation, particularly historical accounts.
- Recognize the contribution of psychological theories/other models.
- Assess the value of survey approaches to travel motivation.
- Appreciate the need for and content of the travel experience ladder as a blueprint for travel motivation study.

A FOCUS ON CONSUMERS

An understanding of the consumer is at the core of successful business practice in the tourist industry. If the various facets of the tourism, travel, and hospitality world can meet the needs of the consumer, some chance of business success is possible provided that other financial and managerial inputs are appropriate. Thus if a theme park can meet the needs of its customers, if a wilderness lodge can provide the kind of accommodation its users expect, and if an adventure tour operator can organize an exciting white-water rafting trip, there is the basis for a successful tourism business. When consumer expectations are met or exceeded by tourism operations, one can expect repeat business and positive word-of-mouth advertising, as well as the ability to maintain or even increase the current level of charging for the existing tourism service. Clearly, consumers matter to tourism businesses.

The general issue of understanding consumer needs falls within the area of the psychology of tourists' behavior. This study area is concerned with what motivates tourists, how they make decisions, what tourists think of the products they buy, how much they enjoy and learn during their holiday experiences, how they interact with the local people and environment, and how satisfied they are with their holidays.

Asking the Question

A major focus of consumer studies in the psychology of tourist behavior is the study of travel motivation. The question is often expressed simply as, "Why do tourists travel?" One of the lessons of social science research is to learn to ask good questions, that is, questions which are stimulating and challenging to our understanding of the world but

---

[1]This chapter was prepared by Phillip L. Pearce, Department of Tourism, James Cook University, Queensland, Australia.

which can be answered with enough specificity and information to enhance our knowledge. The question "Why do tourists travel?" is not a good question. Instead, we need to think of why certain groups of people choose certain holiday experiences, as this more specific question focuses attention on the similarities among groups of people and the kinds of experiences they seek. It should be noted that we are not asking the question of why groups of people travel to a specific destination, such as Las Vegas or central Africa. It can be argued that destinations offer many kinds of holiday experiences, and it oversimplifies the world to assume that areas as diverse as resort cities or countries are going to attract just one group of visitors with a certain narrow range of motivations. Additionally, the focus of this chapter is on pleasure travel rather than travel for sporting, military, political, or predominantly business reasons.

Background

There are three main sources of ideas that assist in answering questions concerning travel motivation. Historical and literary accounts of travel and travelers provides one such source. Additionally, the discipline of psychology and its long history of trying to understand and explain human behavior is a rich vein of writing for travel motivation. Finally, the current practices of tourism industry researchers, particularly those involved in surveying visitors, offer some additional insights concerning how we might approach travel motivation.

HISTORY AND LITERATURE   Historians provide a range of accounts concerning why travelers have set about their journeys over the centuries. Casson[2] and Wolfe[3] point out that the wealthier members of Athenian and Roman society owned summer resorts and used to holiday there to avoid the heat of the cities and to indulge in a social life characterized by much eating and drinking. The stability of the Roman world permitted its citizens to interest themselves in some long-distant travel, and Anthony[4] reports that visiting the Egyptian monuments and collecting souvenirs from these sites was a well-accepted and socially prestigious practice. If motives such as escape, social interaction, and social comparison were popular in Roman times, the emergence of the pilgrimage in the Middle Ages can be seen as adding a serious travel motive to our historical perspective. The original pilgrimages were essentially journeys to sacred places undertaken because of religious motives. Travelers sought the assistance or bounty of their God and journeyed long distances to revere the deity. Rowling[5] has noted that later in the Middle Ages revelry and feasting became important accompaniments to the journey and "licentious living" among the pilgrims was not unknown. The legacy of the pilgrimage for understanding modern traveler motivation is not insignificant. The pilgrimage elevated the importance of travel as an activity in one's life and created the idea that certain key sites or attractions were of long-lasting spiritual benefit to the sojourner. Good times and spiritual times were, however, not always separate.

The seriousness of travel was further enhanced by the Grand Tour, an activity intended principally as a training ground for the young and wealthy members of the English courts of the Tudor times. By the end of the eighteenth century the Grand Tour

[2]L. Casson, *Travel in the Ancient World* (London: Allen & Unwin, 1974).
[3]R. I. Wolfe, "Recreational Travel: The New Migration," *Geographical Bulletin,* Vol. 2 (1967). pp. 159–167.
[4]I. Anthony, *Verulamium* (Hanley, Staffordshire, England: Wood Mitchell, 1973).
[5]M. Rowling, *Everyday Life of Mediaeval Travellers* (London: B. T. Batsford, 1971).

had gained favor as an ideal finishing school for a youth's education, a theme not inconsistent with the analysis of much contemporary youth travel.

The effects of industrialization, urbanization, and improved transportation possibilities brought travel to the middle classes in the mid-nineteenth century and strong elements of social status and class consciousness characterize the fashions of the railway and spa resorts of nineteenth-century Europe.[6] One of the first tourism scholars, Pimlott,[7] writing in 1947, noted: "In the present century holidays have become a cult. . . . For many they are the principal objects for life—saved and planned for during the rest of the year and enjoyed in retrospect when they are over."

Now, of course, tourism is a worldwide phenomenon with enormous differentiation in its available environments, host cultures, and types of visitors. Nevertheless, some of the chief motivations noted in this brief historical review—such as travel for escape, cultural curiosity, spirituality, education, and social status—must be accounted for in any summary of contemporary travel.

Much of the contemporary travel scene is eloquently described by literary figures and professional travel writers. Their accounts of travel motivation, both of themselves and others, is subjective rather than professional but can also be considered as a background for our understanding. The noted American John Steinbeck conceived of travel as an "itch," a disease or pseudomedical condition—"the travel bug"—which periodically drove him to "be someplace else." Additionally, the theme of traveling to discover oneself has a long literary tradition and is present in the works of Ovid, Chaucer, Spenser, and Tennyson, as well as in twentieth-century fiction such as that by Jack Kerouac, E. M. Forster, D. H. Lawrence, and Joseph Conrad. The professional travel writers of the last two decades, such as Paul Thoreaux, Jan Morris, and Eric Newby, have emphasized discovery and curiosity in their analysis of the motives of travelers.

The rich tapestry of ideas about travel motivation from historical accounts and literary sources can be supplemented by theories of motivation from the discipline of psychology.

THE CONTRIBUTION OF PSYCHOLOGICAL THEORY   Psychology, as a separate area of inquiry, is often considered as originating in 1879 with the creation of the first laboratory for the scientific study of behavior by Wilhelm Wundt in Germany. During their own travels as study tours of human behavior, psychology writers and researchers have frequently addressed the topic of human motivation. The scope of this research is impressive, as it includes detailed studies of human physiology and the nervous system, through to approaches with a more cultural and anthropological orientation.

Many well-known theories in psychology have a strong motivational component. In many instances the discussion or study of motivation is a part of a broader theory directed at understanding human personality or, more simply, what makes individuals different. A summary of some major theories in psychology that have been concerned in part with the topic of motivation is presented in Table 9.1. It must be noted that these psychology researchers and thinkers were not considering travel motivation directly when formulating these approaches. Nevertheless, the third column of Table 9.1 lists a number of human needs and motives that might usefully be applied to the question of why certain groups of travelers seek particular kinds of holiday experiences.

A direct application of these psychological theories for tourist motivation adds

---

[6]E. Swinglehurst, *The Romantic Journey* (London: Pica Editions, 1974).
[7]J. A. R. Pimlott, *The Englishman's Holiday* (London: Faber & Faber, 1947).

The beauty of an unspoiled natural landscape is a strong travel motivator. (Photo courtesy of the Michigan Travel Bureau)

some new motives to the list obtained from the historical and literary review. In particular, such motives as personal control, love, sex, competence, tension reduction, arousal, achievement, acceptance, self-development, respect, curiosity, security, understanding, and self-actualization can be identified.

CURRENT MARKET RESEARCH PRACTICES   An understanding of travel motivation can also be approached by examining the kinds of motivation questions asked in surveys of travelers. Basic passport questions that are standardized around the world include only broad categories of motivation and are limited to such distinctions such as whether the travel is for business reasons, as a holiday, to visit friends and relatives, for a convention, or for other reasons. More specific market research questions are typified in studies of "travel benefits" or the rewards of travel. It can be argued that these travel benefits or rewards can be seen as the outcomes or satisfactions linked to tourists' motives for traveling.

In a typical study of travel benefits, Loker and Perdue[8] studied visitors to North Carolina and factor analyzed 12 benefit statements as part of a survey of summer travelers to that state. Using the two statistical sorting procedures of factor analysis and cluster analysis, the researchers argued that there were six segments of the market

[8]L. E. Loker and R. Perdue, "A Benefit-Based Segmentation of a Nonresident Summer Travel Market," *Journal of Travel Research,* Vol. 31, No. 1 (Summer 1992), pp. 30–35.

Table 9.1   Human Motives and Needs in Psychology Theory and Research[a]

Theorist/Researcher	Theoretical Approach	Motives or Needs Emphasized
Sigmund Freud	Psychoanalytic theory	Need for sex; need for aggression; emphasis on unconscious needs
Carl Jung	Psychoanalytic approach	Need for arousal; need to create and to self-actualize
Alfred Adler	Modified psychoanalytic	Need for competence; need for mastery to overcome incompetence
Harry Stack Sullivan	Modified psychoanalytic	Need for acceptance and love
Karen Horney	Modified psychoanalytic	Need to control anxiety; need for love and security
Clark Hull	Learning theory	Need to reduce tension
Gordon Allport	Trait theory	Need to repeat intrinsically satisfying behaviors
Albert Bambera	Social learning theory	Need for self-efficacy or personal mastery
David McClelland, John Atkinson	Social approaches	Need for achievement
Carl Rogers	Humanistic	Need for self-development
Abraham Maslow	Humanistic	Hierarchy of needs, from physiological needs to safety needs to love and relationship needs to self-esteem to self-actualization
David Berlyne	Cognitive approaches	Need to satisfy curiosity; need to seek mental stimulation
Ron Harre	Ethogenic (social and philosophical)	Need to earn respect and avoid contempt of others
Stephen Cohen, Laurie Taylor	Sociological theory	Need to escape; need for excitement and meaning
George Kelly	Personal construct theory	Need to predict and explain the world
Mikhail Csikszentmihali	Humanistic approach	Need for peak experiences

[a]For clarity the terms motives and needs are used together in this summary table. Some writers prefer to see needs as more being physiologically based and motives as more socially oriented.

receiving different kinds of benefits from their holidays. The six categories included those who emphasized excitement and escape, pure adrenalin/excitement seekers, family- and friends-oriented group, naturalists (those who enjoyed natural surroundings), a group that emphasized the value of escape by itself, and a group that enjoyed all benefits. This kind of research, which has been repeated by several other scholars with slightly different benefit groups emerging for different settings, represents a summary of travel satisfaction for a particular destination. It is thus not a pure or clean analysis of travel motivation but helps us to understand the importance of travel motivation in tourism studies by emphasizing that for travel motivation analysis to be useful and meaningful, it must be put in a context. Thus, while the list of motives from psychology theories and the history/literature of travel provides a rich source of potential motives, an understanding of travel motivation makes sense only in a particular context, that is, when people are describing why they might seek certain holiday experiences.

Frequently, market survey organizations provide potential travelers with lists of items that the researchers believe are relevant to the question of why people travel to particular destinations. Echtner and Ritchie[9] provide a summary list of 34 attributes used in 14 leading studies of destination image. Of these 34 attributes, 24 were used in at least three studies. These lists are often a mixture of attributes of the destination and select motives of the traveler. Two examples of such lists are provided in Table 9.2. While such lists of motives and destination features mixed together are common in studies trying to explain the appeal of places, they have some limitations. In particular, the lists may not be comprehensive; they may reflect the biases of the researchers and may not explore the relative importance of the various features or reasons for visiting and assume incorrectly that all reasons are equally important. Additionally, the way in which the attributes are interrelated is not often considered. For example, the characteristics of "seclusion" and "exciting nightlife" may be mutually exclusive.

THE NEED FOR A THEORY

This review of travel motivation has stressed that there are three sources of information that can provide a list of motives concerning why people travel. The list of potential travel motivations is a long one and includes a range of needs, from excitement and

Table 9.2   Motives and Destination Features from Market Survey Research

Canadian Government Travel Bureau (1970s)	Queensland (Australia) Domestic Market Segmentation Study (1990s)
Warm, friendly people	Good service
To visit friends or relatives	—
Relaxing atmosphere	—
Scenery	Lots of interesting countryside and wildlife
For oceans and beaches	Good beaches and lots of water activities
Sports facilities	Opportunity for sporting activities: golf, tennis, etc.
Good weather there	—
Not too many tourists	Seclusion
To get better buys	Good shopping
Low cost of vacations	Low-cost accommodation or good camping facilities
Good camp sites	—
Good roads	—
Outstanding food	Good restaurants
Nightlife	Lots of nightlife
Easier to have fun there	—
Attractive customs, life	Wide variety of things to do
Foreigners	—
Cultural activities	Cultural things to do (theater, museums, etc.)
Attractive advertising	—
—	High-quality accommodation
—	Lots of things for the kids to do
—	Opportunity for adventure activities: rafting, rock climbing, etc.

[9]C. M. Echtner and J. R. B. Ritchie, "The Meaning and Measurement of Destination Image," *Journal of Tourism Studies*, Vol. 2, No. 2 (1991), pp. 2–12.

Seeing a moose in its native natural environment is a thrill for any visitor. (Photo courtesy of the Wyoming Division of Tourism)

arousal to self-development and personal growth. Additionally, the brief review of contemporary market research practice concerning destination image indicated that there were further lists of destination features that might be thought of as a mix of travel motives and destination characteristics.

Theories or models in social science research typically summarize or integrate knowledge in an area, as well as organizing existing knowledge into a new perspective. Occasionally, the theory will enable prediction or specifications of future directions for human action and research. The area of tourist motivation requires a theoretical approach. There are lists of motives that need to be summarized; there are connections with other areas of inquiry, such as destination image studies, which need to be made; and there needs to be a new stimulus to challenge and enhance our current understanding. Pearce[10] has outlined seven features that are necessary for a good theory of tourist motivation. These are listed in Table 9.3.

The work of Plog[11] resulted in the psychocentric–allocentric model of travel motivation. This work was historically important in providing one organizing theory of travel motivation. It does not, however, fulfill some of the criteria listed in Table 9.3 and is notably deficient in terms of offering only a single trait: a static and extrinsic account of tourist motivation. Additionally, it is not of universal application and is limited by its formulation in the tourism context of the early 1970s.

There are some new emerging theories of tourist and leisure motivation that fulfill

---

[10]P. L. Pearce, "Fundamentals of Tourist Motivation," in D. G. Pearce and R. W. Butler, eds. *Fundamentals of Tourism Motivation* (London: Routledge, 1991) pp. 113–134.

[11]S. C. Plog, "Why Destination Areas Rise and Fall in Popularity," *The Cornell Quarterly*, Vol. 14, No. 4 (1974), pp. 55–58; and "Understanding Psychographics in Tourism Research," in J. R. B. Ritchie and C. Goeldner, eds., *Travel Tourism and Hospitality Research* (New York: Wiley, 1987) pp. 203–214.

Most parents are motivated to provide their children with wholesome and exciting vacation experiences such as a visit to see Fred Flintstone and Yogi Bear. (Photo courtesy of Great America, Santa Clara, California)

more of the criteria described in Table 9.3. In particular, the intrinsic motivation–optimal arousal perspective of Iso-Ahola[12] and the travel needs model of Pearce[13] both add new perspectives to the tourist motivation field.

Iso-Ahola argues that tourist and leisure behavior takes place within a framework of optimal arousal and incongruity. That is, while individuals seek different levels of stimulation, they share the need to avoid either overstimulation (mental and physical exhaustion) or boredom (too little stimulation). Leisure needs change during the lifespan and across places and social company. He advises researchers to keep the motivation questions for leisure close to the actual participation in time and emphasizes the importance of participants' feelings of self-determination and competence to ensure satisfaction.

The travel needs model articulated by Pearce and co-workers is concerned more explicitly with tourists and their motives rather than with leisure, which is the focus of Iso-Ahola's work. The travel needs model argues that people have a life cycle in their

[12]S. Iso-Ahola, "Toward a Social Psychological Theory of Tourism Motivation: A Rejoinder," *Annals of Tourism Research*, Vol. 9, No. 2 (1982), pp. 256–262.
[13]P. L. Pearce, *The Ulysses Factor: Evaluating Visitors in Tourist Settings* (New York: Springer-Verlag, 1988); and "Fundamentals of Tourist Motivation," in D. G. Pearce and R. W. Butler, *Fundamentals of Tourist Motivation* (London: Routledge, 1991), pp. 113–134.

Table 9.3   Requirements of a Sound Theory of Tourist Motivation

Element	Explanation
1. The role of the theory	Must be able to integrate existing tourist needs, reorganize the needs, and provide a new orientation for future research
2. The ownership and appeal of the theory	Must be appealing to specialist researchers, useful in tourism industry settings, and credible to marketers and consumers
3. Ease of communication	Must be relatively easy to explain to potential users and be universal (not country specific) in its application
4. Ability to measure travel motivation	Must be amenable to empirical study; the ideas can be translated into questions and responses for assessment purposes
5. A multimotive versus single-trait approach	Must consider the view that travelers may seek to satisfy several needs at once; must be able to model the pattern of traveler needs, not just consider one need
6. A dynamic versus snapshot approach	Must recognize that both individuals and societies change over time; must be able to consider or model the changes that are taking place continuously in tourism
7. The roles of extrinsic and intrinsic motivation	Must be able to consider that travelers are variously motivated by intrinsic, self-satisfying goals and at other times are motivated by extrinsic, socially controlled rewards (e.g., others' opinions)

travel behavior which reflects a hierarchy of their travel motives. Like a career at work, people may start at different levels, they are likely to change their levels during their life cycle, and they can be inhibited in their travel needs by money, health, and other people.

The steps or levels on the travel needs model may be likened to a ladder, and this concept is built on Maslow's hierarchy of needs. By expanding and extending the range of specific needs at each ladder level which fit with Maslow's original formulation, a very comprehensive and rich catalog of the many different psychological needs and motives noted earlier in this chapter can be realized (see Figure 9.1). The travel needs ladder retains Maslow's ideas that lower levels on the ladder have to be satisfied before the person moves to higher levels of the ladder. Thus travelers concerned with developing and extending their relationships while traveling will also have needs in terms of safety and physiological level factors but may not yet be particularly concerned with self-esteem and self-development needs. Importantly, the travel needs ladder emphasizes that people have a range of motives for seeking out holiday experiences. For example, a visitor to Canada who attends the Calgary Stampede might be motivated to do so by the pleasant, safe setting, to entertain a child and develop family experiences of togetherness, and to add to knowledge about Canadian culture. That is, several levels of the travel needs ladder are working together for a rich multimotive picture of travel motivation. This flexibility and variability recognizes that motivation may change over time and across situations so that in visiting Britain, the same person might emphasize cultural understanding and curiosity motives more than relationship and family development motives.

In the travel needs model, destinations are seen as settings where vastly different

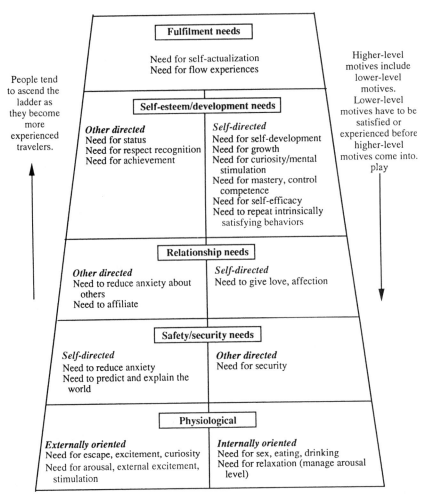

People tend to ascend the ladder as they become more experienced travelers.

Higher-level motives include lower-level motives. Lower-level motives have to be satisfied or experienced before higher-level motives come into play

Figure 9.1 The Travel Needs Ladder

holiday experiences are possible. Thus travelers' motives influence what they seek from a destination, and destinations will vary in their capacity to provide a range of holiday experiences.

In short, travelers do not visit a place with standard objective destination features but, instead, journey to a location where they select activities and holiday experiences among those offered to suit their personal psychological and motivational profile.

The travel needs model was formulated so that a dynamic, multimotive account of travel behavior could serve our understanding of tourism. It acts as a blueprint for the assessment of tourist motives and requires individual tailoring to specific situations. That is, the context or setting helps frame the way in which the travel needs ladder questions are asked. Pearce and McDermott[14] working in a theme park setting, were

[14]P. Pearce and B. McDermott, *Dreamworld Report,* (Townsville, Queensland, Australia: James Cook University of North Queensland, 1991).

Travelers often seek a destination that will reward their fulfillment needs with a place of great beauty, tranquility, and inspiration. (Photo courtesy of the Hawaii Visitors Bureau)

able to use the travel needs ladder to explain the motives of different consumers for that setting. This individual tailoring is done by taking sections of the travel needs ladder (e.g., the physiological level and the need for stimulation) and asking questions about the importance of rides and adventure activities in the theme park. Similarly, questions about the importance of going with friends were asked. In this way a full range of theme park motives is determined by linking travel motivation to other tourism studies.

SUMMARY

In this chapter we have argued that a theory of tourist motivation such as the travel needs ladder helps summarize existing statements and ideas about the motives of travelers. It can also be useful in answering several questions: "Why do certain groups of travelers seek particular holiday experiences?" and the related question "Why do certain groups of travelers travel to destination X?"

In this chapter we have stressed that there will not be one simple answer to these questions but rather, that different groups of individuals will place different weightings on a structured set of answers consistent with their travel needs level. For example, young teenagers emphasize the motives of stimulation and relationships in visiting theme parks, while young couples emphasize developing relationships and the need for relaxation. For travelers exploring exotic locations and participating in more diverse forms of tourism, a wider range of motives, including self-development, mastery, curiosity, escape, and self-fulfilment, will be involved.

Travel motivation studies can be the basis of many consumer analyses in tourism. A good motivational profile of visitors should be of assistance in understanding how well the destination characteristics fit the needs of the travelers. The key to linking travel motivation studies to other tourism studies, such as destination choice, lies in analyzing the activities offered by the destination and the activities that fulfill the travelers' motives. Thus if visitors strongly motivated by the need to enhance their understanding of art and history visit well-managed high-quality cultural attractions, satisfaction is likely. A mismatch can also occur, such as the unfortunate visitor to a tropical island who is seeking rest and relaxation only to be assaulted by a tourism product that is set up for those seeking stimulation, excitement, and new relationships. As tourism grows into an increasingly sophisticated consumer industry, the need to understand the needs of travelers will increase and the motivation of tourists will become a core part of all tourism studies.

About the Reading

The Reading, *Climbing Ayers Rock: Relating Visitor Motivation, Time Perception and Enjoyment,* examines how individual differences in motivation influence the experience of climbing Ayers Rock, a massive geological formation which is a tourist attraction located in north central Australia.

READING 9.1

Climbing Ayers Rock: Relating Visitor Motivation, Time Perception and Enjoyment

BY KERRI-ANNE FIELDING, PHILIP L. PEARCE, AND KAREN HUGHES
James Cook University

▌ Reprinted from *The Journal of Tourism Studies,* Vol. 3, No. 2 (1992).

Many famous tourist sites have become associated with particular activities (Pearce, 1991). Ayers Rock, for example, provides visitors with the opportunity to view magnificent sunsets, examine distinctive geological formations and, of course, climb to the summit. Every year an estimated 200,000 people of all ages and many nationalities attempt the arduous and sometime dangerous 1.5 kilometre trek to the top of the rock. Many of these people come to Central Australia solely for this purpose. The question to be asked is: why do people climb Ayers Rock? and, even more importantly, do individual differences in motivation influence the climbing experience? Currently, consideration is being given to closing the climb, for environmental and cultural reasons. If such a closure takes place it will be important for the local tourism industry to have an understanding of why the climb matters and how individuals perceive it. Armed with such knowledge it might be possible to develop other activities in the vicinity of the rock which meet the tourists' needs and motives.

Additionally, an understanding of the links between visitor motivation and the visitor experience for challenging tourist activities has the potential to be very useful for market segmentation and management purposes. Hsieh, O'Leary and Morrison (1992) claim that

Ayers Rock (Uluru National Park) is a massive conglomerate rock formation rising over 1000 feet above the surrounding plain. It is located in central Australia in Northern Territory. The rock is a popular tourist attraction and climbing to its top a challenging visitor activity. (Photo courtesy of the Northern Territory Tourist Commission)

the psychological benefits which individuals obtain from their tourist experiences represent one of the most subtle and innovative ways of segmenting the visitor market, thus enhancing promotional efforts and facilitating product design and management for target groups.

The importance of motivation to the quality of general leisure experience is not new. In 1974 Neulinger proposed that individual differences in motivation play a major role in determining the intensity of leisure involvement. Ruskin and Shamir (1984) also pointed to the possibility that the activities engaged in and level of involvement may vary according to the individual's prime motivation. There have, however, been few empirical attempts to examine how individual differences in motivation influence the nature and quality of the leisure experience particularly in tourism settings (Hull & Harvey, 1989).

The purpose of the present study, therefore, is to examine whether individual differences in motivation influence the experience of climbing Ayers Rock. In particular, this study examines the differences in task enjoyment and time perception between tourists who are intrinsically motivated (that is, those climbing the rock for the sake of it) and tourists who are achievement motivated (that is, those climbing for the sole purpose of reaching the summit).

Intrinsically motivated activities are those for which there is no apparent reward other than the activity itself. That is, the activities are engaged in for their own sake, and not because they lead to an external reward (Deci, 1975). The rewards for behaviour motivated by intrinsic needs are inherent in the activity itself (e.g., the enjoyment derived from simply participating in the activity). Most leisure researchers argue that leisure is intrinsically motivated, that one does it for the sake of it, and does not expect a reward (Neulinger, 1974).

Several attempts have been made to examine the relationship between intrinsic motivation and leisure. Dichotomising motivation into intrinsic and extrinsic dimensions, these studies have consistently supported the notion that intrinsically motivated activities are more positively experienced than extrinsically motivated activities (Graef, Csikszentmihalyi, & Giannino, 1983; Samdahl, 1988).

The relationship between intrinsic motivation and loss of awareness of the passage of time has also been examined within the context of leisure. Mannell and Bradley (1986) found that people who were intrinsically motivated were more likely to experience time as passing quickly whereas extrinsically motivated individuals were more likely to perceive time to pass slowly. It appears that the major factor affecting perception of time is the degree to which one's attention is directed toward the passage of time itself. According to Gupta and Cummings (1986), when one is engaged in an absorbing activity, temporal awareness is minimised and time is perceived to pass relatively quickly. Thus, the more absorbing and enjoyable the activity, the less attention paid to temporal cues and the shorter the perceived duration of time (Gupta & Cummings, 1986).

Tourism activities and settings offer few possibilities for the study of extrinsic (that is reward-related) motivation. Instead, a contrast may be drawn between intrinsic motivation and achievement motivation for tourism settings. While similar to intrinsic motivation in the sense that it is self-determined behavior (that is, the source of the motivation lies in the individual), achievement motivated behaviour differs from intrinsically motivated behaviour in a number of important ways. Firstly, unlike intrinsic motivation, the reward is the feelings of competence resulting from success in the activity (Deci, 1975; Atkinson, 1982). Secondly, achievement motivated individuals are especially sensitive to performance evaluation (Harackiewicz, Abrahams, & Wageman, 1987). This makes them more likely to be tense and apprehensive, particularly in situations where task competency is evaluated. Indeed, a number of studies have shown that achievement motivation tends to have a detrimental effect on task enjoyment. For example, Harackiewicz et al. (1987) reported a nonsignificant relationship between achievement motivation and enjoyment for a task (puzzle). Wankel and Kreisel (1985) measured ten factors said to be associated with sports enjoyment and found that while intrinsic motivation contributed mostly to enjoyment, winning the game and getting rewards, items which could be classified as outcome oriented (or achievement motivated) were of lesser importance to enjoyment. Shaw (1985) also found that for activities where the participant felt the outcome was being judged, tested or evaluated (as in the case of achievement situations) they were less likely to perceive that activity as leisure.

In relation to time perception, McClelland (1961) found subjects high in the need for achievement tended to overestimate time (that is perceive time to pass more slowly than it actually does) whereas subjects low in need for achievement tend to underestimate time (perceive time to pass more quickly). According to Brown (1985) situations which involved heightened awareness of time, such as boredom, anticipation and impatience result in an apparent lengthening of time. This occurs because the individual wishes the unpleasant experience to finish, therefore the time passes slowly (Gupta & Cummings, 1986). It could be argued that the achievement situation is one which involves anticipation of achieving that goal and result in overestimation of time duration (Quigley, Combs, & O'Leary, 1984).

The above research suggests that intrinsically motivated tourists will tend to experience higher levels of enjoyment while climbing Ayers Rock than those who are achievement motivated. Furthermore, intrinsically motivated people were expected to perceive time as passing more quickly than actual time, whereas achievement motivated individuals were expected to perceive time as passing more slowly than real time.

This study also examines the relationship between enjoyment and time perception. Studies have repeatedly shown that pleasant psychological states result in underestimation of time while unpleasant experiences produce an overestimation (Krus & Fletcher, 1986). The evidence suggests that regardless of activity, if it is evaluated as enjoyable, time seems to pass quickly, but if it is perceived to be dull or uninteresting, time seems to drag. From these findings it was postulated that tourists who enjoyed the climb would be likely to perceive time as passing quickly, whereas those who did not enjoy the climb would tend to perceive time as passing slowly.

METHOD

Study Site

Ayers Rock was chosen as the place of study because it provided access to large numbers of visitors within a confined area. Other studies in recreation have reported difficulties with sampling visitors at such highly mobile sites, as they tend to disperse over a wide area (Mills, Hodgson, McNeely, & Masse, 1981). At Ayers Rock, however, there is only one path to the summit. This enabled the researchers to position themselves at a point which all climbers must pass at the beginning and at the end of the climb. Secondly, climbing Ayers Rock was considered an appropriate activity to study as tourists were expected to be motivated by both intrinsic and achievement motives.

Participants: 187 tourists (97 males and 90 females) participated in this study. Participants ranged in age from 16 to 69 with a mean age of 26. They were mostly Australian (29%), European (30%), or British (28%).

Apparatus: Each participant was given a coloured, prenumbered ribbon which was attached to their clothing with a safety pin. Watches were used by the researchers to record the time each climber commenced and completed their climb. All other data were collected using a 2-page selfreport questionnaire, administered upon completion of the climb. This was designed to assess visitors' motivation for climbing, their level of enjoyment, and their estimates of the duration of the activity. Demographic details were also obtained.

Hikers descend from their climb to the top of Ayers Rock. The satisfactions and enjoyment of their climbing experience were determined by interviews at both the bottom and top of the rock climbing path. (Photo courtesy of the Northern Territory Tourist Commission)

Procedure: Data was collected on-site over a five day period from the 26th April to the 1st May, 1990. The procedure employed in the present study involved three stages: sampling and tagging of climbers, contact with tagged climbers at the summit, and contact again at the base upon completion of the climb. This procedure is similar to that employed by Mills and his associates in sampling participants at ski resorts (Mills, Hodgson, McNeely, & Masse, 1981) and has been found to result in good cooperation and high response rates.

Stage 1:   Two researchers were situated at the base of the climb. As climbers approached to begin their climb, the researchers introduced themselves as students from James Cook University conducting research on the tourist experience at Ayers Rock. After briefly explaining the study, climbers were asked if they were willing to participate in the study. Those who agreed were given a highly visible coloured ribbon to pin to their clothing. Each ribbon was pre-numbered, and this number, along with the time that the participant began the climb, was recorded.

To obtain the most representative sample possible and maximise the use of the survey team, the researchers were required to sample using the "next to pass" procedure (Gale & Jacobs, 1987). This meant that as soon as the last consenting climber had been tagged, the next individual to pass was sampled. This procedure began at 6.00 a.m. and continued until approximately 10.30 a.m., by which time most of the climbers for that day had already begun their climb.

Stage 2:   Two researchers were situated at the top of Ayers Rock to identify tagged climbers as soon as they reached the summit. Participant's ribbon numbers and the time the climber arrived at the top were recorded.

Stage 3:   The final stage involved distributing selfadministered questionnaires to tagged participants upon completion of the climb. This was done at the base of Ayers Rock.

Operationalisation of Variables

Time Perception: The time it took for each person to climb the rock was calculated by subtracting the time they started from the time when they reached the summit. This was labelled 'actual time.' 'Perceived time' was determined by asking the subjects to indicate on the post-climb questionnaire how long they felt it took them to reach the top of the rock. Time judgements were then transformed into a ratio measure by dividing perceived time by actual time (see Brown, 1985). A value less than 1 represented a judgement shorter than the actual duration, while a value greater than 1 represented a judgement longer than the actual duration. This ensured that all scores existed on the same relative scale (Brown, 1985) and were not influenced by the actual time it took to reach the top.

Enjoyment: Enjoyment was measured using a 9 point graphic scale, ranging from very enjoyable to not at all enjoyable. Participants were asked to describe the climb by placing a tick next to the statement which best described their feelings about the climb.

Motivation: The method used to determine climbers' underlying motivation was similar to the one employed by Pearce and Caltabiano (1983) in that climbers' motives were measured indirectly on the basis of their response to an open-ended question. As the most significant distinction to be made in the present study was between intrinsic and achievement motivation, their coding scheme, based on Maslow's hierarchy, was not considered appropriate. For this study the following assessment procedure was implemented.

   The present approach is closely related to the work of Pearce (1988, 1991) who has been developing a travel career ladder model of motivation. This particular study is seen as working within one rung or at one level of the ladder- the self-esteem, self-development level and contrasting an intrinsic versus an external (achievement) oriented approach at that level.

   To determine climbers' underlying motivation, participants were asked to describe the best thing about the climb. The coding of responses into achievement motivation or intrinsic motivation involved a number of stages in an attempt to enhance both the reliability and validity of coding. Firstly, the researchers developed a list of potential reasons for wanting to climb Ayers Rock. This was done by asking one hundred first-year university students enrolled in psychology to provide five reasons why they would want to climb Ayers Rock. A list of 50 different reasons were obtained, most of which were consistent with motives for outdoor recreation found in the literature (Driver & Brown, 1978; Crandall, 1980).

   Twenty-three third year psychology students were then asked to rate each reason on a seven point Likert-type scale (with a score of 1 indicating "not at all", and a score of 7 indicating "very much so") the extent to which they felt each reason represented an example of intrinsic motivation and an example of achievement motivation. The modal scores for both types of motivation were calculated for each of the fifty reasons. Each reason was then classified as either intrinsic or achievement motivation depending on the highest modal score.

   Finally, participants' responses were then matched with the reasons given in Step 1, and the participant was identified as either intrinsically motivated or achievement motivated, based upon the coding in Step 2. If participants' responses were more elaborate and clearly did not fit into any one or combinations of the 50 listed reasons, two independent judges (fourth year psychology students) were asked to code the responses. The level of agreement reached between the judges was 86%. If responses belonged to both motivational categories, they were identified as multi-motivated and were excluded from the analysis.

   On the basis of the above coding system, 52 participants were identified as being intrinsically motivated and 66 participants were identified as being achievement motivated.

RESULTS

A regression analysis was used to assess the relationship between motivation and enjoyment. A moderate but significant correlation of $-.296$ ($p = .0012$) was found between motivation and enjoyment with motivation accounting for 9% of the variance in enjoyment. These results indicate that intrinsically motivated people were more likely to experience higher levels of enjoyment whereas achievement motivated people were more likely to experience lower levels of enjoyment. The relationship between motivational type and enjoyment was further examined using a contingency table, presented in Table 1.

From Table 1 it can be seen that 82.7% of intrinsically motivated climbers reported high levels of enjoyment, whereas only 61.5% of achievement motivated individuals reported this level of enjoyment. 73.5% of those who reported low levels of enjoyment were achievement motivated, whereas only 26.5% were intrinsically motivated. In the group experiencing high levels of enjoyment, 51.8% were intrinsically motivated and 48.2% were achievement motivated. While the differentiation between the motivational types was minimal, these findings do support the hypothesis that intrinsically motivated climbers would be more likely to experience higher levels of enjoyment than would achievement motivated individuals.

The relationship between motivation and time perception was examined in a similar manner. A regression analysis revealed a significant correlation of .312 ($p = .0011$) between motivation and time perception, indicating that people who were intrinsically motivated were more likely to perceive time as passing quickly, whereas people who were achievement motivated were more likely to perceive time as passing slowly. Motivation accounted for 9.7% of the variance in time perception. This relationship is further clarified in Table 2.

It can be seen that 56% of those who perceived time as passing quicker than it actually did were intrinsically motivated, while 44% were achievement motivated. Conversely, of those who perceived time to pass slowly, 70% were achievement motivated whereas only 30% were intrinsically motivated. These results suggest that intrinsically motivated people tended to perceive time as passing more quickly than it actually did, whereas those who were achievement motivated were more likely to perceive time as passing more slowly.

Finally, the relationship between time perception and enjoyment was examined. A weak but significant correlation of $-.148$ ($p = .0462$) was found between enjoyment and time perception, a relationship which is further clarified in Table 3.

Table 3 indicates that 78.2% of climbers who perceived time to pass quickly reported the highest levels of enjoyment. However, the prediction that people who perceived time to pass more slowly would report low levels of enjoyment was not supported, with 56.2% of these people also reporting high levels of enjoyment. Nevertheless, it can be seen that the

Table 1   Relationship Between Motivation and Enjoyment

| | | *Motivation* | | |
		Intrinsic	Achievement	Total
Low enjoyment		**9**	**25**	**34**
	(row)	26.5%	73.5%	
	(col)	17.3%	38.5%	
High enjoyment		**43**	**40**	**83**
	(row)	51.8%	48.2%	
	(col)	82.7%	61.5%	
		52	**65**	**117**

Chi square = 6.271; $p = 0.0123$.

Table 2   Relationship Between Motivation and Time
Perception

		Motivation		
		Intrinsic	Achievement	Total
Perceived time		**28**	**22**	**50**
less than	(row)	56.0%	44.0%	
actual time	(col)	54.9%	34.9%	
Perceived time		**8**	**6**	**14**
equal to	(row)	57.1%	42.9%	
actual time	(col)	15.7%	9.5%	
Perceived time		**15**	**35**	**50**
greater than	(row)	30.0%	70.0%	
actual time	(col)	29.4%	55.6%	
		52	65	117

Chi square = 7.829; p = 0.0199.

majority (55.1%) of those who reported low levels of enjoyment felt that time has passed slower than it actually did.

DISCUSSION

The results of the present investigation indicated a relationship between motivation and enjoyment, with intrinsically motivated people reporting higher levels of enjoyment than achievement motivated individuals (see Table 1). The close association between intrinsic motivation and enjoyment has been previously demonstrated (Roadburg, 1983; Shaw, 1985), however, few studies have examined the relationship between achievement motivation and task enjoyment. The present study indicates no significant relationship between achievement motivation and task enjoyment, supporting the findings of Harackiewicz et al. (1987). Furthermore, this research supports the argument that achievement motivation may have a detrimental effect on enjoyment of the leisure experience.

The relationship between motivation and perception of time was as hypothesised, with intrinsically motivated tourists perceiving time as passing quickly, and achievement moti-

Table 3   Relationship Between Perception and
Enjoyment

		Enjoyment		
		Low	High	Total
Perceived time		**19**	**68**	**87**
less than	(row)	21.8%	78.2%	
actual time	(col)	32.8%	54.8%	
Perceived time		**7**	**15**	**22**
equal to	(row)	31.8%	68.2%	
actual time	(col)	12.1%	12.1%	
Perceived time		**32**	**41**	**73**
greater than	(row)	43.8%	56.2%	
actual time	(col)	55.1%	33.1%	
		58	124	182

Chi square = 8.846; p = 0.012.

vated tourists experiencing time as passing slowly. These findings support the notion forwarded by Harackiewicz et al. (1987) that achievement motivated people tend to be apprehensive, tense, and aware of time passing, and are thus less able to become absorbed by the leisure experience. This occurs because participation in the activity is regarded as a means to an end, rather than an enjoyable experience in itself. Consequently, the time taken and actual involvement in the activity is seen as something of a barrier rather than an enjoyable aspect of the leisure experience. Several researchers (e.g. Harackiewicz et al., 1987; Shaw, 1985) have argued that achievement motivated individuals are particularly aware of their actions in situations where performance is evaluated.

Climbing Ayers Rock could be interpreted as such a situation involving performance evaluation. An obvious gauge of success is one's ability to reach the summit. Furthermore, almost all tourists climb between 7 a.m. and 11 a.m. and thus the activity is performed in the company of others. Additionally, the Ayers Rock climb takes place along a defined track and on busy days there is virtually a chain of human activity with climbers closely monitoring the efforts of others around them in the corridor of ascent. It is likely that achievement motivated people might interpret this setting as a competitive situation in which their performance was being evaluated by other climbers. Such an evaluation would heighten their awareness of performance which, in turn, would focus their attention on the time taken to complete the task. In this context achievement motivated climbers would be keenly anticipating attaining the summit, therefore time taken would be regarded as a barrier to achievement of this goal (Quigley et al., 1984). This argument is also supported by the notion that events which induce anticipation engender overestimation of time involvement (Brown, 1985).

Intrinsically motivated individuals on the other hand, may have been involved in the activity itself. It has been argued that this group undertakes leisure activities because participation is enjoyable (e.g. Graef et al., 1983; Neulinger, 1974). Consequently, it seems logical to suggest that during participation, intrinsically motivated people will focus on other cues and perceive time to pass quickly. This supports the notion proposed by Gupta and Cummings (1986) that the more enjoyable the activity, the more quickly time passes.

The importance of the above findings in terms of tourism and leisure research lies in demonstrating that individual differences in motivation appear to have an influence on the quality of the visitor experience. In particular, people who are intrinsically motivated tend to become absorbed in the activity, experience higher levels of enjoyment, and perceive time as passing quickly. Conversely, achievement motivated individuals tend to report lower levels of enjoyment and perceive time to pass more slowly. From this, it would seem that the quality of the leisure experience is much greater for intrinsically motivated individuals than it is for achievement motivated individuals. These findings have important ramifications for the tourism industry, as they suggest that unless people are encouraged to involve themselves in the activity itself (that is, participate for the experience rather than merely achieving a goal), their enjoyment will be less than optimal. The management implications of these kinds of findings might extend to encouraging visitors to pay attention to sub goals of the total activity as well as heightening the need for interpretive information to add to all visitors' understanding of the settings being encountered. In particular tourism organisers, whether they be promoting long distance walks, white water rafting or managing the climb at Ayers Rock should pay attention to the work of Langer (1989). In her work on mindfulness, Langer notes that one can escape habitual behavioural routines and an achievement goal oriented approach to life by paying attention to the novel and unfamiliar and by adopting a questioning, analytic style to all our experiences. In brief, there may well be a case that some individuals have to learn to enjoy their leisure. Tourism managers can play a role in this process by creating mindfulness inducing opportunities. Such an emphasis on interpretation and mindfulness might be necessary if the climb is closed and an alternate Ayers Rock walk is developed as a substitute experience for the climb.

It is also vital that tour operators, particularly those designing coach tour itineraries, provide visitors with enough time to pursue visitor activities in a relaxed, unhurried and mindful manner. Tight bus schedules and tour guide edicts that the activity must be completed in a short time (and this applies to the Ayers Rock climb) may artificially turn the setting into one where achievement motives emerge. As has been demonstrated in this study, visitors working to achievement oriented goals are less satisfied, overestimate the time they are taking and are likely to be more tense and anxious about their tourist activity. Reversing these trends would be a positive management step and allowing visitors ample time to experience the setting is a key tactic in this better management.

Finally, the methodological implications of this research should be addressed. As previously mentioned, one of the major difficulties in tourism and leisure research has been the practical difficulty of measuring the on-site leisure experience. This study revealed that the relationship between time perception and enjoyment was similar to that between time perception and motivation. This suggests that the time perception measure is a good indicator of enjoyment and intensity of involvement during leisure participation. Time measures have, of course, been used in behavioural observation studies in museums and visitor centres (Hockings & Moscardo, 1991) but the further development of time estimation, time perception and time ratio measures for on site tourist field settings offers much promise. In particular, the application of these motivational, satisfaction and time based studies with the emerging new tourism products in the eco-tourism and adventure travel areas could develop a new body of tourist and leisure studies in the near future.

REFERENCES

Atkinson, J. W. (1982). Attribution theory. In N. T. Feather (Ed.), *Expectations and actions.* Hillsdale, New Jersey: Lawrence Erlbaum.

Brown, S. W. (1985). Time perception and attention: The effects of prospective versus retrospective paradigms and task demands on perceived duration. *Perception and Psychophysics, 38*(2), 115–124.

Crandall, R. (1980). Motivations for leisure. *Journal of Leisure Research, 12*(1), 45–54.

Deci, E. L. (1975). *Intrinsic motivation.* New York: Plenum Press.

Driver, B. L., & Brown, P. J. (1978). The opportunity spectrum concept and behavioral information in outdoor recreation resource supply inventories: A rationale. In *Integrated inventories and renewable natural resources: Proceedings of workshop.* Fort Collins, Colo.: Rocky Mountain Forest & Range Experiment Station.

Gale, F., & Jacobs, J. (1987). *Tourists and the national estate.* Canberra: Australian Government Publishing Service.

Graef, R., Csikszentmihalyi, M., & Giannino, S. M. (1983). Measuring intrinsic motivation in everyday life. *Leisure Studies, 2,* 155–168.

Gupta, S., & Cummings, L. L. (1986). Perceived speed of time and task affect. *Perceptual and Motor Skills, 63,* 971–980.

Harackiewicz, J. M., Abrahams, S., & Wageman, R. (1987). Performance evaluation and intrinsic motivation: The effects of evaluative focus, rewards, and achievement orientation. *Journal of Personality and Social Psychology, 53*(6), 1015–1023.

Hockings, M., & Moscardo, G. (1991). The Cardwell Visitor Centre: Combining evaluation and design. In G. Moscardo & K. Hughes (Eds.), *Visitor centres: Exploring new territory* (pp. 121–237). Townsville: JCU Department of Tourism.

Hull, B. R., & Harvey, A. (1989). Explaining the emotion people experience in suburban parks. *Environment and Behavior, 21*(3), 323–345.

Hsieh, S., O'Leary, J. T., & Morrison, A. M. (1992). Segmenting the international travel market by activity. *Tourism Management, 13*, 209–223.

Krus, D. J., & Fletcher, S. H. (1986). Time: A speeding train or wind-driven sand? The estimation of fixed temporal intervals as related to images of time. *Perceptual and Motor Skills, 62*, 936–938.

Langer, E. J. (1989). *Mindfulness.* Reading, Mass.: Addison-Wesley Publishing.

McClelland, D. C. (1961). *The achieving society.* Princeton: Van Nostrand.

Mannell, R. C., & Bradley, W. (1986) Does greater freedom always lead to greater leisure? Testing a person x environment model of freedom and leisure. *Journal of Leisure Research, 18*(4), 215–230.

Mills, A., Hodgson, R. W., McNeely, J. G., & Masse, R. F. (1981). An improved visitor sampling method for ski resorts and similar settings. *Journal of Leisure Research, 13*(3), 219–231.

Neulinger, J. (1974). *The psychology of leisure: Research approaches to the study of leisure.* Springfield: Charles C Thomas.

Pearce, P. L. (1988). *The Ulysses Factor.* New York: Springer Verlag.

Pearce, P. L. (1991). Analysing tourist attractions. *Journal of Tourism Studies, 2*(1), 46–55.

Pearce, P. L., & Caltabiano, M. L. (1983). Inferring travel motivation from travellers' experiences. *Journal of Travel Research, XXII*, 16–20.

Quigley, J. J., Combs, A., & O'Leary, N. (1984). Sensed duration of time: Influence of time as a barrier. *Perceptual and Motor Skills, 58*, 72–74.

Roadburg, A. (1983). Freedom and enjoyment: Disentangling perceived leisure. *Journal of Leisure Research, 15*(1), 15–26.

Ruskin, H., & Shamir, B. (1984). Motivation as a factor affecting males' participation in physical activity during leisure time. *Society and Leisure, 7*, 141–161.

Samdahl, D. M. (1988). A symbolic interactionist model of leisure theory and empirical support. *Leisure Sciences, 10*, 27–39.

Shaw, S. M. (1985). The meaning of leisure in everyday life. *Leisure Sciences, 7*(1), 1–25.

Wankel, L., & Kreisel, P. S. (1985). Factors underlying enjoyment of youth sports: Sport and age group comparisons. *Journal of Sport Psychology, 7*, 51–64.

Key Concepts

consumers
destination attributes
discipline of psychology
Freud
fulfillment needs
Grand Tour
history
Maslow
motivation

needs
physiological needs
psychological theory
relationship needs
safety/security needs
self-esteem needs
travel motivation analysis
travel needs model

For Review and Discussion

1. Why is it so important for tourism people to have a good understanding of travel motivation?

2. Explain the relationship of customer (tourist) satisfaction and travel motivation.

3. The author states that the question, "Why do tourists travel?" is not a good starting point for research on this subject. Comment.

4. "Why do certain groups of people choose certain holiday experiences?" is a much better question. Why?

5. Identify five motivations for travel of Europeans during Roman times, the Middle Ages, and Tudor times. Do such motivations exist today?

6. How important are the motives of discovery and curiosity?

7. Are your travel benefits or rewards linked closely to your travel motives? Elucidate.

8. Provide a few examples of how a person's travel needs change over a lifespan.

9. Give an example of travel experience overstimulation (mental or physical exhaustion or both). Similarly, give an example of boredom (too little stimulation).

10. Thinking about Pearce's five-level travel needs ladder provides some examples of externally and internally oriented physiological needs. Why are these needs at the bottom of the ladder?

11. Referring to the preceding question, provide similar representations of safety/security needs, relationship needs, self-esteem/development needs, and fulfillment needs.

12. Assume that you were employed by a nature (ecotour) company, and were planning a new tour to a newly established national park. Describe several ingredients of such a tour that meet most of these needs as shown in question 11.

13. How could a resort hotel's activities or social director help guests with their fulfillment needs? Give several cases in point.

14. Below is a short list of travel motivations. Suggest a travel experience or product that would match each motivation.

   - Rest/relaxation
   - Unspoiled natural environment enjoyment
   - Interesting countryside and wildlife study opportunities
   - Lots of nightlife and entertainment
   - Adventure activities
   - Good shopping and browsing

15. How important are a variety of available experiences at a destination?

16. Why would *you* want to climb Ayers Rock?

17. What were the climbers' motivational differences?

Case Problems

1. You have been promoted to director of training of the Cruise Lines International Association. Reviewing the listed travel motivations, which would you select for a group of travel marketing sales seminars that will be sponsored by CLIA? (Attending would be travel agents and tour company reps.)

2. Referring to the preceding problem, after selecting the motivations, what kinds of instructional materials and teaching methods would you employ? Why?

3. Your first assignment after joining a tour company staff was to design a tour that would appeal to young singles. Obviously, you must create a tour that would probably motivate a market sufficiently large for your company to make a profit on it. Identify the motivation(s) selected, then describe briefly your tour concept and the specific marketing elements you would feature in its promotion to reach this very promising market.

4. Pleasure travel motivation is often added to a business trip such as attending a convention. Give an example of such a combination. Identify the principal motivations involved. How would you sell this idea to the convention planning committee?

5. The holiday season is approaching. Jeff R. is trying to compose a direct-mail promotion letter to be sent to each person on his travel agency's mailing list. He's convinced that giving a gift of travel would be very appealing to many of his clients. What key phrases should he embody in this letter to motivate such giving?

Selected References

Anthony, I. *Verulamium*. Hanley, Staffordshire, England: Wood Mitchell, 1973.

Casson, L. *Travel in the Ancient World*. London: Allen & Unwin, 1974.

Echtner, C. M., and J. R. B. Ritchie. "The Meaning and Measurement of Destination Image." *Journal of Tourism Studies*, Vol. 2, No. 2 (1991), pp. 2–12.

Hill, Brian J., Cary McDonald, and Muzaffer Uysal. "Resort Motivations for Different Family Life Cycle Stages." *Visions in Leisure and Business*, Vol. 8, No. 4 (Winter 1990), pp. 18–27.

Iso-Ahola, S. "Toward a Social Psychological Theory of Tourism Motivation: A Rejoinder." *Annals of Tourism Research*, Vol. 9, No. 2 (1982), pp. 256–262.

Loker, L. E., and R. Perdue. "A Benefit-Based Segmentation of a Nonresident Summer Travel Market." *Journal of Travel Research*, Vol. 31 (Summer 1992), pp. 30–35.

Pearce, P., and B. McDermott. *Dreamworld Report*. Townsville, Queensland, Australia: Department of Tourism, James Cook University of North Queensland, 1991.

Pearce, P. L. "Fundamentals of Tourist Motivation." In D. G. Pearce, and R. W. Butler, eds., *Fundamentals of Tourist Motivation*. London: Routledge, 1991, pp. 113–134.

Pearce, P. L. *The Ulysses Factor: Evaluating Visitors in Tourist Settings*. New York: Springer-Verlag, 1988.

Pearce, P. L., and Peter Stringer. "Psychology and Tourism." *Annals of Tourism Research*, Vol. 18, No. 1 (1991), pp. 136–154.

Pimlott, J. A. R. *The Englishman's Holiday*. London: Faber & Faber, 1947.

Plog, S. "Understanding Psychographics in Tourism Research." In J. R. B. Ritchie and C. Goeldner, eds., *Travel Tourism and Hospitality Research*. New York: Wiley, 1987, pp. 203–214.

Plog, S. "Why Destination Areas Rise and Fall in Popularity." *Cornell Hotel Restaurant and Quarterly*, Vol. 14, No. 4 (1974), pp. 55–58.

Rowling, M. *Everyday Life of Medieval Travellers*. London: B. T. Batsford, 1971.

Swinglehurst, E. *The Romantic Journey*. London: Pica Editions, 1974.

U.S. Travel Data Center. *Gender's Power over Pleasure Travel: A Look at Men's vs. Women's Motivations for Pleasure Travel*. Washington, D.C.: Travel Industry Association of America, 1992.

Waryszak, Zbigniew R. "The Importance of Psychology in Educating Future Hospitality and Tourism Managers." *International Journal of Hospitality Management*, Vol. 9, No. 1 (1990), pp. 9–13.

Wolfe, R. I. "Recreational Travel: The New Migration." *Geographical Bulletin*, Vol. 2 (1967), pp. 159–167.

CHAPTER 10

Cultural
and International Tourism
for Life's Enrichment

LEARNING OBJECTIVES

- Recognize that travel experiences are the best way to learn about other cultures.
- Identify the cultural factors in tourism.
- Appreciate the rewards of participation in life-seeing tourism.
- Become aware of the most effective promotional measures involving an area's cultural resources.
- Realize the importance of cultural attractions to any area promoting itself as a tourist destination.

The highest purpose of tourism is to become better acquainted with people in other places and countries, as this furthers the understanding and appreciation that builds a better world for all. International travel also involves the exchange of knowledge and ideas—another worthy objective. Travel raises levels of human experience, recognition, and achievements in many areas of learning, research, and artistic activity. In this chapter we discuss travel as it enriches our lives.

IMPORTANCE

Cultural tourism covers all aspects of travel whereby people learn about each other's ways of life and thought. Tourism is thus an important means of promoting cultural relations and international cooperation. Conversely, development of cultural factors within a nation is a means of enhancing resources to attract visitors. In many countries, tourism can be linked with a "cultural relations" policy. It is used to promote not only knowledge and understanding but also a favorable image of the nation among foreigners in the travel market.

The channels through which a country presents itself to tourists can be considered its cultural factors. These are the entertainment, food, drink, hospitality, architecture, manufactured and handcrafted products of a country, and all other characteristics of a nation's way of life.

Successful tourism is not simply a matter of having better transportation and hotels but of adding a particular national flavor in keeping with traditional ways of life and projecting a favorable image of the benefits to tourists of such goods and services.

A nation's cultural attractions must be presented intelligently and creatively. In this age of uniformity, the products of one nation are almost indistinguishable from those of another. There is a great need for encouraging cultural diversity. Improved techniques of architectural design and artistic presentation can be used to create an expression of originality in every part of the world.

Taken in their narrower sense, cultural factors in tourism play a dominant role chiefly in activities that are specifically intended to promote the transmission or sharing of knowledge and ideas. Consider the following factors:

1. Libraries, museums, exhibitions
2. Musical, dramatic, or film performances
3. Radio and television programs, recordings
4. Study tours or short courses
5. Schools and universities for longer-term study and research
6. Scientific and archaeological expeditions, schools at sea
7. Joint production of films
8. Conferences, congresses, meetings, seminars

In addition, many activities that are not educational or cultural in a narrow sense provide opportunities for peoples of different nations to get to know each other.

LIFE-SEEING TOURISM

Traditionally, a person "sees the high points" of a given location and thus feels that he or she has "seen" this area. However, there is a growing belief among tourism specialists that such an approach, although traditionally valid, is by no means the best approach. Purposeful activities that match the travelers' interests are becoming more commonly accepted and recognized. (In popular tourist areas, such arrangements may have to be limited to the off-season periods of the year.) For example, a physician on a vacation might be interested in talking with local physicians and viewing interesting or progressive medical installations or facilities. He or she may wish to participate in a symposium or some type of educational endeavor there or have lunch with a group of physicians interested in the same particular specialty or in public health or medical practices in general. The visitor may also wish to visit the home of a well-known physician to exchange ideas.

Suggestions made by the travel agent and machinery provided to make such experiences come about are of growing importance to successful tourism. Any place that wishes to become a successful tourist destination must have more activities for visitors than the traditional recreational activities such as lying on the beach or patronizing a night club or visiting popular tourist attractions.

Axel Dessau, former director of the Danish National Tourist Office, is credited with this concept of "life-seeing tourism." In Denmark, for example, the visitor is met by a graduate student or other person who is technically familiar with the field of interest that a visitor may have. This guide then arranges for purposeful visits in a schedule suited to the visitor.

For example, the visitor might be interested in reviewing social problems and city

Pago Pago Resort Hotel, American Samoa. The architectural design reflects the indigenous style of construction. When guests arrive at this hotel, they know they are in Polynesia! (Photo courtesy of Wimberly, Allison, Tong and Goo, Architects, Honolulu, Hawaii)

government. An expert in these matters would plan to visit city planning offices, schools, social welfare establishments, and rehabilitation centers; to attend meetings or seminars at which problems of this nature are discussed; and to provide other opportunities for the visitor to learn firsthand what is happening in his or her field in Denmark.

The plan is usually set up on a half-day basis, with the visitor spending afternoons to visit tourist highlights, go shopping, and pursue other traditional recreational activities. The mornings would be devoted to making visits to organizations and establishments with programs planned by a special expert guide. A travel agent can make these arrangements.

Another aspect of life-seeing tourism is the opportunity to have social intercourse with families. These families host the visitor or the visitor's family in the evening after dinner for conversation and sociability. Or the visitor can stay in a private home—an excellent way in which to become acquainted with the culture and lifestyle of persons in a different locality.

In the Bahamas, visitors can discover the island group's people and culture in a very personal way through their People-to-People Program. This stimulating and exciting program is organized by the Ministry of Tourism. It matches visitors with Bahamian volunteers who host visitors having similar professions or interests. The Bahamian host or host family may choose to take guests to a local theater performance, a Sunday church service, or invite them to a home-cooked Bahamian dinner. A wide variety of other activities may be included, depending on the interests of the visitor(s). Such opportunities substantially increase visitor appreciation and understanding of the culture they are visiting, and often bring about lasting friendships.

THE ROMANCE OF PLEASURE TRAVEL

Perhaps the strongest of all individual travel motivations is simply that of satisfying a need for pleasure. Travel has the unique quality of being able to satisfy this desire to an extremely high degree. Not all trips are pleasurable, but some are more pleasurable than anticipated. The planning and anticipation period prior to the trip can be as enjoyable as the trip itself. Discussing prospects of the trip with friends and pursuing research, educational, and shopping activities relating to the trip and the area to be visited is a most important part of the total pleasure travel experience. In the formulation of marketing programs and advertising, in particular, the pleasurable aspects of the trip need to be emphasized. The prospective traveler should be told how much fun it is to go to the popular, as well as some of the most uncommon, destinations.

The romance of the trip is also a strong motivation, particularly in relation to honeymoon travel and for those who are thrilled with the romantic aspects of seeing, experiencing, and enjoying the culture of strange and attractive places. Thus the romance and pleasure of the trip are primary attributes of the travel experience and need to be emphasized far more than they have been in the past. Sharing experiences with members of the family or friends is another integral part of the enjoyment of the trip. A trip can become a fine medium through which additional pleasure, appreciation, and romance is experienced.

DEVELOPMENTAL AND PROMOTIONAL MEASURES

Measures taken to develop and promote the cultural elements in tourism through special activities can be considered from several different points of view.

Development of Methods and Techniques

The examples just listed involve specialized methods, techniques, and skills, all of which can be developed in their own right, without any direct reference to the promotion of tourism. Theaters, libraries, museums, and other such national institutions are not usually created with tourism in mind, but they are a great asset in attracting the interest of visitors. Museums and monuments, especially, are among the expected features of a tourist itinerary. These and other activities that can assist in the development of tourism may also be desirable elements in the cultural development of the nation. The methods and techniques associated with each of the examples listed constitute a whole field of specialized knowledge. As in most other fields of expert knowledge, information and ideas can be acquired from abroad and adapted to national situations.

Even when the necessary facilities exist, it may be desirable to adapt them to the needs of tourism. Special courses will often have to be created for foreigners. Multilingual guides must be trained. Captions and instructions in museums and cinemas should be provided in at least two languages. Special arrangements may be made for tourists to be given free or inexpensive access to institutions of interest to them. Life-seeing arrangements can also be made.

Improvement in Educational and Cultural Content of Tourism

There is always room for improvement in what a tourist may learn abroad. This applies chiefly to books, pamphlets, films, and all types of illustrated information material. There is a great need for the services of experts in such matters, not only in assembling material on the history or geography of a country, but also in the attractive and accurate presentation of the material in several languages.

Consideration might be given to the development, on a regional basis, of "cultural identity card" systems, such as that operated successfully by the Council of Europe, which would introduce the tourist to experts in the fields of education, science, and the arts.

Heritage interpretation as an academic discipline can be very useful in tourism. Courses can be developed to enable local citizens to become authentic interpreters of their area's cultural, historical, and natural heritage. Achievement of such knowledge builds a person's ability to become a fully qualified interpreter. One example might be a 40-hour course entitled "Tourism—Keeper of the Culture." Those who successfully complete the course would be fully aware of their area's resources and thus would be capable of providing guide services or other services in which their knowledge can be useful. All forms of tourism, from group to individual, can, in various ways, benefit from the assistance of such informed, enthusiastic individuals.

Such an educational effort, when publicized, also creates a new self-awareness and pride in the community and a resulting improvement in the quality of life. Local art events, for example, can be organized to be attractive to the community and tourists alike. "Heritage Trails" or "Cultural Highways" can be designated. "Art in the Park" and festivals with various cultural themes help show off the area's resources and help to lengthen the season or fill in low spots in visitor demand. From the tourist's standpoint, engaging in such culturally oriented activities builds a heightened appreciation and respect for the qualities and abilities of their hosts.

Concentration of Activities Around Important Themes

In recent years, much has been done to link up tourist-related activities with themes or events of widespread interest, as in the case of festivals that bring together a variety of dramatic, musical, or cinema performances. An example is the successful Seattle Ring Festival of Wagner's music and the Quebec, Canada, Winter Festival. Another way is to focus attention on large exhibitions or fairs. Events such as these give an opportunity for the combined sponsorship of many different types of activity. International congresses or meetings can be held at the same time as the exhibitions or festivals. Youth festivals or "jamborees" can take place to coincide with important sporting events or large conventions.

Another way of stimulating interest is through "twinning," whereby towns, communities, or regions in different countries establish relations with each other and send delegations to events arranged by their partners. Special attractions such as EPCOT near Disney World in Florida bring together in one location large-scale cultural exhibits and entertainment of several countries. Another example is the Polynesian Cultural Center in Hawaii. A map of the center is shown in Figure 10.1.

Uses of Mass Media

Mass media are always important in the development of tourism. Whether for use outside a country as a means of attracting tourists or to inform and entertain them after their arrival, there is a great need for high-quality products by journalists, film producers, and artists. In many countries there are some who already specialize in the field of tourism whose services can be used to advantage. The Society of American Travel Writers is one professional group dedicated to good travel journalism.

Development of Out-of-Season Tourism

Educational and cultural activities are particularly well adapted to the "out-of-season" tourism development. International meetings and study courses do not depend on good

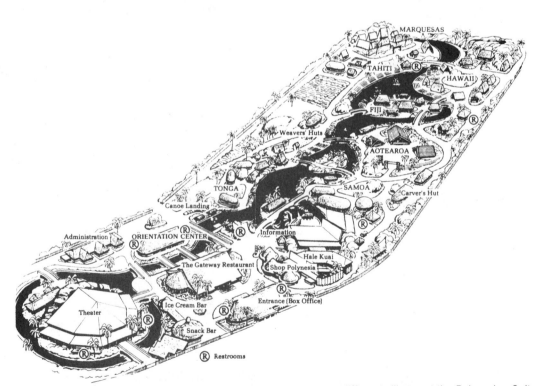

Figure 10.1   Polynesian Cultural Center, Hawaii. There are many different villages at the Polynesian Cultural Center. Each is a combination of buildings, gardens, activities, and people as you would find them if you were to travel to the various island groups represented.

weather and entertainment. Often, their sponsors are glad to take advantage of off-season rates in hotels. Efforts should therefore be made to develop facilities and publicity to attract suitable activities and events. Theater tours are a good example.

ANTHROPOGRAPHY (GEOGRAPHY OF HUMANKIND)

Anthropography is defined as the branch of anthropology that describes the varieties of humankind and its geographical distribution. One of the most important motivations for travel is interest in the culture of other peoples. The Mexicans are not like the Swiss, and the Balinese are not like the Eskimos. Our natural curiosity about our world and its peoples constitutes one of the most powerful travel-motivating influences. A travel agent or other travel counselor must be familiar with the basic differences in culture among the peoples of the world, where accessible examples of such cultures are located, and which of these cultures (or groups of culture) would be most interesting to a particular would-be traveler.

Most of the earth's 5 billion people are concentrated in a limited number of geographical areas. These population concentrations provide attractions in themselves. On the other hand, areas of the earth that are largely empty—such as Canada, parts of western United States, Siberia, western China, Australia, most of Africa, and much of South America—have appeal because of the absence of humans. The landscape, with its towns and villages and rural, and perhaps nomadic cultures, provides interesting contrasts to urban centers. Visits to primitive cultures are enriching and exciting travel experiences. In the United States, such cultural groups as the Amish in Pennsylvania or the American Indian have tourist appeal.

TYPES OF DESTINATIONS— TRAVEL EXPERIENCES

The spatial and characteristic diversity among destinations has become so great that it is important to classify destinations so that a systematic discussion of tourism psychology and motivation can be undertaken. One way to do this is to build on Valene L. Smith's identification of several types of tourism.[1] That is, a classification of destinations can be developed on the basis of the types of travel experience provided at the various destinations.

Smith identified six categories of tourism:

1. *Ethnic tourism*   is traveling for the purpose of observing the cultural expressions and lifestyles of truly exotic peoples. Such tourism is exemplified by travel to Panama to study the San Blas Indians or to India to observe the isolated hill tribes of Assam. Typical destination activities would include visits to native homes, attending dances and ceremonies, and possibly participating in religious rituals.

2. *Cultural tourism*   is travel to experience and, in some cases, participate in a vanishing lifestyle that lies within human memory (Fig. 10.2). The picturesque setting or "local color" in the destination area are the main attractions. Destination activities,

[1] Valene Smith, *Hosts and Guests* (Philadelphia: University of Pennsylvania Press, 1977), pp. 2–3.

Of great interest to Americans and foreign visitors alike is the restored Statue of Liberty, located in New York harbor. This dramatic statue and grounds are maintained by the National Park Service. (Photo courtesy of the New York Division of Tourism)

typically, include meals in rustic inns, costume festivals, folk dance performances, and arts and crafts demonstrations in "old-style" fashion. Visits to Williamsburg, Virginia, and Greenfield Village in Dearborn, Michigan, or to Mystic Seaport, Connecticut, are examples of cultural tourism.

3. *Historical tourism*   is the museum-cathedral tour that stresses the glories of the past—Rome, Egypt, and Greece. Civil war sites in the United States such as Gettysburg, Pennsylvania, and Chancellorsville, Virginia, are other examples. Guided tours of monuments, visits to churches and cathedrals, sound and light performances that encapsulate the lifestyle of important events of a bygone era are favored destination activities. Such tourism is facilitated because the attractions are either in or are readily accessible from large cities. Typically, such attractions seem particularly adaptable to organized mass tourism.

4. *Environmental tourism*   is similar to ethnic tourism, drawing tourists to remote areas. But the emphasis here is on natural and environmental attractions, rather than ethnic ones. Travel for the purposes of "getting back to nature" and to appreciate (or become sensitive to) people-land relationships falls in this category. Environmental tourism is primarily geographic and includes such destinations as Niagara Falls, the Grand Canyon, Yellowstone National Park, and other natural wonders. Typical destination activities include photography, hiking, mountain climbing, canoeing, and camping.

5. *Recreational tourism*   centers on participation in sports, curative spas, sun bathing, and social contacts in a relaxed environment. Such areas often promote sand, sea, and sex through beautiful color photographs that make you want to be there on the ski slopes, on palm-fringed beaches, on championship golf courses, or on tennis courts.

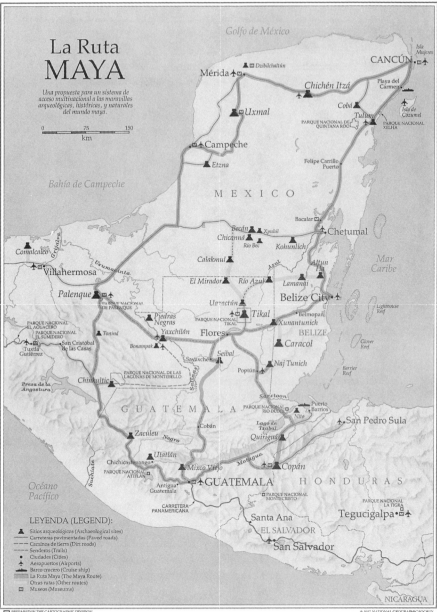

Figure 10.2   The Maya Route is a proposed system of paved roads, dirt roads, and trails connecting archeological sites of the magnificient culture shaped by people called the Maya. Between C.E. 250 and 900 "the Maya created one of the most distinguished civilizations of all antiquity" according to *National Geographic* author George Stuart. How the Maya raised their enormous pyramids and stone temples is one of the many mysteries confronting investigators. The Maya Route plan would also introduce visitors to Spanish Colonial architecture, marvelous tropical forests teeming with wildlife, miles of pristine beaches, excellent snorkeling, and villages of great charm. Preliminary work is now under way for creating and promoting this four-nation ecocultural tourism circuit. (Map courtesy of *National Geographic* magazine)

The opportunity to engage in unique, exciting activities such as scuba diving is a prime tourism motivator. Reef dives, wreck dives, night dives, share dives, wall dives, and cave and tunnel exploring provide exhilarating experiences. (Photo courtesy of the Cayman Islands News Bureau)

Such promotion is designed to attract tourists whose essential purpose is to relax. Las Vegas epitomizes another type of recreational travel—gambling, spectacular floor shows, and away-from-home freedom.

6. *Business tourism* as characterized by conventions/meetings/seminars is another important form of travel. (The United Nations includes the business traveler in its definition of a tourist.) Business travel is frequently combined with one or more of the types of tourism already identified.

This classification system is by no means unassailable. Destination areas can, and in most cases do, provide more than one type of tourism experience. For example, Las Vegas, which essentially provides recreational tourism, is also a popular convention destination. Resorts in Hawaii provide recreational, environmental, and cultural tourism, depending on what types of activities the tourist desires. A tourist vacationing in India, in addition to recreational tourism on one of the spectacular beaches in that country has the opportunity for ethnic tourist experiences. Visits can be made to the villages to observe the life-styles of remote populations.

Conversely, a tourist can select from myriad destinations that provide the same basic type of tourism. For instance, a tourist with an interest in historical tourism may travel to any country that has historical appeal.

OTHER TOURIST APPEALS

Other representative expressions of a people provide powerful attractions for travel. Art, music, architecture, engineering achievements, and many other areas of activity have tourist appeal (see Figure 10.3).

Conventions and trade show exhibits attract many travelers. (Photo courtesy of the Las Vegas Convention Center)

Fine Arts

Such cultural media as painting, sculpture, graphic arts, architecture, and landscape architecture constitute an important motivation for travel. As a specific example, recall the beauty of art forms such as cloisonné or scroll paintings.

A recent trend in resort hotel operations has been the display of local art and craft objects within the hotel or in the immediate vicinity so that the guests may become acquainted with the art of the local people. These objects may be for sale and thus become valued souvenirs. Art festivals often include various types of fine arts together with other cultural expressions to make them more broadly appealing. There are many examples of these, such as the Edinburgh Festival in Scotland. This festival features not only displays of art, but also other forms of craft work, music, pageants, ceremonial military formations, and other cultural attractions.

Music and Dance

The musical expression and resources of a country are among its most appealing and enjoyable aspects. In fact, in some countries or states the music is a major source of enjoyment and satisfaction to visitors. Hawaii, Mexico, Haiti, Spain, various sections of the continental United States, and the Balkan states are examples.

Resort hotels, particularly, can bring to the guests opportunities for enjoyment of local music at its best. Evening entertainment programs, concerts, recordings, and sound

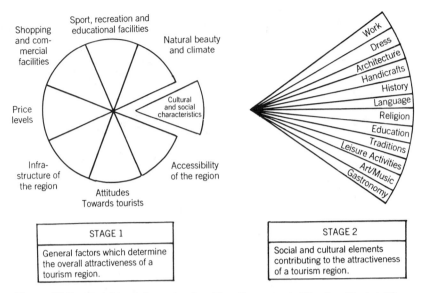

Figure 10.3 Variables Influencing the Attractiveness of a Tourism Region [*Source:* J. R. Brent Ritchie and Michel Zins, "Culture as Determinant of the Attractiveness of a Tourism Region," *Annals of Tourism Research* (April–June 1978), p. 256]

reproduction systems all aid in presenting this aspect of the art of the country. Community concerts, parades, and welcoming ceremonies are appreciated by visitors. Phonograph or tape recordings that the visitor can purchase provide another effective means of keeping in touch with the culture of a particular area.

Ethnic dancing is another exciting and appealing aspect of a country's culture. The color, costumes, music, setting, and skill of forms and execution add to the appeal. Almost all countries have native or ethnic dancing. Local shows, nightclubs, and community programs present additional opportunities. Illustrations show a popular community festival scene and an example of ethnic dancers.

Notable examples of dance as a cultural expression are those of Polynesian dancers, the Ballet Folklorico of Mexico, the Russian ballet, folk dances of the Eastern European countries, dances of many African nations, Thai dancing, the Kabuki dancers of Japan, and Philippine country dancing.

Handicraft

To satisfy tourists, gifts and souvenirs offered for sale should be handcrafted or manufactured in the country or region where the purchase is made. There is much dissatisfaction in purchasing a craft article that you later discover was made in another country thousands of miles away. There is no substitute for genuineness. If the locally produced article is useful and appealing, it should be made available in conveniently located shops. A visit to shops where handicraft products for sale are actually being made is another effective form of guest entertainment.

Keeping alive memories and sentiments of days gone by is the main purpose of the Old Fiddlers' Convention, Galeax, Virginia. (Photo courtesy of the Virginia Tourism Development Group)

Industry and Business

The industrial aspects of an area provide important motivation for travel. A large proportion of travelers, particularly international travelers, are intellectually curious about the economy of any state or country. They are interested in the country's industry, commerce, manufactured products, and economic base.

Industry tours are a good way to develop an interest in the culture of the area and provide a potential market for the product being made. Tourist organizations should encourage tours to factories or processing plants when such visits are appropriate and pleasant experiences. Lists of such industrial installations can be maintained by tourist promotional organizations, chambers of commerce, resort hotels, motels, restaurants, or other establishment or service organizations where tourist contacts are made.

Industrialists from one country are often interested in the industry of another. Group tours can be organized for manufacturers of a particular product who visit another country to see how the manufacture of that or a similar product is accomplished.

Seeing handcrafted baskets created by skilled artisans is a rewarding experience for visitors to Silver City, Missouri. (Photo courtesy of the Missouri Division of Tourism)

Such visits are mutually beneficial as each country's representatives learn from the other.

Chambers of commerce or other business or industrial groups often conduct tours to become acquainted with markets and processors in other countries in an effort to develop more interest in their products and to increase sales in various market areas.

Business establishments, particularly retail stores, are of considerable interest to visitors. Excellent examples are shopping centers near resort areas, where a wide variety of stores is concentrated so that the visitor can readily find the products or services desired.

Shopping is one of the most important elements in tourism. Attractiveness, cleanliness, courtesy, and variety of products are among the most significant elements of the success of any shopping area. In fact, much goodwill can be created by courteous and devoted store clerks who assist the visitor in finding just what is being sought. Probably the world's most notable example of businesses that cater to the tourist is Hong Kong, where shopping and business activity are probably the most important aspect of any visitor's experience.

Agriculture

The agriculture of an area may be of interest to visitors. The type of farming conducted—livestock, poultry, dairy, crops, vineyards and wine production, fresh fruits and vege-

Visitors can observe the making of handcrafted quilts at the Ozark Folk Center. (Photo courtesy of the Arkansas Department of Parks and Tourism)

tables—is an interesting aspect of the culture. Farmer's markets such as the well-known Los Angeles Farmer's Market or roadside stands that offer local agriculture products are also an important part of tourist services in many areas. This is particularly true of stands selling fresh fruits, vegetables, honey, wine, cider and other drinks, and products from nearby farms readily enjoyed by the traveler.

Exemplary agricultural systems provide a point of interest for farm groups who may wish to visit a particular industry from another part of the country. Denmark, with its outstanding pork industry, is of great interest to hog farmers in many parts of the world.

Local tours should include agricultural developments and services so that visitors can see the agricultural products and operations within the country and perhaps try some of the products. On the one-day tour of Oahu in Hawaii, visitors have a chance to sample field-ripened pineapple at a stand adjacent to a great pineapple plantation. State and country fairs and livestock shows also have interesting tourist attractions.

Education

Citizens of one country are concerned with education systems of another. The college and university campuses of any country provide important attractions to tourists. Many of these are beautifully landscaped and attractively situated for a pleasant and enlightening visit. Well-known universities in England such as Oxford or Cambridge are in themselves important tourist attractions.

The operation of high schools and grade schools as well as private schools and other types of vocational training institutions are features of the culture of the area that can be utilized to a considerable degree as attractions for visitors. International education centers provide still another dimension of the relationship between tourism and education. Many universities conduct adult education programs within the university's continuing education service. Such educational opportunities attract learners from other states within their own country or from many countries around the world. This provides an incentive for travel. International conferences of business and industrial groups as well as scientific and educational organizations are often held on the campuses of colleges, universities, or other educational institutions.

Outstanding examples of this type of operation are the adult education centers similar to Kellogg Center at Michigan State University and the East-West Center at the University of Hawaii. These centers attract thousands of adults each year for continuing education courses, conferences, and meetings of an educational nature. "Elderhostel" educational programs for senior citizens are held at many U.S. colleges and universities. These are short programs embracing a wide range of subject matter.

Literature and Language

The literary achievements of a state or country, though having more limited appeal than some cultural aspects, still constitute a significant element of travel motivation. Books, magazines, newspapers, booklets, pamphlets, and other printed literary works are among the most important expressions of the culture of the country. Interestingly, the availability or absence of certain literature is indicative of the political system of the area. Consider the restriction on distribution of literature from various areas of the world practiced by some countries.

Libraries are favorite cultural institutions for the visitor. Many have well-appointed reading lounges and comfortable, attractive surroundings. Particularly on rainy days, the visitor can enjoy reading about the history, culture, arts, and folkways of the host area. Often guest entertainment programs will feature the reading of poetry or the discussion of various books or other literary works as a cultural enrichment opportunity for visitors.

A well-educated person is likely to speak or at least have studied more than one language. Interest in the language of another nation or state is a motivating force for travel. This is particularly true of students traveling to a particular area to practice the language and to become better acquainted with its colloquial usage.

Travel-study programs are particularly valuable learning experiences. Receiving instruction in a foreign language abroad might well be integrated into any comprehensive travel-study curriculum. Language study institutes flourish all over the world. They can be private or associated with universities. Some examples of the latter are the University of Geneva, Switzerland; University of Grenoble, France; and the University of California at Berkeley in the United States. Sophomore or Junior Year Abroad programs for college students provide excellent opportunities to learn a different language. Such programs are numerous in Europe and in other parts of the world. Elderhostel learning opportunities for senior citizens provide another example of travel-study in which a foreign language can be pursued.

Most travelers like to learn at least some of the language to use while they are in a foreign country. Usually, this is in the form of expressions related to ordering food in a restaurant or in talking with hotel or other tourism employees. Classes in language could be included in an entertainment or activities program within a tourist area.

Science

The scientific activities of a country constitute an interest to visitors, particularly those in technical industries, education, or scientific research. Organizations responsible for tourist promotion can serve the scientific community by offering facilities for the exchange of scientific information, organization of scientific seminars, visits to scientific installations, and other activities that provide access to scientific information by visitors.

The most popular scientific appeals include museums of science and industry, planetariums, and visits to unusual scientific installations such as atomic power plants and space exploration centers. Zoos and aquariums are also popular.

An outstanding example is the John F. Kennedy Space Center in northeastern Florida. This installation attracts substantial numbers of visitors each year and provides educational and scientific knowledge for even the most unsophisticated visitor. Another is the Air and Space Museum in Washington, D.C.

Government

Systems of government vary throughout the world. Persons interested in political science and government find visits to centers of government, such as capitals, particularly valuable and highly motivating. Whenever a person visits another area, he or she is made aware of the type of government system in effect and notes the differences

Pathfinder, NASA's full-scale Space Shuttle orbiter mockup, bottom left, points the way to the new U.S. Space Camp Training Center. Built at a cost of $4.5 million, the 70,000-square-foot Training Center is part of the Space and Rocket Center complex—the earth's largest space museum. More than 23,000 young people have attended Space Camp, which has programs for youngsters 11 years old through adults. Space Camp and U.S. Space Academy programs for young people begin each spring and continue through the summer. The adult program is held each fall, and a special orientation program for teachers is conducted each summer. (Photo courtesy of the Space and Rocket Center, Huntsville, Alabama)

between this and the home country. Persons from Western countries are particularly aware of the differences between their form of government and that of Eastern Europe or the former Soviet Union, for example. Probably the world's best example of this was the city of Berlin, which was divided between a Western democratic government and an Eastern totalitarian government before the wall came down.

Persons interested in politics and the ways in which other countries and areas solve their political problems represent another part of the market. Lawmakers often visit another state or country to observe the procedures developed to solve social or economic problems.

A visit to Washington, D.C., can show visitors the lawmaking process in the House of Representatives and in the Senate. Hearings on various proposed regulations or statutes are often open to visitors. As the center of the government of the United States, this city provides educational opportunities in many areas to both American and foreign travelers.

Religion

Another motivation for travel through all of recorded history is the religious pilgrimage. Probably the best known are those to Mecca. Large numbers of people go to the headquarters of their church organizations and to areas well known in their religious literature. Often these are group trips, for example, a group of Protestants visiting magnificent churches and headquarters of various church denominations in different parts of the world. Similarly, missionaries travel with a religious mission. The large amount of travel to Israel is in part based on religious motivation, as are travels to the Catholic centers at Vatican City in Rome, Oberammergau, Lourdes, and Mexico City. Visits to prominent houses of worship of all forms of religious doctrine are an important motivation for travel. Notre Dame cathedral in Paris, Saint Peter's basilica in Rome, and the sacred mosque at Mecca are examples.

Food and Drink

Food and drink of a country are among its most important cultural expressions. The tourist enjoys native foods, particularly items of a local or ethnic nature. When traveling, trying out local dishes is part of the fun.

Restaurants and hotels can make a favorable impression on the tourist if they feature local dishes and also perhaps an explanation on the menu about what the dish consists of and how it is prepared. Of particular appeal is the type of restaurant in which the atmosphere is conducive to the type of food being served, such as seafood restaurants on the wharf.

The purchase of local food and drink is another source of tourist revenue. Advertising messages that include reference to local food are highly effective. The tourist considers eating and drinking important aspects of a vacation. How these foods and drinks are prepared and presented are of great importance. Among the happiest memories may be the experience of dining in a particularly attractive or unusual eating place where local foods were prepared and served.

Encouragement from tourist organizations for restaurants and hotels to feature local foods is highly recommended.

The very best way of learning about any destination's people is to participate in a local cultural event. Enjoying a Maine clambake is a tasty example. (Photo courtesy of the Maine Office of Tourism)

History and Prehistory

The cultural heritage of an area is expressed in its historical resources. See Figure 10.2. Some tourist destination areas are devoted to history such as the Mackinaw City area of northern Michigan, St. Augustine, Florida, the Alamo and San Juan Mission in San Antonio, Texas, old gold mining tours in many western states, Machu Picchu in Peru, and the spectacular archeological find at Xian in east central China.

The preservation of history and the quality and management of museums is of utmost importance for successful tourism. Becoming familiar with the history and prehistory (archaeology) of an area can be one of the most compelling of all travel motivations. One of the principal weaknesses observed in historical museums is that the explanations of the exhibits are provided in only one language. This is a serious limitation to many tourists' enjoyment of such historical exhibits.

The hours of operation of historical points of interest and museums are significant

San Jose Church in Old San Juan dates from 1532 and is the second oldest church in the western hemisphere. (Photo courtesy of the Puerto Rico Tourism News Bureau)

and should be arranged to provide access for visitors at convenient times. Admittance fees to museums and points of historical interest should be kept as low as possible to encourage maximum attendance. Promotion is necessary, and tourist contact organizations such as chambers of commerce, tourist information offices, hotels, resorts, restaurants, and other businesses should have available literature that describes the point of interest, hours, admittance fees, special events, and any other information needed by the tourist to visit this historical attraction.

Some notable examples of museums include the National Museum of Anthropology at Mexico City, the American Museum of Natural History of New York City, the various branches of the British Museum in London, the Hermitage in Leningrad, and the various museums of the Smithsonian in Washington, D.C.

Other types of historical preservation are national historic parks and monuments and national parks with a history or prehistory theme, such as Mesa Verde National Park, Colorado. Another are the "living history" farms in Iowa and Illinois.

Among the most outstanding innovations in the presentation of history are the "sound and light" programs found mainly in Europe, the Mediterranean countries, and Mexico. A series of loudspeakers, broadcasting recorded voices in several languages with sound effects, tell the history of an unusually significant structure or place. Varying lights intensify the effect and focus the attention of the audience on various parts of the location.

At the Forum in Rome, the history of Rome is presented at night in half a dozen languages. Visitors can hear the voices of the emperors and hear the crackling flames as Rome burns. At the pyramids of Teotihuacan, about 20 miles northeast of Mexico City, famous actors relate the history of the area in another sound and light presentation given in Spanish and English language versions. Egypt offers similar programs at its ancient monuments.

SUMMARY

The cultural expressions of a people are of great interest to most travelers. These include fine arts, music and dance, handicrafts, food and drink, industry and business, agriculture, education, literature and language, science, government, religion, history, and prehistory. Tourists' experiences are enriched when they make a sincere effort to become better acquainted with local people.

Any country or area that seeks to attract tourists must plan and develop facilities and promote programs that invite access to such cultural expressions. A useful concept is "life-seeing tourism," a structured local program that arranges evening visits to local homes by tourists or, alternatively, a plan whereby interested tourists are accommodated for a few days in local homes.

Cultural interpretation in any area that hosts foreign tourists requires bilingual provisions. These include foreign language ability by guides, bilingual signs, labels, and literature.

Examination of the interrelationships of the cultural backgrounds of visitors and cultural expressions of the host society as provided by this chapter should provide useful guidance to hosts.

About the Reading

In this section the concept of community interpretation and appropriate tourism through heritage interpretation is outlined. Based on the application of heritage interpretation skills, these concepts are proposed as an approach to aid in the perpetuation of an area's unique heritage. The writer gives examples of the empowerment of local hosts in facilitating heritage experiences for guests. Also discussed is the potential applicability of the appropriate tourism concept at all levels of tourism development.

READING 10.1

Community Interpretation:
The Key to Appropriate Tourism ("Stories New and Stories Old, Stories Kept and Stories Told")

BY GABRIEL J. CHEREM
Department of Geography and Geology, Eastern Michigan University

PERPETUATING COMMUNITY STORIES

I would like to outline two closely related concepts today: community interpretation and appropriate tourism. A decade ago, Barbara Cherem and I, having given the broad applicability of heritage interpretation a great deal of thought, asked the questions: "Why should we confine interpretation only to sites (Cherem, 1977) such as parks, museums, historic sites, and zoos? Why couldn't we interpret the heritage of an entire community to its residents and to its visitors? In response to these questions the concept of "community interpretation" was created in 1980 (B. Cherem, 1981; G. Cherem, 1982; McLennan, 1984; Cherem, 1988b; Gee et. al., 1989).

We defined community interpretation as "telling the natural and cultural stories of a community to its residents and visitors." The term *story* is key here, because we believe that the *story* is the basic unit or building block of community interpretation programs. Indeed, psychologist Rene Fuller has suggested "that the story may be the basic building block, the engram . . . of human learning" (Zemke, 1990). We use the term *story* to mean a narrative of factual content embedded into "vivid events and images that carry strong emotional coloring" (Egan, 1989).

In 1982 we were able to apply the community interpretation concept to Rochester, New York, and spent 18 months preparing a community interpretation plan for that city of 250,000 people. We then were able to produce a community interpretation plan for Chelsea, Michigan, which is a small town of 5,000.

In 1984, I was invited by Ray Tabata and Jane Yamashiro of the University of Hawaii to come to Hawaii to deliver two seminars on the community interpretation concept. One seminar was delivered in Honolulu, and one on the Big Island (Klemm, 1984). Interest in the concept was very strong in Hawaii. As one result a program called "Interpret Hawaii" was initiated by Glen Grant at Kapiolani Community College. The program was designed to empower local hosts to interpret their own heritage. Tour guides, docents, hotel activity coordinators, and others were provided a background in Hawaiian natural and cultural heritage. Many of these local hosts, albeit growing up in the islands, did not have this heritage background. Training was also provided for these hosts in presentational and interpretive skills. The local hosts were thus empowered to become their own best ambassadors for Hawaii when working with visiting guests.

As development of the community interpretation concept progressed, I wanted to more directly link community interpretation to tourism. In 1987, I developed the concept of "appropriate tourism" (Cherem, 1988a; Cherem, 1990). Appropriate tourism was envisioned as the analog of the appropriate technology concept that was popular in the 1960s. It was envisioned as tourism that was appropriate to the scale, values, and unique heritage of a community or locality. It was defined as "tourism that springs from and helps perpetuate the heritage identity of an area." The area's *heritage identity* (Cherem, 1988a) includes both its cultural heritage and its natural heritage—in other words, its "sense of place."

In 1989, I was asked by Glen Grant of the Interpret Hawaii program to lead an Interpretation Institute in Honolulu on the appropriate tourism concept as applied to Pacific tourism. Attendees were working professionals at museums, hotels, parks, visitor attractions, historic sites, and academic institutions in Hawaii. A preliminary listing of 11 principles of appropriate tourism was produced.

Appropriate Tourism Principles

1. Actively aids in the perpetuation of an area's heritage—cultural, historical, and natural
2. Emphasizes and showcases the heritage identity of an area as unique in the world
3. Is based on the application of heritage interpretation skills
4. Empowers local hosts to interpret their own heritage to guests
5. Builds the pride of local hosts in their heritage and improves their guest relations and service skills
6. Helps perpetuate local life-styles and values
7. Empowers local hosts to plan and facilitate authentic and meaningful multidimensional heritage experiences for their guests
8. Is "transcultural," in that both host and guest receive a mutually rewarding enrichment experience
9. Represents programming that can be implemented at any level of tourism development and in virtually any tourism setting
10. Represents a "value-added" approach to tourism, in that it increases the level and depth of genuine service provided to guests
11. Represents an approach to sustainable tourism development, because it respects and emphasizes an area's heritage and empowers its people as the true basis for tourism development

Taken together, the concepts of community interpretation and appropriate tourism were at the very core of the Honolulu Charter (see the box), which was drafted for delegate signature at the 1991 Third Global Congress of Heritage Interpretation International. The Charter outlined the relationship of heritage interpretation and the perpetuation of community place identities to the international travel industry. Two hundred and thirty delegates from thirty countries signed the document, and in January of 1992 the Charter was transmitted to the United Nations Educational, Scientific and Cultural Organization and to the United Nations Environment Program.

THE STORY MATRIX

Every community, area, or locality of the world has a *unique* heritage identity—which includes both its cultural heritage and natural heritage, through time and into the future. To help document and organize the cultural and natural stories of an area, I have developed a tool called the heritage identity matrix, or more simply the "story matrix" (Figure 1). It is divided into cultural heritage (or cultural tourism resources) and natural heritage (or ecotourism resources). The matrix also has a timeline, so we are able to look at cultural heritage, for example, as either in the future, contemporary, historic, or pre-historic. We can do the same thing for the natural heritage of an area.

The cultural heritage portion of the story matrix is broken into four categories. The *first* of these is "non-material culture." By this is meant all of the values, attitudes, beliefs, norms,

HONOLULU CHARTER

The Honolulu Charter was drafted by the Congress organizers as a statement to the international travel industry of the relationship of heritage interpretation and preservation. A total of 230 Congress attendees from 35 countries supported the intent of the Charter and signed the document. In January 1992, the following Honolulu Charter was transmitted to the United Nations:

The undersigned—having gathered in Honolulu, Hawaii, during November 3–8, 1991 for the "Joining Hands for Quality Tourism" Congress of Heritage Interpretation International—do hereby assert and endorse the indispensable roles of heritage interpretation and preservation in the provision of quality tourism experiences for visiting guests at every community and locality in the world.

We assert and endorse that the unique heritage identity of each community and locality, including its natural and cultural resources, must be perpetuated to maintain the biological and cultural diversity, and thereby the diversity of place identities, of the entire planet. Further, such unique local heritages must be interpreted, not only to visiting guests, but to community residents themselves.

We assert and endorse that heritage interpretation principles and practices, and heritage identity preservation, are at the very core of tourism development approaches such as cultural tourism and ecotourism.

We hereby call upon and encourage both public and private groups to join hands in the perpetuation of global diversity and unique place identities— through the application of heritage interpretation principles and practices in all communities and localities of the world. We transmit this document to the United Nations Educational, Scientific and Cultural Organization (UNESCO) and to the United Nations Environment Program (UNEP) with a call for governments to take actions that permit and encourage the implementation of the principles of this Charter.

and other aspects of culture that are held within the heads and within the hearts of a particular group of people. Those non-material elements help define that culture and make it unique in the world.

The *second* category is "selected persons." By this is meant a selected individual, either well known or not, who in some way embodies an important element of that culture. The selected person could be a master artist or a master craftsperson. The selected person could be a well known figure, male or female, who embodies characteristics highly valued by that culture. The selected person could also be an everyday individual who through his work habits, living patterns, and/or religious habits embodies what is seen as being very valued in that culture. Selected persons are embodiments of the non-material culture.

The *third* category, "material culture," is the easiest to grasp. Material culture represents the tangible objects, artifacts, buildings and various other structures that a culture produces. All of the material culture elements are totally dependent on the non-material culture. Different non-material cultures, ways of believing, ways of thinking, will give us different material cultures.

The *last* category is that of "cultural landscapes," which is really an intersection category between cultural heritage and natural heritage. Put very simply the cultural landscape is the imprint of humankind on the land. It is another expression of the non-material culture. The

	Nonmaterials Culture	Selected Persons	Material Culture	Cultural Landscapes	Plants	Animals	Land	Water	Climate
Future	1	5	9	13	17	21	25	29	33
Contemporary	2	6	10	14	18	22	26	30	34
Historic	3	7	11	15	19	23	27	31	35
Prehistoric	4	8	12	16	20	24	28	32	36

Cultural Heritage (Cultural Tourism Resources)

Natural Heritage (Ecotourism Resources)

Figure 1 Story (Heritage Identity) Matrix

cultural landscape is the configuration of buildings, structures, farmscapes, and other landscape features that the particular culture superimposed upon the natural environment. The cultural landscapes category bridges us into the natural heritage portion of the story matrix.

The natural heritage categories of the story matrix are fairly straightforward. Flora and fauna are addressed by the categories of "plants" and "animals." The category of "land" takes in topographic elements, landform, and soils of the area. The category of "water" takes in not only open bodies of water, whether they be ocean coastlines or lakes or streams or rivers, but also the situation underneath the ground in terms of the availability of water resources in the groundwater table. The last category of "climate" involves the broad sun/cloud and temperature patterns, weather patterns, precipitation patterns, and other regular seasonal variations of the area.

(While expressed as separate categories for organizational purposes, all the natural heritage categories are obviously interrelated in the ecosystems of the area. Further, the evolution of any area's cultural heritage is inextricably tied to the natural heritage of the area.)

STORYKEEPERS AND STORYTELLERS

The story matrix is an organizing tool to document and categorize in a balanced manner all of the heritage identity stories of an area through time. In categorizing an area's stories, it is further necessary to say that all areas have living stories, sleeping stories, and dying stories. It is the purpose of community interpretation and appropriate tourism programs to discover, to revive, to tell, and to perpetuate as many of these stories as possible—because collectively those stories define the area's unique sense of place. I call people who are responsible for discovering, rediscovering, and reviving an area's stories "storykeepers." These are people who are actively involved in the study, documentation, preservation, and conservation of both the natural and the cultural stories of an area.

Traditionally, most societies have had persons responsible for safeguarding its stories. As an example, Alex Haley in *Roots* refers to the "griot" as serving this role in certain African cultures. In contemporary times, anthropologists, biologists, historians, ecologists, preservationists, and conservationists are among those serving roles of "storykeepers."

"Storytellers," by extension then, are those persons who are involved as interpreters, as local hosts and guides, as writers and photographers in community interpretation and appropriate tourism programs. They take the stories that have been revived and kept by the storykeepers, and they tell those stories to both area residents and visiting guests.

When the unique heritage identity stories of an area are realized, organized, kept and told—to residents and visitors alike—we have the sound basis of a community interpretation and appropriate tourism program.

LITERATURE CITED

Cherem, Barbara. 1981. "Community Interpretation in Chelsea." *The Historical Society of Michigan Newsletter,* Vol. 7, No. 2 (July–August 1981).

Cherem, Gabriel J. 1977. "The Professional Interpretor: Agent for an Awakening Giant." *Journal of Interpretation,* Vol. 2, No. 1, 3–16.

Cherem, Gabriel J. 1982. "Life Space Analysis in Interpretation." *Proceedings of the Interpretation Canada National Workshop.* Banff, Alberta.

Cherem, Gabriel J. 1988a. "Interpretation as the Vortex: Tourism Based on Heritage Experiences." *Proceedings of the Interpretation Canada National Conference.* Ottawa, Ontario.

Cherem, Gabriel J. 1988b. "Community Interpretation and Tourism." Presented at the Second World Congress on Heritage Presentation and Interpretation. Warwick, England (August–September).

Cherem, Gabriel J. 1990. "Appropriate Tourism Through Heritage Interpretation." In McIntosh, Robert W. and Goeldner, Charles R., *Tourism Principles, Practices, Philosophies, Sixth Edition.* New York, New York.

Egan, Kieran. 1989. "Memory, Imagination, and Learning: Connected by the Story." *Phi Delta Kappan* (February).

Gee, Chuck Y., Makens, James C., and Choy, Dexter J. L. 1989. "The Travel Industry." Library of Congress. Van Nostrand Reinhold.

Haley, Alex. 1976. *Roots.* Doubleday.

Klemm, R. 1984. "Community Interpretation—Not Just Another Tourist Trap." *Makai 6(11)* (November). University of Hawaii.

McLennan, Marshall. 1984. "New Opportunities in Historical Geography." *The Geographical Bulletin,* Vol. 26 (November).

Zemke, Ron. 1990. "Storytelling: Back to a Basic." *Training* (March).

Key Concepts

achievements
agriculture
appreciation
appropriate tourism
artistic activity
attractiveness
communication
community interpretation
cultural attractions
cultural identity card
cultural tourism
education
festivals
fine arts
food and drink
government
handicraft
heritage interpretation
history and prehistory

Honolulu Charter
industry and business
international travel
learning
life-seeing tourism
literature and language
multilingual guides and signs
music and dance
peace
pleasure travel
religion
recognition
research
science
sound and light programs
story matrix
twinning principle
understanding
ways of life and thought

For Review and Discussion

1. Evaluate culture as a travel motivator.
2. Give an example of a cultural experience that would be most satisfying to a visitor in a country much different from his or her own.
3. Create a life-seeing tourism program in a familiar community.
4. What type of life-seeing experience would you particularly enjoy?
5. How much cultural difference can most tourists tolerate? Give examples.
6. Identify some of the rewards that international travel can bring to a perceptive, sensitive traveler.

7. For what reasons did the Minister of Tourism for the Bahamas promote their People-to-People Program?

8. Referring to question 7, identify some other countries where a similar program would be equally successful.

9. A philosopher states that culture is what we know. Research changes our viewpoint. Thus new discoveries make us change. Do you agree?

10. Does your community possess some distinctive cultural attraction?

11. Can you apply the concept of "appropriate tourism" to any tourist destination area? Give examples.

12. Explain the benefits tourists would enjoy if they participated in a heritage experience led by a graduate of a heritage interpretation training program of excellent quality.

13. How significant will be the Honolulu Charter?

Case Problems

1. An attractive lakeside community of 5000 persons is presently a popular tourist center, primarily due to its appeal to sports enthusiasts and its proximity to a magnificent state park. However, tourist expenditures are low due principally to the lack of entertainment in the community. The movie theater closed three years ago, and there is virtually no entertainment except that to be found in a couple of beer taverns. The town and surrounding countryside are rich in history, but the only museum is a small one in the front part of a bar. How could a museum and other entertainment be provided?

2. As the director of an area tourism organization, you have been approached by a fine arts group to consider the feasibility of promoting a Shakespearian Festival in your community similar to the long-established festival at Stratford, Ontario, Canada. What factors would you consider in evaluating this request, and how would you work with your state and national tourism organizations to determine how this cultural event could be publicized?

Selected References

Alley, Kelly D. "Heritage Tourism and Urban Development in India." *Practicing Anthropology*, Vol. 14, No. 2 (Spring 1992).

Bohnet, Gerald V. "The Polynesian Cultural Center: A Multi-cultural Theme Park Experience." *Visions in Leisure and Business*, Vol. 9, No. 1 (Spring 1990), pp. 51–60.

Boniface, Brian G., and Christopher P. Cooper. *The Geography of Travel and Tourism*. London: Heinemann, 1987.

Brokensha, Peter, and Hans Guldberg. *Study of Cultural Tourism in Australia*. Canberra, Australia: Government Printing Office, 1992.

Cohen, Erik. "Pilgrimage Centers: Concentric and Eccentric." *Annals of Tourism Research*, Vol. 19, No. 1 (1992), pp. 33–50.

Davis, Derrin, and Betty Weiler. "Kakadu National Park: Conflicts in a World Heritage Area." *Tourism Management*, Vol. 13, No. 3 (September 1992), pp. 313–320.

Dernoi, Louis A. "Farm Tourism in Europe." *Tourism Management*, Vol. 4, No. 3 (September 1983), pp. 155–166.

Evans-Pritchard, Deirdre. "Ancient Art in Modern Context." *Annals of Tourism Research*, Vol. 20, No. 1 (1993), pp. 9–31.

Farrell, Bryan H. *Hawaii, the Legend That Sells*. Honolulu: University Press of Hawaii, 1982.

Graburn, Nelson H. H. "The Anthropology of Tourism." *Annals of Tourism Research,* Vol. 10, No. 1 (1983), pp. 9–33. Special Issue on the Anthropology of Tourism.

Graburn, Nelson H. H. *Ethnic and Tourist Arts.* Berkeley, Calif.: University of California Press, 1976.

Hall, Derek R. "The Challenge of International Tourism in Eastern Europe." *Tourism Management,* Vol. 13, No. 3 (September 1992), pp. 313–320.

Haukeland, Jan Vidar. "Sociocultural Impacts of Tourism in Scandinavia." *Tourism Management,* Vol. 5, No. 3 (September 1984), pp. 207–214.

Hughes, Howard L. "Tourism and the Arts." *Tourism Management,* Vol. 10, No. 2 (June 1989), pp. 97–99.

International Association of Scientific Experts in Tourism. *Tourism and the Architectural Heritage: Cultural, Legal, Economic and Marketing Aspects.* St. Gallen, Switzerland: The Association, 1984.

Johnson, Barbara R. "Anthropology's Role in Stimulating Responsible Tourism." *Practicing Anthropology,* Vol. 14, No. 2 (Spring 1992).

Lew, Alan A. "Authenticity and Sense of Place in the Tourism Development Experience of Older Retail Districts." *Journal of Travel Research,* Vol. 27, No. 4 (Summer 1989), pp. 15–22.

Lundberg, Donald E., and Carolyn B. Lundberg. *International Travel and Tourism.* New York: Wiley, 1993.

Mitchell, Lisle S., and Peter E. Murphy. "Geography and Tourism." *Annals of Tourism Research,* Vol. 18, No. 1 (1991), pp. 57–70.

Moscarfdo, Gianna M., and Phillip L. Pearce. "Historic Theme Parks: An Australian Experience in Authenticity." *Annals of Tourism Research,* Vol. 13, No. 3 (1986), pp. 467–479.

Nash, Dennison, and Valene L. Smith. "Anthropology and Tourism." *Annals of Tourism Research,* Vol. 18, No. 1 (1991), pp. 12–25.

Sinclair, Thea M., and M. J. Stabler. *The Tourism Industry: An International Analysis.* Tucson, Ariz.: University of Arizona Press, 1991.

Smith, Valene L. *Hosts and Guests: The Anthropology of Tourism.* Philadelphia: University of Pennsylvania Press, 1989.

Smith, Valene L. "Managing Tourism in the 1990s and Beyond." *Practicing Anthropology,* Vol. 14, No. 2 (Spring 1992).

Toops, Stanley. "Xingiang's Handicraft Industry." *Annals of Tourism Research,* Vol. 20, No. 1 (1993), pp. 88–106.

Weiler, Betty, and Michael Hall. *Special Interest Tourism.* New York: Wiley, 1992.

Zeppel, Heather, and C. Michael Hall. "Selling Art and History: Cultural Heritage and Tourism." *Journal of Tourism Studies,* Vol. 2, No. 1 (May 1991), pp. 29–45.

CHAPTER 11

Sociology of Tourism

LEARNING OBJECTIVES

- Appreciate the inordinate social impact that travel experiences make on the individual, the family or group, and society as a whole—especially the host society.
- Recognize that a country's indigenous population may resent the presence of visitors, especially in large numbers. Also recognize that the influence of these visitors may be considered detrimental—both socially and economically.
- Discover that travel patterns change with changing life characteristics and social class.
- Become familiar with the concept of social tourism and its importance in various countries.
- Perceive that there are four extremes relating to the travel preferences of international tourists. Also, recognize that a sociologist has identified a typology of four tourist roles in international tourism.

Sociology is the science of society, social institutions, and social relationships. Visitors to a community or area create social relationships that typically differ greatly from the affiliations among the indigenous population. In this chapter we identify and evaluate tourist–host relationships and prescribe methods of managing these to create significant advantages for both groups. The ultimate effects of travel experiences on the population in areas of origin as well as in places of destination should determine to what extent societies encourage or discourage tourism.

EFFECTS ON THE INDIVIDUAL

Someone who travels, particularly to a strange location, finds an unfamiliar environment not only geographically but personally, socially, and culturally. Thus the traveler faces problems for which a solution must be found if the trip is to be fully enjoyable and rewarding. Travelers must manage their resources of money and time in situations much different from those at home. They also must manage their social interactions and social relations to obtain sustenance, shelter, and other needs and possibly to find companionship. Determining the extent of the "cultural distance" they may wish to maintain results in decisions as to just *how* unfamiliar the traveler wants his or her environment away from home base to be. People who travel do so with different degrees of contact with the new cultures in which they may find themselves. Life-seeing tourism, for example, is a structured method for those who wish deeper immersion in local ways of life to acquire such enrichment. Some travelers prefer a more selective contact experience as might be arranged by a tour company. Tours designed around cultural subjects and experiences such as an anthropological study tour or participation in an arts and crafts festival are examples. Regardless of the degree of local participation, the individual traveler must at least superficially study the country to be visited and reach some level of decision on how these problems in environmental differences are to be resolved. Advance preparation is an intelligent approach. Travel experiences have a profound effect on the traveler as well as on society, as travel experiences often are among the most outstanding memories in the traveler's life.

EFFECTS ON THE FAMILY

As a family is growing and the children are maturing, the trips taken as a family are highlights of any year. The excitement of preparation and anticipation and the actual

Ten miles of beach and almost 12 miles of paved bicycle paths are ideal for family cycling on Kiawah Island, South Carolina. (Photo courtesy of Kiawah Island)

Father and son find companionship and enjoyment viewing this elaborate 20-train model railroad and model ship display at Cypress Junction. (Photo courtesy of Cypress Gardens, Florida)

travel experience are memorable occasions of family life. Travels with a measure of adventure are likely to be the most memorable. Family travel may also be educational. The more purposeful and educational a trip becomes, the more beneficial it is. Study before taking the trip and expert travel counseling greatly add to a maximization of the trip's benefits.

EFFECTS ON SOCIETY

Travel has a significant influence on national understanding and appreciation of other people. Government policies in progressive and enlightened nations encourage travel, particularly domestic travel, as a means of acquainting citizens with other parts of their country and building appreciation for the homeland.

The presence of visitors in a country affects the living patterns of indigenous peoples. The way visitors conduct themselves and their personal relationships with citizens of the host country often have a profound effect on the mode of life and attitudes of local people. Probably the most pronounced effects of this phenomenon are noted when visitors from North America or Western Europe travel in an emerging country that has a primitive culture or a culture characterized by a low (economic) standard of living and an unsophisticated population.

Conversely, the visitor is influenced by the contrast in culture. Generally, however, this brings about an increased appreciation for qualities of life in the society visited that may not be present at home.

A favorable situation exists when visitors and those of the host country mingle socially and become better acquainted. This greatly increases the awareness of each other's character and qualities, building appreciation and respect in both groups.

Tourism and Crime

Unfortunately, tourists can be easy prey for criminals. Tourists do not know about dangerous areas or local situations in which they might be very vulnerable to violent crimes. They become easy marks for robbers and other offenders as they are readily identified and are usually not very well equipped to ward off an attack.

Sometimes popular tourist attractions such as parks or beaches are within walking distance from hotel areas. However, a walking tour from the hotel may bring the tourist into a high-crime area lying directly in the path taken to reach this attraction. If such high-crime areas exist, active efforts must be made to inform visitors and guests. Hotels and others that publish maps of walking tours should route such tours into safe areas only. Also, they should warn guests of the danger that could arise if the visitor undertakes certain activities.

Crimes against tourists result in bad publicity and create a negative image in the minds of prospective visitors. So tour companies tend to avoid destinations that have the reputation for crimes against tourists. Eventually, no matter how much effort is applied to publicize the area's benefits and visitor rewards, decreasing popularity will result in failure.

Pizam, Reichel, and Shieh found that tourism expenditures had a negligible effect on crime.[1] However, they suggested that tourism could be considered a potential determinant of crime, negatively affecting the quality of the environment. The tourist industry cannot be held responsible for the occurrence of crime. But one must be aware that tourists are a potential target of crime. Protecting them from offenders is essential to the survival and growth of the industry.

Resentments

Resentment by local people toward the tourist can be generated by the apparent gap in economic circumstances, behavioral patterns, appearance, and economic effects. Resentment of visitors is not uncommon in areas where there is conflict of interests because of tourists. For example, in North America, local people may resent visiting sports enthusiasts because they are "shooting our deer" or "catching our fish." The demand for goods by tourists may tend to increase prices and cause bad feelings.

Another form of resentment may result in a feeling of inferiority among indigenous groups because of unfavorable contrasts with foreign visitors. Local persons employed in the service industries catering to visitors may be better paid and, thus, exhibit feelings of superiority toward their less fortunate fellow citizens. This creates a poor attitude toward the entire visitor industry.

---

[1]Abraham Pizam, Arie Reichel, and Chia Fian Shieh, "Tourism and Crime: Is There a Relationship?" *Journal of Travel Research,* Vol. 20, No. 3 (Winter 1982), pp. 7–10.

Financial dislocations can also occur. While a tourist may give a young bellhop a dollar tip for delivering bags, the bellhop's father may be working out in the fields as a farm laborer for a total daily wage of only a dollar or a dollar and a half.

Sensitive tourists become aware of another society's ways of life during a visit. For example, tourists might be interested in observing how different societies find solutions to common problems. An example of this is "welfare square" in Salt Lake City, Utah, where members of the Mormon Church work to recondition used clothes and other necessities of life for use by less fortunate members of the church. Publicly financed welfare is not welcome; they prefer to help each other.

As a rule, both hosts and guests in any society can learn from each other. Beneficial social contact and planned visits to observe local life and culture do much to build appreciation for the indigenous culture. At the same time, the visitors' interest in their ways of life increases the local people's respect for these visitors and gives them a feeling of pride in their own accomplishments.

Tourism, especially in-tourism, often facilitates a transition from rigid authoritarian social structure to one that is more sensitive to the individual's needs. When societies are "closed" from outside influences, they tend to become rigid. By encouraging visitors, this policy is changed to a more moderate one, for the benefit of hosts and guests. The preservation of wildlife sanctuaries and parks as well as national monuments and other cultural resources is often encouraged when tourism begins to be a force in the society.

One-to-one interaction between hosts and guests can break down stereotypes, or the act of categorizing groups of people based upon a single dimension. By "labeling" people, often erroneously, individualism is lost. When a visitor gets to know people personally and is aware of their problems, hopes, and ways in which they are making life more pleasant, this visitor becomes much more sensitive to the universality of humankind. It is much easier to distrust and dislike indistinguishable groups of people than individuals one has come to know personally.

Some problems are often rooted in economic problems, such as unemployment or underemployment. The economic contributions of tourism can help to moderate such social difficulties. Negative social effects on a host society have been identified as follows:

1. Introduction of undesirable activities such as gambling, prostitution, drunkenness, and other excesses
2. The so-called "demonstration effect" of local people wanting the same luxuries and imported goods as those indulged in by tourists
3. Racial tension, particularly where there are very obvious racial differences between tourists and their hosts
4. Development of a servile attitude on the part of tourist business employees
5. "Trinketization" of crafts and art to produce volumes of souvenirs for the tourist trade
6. Standardization of employee roles such as the international waiter—same type of person in every country
7. Loss of cultural pride, if the culture is viewed by the visitor as a quaint custom or as entertainment

8. Too rapid change in local ways of life due to being overwhelmed by too many tourists
9. Disproportionate numbers of workers in low-paid, menial jobs characteristic of much hotel and restaurant employment

Many, if not all these negative effects can be moderated or eliminated by intelligent planning and progressive management methods. Tourism can be developed in ways that will not impose such a heavy social cost. Strict control of land use by zoning and building codes, enlightened policies on the part of the minister of tourism or similar official organization, proper phasing of supply components such as infrastructure and superstructure to match supply with demand for orderly development are some of the measures needed. Education and good public relations programs can accomplish much. Enforcing proper standards of quality in the marketing of local arts and crafts can actually enhance and "rescue" such skills from oblivion. As cited in the book *Hosts and Guests*,[2] the creative skills of America's Indians of the Southwest were kept alive, enhanced, encouraged, and ultimately expanded to provide tourists with authentic Indian rugs and turquoise jewelry particularly, but other crafts as well. The Fred Harvey Company, which still bears his name, is credited with encouraging Indians to continue these attractive crafts so that he could market them in his hotels, restaurants, and gift shops.

Changing Population and Travel Interests

People change, group attitudes change, and populations change. All these factors affect travel interests. Travel interests also change. Some countries grow in travel popularity; others wane. World events tend to focus public attention on particular countries or regions of the world. The emergence of Japan and Korea as travel destinations following World War II and the Korean War and interest in visiting the Caribbean area, as well as Israel, Spain, Morocco, and East Africa are examples. Currently, travel to China and Australia is of great interest. There is an old saying among travel promotors that "mass follows class." This has been proven beyond a doubt. Travel page publicity concerning prominent persons visiting a particular area inevitably produces a growth of interest in the area and subsequent increases in demand for travel to such well-publicized areas.

The growth of communication systems, particularly network and cable television, has broadened the scope of peoples' interests in other lands and other peoples. To be able to see, as well as hear, has a powerful impact on the viewer's mind and provides acquaintanceship with conditions in another country that may develop a desire for a visit. As communications resources grow, awareness and interest also grow.

LIFE CHARACTERISTICS AND TRAVEL

Rising standards of living, changes in the population age composition, the increasing levels of educational attainment, better communication, increased social consciousness of people relating to the welfare and activities of other people throughout the world,

---

[2]Valene L. Smith (Ed.) *Hosts and Guests* (Philadelphia: University of Pennsylvania Press, 1977), p. 176.

and the psychological shrinking of the world by the jet plane have combined to produce an interest among nations in all other nations.

Travel Patterns Related to Age

With age (late sixties and upward) the traveler may become more passive. Family recreation patterns are associated with life stages of the family. The presence of young children tends to reduce the number of trips taken, whereas married couples with no children are among the best travel prospects. As the children mature, however, families increase their travel activities, and families with children between the ages of 15 and 17 have a much higher family travel pattern than do those with younger children. As the children grow up and leave home, the married couple (again without children) renews interest in travel. Also, couples in this life stage are more likely to have more discretion-

Motorcoach tours have the advantage of allowing passengers to see the countryside without the responsibility of driving. Today's motorcoaches have rest rooms, air conditioning, reclining seats, and large tinted windows to ensure comfortable traveling. (Photo courtesy of the National Tour Association)

ary income and are financially able to afford more travel. Persons living in urban centers are more travel inclined than are those in rural areas.

SENIOR CITIZEN MARKET   A major trend is the growth of the over-65 senior citizen market and semi-senior citizen market, the over-55-year-olds. Many have dubbed this the mature market, senior market, retirement market, or elderly market. Others look at it as the 50-plus market because 50 is the age for American Association of Retired Persons (AARP) membership.

Whatever it is called, it is an important and growing market. The over-65 group totaled 25.7 million in 1980 and 31.7 million in 1990. This segment is expected to grow to 33.9 million in 1995; then, because of the small birth cohorts of the Great Depression, the group will grow more slowly to 36.2 million in 2005. After that it is expected to grow rapidly to 64.6 million in 2030 as the baby boomers reach this age (see Figure 11.1).

Income

Buying power is another factor for the tourism manager to consider. People must have buying power to create a market. There is no question that a large and increasing percentage of the population today has sufficient discretionary income to finance business and pleasure travel, although some families may be limited to inexpensive trips. The frequency of travel and the magnitude of travel expenditures increase rapidly as income increases. All travel surveys, whether conducted by the Census Bureau, U.S. Travel Data Center, market research firms, or the media, show a direct relationship between family income and the incidence of travel. The greater the income, the more likely a household will travel. The affluent spend more on just about everything, but spending on travel is particularly strong. The value placed on time increases with household income, which is one of the reasons air travel attracts the higher-income consumer.

How the travel dollar is spent obviously depends on income. When the income of

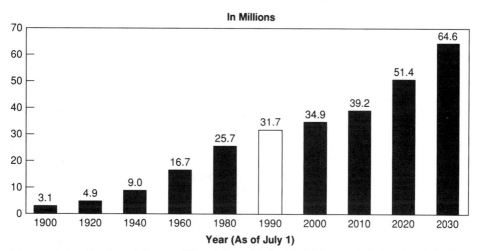

Figure 11.1   Number of Persons 65 and Over, 1900–2030 (*Source:* U.S. Bureau of the Census and AARP)

the population is divided into fifths, less than 33 percent of the lowest fifth report an expenditure for travel, whereas 85 percent of those in the top fifth report a travel expenditure. Almost half of all consumer spending for vacation and pleasure trips comes from households in the top fifth of the income scale. The affluent spend more on lodging, all-expense-paid tours, food, and shopping, but transportation expenditures are a smaller share of their total travel outlays than with those at the bottom of the income scale—32 percent versus 43 percent. This results from the fact that it is more difficult to economize on transportation than on food, lodging, and miscellaneous expenses.[3]

If current trends continue, the U.S. population will be wealthier by the year 2000. The Bureau of the Census reports that median family income rose to $30,850 in 1987. Since 1982, real median family income (after adjusting for inflation) increased by 11.8 percent. In addition to a rise in real wage rates, an exceedingly important factor was the growth in dual wage earners. The increase in the number of women who work outside the home has been dramatic and has boosted household income. Both husband and wife are employed in about half of all marriages (51 percent), an increase over the less than 29 percent in 1960. This trend is expected to continue, 57 percent of families having both partners working by the year 2000. As incomes increase, it bodes well for travel, but with husbands and wives both working, it may be more difficult to find time for travel and vacation. It is believed that this is one of the reasons for the trend toward shorter and more frequent vacations.

Travel expenditures historically have had an income elasticity exceeding unity; as per capita real incomes continue to rise, consumers should spend an increasing proportion of their incomes on travel. Besides making more trips in the future, increasing numbers of consumers can be expected to choose air travel over other modes of travel. Income and education are closely correlated. We discuss this relationship below.

Education

Another factor deserving attention from tourism managers is education because it tends to broaden peoples' interests and thus stimulate travel. People with college educations take more pleasure trips than do those with high school educations, and those with high school educations take more trips than do those with grade school educations. Educators are forecasting continued increases in the average educational level, which would result in a continued positive impact on pleasure travel.

Studies uniformly show that the well educated account for the most travel and the most dollars spent for vacation and pleasure trips. Only about 50 percent of the homes where the household head did not earn a high school diploma report an expenditure for vacation trips. Where the head holds a high school diploma, about 65 percent report vacation expenditures; where the head has some college, 75 percent spend on vacations; and where the head has a degree, 85 percent report vacation expenditures. Income accompanies education as an important factor. In the approximately 35 percent of the homes where the head of the household has had some college, approximately 55 percent of the expenditures for vacation travel are made. Where the head has more than four years of college, vacation expenditures run two to three times the U.S. average. There

[3]Fabian Linden, "The Business of Vacation Traveling," *Across the Board*, Vol. 27, No. 4 (April 1980), pp. 72–75.

appears to be no question that increased education levels heighten the propensity to travel, and with expanding higher education levels within the population, air travel should also expand.

The nation's educational level continues to rise. Fifty years ago, a high school diploma was nearly as rare a credential as a four-year college degree is today. As of 1992, 79.4 percent of all adults 25 years of age and older had completed four years of high school. The proportion of the population completing college has also increased considerably. In 1950 only 7.3 percent of men and 5.2 percent of women had completed college. In 1992 the proportion of persons 25 and over completing four years of college or more grew, so that 24.3 percent of men and 18.6 percent of women were college graduates. Today, the majority of college students (54.2 percent) are women.[4] Education is closely correlated with income and occupation, so the rising level of education should help to increase the demand for travel.

Travel and the Handicapped

In the United States alone there are about 47[5] million physically handicapped people—almost twice the total population of Canada. This group constitutes an excellent potential market for travel if the facilities and arrangements are suitable for their use and enjoyment. Woodside and Etzel made a study of the degree to which physical and mental conditions restricted travel activities by households and how households with one or more handicapped persons were likely to adjust their vacation travel behavior.[6]

Findings in Table 11.1 indicate that many of the physical or mental conditions that limited travel were unobservable (such as heart condition or diabetes) by other travelers or by employees of tourist facilities. But this high percentage of disabled persons creates a substantial potential for emergency situations, and the planning and management of travel equipment and facilities must aim for a major reduction or elimination of such possibilities.

The effect of the presence of handicapped persons in a family on lengths of stays is summarized in Table 11.2. The number of nights away from home differed considerably between those traveling with handicapped persons and those without handicapped persons.

Many households reported little difficulty in using accommodations due to careful planning before making the trip. The majority of difficulties encountered seemed to be at recreational facilities. However, as shown in the Winter Park, Colorado, photo the handicapped can participate in difficult recreation activities. Winter Park is famous for its handicapped and blind skier programs. Over 250 handicapped competitors of all ages and disabilities participate in the annual Handicap National Championships.

[4]U.S. Bureau of the Census, *Statistical Abstract of the United States, 1993,* 112th edition (Washington, D.C.: U.S. Government Printing Office, 1993), pp. 153–174.
[5]Michael Quigley, "Cruise Lines Under Jurisdiction of Americans with Disabilities Act," *Handicapped Travel Newsletter* (June/July/August 1993), p. 1.
[6]Arch G. Woodside and Michael J. Etzel, "Impact of Physical and Mental Handicaps on Vacation Travel Behavior," *Journal of Travel Research,* Vol. 18, No. 3 (Winter 1980), pp. 9–11.

Table 11.1   Physical or Mental Conditions Limiting Travel

Condition	Number of Conditions	Percentage of Respondents
Heart condition	20	33%
Crutches	6	10
Old age	5	8
Wheelchair	3	5
Stroke victim	3	5
Recent major surgery	3	5
Diabetes	3	5
Leg braces	2	3
Blindness	2	3
Other[a]	15	23
	62	100%
		(n = 60)

[a]For example, phobia of mountains, mental retardation, pregnancy, bad leg, dizziness, sprained back, flu, and stomach virus.

Americans with Disabilities Act

Substantial improvements have been made by the tourist industry to serve this segment of the market over the years. Activity accelerated with the enactment of the Americans with Disabilities Act (ADA) on July 26, 1990. ADA contains five titles, or sections: Employment, Public Services, Public Accommodations and Services Operated by Private Entities, Telecommunications, and Miscellaneous Provisions. Included in these titles are mandates for accessible public transit and complementary paratransit; accessible intercity (AMTRAK) and commuter rail; accessible stations; accessible public accommodation (private entities), including inns, hotels, motels, restaurants, bars, theaters, concert halls, auditoriums, convention centers, all kinds of stores, service establishments, offices, terminals and depots, museums, libraries, galleries, schools, and so on; and telecommunications relay services for hearing- and speech-impaired persons.

Table 11.2   Number of Nights away from Home (as a Percentage of Total)

Nights	Travel Parties	
	With Handicapped Persons	Without Handicapped Persons
1–3	37	42
4–6	24	31
7–9	15	15
10–12	5	5
13–15	7	3
16 or more	12	4
Number of respondents	60	530

A handicapped skier participating in the Handicap National Championships at Winter Park Colorado. (Photo courtesy of Colorado Ski Country, USA)

Although the act is not specifically a travel law, travel agencies, lodging establishments, motorcoach operators, museums, and restaurants fall into the broad category of public accommodation that are required to make their facilities accessible to disabled persons. As the Justice Department and the Transportation Department issue final regulations and firms comply, easier travel for the disabled will result.

EMERGENCE OF GROUP TRAVEL PATTERNS

Travel Clubs

These are groups, sometimes with a common interest (if only in travel), that have formed travel organizations for their mutual benefit. For example, some purchase an aircraft and then arrange trips for their members. Others join international membership clubs such as Club Méditerranée, which owns resort properties in many countries and provides package-type holidays at usually modest cost.

Low-Priced Group Travel

Many tour companies cater to common interest groups such as the members of a religious group or professional or work group. A tour is arranged, often at reasonable cost, and is promoted to members of the group.

Public Carrier Group Rates and Arrangements

Airlines and other public carriers make special rates available for groups—a common number is 15 at discounted rates. A free ticket is issued to the group's escort or leader. Chartering all or part of a public transportation vehicle, aircraft, or ship is also a special effort on the part of the carrier to accommodate travel groups.

Incentive Tours

One of the fastest-growing group arrangements is that of incentive tours provided by a company to members and their spouses who are successful in achieving some objective, usually a sales goal. At the destination, the group is sometimes asked to review new products and receive some company indoctrination.

Special-Interest Tours

Special-interest group travel is another segment growing in importance. Tours are arranged for those interested in agriculture, archaeology, architecture, art, bird watching, business, industry, castles and palaces, ethnic studies, fall foliage, festivals, fishing, hunting, flower arranging, gardening, gems and minerals, music, golf, history, literature, nature, opera, photography, professional interests, psychic research, safaris, skiing, skin diving, social studies, sports, study, theater, and wine, to name a few examples.

Social and fraternal organizations also are traveling more in groups. Some private clubs are taking group trips. Some are extensive trips around the world or trips lasting up to 60 days. Women's groups, social groups, youth groups, alumni, and professional societies commonly take extended trips together as a group. Preconvention and postconvention trips are also popular.

SOCIAL (SUBSIDIZED) TOURISM

Although there is as yet no agreed definition of social tourism there has been considerable study of the question. W. Hunziker at the Second Congress of Social Tourism held at Vienna and Salzburg in 1959 proposed the following definition: "Social tourism is a type of tourism practiced by low income groups, and which is rendered possible and facilitated by entirely separate and therefore easily recognizable services." Another defintion, that of M. Andre Poplimont, is as follows: "Social tourism is a type of tourism practiced by those who would not be able to meet the cost without social intervention, that is, without the assistance of an association to which the individual belongs."

From these definitions and from the reports of the three International Congresses on Social Tourism, it is clear that certain elements may be described. First is the idea of "limited means." Second, social tourism is subsidized by the states, local authorities, employers, trade unions, clubs, or other associations to which the worker belongs. Third, it involves travel outside the normal place of residence, preferably to a different environment that is usually within their own country or sometimes to a country nearby.

Holidays with Pay

Paid holidays are now established all over the world, and in most countries a minimum duration (one, two, or three weeks) is specified either by law or by collective agreement. Some, however, consider this institution only a first stage, and believe that attention should now be turned to the way in which these holidays are used. One of the great subjects of discussion by twentieth-century sociologists is the use of the increased leisure time now available to workers and the cultural and educational development that such leisure time makes possible.

Large numbers of workers are obliged to spend their holidays at home, partly because of their lack of means or tourist experience and partly because of lack of information, transport difficulties, or shortage of suitable accommodation. Organized social tourism, if efficiently managed, can overcome most of these problems: finance through subsidies and savings schemes, experience and information through contacts elsewhere in the country concerned or abroad, transport problems through package deals with carriers, and accommodation through contracts with resorts. Thus organizations can bring tourism within the reach of many who would otherwise be unable to travel. There will be some, however, who for reasons of age, health, family responsibility, or disinclination are unwilling to join in such holidays even when all arrangements are made for them.

Determination of Needs

Some countries carry out research in this field. In Belgium it was discovered that almost 60 percent of the respondents to an inquiry preferred a continuous stay to moving from place to place, but this preference was more marked among older than younger people. In the Netherlands, another inquiry revealed that about a million holiday makers preferred not to rely on the hospitality of relatives if other facilities within their means were provided. It was evident that existing facilities of this kind were inadequate.

It was also found that the tendency to take holidays away from home was increasing and that more attention should be given to the educational and cultural aspects of tourism. Studies in France and Italy have found orders of preference between the countryside, the seaside, the mountains, health resorts, and other places, and in Sweden and Italy, inquiries have been carried out into the types of accommodations favored.

Examples of Social Tourism

Leysin, in Switzerland, is one of the best known examples of holiday centers for social tourism. Originally a famous health resort, advances in medicine meant that its clientele would gradually diminish, but with the cooperation of certain organizations, including the Caisse Suisse de Voyage, the resort was adapted to attract a new type of tourist. A small golf course, a swimming pool, tennis courts, and arrangements for skiing were established, and sanatoria and hotels were converted to meet the new demands. A publicity campaign was begun, and in its first year over 2000 tourists arrived and spent more than 50,000 bed-nights in the resort.

Camping and staying at hostels are popular with younger tourists and are also used by families. In recent years there has been a considerable development of caravan camps, particularly in Great Britain. Camping has the advantage of being one of the least expensive forms of holiday and makes possible more mobility. Financial aid is given to camps by the state in France and other countries. In Greece, camps are operated by some large industrial firms for the benefit of their employees, and in most countries, they are run by camping clubs and youth associations.

Provision of Information

In the development of social tourism, other problems arise, but these are largely common to tourism in general. The provision of information, however, deserves brief mention here, as many of the beneficiaries of social tourism will have little knowledge of the special attractions of different resorts. In some countries, government authorities, trade unions, national tourist organizations, and other bodies have given attention to this question. In the United States, for example, there are tourist information offices in the large cities, and publications are issued advising workers how they can spend their holidays. In Canada, bulletins are sent to the trade union offices and other organizations.

To date, most progress has been made in domestic tourism only, and although many workers are already traveling abroad, there is great opportunity for joint action between the official travel organizations of different states. Proposals have been made in some regions as how best to promote foreign travel by the lower-income groups, and the Argentine national tourist organization has invited the correspondent bodies in other South American states to arrange programs on a reciprocal basis.

SUMMARY OF THE PRINCIPAL SOCIAL EFFECTS OF TOURISM

1. The vacation and special business trips a person takes are often among life's most vivid memories.
2. For families, vacation trips taken together are among the highlights of the year's activities.
3. The presence of visitors in a particular area can affect the living patterns of local people. The extent to which a local population is affected depends on the diversity of the mixing groups, including factors such as obvious differences in wealth, habits, appearance, and behavior.
4. On a national basis, people of a particular country can have their lives changed by tourism, particularly if there are large numbers of tourists in proportion to the indigenous population. Visitors may influence ways of dressing, consumption patterns, desire for products used by tourists, sexual freedoms, and a broadening outlook on the world.
5. For both hosts and guests, the most satisfying relationships are formed when they can meet and interact socially at a gathering such as a reception, a tea, or a cultural event; in "people to people" programs (home visitation); or in life-seeing tourism (a structured learning-leisure program).
6. Tourism's effects on crime are negligible, but tourists can become easy victims of crime. Hosts must help them avoid dangerous places and areas.
7. Resentment of visitors by local (indigenous) people can occur. There may be

conflicts over the use (or abuse) of local facilities and resources. Consumer prices may rise during the "tourist season."

8. Extensive tourism development can bring about undesirable social effects such as increased prostitution, gambling, drunkedness, rowdyism, unwanted noise, congestion, and other excesses.

9. Domestic and international tourism increases for people in a country that has a rising standard of living, a population age distribution favoring young adults or young marrieds with no children, and an increasing population of older, affluent adults.

10. People living in cities are more interested in travel than those living in small towns or rural areas.

11. Wealthy people and those in higher social classes are greatly inclined to travel.

12. Increase in the educational level in a population brings about an increase in travel.

13. Catering to handicapped persons substantially increases markets.

14. Group travel and tours are popular ways to travel.

15. Social tourism is a form of travel wherein the cost is subsidized by the traveler's trade union, government, public carrier, hotel, or association. Travelers thus assisted are in low-income groups, older age groups, or workers in organizations authorized to receive such subsidies or vacation bonuses.

THE INTERNATIONAL TOURIST

International travel largely emanates from countries with a comparatively high standard of living, with high rates of economic growth, and with social systems characterized by declining inequality of incomes and a sizable urban population. In addition these international travelers come from countries where large-scale industry and commerce comprise the foundations of the economy and where the communications and information environment is dominated by the mass media. The international market is largely made up of middle-income people, including the more prosperous minority of the working class, who normally live in large cities and earn their living in managerial, professional, white-collar, supervisory, and skilled occupations.

There are four extremes relating to the preferences of the international tourist: (1) complete relaxation to constant activity, (2) traveling close to one's home environment to a totally strange environment, (3) complete dependence on group travel to traveling alone, and (4) order to disorder. These extremes are not completely separate, and for most travelers there may be any number of combinations on any given trip. For example, a traveler may take a peaceful river cruise and then enjoy a strenuous swim in a quiet pool.

Relaxation Versus Activity

Historically, the first wave of mass international travel (the interwar and postwar years) occurred at a time when there was a sharp differentiation between work and leisure and when the working week for most people, including the middle class, was long and exhausting. Under these circumstances it was not surprising the demand concentrated on holidays that offered relaxation, recuperation, rest. Essentially they provided an

A cruise vacation allows participants both relaxation and activity. Here Royal Caribbean Cruise Line passengers enjoy an early morning workout on the sports deck. (Photo courtesy of the Royal Caribbean Cruise Lines)

opportunity for winding down and getting fit for the next 49 weeks of arduous activity. Since then the balance between work and leisure has shifted sharply in favor of the latter. Usually the weekend is free, and the annual holiday leave for some workers has been lengthened. In other words, over the past decade people have become used to greater slices of leisure time. Relaxation is possible throughout the year, and there is less need to use a holiday exclusively for this purpose.

With the arrival of year-round leisure, there seems to be a surfeit of opportunities for relaxation, so that increasingly the people have started to use their nonholiday leisure time to acquire and exercise new activity skills: sailing, climbing, sports, horseback riding. It is reasonable to forecast that the balance between leisure and work will continue to move in the direction of leisure and that the relative demand for activity-oriented travel will increase.

Familiarity Versus Novelty

Most people, when they make their first venture abroad, tend to seek familiarity rather than novelty: people speaking the visitors' language, providing the meals and beverages they are accustomed to, using the same traffic conventions, and so on. Having found a destination where the traveler feels at home, this sort of tourist, at least for the first few ventures abroad, will be a "repeater," going back time and again to the same place. Not until more experience is gained will the traveler want to get away from a normal environment—to mix with people who speak differently, eat differently, dress differently.

In the Western world the general change in social conditions seems to be in the direction of speeding up the readiness for novelty. Where previously the social climate and rigid structure of society had reinforced a negative attitude to change, we now find increasingly a positive attitude to change. People accept and seek innovation in industry, education, family life, the arts, social relationships, and the like.

In particular, in countries with high living standards, manufacturers faced with quickly saturated markets concentrate on developing new products and encouraging the consumer to show greater psychological flexibility. More and more markets are dependent on the systematic organization of rapid change in fashion to sustain and expand. With the blurring of class differences and rising standards of living, travel demand will likely reflect this climate and express fragmentation of the total market as people move away from the traditional resorts to a succession of new places.

Dependence Versus Autonomy

A widely accepted analysis of modern industrial society is based on the concept of alienation in work. Briefly, this view states that most people are inevitably employed in work that, though perhaps well paid, is not intrinsically rewarding and satisfying and that from this frustration results, among other things, a general sense of powerlessness, a withdrawal from political and social activities, and the pursuit of status symbols. In the field of leisure, this work alienation should lead to a demand for either passive, time-killing holidays or for holidays where the main gratification is the achievement of easily recognized status. Fundamental absence of significance in work, in other words, would lead to holidays during which the same sense of powerlessness and dependence would prevail—organized holiday camps, organized package trips, mass entertainment, and so forth.

In fact, there has been very little empirical research to substantiate this description of an industrialized society. Indeed, the data available suggest the very contrary—that many industrial workers, backed by strong trade unions and state-created full employment, feel that as workers they wield considerable power. Certainly, industry and social organization is moving in the direction of providing work that is intrinsically rewarding and satisfying, which should enhance life for today's workers, leading to a sense of personal autonomy in all aspects of their lives, including their leisure time. They are likely to seek holidays during which they feel independent and in control of what they do and how they do it. One would expect that for some time ahead, economic and social circumstances should generate a greater proportion of autonomous participants in the total demand for travel.

Order Versus Disorder

Until recently in most Western societies, the training of children has been based on control and conformity, defined and enforced by an all-embracing circle of adult authority figures: parents, teachers, police officers, clergy, employers, civil authorities. With such a background, it is not surprising that most tourists sought holidays that reinforced this indoctrination: set meals at fixed times, guide books that told them the

Hands-on learning is the focus of many area cultural centers, such as the Cabrillo Marine Museum in San Pedro, one of many family-oriented museums in the Los Angeles area. (Photo courtesy of the Los Angeles Convention and Visitors Bureau/Michele and Tom Grimm)

"right" places to visit, resorts where their fellow-tourists were tidy, well-behaved, "properly" dressed, and so on. They avoided situations where their sense of orderliness might be embarrassed or offended.

More recently child-rearing practices have changed in the direction of greater permissiveness, and the traditional incarnations of authority have lost much of their Victorian impressiveness. The newer generation of tourists no longer feels inhibited about what to wear and how to behave when on holiday; differences of others, opportunities for unplanned action, and freedom from institutionalized regulations are distinctive characteristics of the contemporary traveler.

Summing up, then, one would predict that because of deep and persisting social and economic changes in modern Western society, the demand for travel will be based less on the goals of relaxation, familiarity, dependence, and order and increasingly on activity, novelty, autonomy, and informality. One should not, of course, ignore the fact that, since international travel is a rapidly growing market, each year's total consumers will always include a minority who value familiarity, dependency, and order.

BARRIERS TO TRAVEL

While travel has become a popular social phenomenon, there are a number of reasons why people do not travel extensively, or do not travel at all. The reasons, products of psychological analysis, are not meant to be ultimate answers as to why people travel where they do. We can, however, look at the more concrete reasons why those studied did not go on a trip during a certain period of time. For most of these studies, barriers to travel fall into six broad categories:

1. *Cost.* Consumers operate within monetary constraints, and travel must compete with other allocations of funds. Saying that travel is too expensive is an indirect way of saying that travel is not important, but, even allowing this interpretation, costs are a principal reason for staying home.
2. *Lack of time.* Many people cannot leave their businesses, jobs, or professions for vacation purposes.
3. *Health limitations.* Poor health and physical limitations keep many persons at home.
4. *Family stage.* Parents of young children often do not travel because of family obligations and inconveniences in traveling with children. Widows and singles sometimes do not travel because of the lack of a traveling companion.
5. *Lack of interest.* Unawareness of travel destinations that would bring pleasurable satisfaction is a major barrier.
6. *Fear and safety.* Things unknown are often feared, and in travel, much is often not familiar to the would-be traveler. Wars, unrest, and negative publicity about an area will create doubt and fear in the mind of the prospective traveler. Terrorism has reared its ugly head in the last decade and is a deterrent to travel.

When motivation to travel is sufficiently powerful, the barriers may be overcome, but these forces may still influence means of travel and destinations selected.

Although travelers may be able to overcome the first four variables listed, tourism marketers need to modify the fifth barrier—lack of interest. This is a challenge for tourism marketing managers. To illustrate just how widespread this barrier is, the following approach was taken where the cost barrier was eliminated. The respondents were asked this incomplete sentence: "Mr. and Mrs. Brown were offered an expense-free tour of the United States, but they didn't want to go because . . ." Forty-two percent of the respondents said that the Browns wanted to go on the trip but couldn't due to job reasons, poor health, age, or responsibilities for children. However, 26 percent indicated that the Browns did not want to go on the trip at all; they would rather stay home, or they did not like to travel, or they were afraid to travel. It is evident that in spite of widespread desires to travel, some people would rather stay home. For others, a weak desire to travel is compounded by nervousness or fear of what the experience may bring. Such a reluctance to travel runs counter to the tide, but this segment is too large a group to be overlooked. With the proper motivational tools, a significant percentage of this untapped group of potential travelers might be convinced that there are places or things of interest outside the world in which they are now existing.

When analyzing some of the psychological reasons contributing to the lack of interest in travel, at least some are related to conflicts between exploration and safety needs. A person's home is safe, a place thoroughly known, and he or she is not required to maintain a facade there. On the other hand, the familiarity of home can also produce boredom and the need to explore. A person is thus possessed of two very strong drives—*safety* and *exploration*—and he or she needs to reduce this conflict.

One way to do this is by traveling in areas that the person knows well. He or she may to go the same cottage at the same lake with the same people he or she has known for years. Thus, a new experience that may threaten the need for safety is avoided, but this approach reduces the exploration need by the person's leaving home and traveling to a different place even though it is familiar.

SUMMARY

Sociologists are interested in tourism because travel profoundly affects individuals and families who travel, inducing behavioral changes. The new insights, understandings, and appreciations that travel brings are enlightening and educational.

A person who travels to a strange environment encounters problems that must be resolved. How well the traveler solves these problems will largely determine the degree of the trip's success. In planning a trip the traveler must decide how much cultural distance (from the home environment) he or she desires. Tourists differ greatly in this regard.

In this chapter we have described various social phenomena related to mass tourism. Included are social tourism, international travel behavior extremes, barriers to travel, and a typology of four tourist roles. Your understanding of these can help to provide a basis for determining tourist volume policy. Consideration must be given to the likely influence that masses of tourists will have on their hosts. Furthermore, applying the procedures explained in this chapter should minimize the negative sociological influences and enhance the positive effects of large numbers of tourists on their host society. Although tourism expenditures have a negligible effect on crime, tourists are potential targets for crime. It is essential that they be protected as much as possible.

About the Readings

As you become educated in tourism, you will develop a growing awareness that international tourists differ greatly in their travel objectives, their manner of traveling, their spending habits, and their relationship to the tourist business establishment and to the citizens of the host country.

Each tourist must decide to what extent he or she wishes to become immersed into a different society when on a vacation trip. The degrees of involvement are divided or classified into a typology of four tourist roles by a sociologist, and these are described in detail in Reading 11.1, which has become a classic. Once understood, the classifications become very useful criteria for making decisions about who we wish to attract as tourists and what kinds of supply components are appropriate for each type of tourist.

Reading 11.2, "Social Impacts of Tourism, Host Perceptions," is a report about how local people in an area benefiting economically from tourism also recognize that there are social costs as well. Even so, they favor further tourism development and are very positive in their attitudes toward tourists. An unusual finding was that over half of the survey respondents claimed that they or their families maintain correspondence with their tourist visitors.

READING 11.1

Toward a Sociology of International Tourism

By Erik Cohen
Department of Sociology and Social Anthropology
The Hebrew University of Jerusalem

Reprinted from *Social Research,* Vol. 39, No. 1 (Spring 1972).

In recent years, there has been an enormous rise in both the number of people traveling for pleasure and the number of countries and places visited regularly by tourists.[1] Sociologists, however, seem to have neglected the study of tourism as a social phenomenon of international tourism, one which includes a typology of tourists on the basis of their relationship to both the tourist business establishment and the host country.[2]

> *Varieties of Tourist Experience*
> "After seeing the jewels of Topkapi, the fabled Blue Mosque
> and bazaars, it's awfully nice to come home to
> the Istanbul Hilton"
> (Advertisement in *Time* magazine)

Tourism is so widespread and accepted today, particularly in the Western world,[3] that we tend to take it for granted. Traveling for pleasure in a foreign country by large numbers of people is a relatively modern occurrence, however, dating only from the early nineteenth century.[4]

It seems that mass tourism as a cultural phenomenon evolves as a result of a very basic change in man's attitude to the world beyond the boundaries of his native habitat. So long as man remains largely ignorant of the existence of other societies, other cultures, he regards his own small world as the cosmos. What lies outside is mysterious and unknown and therefore dangerous and threatening. It can only inspire fear or, at best, indifference, lacking as it does any reality for him.

A tremendous distance lies between such an orientation and that characteristic of modern man. Whereas primitive and traditional man will leave his native habitat only when forced to by extreme circumstances, modern man is more loosely attached to his environment, much more willing to change it, especially temporarily, and is remarkably able to adapt to new environments. He is interested in things, sights, customs, and cultures different from his own, precisely *because* they are different. Gradually, a new value has evolved: the appreciation of the experience of strangeness and novelty. This experience now excites, titillates, and gratifies, whereas before it only frightened. I believe that tourism as a cultural phenomenon becomes possible only when man develops a *generalized* interest in things beyond his particular habitat, when contact with and appreciation and enjoyment of strangeness and novelty are valued for their *own sake.* In this sense, tourism is a thoroughly modern phenomenon.

An increased awareness of the outer world seems to lead to an increased readiness to leave one's habitat and to wander around temporarily, or even to emigrate to another habitat. Although we have little real knowledge of the way in which this awareness grows, it would seem that the technological achievements of the past two centuries have been prime determinants. While the invention of increasingly effective means of communication and the increasingly widespread availability and use of these means helped make man more aware of the outside world, at the same time a parallel phenomenon occurred in transportation, making travel less arduous, less dangerous, and less time-consuming. Also, the creation and growth of a monied middle class in many societies made traveling for pleasure a possibility for large numbers of people, whereas even as recently as the early nineteenth century only the aristocracy could afford the necessary expenditure in money and time.

Though novelty and strangeness are essential elements in the tourist experience, not even modern man is completely ready to immerse himself wholly in an alien environment. When the experience becomes too strange he may shrink back. For man is still basically molded by his native culture and bound through habit to its patterns of behavior. Hence, complete abandonment of these customs and complete immersion in a new and alien environment may be experienced as unpleasant and even threatening, especially if prolonged. Most tourists seem to need something familiar around them, something to remind them of home, whether it be food, newspapers, living quarters, or another person from their native country. Many of today's tourists are able to enjoy the experience of change and novelty only from a strong base of familiarity, which enables them to feel secure enough to enjoy the strangeness of what they experience. They would like to experience the novelty of the macroenvironment of a strange place from the security of a familiar microenvironment. And many will not venture abroad but on those well-trodden paths equipped with familiar means of transportation, hotels, and food. Often the modern tourist is not so much abandoning his accustomed environment for a new one as he is being transposed to foreign soil in an "environmental bubble" of his native culture. To a certain extent he views the people, places, and culture of that society through the protective walls of his familiar "environmental bubble," within which he functions and interacts in much the same way as he does in his own habitat.[5]

The experience of tourism combines, then, a degree of novelty with a degree of familiarity, the security of old habits with the excitement of change.[6] However, the exact extent to which familiarity and novelty are experienced on any particular tour depends upon the individual tastes and preferences of the tourist as well as upon the institutional setting of his trip. There is a continuum of possible combinations of novelty and familiarity. This continuum is, to my mind, the basic underlying variable for the sociological analysis of the phenomenon of modern tourism. The division of the continuum into a number of typical combinations of novelty and familiarity leads to a typology of tourist experiences and roles. I will propose here a typology of four tourist roles.[7]

The Organized Mass Tourist: The organized mass tourist is the least adventurous and remains largely confined to his "environmental bubble" throughout his trip. The guided tour, conducted in an air-conditioned bus, traveling at high speed through a steaming country-side, represents the prototype of the organized mass tourist. This tourist type buys a package tour as if it were just another commodity in the modern mass market. The itinerary of his trip is fixed in advance, and all his stops are well-prepared and guided; he makes almost no decisions for himself and stays almost exclusively in the microenvironment of his home country. Familiarity is at a maximum, novelty at a minimum.

The Individual Mass Tourist: This type of tourist role is similar to the previous one, except that the tour is not entirely preplanned, the tourist has a certain amount of control over his time and itinerary and is not bound to a group. However, all of his major arrangements are still made through a tourist agency. His excursions do not bring him much further afield than do those of the organized mass tourist. He, too, does his experiencing from within the "environmental bubble" of his home country and ventures out of it only occasionally—and even then only into well-charted territory. Familiarity is still dominant, but somewhat less so than in the preceding type; the experience of novelty is somewhat greater, though it is often of the routine kind.

The Explorer: This type of tourist arranges his trip alone; he tries to get off the beaten track as much as possible, but he nevertheless looks for comfortable accommodations and reliable means of transportation. He tries to associate with the people he visits and to speak their language. The explorer dares to leave his "environmental bubble" much more than the previous two types, but he is still careful to be able to step back into it when the going becomes too rough. Though novelty dominates, the tourist does not immerse himself completely in his host society, but retains some of the basic routines and comforts of his native way of life.

The Drifter: This type of tourist ventures furthest away from the beaten track and from the accustomed ways of life of his home country. He shuns any kind of connection with the tourist establishment, and considers the ordinary tourist experience phony. He tends to make it wholly on his own, living with the people and often taking odd-jobs to keep himself going. He tries to live the way the people he visits live, and to share their shelter, foods, and habits, keeping only the most basic and essential of his old customs. The drifter has no fixed itinerary or timetable and no well-defined goals of travel. He is almost wholly immersed in his host culture. Novelty is here at its highest, familiarity disappears almost completely.

The first two tourist types I will call *institutionalized* tourist roles; they are dealt with in a routine way by the tourist establishment—the complex of travel agencies, travel companies, hotel chains, etc., which cater to the tourist trade. The last two types I will call *noninstitutionalized* tourist roles, in that they are open roles, at best only very loosely attached to the tourist establishment.

> *The Institutionalized Forms of Tourism:*
> *The Organized and the Individual Mass Tourist* [8]
> "Where were you last summer?"
> "In Majorca."
> "Where is that?"
> "I don't know, I flew there."
> (Conversation between two girls, reprinted in a German journal)

Contemporary institutionalized tourism is a mass industry. The tour is sold as a package, standardized and mass-produced.[9] All transportation, places to be visited, sleeping and eating accommodations are fixed in advance. The tourist establishment takes complete care of the tourist from beginning to end. Still, the package tour sold by the tourist establishment purportedly offers the buyer the experience of novelty and strangeness. The problem of the system, then, is to enable the mass tourist to "take in" the novelty of the host country without experiencing any physical discomfort or, more accurately, to observe without actually experiencing.

Since the tourist industry serves large numbers of people, these have to be processed as efficiently, smoothly, and quickly as possible through all the phases of the tour. Hence, it is imperative that the experience of the tourist, however novel it might seem to him, be as ordered, predictable, and controllable as possible. In short, he has to be given the illusion of adventure, while all the risks and uncertainties of adventure are taken out of his tour. In this respect, the quality of the mass tourist's experiences approaches that of vicarious participation in other people's lives, similar to the reading of fiction or the viewing of motion pictures. The tourist establishment achieves this effect through two interrelated mechanisms that I will call the *transformation of attractions* and the *standardization of facilities.*

Every country, region, or locality has something which sets it apart from all others, something for which it is known and worth visiting: scenic beauty, architecture, feasts or festivals, works of art, etc. In German there is a very appropriate term for these features, *Sehenswurdigkeiten,* or "things worth seeing," and I will call them "attractions." Some attractions are world renown, and become the trademark of a place; these attract tourists naturally. In other cases, they are created artificially—they are contrived "tourist attractions."[10]

The main purpose of mass tourism is the visiting of attractions, whether genuine or contrived. However, even if they are genuine, the tendency is to transform or manipulate them, to make them "suitable" for mass tourist consumption. They are supplied with facilities, reconstructed, landscaped, cleansed of unsuitable elements, staged, managed, and otherwise organized. As a result, they largely lose their original flavor and appearance and become isolated from the ordinary flow of life and natural texture of the host society.[11] Hawaiian dancing girls have to be dressed for public decency—but not much, so that they remain attractive; natural sights have to be groomed and guarded until they look like well-kept parks; traditional festivals have to be made more colorful and more respectable so tourists will be attracted but not offended. Festivals and ceremonies, in particular, cease being spontaneous expressions of popular feelings and become well-staged spectacles.[12] Even still-inhabited old quarters of otherwise modern cities are often turned into "living museums" to attract tourists, like the old town of Acre in Israel, Old San Juan, and Old Town in Chicago.

While the transformation of attractions provides controlled novelty for mass tourist, the standardization of facilities serves to provide him with the necessary familiarity in his immediate surroundings. The majority of tourists originate today from the affluent Western countries, the U.S. and Western Europe, and increasingly from Japan. Hence, whatever country aspires to attract mass tourism is forced to provide facilities on a level commensurate with the expectations of the tourists from those countries. A tourist infrastructure of facilities based on Western standards has to be created even in the poorest host countries. This tourist infrastructure provides the mass tourist with the protective "ecological bubble" of his accustomed environment. However, since the tourist also expects some local flavor or signs of foreignness in his environment, there are local decorations in his hotel room, local foods in the restaurants, local products in the tourist shops. Still, even these are often standardized: the decorations are made to resemble the standard image of that culture's art, the local foods are made more palatable to unaccustomed tongues, the selection of native crafts is determined by the demands of the tourist.[13]

The transformation of attractions and the standardization of facilities, made necessary by the difficulties of managing and satisfying large numbers of tourists, have introduced a basic uniformity or similarity into the tourist experience. Whole countries lose their individuality to the mass tourist as the richness of their culture and geography is reduced by the tourist industry to a few standard elements, according to which they are classified and presented to the mass tourist. Before he even begins his tour, he is conditioned to pay attention primarily to the few basic attractions and facilities advertised in the travel literature or suggested by the travel agent, which are catalogued and sometimes even assigned a level of "importance."[14] This induces a peculiar kind of selective awareness: the tourist tends to become aware of his environment only when he reaches spots of "interest," while he is largely oblivious to it the rest of the time.[15] As a result, countries become interchangeable in the tourist's mind. Whether he is looking for good beaches, restful forests, or old cities, it becomes relatively unimportant to him where these happen to be found. Transportation by air, which brings him almost directly to his destination without his having to pass through other parts of the host country, contributes to the isolation of the attractions and facilities from the rest of the country—as well as the isolation of the tourist. And so mass tourism has created the following paradox: though the desire for variety, novelty, and strangeness are the primary motives of tourism, these qualities have decreased as tourism has become institutionalized.

In popular tourist countries, the tourist system or infrastructure has become separated from the rest of the culture and the natural flow of life. Attractions and facilities which were previously frequented by the local population are gradually abandoned. As Greenwich Village became a tourist attraction, many of the original bohemians moved to the East Village. Even sites of high symbolic value for the host society may suffer a similar fate: houses of government, churches, and national monuments become more and more the preserve of the mass tourist and are less and less frequented by the native citizen.

The ecological differentiation of the tourist sphere from the rest of the country makes for social separation; the mass tourist travels in a world of his own, surrounded by, but not integrated in, the host society. He meets the representatives of the tourist establishment—hotel managers, tourist agents, guides—but only seldom the natives.[16] The natives, in turn, see the mass tourist as unreal. Neither has much of an opportunity to become an individual to the other.

A development complementary to the ecological differentiation of the tourist sphere is the gradual emergence of an international tourist system, reaching across political and cultural boundaries. The system enjoys a certain independence and even isolation from its immediate surroundings, and an internal homogeneity in spite of the wide variations between the countries with which it intersects. The autonomy and isolation can be most clearly seen in those cases where tourists enjoy some special facilities that are out of bounds to the members of the host society, such as spas and nightclubs in Eastern European countries serving exclusively foreigners or the Berionka (dollar shop) in the Soviet Union, which caters only to tourists.

The isolation of the mass tourist from the host society is further intensified by a general communication gap. Tourist publications and travel literature are ordinarily written in the spirit of the tourist establishment—and often not by a native of the country—whose prime motive is selling, not merely informing. Such literature colors the tourist's attitudes and expectations beforehand. But probably more responsible than any other single factor mentioned thus far in creating and maintaining the isolation of the tourist is the fact that he seldom knows the language of the country he is traveling in. Not knowing the language makes forming acquaintances with the natives and traveling about on one's own so difficult that few tourists attempt it to any extent. Even worse, it leaves the tourist without any real feel for the culture of people in the country.

The sad irony of modern institutionalized tourism is that, instead of destroying myths between countries, it perpetuates them. The tourist comes home with the illusion that he has "been" there and can speak with some authority about the country he has visited. I would hypothesize that the larger the flow of mass tourists becomes, the more institutionalized and standardized tourism becomes and consequently the stronger the barriers between the tourist and the life of the host country become. What were previously formal barriers *between* different countries become informal barriers *within* countries.

THE NONINSTITUTIONALIZED FORMS OF TOURISM: THE EXPLORER AND THE DRIFTER

Boorstin's vivid description of the evolution of the aristocratic traveler of yesterday into the tourist of modern times oversimplifies the issue to make a point. For Boorstin, there exists either the mass tourist or the adventurer, who contrives crazy feats and fabricates risks in order to experience excitement.[17] Even Knebel's less tendentious analysis postulates little variety in the role structure of the contemporary tourist. Both writers seem to have overlooked the noninstitutionalized tourist roles of explorer and drifter.

While the roles of both the explorer and the drifter are noninstitutionalized, they differ from each other chiefly in the extent to which they venture out of their microenvironment and away from the tourist system, and in their attitudes toward the people and countries they visit.

The explorer tries to avoid the mass tourist route and the traditional tourist attraction spots, but he nevertheless looks for comfortable accommodations and reliable means of transportation. He ventures into areas relatively unknown to the mass tourist and explores them for his own pleasure. The explorer's experience of the host country, its people, places and culture, is unquestionably much broader and deeper than that of the mass tourist. He tries to associate with the people he visits and to speak their language, but he still does not wholly immerse himself in the host society. He remains somewhat detached, either viewing his surroundings from an aesthetic perspective or seeking to understand the people on an intellectual level. Unlike the drifter, he does not identify with the natives emotionally or try to become one of them during his stay.

Through his mode of travel, the explorer escapes the isolation and artificiality the tourist system imposes on the mass tourist. Paradoxically, though, in his very attempts at escape he serves as a spearhead of mass tourism; as he discovers new places of interest, he opens the way for more commercialized forms of tourism, the managers of which are always on the lookout for new and unusual attractions. His experiences and opinions serve as indicators to other, less adventurous tourists to move into the area. As more and more of these move in, the tourist establishment gradually takes over. Thus, partly through the unwitting help of the explorer, the scope of the system expands.

As the tourist system expands, fewer and fewer areas are left that have mass tourist potential in terms of the traditional kinds of attractions. Recently, however, the ability of an area to offer a degree of privacy and solitude has, in itself, become a commodity of high value. Indeed, much of the mass tourist business today seems to be oriented to the provision of privacy *per se.* Obviously, mass tourism here reaches a point at which success is self-defeating.

While the explorer is the contemporary counterpart of the traveler of former years, the drifter is more like the wanderer of previous times. The correspondence is not complete, though. In his attitude toward and mode of traveling, the drifter is a genuine modern phenomenon. He is often a child of affluence, who reacts against it. He is young, often a student or a graduate, who has not yet started to work. He prolongs his moratorium by moving around the world in search of new experiences, radically different from those he has been accustomed to in his sheltered middle-class existence. After he has savored these experiences for a time, he usually settles down to an orderly middle-class career.

The drifter seeks the excitement of complete strangeness and direct contact with new and different people. He looks for experiences, happenings, and kicks. His mode of travel is adapted to this purpose. In order to preserve the freshness and spontaneity of his experience, the drifter purposely travels without either itinerary or timetable, without a destination or even well-defined purpose. He often possesses only limited means for traveling, but even when this is not true, he usually is concerned with making his money last as long as possible so as to prolong his travels. Since he is also typically unconcerned with bodily comfort and desires to live as simply as possible while traveling, he will travel, eat, and sleep in the most inexpensive way possible. He moves about on bicycle or motorcycle or hitchhikes rides in autos, private planes, freighters, and fishing boats. He shares rooms with fellow travelers he has met along the way or stays with a native of the area who has befriended him. When necessary, and often when not, he will sleep outdoors. And he will cook his own meals outdoors or buy food on the street more often than eat in a restaurant. If, in spite of such frugality, his money runs out before his desire to travel does, he will work at almost any odd-job he can get until he has enough to move on.

The particular way of life and travel of the drifter brings him into contact with a wide variety of people; these usually belong to the lower social groups in the host society. Often the drifter associates with kindred souls in the host society. In my study of a mixed

Jewish-Arab town in Israel, I encountered a great deal of association between drifters and local Arab boys who also wanted to travel.[18]

An international subculture of drifters seems to be developing. In some places drifters congregate and create an ecological niche of their own. On the shore of the Red Sea in Eilat, Israel's southernmost port, there is a "permanently temporary" colony of squatters locally called "beatniks," who drifted there from many parts of the world. Similarly, the National Monument on the Dam, in the very center of Amsterdam, serves as a mass meeting place for young people who flock there from all over Europe and the U.S.

The drifter discards almost completely the familiar environment of his home country and immerses himself in the life of the host society. Moreover, as explained above, the drifter differs significantly from the explorer in the manner in which he relates to the host society. The drifter is, then, the true rebel of the tourist establishment and the complete opposite of the mass tourist.

DISCUSSION

So far I have formulated a general approach to the sociology of tourism based on a typology of tourist roles. Here I will develop some implications of this approach and propose several problems for further research.

The fundamental variable that forms the basis for the fourfold typology of tourist roles proposed here is strangeness versus familiarity. Each of the four tourist roles discussed represents a characteristic form of tourist behavior and a typical position on the strangeness/familiarity continuum. The degree to which strangeness or familiarity prevail in the tourist role determines the nature of the tourist's experiences as well as the effect he has on the host society.

Initially, all tourists are strangers in the host society. The degree to which and the way they affect each other depends largely on the *extent* and *variety* of social contacts the tourist has during his trip. The social contacts of the mass tourist, particularly of the organized mass tourist, are extremely limited. The individual mass tourist, being somewhat more independent, makes occasional social contacts, but his conventional mode of travel tends to restrict them to the close periphery of the tourist establishment, thus limiting their number and their nature. The social contacts of the explorer are broader and more varied, while those of the drifter are the most intensive in quality and the most extensive in quantity.

The extent to which the tourist role is predefined and the social expectations of it spelled out determines to a large degree the *manner* in which tourists interact with members of the host society, as well as the images they develop of one another. The mass tourist generally does not interact at all, but merely observes, and even that from within his own microenvironment. The explorer mixes but does not become involved in the lives of members of the host society. Here the length of *time* spent in one place is as important a determinant of social involvement as attitude. The drifter, unlike the mass tourist, does not set a limit beforehand on the length of time he will spend in any one place; if he finds an area that particularly pleases him, he may stop there long enough for social involvement to occur.

Tourism has some important aggregate effects on the host society, in terms of its impact on the division of labor and on the ecology or the land-use patterns of that society. As the tourist role becomes institutionalized, a whole set of other roles and institutions develop in the host country to cater to his needs—what we have called the tourist establishment. This development gradually introduces a new dimension into the ecology of the host society, as attractions and facilities are created, improved, and set aside for tourist use. This primary impact of tourism has important secondary and tertiary consequences.[19] Predominantly agricultural regions may become primarily tourist areas, as agriculture is driven out by tourist facilities, and the local people turn to tourist services for their living. The "tourist villages" in the Austrian Alps are an example. Conversely, stagnant agricultural areas may receive a boost from increased demands for agricultural products in nearby tourist regions, such as the agricultural boom that has occurred in the hinterland of the Spanish Costa Brava. Without doubt, the impact of large-scale tourism on the culture, style of life, and world-view of inhabitants of tourist regions must be enormous. To my knowledge, however, the problem has not yet been systematically studied.[20]

The explorer and the drifter do not affect the general division of labor in the host society to the same degree as the mass tourist does, and consequently do not have the same aggregate impact on that society. Their effect on the host society is more subtle, but sometimes considerable, as I found in my own study of the impact of drifting tourist girls on Arab boys in a mixed Jewish-Arab city.

It is understood that foreign travel can have a considerable impact upon the traveler himself, and, through him, on his home country. In premodern times, travelers were one of the chief means through which knowledge and innovations were diffused and information about other countries obtained. How does the impact vary with the different kinds of experiences yielded by each type of tourist role, on the tourist himself, and, through him, on his own society? Is his image of his own society and his own style of life changed? In what ways? These are some of the questions that future studies of tourism might be organized around.

We also know very little about the way preferences for countries and localities are formulated in the mind of the tourist and later translated into the ways the tourist system expands or contracts geographically.[21] I have dealt with the role of the explorer in the dynamics of growth of the tourist system, but other mechanisms are undoubtedly at work, such as the planned creation of new attractions to foster mass tourism, like the building of Disneyland. It might be worthwhile to differentiate between the organic and the induced growth of the tourist system and look into the differential effect of the modes of expansion on the workings of the tourist system and the host society.

The problems raised in this paper have been dealt with in a most general form; any attempt to explore them in depth will have to make use of a comparative approach. Though tourism could be studied comparatively from several angles, the most important variables of comparison are probably the differences between the cultural characteristics of the tourist and the host[22] and the manner in which tourism is embedded in the institutional structure of the host country.[23]

CONCLUSION

Growing interaction and interpenetration between hitherto relatively independent social systems is one of the most salient characteristics of the contemporary world. In K. Deutsch's phrase, the world is rapidly becoming a "global village." No far-off island or obscure primitive tribe manages to preserve its isolation. Tourism is both a consequence of this process of interpenetration and one of several mechanisms through which this process is being realized. Its relative contribution to the process—in comparison to that of the major transforming forces of our time—is probably minor, though it seems to be increasing rapidly. Tourism already serves as the chief source of foreign currency in several countries, and its scope is growing at an accelerating rate.

It is interesting to speculate, then, about some of the broader sociological consequences of the increase in the scope of tourism for the society of the future. The picture which emerges is complex. On the one hand, as the numbers of mass tourists grow, the tourist industry will become more and more mechanized and standardized. This, in turn, will tend to make the interaction between tourist and host even more routinized. The effect of the host country on the mass tourist will therefore remain limited, whereas his effect on the ecology, division of labor, and wealth of the country will grow as his numbers do. On the other hand, as host societies become permeated by a wide variety of individually traveling tourists belonging to different classes and ways of life, increased and more varied social contacts will take place, with mixed results for international understanding.[24] Like-minded persons of different countries will find it easier to communicate with each other and some kind of new international social groupings might appear. Among the very rich such groups always existed; the fashionable contemporary prototype is the international "jetset." And only recently drifter communities have emerged in many parts of the world, comprised of an entirely different kind of social category. The effect of such developments may well be to diminish the significance of national boundaries, though they also create new and sometimes serious divisions within the countries in which such international groups congregate. Some indication of the emergence of new foci of conflict can already be seen in the recent riots between drifters and seamen in Amsterdam, the hub of the European "drifter community."

Finally, the differential impact of tourism on various types of societies should be noted. As Forster pointed out,[25] the impact of tourism on a society with an unbalanced, developing economy might be much more serious than its impact on a mature, well-developed society. As tourism is eagerly sought for by the developing nations as an important source of revenue, it may provoke serious disruptions and cause ultimate long-range damage in these societies. The consequences cannot yet be fully foreseen, but from what we already know of the impact of mass tourism it can safely be predicted that mass tourism in developing countries, if not controlled and regulated, might help to destroy whatever there is still left of unspoiled nature and of traditional ways of life. In this respect, the easy-going tourist of our era might well complete the work of his predecessors, also travelers from the West—the conqueror and the colonialist.

READING ENDNOTES

1. This paper was first written while I was a visiting scholar at the Institute of Urban Environment, Columbia University, New York. Thanks are due to the Institute as well as to Dr. R. Bar-Yoseph, Prof. Elihu Katz, and Dr. M. Skokeid, for their useful comments.
2. There exist very few full-length studies of tourism. One of the most comprehensive studies is that by H. J. Knebel, *Soziologische Struckturwandlungen in Modernem Touriusmus* (Stuttgard: F. Enke Verl, 1960). By far the most incisive analysis of American tourism has been performed by D. Boorstin, *The Image* (New York: Atheneum, 1961), pp. 71–117. There is a chapter on tourism in J. Dumazedier, *Towards a Society of Leisure* (New York: Free Press, 1967), pp. 123–128, and in M. Kaplan, *Leisure in America: A Social Inquiry* (New York: Wiley, 1960), Ch. 16.
3. For the contemporary tourist boom see S. K. Waters, "The American Tourist," The Annals of the American Academy of Social Science, 368 (November 1966), pp. 109–118.
4. Dumazedier, op. cit., p. 125n. For the scarcity of tourists even as late as 1860, see Boorstin, op. cit., p. 84.
5. Knebel speaks, following von Uexkull, of a *"touristische Eigenwelt,"* from which the modern tourist can no longer escape; op. cit., p. 147.
6. For a similar approach to modern tourism, see Boorstin, op. cit., pp. 79–80.
7. For a different typology of tourist roles ("travelers"), see Kaplan, op. cit., p. 216.
8. For a general description of the trends characteristic of modern mass tourism, see Knebel, op. cit., pp., 99ff.

9. See Boorstin, op. cit., p. 85.

10. Ibid., p. 103.

11. In Boorstin's language, they become "pseudo-events."

12. "Not only in Mexico City and Montreal, but also in the remote Guatemalan Tourist Mecca of Chichecastenango, out in far-off villages of Japan, earnest honest natives embellish their ancient rites, change, enlarge and spectacularize their festivals, so that tourists will not be disappointed." Ibid., p. 103.

13. Boorstin, talking of the Hilton chain of hotels, states: "Even the measured admixture of carefully filtered local atmosphere [in these hotels] proves that you are still in the U.S." Ibid., pp. 98–99.

14. For an analysis of travel literature, see Knebel, op. cit., pp. 90–97. On the development of the guidebook, particularly the Baedeker, see Boorstin, op. cit., pp. 109ff, and Knebel, op. cit., pp. 24–26.

15. The tendency of the mass tourist to abide by the guidebook was noticed a hundred years ago by "A Cynic" who wrote in 1869: "The ordinary tourist has no judgment; he admires what the infallible Murray orders him to admire. . . . The tourist never diverges one hair's breadth from the beaten track of his predecessors, and within a few miles of the best known routes in Europe leaves nooks and corners as unsophisticated as they were fifty years ago; which proves that he has not sufficient interest in his route to exert his own freedom of will." "A Cynic: Vacations," *Cornhill Magazine, August 1869, reported in Mass Leisure,* E. Larrabee and K. Meyersohn (eds.), (Glencoe, Ill.: Free Press, 1952), p. 285

16. Boorstin, op. cit., pp. 91ff.: Knebel, op. cit., pp. 102–104; see also Knebel's discussion of the primary tourist group, op. cit. pp. 104–106.

17. Boorstin, op. cit., pp. 116–117.

18. E. Cohen, "Arab Boys and Tourist Girls in a Mixed Jewish-Arab Community," *International Journal of Comparative Sociology,* Vol. 12, No. 4 (1971), pp. 217–233.

19. For some of these see J. Forster, "The Sociological Consequences of Tourism," *International Journal of Comparative Sociology,* Vol. 5, No. 2 (1964), pp. 217–227.

20. A study of this problem is in progress now in the region of Faro in southern Portugal; this is a backward region in which the sudden influx of mass tourism seems to have some serious disruptive effects.

21. This problem is discussed with reference to the rather special conditions of Hawaii and other Pacific Islands, by Forster, op. cit.

22. W. A. Sutton, "Travel and Understanding: Notes on the Social Structure of Touring," *International Journal of Comparative Sociology,* Vol. 8, No. 2 (1967), pp. 218–223, touches upon this point in a discussion of factors which make for harmony and tension in the tourist-host encounter.

23. Forster's argument about the differential impact of tourism on a society with an underdeveloped as against an advanced economy is one example of such an approach. Another would be to compare the effects of tourism on closed (totalitarian) as against open (democratic) societies.

24. See Sutton, op. cit.

25. See Forster, op. cit.

READING 11.2

Social Impacts of Tourism: Host Perceptions

BY BRIAN KING
Victoria University, Australia

ABRAHAM PIZAM AND ADY MILMAN
University of Central Florida, USA

Reprinted from *Annals of Tourism Research,* Vol. 20, No. 4 (1993).

INTRODUCTION

The responses of local residents to tourism development and to the impacts of tourism have been extensively studied over the last two decades. Most research has focused on how various sections of the community have differed in their reactions to the impacts of tourism and most have concentrated on either a single or else a small number of neighboring communities.

Perdue, Long and Allen (1990) examined the relationship betwen what residents perceived to be the positive and negative impacts of tourism and the extent to which they supported tourism development in 16 rural communities in the state of Colorado, USA. They concluded that where the variable of personal benefits was controlled (i.e., ensuring that respondents did not have a direct and pecuniary interest in tourism development), percep-tions of tourism impacts were unrelated to sociodemographic characteristics. Furthermore, support for additional development was positively related in the case of those who perceived positive impacts to dominate, and negatively correlated in the case of those who perceived negative impacts to dominate.

Dogan's review (1989) of the consequences of international tourism concluded that in many "touristic countries" sociocultural structures have changed considerably under the influence of tourism. In addition, a previously homogenous community characterized by a particular response to tourism becomes diversified as a result of the presence of tourism, and groups exhibiting different responses to tourism emerge within the community as a result of touristic developments. Husbands (1989) investigated the perception of tourism by residents who live near the world-famous Victoria Falls in Zimbabwe. Analysis of the data revealed that, broadly speaking, respondents do not have an enthusiastic view towards tourism. Differences of opinion on the subject that are evident within the community are associated with social status and with differences in social class. Schluter and Var's study of residents attitudes toward tourism in Argentina (1988) indicated that while local residents did not have a strong perception of the economic benefits of tourism, they recognized a number of positive sociocultural benefits brought about by tourism. The study also identified a strong relationship between the level of economic dependency on tourism and the extent to which perceptions of the economic effects of tourism were positive.

Ross's (1992) study of residents in an Australian city indicated that residents recognized the existence of major positive impacts of tourism on the economy and major negative impacts on housing and crime levels. The major concern for residents concerning personal impacts was the fact that local residents appeared to be less friendly than previously. A study of residents and entrepreneurs in a South Dakota community by Caneday and Zeiger (1991) concluded that while respondents acknowledged the importance of tourism, they were con-cerned with the potential impacts caused by the reintroduction of gambling into the community.

According to some other studies, intervening variables, such as participation in formal tourism education and participation in outdoor recreation, are believed to result in perceptual differences among local residents. Brayley, Var and Sheldon (1990) examined the results of exposure to tourism education on student perceptions towards the influence of tourism on four social issues. The study identified a generally positive view towards the influence of tourism on both economic and social conditions. It also highlighted major perceptual differences between separate groups of students with and without tourism education. Brayley and Var (1989) suggested that the strongest held view by students was as a positive economic influence. The positive social and cultural influence was acknowledged but regarded as being of secondary significance. The study examined both French and English speaking Canadian students and observed some differences between the subsamples. Perdue, Long and Allen (1987) examined the influence of participation in outdoor recreation on the tourism perceptions and attitudes of rural residents of Colorado, USA. They found that there were no significant differences identifiable between the tourism perceptions and attitudes of the participants and non-participants in outdoor recreation activities.

Allen, Long, Perdue and Kieselbach (1988) investigated the extent to which residents perceived satisfaction levels with life in their particular neighborhood varied according to the extent of tourism development in their community. They found that the relationship between the two issues was generally nonlinear. Issues such as the extent to which respondents were involved in community activities, public service, and environmental issues were identified as being most sensitive to tourism development.

A number of studies have identified quite specific and measurable impacts of tourism (Ross 1992). Others have proposed models that attempt to cluster and summarize such impacts. Davis, Allen and Consenza (1988) identified five clusters of attitudes towards tourism development in Florida, USA. A strong antitourism cluster was identified as a source of concern and it was suggested that the state government should direct increased promotion effort towards raising resident awareness of the positive multiplier effects of tourism. A broad overview of tourism social impact studies was undertaken by Ap (1990) and included a comparison of four studies by (Belisle and Hoy 1980; Liu and Var 1986; Milman and Pizam 1988; and Pizam 1978).

Other studies have involved the development of new research methodologies. Ritchie's research on residents of Alberta, Canada (1988) attempted to draw up a methodology capable of providing an operational basis for consensus policy formulation in tourism. To underpin such a process, it sought to recognize and identify the significant differences that exist within the host population. Maddox (1986) used the critical incident technique to study residents' satisfaction with local tourism programs in Halifax, Canada. His analysis concluded that local residents expressed a great interest in tourists to the area as individuals. Respondents wanted tourists to be well treated. A survey by Andressen and Murphy (1986) investigated the reaction of residents to possible future tourism development in British Columbia, Canada. Resident input to the tourism planning process in two travel corridors within the province was the focus of a second study (Andressen and Murphy 1986).

Recently, an attempt has been made to compare the social impact of tourism in various geographical locations. Jafari, Pizam and Przeclawski (1990) reported on a preliminary study by the Vienna Center on the social impact of tourism in several countries. Countries selected for study were Bulgaria, Hungary, Poland, Spain, the United Kingdom, the United States, and former Yugoslavia.

Studies on the social dimensions of tourism in Fiji have noted the warm welcome extended to tourists by ethnic-Fijian natives who make up just over 50% of the population (Plange 1984; Vusoniwailala 1980). Referring specifically to the ethnic population, Vusoni-wailala has stated that "although Fijian hospitality has changed, the tourist still receives a degree of friendliness not found in a metropolitan area" (1980:104). While Samy (1980) pointed to disenchantment among both racial populations, particularly the Indians, a study by Plange found a high level of support for tourism by both the Fijian and Indian populations. He stated that "within the country and amongst the various races and ethnic groups, there exists an overwhelming feeling of friendliness and receptivity towards tourists" (1984:46). He did, however, identify a major concern among residents that tourism was leading to a commercialization of culture. Britton (1982) identified resentment by sections of the resident population to the predominance of expatriate staff in the higher status tourism management positions. He likened both industry structure and local attitudes to a form of neocolonialism. Varley (1978) identified some of the social problems encountered in Fiji due to the impact of relatively wealthier overseas tourists on a developing country with a relatively lower standard of living.

Tourism Development in Fiji

Fiji is a republic of approximately 725,000 people (mid-1990 estimate), located just West of the International Dateline, 15–22° South of the Equator and 177° west and 175° east of the Greenwich Meridian. It consists of 332 islands, of which one-third are inhabited. Of the total land mass of 18,272 square kilometres, the two largest islands Vita Levu (10,429 square kilometres) and Vanu Levu (5,556 square kilometres) make up the bulk. Situated in the South West Pacific, Fiji developed historically as a significant refueling stop for air and sea transport between North America, Australia, and New Zealand though the advent of nonstop flights from North America to Australasia has reduced such traffic (Main 1990). The bulk of air travelers enter the country through the international airport at Nadi in the West of Viti Levu. A much smaller number enter through Nausori airport, which serves the national capital of Suva. The population is made up of two major ethnic groups, namely Fijians and Indians, with smaller numbers of Chinese, Europeans, and other Pacific islanders.

Tourism is the principal foreign exchange earner for Fiji, followed by sugar. Fiji attracted 278,996 international visitors in 1990, accounting for 43% of total arrivals to the 12 countries in the region (Tourism Council of the South Pacific 1991). Its nearest competitor in terms of volume was French Polynesia with 132,361. In 1990, tourism receipts totalled 335.9 million Fiji dollars (approximately AUS$314 million). Tourism policy and development is the responsibility of the Ministry of Tourism and marketing of the country is directed by the Fiji Visitors' Bureau (FVB).

The main resort zones are located within easy reach of Nadi. The largest integrated resort (a large village-like area consisting of accommodations, food and beverage, recreation, entertainment, sports, and shopping facilities) in Fiji is Denarau, which is a few kilometres from the town. The popular Mamanuca Islands and Coral Coast are located between 30 minutes and 2 hours from Nadi airport by sea or by land transfer. Nadi, the Coral Coast and the Mamanucas were identified as key areas for development in Fiji's first Tourism Master Plan (Belt and Collins 1973) and remain the country's most developed tourist zones. According to FVB, the Nadi area accounted for 31.4% of the country's room capacity in 1991, with the Mamanucas and the Coral Coast making up a further 10.86% and 22.14%, respectively. Apart from the nearby Denarau complex (which is included in the Nadi figure), Nadi functions as a tourist transit town. Most visitors stay for a night and then head off to the resorts. Local residents have a high level of exposure to tourists though the typical encounter is fleeting in view of the short average length of stay by visitors.

Study Methodology

The questionnaire used to investigate perceptions held by residents of Nadi was based on a similar instrument developed for a tourism research on Central Florida several years ago (Milman and Pizam 1988). The revised questionnaire included the distinct Fijian cultural and environmental settings. The study was exploratory in nature and no formal hypotheses were developed.

This questionnaire was used to survey the residents of the immediate Nadi area. Interviews (199, one per household) were conducted from a total population of approximately 7,500, constituting a sample size of 2.65%. The nature of the local community demanded that a cluster sample be undertaken, since the town consists of a central business area, a number of adjoining communities, and some villages located at some distance from the main town, mainly in the vicinity of the airport. The sample selection allowed for an equal split between three areas. These were the town center, the adjoining localities of Namotomoto and Navoce villages and the more detached communities near Nadi airport. The dispersal of the sample between the three areas ensured a balance between localities at varying distances from the main tourism shopping area and the airport; different income earners; occupants of traditional and modern housing; and between Fijians (approximately 60%) and ethnic Indians (40%).

Interviews were conducted by experienced interviewers who were part-time students at the University of the South Pacific, where one of the authors of this article was on sabbatical leave. The interviewers, half of whom were Indians and half Fijians, were both English and Fijian language speakers, thereby minimizing any language difficulties. The interviewers introduced themselves as working for the University of the South Pacific at Suva, Fiji. Calls were made to households between 3 and 9 in the afternoon, with a view to obtaining a balance between day and night workers. Interviewers asked to speak with adult male or female households. Where such a person was not available at the time, an appointment was made to return later. Respondents were prompted with the assistance of visual aids identifying the scales being used for each question. Each third property on one side only of each street was incorporated into the sample, in order to achieve a representative group within the relevant communities. The interviewers sketched out target households, prior to the commencement of fieldwork.

Several limitations in the research methodology should, however, be noted. The practice of interviewing only willing respondents may have created problems of representation. There was no control over who participated in the study and the results could have been biased by either favorable or unfavorable responses.

Furthermore, Nadi and its surrounding villages benefit financially from the Fijian tourism industry through the payment of direct royalties (i.e., commission on sales) by tourism enterprises to the local communities. It is possible that respondents' opinions have been positively biased and less inclined to express dissatisfaction with various aspects of tourism development in the area.

The initial purpose of this study was to examine the attitudes of Nadi residents towards tourism. In practice, an extremely high proportion of sample respondents were found to be either employed in or associated with the tourism industry. One might then suggest, that this study is representative only of those residents who are employed in or associated with the tourism industry.

As another research shortcoming, due to an unintentional oversight, the interviewers did not mark the ethnic origin of the respondents. Consequently, it was impossible to do any detailed analyses distinguishing between the attitudes of ethnic Fijians and ethnic Indians. Hence, this study is representative of the sample population as a whole and may not be representative of each separate ethnic group.

STUDY FINDINGS

General Profile of Respondents

Most of the respondents (97%) have residence in the Nadi area over 10 years, possess a secondary school certificate (72%), and are aged between 40 and 50 years (median figure). Most were married (83%) and had children under 18 living at home (79%). Of those reporting dependents, the average number of children was 3.3.

Almost all of the respondents (99%) were either employed or self-employed on a full-time basis. Of those respondents who were employed, 94% declared themselves as being employed by or associated with the tourism industry. Since the above proportion represented an extremely high number of people, the interviewers were questioned as to its validity. It transpired that those respondents who were employed in occupations serving tourists, defined themselves as part of the industry. For example, tailors and grocers who engaged in a significant volume of selling merchandise to tourists declared themselves as being associated with tourism. About 67% of the respondents also indicated that at least one family member was employed in the industry. The reported median annual income of respondents was in the range of F$5,000–7,000 (AUS$4,673–6,542). The demographic profile of this sample represents the population of the Nadi and its surrounding villages as attested by demographers at the University of the South Pacific Department of Sociology.

Overall Attitude Towards Tourism in Nadi

In general, respondents expressed a very positive attitude towards tourism. About 80% of the respondents favored somewhat or strongly favored the presence of tourism in Nadi (Table 1). A very large proportion (90.7%) also stated that the image of Nadi improved somewhat or significantly improved as a result of tourism activities (Table 2).

Respondents were asked to express opinions about the impact of tourism on a variety of social and economic activities and concerns. Sixteen areas (variables) were evaluated with regard to the impact of tourism, where 1 indicated that the variable had been "significantly worsened" as a result of the presence of tourism and 5 "significantly improved."

As Table 3 shows, a number of improvements were identified as having been brought about by tourism. These included the town's overall tax revenue, income, and standard of living, work attitudes, quality of life, courtesy and hospitality to strangers, and confidence among people. A number of negative effects were also recognized. These were the increased incidence of alcoholism, individual crime, drug addictions, organized crime, openness to sex, and traffic conditions.

Table 1.   Attitude Towards Tourists in Nadi[a]

Attitude Towards Tourism	Percentage
Strongly oppose the presence of tourism	0.0
Oppose somewhat the presence of tourists	0.0
Neither oppose nor favor	19.9
Favor somewhat	22.0
Strongly favor	58.2
Total percentage	100.0
Mean: 4.3	
Std. dev: 0.6	

[a]"What are your feelings about the presence of tourists in Nadi?"

Table 2. Perceptions About the Impact of the Presence of Tourism on the Image of Nadi[a]

Attitude Towards Tourism	Percentage
Significantly worsen	0.0
Worsen somewhat	0.0
Not make any difference	9.3
Improve somewhat	45.0
Significantly improve	45.7
Total percentage	100.0
Mean: 4.4	
Std. dev: 0.6	

[a]"What impact do you think the increased presence of tourism would have on the image of Nadi?"

In the case of the remaining variables, the mean of around 3.0 may indicate that residents perceived the current level of tourism as having no significant impact. These variables included morality, politeness, and manners, and people's honesty.

When asked whether local residents would willingly take jobs in the tourism hospitality industry, 97% of the respondents said they would do so. About 90% of the respondents said that they would suggest to their friends or relatives to take jobs in the tourism industry. This result was of no surprise once it was found that practically all respondents were employed in or associated with the tourism industry.

The survey set out to also investigate attitudes to tourism employment. Respondents were asked to choose their preferred occupation from a limited list that included one category of work clearly identified as being within the tourism industry, namely hotel worker, which

Table 3. Tourism Impacts[a]

Benefits of Tourism	Mean[b]	Std. Dev.
Employment opportunities	4.4	0.7
Town's overall tax revenue	4.2	0.8
Income and standard of living	4.1	0.9
Attitude toward work	3.9	0.9
Quality of life in general	3.7	0.6
Courtesy and hospitality toward strangers	3.7	0.5
Mutual confidence among people	3.6	0.5
Politeness and good manners	3.1	0.9
Morality	2.9	1.2
People's honesty	2.8	1.2
Traffic conditions	2.4	1.0
Sexual permissiveness	2.3	1.2
Organized crime (crimes that are the products of groups or organizations)	2.2	1.0
Drug addiction	2.1	1.0
Individual crimes (planned and conducted by individuals)	2.1	1.0
Alcoholism	1.9	0.9
Grand mean	3.1	

[a]"What impact do you think the current level of tourism would have on the following issues?"
[b]1 = Significantly worsen; 2 = Worsen somewhat; 3 = Not make any difference; 4 = Improve somewhat; 5 = Significantly improve.

Table 4.   Preferred Occupation[a]

Preferred Occupation	Percentage
Hotel worker	67.4
Shop owner	11.3
Office worker	4.3
Field worker	0.7
Foreman in a factory	0.7
Other	15.6
Total percentage	100.0

[a]"If you were to select for yourself an occupation from the following, which one would you select?"

was chosen by 67%. The other notable categories were shop owner for 11%, office clerk for 4%, and factory foreman for 1% (Table 4). One can surmise that Nadi residents regard hotel occupations as being relatively more desirable than the other four listed occupations, though it should be acknowledged that the range of occupations offered to respondents in the questionnaire was limited.

General Attitude Towards Tourists

A number of questions attempted to gauge the perceptions of residents towards tourists. A majority of respondents described tourists in general and overseas tourists in particular as being very different from Fijians. About three quarters of respondents stated that tourists to the Nadi area were very different from people in their locality (Table 5). Almost three quarters also described international tourists as being very different from domestic tourists (Table 6).

   Respondents were asked about the extent to which they had developed social relationships with tourists. A majority (about 88%) indicated that they had contact with tourists (Table 7). Furthermore, more than half of the respondents (about 58%) claimed that they or their families maintained correspondence with tourists. Given that an overwhelming proportion of tourists to Nadi are residents of foreign countries, this a remarkably high figure. Several alternative explanations can be given. The issue of "social desirability," namely a tendency to answer questions in a "proper" or "socially desirable" manner is one possible explanation. The much publicized friendliness of the people of Fiji and the consequent interest that they share in people from other places is a second possibility. Finally, a third

Table 5.   Difference Between Tourists and Locals[a]

Perceptions of Tourists	Percentage
Very different	75.9
Somewhat different	7.8
In some ways different and in others similar	1.4
Somewhat similar	0.7
Very similar	14.2
Total percentage	100.0
Mean: 1.7	
Std. dev: 1.4	

[a]"Do you think that tourists visiting your area are different from people in your locality?"

Table 6.   Difference Between International and
Domestic Tourists[a]

Domestic vs. International Tourists	Percentage
Very different	73.8
Somewhat different	22.7
In some ways different and in others similar	2.8
Somewhat similar	0.7
Very similar	0.0
Total percentage	100.0
Mean: 1.3	
Std. dev: 0.6	

[a]"How would you regard tourists from other countries compared to Fijian
tourists?"

Table 7.   Social Contacts Between Locals and
Tourists[a]

Contact with Tourists	Percentage
Have no contact with tourists	12.1
Have some contact with tourists	23.4
Have constant contact with tourists	64.5
Total percentage	100.0
Mean: 2.5	
Std. dev: 0.7	

[a]"What kind of social relationships do you have with tourists?"

Table 8.   Overall Opinion About the Nadi
Tourism Industry[a]

Attitude Towards Tourism	Percentage
Strongly oppose it	1.4
Oppose somewhat	1.4
Neither oppose nor favor it	19.9
Favor it	32.6
Strongly favor it	44.7
Total percentage	100.0
Mean: 4.2	
Std. dev: 0.9	

[a]"What is your overall opinion of the tourism industry in Nadi
and vicinity?"

possibility might be correspondence with tourists who are friends or relatives and reside in foreign countries, such as India.

Current Attitudes Towards Tourism in Nadi

Respondents were asked to express their overall attitude towards tourism activity in Nadi and its immediate vicinity. Some 77% stated that they either favored or strongly favored tourism (Table 8). Only about 3% of the respondents were opposed to the existence of

Table 9. Perceptions about the Volume of Tourists Visiting the Nadi Area[a]

Volume of Tourism	Percentage
Should significantly decrease	0.7
Should decrease somewhat	4.3
Not change	12.8
Should increase somewhat	42.6
Should significantly increase	39.7
Total percentage	100.0
Mean: 4.2	
Std. dev: 0.9	

[a]"How do you feel about the volume of tourists visiting this area?"

tourism in Nadi. Most respondents were supportive of an expansion of tourism in the area. Approximately 82% answered that the number of tourists visiting the area should increase, with 13% saying that it should not change, and 5% that the number of tourists should decrease (Table 9).

VARIANTS RELATIONSHIPS ANALYZED

The Relationship Between Respondents' Demographic Characteristics and Their Level of Support for the Tourism Industry

A series of one-way analyses of variance, t-tests, and Pearson correlations were conducted. Such tests were undertaken to isolate any significant differences that might be evident between the socioeconomic characteristics of respondents and their level of support for tourism.

The results indicated only a limited statistical difference between the various demographic groups in their attitude towards tourism. The results indicated that residents in the 51–61 age group had a more positive opinion about tourism in the Nadi area (mean = 4.6) than respondents in the 29–39 age group (mean = 4.1); that the higher the number of children under 18 living in the household, the less the support for tourism ($r = -0.42$); and that respondents who had children under 18 living in their household were disposed more favorably to tourism in the Nadi area (mean = 4.3) than respondents who did not have children under the age of 18 in their household (mean = 3.6).

Respondents' Support for Nadi Tourism

A stepwise multiple regression was conducted to determine what factors affect expressed support by residents for tourism in Nadi. The dependent variable was "overall opinion about the tourism industry in Nadi" (Table 8). As shown in Table 10, and unlike a number of earlier studies (Milman and Pizam 1988), this variable was not highly correlated with two other key ones, namely "feeling about the presence of tourists in Nadi" (Table 1) and "feelings about the volume of tourists" (Table 9). In the light of this apparent inconsistency, it was decided to use it as the sole dependent variable without combining the three into an index.

Twenty-three independent variables were included in the regression: four tourism impact variables; eight sociodemographic variables; eight describing the issues of percep-

Table 10. Correlation Matrix between Variables Explaining Overall Opinion of Tourism in Nadi

	Q4	Q9	
Q1	0.25	0.22	Q1 = Feeling about presence of tourists (Table 1)
Q4	—	0.34	Q4 = Controlling number of tourists (Table 9)
Q9		—	Q9 = Overall opinion of tourism industry (Table 8)

tions of tourists, social relations with tourists, and willingness to work in tourism; and three impact indexes.

The 16 impact variables were identified as being highly intercorrelated. Three indexes were created: (a) *Legal/Environmental Impacts*—consisting of the variables used to measure the impacts of tourism on crime, organized crime, alcoholism, drug addiction, and traffic conditions; (b) *Social Conduct Impacts*—consisting of the variables of politeness and good manners, openness to sex, honesty, and confidence among people; and (c) *Economic Impacts*—consisting of the variables of income and standard of living, employment opportunities, and the town's tax revenue.

Table 11 shows the results of the multiple regression with "overall opinion of the tourism industry" as the dependent variable. As can be seen from the above, 9 out of the 23 independent variables were significant in explaining 69% of the variance in respondent attitudes towards the tourism industry in Nadi.

Residents whose overall opinion of tourism in Nadi was positive were found to have a number of personal characteristics and perceptions of tourism. They believed that tourism was having a negative impact on morality; that tourism was creating a negative impact on work attitudes; that local residents were willing to take work in the tourism industry; that tourism was improving the image of their community; that tourists were different from themselves; that tourism was impacting negatively on their quality of life; had more children under the age of 18 living in their households; that tourism was having a negative impact on legal/environmental factors; and that they did not have family members employed in the tourism industry.

Table 11. Multiple Regression of Level of Support for Nadi's Tourism on Specific Opinions and Personal Characteristics

Variable	Standardized Regression Coefficient	F	Zero Order Correlation Coefficient	Cum R^2
Morality	−.57	71.4[a]	−.55	.30
Work attitudes	−.14	57.9[a]	−.20	.37
Inhabitants willing to work in tourism	.26	53.4[a]	.23	.50
Town image	.28	54.0[a]	.43	.57
Difference between tourists and residents	−.34	50.0[a]	−.10	.61
Quality of life	−.33	48.0[a]	.01	.64
Children under 18 at home	.34	42.6[a]	.29	.66
Legal factors index	−.31	41.6	−.13	.68
Family employed in tourism	−.14	38.3[a]	.09	.69

$N = 165$.
$R^2 = 0.69$.
[a]$p < .001$.

One might have expected that in a population highly dependent on the tourism industry, and where most of the residents are employed in it, support for tourism would be associated with the belief that it causes only positive impacts or benefits. The results of this study suggest something different. In Nadi, tourism was not thought of as an activity whose impacts are positive in all respects, and was not perceived as "manna from heaven." On the contrary, though most respondents were highly dependent on tourism for employment, they recognized its shortcomings and negative impacts. Awareness of the negatives did not lead to reduced support. This is an important finding that suggests that residents of communities that are dependent on tourism can be highly discriminating in their opinions towards tourism and can differentiate between economic benefits and social/legal costs, while still remaining predominantly supportive of tourism.

CONCLUSIONS

The results of the study have indicated that support for the tourism industry in Nadi is strong among its residents. Residents were not opposed to tourism at its current levels and even favored its expansion.

Residents of Nadi regarded tourists as being very different from themselves, but expressed no negative feelings towards them. They demonstrated a predominantly positive feeling towards tourists and towards the industry. Despite this, they were able to point out some specific negative impacts that, in their opinion, were brought about by tourism. Such negative impacts were alcoholism, drug addictions, individual crimes, organized crimes, openness to sex, and traffic conditions. The positive impacts that they pointed out were predominately economic, but included a few social factors. The positive impacts were employment opportunities, town's overall tax revenue, income, and standard of living, work attitudes, quality of life, hospitality to strangers, and confidence among people.

This study has attempted to contribute to the body of knowledge concerning the perceptions of local residents, particularly those employed in or associated with the tourism industry, towards the presence of tourism. Until now, it was commonly believed that resident perceptions of such impacts were subjective, inconsistent, and affected by some factors more than others. A typical view has been that residents who benefit economically from tourism are supportive of it and that such support is associated with a belief that tourism causes *mostly* positive benefits. Following the same logic, those without a pecuniary interest in tourism would tend to regard its impacts in a negative light. Residents who expressed the view that tourism causes drug addiction or attracts organized crimes, for example, would almost automatically be opposed to tourism, so the argument goes.

The results of this study suggests that this state of affairs is not always the case and that support for tourism can be associated with a belief that it induces negative as well as positive impacts. Should the results noted above be confirmed in studies in other geographical areas, then these observations may form the foundation of some new hypotheses in the development of a theory of the social impacts of tourism.

In the past, tourism leaders have strongly denied the negative impacts that the industry can bring about in host communities. This denial has been based on a belief that if such an admission were to be made, then tourism would lose its vital support from residents, employees, and politicians. This study, if confirmed by others, suggests that even the industry's "best friends" are aware of its negative impacts and that support for tourism is not based on a belief that it causes *only* positive impacts on host communities. In the light of these findings, it would be wise for the private and public officials and leaders, worldwide, to admit candidly that the industry *can* cause negative impacts. Such an admission should allow industry members to work side by side with other concerned citizens to minimize the negative impacts.

Acknowledgement: The authors wish to acknowledge the assistance of Dr. Nii-K Plange, Head of the Department of Sociology, University of the South Pacific, in preparing a representative sample of the Nadi community.

REFERENCES

Allen, Lawrence R., P. T. Long, R. R. Perdue, and S. Kieselbach. 1988. The Impact of Tourism Development of Residents' Perceptions of Community Life. Journal of Travel Research 27(1):16–21.

Andressen, B., and P. E. Murphy. 1986. Tourism Development in Canadian Travel Corridors: Two Surveys of Resident Attitudes. World Leisure and Recreation 28(5):17–22.

Ap, John. 1990. Residents' Perceptions Research on the Social Impacts of Tourism. Annals of Tourism Research 17:610–615.

Belisle, Francois J., and Don R. Hoy. 1980. The Perceived Impact of Tourism by Residents: A Case Study in Santa Maria, Columbia. Annals of Tourism Research 7:83–101.

Brayley, Russ, and Turgut Var. 1989. Canadian Perceptions of Tourism's Influence on Economic and Social Conditions. Annals of Tourism Research 16(4):578–582.

Brayley, Russ, Turgut Var, and Pauline Sheldon. 1990. Perceived Influence of Tourism on Social Issues. Annals of Tourism Research 17:285–289.

Britton, S. 1982. Tourism and Underdevelopment in Fiji. Canberra: Development Studies Centre Monograph.

Caneday, Lowell, and Jeffery Zeiger. 1991. The Social, Economic, and Environmental Costs Tourism to a Gaming Community as Perceived by Its Residents. Journal of Travel Research 27(2):2–8.

Davis, Duane, Jeff Allen, and Robert M. Consenza. 1988. Segmenting Local Residents by Their Attitudes, Interests, and Opinions Toward Tourism. Journal of Travel Research 30(2):45–48.

Dogan, Hasan Zafer. 1989. Forms of Adjustment: Sociocultural Impacts of Tourism. Annals of Tourism Research 16:216–236.

Fiji Visitors Bureau. 1991. An Analysis of Fiji's Tourist Accommodation Structure and Room Constraints: 1991–1996. Suva: Fiji Visitors Bureau.

Husbands, Winston. 1989. Social Status and Perception of Tourism in Zambia. Annals of Tourism Research 16:237–253.

Jafari, Jafar, Abraham Pizam, and Krzysztof Przeclawski. 1990. A Sociocultural Study of Tourism as a Factor of Change. Annals of Tourism Research 17:469–472.

Liu, Juanita C., and Turgut Var. 1986. Resident Attitudes Toward Tourism Impacts in Hawaii. Annals of Tourism Research 13:193–214.

Maddox, R. N. 1986. Factors Contributing to Satisfaction with Tourism: The Resident View. *In* Tourism Services Marketing: Advances in Theory and Practice (Special Conference Series), pp. 76–84. Academy of Marketing Science, University of Miami, USA.

Main, Kathy A. 1989. Airline Development in the South Pacific: A Turning Point. Thesis, Victoria University of Technology, Australia.

Milman, Ady, and Abraham Pizam. 1988. Social Impacts of Tourism on Central Florida. Annals of Tourism Research 15:191–204.

Perdue, Richard, R., Patrick T. Long, and Lawrence Allen. 1987. Rural Resident Tourism Perceptions and Attitudes. Annals of Tourism Research 14:420–429. 1990. Resident Support for Tourism Development. Annals of Tourism Research 17:586–599.

Pizam, Abraham. 1978. Tourism Impacts: The Social Costs to the Destination Community as Perceived by its Residents. Journal of Travel Research 16(4):8–12.

Plange, N.-K. 1984. Tourism: How Fiji People See It and What They Think of It. Suva: Fiji Tourism Education Council.

Ritchie, J. R. B. 1988. Consensus Policy Formulation in Tourism: Measuring Resident Views via Survey Research. Tourism Management 9:199–212.

Ross, Glenn F. 1992. Resident Perceptions of the Impact of Tourism on an Australian City. Journal of Travel Research 30(4):13–17.

Samy, J. 1980. Crumbs from the Table? The Workers' Share in Tourism. In Pacific Tourism as Islanders See It, Crocombe, R., and F. Rajotte, eds., pp. 67–82. Suva: Institute of Pacific Studies, University of the South Pacific.

Schluter, Regina, and Turgut Var. 1988. Resident Attitudes Toward Tourism in Argentina: A Research Note. Annals of Tourism Research 15:442–445.

Tourism Council of the South Pacific. 1991. South Pacific Tourism Statistics 1985–1990. Suva: Tourism Council of the South Pacific.

Varley, R. 1978. Tourism in Fiji: Some Economic and Social Problems. Cardiff: University of Wales Press.

Vusoniwailala, L. 1980. Tourism and Fijian Hospitality. In Pacific Tourism as Islanders See It, Crocombe, R., and F. Rajotte. Suva: Institute of Pacific Studies, University of South Pacific.

Key Concepts

appreciation of strangeness and novelty
beneficial social contacts
conduct of visitors
contemporary institutionalized tourism
contrasting cultures and cultural distance
democratization of travel
drifter
effects of travel experiences
environmental bubble
group travel arrangements
handicapped travelers
income
individual mass tourist
isolation of the mass tourist
mass follows class
national understanding

negative social effects on host society
organized mass tourist
population changes and travel interests
reduced fare schemes
resentment toward visitors
social tourism
standardization of facilities
strangeness versus familiarity
tourism and crime
transformation of attractions
travel patterns change with age, family life stages
travel preferences of international tourists
trips as family highlights
world as a global village

For Review and Discussion

1. As a manager of a resort hotel popular with families, what social and/or educational activities would you offer your guests?
2. You have decided to take a trip to a country whose culture is very much different from your own. Would you participate in a group tour or go alone? Why?
3. Would a child's learning experience during a trip to another part of his or her country be comparable to school learning for that period of time? In what ways might parents maximize the educational benefits of such a trip?
4. Describe how a hotel's food and beverage manager might avoid the "universal waiter uniform" image.
5. Discuss the effects of television news coverage of global and national events on tourism.

6. Give some examples of how tourism suppliers accommodate handicapped travelers. How important is this segment of the market?
7. Is there a potential for increased social tourism in your country?
8. How might the four extremes relating to the preferences of present-day international tourists affect a resort hotel's social and recreational program? Give some specific examples.
9. How do your travel interests differ from your parents'? from your grandparents'?
10. You are president of a tourist promotion association. Which of Cohen's four tourist types would you try to attract? Why?

Case Problems

1. Alfred K. is a widower 67 years old. He has not had an opportunity to travel much, but now as a retiree he has the time and money to take extensive trips. As a travel counselor, what kinds of travel products would you recommend?
2. Sadie W. is president of her church missionary society. She has observed that many visitors to her fairly small city in England are interested in the local history. Her church is a magnificent cathedral, the construction of which began in the year 1083. Mrs. W. and her colleagues believe that missionary work begins at home. By what methods could her group reach and become acquainted with the cathedral visitors?
3. A U.S. group tour conductor wishes to maximize the mutual social benefits of a trip to an underdeveloped country. Describe possible kinds of social contacts that would be beneficial to the hosts and to the members of the tour group.
4. A popular beach resort hotel is located in a tropical country which, unfortunately, has a high crime rate. One section of the city nearby has some "South Seas" atmosphere gambling casinos. Many guests would like to visit them. How might the hotel's staff control this situation?
5. Nadia P. is Minister of Tourism for a small West African country. This country has become a very popular winter destination for Scandinavians. The tourists seem to be mainly interested in the beaches, which are among the finest in the world. However, it is customary for these visitors to wear very scanty clothing, especially when bathing. In fact, nude bathing is occasionally practiced. About 90 percent of the indigenous population of the host country are Moslems. The appearance and sometimes behavior of the visitors, especially when shopping and otherwise contacting local citizens, often seems improper to their hosts. Tourism is increasing each year. The economic benefits are considerable and are very much needed. However, the social problem is becoming more acute. What should Ms. P. do about this?

Selected References

Buck, Roy C. "Boundary Maintenance Revisited: Tourism Experience in an Old Order Amish Community." *Rural Sociology*, Vol. 43, No. 2 (Summer 1978), pp. 221–234.

Canadian Broadcasting Corporation. *Welcome to Paradise*. Ottawa: The Corporation.

Cohen, Erik. "Rethinking the Sociology of Tourism." *Annals of Tourism Research*, Vol. 6, No. 1 (January/March 1979), pp. 18–35. Special Issue on Sociology of Tourism.

Cohen, Erik. "Traditions in Qualitative Sociology of Tourism." *Journal of Travel Research*, Vol. 15, No. 1 (1988), pp. 29–46.

Dann, Graham, and Erik Cohen. "Sociology and Tourism." *Annals of Tourism Research,* Vol. 18, No. 1 (1991), pp. 155–169.

deKadt, Emanuel. "Social Planning for Tourism in the Developing Countries." *Annals of Tourism Research,* Vol. 6, No. 1 (January/March 1979), pp. 36–48. Special Issue on Sociology of Tourism.

Farrell, Bryan H. *The Social and Economic Impact of Tourism on Pacific Communities.* Santa Cruz, Calif.: Center for South Pacific Studies, University of California at Santa Cruz, June 1977.

Getz, Donald, and Wendy Frisby. "Evaluating Management Effectiveness in Community-Run Festivals." *Journal of Travel Research,* Vol. 27, No. 1 (Summer 1988), pp. 22–27.

Goodrich, Jonathan N. "Socialist Cuba: A Study of Health Tourism." *Journal of Travel Research,* Vol. 32, No. 1 (Summer 1993), pp. 36–41.

Haukeland, Jan V. "Non-travelers: The Flip Side of Motivation." *Annals of Tourism Research,* Vol. 17, No. 2 (1990), pp. 172–184.

Hornback, Kenneth E. "Social Trends in Outdoor Recreation." *Proceedings of the National Outdoor Recreation Trends Symposium II,* Vol. 1. Atlanta, Ga.: National Park Service Science Publications Office, 1985, pp. 37–48.

Jafari, Jafar. "Tourism and Social Science: A Bibliography." *Annals of Tourism Research,* Vol. 6, No. 2 (April/June 1979), pp. 149–195. Special Issue on Sociology of Tourism.

MacCannel, Dean. *The Tourist: A New Theory of the Leisure Class.* New York: Schocken Books, 1976.

Milman, Ady, and Abraham Pizam. "Social Impacts of Tourism in Central Florida." *Annals of Tourism Research,* Vol. 15, No. 2 (1988), pp. 191–205.

Murray, M., and J. Sproats. *The Disabled Traveler: Tourism and Disability in Australia.* Townsville, Australia: James Cook University, 1990.

O'Leary, Joseph T. "Social Trends in Outdoor Recreation." *Proceedings of the National Outdoor Recreation Trends Symposium II,* Vol. 1. Atlanta, Ga.: National Park Service Science Publication Office, 1985, pp. 24–36.

Pizam, Abraham, and Ady Milman. "The Social Impacts of Tourism." *Tourism Recreation Research,* Vol. 11, No. 2. Lucknow, India: Lucknow Publishing House, 1986.

Ryan, C. "Crime, Violence, Terrorism, and Tourism: An Accidental or Intrinsic Relationship." *Tourism Management,* Vol. 14, No. 3 (1993), pp. 173–183.

Salmon, J. P. S. *Accommodating All Guests: The Americans with Disabilities Act and the Lodging Industry.* Washington, D.C.: American Hotel and Motel Association, 1992.

Schroeder, Tim. "Preliminary Assessment of the Social Impacts of Tourism on Flagstaff, Arizona." *Visions in Leisure and Business,* Vol. 9, No. 2 (1990), pp. 26–39.

Smith, Ralph W. "Leisure of Disabled Tourists: Barriers to Participation." *Annals of Tourism Research,* Vol. 14, No. 3 (1987), pp. 376–389.

"Social Tourism for All: The Swiss Travel Saving Fund." *Tourism Management,* Vol. 4, No. 3 (September 1983), pp. 216–219.

Transport Canada. *Access for All.* Ottawa: Transport Canada, 1991.

Turner, Louis, and John Ash. *The Golden Hordes.* London: Constable, 1975.

Van Doren, Carlton S. "Social Trends and Social Indicators: The Private Sector." *Proceedings of the National Outdoor Recreation Trends Symposium II,* Vol. 1. Atlanta, Ga.: National Park Service Science Publication Office, 1985, pp. 13–23.

Woodside, Arch, G., Ellen M. Moore, Mark A. Bonn, and Donald G. Wizeman. "Segmenting the Timeshare Resort Market." *Journal of Travel Research,* Vol. 24, No. 3 (Winter 1986), pp. 6–12.

PART FOUR

TOURISM SUPPLY, DEMAND, PLANNING, AND DEVELOPMENT

CHAPTER 12

Tourism Components and Supply

LEARNING OBJECTIVES

- Know the four major supply components that any tourist area must possess.
- Become familiar with the newer forms of accommodations: condominium apartments and timesharing arrangements.
- Be able to use the mathematical formula to calculate the number of guest rooms needed for the estimated future demand.
- Develop the ability to perform a task analysis in order to match supply components with anticipated demand.
- Discover methods of adjusting supply components in accordance with fluctuating demand levels.

Considering that tourism is a composite of activities, services, and industries that deliver a travel experience, it is important to identify and categorize its supply components. The quality and quantity of these determine considerably tourism's success in any area.

COMPONENTS

Tourism supply components can be classified into four main categories:

1. *Natural resources.* This category constitutes the fundamental measure of supply—the natural resources that any area has available for the use and enjoyment of visitors. Basic elements in this category include air and climate, land forms, terrain, flora, fauna, bodies of water, beaches, natural beauty, and water supply for drinking, sanitation, and similar uses.
2. *Infrastructure.* The infrastructure consists of all underground and surface developmental construction such as water supply systems, sewage disposal systems, gas lines, electrical and communications systems, drainage systems, other constructed facilities such as highways, airports, railroads, roads, drives, parking lots, parks, night lighting, marinas and dock facilities, bus and train station facilities, resorts, hotels, motels, restaurants, shopping centers, places of entertainment, museums, stores, and similar structures.
3. *Transportation.* Included are items such as ships, airplanes, trains, buses, limousines, taxis, automobiles, cog railroads, aerial tramways, and similar passenger transportation facilities.
4. *Hospitality and cultural resources.* These are all the cultural wealth of an area that makes possible the successful hosting of tourists. Examples are the tourist business

269

employees' welcoming spirit ("aloha" in Hawaii, for example), attitude of the residents toward visitors, courtesy, friendliness, sincere interest, willingness to serve and to get better acquainted with visitors, and other manifestations of warmth and friendliness. In addition, the cultural resources of any area are included here—fine arts, literature, history, music, dramatic art, dancing, shopping, sports, and other activities.

There is a wide range of tourist resources created by combining cultural resources. Such examples would be sports events and facilities, traditional or national festivals, games, and pageants.

NATURAL RESOURCES

A great variety of combinations of natural resource factors can create environments attractive to tourism development. Thus, no general statements can be formulated. Probably the most noticeable are the pronounced seasonal variations of temperature zones and the changes in demand for recreational use of such areas. To even out demand, the more multiple-use possibilities, the better. For example, it is more desirable that an area be used for golf, riding, fishing, hunting, snow skiing, snowmobiling, mushroom hunting, sailing and other water sports, nature study, and artistic appreciation such as painting and photography than for hunting alone. The wider the appeal throughout the year, the greater the likelihood of success.

Another highly important consideration is that of location. As a rule, the closer an area is to its likely markets, the more desirable it is and the more likely to have a high demand. User-oriented areas (e.g., golf courses) should be close to their users. By contrast, an area of superb natural beauty such as a U.S. national park could be several thousand miles from major market areas and yet have very satisfactory levels of demand.

Productivity of the natural resources of the area for tourism is a function of the application of labor and management. The amounts and proportions of these inputs will determine the quality and quantity of the output. The terrain, vegetation, and beaches of the natural resource will be affected by the intensity of use. Proper planning, taking such concentrations of use under consideration, and planning accordingly for permanent aesthetic appreciation will help to maintain the quality of the natural resources for the enjoyment of present and future users.

The quality of the natural resources *must* be maintained to sustain tourism demand. Proper levels of quality must be considered when planning is undertaken, and the maintenance of quality standards after construction is undertaken is absolutely necessary for continued satisfaction of the visitor. In fact, tourism is very sensitive to the quality of recreational use of natural resources, and unless high standards are maintained, a depreciation of the demand will inevitably result. Thus ecological and environmental considerations are vital.

INFRASTRUCTURE

The ground and service installations described as infrastructure are of paramount importance to successful tourism. These installations must be adequate. For example,

Vail, Colorado, is an example of how a world-class resort can be developed using natural resources. (Photo by David LoKey; courtesy of Vail Associates)

the diameters of the pipes in various utility systems should be ample for any future increase in use. Electrical installations, water supply systems, communications installations, waste disposal, and similar service facilities should be planned with a long-term viewpoint so that they can accommodate future expansion. Airport runways should be built to adequate standards for use by the newest group of jets so that future costly modifications will not be necessary.

Hotel or lodging structures are among the most important parts of the infrastructure. The goal should be to produce an architectural design and quality of construction that will result in a distinctive permanent environment. A boxlike hotel typical of any modern city is not considered appropriate for a seaside resort dominated by palms and other tropical vegetation, nor is it likely to attract tourists.

A tourist is often more attracted by a facility designed in conformance with local architecture as a part of the local landscape than the modernistic hotel that might be found at home. Attention must be given to this subject since people often travel to immerse themselves in an environment totally different from their own. Modern amenities such as air conditioning, central heating, and plumbing, however, should be used in buildings otherwise characteristic of a particular region.

Interior design should also be stimulating and attractive. Lodging structures need local decor and atmosphere as well as comfort. To minimize the expense of obsolescence, high-quality materials and furnishings and first-rate maintenance are necessary. Infrastructure is expensive and requires considerable time to construct.

Auto Traveler Service

In developed countries, automobile transportation is most common. As the economy of a country develops, the usual pattern is from walking, to using horses or other working animals, to bicycles, to motorcycles, and finally to small and then larger automobiles, augmented by public transport. In the case of roads, they should be hard, all-weather surfaced, be properly graded and drained, and be built to international standards for safe use. Small, inadequate roads will only have to be torn up and replaced with better and more adequate systems.

Auxiliary services, such as gasoline stations, roadside eating facilities, motels, roadside parks, roadside picnic facilities, rest parks that have toilet facilities, scenic turnouts, marked points of interest within easy access of the road, and auto repair and service facilities are all needed for successful auto tourism. The number and spacing of essential services depend on the nature of the area, but a spacing of about one hour's driving distance is recommended.

A trained travel counselor provides advice to visitors at an official travel information welcome center. Travelers may call, free of charge, anywhere in Michigan to make reservations or obtain information. These centers are part of Michigan's integrated system of highway signing, travel information, and service for motorists. (Photo courtesy of the Michigan Department of Transportation)

Attractive road signs giving historical information enhance the visitors' enjoyment of an area. This historical marker tells of the difficulties pioneers faced in their efforts to pass Mt. Hood. (Photo courtesy of the Oregon Department of Transportation)

Road Planning and Road Signs

In the planning of new roads, long-term consideration must be given to "tourist" or "scenic routes" that present the most impressive scenery. A good example is the scenic Mississippi River route in the United States. Such routes should have specially colored markers and be indicated on road maps as "scenic tourist routes" or some similar designation. The marking or sign program for the roads should show points of interest—including directions—and have sufficient information concerning availability of food, lodging, and gasoline.

Some type of classification for such signs indicating the nature of the accommodations and services available is desired. One method is to provide signs with the logos of the various hotel, motel, restaurant, and gasoline service stations. This type of sign identifies for the traveler the type of facilities he or she can expect. Adequate sign facilities including the international auto-road symbols are essential as are adequate supplies of maps that translate road signs into the most needed language of visitors.

Another aspect of signs concerns their control along the highways. It is the authors' belief that the most satisfactory way to provide information (and advertising) for the tourist and at the same time protect the beauty of the countryside is to control the placement of signs as follows:

Within one mile (1609 meters) from the outskirts of the city or community, signs along the highways will be permitted. These signs will be located in any convenient place, with one stipulation—that signs be maintained in excellent physical condition. No obvious deterioration of the signs will be allowed, and if such deterioration takes place, the highway authorities would have the mandate to remove the sign at the expense of the owner. The countryside between cities beyond the one-mile radius of each city would have no advertising signs. Only highway marker signs to indicate road conditions, curves, warning signs, and similar highway directional information would be found in this area.

An exception to these rules might be made in the case of major intersections where highway directional signs exist and a cluster of informational signs of tourist accommodations and other tourist services could be permitted.

Roadside Parks

Auto tourists use and enjoy roadside parks, picnic tables, rest areas, scenic turnouts, and similar roadside facilities. These facilities are sometimes abused by inconsiderate motorists who litter the area with their trash. Thus the rule "If you can't maintain it, don't built it" is a cardinal principle of tourism development, and regular maintenance to keep the park in an orderly condition is essential. If the parks are not properly maintained, the tourist is disappointed and the investment in the park is largely wasted.

Some states provide deluxe roadside parks with a fine information building, free refreshments, tourist hosts and hostesses, and rest rooms. These parks are equipped with supplies of folders, maps, pictures, and other amenities for a refreshing informative stop.

Gasoline Stations

Service stations should be provided in sufficient quantity to avoid delays for service. An automobile patron should not wait more than five minutes for service. Station attendants need to be schooled in courteous service and in the importance of friendliness, hospitality, and knowledge of the tourist attractions in the immediate vicinity (such as within a radius of 50 miles). They should be knowledgeable concerning accommodations, shopping, and entertainment in their community.

Accommodations

For successful tourism, accommodations must be available in sufficient quantity to match the demand of the travelers who arrive at the destination. Accommodations should precede any other type of development; their importance cannot be overemphasized.

Hotels vary tremendously in their physical facilities, level of maintenance and cleanliness, and services provided. Unless all of these factors are at satisfactory levels, tourism cannot succeed. The hotels must provide the physical facilities, price ranges, locations, and services that meet the expectations, wants, and needs of the travelers. Should the quality of facilities and services drop, demand will fall off—a serious blow to the tourism industry in the area.

Types of Accommodations

HOTELS   Hotels are of several types: commercial, resort, motor, airport, and residential. In relation to tourism, residential hotels are probably not important, although there

This elaborate beachfront hotel supplies resort, commercial, and convention accommodations. It is a good example of skilled design, engineering, and construction in an attractive location and setting. (Photo courtesy of Hyatt Hotels Corporation)

are usually some rooms available to tourists in most residential hotels. The primary type is the resort hotel situated in attractive surroundings and usually accompanied by a large mix of services, including entertainment and recreational activities for the traveler and vacationer. The commercial hotel is usually a downtown structure located conveniently for the business traveler, convention attender, and vacationer.

The demand for accommodations varies according to the price guests are willing to pay, services required, and similar considerations. Many successful tourism areas have no multistoried, expensive, contemporary-looking hotels. For example, a bungalow-type accommodation constructed with native materials, built to modern standards of comfort and safety, and kept immaculately clean will be acceptable to a large segment of the market.

The motor hotel is of primary importance for tourists traveling by car and is of major importance in the United States, Canada, and Mexico. Suitable accommodations should be available for all segments of the market. American companies such as Marriott, Ramada, Holiday Corporation, and Quality International now offer accommodations under different names that are aimed at specific price levels of the market. Thus they compete for various segments of the travel market. Expensive hotel accommodations may be demanded by those who "want the best" and are willing and able to pay accordingly. On the other hand, youth tourism and adults unable or unwilling to pay for top-level accommodations should have facilities available, such as hostels, pensions, and bed and breakfast. Camping or caravanning facilities are often needed. Other types of accommodations include marina hotels, airport hotels, gambling resort hotels, and rustic cabins in wilderness areas. All accommodations should be harmonious with one another.

Certain places are known as expensive destination areas, and travelers expect to find higher-quality accommodations there. Conversely, other areas are expected to be inexpensive, and the high-priced hotel would be out of place in such a locality.

CONDOMINIUM APARTMENTS   Individual buyers of condominium units typically use the apartment for their own enjoyment, or they rent it to tourists for all or part of the year. This form of accommodation has become increasingly important and, in some resort areas, constitutes considerable competition to the resort hotels. Real estate management firms often manage such apartments or groups of "condos" within a building or complex and thus serve as agents for the owners. They rent the condos as managers of the group, charging a fee for this service to the absent owner. Such arrangements can be made through a local travel agent in the prospective traveler's home city. The agent will book the reservation through the real estate management firm.

TIMESHARING   Timesharing is a technique for the multiple ownership and/or use of resort and recreational properties. Timesharing has been applied to hotels, motels, condominiums, townhouses, single-family detached homes, campgrounds, and even boats and yachts. It involves both new construction and conversion of existing structures, along with properties devoted solely to timesharing and projects that integrate timesharing and nontimesharing properties. While most programs may be classified as either ownership or nonownership (right to use), there are wide variations in program and legal format.

The attraction of timesharing is simple: it permits purchasers to own or have occupancy rights at a resort accommodation for a period of time each year for a fraction of the purchasing price of the entire unit. Timeshare owners pay for exactly what they plan on using, and when they leave they don't have to think about where they'll be vacationing next year. Another option or advantage of timesharing is the exchange program. The exchange system affords vacation flexibility by allowing owners to trade or swap their timeshares for other locations and times. Finally, a well-designed timeshare program can be a hedge against inflation in resort accommodations.

The benefits of timesharing are substantially borne out by the high degree of consumer satisfaction it has achieved. In a survey of approximately 10,000 timeshare buyers, conducted by the National Timesharing Council of the American Land Development Association, 86.3 percent of the respondents said they were "very satisfied" or "satisfied" with their purchase. About 40 percent indicated that they were interested in purchasing additional timeshares. Additional information on timesharing is available from the National Timesharing Council, 1220 L Street N.W., Suite 510, Washington, D.C. 20005. Also see the discussion in Chapter 6.

Hotel Management

As mentioned in the preceding section, the management of a hotel should ideally be the same group that was involved in the planning and construction of the hotel. To do otherwise is unadvisable because the hotel business is not overly profitable, and any efficiency that can be built into the design or layout of the hotel as recommended by an experienced management group helps to assure a better chance of success. For best results, the manager should be a graduate of a hotel school so there is a proper depth of understanding and appreciation of the industry as well as training for the job.

All decisions pertaining to the management of the hotel should begin with the customers and guests. What is the likely reaction to each management decision? Implementation of such a policy favors success for the hotel as the policy most likely to produce a high measure of guest satisfaction.

Success in hotel management also depends on organization and the functioning of each department. Each department head should be considered a manager of his or her own department. The goals of each should affect and support the overall goals of the hotel. The personal goals of each employee should contribute to and buttress the goals of the department. Each employee should be taught high standards of service, sanitation, and personal conduct, essential for the success of the hotel.

Thorough training sessions must be conducted for new employees, and recurring training should be provided for all employees. A wide selection of home study courses (also suitable for group use) is available, in English, from the Educational Institute of the American Hotel and Motel Association, 1407 S. Harrison Road, East Lansing, Michigan 48826.

Assistance in training staff and managers can also be obtained from colleges and universities, state departments of education and public instruction, trade associations, and private management institutes or associations as well as from resources from within the organization or from larger affiliates or chain staff personnel.

LOCAL CHARM   A principal appeal of travel is the enjoyment of people of other cultures, and guests will inevitably become acquainted with the staff of the hotel. In fact, at a resort hotel, the guest probably gets to know his or her waiter or waitress better than anyone else in the hotel or local area.

Tourists expect all hotel personnel to serve them with courtesy and efficiency. Thus all hotel employees should be indoctrinated into the importance of this relationship and its success-building potential. The use of local costumes, the retention of unsophisticated charm, and the practice of friendliness and cleanliness are integral to achieving good hotel management.

INSPECTION   The most common types of hotel inspection relate to water supplies, sewage and waste disposal, general cleanliness, kitchen and food storage, and safety. Such inspection can be accomplished by local-, area-, or state-level authorities. Inspections of these conditions should be made no less than annually, and semiannually would be preferred.

Inspection to prevent fires is also important. Rigid inspections of electrical systems, heating systems, ventilating systems, air-conditioning systems, fuel storage, elevators, and storage areas are all important. Cleanliness and orderliness are essential ingredients in the prevention of fires. Fire prevention systems such as automatic sprinklers or similar warning devices should be inspected, and installation of fire prevention devices should be encouraged, if not required.

REGULATIONS   Regulations of hotels take many forms depending on local conditions and requirements. Regulations often relate to fairness and minimum standards of wages, hours, and ages of employees. Others relate to the licensing for selling alcoholic beverages; various tax structures for hotels; the disposal of wastes; hours of operation for public eating and drinking facilities; registration of guests; the importation of various food and drink items; equipment, unemployment, and disability insurance and other staff benefits; passport identification; zoning and building regulations; and fair employment and civil rights regulations. Many states regulate the sale of alcoholic beverages and the licensing of serving establishments, usually via a special agency.

HOTEL CLASSIFICATION   Hotels are classified using a number of different systems. Then, too, many tourist countries have no classification system whatsoever. Many in the industry prefer the five-star rating system, which grades hotels according to specific criteria (usually by the national tourist organization) from the highest (five stars) to the most modest accommodations (one star) suitable for travelers. Countries such as Spain also classify nonhotel accommodations, such as pensions. Criteria used for star ratings are public rooms, bathrooms, climatization, telephone, bar, dining rooms, and other characteristics. The inspections and classifications in Spain are conducted by the director general of Touristic Enterprise and Activities.

Other classifications are *deluxe, superior,* and *good,* or *super deluxe,* and *first-class reasonable.* Still another classification is A, B, C, D, or E. A uniform worldwide classification truly indicative of the grades of hotels in any country would be a real plus to tourism. Of course, differences in general standards of development in various countries would be understood. A five-star hotel in a highly developed country would likely be more deluxe than would a five-star hotel in a less developed area.

PROMOTION THROUGH REFERRAL AND FRANCHISE GROUPS   A substantial number of U.S. hotels and motels belong to some kind of an endorsing or referral association. Examples are Best Western, American Automobile Association (AAA), or Preferred Hotels. The main purpose of group membership is to obtain substantial numbers of reservations from other properties in the group and from the association's computerized reservation system.

Accommodations firms can also hold a franchise such as Holiday Inns, Hilton Inns, or Marriott Inns. All members of the franchise encourage their guests to make free reservations at another property in the group. Franchise companies operate sales offices in major cities (called hotel rep firms) and also provide national and international reservations services. All of this effort is aimed at increasing members' annual volume of reservations.

TRANSPORTATION

All factors concerning transportation should be considered in developing tourism, beginning with taxis, limousines, and bus service from the place of lodging to the departure terminals. Such services must be adequate and economical.

Air

As described in Chapter 5, the airline industry dominates public intercity transportation systems, capturing over 92 percent of the common-carrier passenger mile market. Thus, planners looking to improve tourism must evaluate the adequacy of air transportation. Flight frequencies as well as size and type of aircraft are important. Air service from important origins for tourists is, of course, essential.

Airport facilities must be adequate. Major problems frequently encountered are the accessibility to the airport and the loading-unloading-parking space sequence. Newly built airports seem to have solved these to a considerable degree and also reduced

The Dallas–Fort Worth airport exemplifies good planning for traveler convenience. Note the narrow terminal buildings, requiring only a short walk to taxi and parking areas. There are airport hotels, multilevel parking ramps, and elevated highways connecting each terminal complex. An automated shuttle train provides passengers with transportation to the other terminals. Land area for future expansion has been included. (Photo courtesy of American Airlines)

walking distances due to design improvements. There is also frequent shuttle bus service for interline passengers.

Motorcoach

Motorcoaches intended for tour use should have large windows, air conditioning, comfortable seats, and rest room facilities. Springs or other suspension systems in the coaches should be designed so that the joggling of passengers is kept to a minimum or eliminated. Multilingual guide service or multilingual tape recording facilities with earphones for each passenger are desirable in communities or on tours where an interpretation of the points of interest is desirable.

Personnel assigned to buses should be selected for suitable temperament, courtesy, and spirit of hospitality. For example, if a bus is staffed by a driver and an interpreter, the interpreter can assist passengers on and off the bus as well as inform them of local environment, particularly attractions of interest. Interpreters or guides should be trained and educated for this duty. Too often, the interpretation of points of interest is superficial (and inaccurate). A program of certification for guides should be conducted by a special school or provided in the curriculum of an institution of higher learning. In such a program, competent instructors should educate potential guides in the history, archeology, ethnology, culture, and economic system of the area in which the tour is being conducted. Competency in the various languages commonly encountered with tourists is also an essential qualification.

Ship and Boat

Water travel is a major part of tourism and contributes considerably to the development of travel on land and by air. Forms of water travel include cruise ship, passenger travel

Breathtaking Glacier Bay is one of the scenic attractions that draw many people to Holland America's flagship Rotterdam for Alaska Inside Passage cruises. (Photo courtesy of Cruise Lines International Association)

The Superliner deluxe bedroom contains a long sofa and swivel chair for day use, as well as two beds for sleeping. Located on the upper level of the bilevel cars, the deluxe bedroom features a folding table, a vanity shelf and mirror, a coat closet, a small overhead luggage rack, and storage space for three suitcases. Private toilet facilities, including a toilet, basin and mirror, are also featured. (Photo courtesy of Amtrak)

on freighters, ferryboats, river stern wheelers, chartered boats and yachts, houseboats, and smaller family boats and canoes.

Cruise ships and other large vessels need convenient piers and good land-air transportation connections for their passengers. Smaller boats need docks and loading-unloading ramps for easy accessibility to water. Charter boat operators must have reliable weather forecasting and ready availability of needed supplies and repair services. Where rental canoes are popular, delivery and pickup services are often necessary as are campgrounds in wilderness areas where canoeists can stay overnight. Persons owning their own boats appreciate good public access points for launching.

Rail

Travelers worldwide often prefer rail travel, particularly because of its unparalleled safety record and the convenience and comfort of viewing the scenery from an air-conditioned car. Also the frequent schedules of trains in many countries appeal to travelers. The recent advent of high-speed trains further enhances their appeal. Some trains have stewardesses or hostesses, which travelers seem to appreciate.

Adequate taxi, limousine, or bus service from the railroad station to hotels and downtown points is essential. Such transportation service must be frequent enough to get the traveler to the destination promptly. Conversely, the traveler should be able to get to the railroad station in ample time to make connections with the train as well.

An interior view of the refurbished Metroclub car shows the rich-looking seats that are arranged in 2–1 fashion for passenger comfort. Metroclub cars will be used in high-speed Northeast Corridor travel between New York and Washington. (Photo courtesy of Amtrak)

Taxis

Adequate taxi and limousine services are essential in a tourist area. Ideally, taxis should have removable and washable seat covers so the car always presents a clean appearance to the passenger. Also, the taxi driver, to make the best impression, should dismount from the driver's seat and open the door for the passenger. He or she also should assist in stowing the luggage in the trunk or elsewhere in the cab and be courteous at all times.

Taxi drivers that are multilingual are highly desirable and, in fact, essential if tourism is to be an important element of the economy of the state. Training taxi drivers in foreign languages should be no more difficult than training of tourist guides or front desk clerks. Where taxi drivers have no foreign language ability, hotels may provide written directions for the tourist to give to the driver concerning the destination and the return to the hotel at the end of the excursion.

HOSPITALITY AND CULTURAL RESOURCES

The development of hospitality resources is perhaps the most important factor in tourism. The finest physical facilities will be worthless if the tourist feels unwelcome. For example, we suggest having a welcoming sign and a special reception area for visitors at airports and other entry points. A favorable attitude toward the visitor can be created through programs of public information and propaganda. Public relations and publicity designed to convince local citizens of the importance of tourism are helpful. Courses at tourist hospitality schools for all persons who have direct contact

A group of youngsters learn about shipbuilding in olden times at the Maritime Museum, Basin Harbor, Vermont. Such cultural experiences make deep impressions on their young minds and help them appreciate their rich heritage. (Photo courtesy of the Vermont Travel Division)

with visitors are useful. In these schools, store clerks, gasoline station attendants, hotel clerks, and other persons who are directly in contact with the visitor are given indoctrination on the importance of tourism to their community and are taught the location of important points of interest. Other parts of the program include the importance of appearance and good grooming, greeting of visitors, providing information, and being helpful, gracious, friendly, and cooperative.

Cultural programs such as "Meet the Danes" (home visitation arrangements) help greatly in this respect. Adequate training of personnel by tourist hospitality businesses can also create the desired hospitable attitude.

Activities Tourists Enjoy Most

One of the most important functions of a tourism promotion organization is to ascertain what activities visitors would enjoy. When substantial data are accumulated, the findings should be reported to those who accommodate and entertain. They are thus guided into more successful methods and programs.

The best method of obtaining this information is by interviewing both the visitors and their hosts. Questionnaires can also be placed in guests' rooms. Public contact employees can be instructed to inquire politely as to guests' interests and entertainment preferences. Careful recording and thorough analysis of these data will result in findings of real value. When those responsible for attracting and hosting visitors provide the requested entertainment activities, the community will likely be a preferred destination area. There is no better advertising than a satisfied visitor (see Chapter 17).

Shopping

Shopping is an important tourist activity and thus an essential element in the tourism supply as it affects the success of the tourist destination area. The most important single element in shopping is the authenticity of the products offered for sale as they relate to the local area. A product that is supposedly a "native handicraft" should be that. If it is an import, the purchaser may be disappointed if he or she expected an authentic, locally made item.

Tourists who are shopping are particularly interested in handicraft items that are typical or indigenous to the particular locale or region. Of course, they are also interested in essential items such as toothpaste, but our discussion here is confined to purchases that tourists make as souvenirs or special gifts.

Tourists can be encouraged to spend more money on shopping if displays are high quality, imaginative, and attractive. Hotels are excellent places for shops, and if these shops are exquisitely furnished and stocked, the tourist is attracted to the shop and is more likely to make purchases.

NATIVE MARKETPLACES   Another shopping experience concerns the local market or so-called "native marketplace." Such areas are rich in ethnicity and have much local color. They are popular with visitors, even though the visitor may not understand the language and may have trouble making a purchase. Although many persons in native shopping places do not understand any foreign languages, the sign language of bargaining is fairly universal.

SHOPS AND CLERKS   Shopkeepers and clerks themselves should be amiable and courteous. Furthermore, the shopkeeper should not be so anxious to close a sale that the

Tourism is a "people" industry, and cheerful, friendly service makes visits memorable. (Photo by Fred W. Marvel; courtesy of Oklahoma Tourism Department)

tourist is pressured. A tourist who is courteously served in a store and who makes a good purchase will tell friends back home. Thus, future business can be developed in this way. Salespeople should also take the time to explain the value of the item and relate something of its history that would be otherwise unknown to the purchaser. Of course, this information should be accurate and truthful.

Salespersons must have sufficient language ability to conduct conversations with the visitors. The most common language is English, but a knowledge of other languages that are commonly spoken by tourists who visit a particular area is a necessary qualification of clerks who serve these visitors. Salespersons must be patient and understanding and try to help the prospective purchaser cheerfully at all times.

PRICES AND UNETHICAL PRACTICES   One of the most important considerations in shopping is the pricing of the goods. Probably resented more than any other single factor of tourism is higher prices for tourists than for local residents. Since many shoppers compare prices from one store to another, prices should be as consistent as possible and in line with costs.

If the shopkeeper resorts to unethical methods of selling such as deception, selling imitation goods or products of inferior quality, refusing to exchange damaged goods, or short-changing or short-weighting, the seller is hurting the tourist trade and should be prosecuted by local authorities.

Entertainment, Recreation, and Other Activities

The recreation and other activities engaged in by tourists at their destination comprise a major component of tourism. Thus considerable thought and effort should be devoted to the type of activities that visitors are likely to enjoy.

ENTERTAINMENT   The most satisfying entertainment for visitors is native to the area. In any country, there are expressions of the culture in the music, dance, drama, poetry, literature, motion pictures, television, ceremonies, festivals, exhibits, shows, meetings, food and beverage services, and tours (or local excursions) that portray the best the area has to offer.

Not all forms of entertainment can be successfully described or illustrated in tourist promotional literature. One of the best ways to bring these entertainment opportunities to the attention of the visitor is with a social director whose desk is in the lobby of hotels, resorts, and other forms of accommodation so that the visitor can readily find out what is going on and make arrangements to attend. In European hotels this desk is traditionally staffed by the concierge who provides an amazing amount of information concerning all types of entertainment and activities available. An appropriate substitute is a knowledgeable person at the front desk to provide information concerning recreation and entertainment.

Bulletin board displays or posters and verbal announcements of outstanding events made in the dining room or other areas where guests gather can also provide entertainment information. A local newspaper that features articles concerning everyday as well as special entertainment events and opportunities is a valuable method of distributing information. These newspapers or bulletins are presently provided in popular vacation destination areas such as Miami Beach and Honolulu, but the idea is not widespread. In metropolitan centers, a weekly magazine is normally provided

An important component of supply is the availability of entertainment and historical resources. The Yukon Follies Review features a cast of Yukon characters, including Klondike Kate and Sergeant Preston. (Photo courtesy of the Disneyland Hotel)

to hotel guests to give current information on entertainment, recreational, and cultural opportunities in the city.

SPECIAL EVENTS   Entertainment can be provided very effectively as a special promotional event to attract visitors during an off-season. One of the best examples of this is "Aloha Week," which was inaugurated in Hawaii in the early 1960s to bolster tourist traffic in the fall. This festival is enthusiastically supported by local tourism interests and is very successful in attracting tourists. Musicians, dancers, exhibits, floral displays, and special programs are assembled and give the visitor an unusual opportunity to enjoy the beauty and excitement of cultural expression that this state offers. Once created, such events become annual and typically grow in visitors and importance. Expositions and festivals are very attractive to visitors and deserve adequate promotion.

MUSEUMS AND ART GALLERIES   Museums and art galleries are another major attraction for tourists. They provide some of the highlights in many of the world's most important tourist destinations such as New York, Washington, D.C., Chicago, Paris, London, Madrid, Rome, Singapore, Tokyo, Buenos Aires, Mexico City, and many others. The quality and magnitude of these institutions are an important consideration for attracting and satisfying tourists.

SPORTS   Golf and sports such as tennis, surfing, swimming, mountain climbing, skiing, hunting, fishing, hiking, prospecting, or any other outdoor sports activity require properly publicized facilities and services. Guides, equipment, charter boats, and other

The musical productions at Opryland theme park feature Country Music U.S.A., tracing the history of country music. (Photo courtesy of the Tennessee Tourist Development)

Western culture in Canada and the United States provides resources of great interest to most visitors. Bareback bronco riding is a featured event in many localities. (Photo courtesy of the Wyoming Division of Tourism)

Located in the San Jose Plaza, the Pablo Casals Museum is a tribute to the renowned cellist/composer Pablo Casals, who spent the last 20 years of his life in Puerto Rico. The museum houses his cello, manuscripts, photographs, and library of videotapes of Casals Festival concerts. (Photo courtesy of the Puerto Rico Tourism News Bureau)

services needed to enjoy these sports must be readily available at fair prices. Convenience and accessibility are key factors in this type of entertainment.

MATCHING SUPPLY WITH DEMAND

Providing an ample tourism supply to meet anticipated demand is a challenge for the planner. Supply functions are always constrained by demand. The following formula can be used to calculate the number of hotel rooms (or other types of lodging) required:

$$\text{room demand per night} = \frac{\text{no. tourists} \times \% \text{ staying in hotels} \times \text{average length of stay}}{365 \times \text{average no. persons per room}}$$
(100% occupancy)

$$R = \frac{T \times P \times L}{S \times N}$$

where

T = number of tourists

P = percentage staying in hotels

N = average number of persons per room (obtained from hoteliers); this is the total number of guest nights divided by the number of guests, during any period of time

R = room demand per night, at 100 percent occupancy

O = hotel occupancy used for estimating (for 70 percent occupancy); divide number of rooms needed at 100 percent occupancy by 70 percent

S = number of days per year in business

L = average length of stay

Illustration of application of the formula:

T = 1,560,000 visitors

P = 98%

L = 9 days

N = 1.69

O = 70%

S = 365 days per year open for business

$$R = \frac{1{,}560{,}000 \times 0.98 \times 9}{365 \times 1.69} = \frac{13{,}759{,}200}{616.85} = 22{,}306 \text{ (rooms needed at 100\% occupancy)}$$

$$= \frac{22{,}306}{0.70} \text{ (as more rooms will be needed at 70\% occupancy than at 100\%)}$$

$$= 31{,}866 \text{ rooms needed}$$

Infrastructure factors in supply will be determined largely by the number of guest rooms as well as restaurants, stores, and similar installations. Infrastructure appropriate to the size of the development is an engineering problem and is readily ascertained as the plans are developed. Transportation equipment is generally supplied by commercial firms as well as publicly owned or quasi-public transportation facilities and services.

Regarding hospitality resources, the recruiting and training of staff for the various elements of supply is a critical one. The traveler generally enjoys being served by unsophisticated local persons who have had proper training and possess a hospitable attitude. Such persons may be recruited through government and private employment agencies as well as through direct advertisement to the public. Newly hired employees must be indoctrinated in the importance of tourism, how it affects their own personal welfare as well as that of their community, the importance of proper service to the visitors, and how their economic welfare is closely related to their performance.

Museums, art exhibits, festivals, craft shows, and similar cultural resources are usually created by community cooperation and the willing assistance of talented people. A chamber of commerce or tourism body is the best mechanism for organizing the creation of these hospitality resources.

Task Analysis

The procedure used in matching supply with demand is called a task analysis. Suggested steps are as follows:

1. *Identification of the present demand*
   a. By mode of transportation and by seasons of the year
   b. For various forms of tourism such as activities, attendance at attractions, and similar categories
   c. For special events such as conventions, celebrations, fairs
   d. Group and tour visitors

      e. Family and individual visitors

      f. Business visitors

2. *A quantitative and qualitative inventory of the existing supply*
3. *The adequacy of present supply with present demand*
   a. Natural resources
   b. Infrastructure
   c. Transportation and equipment
   d. Hospitality and cultural resources
4. *Examination of present markets and the socioeconomic trends*
   a. Geographic market segmentation and orientation
   b. Demographic market segmentation and orientation
     (1) Population age, sex, occupation, family life stages, income, and similar data
     (2) Leisure time and work patterns
   c. Psychographic market segmentation
     (1) Motivations, interests, hobbies, employment orientation, skills, professional interests
     (2) Propensity to travel, responsiveness to advertising
5. *Forecast of tourism demand*
   a. Computer systems simulation method
   b. Trend analysis
   c. Simple regression—linear least squares
   d. Multiple regression—linear least squares
   e. Executive judgment or Delphi method
6. *Matching supply with anticipated demand*
   a. If adequate, no further action necessary
   b. If inadequate, inauguration of planning and development procedures

To perform the task analysis, certain skills are required, with statistical research techniques employed to identify and quantify the present demand. Suggestions for doing this are provided in Chapter 13.

When making a quantitative and qualitative inventory of the existing supply, the aid of specialists and experts is usually needed. For example, the adequacy of the present supply in relation to present demand requires the work of tourism specialists such as travel agents, tour company and hotel executives, tourism promotion people, ground operators (companies that provide baggage transfers, taxi services, local tours, and similar services), shopkeepers, and perhaps a sample of the tourists themselves.

Examining the present markets and the socioeconomic trends that will affect future markets requires specialized market research activities. These should include determination of market characteristics, development of market potentials, market share analysis, sales analysis, competitive destination studies, potentials of the existing and possibly new markets, short-range forecasting, and studies of travel business trends. A number of sophisticated techniques are now available. The engagement of a reputable market research firm is one way to obtain this information.

Forecasting tourism demand is a perilous business. However, a well-structured statistical analysis coupled with executive judgment is most likely the best approach to this difficult problem. See Chapter 13 for several methods for accomplishing this.

Finally, matching supply with the anticipated demand must be done by knowledgeable planners. A tourism development plan within the master plan is recommended. Supply items are essentially rigid. They are elaborate and expensive and, thus, cannot be expanded rapidly. An exception would be transportation equipment. Additional sections of planes, buses, trains, or cars could be assembled quite rapidly to meet an unusually high-demand situation.

Peaks and Valleys

The foregoing discussion dealt with matching supply and demand in a long-run context. Another important consideration is that of fluctuations in demand in the short run (seasonality) and the resulting peaks and valleys in demand. This is a vexing problem.

The reason for this is simply that tourism is a service and services cannot be placed in inventory. If a 400-room hotel rents (sells) 350 rooms on a particular night, it cannot place the other 50 rooms in inventory, for sale the following night. Regardless of how many rooms went unoccupied in the past, a 400-room property can only rent up to 400 rooms on any given night. By way of contrast, consider the case of some tangible good, say, television sets. If some television sets are not sold in one month, the storekeeper can keep them in inventory and sell them the next month. Of course, the storage charges, interest payments, and other expenses incurred in inventorying a particular item reduces the item's economic value. But in tourism, the economic value of unsold items such as the 50 hotel rooms mentioned is exactly *zero*.

It should be clear then, that while in most cases, firms selling tangible goods can deal with demand fluctuation through the inventory process, this option is not available to firms providing travel services. In the travel industry, an effort must be made to reduce seasonal fluctuations as much as possible. Because of the high economic cost involved, no effort should be spared in attempting to limit the amount of seasonal variations in demand. Nor can the problem be dealt with by simply selecting an appropriate supply level. The following charts illustrate various supply situations associated with fluctuating demand levels.

Suppose that the demand for a particular destination exhibits the seasonal pattern depicted in Figure 12.1a. If no action is taken to "level off" the demand, then three possible levels of supply can be considered. In Figure 12.1b, the level of supply is provided so that demand in the peak season is fully satisfied. This implies that tourists coming to the destination in the peak season will be accommodated comfortably and without overcrowding. However, during the slack season, the destination will suffer from extremely low occupancy levels, with obvious implications for profitability. If, on the other hand, the supply is set at a low level (Figure 12.1c), the facilities during the peak season will be overcrowded enough to detract from the tourist experience. Visitor satisfaction will be at a low level, and the future of such a resort area will be doubtful. Last, if supply is set in between the level of demand during the peak and the off season (Figure 12.1d), the problems are somewhat mitigated. Nevertheless, low occupancy will result during low demand periods, and overcrowding will result in peak periods—neither is desirable. To maximize customer satisfaction and to utilize the facilities year around, some action must be taken. Two strategies for dealing with this situation are:

1. *Multiple use.* This involves supplementing peak-season attractions of a destination with other attractions that would create demand for travel to that destination during off-season periods. In effect, the peak season for the destination is extended.

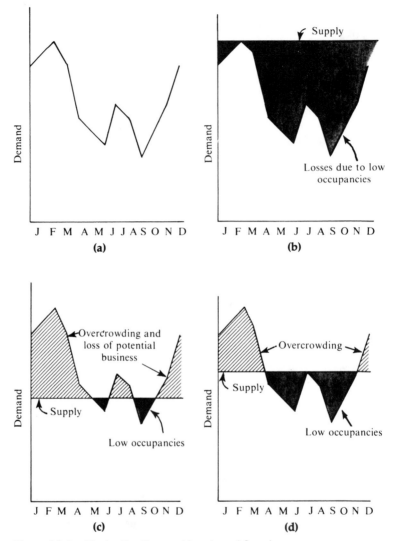

Figure 12.1   Fluctuating Demand Levels and Supply

Examples of such efforts abound. In Michigan, for example, the current demand for off-season travel (during the fall, winter, and spring) has been successfully increased and sustained at much higher levels than 10 years ago. While Michigan was once viewed primarily as a summer destination, the development and promotion of winter sports in resort areas, foliage tours, and superb salmon fishing in the fall and spring have created new markets for these off-season periods. Festivals, special celebrations, conventions, and sports activities sponsored and promoted during off-seasons are other examples of multiple-use strategies.

2. *Price differential.* This technique, as contrasted with the multiple-use strategy, creates new markets for the off-season periods by employing price differentials as a strong

tool to shift demand away from the peak season in favor of the off-season. Florida and destinations in the Caribbean have used this strategy rather effectively. The prices in these destinations during the off-seasons are considerably less than during the peak seasons. In addition, the development of promotional fares by airlines and other carriers, and the expansion of the number, timing, and variety of price-discounted tours have all helped to stimulate demand in the off-season. Increased efficiency and effectiveness of promotional campaigns and better marketing also tend to offset the traditional seasonal patterns of demand.

In addition to these strategies implemented by destination areas, some trends in the employment and leisure patterns of Western societies contribute further to the leveling of demand between off and peak seasons. The staggering of holidays, the increasing popularity of three-day weekends with a holiday on Friday or Monday, the splitting of vacations between various seasons of the year all lend themselves to leveling the demand for travel. Once the demand is evened out, the destination is then able to maximize customer satisfaction during the peak season *and* during the off-season. Also, facilities are utilized at a considerably higher level than previously. The importance of boosting off-season demand and, therefore, utilization level is further underscored by the fact that in most tourist service businesses, fixed costs are quite high in relation to operating costs. This implies that increasing total yearly revenue, even modestly, produces proportionally larger profits. There may be some softening of demand during the peak season due to those who might switch to the off-season because of the lower prices (see Figure 12.2). However, this is believed to be minimal. When off-season demand is boosted by the multiple-use strategy, peak season demand is unaffected. Therefore, overall demand for the entire year will be substantially higher (see Figure 12.3).

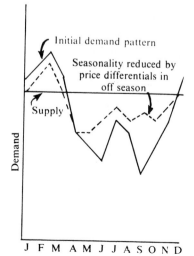

Figure 12.2   Reducing Seasonality Through Price Differentials

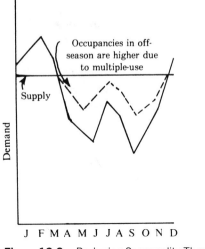

Figure 12.3 Reducing Seasonality Through Multiple Use

SUMMARY

Certain broad classifications of supply components must be provided by any area that is attractive to tourists. The components consist of natural resources, infrastructure, transportation-transport equipment, and hospitality and cultural resources. These factors may be combined in many ways to create the environment, facilities, and services that the planners hope will attract and please the customers.

Creation of supply components necessarily involves financing—a critical element. Ideally, all the supply components perfectly match the demand at any given time. However, this is unrealistic. Too much supply means unused facilities, which is uneconomic. Too little supply results in overcrowding with resultant depreciation of the vacation experience. A moderate supply level is recommended.

Supply can be matched with demand using a mathematical formula. When confronted with a supply problem, the proper level of supply to meet the anticipated demand can be estimated by using the formula provided in this chapter. The process is refined and completed by a six-step task analysis.

Key Concepts

accommodations

cultural resources

entertainment, recreation, and other activities

financing

government-financed components

hospitality resources

hotel management

infrastructure

multiple use

natural resources

peaks and valleys of demand

price differentials

reducing seasonality

regional planning

seasonality

shopping

supply components   total planning effort
task analysis   transportation
timesharing

For Review and Discussion

1. In planning supply components for a development in an entirely new area, which one of the four components should be considered first? Last? Why?
2. When a gorgeous new hotel is opened for business, are the attractive physical facilities more important than the quality and training of the staff?
3. As a resort hotel manager, do you believe there is any need to educate your guests about environmental protection? Is there a need to educate your staff?
4. In a poor, developing country, a world-class hotel uses about half of the community's water supply. This requires rationing of water by the local people, which creates resentment. Suggest a partial solution to this problem.
5. For new developments, should the access roads be supplied by a government agency, the developer, or both? If both, who should supply what?
6. What might be appropriate costumes and uniforms for waiters and waitresses in various localities?
7. A motor hotel manager states, "I can't seem to sell any souvenirs that cost over $5." How could this situation be improved?
8. The sports director of a large resort hotel has been instructed to upgrade the hotel's physical fitness program. Provide some suggestions as to how this might be done.
9. Is changing the prices of hotel rooms, meals, and entertainment the best way to mitigate fluctuating levels of demand? Are there nonprice methods? Could combinations of methods be used?

Case Problems

1. To maintain and hopefully enhance the appeal and quality of its area's natural resources, the city council had decided it needs to enact protective laws to help ensure its future tourism success. What specific laws and regulations might these be?
2. Resort City is anxious to attract more tourists. The chamber of commerce has been successful in attracting several new tourist firms to the community. These firms plan to develop new hotels, motels, shops, and restaurants. However, an influential member of the chamber of commerce expresses the viewpoint that the community should enact some strict zoning and building code laws before these construction projects get under way. The prospective developers and many other members of the chamber disagree. What do you think should be done to resolve this situation, and why?
3. A national tourism organization is seeking ways in which to improve the proficiency of accommodations management. It is exploring the possibility of installing a computer-based accommodations information system. This system provides data comparisons between similar operations considering size, location, and countrywide averages. What do you see as advantages for implementing such a system? How might the system be implemented in your country? What other management improvement incentives or programs could be provided?

Selected References

Arbel, Avner, and Abraham Pizam. "Some Determinants of Urban Hotel Location: The Tourist Inclinations." *Journal of Travel Research*, Vol. 15, No. 3 (Winter 1977), pp. 18–22.

Bonn, Mark A., H Leslie Furr, and Muzaffer Uysal. "Seasonal Variation of Coastal Resort Visitors: Hilton Head Island." *Journal of Travel Research*, Vol. 31, No. 1 (Summer 1992), pp. 50–56.

Clawson, Marion, and Jack L. Knetsch. *Economics of Outdoor Recreation.* Baltimore: Johns Hopkins University Press, 1966.

Maguire, Patricia A. "Tourism Supply: A U.S. Perspective." *Tourist Review*, No. 3 (July/September 1990), pp. 2–6.

Manning-Shaw, Janet. "The Channel Tunnel." *Tourism Management*, Vol. 12, No. 1 (March 1991), pp. 5–7.

McCool, Stephen F. "Recreation Use Limits: Issues for the Tourism Industry." *Journal of Travel Research*, Vol. 17, No. 2 (Fall 1978), pp. 2–7.

Smith, Stephen L. "Room for Rooms: A Procedure for the Estimation of Potential Expansion of Tourist Accommodations." *Journal of Travel Research*, Vol. 15, No. 4 (Spring 1977), pp. 26–29.

Travel Signing in Oregon. Salem, Oreg.: Oregon Tourism Division, 1989.

Trowbridge, Keith W. *Resort Timesharing.* New York: Simon and Schuster, 1981.

Var, Turgut, R. A. D. Beck, and Patrick Loftus. "Determination of Tourist Attractiveness of the Tourist Areas in British Columbia." *Journal of Travel Research*, Vol. 15, No. 3 (Winter 1977), pp. 23–29.

Waddell, Joseph M. "Hotel Capacity: How Many Rooms to Build?" *Cornell Hotel and Restaurant Administration Quarterly*, Vol. 18, No. 2 (August 1977), pp. 35–47.

World Bank. *Tourism Supply in the Caribbean Region.* Washington, D.C.: The Bank, November 1974.

CHAPTER 13

Measuring and Forecasting Demand

LEARNING OBJECTIVES

- Know the definition of demand and its application and importance in tourism development planning.
- Understand the factors determining the magnitude and fluctuations of demand.
- Become able to apply various methods to measure and forecast demand.

Economists define demand as a schedule of the amount of any product or service that people are willing and able to buy at each specific price in a set of possible prices during some specified period of time. Thus there exists at any one time a definite relationship between the market price and the quantity demanded.

WHY DEMAND IS IMPORTANT

The amount of demand for travel to a particular destination is of great concern to anyone involved in tourism. Vital demand data include (1) how many visitors arrived, (2) by what means of transportation, (3) how long they stayed and in what type of accommodations, and (4) how much money was spent. There are various measures of demand; some are much easier to obtain and are usually of more general interest than are others. Techniques also exist for making forecasts of future demand. Such estimates are of great interest to anyone planning future tourism developments. The availability of financing will depend largely on reliable forecasts of the future gross sales or revenues from the project to determine if the proposal will be financially feasible.

Marketing and sales promotion programs are, of course, aimed at increasing demand. Sometimes this effort focuses on increasing demand at certain times of the year or to a particular market. But the basic purpose is the same—to increase demand.

DEMAND TO A DESTINATION

In somewhat more specific terms, the demand for travel to a particular destination will be a function of the person's propensity to travel and the reciprocal of the resistance of the link between origin and destination areas. Thus

$$D = f(\text{propensity, resistance})$$

where D is demand.

Propensity can be thought of as a person's predisposition to travel: in other words, how willing the person is to travel, what types of travel experiences he or she prefers, and what types of destinations are considered. A person's propensity to travel will, quite obviously, be determined largely by his or her psychographic profile and travel motivation, as discussed in previous chapters. In addition, a person's socioeconomic status will have an important bearing on propensity. It follows that to estimate a person's propensity to travel, we must understand both psychographic and demographic variables concerning the person. Propensity is *directly* related to demand.

Resistance, on the other hand, relates to the relative attractiveness of various destinations. This factor is, in turn, a function of several other variables, such as economic distance, cultural distance, the cost of tourist services at destination, the quality of service at destination, effectiveness of advertising and promotion, and seasonality. Resistance is *inversely* related to demand.

Economic Distance

Economic distance relates to the time and cost involved in traveling from the origin to the destination area and back. The higher the economic distance, the higher the resistance for that destination, and consequently, the lower the demand. It follows, conversely, that between any origin and destination point, if the travel time or travel cost can be reduced, demand will increase. Many excellent examples of this are available, such as the introduction of the jet plane in 1959 and the introduction of the wide-bodied jets in the late 1960s. They first cut travel time between California and Hawaii, for example, from 12 hours to 5 hours, and demand grew dramatically. A similar surge in demand was experienced with the introduction of the wide-bodied planes for transatlantic flights. The introduction of these planes cut the travel cost by almost 50 percent between the United States and most countries of the European continent.

Cultural Distance

Cultural distance refers to the extent to which the culture of the area from which the tourist originates differs from the culture of the host region. In general, the greater the cultural distance, the greater will be the resistance. In some cases, however, the relationship might be the opposite. For example, the higher the cultural distance between particular origin and destination areas, the more an allocentric person may wish to travel to that destination, to experience this extreme difference.

Cost of Services

The higher the cost of services at a destination, the higher the resistance to travel to that destination will be and, therefore, the lower the demand. This variable captures the familiar inverse relationship between the price of a good or service and demand for it.

Quality of Service

Clearly, the higher the quality of service at a destination, the lower the resistance will be for travel to that destination. Although the relationship between quality of service and demand is straightforward enough, a difficulty arises in the interpretation and evaluation of "quality." Evaluation of quality is a highly personal matter, and what is quality to one tourist is not necessarily quality to another. Second, if a tourist does not have previous travel experience at a destination, can the tourist accurately judge the quality of services there? In such a case, the tourist must select a destination based on what the quality of service is *perceived* to be. Often, due to misleading advertisements or inaccurate input from others, the tourist's perception of the quality of service may not be realized at the destination. Such a situation has serious implications for establishing a repeat clientele, which is an important ingredient for success in the tourist business. Consequently, a destination area must be meticulous in projecting an accurate image.

Seasonality

The effect of seasonality on demand is quite apparent. The relative attractiveness of a given destination will depend on the time of year for which a vacation is planned. For a ski resort, for example, the demand will be at the highest level during the winter months. Resistance is at a minimum in this season.

The following illustrates the relationship between propensity, resistance, and demand, in terms of these variables as just described:

$$\text{demand} = f(\text{propensity, resistance})$$

Propensity depends on:
Psychographics
Demographics (socioeconomic status)
Marketing effectiveness

Resistance depends on:
Economic distance
Cultural distance
Cost of tourist services
Quality of service
Seasonality

MEASURING DEMAND

Demand is strongly affected and limited by the supply. If the supply aspects are not taken into consideration when using demand figures, planners might be led into false assumption that in a particular area, the supply should be increased to meet the demand when, in actuality, the increased supply may be needed much more elsewhere.

There are several measures of actual demand:

1. Visitor arrivals
2. Visitor-days or visitor-nights
3. Amounts spent

Visitor Arrivals

Simply counting the number of people who arrive at a destination is a measure of demand, although not a particularly adequate one. However, when visitors arrive by ship or aircraft, for example, to an island, quite accurate data are obtainable. Those who

Convenience creates demand. Visitors are shown bound for the slopes of Steamboat, Colorado, after deplaning from their direct flight to Yampa Valley Regional Airport. Three carriers, American Airlines, Northwest Airlines, and American West Airlines, fly nonstop to Steamboat from six different cities, helping Steamboat increase skier visits. (Photo by Larry Pierce; courtesy of Steamboat)

are en route to someplace else should not be included in the arrival data. Visitor arrivals are the easiest type of data to obtain, especially if public transportation is the principal mode used. Regular reporting of visitor arrivals is of value in measuring broad changes in demand. Variation in the number of arrivals month by month is quite significant as it indicates the rise and fall of demand during the course of a year.

Arrival data become more of a problem if a large proportion of visitors arrive by private automobile on many major highways. In this case, a sampling method is employed, sometimes involving a tourist information center. Those stopping at the center are asked to fill out a card with data about their trip. The total number of visitors is then estimated, based on the sample obtained.

Visitors coming through seaports should be classified according to the United Nations' definition of tourists and excursionists. Excursionists remain in an area for less than 24 hours; tourists stay 24 hours or longer. Arrival statistics should not include those who illegally enter the country, air travelers who do not leave the airport transit area, or analogous cases.

Visitor-Days or Visitor-Nights

Data on visitor-days and visitor-nights are much more valuable to tourism planners than are data on the number of arrivals. To calculate the former, the number of visitors is multiplied by their average length of stay. Public park planners and beach managers are interested in visitor-day figures. Hotel and other accommodations people want data on visitor-nights. When such data are obtained, it is not difficult to make an estimate of the likely expenditures made per visitor per day or night. But these expenditure figures are at best only estimates and need to be used carefully. Data on visitor-days and visitor-nights are of great benefit to planners who are working on public facilities for tourists such as utility systems, parking, and recreation areas. Similarly, private developers planning new hotels or other accommodations or services want and need visitor-night information. Thus visitor-days and/or visitor-nights are the most practical data to obtain and are useful to tourism people.

$$D = \text{no. of visitors} \times \text{av. no. of days or nights at destination}$$

Amounts Spent

Amount spent is the most meaningful measure of demand if determined accurately. However, it is the *most difficult measure* to obtain. Statistics of this type tend to be hidden or partially forgotten by the visitor. Thus they are not as accurate as desired. However, to members of legislatures and the public, total tourist expenditures are the most easily understood and the most impressive.

The most common method of estimating tourist expenditures is to multiply visitor-days or visitor-nights by the average per day or per night expenditure. Thus

$$D(\$) = \text{no. of visitor-days or visitor-nights} \times \text{avg. expenditures per day/night}$$

Total expenditures in an area consists of the visitor-day and visitor-night total expenditures over a specified period of time.

Measuring Tourism Expenditures Through Tax Collections

Many states have a sales and use tax on consumer items. These tax collections provide a statistical base for calculating tourist expenditures. Suppose that a state has a 4 percent use tax on hotel and motel rooms. If we know what percentage of the average tourist dollar is spent for lodging, we could make an estimate of how much is spent on lodging and total expenditures, as illustrated in the following hypothetical example:

Rooms tax collections   = $5 million
Rooms use tax rate   = 4 percent
Total lodging spending = $5 million ÷ 0.04 = $125 million
Lodging expenditures   = 25 percent of total spending
Total expenditures   = $125 million ÷ 0.25 = $500 million (visitor-nights)

Estimated spending of those not using commercial lodging
+ visitor-day spending   = $600 million

$$\text{Total } D(\$) = \$500 \text{ million} + \$600 \text{ million} = \$1.1 \text{ billion}$$

Research in Measuring Demand

Considerable interest exists in improving methods of measuring current demand. Tourism is a labor-intensive service industry. As such, it is looked upon by state governments as a promising business to relieve unemployment. But one of the main problems is to determine its present financial dimensions.

Official tourism organizations are typically charged with the responsibility of undertaking research to measure economic impact and current demand. In this task they are assisted greatly by the U.S. Travel Data Center. Details on research are provided in Chapter 17. The next research task is to make an estimate of what the future demand might be should certain steps be taken by the destination area.

PROJECTION METHODOLOGY

Several statistical methods or econometric analyses can be used to project demand. All require a degree of statistical or mathematical sophistication, familiarity with computers, and a clear understanding of the purpose (and limitations) of such projections. Listed are several such methods with brief explanations. (For a more complete review, see the references at the end of this chapter.)

Trend Analysis Method

This method involves the interpretation of historical demand data. For instance, if a record of the number of tourist arrivals in an area on an annual basis is available, then demand for future years can be projected using this information. The first step is to plot the available data on a graph—time (in years) against the tourist arrivals. Once this has been done, a linear trend can be established, which best captures the changes in demand levels in the past. Demand projections for future years can now be made by extending the trend line up to the relevant year and reading the demand estimate off the graph. Figure 13.1 illustrates this procedure. The points represent the levels of demand for the six-year period for which data are available.

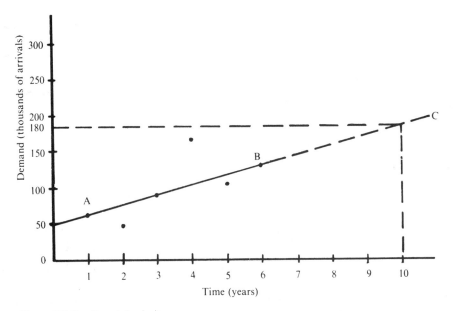

Figure 13.1 Trend Analysis

A linear trend in demand levels can then be determined (say, line *AB*). If a demand projection for year 10 were needed, the trend line *AB* can be extended to a point such as *C*. Finally, the projected demand level in year 10 can be determined to be approximately 180,000 arrivals as shown in Figure 13.1.

The advantage of using trend analysis is that the data needed are rather basic and easy to obtain. Only one data series is required—visitor arrivals, or some other measure of demand on a quarterly or on an annual basis for the past few years. In addition, the method is simple and does not require a great deal of mathematical sophistication. Characteristically, however, the simplicity of the model is to a large extent a trade-off for the usefulness of the results. For instance, the future demand estimates obtained in this manner should be interpreted with a great deal of caution. There are several reasons for this. First, trend analysis does not "explain" demand in any way. In other words, if demand changes from year to year, we would expect this to be due to changes in the components of demand (propensity and resistance, as discussed earlier in this chapter). Trend analysis does not acknowledge the influence that these variables have on demand levels and, therefore, cannot explain why it changed. Second, to *extrapolate* from a linear trend (extending the trend line *AB* to point *C*) is to assume that past growth trends will continue without change. Such an assumption is tentative at best. Estimates based on a constant growth rate tend to become very unrealistic in rather short periods of time, due to the nature of compounding.

Simple Regression: Linear Least Squares Method

In this method, information on demand levels for past years is plotted against one important determinant of demand, say, income or prices. Then, through the application of a statistical technique called least squares regression, a straight line is used to "explain" the relationship between demand and the particular variable being considered (such as income levels of tourists). Consider, for example, the hypothetical data in Table 13.1 for demand levels for 10 years and the income levels of tourists for these same years.

By plotting the pairs of arrivals—income data on a graph—we obtain a relationship

Table 13.1   Demand and Income Data

Year	Number of Tourist Arrivals (thousands)	Per Capita Income of Tourists
1	75	$6300
2	90	7200
3	100	7000
4	105	7400
5	95	6800
6	110	7500
7	105	7500
8	100	7200
9	110	7600
10	120	7900

between income and travel demand, illustrated in Figure 13.2. The points represent the annual observations, and the line *AB* represents the line of "best fit." It is obtained by the least squares method.

We can now obtain demand projections from this method based on what we *expect* income levels to be in the future. Suppose we wish to estimate demand for year 15. In this year, income is projected to be $8300 per capita. As shown in the figure, the estimate of demand for this income level is 128,000.

Since income is a major determinant of demand, simple regression "explains" demand to some extent. It is superior to trend analysis for this reason. Besides, the methodology is still relatively simple and can be presented visually. Data needed for this method are relatively easy to collect, when compared to the data needs of the two following projections methods.

Multiple Regression—Linear Least Squares Method

The major drawback of simple regression is that only one variable can be considered at a time. In reality, demand is affected by all the factors that influence propensity and

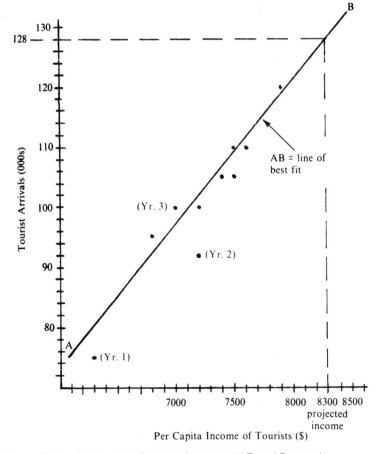

Figure 13.2   Relationship Between Income and Travel Demand

resistance, as discussed earlier. It may not be feasible to include all these variables at one time, but it is certainly practical to isolate a few that are particularly relevant to determining demand and deal with these in one model. Multiple regression is one way to do this. It is essentially the same as simple regression, except that now more than one variable can be used to explain demand. Through a mathematical formula, a relationship is established between demand and the variables that we have chosen to consider in the model. For example, suppose that we had data on the prices of tourist services at a destination in addition to the incomes of the tourists. We could then regress demand on these two variables (income and prices) and obtain a mathematical relationship between them. To estimate future demand, projected income and price levels for the relevant year can simply be substituted into the mathematical formula. The resulting estimate of demand will be more reliable than will one obtained by the simple regression method, since the former incorporates the *combined* effect of income and price on demand.

Indeed, the analysis is not restricted to these two variables alone. Conceptually, any number of variables can be used to explain and predict demand levels. But there are some practical limitations. As the number of "explanatory" variables increases, the calculations become increasingly complex. In addition, the costs involved in collecting the additional data and solving the mathematics of the technique are considerable. In some instances, the incremental reliability of the estimates may not justify these expenses, because estimates are after all estimates, and not certain to materialize—no matter how comprehensibly they may be calculated.

In addition to the expense involved, another drawback of multiple regression is that the relationships cannot be depicted graphically, as the results of the two earlier methods

Greatly increased demand for cruising has brought about a remarkable expansion in the number of cruise ships. (Photo courtesy of Cruise Lines International Association)

can be. The reason is, of course, that we get into multidimension planes. Up to three dimensions can be depicted visually, but beyond that, it becomes impossible.

Computer Simulations and Models

The essence of this approach is building a computer model that will simulate tourist demand. Typically, the demand for tourism to a particular area is a function of factors such as levels of income of tourists, the cost of travel from the tourists' homes to the destination, price levels, competition, currency exchange rates, and distance or journey time. These relationships are usually identified using multiple regression, as discussed above.

Simulation models include a complex set of equations that will usually combine both the trend-line extrapolation methods and the regression techniques models into a more comprehensive systems simulation. Relationships between many variables are specified through interrelated equations. Simulation models rely on historical data for input and model calibration. Once a model gives reasonably accurate distributions for past years, it can be used to predict probable future distributions.

Simulation models require specially trained personnel with a high degree of technical expertise to set up original model and data processing programs. Knowledge of time-series, cross-sectional, and causal relationships and change processes is required. Also, powerful computing resources and high data precision are necessary. These are

A primary factor in creating travel demand is satisfaction (and even enthusiasm) concerning the services received. If these have been top-notch, the traveler is likely to go again as soon as feasible and recommend the experience to friends and relatives. (Photo courtesy of United Airlines)

serious problems that have to be faced by any tourism organization that might consider using this approach. Simulation forecasting is best suited for a problem that is complex with known and quantifiable relationships and some feedback effects. It is also suitable for long forecast horizons.

Executive Judgment (Delphi) Method

Mathematical and statistical models are most useful and often produce accurate results. However, the combined experience of tourism executives is also valuable. The Delphi method, in essence, consists of a systematic survey of such experts. A series of questions is asked, and then the results, as a consensus, are reached.

Mathematical-statistical tools cannot incorporate the influences of variables not explicitly included in the model. For example, under multiple regression, income and travel prices were the only two variables used to predict demand. However, other factors such as the political situation, fuel situation, changes in taste, amounts of leisure, and the effectiveness of promotion campaigns obviously have an impact on demand levels. By the Delphi method, the combined effects of all such factors are carefully considered from the base of the executive's experience. For estimating tourism demand, then, *a combination of various mathematical statistical methods and the Delphi method* is believed to produce the most reliable demand estimates in any given situation.

SUMMARY

Demand, without doubt, is the fundamental measure of any area's success in attracting visitors. All planning activities are ultimately intended to increase or control demand. Marketing programs are aimed at increasing demand, sometimes at certain periods during the year, and/or to attract particularly identified market segments.

Understanding demand requires a knowledge of its definition, what comprises demand, what affects the levels of demand, and how future demand can be identified and estimated. Thus, use of demand data is essential in any tourist business situation.

Development of a destination area, whether by public authority, private developers, or both requires demand data that are as accurate as possible. Providing such data is one of the most important responsibilities of an official tourism organization. Similar data are provided by research organizations and consulting firms, usually when commissioned to make feasibility studies. Any development proposal must have ample estimates of expected demand before any financing can be committed.

Becoming familiar with methods of measuring or estimating present and future demand, as described in this chapter, should enable you to produce such data. With the current high cost of land and construction, reasonably accurate demand statistics are of paramount importance.

Key Concepts

amounts spent	cost of services
arrivals	cultural distance
computer simulation	demand forecasts (projection)

demand measures	resistance
economic distance	seasonality
executive judgment (Delphi method)	simple regression
increasing demand	tax collections
linear least squares method	trend analysis
multiple regression	visitors
projection methodology	visitor-days
propensity	visitor-nights
quality of service	

For Review and Discussion

1. Why are demand data so important? Give examples. By whom are demand data used?
2. Explain why resistance to make a trip is inversely related to demand. Are there situations with which you are familiar? Explain.
3. Describe in detail the three factors that determine propensity. Create an example using all three of these major elements.
4. What determines the degree of resistance to travel experiences? Considering the five factors described in this chapter, give an example involving (1) an irresistible travel offer, and (2) a seasonal travel product.
5. Using the three measures of demand presented, describe a situation in which each one of these would be the most meaningful.
6. A state tourism director wants to convince the legislature to increase the promotion budget for the next fiscal year. What measure of demand should be used? How might these data be obtained?
7. How much faith should be placed in mathematical models of demand projection? What characteristics of input data affect the degree of reliability?
8. A national lodging chain is planning expansion. What are the best methods for estimating future demand?
9. How valuable is trend analysis?
10. What is the Delphi method?
11. How would a free-trade zone affect travel demand?

Case Problems

1. The federal government has imposed an increase in the gasoline tax of 50 cents per gallon, effective in three months. How might a motel franchise headquarters organization estimate the effect on demand that this new tax would have for their member motels, which are located in all parts of the country? How could a restaurant chain organization operating turnpike food services make such an estimate? How could a regional airline?
2. Byron C. is director of development for a major hotel systems firm. His company has formulated a new concept in resort-type overnight and longer-stay accommodations. The new suites will possess an exciting array of electronic entertainment features, including a large screen, stereo sound, movies, compact discs, and cassette players. Understandably, these suites are quite expensive to build. Thus reasonably accurate

demand forecasts are essential. Byron C. has tentatively selected your city as a location for the first of these new suite concepts. As executive vice-president of your city's convention and visitors bureau, what method would you use to assist Mr. C. in making these crucial demand estimates?

Selected References

Calatone, Roger J., Anthony Di Benedetto, and David Bojanic. "A Comprehensive Review of the Tourism Forecasting Literature." *Journal of Travel Research,* Vol. 26, No. 2 (1987), pp. 28–39.

Johnson, Peter, and Barry Thomas. *Choice and Demand.* London: Mansell Publishing, 1992.

Mak, James. "Taxing Hotel Room Rentals in the U.S.?" *Journal of Travel Research,* Vol. 27, No. 1 (Summer 1988), pp. 10–15.

Morley, Clive L. "A Microeconomic Theory of International Tourism Demand." *Annals of Tourism Research,* Vol. 19, No. 2 (1992), pp. 250–267.

Ritchie, J. R. Brent, and Michael Sheridan. "Developing an Integrated Framework for Tourism Demand Data in Canada." *Journal of Travel Research,* Vol. 27, No. 1 (Summer 1988), pp. 3–9.

Smeral, Egon, and Stephen F. Witt. "The Impacts of Eastern Europe and 1992 on International Tourism Demand." *Tourism Management,* Vol. 13, No. 4 (December 1992), pp. 368–376.

U.S. Travel Data Center. *National Travel Survey: Full-Year Report.* Washington, D.C.: USTDC, annual.

U.S. Travel Data Center. 1994 *Outlook for Travel and Tourism.* Washington, D.C.: USTDC, 1993.

U.S. Travel Data Center. *Travel Printout.* Washington, D.C.: USTDC, monthly.

Uysal, Muzaffer, and John L. Crompton. "An Overview of Approaches Used to Forecast Tourism Demand." *Journal of Travel Research,* Vol. 23, No. 3 (Spring 1985), pp. 7–15.

Waters, Somerset R. *Travel Industry World Yearbook: The Big Picture.* New York: Child and Waters, annual.

Witt, Stephen F. "Tourism Forecasting: How Well Do Private and Public Sector Organizations Perform?" *Tourism Management,* Vol. 13, No. 1 (March 1992), pp. 79–84.

Witt, Stephen F., and Christine A. Martin. "Econometric Model for Forecasting International Tourism Demand." *Journal of Travel Research,* Vol. 25, No. 3 (Winter 1987), pp. 23–30.

Witt, Stephen F., and Christine A. Witt. *Modeling and Forecasting Demand in Tourism.* London: Academic Press, 1992.

Witt, Stephen F., Gerald D. Newbould, and Alan J. Watkins. "Forecasting Domestic Tourism Demand: Application to Las Vegas Arrivals Data." *Journal of Travel Research,* Vol. 31, No. 1 (Summer 1992), pp. 36–41.

14
Tourism's Economic Impact

LEARNING OBJECTIVES

- Know the economic generators and impact of tourism.
- Perceive the relationship between tourism, employment, and taxes.
- Understand multipliers.
- Know about balance of payments.
- Comprehend elasticity and inelasticity.

GENERATORS OF ECONOMIC IMPACT

The economic impact of tourist spending is a function of the numbers of domestic plus international visitors, their expenditures, and the various multipliers in that particular definition area.

NUMBER OF VISITORS

Figure 14.1 documents the number of person-trips of U.S. residents. Americans took nearly 1.06 billion person-trips during 1993, a decline of 0.5 percent from 1992. Person-trips basically leveled off after showing steady growth since 1984.

As in previous years, many 1993 travelers used auto/truck/RV transportation (75 percent), stayed in hotels and motels (49 percent), and ventured more than 900 miles round trip on an average trip. They traveled most often for pleasure: visiting friends and relatives, outdoor recreation, or entertainment (70 percent). In 1993, more than one-fourth of all person-trips (26 percent) were classified as business or convention travel, 60 percent were classified as vacation, and 54 percent were classified as weekend or long weekend trips.

Seven percent of all trips were day trips. On average, the traveler was away 3.9 nights per trip. The South Atlantic (22 percent) region was the most popular destination among 1993 travelers.

Figure 14.2 provides data on international visitors to the United States. International visitors have been one of the strongest growth areas in tourism. From 1986 to 1992, international visitors increased 71.5 percent. Preliminary estimates for 1993 predict 46.0 million visitors.

Expenditures

In 1992, domestic and international travelers spent $361.8 billion in the United States, for an increase of 5 percent over 1991 (Figure 14.3). This amount does not include $17.4 billion in international visitor spending on U.S. air carriers for transactions made outside

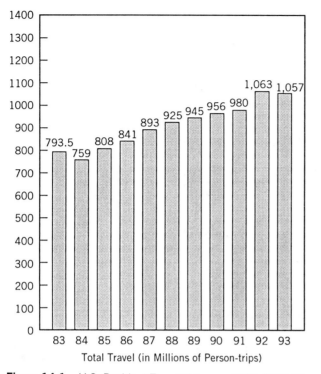

Total Travel (in Millions of Person-trips)

Figure 14.1 U.S. Resident Travel Volumes: 1983–1993 (*Source:* U.S. Travel Data Center's National Travel Survey)

the country. If these were included, spending would total almost $380 billion. International visitor spending continues to rise, increasing 11 percent in 1992 to $53.9 billion. Domestic expenditures rose by 4 percent, to a total of $307.9 billion. Based on expenditures, travel and tourism continues to be the nation's third largest retail industry after automotive dealers and food stores (see Table 14.1). Figure 14.3 shows the rise in U.S. travel expenditures from 1987 to 1992. Preliminary estimates for 1993 have been released by the U.S. Travel Data Center, indicating that tourism generated an estimated $397 billion in expenditures, with $75 billion attributed to international visitors.

Direct and Indirect Impact of Travel

Direct payments to supply components subsequently produces indirect economic impact on businesses that serve these suppliers. A good example would be a food jobber who provides food to a hotel. Figure 14.4 illustrates this impact in the United States for 1992.

Tax Receipts

Taxes imposed by federal, state, and local governments continue to make up a large share of travel expenditures. Domestic travelers generated $44.4 billion in tax receipts in 1992. Domestic travel expenditures produced $25.3 billion in federal taxes, $12.1

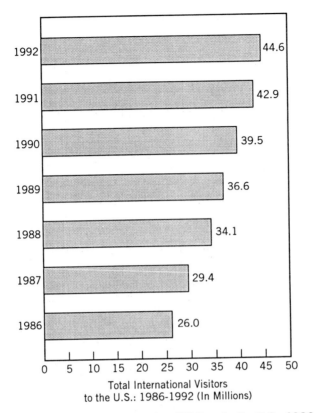

Year	Total International Visitors (Millions)
1992	44.6
1991	42.9
1990	39.5
1989	36.6
1988	34.1
1987	29.4
1986	26.0

Total International Visitors
to the U.S.: 1986-1992 (In Millions)

Figure 14.2 Total International Visitors to the U.S.: 1986–1992 (Millions) (*Source:* United States Travel and Tourism Administration)

billion in state taxes, and $7 billion in local taxes. International travelers produced another $7.2 billion in tax receipts, totaling $51.6 billion in revenue for federal, state, and local governments.

Employment

In 1992, the travel and tourism industry generated more than 6 million jobs in the United States, more than 5.5 percent of the total nonagricultural employment within the United States. Over 5.1 million of these jobs were supported by domestic tourism, while the spending of 44.6 million international visitors to the United States generated an additional 884,100 American jobs. This makes the travel and tourism industry a leading private employer, second only to health care services.

Table 14.2 illustrates employment by industry. The foodservice and lodging sectors provide the most jobs, with foodservice generating nearly 1.8 million, or about 35 percent of the total. Spending on lodging generated over 1 million jobs, or about 21 percent of the total.

Employment directly generated by travel has grown 56.3 percent in the last 10 years, more than twice as fast as the more modest 21 percent increase in total nonagricultural U.S. employment.

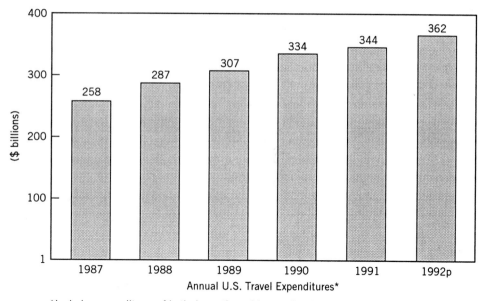

*Includes expenditures of both domestic and international visitors in the U.S.; does not include $17.4 billion in international visitor spending on U.S. carriers for transactions made outside the U.S. p = preliminary.

Source: U.S. Travel Data Center's Travel Economic Impact Model

Figure 14.3 Annual U.S. Travel Expenditures

Table 14.1. 1992 Preliminary U.S. Travel Expenditures

Expenditure Category[a]	Expenditures ($ billions)	Percent of U.S. Total	Percent Change from 1991
Food service	$75.76	24.6	6.4
Public transportation	70.90	23.0	2.9
Auto transportation[b]	52.77	17.1	−0.1
Lodging	52.24	17.0	4.0
Entertainment and recreation	29.85	9.7	7.0
General retail trade	26.40	8.6	6.9
U.S. Total	$307.92	100.0	4.1
International visitor generated	$53.90		11.3
Grand[c] Total	$361.82		5.1

[a]Does not include spending by international visitors and local residents.
[b]The auto transportation industry includes automotive dealers, gasoline service stations, automotive rental, and leasing without drivers.
[c]Does not include $17.4 billion in international visitor spending on U.S. air carriers for transactions made outside the U.S.
Source: U.S. Travel Data Center, U.S. Travel and Tourism Administration.

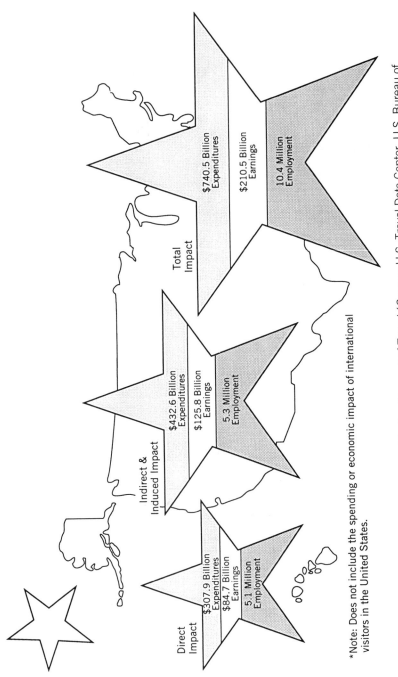

Figure 14.4 1992 Predicted Total Direct and Indirect Impact of Travel (*Source:* U.S. Travel Data Center, U.S. Bureau of Economic Analysis, Department of Commerce)

Total Impact

$740.5 Billion Expenditures

$210.5 Billion Earnings

10.4 Million Employment

Indirect & Induced Impact

$432.6 Billion Expenditures

$125.8 Billion Earnings

5.3 Million Employment

Direct Impact

$307.9 Billion Expenditures

$84.7 Billion Earnings

5.1 Million Employment

*Note: Does not include the spending or economic impact of international visitors in the United States.

Table 14.2 Direct Travel-Generated Employment by Industry Category (Employees in Thousands)

Category	Employment	Percent
Public transportation	843.7	16.4
Auto transportation	231.8	4.5
Lodging	1,068.9	20.8
Foodservice	1,779.7	34.6
Entertainment/Recreation	755.9	14.7
General retail	269.0	5.2
Travel planning	189.7	3.7
U.S. Total	5,138.4	100.0
International Visitors[a]	884.1	
Grand Total	6,022.5	

[a]International visitor spending data not available by category.
Source: U.S. Travel Data Center, U.S. Travel and Tourism Administration, 1992 preliminary figures.

Employment in major travel industry sectors has been forecast to grow in excess of 30 percent during the next 12 years. This compares very favorably to other major industries in the economy.

Table 14.3 shows U.S. domestic travel expenditures and employment by state for 1991, which is the latest information available on the state level.

OPTIMIZATION

Economics is concerned with the attainment of an optimum return from the use of scarce resources. Whether it is a person seeking psychological benefit from travel, or a business interested in providing tourists goods and services at a profit, or a host community government viewing tourism in terms of the economic benefits resulting from tourist expenditures, the principle is the same. Economic agents seek to fulfill psychological and physical wants (which, as a rule, are limited). The problem that economics attempts to solve is how these scarce resources should be allocated in the pursuit of a variety of unfulfilled needs and wants.

Goals

As indicated, at least three major goals can be identified in tourism:

1. Maximize the amount of psychological experience for tourists.
2. Maximize profits for firms providing goods and services to t+ourists.
3. Maximize the direct (primary) and indirect (secondary) impacts of tourist expenditures on a community or region.

These goals are often compatible; maximizing psychological experience creates happy clientele, which causes them to return, to spend money, and to make everyone in the industry and the region satisfied. In certain situations, they can also be incompatible. A short-run profit-maximizing goal may cause the development of facilities beyond

Table 14.3 1991 U.S. Domestic Travel Expenditure and Employment by State[a]

State	Spending ($ Millions)	Employment (Thousands)
Alabama	3,372.5	52.7
Alaska	1,064.5	20.1
Arizona	4,890.5	94.9
Arkansas	2,386.2	42.3
California	41,572.5	593.4
Colorado	5,615.7	109.5
Connecticut	3,166.9	37.5
Delaware	806.5	12.4
Florida	25,970.2	442.4
Georgia	7,760.8	166.8
Hawaii	5,700.0	88.4
Idaho	1,324.8	20.5
Illinois	11,990.0	207.9
Indiana	3,928.6	76.0
Iowa	2,680.7	46.0
Kansas	2,258.2	36.8
Kentucky	3,208.7	67.2
Louisiana	4,424.0	75.6
Maine	1,430.1	22.7
Maryland	4.494.9	70.5
Massachusetts	6,520.9	90.8
Michigan	6,740.9	114.5
Minnesota	4,040.5	93.4
Mississippi	1,946.8	36.4
Missouri	5,720.1	106.6
Montana	1,363.5	20.5
Nebraska	1,633.0	30.7
Nevada	11,292.0	247.3
New Hampshire	1,302.4	17.4
New Jersey	10,093.5	156.7
New Mexico	2,328.7	37.8
New York	18,718.5	273.9
North Carolina	6,985.6	142.8
North Dakota	830.6	16.5
Ohio	7,947.8	139.7
Oklahoma	2,591.5	58.3
Oregon	3,507.6	58.6
Pennsylvania	9,129.9	156.2
Rhode Island	658.9	8.4
South Carolina	4,525.6	85.7
South Dakota	757.8	15.8
Tennessee	6,010.3	125.7
Texas	17,756.9	350.7
Utah	2,371.9	46.7
Vermont	919.6	15.5
Virginia	8,192.4	154.6
Washington	5,008.2	80.1
West Virginia	1,255.5	21.6
Wisconsin	4,050.9	79.3
Wyoming	1,054.7	21.4
Washington,DC	2,867.3	38.7
Total	$296,162.4	5,124.0

[a]Estimates are based on travel 100 miles or more away from home or overnight trips with one or more nights in paid accommodations.
Source: U.S. Travel Data Center.

capacity of the site, thus leading to overuse and a decline in psychic enjoyment. Extreme emphasis on tourism as an element in economic development might have the same result. There can also be clashes between use of resources for tourism and for other kinds of development.

Constraints

The second half of the optimizing situation is occupied by those factors that place obstacles in the way of goal attainment. We assume that it is desirable to have unlimited amounts of psychic enjoyment, profits, and local impacts. But that is not possible because something is always getting in the way. Tourism, being extremely broad and diverse, must deal with a large number of constraints. To make an analysis of relationships, it will be necessary to classify them.

DEMAND Every firm providing goods and services to tourists is constrained by the demand functions of its customers. These relate quantity purchased to price, wealth, and income.

SUPPLY OF ATTRACTIVE RESOURCES Possibly one of the most important constraints faced by the industry as a whole is the limited amount of resources available for tourist enjoyment. This is particularly true when geographic distribution of these sites is considered. Some areas are simply better attractions for tourists than others.

TECHNICAL AND ENVIRONMENTAL CONSTRAINTS These are usually related to a particular site or situation. They involve such things as the relationship between sewage effluent disposal and the environment, numbers of fish and numbers of fishermen, number of people who can walk in a given area without causing unacceptable damage, number of elephants supportable on a wildlife range, impact on lions' behavior of observing them from a car, number of campsites possible in a given area without harming the environment, and so on.

TIME CONSTRAINTS The amount of vacation time available limits what the vacationer can do. The length of the tourist season influences profitability of tourist-oriented businesses and the impact of tourist expenditures on the local economy.

INDIVISIBILITIES Many times it is necessary to deal with all of something or nothing. It is not possible to fly half an airplane, even though the seats are only half filled. It may not be profitable to build a hotel under a given size. A road has to be built all the way from one point to another.

LEGAL CONSTRAINTS There are several types of legal constraints affecting tourism. Activities of the government tourist bureau might be one. Laws concerning environmental problems could be another. Zoning and building codes may influence the construction of facilities. Laws concerning contractual relations may limit activities.

SELF-IMPOSED CONSTRAINTS This type of constraint arises from a need to reconcile conflicting goals. The conflicts may arise within a firm or among firms, government agencies, and so on that are seeking to develop a particular area or concept.

LACK OF KNOWLEDGE   Many activities are limited because little is known about particular situations. Businesspeople are used to living with a certain amount of uncertainty, but there are inevitable limits to the amount they are willing to countenance. Ignorance influences governmental operations as well.

LIMITS ON SUPPORTIVE RESOURCES   There are always limits to the amount of money, managerial talent, workers, construction materials, social capital, and so on. And these, in turn, limit chances to provide psychic experiences, take advantage of profit-making opportunities, or develop local attractions.

Many times these individual constraints interact, creating compound constraints on given activities.

Optimizing the Experience

Maximization of the tourist experience is subject to a number of constraints and is manifested in the demand function. Demand for tourist experience is peculiar in the sense that the product being purchased is not easy to identify directly and is frequently purchased sight unseen.

The tourist is particularly constrained by time and budget. To optimize the experience, it is necessary to determine the combination of destinations preferred and then the possibilities within the money and time constraints. This explains some of the popularity of package tours, where both time and cost can be known in advance. There are some exceptions. Retired persons and young people often have time but limited resources. A few people have neither constraint.

Optimizing Returns to Businesses

Since goods and services provided to tourists are really inputs to the process of producing the experience, demand for them is derived from demand for tourism as a whole. Some goods and services are complementary, and their demand is interrelated in a positive fashion. Others are substitutes and are characterized by limited area competition.

Packaged tours have the characteristic of putting all parts and services together, so they become complementary. Competition occurs among tours. Tour operators can maximize profits by selling tours of different value and costs, in order to cater to as many people as possible along the demand curve. The number of people to be accommodated can be determined from the marginal cost of the tour and the marginal revenue to be derived from a given price level.

Goods and services sold to tourists are subject to severe peaking in demand. That is, the heaviest tourist season is usually limited. During that period, demand is intense and must be met with facilities that are excess in the off-season. This means that investment necessary to provide the excess capacity must be paid for from revenues received during the peak period. During off-peak periods, only variable cost is of interest, but, since demand is low, some capacity will not be utilized.

As owner of the facilities, firms are concerned with providing adequate long-run capacity and with choosing those investments that will give optimum returns. In the tourist industry, a number of interrelationships must be considered. Sometimes, low benefit–cost investments are made so that higher yielding investments can succeed. Consequently, it is not always true that investors choose the highest-yielding opportunities.

Generally, it is considered the long-run business of the firm to remove constraints on operations. But in tourism there are a number of constraints to expansion. These include demand for the tourist experience and environmental constraints.

Optimizing for the Local Economy

Tourism affects a region during periods of intense investment activity and afterward when the investments are producing. The effects depend on linkages among economic units. Money spent for investment will go to construction and a few other industrial sectors. These will have links to economic units varying from households to manufacturing plants. Money spent by tourists will also be introduced through a few sectors that will also be linked to the economy.

The multiplier effects in both cases are dependent upon the strength of the linkages. The multiplier reflects the amount of new economic activity generated as basic income circulates through the economy. Some sectors have strong links to other sectors in an economy and a large multiplier effect. Others have weak links and small multipliers. It is possible to have a thriving tourist industry and abject poverty in the local populace, if there are not links. For example, linkages will be strong and the income multiplier high if the year-round resorts in a particular destination area hire all local labor; buy their flowers, fruit, and vegetables and poultry products from local farmers; hire local entertainers; and buy furnishings for guest rooms from local manufacturers. Linkages would be weak if most of these goods and services were imported from another state or country.

Tourism Exports and Imports

The host region is defined loosely as a country, a state, or a nation, depending on the level at which the problem is being considered. For a county-level government, the income of the county is of primary interest. A state government would perceive the maximization of the combined income of the entire state to be its objective and so on. Regardless of which definition of host region is being considered, expenditures in this area by tourists coming from another region represent *injections* into the area's economy.

Japanese traveling to the United States presumably earned their income in Japan. When spending money in the United States as tourists, they are "injecting" money into our economy that wasn't here before. As such, expenditures by foreigners in this country (for travel purposes) represent *tourism exports* for the United States. This may be somewhat confusing since we are accustomed to thinking of something leaving the country as an export. When we export computers or cars, for example, these commodities are sent out of the United States. In the example of the Japanese tourists, the tourists are coming *into* this country. So how is it an export? There seems to be a contradiction in terminology. As the astute student would note, however, when tourists come into this country, they are purchasing travel experiences. When they leave, they take these experiences back with them. We have exported travel experiences, which are, after all, what tourism is all about.

Tourists arriving from Japan will spend money in the United States and take travel experiences home with them. These tourists create export income. (Photo courtesy of the Boeing Company)

Figure 14.5 clarifies this concept. When U.S. tourists travel to Japan and spend money there, this becomes a tourism *import* to the U.S. economy. For the Japanese, their money spent in the United States is a tourism *import* for the Japanese economy.

In tourism exports, the flows of tourists and payments are in the same direction, whereas in commodity exports, the two flows are in opposite directions. Therein lies the confusion. However, if one were to look at the *direction of payment flow* to determine what is an export, there is no contradiction between the two cases. When payment flows

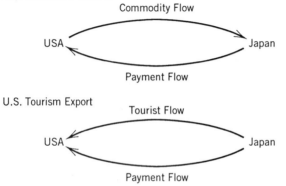

Figure 14.5 Economic Comparison—Commodity Flows and Tourist Flows

into the United States, something has been exported—travel experiences, for instance, or commodities. Both payment flows are in the same direction.

Balance-of-Payments Effects

Tourism is one of the world's largest international industries. As such it has a noticeable impact on the balance of payments of many nations. We have heard much about the balance-of-payments problems of the United States, and, indeed, tourism imports do affect the balance of payments and economic conditions generally. We define tourism imports as those expenditures made by American tourists in foreign countries. An easy way to remember this is "Who got the money?" If, for example, Britain received American funds, it makes no difference whether we bought some English china or an American tourist visited England.

Our balance-of-payments situation directly affects the gross national product of the United States (Y). The formula is

$$Y = C + I + G + (X - M)$$

where

$$
\begin{aligned}
Y &= \text{GNP} \\
C &= \text{consumer expenditures} \\
I &= \text{investments} \\
G &= \text{government expenditures} \\
X &= \text{exports} \\
M &= \text{imports}
\end{aligned}
$$

By looking at the formula, we can see that if imports (M) exceed exports (X), it will be a negative number and Y will thus be smaller. So it is advantageous to us in our American economy to attract more visitor spending in the United States. These "tourism exports" are like credits and help our economy. It is economically better to have foreign visitors come to the United States than it is to have U.S. citizens travel abroad. However, this should be tempered with the realization that the situation is not entirely positive or negative.

Expenditures by U.S. tourists abroad make possible purchasing power in foreign countries for those countries to buy American-made products. For example, most airlines of the world use American-made equipment. Purchase of these aircraft, parts, supplies, repair services, and so forth makes an important contribution to the export trade of the United States, and thus, we cannot charge the tourist industry with all the problems of our negative balance of payments. The purpose of the foregoing discussion is simply to point out the relationships.

Tourism exports become very desirable as far as the gross national product and the prosperity of the country are concerned. Efforts on the part of the United States Travel and Tourism Administration to attract foreign visitors have a great impact on the balance-of-payments situation. Business firms, which serve the foreign visitor, provide desired services, and stimulate sales, materially help our national economy. However, during periods when the U.S. dollar is high against foreign currencies, a dampening effect occurs on our tourism exports as this situation is seen as unfavorable by prospective foreign visitors. Conversely, if the dollar is low, more foreign tourists will visit the

United States. This increases our tourism exports, improves our balance of payments, and raises the gross national product. These same relationships of comparable currency values exist between any country that exports tourism and the countries of its tourists' origin.

Investment Stimulation

The tourist industry has a unique structure. It is characterized by, and, in fact, is, an agglomeration of a large number of very small units, covering a variety of different service trades—the small restaurants, motels, guest houses, laundries, arts and crafts shops, and others. Thus, investment in infrastructure and sometimes expensive super-structure by the government stimulates investment in numerous smaller businesses. Because of the small size of these businesses, capital requirements are relatively low and investment generally proceeds at a rapid pace. In this respect, too, governments view tourism rather favorably. The initial investment in tourism brings forth a large invest-ment in supporting and tertiary industries. This also includes large investments in major hotels, restaurants, shopping centers, marinas, airports, and so on.

Tourism Increases Tax Revenue

Tourists must pay taxes like most other people. Since they come from other regions or countries, their expenditures represent an increased tax base for the host government. In addition to the usual sales tax, tourists sometimes pay taxes in less direct ways. Airport taxes, exit fees, customs duty, and charges assessed for granting visas are just a few examples of commonly used methods of taxing tourists. The wisdom of imposing such special taxes on tourists is questionable, since it merely serves to reduce demand. In some countries, for instance, the room rate at a hotel can be different for tourists (generally higher) than for residents. This is a questionable practice, for it leaves the tourist with a feeling that he has been "taken." Apart from these special cases, the usual taxes collected from both tourists and residents increase due to tourism expenditures.

Is tourism, then, a panacea for all the economic woes of a region or country? It has been claimed that tourism increases incomes, employment, investment, tax revenues, and so forth, so it might indeed appear to be one. However, there are constraints that limit the extent to which governments can maximize the benefit from these aspects of tourism. These constraints are of two types: social and economic. The social constraints have already been discussed. The economic constraints are in the form of potential economic costs that the tourism industry may impose. These merit further scrutiny to gain a better understanding of the government's optimization problem.

Inflationary Pressure

Tourists inject money (earned elsewhere) into the destination economy. While this increases the income of the region (as discussed earlier), it also might cause inflationary pressures. Tourists typically have a higher expenditure capability than the residents do—either because tourists have higher incomes or because they have saved for the trip and are inclined to "splurge" while on vacation. Hence, they are able to somewhat bid up the prices of such commodities as food, transportation, and arts and crafts. This causes inflationary pressures, which can be detrimental to the economic welfare of residents of the host community. This is particularly true when inflation affects the prices of essentials such as food, clothing, transportation, and housing. Land prices have been known to escalate rapidly in tourist destination areas. The prices that foreigners are willing to pay for "vacation homes" in the area can decrease the demand for "first homes" by residents.

Lundberg[1] notes that as the tourist industry developed in an area, land prices rose sharply. In a particular underdeveloped area, the amount of investment in land constituted just 1 percent of the total investment for a hotel project. By contrast, this ratio increased to 20 percent in an area where tourism was already overdeveloped. With such increases in land prices, it can be expected that local residents (with their lower incomes) are effectively "chased out" of the housing market in a tourism-developing section.

ECONOMIC MULTIPLIERS

Direct Effect

In addition to the direct impact of tourism expenditures on an area, there are also indirect impacts. The indirect or *multiplier* impact comes into play as visitor spending circulates and recirculates. The direct effects are the easiest to understand as they result from the visitor spending money in tourist enterprises and providing a living for the owners and managers and creating jobs for employees.

Tourism has a powerful economic impact because tourists inject money into the destination economy. New York City is one of the world's top tourist destinations as well as the site of the world headquarters for the United Nations Organization (building in foreground). (Photo courtesy of the New York Division of Tourism)

---

[1]Donald E. Lundberg, "Caribbean Tourism," *The Cornell Hotel and Restaurant Administration Quarterly,* Vol. 14, No. 4 (February 1974), pp. 30–45.

This chartered motorcoach tour, carrying 40 people, will generate about $5495 for the local economy. The tourists' expenditure for meals, lodging, shopping, admission fees, discretionary spending, and other expenses will ultimately become widely distributed and will be multiplied during the ensuing year. (Photo courtesy of the National Tour Association)

Indirect Effect

This visitor expenditure gives rise to an income that, in turn, leads to a chain of expenditure-income-expenditure and so on, until leakages bring the chain to a halt. Consequently, the impact of the initial income derived from the tourist's expenditure is usually greater than the initial income, because subsequent rounds of spending are related to it. For example, a skier purchases a lift ticket for $30. This money received by the ski area will be used to pay the wages of the lift operators. The lift operator spends the money on groceries; the grocer uses the money to pay part of his rent to the local landlady; the landlady uses it to pay for her dry cleaning; the dry cleaner spends it in a restaurant for a dinner; the restaurant owner spends it for steaks shipped in from Kansas City; and the cycle stops as the money is lost to the local economy. This last transaction is known as "leakage" from the economy.

The combination of the direct and indirect effects of an expenditure pattern determines the impact. In a typical situation, not all of the income generated in each round of expenditure is respent. Some portion tends to be saved, and some portion tends to be spent outside the local economy. The greater the proportion of income spent locally, the greater will be the multiplier.

The degree to which a local area is able to retain tourist income depends on how self-sufficient the local economy is. If the local economy is able to produce the goods and services tourists buy, the greater will be the multiplier effect. The more goods that have to be imported from outside the region, the smaller the multiplier will be.

From the discussion, it is clear that when a tourist's spending injects funds into the economy of a host area, an economic effect occurs that is a specified number of times what was originally spent. Initially, this effect is thought of as an *income multiplier*, as tourist expenditures become income directly and indirectly to local people. However, there are additional economic phenomena. Increased spending necessitates more jobs, which results in an *employment multiplier*. Because money changes hands a number of times during a year, there is a *transactions multiplier*. This is of particular interest to governmental tax officials where sales taxes are imposed. As business grows in a tourist destination area, more infrastructure and superstructure are constructed. This results in a *capital multiplier*. Examples are provided here of how an *employment multiplier* and an *income multiplier* were determined.

Employment Multiplier

This multiplier varies from region to region depending on its economic base. In a study entitled *Recreation as an Industry,* by Robert R. Nathan Associates, county employment multipliers calculated for the Appalachian region provide a good illustration of what typical multipliers are and how they work.[2]

The multipliers estimated in this study were based on county employment data. They represent the approximate measure of the direct and indirect employment associated with each addition of direct employment to the export sector of a county. There are 375 counties and 3 independent cities for which multipliers were estimated. The smallest multiplier was 1.13 and the highest was 2.63. Thus the county with the smallest multiplier value would provide other employment opportunities for approximately 0.13 person for each person directly employed in servicing export demand, and the county with the highest multiplier value would provide other employment opportunities for approximately 1.63 persons for each person directly employed in servicing export demand. In general, county employment multipliers vary directly with the population or total employment size of the counties: as county population size grows, so does the multiplier value. This relationship is as might be expected, insofar as import leakages would tend to be less where diversity of occupations is greater, and diversity is positively associated with county population or total employment.

Income Multiplier

Jobs mean income, which stimulates the economy of the area in which the development occurs. How much stimulation depends on several factors. Using a hotel as an example, the management takes one of two actions concerning the revenue earned—it either spends the money on goods and services, or it saves part of such funds. Economists refer to such action as *MPC* (marginal propensity to consume) or *MPS* (marginal propensity to save—removing funds from the local economy). Such removal of these marginal (extra) funds can be made in two ways: (1) they can be saved and thus not loaned to another spender, or (2) they can be used to purchase imports. In either case, so doing removes the funds and thus does not stimulate the local economy.

Economic research is needed in a tourist destination area to determine what these income relationships are. If the results of such economic research were made available, many beneficial results might be possible. For example, governmental bodies might be more inclined to appropriate additional funds for tourism promotion to their areas if

[2]*Recreation as an Industry* (Washington, D.C.: Robert R. Nathan Associates and Resource Planning Associates, 1966), p. 57.

they knew more about the income that was generated by tourist expenditures. Also, improved and added developments of facilities to serve tourists might be more forthcoming if prospective investors could have more factual data upon which to base decisions.

To understand the multiplier, we must first make some approximation as to what portion of the tourist dollars that are received in a community are spent (consumed) and saved (leakage). To illustrate this, suppose that we had a total of $1000 of tourist spending in a community and that there was an MPC of 1/2. The expenditure pattern might go through seven transactions in a year. These are illustrated in Table 14.4.

The other formula for the multiplier is $1/MPS$. This is a simpler formula, as it is the reciprocal of the marginal propensity to save. If the marginal propensity to save were 1/3, the multiplier would be 3. This is shown in Table 14.5.

Leakage, as defined, is a combination of savings and imports. If we spend the money outside our country for imports, obviously it does not stimulate the economy locally. Also, if it is put into some form of savings that are not loaned to another spender within a year, it also has the same effect as imports—not stimulating the economy. Thus, to get

Table 14.4 Formula for the Multiplier

$$\text{Multiplier} = \frac{1}{1 - MPC}$$

where
M = marginal (extra)
P = propensity (inclination)
C = consume (spending) MPC
S = savings (money out of circulation) MPS
Suppose $1000 of tourist expenditure and an MPC of 1/2. Then

$1000.00	
+	
500.00	$1/2 \times 1000$
+	
250.00	$(1/2)^2 \times 1000$
+	
125.00	$(1/2)^3 \times 1000$
+	
62.50	$(1/2)^4 \times 1000$
+	
31.25	$(1/2)^5 \times 1000$
+	
15.63	$(1/2)^6 \times 1000$
+	
7.81	$(1/2)^7 \times 1000$
$\cdots$	

$2000.00 (approx.)

Multiply: $\dfrac{1}{1 - 1/2} \times \$1000$, or $2 \times \$1000 = \$2000$

Thus, the original $1000 of tourist expenditure becomes $2000 of income to the community.

Table 14.5 "Leakage"

$$\text{Leakage} = \begin{cases} \text{Savings} \\ \text{Imports} \end{cases}$$

Where
Savings = not loaned to another spender
Imports = spending on tourism needs in sources outside country (state)

$$\text{Multiplier} = \frac{1}{MPS}$$

$$MPS = 1/3$$

$$\text{Multiplier} = \frac{1}{1/3}$$

$$\text{Multiplier} = 3$$

the maximum benefits economically from tourist expenditures, we should introduce as much of the tourist funds as possible into the local economy for goods and services rather than save the proceeds or buy a large amount of imports.

Here, also, more economic research is needed. Some studies have indicated that the multiplier might be as high as 3 in some areas, but economic research in other localities indicate that it may be more typically lower than this.

Economic Benefits Widely Distributed

Using a conceptual approach, you should realize that tourism is characterized by the existence of a large number of very small businesses that support and are ancillary to the industry. The receipts from tourism quickly filter down to an extremely broad cross section of the population, so that the entire community shares the economic benefits. Table 14.6, based on a partial hypothetical example, illustrates how quickly tourism receipts seep through the economy and the diversity of the businesses that benefit from tourism. As the figure indicates, the tourism dollar is shared by over 70 distinguishable types of enterprises in just two rounds of spending.

Structural Changes

In countries that primarily rely on a single industry, such as agriculture, the introduction of tourism has often led to a decrease in the agricultural base of the country. Agriculture is an extremely low-productivity industry in the developing countries. The promise of much higher wages in the tourism industry draws people away from farming. Agricultural output declines as a result, just when the demand for food is increasing due to the influx of tourists. The inflationary pressure on food prices is further aggravated and can lead to considerable social upheaval. In the mid-1970s, some Caribbean countries experienced a wave of protests and even direct attacks on tourists, as the resident population expressed its dissatisfaction over rising prices.

Another major implication of the structural change is that instead of diversifying

Table 14.6 Distribution of Tourism Expenditures

Visitors Spend for	Travel Industry Spends for	Ultimate Beneficiaries
Lodging	Wages and salaries	Accountants
Food	Tips—gratuities	Advertising and public relations
Beverages	Payroll taxes	Appliance stores
Entertainment	Commissions	Architects
Clothing, etc.	Music and entertainment	Arts and crafts producers
Gifts and souvenirs	Administrative and	Attorneys
Photography	general expenses	Automobile agencies
Personal care	Legal and professional	Bakers
Drugs and cosmetics	services	Banks
Internal	Purchases of food,	Beach accessories
transportation	beverages, etc.	Butchers
Tours and	Purchases of goods sold	Carpenters
sightseeing	Purchases of materials and	Cashiers
Miscellaneous	supplies	Charities
	Repairs and maintenance	Chemists
	Advertising, promotion,	Clerks
	and publicity	Clothing stores
	Utilities—electric gas,	Clubs
	water, etc.	Confectioners
	Transportation	Contractors
	Licenses	Cooks
	Insurance premiums	Cultural organization
	Rental of premises and	Dairies
	equipment	Dentists
	Interest and principal	Department stores
	payments of borrowed	Doctors
	funds	Dry cleaning establishments
	Income and other taxes	Electricians
	Replacement of capital	Engineers
	assets	Farmers
	Return to investors	Fishermen
		Freight forwarders
		Garages and auto repairs
		Gardeners
		Gift shops
		Government
		Education
		Health
		Roads and railroads
		Utilities
		Development and others
		Greengrocers
		Grocery stores
		Financiers
		Furniture stores
		Importers
		Insurance agencies
		Landlords
		Laundries
		Manufacturing agents

Table 14.6   Continued

Visitors Spend for	Travel Industry Spends for	Ultimate Beneficiaries
		Managers
		Motion picture theaters
		Newspapers, radio, etc.
		Nightclubs
		Office equipment suppliers
		Painters
		Pastoralists
		Petrol stations
		Plumbers
		Porters
		Printers—sign painters
		Publishers
		Real estate brokers & developers
		Resorts
		Restaurants
		Room maids
		Shareholders
		Sporting events
		Transportation
		Travel brokers
		Taxi—hire car services
		Unions
		Wholesale establishments

Source: Pannell Kerr Forster and Belt Collins and Associates.

its economic base, the country's tourism sector merely "cannibalizes" its other major economic sector. Diversity is the foundation of economic stability. When one sector (or industry) is experiencing a slump, another sector is booming, thus reducing the probability of a severe depression and, indeed, reducing its impact if a depression does occur. Thus tourism, instead of diversifying an economy, sometimes replaces agriculture as a "subsistence" sector.

Dependence on Tourism

Permitting tourism to become the subsistence industry is not desirable for a number of reasons. First, tourism is by its very nature subject to considerable seasonality. While seasonal fluctuations in demand can sometimes be reduced, they cannot be eliminated. Thus, when tourism is the primary industry in an area, the off-season periods inevitably result in serious unemployment problems. Such areas find that the seasonal character of tourism leaves severe economic and social effects on the host region.

Another very important reason relates to the source of demand for tourism. The demand for tourism depends largely on the income and the tastes of tourists, both of which are beyond the control of the host region. If the American economy is going through a slump, demand for travel to a foreign destination by Americans will fall off. There is precious little a destination area can do, in this case, to increase the level of demand. If the tastes of the people in the tourist-generating area change—they decide to travel to a new destination—tourism in the old area will decline, causing economic and social problems. Again, there will be little or nothing the destination can do to avoid this. In fact, as Plog[3] points out, there is reason to believe that such a decline in an area's popularity may be largely inevitable. Quite clearly, then, tourism should not be allowed to grow to an extent that the destination area becomes totally dependent on it.

In other words, total dependence on a single industrial sector is undesirable. If it cannot be avoided, then dependence on domestic agriculture is in many ways preferable to dependence on tourism. The country has presumably adapted itself economically and socially to dependence on agriculture over several centuries. The demand for agriculture output is also unlikely to suffer from a secular decline since people must eat. Also, it is the residents, not foreigners as in tourism, who directly benefit from agricultural production.

Investment Priorities

Sometimes, governments of developing countries take an overly optimistic view of tourism. They undertake aggressive investment programs to develop tourism, assigning it top priority in their development plans. In extreme cases, such an approach can lead to the neglect of more fundamental investment needs of the country. For example, funds can be channeled into tourism development at the cost of education, health, and other social services. The education, health, and other aspects of the social well-being of the population should be of primary concern for a developing country. Not only is undue glamorization of tourism unwise because it usurps this position, but such a strategy only speeds up the process of dependence on tourism, which, as discussed earlier, is itself undesirable. Moreover, investment in tourism at the cost of health and education programs also slows down the rate at which the local population is assimilated into the modern market economy of the country. Under certain circumstances, it may actually retard development rather than enhance it.

The conclusion is that although tourism has tremendous potential as a tool in economic development, it is no panacea. Governments should attempt to optimize (not maximize) the benefits that tourism provides, being ever mindful of the costs that it can impose. It should be noted also that the probability and the intensity of the economic costs of tourism are greater for developing nations (or regions) than for wealthy ones. Wealthy nations, by definition, possess robust economies that can more easily absorb the costs of tourism. Typically, such economies are well diversified, and government investment programs are not so central to development efforts.

The social benefits and costs of tourism should be viewed similarly. While the host community seeks to maximize the benefits, it must weigh these against the social costs. The social costs are likewise higher in both probability and magnitude when tourism is being considered for development in an area that still possesses a traditional social structure.

[3]Stanley C. Plog, "Why Destination Areas Rise and Fall in Popularity," *The Cornell Hotel and Restaurant Administration Quarterly*, Vol. 14, No. 4 (February 1974), pp. 55–58.

Table 14.7   Relationships Between Price Elasticity and Total Revenue (*TR*)

	Elastic Demand (I∈$_p$l > 1)	Unitary Elasticity (I∈$_p$l = 1)	Inelastic Demand (I∈$_p$l < 1)
Price rises	*TR* falls	No change	*TR* rises
Price falls	*TR* rises	No change	*TR* falls

Quantity Demanded and Price Elasticity

For some products, even a large change in price over a certain range of the demand curve results in only a small change in quantity demanded. In this case, demand is not very responsive to price (Table 14.7). For other products, or for the same product over a different range of prices, a relatively small change in price elicits a much larger relative change in quantity demanded. Demand can be classified as inelastic or elastic on the basis of the relative responsiveness of quantity demanded to changes in price. Specifically, price elasticity of demand may be defined as the percentage change in demand resulting from a given percentage change in price. Most tourism products are price elastic. During 1992, when U.S. airlines began offering one-half fares, the number of air travelers increased to record-high levels.

Income Elasticity of Demand

As income rises, more travel is demanded at any given price. Thus the relationship between income and demand is positive. The responsiveness of demand to changes in income is called income elasticity of demand. It is defined as the percentage change in quantity demanded in response to a given percentage change in income, price remaining unchanged.

SUMMARY

Domestic and international tourism are major economic strengths to many of the world's countries, states, cities, and rural areas. Thus, those who live there are affected by the economic results of tourist spending. In this chapter we explain why these resulting effects vary greatly and what brings about a large measure of benefits or possible detriments to a community. The main economic phenomena described are various multipliers, balance of payments, investments, tax consideration, employment, economic impact generators, travel expenditures, dependence on tourism, price and income elasticity as related to buying travel experiences, and optimization.

Many people do not understand or appreciate the economics of tourism. The following list summarizes the principal economic effects:

1. Expenditures by foreign visitors in one's country become exports (mainly of services). The economic effects are the same as those derived from exporting tangible goods. If there is a favorable exchange rate (foreign currency buying

appreciably more of one's own country's currency) the country that has the devalued currency will experience a higher demand for visitor services than before devaluation.

2. If citizens of one's country spend money in foreign countries, these expenditures become imports for the tourists' originating country.
3. Sums of the values of national exports and imports are used when calculating a nation's balance of payments. A plus balance results when exports exceed imports, thus increasing a nation's gross national product (GNP).
4. Tourism developments typically require large investments of capital. Thus, local economies where the developments take place are stimulated by such investments.
5. Tourists pay various kinds of taxes directly and indirectly while visiting an area. Thus tax revenues are increased for all levels of government.
6. As tourists usually spend more per day at a destination than they do while at home, these extra expenditures may cause inflationary pressures and rising prices for consumer goods in the destination area.
7. Tourism expenditures injected into the economy produce an income multiplier for local people. This is due to the diversity of expenditures made by those receiving tourist payments. Tourist receipts are used to buy a wide variety of goods and services over a year's time. The money turnover creates additional local income.
8. The amount of income multiplication, however, will depend on how much leakage takes place. Leakages are a combination of (1) imported goods and services purchased by tourism suppliers, and (2) savings made of tourist receipts not loaned to another spender within one year of receipt. Thus, the more tourist goods that are supplied locally, the higher will be the multiplier.
9. Income multiplication caused by tourist expenditures necessitates hiring more people. Thus, they also effect an employment multiplier.
10. As increased spending produces more financial transactions, they create a transactions multiplier. These are of particular interest to governments that have a sales or value-added tax on such transactions.
11. As a tourist area grows, more capital is invested in new facilities. This results in a capital multiplier.
12. It is an unwise policy for a society to place too much dependency on tourism as a subsistence industry.
13. Although tourism often has an excellent potential in economic development, it is not a panacea for economic ills. Its economic benefits should be optimized rather than maximized.
14. We believe that tourism products are mainly price elastic, meaning that as prices rise, the quantity demanded tends to drop.
15. In general, we believe that tourism is income elastic. This means that as family income rises, or a particular market's income rises, and tourism prices do not rise proportionally, the demand for travel to that particular area will increase.

Key Concepts

balance of payments	demand schedule
demand	direct impact
demand curve	economic base

economic impact
economic impact generators
employment
exports and imports
expenditures
gross national product
income
income elasticity
income inelasticity
inflationary pressure

indirect impact
investment stimulation
leakage
multipliers
number of visitors
optimization
price elasticity
price inelasticity
supply categories
tax revenue

For Review and Discussion

1. What is meant by *optimization?*
2. Discuss how an airline executive might use tourism economics relating to passenger load factors, ticket prices, discounts, frequent flyer programs, joint fares, and flight frequencies.
3. Selecting one form of public transportation, enumerate the economic constraints that affect this business.
4. A full-service restaurant is considering having an elaborate buffet dinner three nights a week. What constraints are likely to bear on this consideration?
5. Define *tourism exports and imports* in terms of national economies.
6. Explain how international tourism could assist in reducing the current sizable U.S. trade deficit. How could it increase the deficit?
7. Give several reasons that a hotel's purchasing director should be familiar with the income multiplier phenomenon.
8. Trace how tourist expenditures in a community provide financial support to the public library.
9. Enumerate various methods by which a tourist-dependent community can at least partially overcome seasonality of tourism demand.

Case Problems

1. Mr. and Mrs. Henry B. are considering taking their first trip abroad. Deciding to buy a group tour, they find that some countries in which they are interested seem to offer a much better value than do others. Assuming that the ingredients of the tours being considered are very similar, what factors are likely to account for this price difference?
2. A western U.S. state is quite popular with tourists, hosting about 6 million visitors per year. The state's director of sales and use taxes has recently advised the governor that a special 5 percent hotel and motel rooms tax should be added to the present 4 percent use tax, making a 9 percent total rooms tax. Currently, the state's budget is in the red. Thus an increase in revenue is badly needed. What economic advice should the governor seek?

Selected References

Archer, Brian. "Tourism in Mauritius: An Economic Impact Study with Marketing Implications." *Tourism Management,* Vol. 6, No. 1 (March 1985), pp. 50–54.

Braun, Bradley M. "The Economic Contribution of Conventions: The Case of Orlando, Florida." *Journal of Travel Research,* Vol. 30, No. 3 (Winter 1992), pp. 32–37.

Briassoulis, Helen. "Methodological Issues in Tourism Input–Output Analysis." *Annals of Tourism Research,* Vol. 18, No. 3 (1991), pp. 485–495.

Bull, Adrian. *The Economics of Travel and Tourism.* Melbourne, Australia: Longman Cheshire, 1991.

Eadington, William R., and Milton Redman. "Economics and Tourism." *Annals of Tourism Research,* Vol. 18, No. 1 (1991), pp. 41–56.

Edwards, Anthony. *Choosing Holiday Destinations: The Impact of Exchange Rates and Inflation.* London: The Economist Intelligence Unit, 1987.

Fesenmaier, Daniel R., Lonnie Jones, Seoho Um, and Teofilo Ozuna, Jr. "Assessing the Economic Impact of Outdoor Recreation Travel to the Texas Gulf Coast." *Journal of Travel Research,* Vol. 28, No. 1 (Summer 1989), pp. 18–23.

Heng, Toh M., and Linda Low. "Economic Impact of Tourism in Singapore." *Annals of Tourism Research,* Vol. 17, No. 2 (1990), pp. 246–267.

Johnson, Daniel G., and Jay Sullivan. "Economic Impacts of Civil War Battlefield Preservation: An Ex-ante Evaluation." *Journal of Travel Research,* Vol. 32, No. 1 (Summer 1993), pp. 21–29.

Johnson, Peter, and Barry Thomas. *Tourism, Museums and the Local Economy: The Economic Impact of the North of England Open Air Museum at Beamish.* Brookfield, Vt.: Ashgate Publishing Co., 1992.

Khan, Habibullah, Chou Fee Seng, and Wong Kwei Cheong. "Tourism Multiplier Effects on Singapore." *Annals of Tourism Research,* Vol. 17, No. 3 (1990), pp. 408–418.

Kottke, Marvin. "Estimating Economic Impacts of Tourism." *Annals of Tourism Research,* Vol. 15, No. 1 (1988), pp. 122–133.

Latimer, Hugh. "Developing-Island Economies: Tourism vs. Agriculture." *Tourism Management,* Vol. 6, No. 1 (March 1985), pp. 32–42.

Liu, Juanita C. "Relative Economic Contributions of Visitor Groups in Hawaii." *Journal of Travel Research,* Vol. 25, No. 1 (Summer 1986), pp. 2–9.

Mak, James. "Taxing Hotel Room Rentals in the U.S." *Journal of Travel Research,* Vol. 27, No. 1 (Summer 1988), pp. 10–15.

Mak, James, and Edward Hishimura. "The Economics of a Hotel Room Tax." *Journal of Travel Research,* Vol. 17, No. 4 (Spring 1979), pp. 2–6.

Mescon, Timothy S., and George S. Vozikis. "The Economic Impact of Tourism at the Port of Miami." *Annals of Tourism Research,* Vol. 12, No. 4 (1985), pp. 515–528.

Milne, Simon S. "Differential Multipliers." *Annals of Tourism Research,* Vol. 14, No. 4 (1987), pp. 499–151.

Schulmeister, Stephan. *Tourism and the Business Cycle.* Vienna: Austrian Institute for Economic Research, 1979.

Summary, Rebecca M. "Tourism's Contribution to the Economy of Kenya." *Annals of Tourism Research,* Vol. 14, No. 4 (1987), pp. 531–540.

Taylor, David T., Robert R. Fletcher, and Trish Clabaugh. "A Comparison of Characteristics, Regional Expenditures, and Economic Impact of Visitors to Historical Sites with other Recreational Visitors." *Journal of Travel Research.* Vol. 32, No. 1 (Summer 1993), pp. 30–35.

U.S. Travel Data Center. *Impact of Travel on State Economies: 1990.* Washington, D.C.: USTDC, 1992.

U.S. Travel Data Center. *1993 Travel Market Report.* Washington, D.C.: USTDC, 1994.

CHAPTER 15

Tourism Planning, Development, and Social Considerations

LEARNING OBJECTIVES

- Discover what the goals of tourism development should be.
- Recognize that there are some serious barriers to tourism development that must be overcome if a desired growth is to occur.
- Learn the political and economic aspects of development, including those related to developing countries.
- Appreciate the importance of architectural design and concern for heritage preservation, local handicrafts, and use of indigenous materials in creating tourist facilities.

WHY TOURISM PLANNING IS NECESSARY

The decision to develop tourism or expand present tourism development in a community, a region, or a country must be studied carefully. The socioeconomic benefits from tourism are powerful. Tourism development looks attractive to both developed and underdeveloped countries with the right preconditions—some combination of natural, scenic, historical, archaeological, cultural, and climate attractions. Tourism is a growth industry, and while that growth may show some slowing in the short run, the long-run prospects are good. The expected continued growth is based on continually rising per capita incomes, lower travel costs, increased leisure time, and changes in consumers' tastes and preferences toward travel, recreation, and leisure goods and services.

Many advocates look at tourism as a panacea for solving an area's development problems. This view is unrealistic because benefits may be accompanied by detrimental consequences. A review of some advantages and disadvantages from Chapter 1 arising from tourism development will indicate why careful planning is necessary.

Major arguments for tourism are that it:

1. Provides employment opportunities, both skilled and unskilled, because it is a labor-intensive industry
2. Generates a supply of needed foreign exchange
3. Increases incomes
4. Creates increased gross national product

5. Requires the development of an infrastructure that will also help stimulate local commerce and industry
6. Justifies environmental protection and improvement
7. Increases governmental revenues
8. Helps to diversify the economy
9. Creates a favorable worldwide image for the destination
10. Facilitates the process of modernization by education of youth and society and changing values
11. Provides tourist and recreational facilities that may be used by a local population who could not otherwise afford developing facilities
12. Gives foreigners an opportunity to be favorably impressed by little-known country or region

Some disadvantages of tourism are that it :

1. Develops excess demand
2. Creates leakages so great that economic benefits do not accrue
3. Diverts funds from more promising forms of economic development
4. Creates social problems from income differences, social differences, introduction of prostitution, gambling, crime, and so on
5. Degrades the natural physical environment
6. Degrades the cultural environment
7. Poses the difficulties of seasonality
8. Increases vulnerability to economic and political changes
9. Adds to inflation of land values and the price of local goods and services

Consequently, tourism is not always a panacea. On the contrary, overdevelopment can generate soil and water pollution and even people pollution, if there are too many visitors at the same place at the same time. Consider automobile and bus traffic congestion, inadequate parking, hotels dwarfing the scale of historic districts, and the displacement of the local community serving businesses by tourist-serving firms leading to degradation of the quality of life rather than improving it.

Then, too, too many visitors can have a harmful impact on life in the host country and on the visitors themselves. A beautiful landscape can suffer through thoughtless and unwise land development and construction methods. And customers and crafts can be vulgarized by overemphasis on quantity and cheapness.

These responsibilities cannot really be blamed on tourism, but rather on overcommercialization. Tourism is one of the world's greatest and most significant social and economic forces. But government officials and business people must weigh the economic benefits against the possible future degradation of human and natural resources.

Tourism development must be guided by carefully planned policy, a policy not built on balance sheets and profit and loss statements alone, but on the ideals and principles of human welfare and happiness. Social problems cannot be solved without a strong and growing economy that tourism can help to create. Sound development policy can have the happy result of a growing tourist business *and* the preservation of the natural and cultural resources that attracted the visitors in the first place.

Planning is critical to having sustainable development and protecting the environment. For that reason the next chapter has been devoted to "Tourism and the Environment" to expand the discussion on how to have development and, hopefully, both protect and enhance the environment.

Viewed comprehensively, the relationship between tourism and the community, state, regions, and countries requires consideration of many difficult issues: the quality of architecture, landscape, and environmental design; environmental reclamation and amenity; natural conservation; land-use management; financial strategies for long-term economic development; employment; transportation; energy conservation; education, information and interpretation systems; and more.

These are the reasons sound tourism planning is essential. Planning can ensure that tourist development has the ability to realize the advantages of tourism and reduce the disadvantages.

THE PLANNING PROCESS

Proper planning—of the physical, legal, promotion, finance, economic, market, management, social, and environmental aspects—will help to deliver the benefits of tourism development.

Good planning defines the desired result and works in a systematic manner to achieve success. The following steps briefly describe a logical sequence:

DEFINE THE SYSTEM   What is the scale, size, market, character, and purpose?

FORMULATE OBJECTIVES   Without a set of objectives the development concept has no direction. The objectives must be comprehensive and specific and should include a timetable for completion.

DATA GATHERING   Fact finding, or research, provides basic data that are essential to developing the plan. Examples of data gathering are preparing a fact book, making market surveys, undertaking site and infrastructure surveys, and analyzing existing facilities and competition.

ANALYSIS AND INTERPRETATION   Once collected, the many fragments of information must be interpreted so the facts gathered will have meaning. From this step results a set of conclusions and recommendations that leads to making or conceptualizing a preliminary plan.

PRELIMINARY PLANNING   Based on the previous steps, alternatives are considered and alternative physical solutions are drawn up and tested. Frequently scale models are developed to illustrate the land-use plans; sketches are prepared to show the image the development will project; financial plans are drafted from the market information, site surveys, and the layout plan to show the investment needed in each phase of the project and the cash flow expected; and legal requirements are met.

APPROVING THE PLAN   The parties involved can now look at plans, drawings, scale models, estimates of costs, estimates of profits, and know what will be involved and what the chances for success or failure will be. While a great deal of money may have been spent up to this point, the sum is a relatively small amount compared to the expenditures that will be required once the plan is approved and master planning and implementation begin.

Sketches show the image a development will project and facilitate the planning process. (Sketch courtesy of Wimberly, Allison, Tong and Goo, Architects, Honolulu, Hawaii)

FINAL PLAN This phase typically includes a definition of land use; plans for infrastructure facilities such as roads, airports, bike paths, horse trails, pedestrian walkways, sewage, water and utilities; architectural standards; landscape plans; zoning and other land-use regulations; economic analysis, market analysis, and financial programming.

IMPLEMENTATION Implementation carries out the plan and creates an operational tourism development. It also follows up and evaluates. Good planning provides mechanisms that give continuing feedback on the tourism project and the levels of consumer satisfaction achieved.

Good planning should eliminate problems and provide user satisfaction. The final user is the judge in determining how successful the planning process has been.

Figure 15.1 shows a model for the tourism planning and development process and illustrates the large number of variables that come into play. The advantage of utilizing such a model is that it requires the planner to view the total picture and guides the thinking process. While no model can depict all interrelated facts of a planning process or eliminate all guesswork, such a model deserves inclusion in the initial phases of planning as a tool that helps to order, coordinate, and control the process.

Table 15.1 shows an integrated approach to planning. Again it serves as a guide to asking the right questions and making sure that the process is complete. It also illustrates that there are a number of approaches to tourism planning. There is no single magic approach.

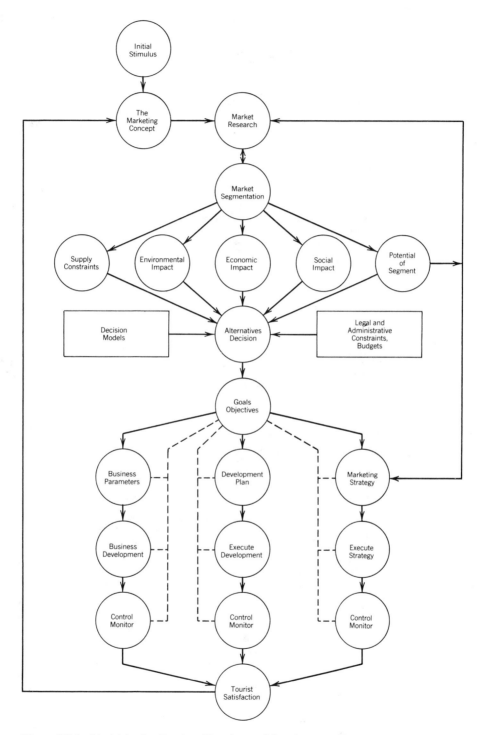

Figure 15.1 Model for the Tourism Planning and Development Process

Table 15.1 Tourism Planning: An Integrated Approach

Planning Activity	Organizational Development	Community Involvement	Tourism Product Development	Tourism Product Marketing
		Where Are We Today?		
1. Gather Information	Evaluate existing group composition. Identify potential represen- tatives that could or should be involved.	Identify both tourism and nontourism interests that may be affected by the proposed tourism development. Determine key issues and concerns of the various stake-holders.	Conduct an inventory and assessment of the area's tourism resources, services, and infrastructure. Estimate existing levels of use and carrying capacity.	Profile the existing markets in terms of geographic origin, demographics, family life-cycle, spending patterns, needs, and interests.
		Where Do We Want To Go?		
2. Identify community values	Tourism organization members express community values by answering questions related to quality of life now and in the future.	Community representatives express their values by answering questions related to quality of life now and in the future.	Values expressed by the tourism organization and community representatives begin to form the foundation upon which future tourism development and resource allocation decisions will be based.	Values expressed by the tourism organization and community representatives begin to form the foundation upon which future tourism marketing decisions will be based.
3. Create a vision	Tourism organization members create an image of how the community should look, feel, and be, now and in the future.	Community representatives create an image of how the community should look, feel, and be, now and in the future.	The descriptive "story" about future de- velopment and quality of life in the community further strengthens the foundation and guides tourism devel- opment and resource allocation decisions.	The descriptive "story" about future de- velopment and quality of life in the community further strengthens the foundation and guides tourism marketing decisions.
4. Identify concerns and opportunities	Tourism organization members brainstorm a list of concerns and opportunities that the group or community may be facing. Similar ideas are combined and narrowed down to reflect those: (1) related to tourism and (2) the tourism organization *should* handle.	Community rep- resentatives brainstorm a list of concerns and op- portunities the com- munity may be facing. Similar ideas are combined and narrowed down to reflect: (1) those related to tourism and (2) those that can be addressed by the tourism orga- nization or through tourism initiatives.	The major concerns and opportunities will provide direction for tourism development initiatives. Ideas expressed should be revisited as more concrete plans for developing or enhancing tourism attractions, services, and infrastructure are being considered.	The major concerns and opportunities will provide direction for tourism development initiatives. Ideas expressed should be revisited as more concrete plans for marketing tourism resources and services are being considered.
5. Develop a mission	Tourism organization members articulate their purpose for existing and determine who they are serving. It is important to recognize not only the visitor, but also community needs during this activity.	The tourism organization's mission serves as a vehicle to inform the community about the group's purpose for existing.	The mission, along with the values, vision, concerns, and opportunities helps guide the tourism development effort.	The mission, along with the values, vision, concerns, and opportunities helps guide the tourism marketing effort

Table 15.1   Continued

Planning Activity	Organizational Development	Community Involvement	Tourism Product Development	Tourism Product Marketing
		Where Do We Want To Go?		
6. Develop goals	Based on the tourism organization's values, vision, concerns, opportunities, and mission, *goals* relative to the structure and administration of the organization are developed.	Goals related to community education and involvement in the tourism development effort are developed. Most likely, goals will center on ways to involve the public in the planning process.	Based on the expressed values, vision, concerns, opportunities, and mission, goals for the physical development and/or enhancement of tourism resources, traveler services, and infrastructure are developed.	Based on the plans for tourism product development and/or enhancement, goals for tourism marketing are developed.
		How Are We Going To Get There?		
7. Develop objectives	Tourism organization members develop action-oriented statements that propose how to achieve each *organizational* goal. The number of objectives for each goal will vary depending on the group's stage of development and available human, physical, and financial resources.	Tourism organization members develop action-oriented statements that propose how to achieve each *community education and involvement* goal. The num- ber of objectives for each goal will vary depending on the community's level of interest and involvement in the tourism initiatives, and the available human, physical, and financial resources.	Tourism organization members develop action-oriented statements that propose how to achieve each *tourism product development* goal. The number of objectives for each goal will vary depending on the community's stage of develop- ment, the quantity and quality of existing tourism resources, services, and infrastructure, and available human, physical, and financial resources.	Tourism organization members develop action-oriented statements that propose how to achieve each *tourism product marketing* goal. The number of objectives for each goal will vary depending on the quantity and quality of existing tourism marketing activities and available human, physical, and financial resources.
8. Develop actions	Tourism organization members define strategies and tactics which outline specifically how each *organizational development* objective will be achieved. This includes exploring funding and technical assistance alternatives, identifying timelines, and assigning tasks.	Tourism organization members define strategies and tactics which outline specifically how each *community education and involvement* objective will be achieved. This includes exploring funding and technical assistance alternatives, identifying timelines, and assigning tasks.	Tourism organization members define strategies and tactics which outline specifically how each *tourism product develop- ment* objective will be achieved. This includes exploring funding and technical assistance alternatives, identifying timelines, and assigning tasks.	Tourism organization members define strategies and tactics which outline specifically how each *tourism marketing* objective will be achieved. This includes exploring funding and technical assistance alternatives, identifying timelines, and assigning tasks.
		How Did We Do?		
9. Evaluate progress	Organization members conduct a periodic review of the organization's activities and progress. A report is written and copies submitted to appropriate governing bodies, funding agencies, and the general public.	Organization members conduct a periodic review of key public involvement activities. A report is written and copies submitted to appropriate governing bodies, funding agencies, and the general public.	Organization members conduct a periodic review of tourism product development and implementation activities and progress. A report is written and copies submitted to appropriate governing bodies, funding agencies, and the general public.	Organization members conduct a periodic review of tourism product marketing activities and progress. A report is written and copies submitted to appropriate governing bodies, funding agencies, and the general public.
10. Update and modify plan	Based on new information or changing circumstances, revisions to the organizational development plan are made.	Based on new information or changing circumstances, revisions to the plan for community involvement are made.	Based on new information or changing circumstances, revisions to the plan for tourism product development are made.	Based on new information or changing circumstances, revisions to the plan for tourism marketing are made.

Source: Jonelle Nuckolls and Patrick Long, *Organizing Resources for Tourism in Rural Areas* (Boulder, Colo.: University of Colorado, 1993).

GOALS OF TOURISM DEVELOPMENT

Tourism development should aim at:

1. Providing a framework for raising the living standard of the people through the economic benefits of tourism
2. Developing an infrastructure and providing recreation facilities for visitors and residents alike
3. Ensuring types of development within visitor centers and resorts that are appropriate to the purposes of those areas
4. Establishing a development program consistent with the cultural, social, and economic philosophy of the government and the people of the host country or area
5. Optimizing visitor satisfaction

Obstacles to Development of Supply

The first obstacle to overcome in turning potential supply into actual supply is the lack or inadequacy of transportation and access routes to the tourist nucleus or center. It is, of course, not enough to get there. The tourist should also be induced to stay. To this end, another basic obstacle to the development of actual supply should be overcome—the lack or shortage of accommodation.

Tourists inevitably require a series of goods and services. Some may be found on the spot and may be economically flexible enough to adapt to the fluctuations of demand. The infrastructure capacity must meet maximum demand. Financing can be a major obstacle. Finally, we cannot overlook the need for sufficiently trained and hospitable personnel.

INTERNAL OBSTACLES   These are the obstacles found within the destination area that can be corrected or eliminated by direct, voluntary means. They may occur in incoming as well as outgoing or internal tourism.

As tourism in all its forms absorbs consumer goods, prices in this field tend to be extremely sensitive to movements in the prices of goods. The rising price of tourism has the same effect as a decrease in the income of the potential tourist. Consequently, when considering costs and planning a holiday, the tourist will choose to go—if the value is the same—where money goes the furthest.

Another major obstacle is the attitude of government and business leaders in the destination area. If this leadership is resistant or even passive toward tourism, development will lag.

POLITICAL ASPECTS OF TOURISM DEVELOPMENT

Like any significant element of an area's economy, there are political aspects that can and often do have major influences on the creation, operation, and survival of tourism projects. Many examples can be cited. One is the land-use regulations (zoning) for commercial or public tourism developments, which can be emotionally and politically sensitive topics. Another is the degree of involvement of governmental agencies in creating and maintaining tourism infrastructure. A third is the type and extent of publicity, advertising, and other promotional efforts.

Land Use (Zoning)

Zoning ordinances specify the legal types of land use. But the final determination of the land use and the administration of the zoning ordinances are typically assigned to a publicly employed zoning administrator and a politically appointed or elected zoning board. Thus, the government decides on how land is to be used and rules on any request for changes in the zoning districts or rezoning to accommodate a nonconforming proposed development.

Attitudes of these public bodies toward tourism development will be influenced by the general public's perception (if any) of the desirability of a specific development. Creating a favorable public image is the responsibility of the developer and the managers of all tourism supply components. The public tourism promotion organization bears responsibility as well. If the public feels that tourism is desirable, rational zoning regulations and administration should result. Furthermore, if principles of tourism planning and development, as presented in this chapter, are faithfully implemented, the result should be well-planned projects. These will be accepted in the community as welcome sources of employment and tax revenues.

Creation and Maintenance of Infrastructure

Any tourism development will need infrastructure. Whether this is provided by government agencies, the private developer, or both, is basically a political question. What troubles many local people is that their taxes are spent in part to provide roads, water systems, sewers, airports, marinas, parks, and other infrastructure that they perceive as benefiting mainly tourism. Is this fair or desirable from their point of view? Those having a common concern in tourism must realize that it is their responsibility to convince the public that such expenditures by government *are* desirable and *do* benefit the local economy. One way to achieve this understanding is through an intelligent lobbying effort. Another approach is to address service clubs, social organizations, and school groups. A third method shows how much money was spent by tourists or convention delegates.

Maintenance policies are also a vital factor in successful tourism development. Any element of infrastructure, once created, needs maintenance. The level of this maintenance can greatly affect successful tourism. An example is the promptness and adequacy of snow removal from public roads servicing ski resorts. Another is the quality and adequacy of public water and sewage systems. Many other examples could be given. Political influence to obtain good maintenance can be brought to bear by hotel and motel associations, chambers of commerce, convention and visitors' bureaus, and promotion groups. Such efforts can be very effective as public service agencies tend to be receptive if the demands are frequent and forceful.

Government and private industry *must* interact cooperatively if tourism development is to be successful. Political friction can develop when government officials think that private industry should do more to help itself and businesspeople believe that the government should do more to assist them. A knowledgeable outside consulting firm can study the situation and make recommendations in the best interests of both factions.

Promotional Efforts

Publicly funded promotional programs are an essential part of the industry. However, the level or degree of participation in such publicity is largely a political process. To convince lawmakers and local political decision makers of the desirability of tourism, produce accurate data on the economic impact of tourism spending. An "investment" concept is the preferred way to view government programs. Pointing out industry diversification in the economy is another good approach. Other benefits cited could be employment, income multipliers, additional investments, preservation and enhancement of local industries, crafts, and the arts, as well as building local pride and recognition.

Lobbying efforts need to be convincing and persistent. Organizations representing tourism must have both moral and monetary support in sufficient measure to bring about successful political influence. Nothing succeeds like success. If tourism booms, the politicians can well take pride in their important contribution. We repeat—as in all other aspects of the tourist business, cooperation pays!

DEVELOPMENT OF TOURIST POTENTIAL

Official Tourism Body

A tourism body or organization should be created to keep abreast of socioeconomic developments in the various market countries or areas to provide a reasonably early forecast of the size, type, and structure of probable tourism demand. It would be equally useful to have a report on developments in the tourist industry of supplying centers or areas and on activities and projects undertaken to promote development.

Since tourism is such a complex phenomenon, distinct ministerial departments are responsible for finding solutions to developmental problems.

The stabilization of general and tourist prices should be a constant objective, as rising prices automatically reduce the volume of demand. Land speculation should be discouraged.

The inventory of potential national tourist resources (parks, attractions, recreational facilities, and so on) should be kept up to date and extended so that these resources may be duly incorporated into actual tourist trade in accordance with quantity and quality forecasts of demand.

Tax pressures that directly affect operating costs also influence prices. Because of the export value of tourism, a fiscal policy similar to that applied to the conventional or classical export trade should be devised.

Publicity campaigns should be organized and implemented every year according to the forecasts. These should be to-the-point, detailed, and constructive and should zero in on socioeconomic developments and activities in the market. Financing to cover this activity should be obtained from annual tourist earnings and other identifiable funds at a rate of not less than 1 percent and perhaps not more than 4 percent of total earnings.

Customs facilities should be as lenient as possible while ensuring control and maintenance of order and avoiding fraud or other crimes.

For their own benefit, host countries should make the tourists' sojourn as agreeable as possible. But proof that tourists have the financial means to cover the costs of their stay may be desired.

The seasonal nature of mass tourism causes congestion in the use of services required by tourists. Some services, such as accommodation, cannot adapt easily to seasonal fluctuation. On the other hand, some, such as transportation and communications, can adapt. Government provision of public services are important for development.

Transportation

Because of its role in tourist development, the following measures with regard to transportation are recommended:

1. Continual, detailed study of transport used for tourism with a view toward planning necessary improvements and extensions.
2. Establishing a national or international plan of roads relevant to tourism, building new roads if necessary, improving those in a deficient state, and improving road sign systems. Such activities should be included in the general road plans with priorities according to economic necessity and the significance of road transport in tourism.
3. Improving rail transport (where needed) for travelers on lines between the boundary and the main tourist centers and regions as well as short-distance services in these regions of maximum tourist influx.
4. Improving road frontier posts, extending their capacity to ensure smoother crossings, organizing easier movement of in- and outgoing tourist flows. Crossing the frontier is always either the prologue or the epilogue to any journey between countries and is therefore important for the favorable impression the tourist will retain.
5. Providing adequate airport services and installations to meet demand. The rapid progress of technology in air transport makes reasonable forecasts possible.
6. Planning for ports and marinas equipped for tourism.
7. Extending car-hire services (with and without drivers) for tourists who arrive by air or sea.

Accommodations

Accommodations must be properly placed in the regional plan. Hotels are permanent structures and grace the landscape for a long time. Planning considerations are vital. Figure 15.2 shows a specific site development plan.

One of the first considerations to be made by any planning body should be where hotels will be located. This can be accomplished by using zoning laws. Hotels are commonly allowed in "commercial" zones. Also to be decided is the number of hotel

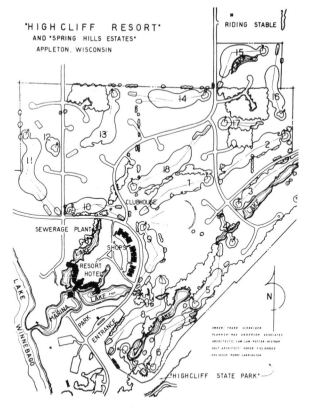

Figure 15.2 Example of Planning for Private Tourism Development Adjacent to a State Park. Note integration of infrastructure and recreational facilities. (Source: Recreational Land Development, Wisconsin Department of Natural Resources, Division of Resource Development, Bureau of Recreation)

rooms needed in relation to the anticipated demand. Then to be considered is a provision for expansion of hotels as demand increases.

One consideration in hotel planning is intelligent spacing of hotels in a given area. Hotels spaced too close together tend to have a mutual value-reducing effect. Views are cut off or inhibited, and structures are lowered in value.

Also important is the ratio of the number of persons on the beach to the number of rooms in the hotel. Research in the Department of Natural Resources of the state of Michigan indicates that the optimum capacity of an average-sized ocean or Great Lakes beach is approximately 1000 persons for each 400 lineal feet of beach. Typically, about 50 percent of those vacationers in a resort or beach area will actually be on the beach, and of this group, 25 percent will be in the water and 75 percent will be on the beach.

Another consideration is the topography. In rolling or hilly country, more accommodations can be placed close together without a feeling of interference with one another than in a flat area. Also, the type of vegetative cover affects the density of the accommodations. A heavy, thick cover tends to obscure the view, and more accommodations can be successfully placed in a limited area than if the vegetation is sparse or absent entirely (see Figure 15.3).

Clusters of accommodations in reasonably close proximity, surrounded by exten-

Universal Studios Florida is an example of a highly complex, integrated development of a tourist attraction. Each component in the planning process was undertaken, culminating in the implementation of the final plan by the actual construction program. (Photo courtesy of the Florida Department of Commerce, Division of Tourism)

sive natural areas, is recognized as superior planning, as opposed to spreading out accommodations over a wide area. The beauty of the natural environment can be more fully appreciated in such an arrangement.

Before any investment in hotels and similar lodging facilities is made, the traveling and vacation habits of the prospective guests should be studied to tailor the facilities to the requirements and desires of guests. This is extremely important and conforms to the "market orientation" concept in which major decisions on investment begin with the desires of the potential customers. Another factor is the harmony required between the various elements of the travel plan, the local environment, and infrastructure.

Finally, when resort development is to be limited (and it usually is), it is best to select the most desirable location and create a hotel of real distinction at this site. Then, later, if proper planning and promotion have been accomplished, expansion to other nearby sites can be achieved. Distinctive design of other hotel sites will encourage the visitor to enjoy the variety, architectural appeals, and other satisfactions inherent in each resort hotel.

Financing

Possible procedures for financing construction include a mortgage guarantee plan and direct loans from a variety of sources.

MORTGAGE GUARANTEE PLAN   Under this plan the government would guarantee mortage loans up to 80 percent of the approved and appraised value of the land,

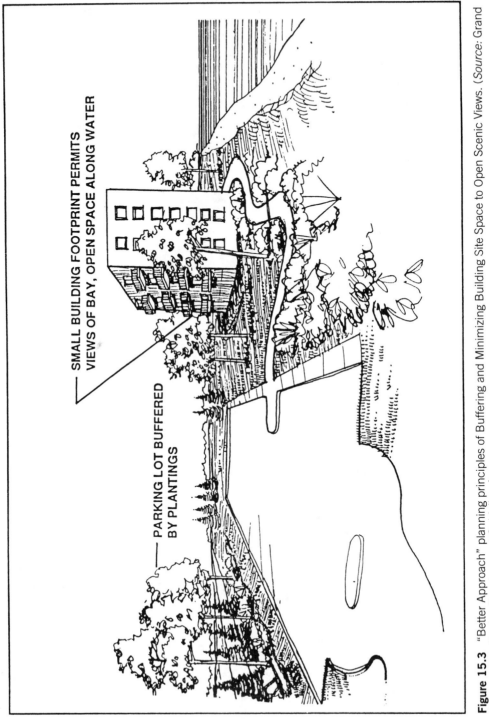

SMALL BUILDING FOOTPRINT PERMITS VIEWS OF BAY, OPEN SPACE ALONG WATER

PARKING LOT BUFFERED BY PLANTINGS

Figure 15.3 "Better Approach" planning principles of Buffering and Minimizing Building Site Space to Open Scenic Views. (*Source:* Grand Traverse Bay Region Development Guidelines)

Hotel accommodations should be planned to blend in with the surrounding environment to enhance the tourist experience. (Photo courtesy of Wimberly, Alison, Tong, and Goo, Architects)

building, furnishings, and equipment when the resort is completed. The approved mortgage would carry interest at prevailing mortgage rates and would require a schedule of amortization for the full retirement of the loan in not more than perhaps 30 years.

A guarantee fund would be established that at all times would be maintained at 20 percent of the total outstanding principal amount of mortgages guaranteed under this plan. The guarantee fund would be managed by trustees who would make any payments of interest and principal certified to them by the agency in charge of the mortgage loan plan. This agency would supervise the status of all approved loans and would investigate the facts and situations whenever it might become necessary to rely upon the guarantee fund to make the required interest and amortization payments. In such cases, an assignment of assets and income would be taken from the resort in default, which would have to be made up from subsequent earnings before any other use could be made of it.

Under this plan, the investor in the resort project would secure a mortgage loan from a lending institution or issue bonds or mortgage certificates to one or more sources of the borrowed capital. With the guarantee of payments of interest and principal and the existence of the guarantee fund for that purpose, mortgage loans under this plan should be attractive to lending institutions and other sources of borrowed capital.

With an approved resort development project and a guaranteed mortgage loan equivalent to 80 percent of the total financing required for land, building, furniture and equipment, 20 percent of the cost could be invested as equity risk capital. The ability to finance on this basis would provide incentive to those directly interested in the business, as well as other investors, to participate in new resort development projects.

FINANCING PROCEDURES   A group interested in building a resort must convince the local city, regional, or national authorities that the resort should be built. The next step is to obtain a suitable site designated for construction under a previously completed tourist developmet plan for the area. A third-party feasibility study should be undertaken.

To indicate that this group is seriously interested in building a resort, architects, engineers, consultants, and other specialists should be contacted during the planning phase. The organization that is to *operate* the resort should be the same group that *builds* the hotel. An important planning ingredient is the recommendation of experienced resort managers concerning design and layout of the project.

The next step is to obtain construction capital either from local sources or from government or foreign sources. Also, capital must be secured for equipment, supplies, and services, including opening expenses and pre–break-even expenses. Government aid in obtaining imported supplies and equipment is often necessary. Governmental consideration should be given for reduction or elimination of taxes for an adequate length of time to help insure the financial success of the resort venture. Elimination of import duties on materials needed to build and run resorts is also desirable.

SUMMARY

The quality of tourism planning and development will determine the ultimate success and longevity of any destination area. Thus, time, effort, and resources devoted to planning are essential investments.

Thoughtful planners have formulated the goals for tourism development, and these should be guiding principles everywhere. Obstacles must be overcome by sound planning augmented by political means, if growth is desired. This is often accomplished by the official tourism body. Tourism development should be a part of the overall regional or urban land-use development plan.

Tourism developments almost always involve both government and private developers. Each sector can best contribute certain parts of a project. Government typically provides the infrastructure, such as roads, water supply, sewers, public transportation terminals, and parks. Private developers supply superstructure, such as hotels, restaurants, recreation facilities, and shopping areas.

Government can also help considerably in making financing available. The private sector must deem an investment in a tourist facility attractive from the standpoint of financial return and risk before funds will be committed.

About the Readings

The first brief reading provides a development example in a small city provided by the organization Partners for Livable Places.

Allison's article emphasizes the wisdom of incorporating local architectural designs, materials, decor, handicraft products, and other manifestations of local culture into tourist facilities. Doing so helps to make the developments an asset to the country instead of a detriment.

The third reading examines an exotic development in southern Africa—The Palace of the Lost City.

READING 15.1

Development Example in a Small City

"Destination? Where? Putting Cities Without Surf, Slopes and Slot Machines on the Map," Partners for Livable Places, Washington, D.C.

Jonesborough (population 3000), Tennessee, is the oldest town in the state, a living historic community and seat of the short-lived State of Franklin that offers a rare glimpse into the past. The restoration of the town's historic district, initiated less than two decades ago, boasts the preservation of many Victorian, Neo-Classical, Federal and Greek Revival style buildings. The cornerstone of the district is the Christopher Taylor House, a log cabin that once housed President Andrew Jackson. Visitors can also view historic churches, the 1779 courthouse in which Jackson was admitted to the bar, charming houses, and can dine and shop along the town's Main Street.

A multi-purpose tourist facility was recently constructed to serve as a welcome and orientation to the preserved historic district. The center provides an introduction to Tennessee's first town through an audiovisual program and museum displaying the city's history and artifacts. As it has no hotels, Jonesborough promotes itself as a day-visitor destination.

Jonesborough's efforts to preserve an important part of American history and culture have added to tourist-related expenditures in the upper East Tennessee region. These funds amounted to $145 million in 1981, and produced $5.7 million in state tax revenues and $2 million in local tax receipts.

READING 15.2

Special Places in Special Places
BY GERALD L. ALLISON, FAIA, RIBA
President, Wimberly Allison Tong and Goo Architects, Ltd.

Special places in special places—redundant? Not really. In the context of resort travel, those words are a fair description of what we all seek when we become travelers for pleasure. Certainly when we head for a resort in anticipation of cherished days of respite, we look forward to finding a special place within a special place.

Furthermore, this expectation often influences travel decisions even when the primary purpose is not an unalloyed holiday. Otherwise, why would resort hotels offer extensive convention facilities or corporate conferences be held in exotic places?

Speaking for myself—with everything else being equal—I am far more likely to accept an invitation to speak in Portugal, for example, over the same opportunity in Chicago. I have never experienced Portugal. It holds great promise of pleasure. I have been to Chicago and experienced Chicago. I stayed in a Chicago hotel. And I also stayed in a Chicago hotel in Hong Kong. And in Tokyo. And in Singapore. A couple of them in Sydney, another in Auckland, and a whole list of other places around the world. Also Athens, the wellspring of architectural history. It is truly amazing how widespread Chicago hotels are. Even in Kuala Lumpur and Bali you can wake up in the morning and say, "What a nice hotel—for Chicago."

That's what I want to talk about—how it is not necessary or even desirable to design Chicago hotels around the world. They belong in Chicago.

Please understand, this is not meant to denigrate Chicago, the city. Or special places appropriate to Chicago, where they reflect the special character of that city.

The repetition of the architecture of any particular place—over and over in other places—and mindlessly superimposed out of context—inevitably adds up to sameness and usually inappropriateness. This homogenizing sameness means, at best, overlooking the vast potential that awaits sensitive, responsible development. Sameness in hotel design has the effect of watering down the individuality of place—the very thing that should be enhanced, spotlighted. This sameness is—by inference—disrespectful of the character and culture of the host community. Further, it tends to limit rather than contribute to guest opportunities to experience the place chosen for special qualities. These clone hotels are anything but special places.

I concede they routinely offer the basics for comfortable travel—plumbing that works, hot water for bathing, safe water for drinking, and clean sheets—but not deeply rewarding travel.

And I would gladly accept a little sag in the bed in exchange for a little lift of the spirit.

Do you think this is a bit overstated? I don't think so. There are highly successful premium priced resorts in which all rooms have views and none have telephones, radios, TVs, or mini-bars. Let's consider the implications of "travel for pleasure." What does it mean? It means that for reasons of pleasure we leave one place to go to another. Why? The expectation of change, relaxation, escape, newness, excitement, enrichment, fantasy. Rejuvenating experience.

A successful resort, then, is one that satisfies these expectations. Put another way: The realization of these expectations is what sells hotel rooms and dining seats. And that's really what spells success in the hospitality industry; because if you don't fill those rooms and those seats, you are destined for failure.

So what are we talking about in terms of satisfying this wish list of expectations?

First—and I know this is repetitive, one thing we are not talking about is cookie cutter sameness, because change, not sameness, is what the pleasure traveler seeks.

Note of caution, however. Never underestimate the power of the cookie cutter. As rich as the possibilities are for individuality and appropriateness in hotel design, the cookie cutter mold is an ever-present temptation. It's always there, available, quick, cost efficient (in the short haul), ready to stamp out more and more copies of itself. It is often sneaked in under the guise of expediency, among other things. Perhaps one of the most heavily weighted reasons for reliance on cookie cutter hotels has been guest acceptance. Fortunately, this is eroding. Discrimination in matters of taste is an acquired, or developed, attribute. Jet travel, growing affluence, the opening up of heretofore undeveloped areas, renovation of the grand old hotels of Europe and America, and a rapidly expanding inventory of truly fine new hotels worldwide all contribute to the growing pool of pleasure travelers who grow more and more discriminating as they amass travel experiences. Thus, the more success the travel industry enjoys, the more dedicated to excellence it must become—to keep pace with the enlightened, discriminating traveler it is in the process of producing.

If we disdain cookie cutter hotels, we endorse hotels that are an expression of their particular environment and its people, that have a vibrant sense of place, and provide guests a rich array of optional pleasures. These hotels work, in part, because they recognize the name of the game is "pleasure" and they do afford guests the means whereby their individual expectations of pleasure can be realized. And because people are as individual in their preferences as in their personalities, the potential for creating uniquely wonderful—special—places is limitless.

While the ideal site for your special place may be in the Swiss or New Zealand Alps or mountains of Colorado, my fantasies may focus on the shores of Bora Bora or Cannes.

Australian rain forests and desert sands of the American Southwest have strong appeal.

Country lanes and, surely, city streets have allure.

Both the exoticism of Bangkok and the familiarity of American apple pie in Memphis attract, as surely as the warmth of the California or Riviera sunshine, or Scandinavia's bracing winds and weather.

History and culture buffs are drawn, as if by a magnet, to Williamsburg and New Orleans, London and Paris, Rome and Lisbon. . . .

How about castles in Spain? Or—Italy? Surely they too capture the imagination.

Fly to the Pacific for safe viewing of primeval furies of Hawaii's volcanoes; or, to the Atlantic for leisure listening to mellifluous songs and vibrant rhythms of the Caribbean.

Sip a Singapore Sling at fabled Raffles Hotel and talk about the tiger that was killed in the bar and the writers who created legends there.

Small jewel-like resorts—simple to sophisticated, informal and formal, each catering to a single facet of recreation—are cutting a nice niche in the marketplace—for example, the European and African resorts of Serena Hotels.

Leave your *istana* (ancient palaces of Malaysian sultans) inspired quarters in Trengganu to watch the ageless ritual of a giant sea turtle lumbering ashore, laying and burying her eggs and then with silent dignity returning to the deep from whence she came.

Is the picture emerging? Growing in your mind's eye?

You ask, am I talking business or am I caught up in my own dreams and imaginations? The answer is—both!

The business of pleasure travel is the business of creativity, creating special places in special places—to translate everyone's dreams into reality. Call it the Pleasure Principle, if you like. But never lose sight of this very real fact: In this business, pleasure is paramount. Believe it—there is a correlation between the degree of success we achieve in pleasing people and the color of the bottom line.

To deviate slightly, I would like to encourage you to feel good about all this "leisure."

Americans as a group are probably burdened excessively with our Puritan work ethic. Hotel management attracts many Germans, who may have originated the super disciplined approach to work. Unless, of course, it was of Chinese derivation. Whatever the roots of our dedication to work, I think we sometimes need reminding that it's OK—even desirable for good health—for humans to indulge, on a regular basis, in periods of pure pleasure. Recreation, in the sense of re-creation.

This business we're engaged in has a very valid *raison d'etre*. It is not simply a modern version of Louis XIV opulence. For all the super rich who can afford to spend their lives doing nothing but trekking from one resort to another, there are thousands of ordinary people who work diligently on a year-round basis, subjected to highly stressed lifestyles. They need and are willing to pay for the rejuvenation that comes from a complete change of pace—pleasure in a special place.

This is our major market segment, our growth potential.

What does it take, in a hotel, to richly reward our travel expectations? What is required to keep it out of the cookie cutter class and assure its role as a destination of distinction?

Keeping in mind that the primary function or service provided is pleasure—although the hotel is eminently practical—attractiveness and the ambiance of the physical structure are vital to its economic success. Every hotel needs thoughtful, imaginative design. Resort hotels, which exist solely for the pleasure of their users, demand it.

But it is not simply a matter of serving up a physically beautiful hotel. We recreational travelers seeking new experiences in exotic places are looking for far more than that. We want to observe and to experience that which makes our destinations different from the places we have left. Universally, we seek that special place in a special place. That is what drives us to other parts of our own countries and to other parts of the world. We seek other cultures, other lifestyles, and the uniqueness of the region we visit.

Toward fulfilling these goals, the hotel design can be a key element. Generally, the first unhurried introduction to a new region is the hotel in which we are to stay. It becomes our temporary home base. The place where we must eat, sleep, exercise, socialize, shop, listen to music, look at art, or simply "hang out" as the younger generation would say. It should be very much a part of our escape objective, not simply where we sleep and change clothes. It is also at our hotel that we may have the closest relationship with natives of the host locale. This offers an opportunity for good social interchange between guest and host. Both benefit. The hotel provides a captive audience eager to learn.

However . . .

Considering the salient and comprehensive role of the hotel in the guest's holiday experience, it naturally follows that hotel design should address the matter as creatively and effectively as possible.

There are other reasons for appropriate design. If the hotel design is sensitive to and appreciative of the culture and arts of the host area, this encourages and reinforces pride of heritage in the native resident and tends to make him or her more receptive to nonresidents. Sensitive, responsible design may also make significant contributions to the preservation and/or enhancement of a region's particular heritage. This works to the benefit of everyone.

From the developer's and operator's points of view, design appropriate to the region will quite likely result in cost savings as the facilities will be easier to construct and maintain. The design will often make use of readily available materials and technology appropriate to local construction techniques. Proper design may even eliminate the need for elevators, air conditioning and numerous other high maintenance building elements.

Designing with this kind of approach should lead to a degree of guest satisfaction that results in solid demand, excellent occupancy rates, enviable room charges, and long stays.

It should also result in return visits and a generous number of referrals, each looking for a special place of escape.

Successfully meeting these goals is not a project confined to design of buildings. It is, rather, a highly complex matter encompassing the whole project continuum from master planning, design, approvals, and financing right through construction to maintenance, management, and even marketing, and in some cases periodic additions and renovations.

Meeting the challenge requires a lot of understanding—understanding by management of the challenges inherent in creating a design that fits the locality and cultural mores, and understanding by the design team of management's problems in providing services to guests and of maintaining the property in top condition. At times, it is difficult for clients, particularly in developing countries, to understand that locally inspired designs and native materials in new buildings can be as marketable as ancient temples.

Generally speaking, America has only recently begun to understand what Europe has long known—saving old landmarks and/or constructing new buildings near landmarks in such a manner as to respect and complement them is a responsibility. And a privilege.

There are many examples of this enlightened philosophy in Europe, where tourism plants are frequently integral parts of the regional cultural heritage. Ironically, many of the most successful projects are, by their very nature, difficult to find—which may be a good part of the reason for their success. They so blend into their immediate environment that they are hardly distinguishable as part of the tourist industry. Many, in fact, originally were not. Villas and houses, taverns and castles, have been converted to hotels, lodges, resorts. That they are, practically speaking, inseparable from the architecture and tapestry of life in their respective communities is a large part of their grace and appeal.

To summarize this relationship between special places and success in the pleasure travel arena: In the long run, the hotel providing the strongest possible sense of place will become the most desirable. The pleasure traveler seeks novel experiences, not a rerun of "Chicago." If the hotel patronized provides all the amenities required, while reinforcing the sense of being in an exotic location, the satisfaction quotient should be high—and this means the traveler will stay longer, return sooner, and pay more for the travel experience.

One price I paid as a traveler, I hadn't really bargained for; but with the added perspective of time, I can now treasure it as a priceless experience. Imagine a business conference in Japan with twelve stark naked men and one equally naked woman—the secretary—sitting chest deep in a steaming hot-spring bath discussing redesign of the world's largest enclosed communal "jungle bath." Also imagine being the only 6'2" blond-haired, blue-eyed Caucasian in the group. The meeting wears on; an hour later you are still sitting stark naked in that steaming bath trying to sketch design solutions before you and the paper wilts into oblivion. Making the challenge even more interesting—you are surrounded by bathers of both genders. They are curious, and slightly amused, about the way you look. Imagination is probably not vivid enough to match the reality that was.

Now, let's bring theory into focus by looking at specific projects, each with its own unique characteristics, challenges, and requirements. Ideally, there is no typical resort.

Much of what has been presented so far can be pulled together in a single case study of a small resort project that relies much less on fantasy for guest satisfaction, than on its integration with the culture of the beautiful east coast of West Malaysia. Exoticism, romance, seclusion, are key words to describe the resort. It is an unusual one, too, in that facilities are split in two sections five miles apart. They are the hotel and resort facilities at Tanjong Jara Beach and visitor center facilities at Rantau Abang.

Genesis of the design process was preparation of a tourism study in which Wimberly, Allison, Tong and Goo Architects participated. The study concluded that the economic success of a Malaysian visitor development program venture would depend in large on the country's ability to maintain and enhance Malaysia's distinctive character—its historic, cultural, and scenic attractions.

Five years later, the Malaysian Tourism Development Corporation engaged WAT&G to transform the development plan from a dream to reality, to create a hotel which would become the first step towards actualization of the master plan. The architects were charged with site selection as well as design and project development of what would become the first major tourist facility on West Malaysia's picturesque east coast.

One of the principal attractions of the area—giant sea turtles in their migration and egg laying rituals—presented both an opportunity and a responsibility. The architects felt visitors should be acquainted with the turtles' delicate life cycle and also the relationship that exists between Malaysia and the surrounding sea. On recommendation of the architects, the Malaysian government agreed to establish, as part of the overall project, a museum and visitor center near the middle of the hatching grounds, five miles from the hotel site. The two separate yet complementary parts of an integrated whole.

Throughout concept development and the working out of details there was strong motivation to create a project so appropriate to its total environment that it would not only look and feel right but seem an inevitable outgrowth of the whole.

Before starting with the actual hotel design, extensive research took place. This involved photographs and sketches and the study of whatever documents we could obtain that dealt with the unique cultural aspects of West Malaysia's east coast.

The design team then searched the area for craftsmen whose work could be incorporated into the construction. Trengganu is fortunate in having an abundance of talent capable of doing excellent wood carving, kite making, fine weaving, and mat making plus other crafts suitable for incorporation into design plans.

Ultimately, work of these craftsmen was well utilized and integrated into the construction and interiors of the facilities. As a side effect, this involvement provided a whole new ongoing economic outlet for their production and encouraged further development of traditional crafts.

The final step in our research was into the historic architectural styles of Trengganu. We determined that the unique and handsome, 100-year-old *istanas* (Sultan's palace) were an architectural form that could be adapted for hotel use. Their design and construction was such that natural ventilation could drastically reduce the need for energy-consuming airconditioning. Using the *istanas* as the architectural theme, we designed a resort master plan facility in the manner of a Malaysian riverside village with an existing stream as a focal point and the hotel placed on a curve of white sand beach at the foot of lush green mountains.

Architecture of the *istana*-like buildings is eminently practical in relationship to local weather conditions, makes use of materials plentiful in the area, and features traditional Malaysian art forms and craftsmanship. A salient feature of the two-story hardwood construction is that buildings are three to five feet above the ground for purposes of security, flood protection, and air circulation. Other ventilating elements are open-sided rooms, lattice soffits, steep pitched roofs with gable grilles, and locally-made bisque roof tiles left exposed "to breathe" on the inside. Buildings are constructed of native hardwood allowed to weather naturally.

Decorative motifs utilize Malaysian arts and crafts including wood carvings, woven mats, baskets, kites, shadow puppets and ceramics that are an integral part of the design and made by local artisans using traditional methods.

Rantau Abang Visitor Centre, with its sea life museum, depicts the strong traditional link between Malaysians and the sea. It serves, further, to protect the giant sea turtle during one step of its migratory life. The site is sandwiched between the coastal road and ocean with the Kabang River lying between the two.

The project consists of a complex of Malaysian-style buildings that include the museum/visitor center, a bazaar featuring Malaysian craftsmen with their wares, a Malaysian cuisine restaurant, a botanical garden featuring Malaysian plants used for food, shelter, and medicinal purposes, and a group of bungalows for overnight guests.

Structures are raised on piers above the river and sand dunes to avoid disruption of the site's natural characteristics. The height also affords a sweeping view of the turtle hatching grounds. Buildings, entirely of native hardwoods from nearby forests, are built in the centuries-old tradition of Malaysian construction by carpenters and craftsmen of the area.

Was the project well received? Very much so. It has been critically acclaimed internationally; the client is well-pleased, Rantau Abang was awarded an American Institute of Architects Excellence in Design citation, and in 1983 Tanjong Jara/Rantau Abang captured the prestigious Aga Khan Award for Architecture. The jury commended WAT&G for having "the courage to search out and successfully adapt and develop an otherwise rapidly disappearing traditional architecture and craft, to meet the demands of contemporary architecture. The consistency and seriousness with which this approach has been pursued at all levels of design and execution has generated an architecture that is in keeping with traditional values and esthetics, and of an excellence matching the best surviving traditional examples."

By the way, sometimes the process of learning foreign customs can be embarrassing—if somewhat humorous. A personal example happened while I was designing the project in Malaysia, where it is the usual Muslim custom in an Islamic country to wash your hands prior to partaking of food. At a business meeting, we were all served tea and each received an individual dish of delicacies. Folded neatly at the side of the dish was a thin, damp, chartreuse green sponge. I unfolded it and was diligently wiping my hands when I was shocked to see the Malaysian across from me eating his. A closer look at my ritual hand washing "sponge" revealed that it was, in fact, a coconut filled crepe.

Among WAT&G's work is a group of resort projects in several countries of the South Pacific. These projects have been extremely successful. Each is uniquely different from the others, and without exception—design for these hotels was derived from the culture of the particular host area.

Let's consider a few of them, briefly.

First, the Fijian Hotel, on Yanuca Island. The site plan of this hotel reflects the traditional Fijian village layout, with buildings clustered around a central court. Design and construction of the public rooms drew heavily on the indigenous architectural style of the Fijian *bure* (house), which is characterized by a high, steep roof and projecting ridge pole. Construction throughout was done by local natives using techniques familiar to them. The architectural firm sent a sculptor, Mick Brownlee, to work with natives in reestablishing the all but lost art of Fijian wood carving. As a result, newly trained artisans were employed to carve Fijian-motif artifacts to be used in the public rooms and established a shop on the site to sell their wares to the visitor.

One of WAT&G's most spectacularly romantic and equally as understated projects is the world renowned Hotel Bora Bora in French Polynesia. On a palm-studded promontory facing Bora Bora Lagoon are 65 beach and garden bungalows designed in the manner of the traditional Tahitian *fare* (house). Fifteen over-water luxury bungalows are perched at the reef's edge. Each unit has a view of the azure lagoon and reef, white sand beach, tropical flowers, and distant mountains. The open-air buildings, cooled by prevailing tradewinds, have bamboo walls with screened openings and roofs constructed of *lauhala* thatching. At Hotel Bora Bora, don't expect such intrusions as radios and televisions.

In almost every instance, native solutions to climatic problems—representing centuries of trial and error—are good responses to local conditions. We found this to be particularly true in American Samoa while working on design solutions for the Hotel Pago Pago Intercontinental. The Samoan *fale* (house) effectively solves the problems of building in a hot, humid climate. The traditional thatched roof protects from rain without impeding air movements; the open sides let prevailing winds pass through; palm-leaf "blinds" can be lowered to keep rain out. To base our design on this vernacular architecture and yet speak to modern requirements for comfort and sanitation, we devised a contemporary version of the *fale* combining its form and response to climate with modern materials to obtain a simple and economical structure adaptable to a variety of conditions. Our hotel *fales* were constructed by native workmen using traditional methods. Timbers were hand hewn by adzes, fitted together with wooden pegs and lashed with coconut fiber sennet. The project won a Hawaii Society American Institute of Architecture Design Award.

READING 15.3

Creating a Fantasy, Retaining a Culture:
The Palace of the Lost City
BY BETH VINCENT
Wimberly Allison Tong and Goo Architects, Ltd.

A landmark phase of Sol Kerzner's Sun City Development, the 350-room hotel extravaganza called The Palace of The Lost City, opened recently in Bophuthatswana in southern Africa. The press heralded the resort for its unprecedented opulence, for introducing an original architectural form and for implementing new technology in the Republic of Bophuthatswana. All of this was achieved in a record-breaking time span—less than twenty-eight months from beginning of design to opening date.

What is perhaps more amazing is that a themed, fantasy resort of this magnitude and complexity has retained a strong sense of the ethnic and cultural magic that is Africa. The Palace has emerged as a visible folk memory, a drama in which the wisdom and elusive spirit of Africa astonish the guest at every turn, every vista.

The story of how the design and completion of The Palace was accomplished is an adventurous expedition in itself, and a very revealing one. It is the story of two Americans working in a remote country far from their home base: the design architect, Gerald Allison of Wimberly Allison Tong & Goo (WAT&G) Architects and Planners, and the interior architectural designer, Trisha Wilson of Wilson & Associates. The adventure began with the vision of the developer Sol Kerzner.

For years, Sun City, Kerzner's brainchild, has been one of the most magnetic tourist destinations on the continent. Kerzner decided in the late 1980's to add a new dimension to the project: an ultra-luxurious hotel for the most sophisticated traveler and a surrounding world of fantasy attractions that would double the influx of day-visitors.

After a lengthy search for the conceptual and design architect he believed would best bring his dream hotel to life, Kerzner chose Gerald L. Allison, FAIA, of the Newport Beach, California office of Wimberly Allison Tong & Goo.

Allison and WAT&G have a forty-eight-year history of creating resorts well-matched to their specific locations. But the commission Kerzner gave to Allison and WAT&G was daunting: Kerzner wanted to build a fantasy-resort hotel that in its opulence and originality would be unrivaled anywhere in the world, and he wanted this project to be designed, constructed and open for business in under three years.

In designing the project, the WAT&G architects followed three self-imposed dictates. First, The Palace was internalized as an idea and designed as a palace, not as a hotel. Second, the real storehouse to be mined for concept and decorative elements was the lore of southern Africa—its cultural history, diversity of flora and fauna, and its deep-rooted traditions. Third, the project was to be a serious project; the fantasy would have an underlying sense of authenticity and would be created in a way that would bring a focus and a greater economic strength to the small nation of Bophuthatswana in which it was to be built.

The strength of the design concept held the project together from beginning to end and gave flavor and meaning to the result. For Allison, the first design tool was the creation of a legend.

In December, 1989, Allison flew to Bophuthatswana to meet Kerzner. The two visited the site, a rather unremarkable location in the midst of a centuries-old volcanic crater. What Allison and Kerzner saw was an opportunity to create something totally new: they imagined the re-creation of an ancient lost city, newly rediscovered, and of a palace which would

Facade of the Fantasy resort hotel, Palace of the Lost City, in southern Africa. (Photo courtesy of Wimberly, Allison, Tong and Goo, Architects)

become a royal residence for guests to explore and enjoy. This palace would serve as a smoothly functioning hotel, but be conceived and designed as the remaining intact building amid the ruins of a previously unknown civilization. The entire project would call for an architecture never before seen by modern man.

With this idea in mind, the actual design adventure began.

A rough script about this legendary place, which eventually evolved into The Legend of The Lost City, was crafted by Allison on that first day. He and his associate designer Eduardo Robles, also began making preliminary on-site design studies, working late into the night.

By the next morning they had produced over a dozen sketches and plans. The client reviewed these ideas and asked for a concept presentation the next afternoon for his board members. Allison and Robles again worked all night.

"By noon the following day, we had produced another dozen sheets of presentation drawings, including site plans, basic building plans and 14 vignette renderings," Allison remembers.

The project was approved.

"Our next step was to return to the California office and put a strong architectural design team together to develop the concept," says Allison. "We got together, as part of the design process, in role-acting sessions; we'd conjure up what might have happened in an isolated civilization in which an architecture based on ancient stories and distant memories evolved."

Central to the development of this architecture was the idea that it would reflect the surrounding environment.

"Our challenge was an odd one," says Allison. "We were trying to re-create an architecture that never existed."

This rather nebulous concept had to be grounded in reality.

"The most natural choice was to use the symbols of southern Africa," says Allison. "Its colors, traditions and the rich world of plant and animal life would define all of our design and planning."

Reams of sketches, plans and detail drawings were studied as WAT&G sought this new architecture. Exotic directions were researched: "We looked at Middle Eastern, North African, Southeast Asian, Aztec, Incan, every form—you-name-it—of ancient architecture imaginable," says Allison.

Some ideas were rejected as inconsistent with the theme. Others were accepted because they suited the topography and the climate of Bophuthatswana.

"Once positioning on the site was determined," Allison explains, "the plan of The Palace developed more rapidly. Because the climate of this region can be quite warm at times, we designed around courtyards; open, single-loaded corridors; and high, lofty, shaded spaces with walls that could be left open. We also introduced the cooling effect of water running around and cascading within the building."

"We decided early in the project that we would not design a hotel," Allison says. "We would design a true palace and then convert it to hotel use."

This decision further defined the design. The architectural character of this true palace—its towers, domes, arches—emerged clearly with more and more renderings. A series of block models were built, and the decision was made to endow The Palace with an enormous amount of detailing to depict the particular flora and fauna of the surrounding countryside and to convey a feeling of the immensity and diversity of species inhabiting the area.

Some of this detail work was to be in large form: domes would be shaped with man-made elephant tusks and palm fronds. At this point, Trisha Wilson of the Texas-based firm of Wilson & Associates had joined the effort and was working along with the WAT&G team to continue the development of the interior architectural details, as conceived, in a way that would seamlessly meld them with the exterior design.

"Their talents generated new, exciting features," says Allison, "such as the Tusk Lounge and the Grand Stair, as well as ceiling components and layouts."

Thousands of details were intricate, designed to express the abundance of biological wonders found in the bush country. The African protea blossom, for instance, became a distinguishing feature of The Palace in a variety of forms from concrete finials that adorn the top of columns to door-frame embellishments.

"Throughout this process of research, discussion and changing ideas, we continued

View of a guest lounge in the Palace of the Lost City. Note the use of reproductions of locally found palms as interior decor. (Photo courtesy of Wimberly, Allison, Tong and Goo, Architects)

our design studies, always relating all the architectural motifs to the local environment," says Allison.

Once the final design was developed, the question loomed: could this remote section of southern Africa provide the skilled artisans and high level of technology required to produce the elaborate ornamentation that the architects were creating?

Basic construction of the building began and proceeded at a rapid pace. Production of the precast decorative elements, however, lagged behind. Both project managers and local workers, who were eager to advance their technology, were anxious to find a solution to this delay.

The team's solution was to bring together 25 artists from the United States and Africa to set up an on-site warehouse studio. A precasting plant was built on site for the execution of precast concrete features; sculptural studios were also erected on site to sculpt the daily changes.

"This team, led by Bernardo Munoz, was a Godsend," says Allison. "Soon they were carving the molds for the precast elements as shown on our detail drawings, and we were catching up with production. Animal and plant forms merged from dead blocks of foam. The fantasy was coming alive."

As construction proceeded, more mock-ups of major structural components of The Palace were made. Kerzner ordered a final model to illustrate what The Palace would look like when completed and the project leapt swiftly toward that goal.

While the development of the architecture continued, Wilson & Associates was formulating ideas that would continue the linkage of the interior to the exterior and to the surroundings.

"To give a particular African vibrancy to our work, we sought out local materials and artisans," says Wilson. "The region was isolated, but there was a rich lore of talent and materials; we found them everywhere."

On one occasion when she had gone on safari to a game lodge in the Eastern Transvaal bushveld, Wilson noticed some extraordinary carved wooden panels covered with a frieze of African animals—lions, elephants, buffalo, zebra and antelope. After investigating, she discovered that the artist, Alson Zuma, was a night guard on a farm in the Natal Province some 1000 km. away. Zuma was later commissioned to do a number of panels for The Palace.

Wilson also set out to train a local work force of artisans.

"The positive response was incredible," says Wilson. "And everyone benefited. Once we taught the local furniture makers how to create a four-poster bed, all four posts would be hand-carved beautifully from a single piece of mahogany."

Wilson says that in locating and working with local consultants in a foreign environment she found several steps particularly helpful. First, she advises networking.

"Don't go to tried and true sources; ask everyone questions explore every lead."

Her second step was assessment; she always scrutinized the actual skills and potential in addition to past work performed.

"Past work may have been influenced by market need. With new instruction I've found this can be modified or improved drastically."

Wilson said that a third pointer she would give to any designer working in a foreign environment with limited resources was to offer personal encouragement.

"Encourage people to do work they didn't think possible; let them feel that anything can be done and take a personal interest in their progress," she adds.

Part of her logistics for securing superior designs was to take highly specialized samples, such as tapestry work or wood carving from the United States or Europe, to Bophuthatswana. This way she could demonstrate to the local workers exactly how to bring their work up to five-star standards.

Manufacturers in the States would sometimes do prototypes. For instance, Wilson

A guest suite at the Palace of the Lost City. All of the furniture was crafted locally. Wildlife of the area is depicted in the bedspreads and furniture upholstery. (Photo courtesy of Wimberly, Allison, Tong and Goo, Architects)

wanted a console with wooden-monkey legs in the guest rooms but was concerned that the level of detail conveyed by furniture modelers in southern Africa was unrefined. A model was carved in Dallas and transported to Africa to illustrate a less roughhewn approach.

"We'd say, this is the quality we want. The locals were thrilled and cooperative. They studied the model piece, examined how the details were carved, and, after a lot of going back and forth about the scale and intricacies of the carving, they were able to reproduce what we needed."

In other situations, such as tapestry weaving, native artisans had a high level of proficiency. Large tapestries in the rotunda lobby of The Palace depict African savannah scenes with animals, water, trees and grass. The tapestry designs were done by an artist in the United States; the tapestries were woven by a local South African artist who employs native weavers and uses South African mohair and local dyes.

When imported materials and furnishings were used, the African theme was still a central consideration. The Tusk bar in the Palace has Ndebele-influenced fabric. The Ndebele are a southern African tribe who use brightly-colored geometric designs in the decoration of their houses and in their beadwork for personal adornment. Even the hardware on all doors is custom-designed with African themes. The handles of the doors leading off the Tusk Lounge, for example, are cast elephant heads.

"The dominating influence behind all decision-making for all the guestrooms was the African feeling in which I wanted to immerse the guests. To me, that meant carved woods; rich, earthy colors; and animal motifs."

A typical guestroom serves as a good example of how a number of unusual features were used and pulled together to create a whole. The bedside lamp is a monkey designed by Wilson & Associates and hand-carved by local African craftsmen. In the entrance foyer is another hand-carved mahogany piece, a console with legs rendered in monkeys and vines. The drapery fabric has a design motif of large cat paw-prints, and this is complemented by the same design on the coverlets with added images of lions and lizards.

"Just as WAT&G was doing, we used the animal and flora imagery everywhere—in all areas of the hotel and for all purposes; all custom carpet patterns are original and feature various animal and vegetation themes, as do the fabrics and furniture carving," Wilson says.

The years of practical experience that the imported architect and designer and their firms brought to Africa has led to a highly-practical, highly-functional Palace turned hotel. The fantasy concept has been conveyed in intricate, baroque detail derived from the biological vigor that is southern Africa.

By the December 1, 1992, opening, every aspect of the project—including the almost 15,000 pieces of pre-cast, custom-made ornamentation—was planned and built to give the effect of a venture into a newly-discovered world that will bring a bristling, constant sense of Africa and its magical, distant past to all who see it.

Now complete, The Palace of The Lost City tells its own story.

Key Concepts

architectural recommendations
area tourism development plan
creating infrastructure
economic and financial aspects
economic dependence on tourism
goals of tourism development
government tourism program
heritage preservation
land use
management of government tourism
   program

obstacles to development
official tourism body
policy formulation
political aspects
preservation and environmentalism
problems of unplanned growth
promotional efforts
role of local or state governments
total planning effort
transportation
zoning

For Review and Discussion

1. Basically, what is the purpose of planning?
2. Discuss the importance of transportation to tourism development.
3. Discuss the most important factors that would influence the success of a newly built resort.
4. Why is tourism developmental planning so necessary?
5. What are some of the most significant relationships between a large-sized resort development and its nearby community?
6. Referring to the previous question, if the community is a rather small one, should any input be solicited from residents of the community before major remodeling or new construction is undertaken?
7. What goals should guide the land use plan of a small lakeshore village that is popular with summer visitors?
8. Provide some descriptions of the importance of infrastructure to the following: ski resort, summer campground, fishing pier, public marina, shopping center, resort apartment condominium project.
9. From planning to completed project, name the principal individuals and organizations that would be involved.
10. Do you agree with the statement that if a community's government and business leaders are resistant or passive toward tourism, development will lag?

11. Currently, heritage preservation is a popular trend. Is it a desirable one?

12. Would you encourage tourism development if your community and area were already very prosperous ones?

13. Enumerate various kinds of environmental pollution that unwise developments can create.

14. How could greater emphasis be placed on the importance of a development process in which meticulous attention is given to the environment to create a harmonious combination of natural assets and human-made facilities?

15. Architect Gerald Allison states that he would "gladly accept a little sag in the bed for a little lift in the spirit." What does he mean by this? Do you agree? Explain.

16. Explain nature tourism and enumerate its advantages for a developing country.

Case Problems

1. A real estate developer, aware of a growing demand for a lakeshore resort condominium, planned for 126 apartments plus a 56-slip marina. Upon submission of his plan, the township planning board informed him that only one apartment and one boat slip would be allowed for each 100 feet of lakeshore. As he did not own that much lakeshore, plans were redrawn to construct the planned development back from the lakeshore. Access to the lake would be provided via a canal, using one of the lakeshore lots—a "keyhole" plan. This proposal was also rejected. The developer then sued the township board to force approval. What should the court or judge decide?

2. You have accepted a United Nations Development Program assignment in tourism to a small Central American country. Your first task is to make financial calculations concerning the economic feasibility for such development. What factors do you consider when beginning this process? Assuming your findings result in a favorable conclusion, what would your next step be?

3. Hotels built in a box-like manner are cheaper to construct and maintain than those with more elaborate designs. Hotel companies normally aim to maximize profits. Thus, should all hotels be built in that manner?

Selected References

Allen, Lawrence R., Harry R. Hafer, Patrick T. Long, and Richard R. Perdue. "Rural Residents' Attitudes Toward Recreation and Tourism Development." *Journal of Travel Research,* Vol. 31, No. 4 (Spring 1993), pp. 27–33.

Arnold, David E., et al. *Hotel/Motel Development.* Washington D.C.: The Urban Land Institute, 1984.

Baud-Bovy, Manuel, and Fred Lawson. *Tourism and Recreation Development.* London: Architectural Press; Boston: CBI, 1977.

Bell, Charles Anderson. "Crosscultural Construction: Designing Hotels Overseas." *Cornell Hotel and Restaurant Administration Quarterly,* Vol. 27, No. 2 (August 1989), pp. 25–28.

Butler, R. W., and L. A. Waldbrook. "A New Planning Tool: The Tourism Opportunity Spectrum." *Journal of Tourism Studies,* Vol. 2, No. 1 (May 1991), pp. 2–14.

Canestrell, Elio, and Paolo Costa. "Tourist Carrying Capacity: A Fuzzy Approach." *Annals of Tourism Research,* Vol. 18, No. 2 (1991), pp. 295–311.

Cater, Erlet A. "Tourism in the Least Developed Countries." *Annals of Tourism Research*, Vol. 14, No. 2 (1987), pp. 202–226.

Culpan, Refik, "International Tourism Model for Developing Economies." *Annals of Tourism Research*, Vol. 13, No. 4 (1986). pp. 541–552.

Davies, E. T., and D. C. Gilbert. "A Case Study of the Development of Farm Tourism in Wales." *Tourism Management*, Vol. 13, No. 1 (March 1992), pp. 56–63.

deKadt, Emanuel. *Tourism: Passport to Development?* Washington, D.C.: Oxford University Press for UNESCO and the International Bank of Reconstruction and Development/The World Bank, 1979.

Dieke, U.C. "Policies for Tourism Development in Kenya." *Annals of Tourism Research*, Vol. 18, No. 2 (1991), pp. 269–294.

Dorwood, Sherry. *Design for Mountain Communities.* New York: Van Nostrand Reinhold, 1991.

Dowling, Ross K. "Tourism Planning: People and the Environment in Western Australia." *Journal of Travel Research*, Vol. 31, No. 4 (Spring 1993), pp. 52–58.

Dredge, Dianne, and Stewart Moore. "A Methodology for the Integration of Tourism in Town Planning." *Journal of Tourism Studies*, Vol. 3, No. 1 (May 1992), pp. 8–21.

Gee, Chuck Y. *Resort Development and Management.* East Lansing, Mich.: Educational Institute of the American Hotel and Motel Association, 1988.

Getz, Donald. "Models in Tourism Planning." *Tourism Management*, Vol. 7, No. 1 (March 1986), pp. 21–32.

Gill, Alison, and Rudi Hartman. *Mountain Resort Development.* Burnaby, British Columbia, Canada: Simon Fraser University, 1992.

Gunn, Clare A. *Vacationscape: Designing Tourist Regions.* New York: Van Nostrand Reinhold, 1988.

Gunn, Clare A. *Tourism Planning.* New York: Taylor & Francis, 1994.

Hall, Derek. *Tourism and Economic Development in Eastern Europe and the Soviet Union.* New York: Wiley, 1991.

Inskeep, Edward. *Tourism Planning: An Integrated and Sustainable Development Approach.* New York: Van Nostrand Reinhold, 1991.

Kariel, Herbert. "Tourism and Development: Perplexity or Panacea?" *Journal of Travel Research*, Vol. 28, No. 1 (Summer 1989), pp. 2–6.

Mak, James. "Exacting Resort Developers to Create Non-tourism Jobs." *Annals of Tourism Research*, Vol. 20, No. 2 (1993), pp. 250–261.

Milne, Simon. "Tourism and Development in South Pacific Microstates." *Annals of Tourism Research*, Vol. 19, No. 2 (1992), pp. 191–212.

Nuckolls, Jonelle, and Patrick Long. *Organizing Resources for Tourism Development in Rural Areas.* Boulder, Colo.: University of Colorado, 1993.

O'Reilly, A. M. "Tourism Carrying Capacity: Concept and Issues." *Tourism Management*, Vol. 7, No. 4 (December 1986), pp. 254–258.

Pearce, Douglas. *Tourist Development*, 2nd edition. New York: Wiley, 1989.

Phillips, Patrick. *Developing with Recreational Amenities.* Washington, D.C.: The Union Land Institute, 1986.

Portman, John, and Jonathan Barnett. *The Architect as Developer.* New York: McGraw-Hill, 1976.

Richter, Linda K. *Land Reform and Tourism Development.* Cambridge, Mass.: Schenkman, 1982.

Smart, J. Eric. *Recreational Development Handbook.* Washington, D.C.: The Urban Land Institute, 1989.

Smith, Valene, and William Eadington. *Tourism Alternatives: Potentials and Problems in the Development of Tourism.* Philadelphia: University of Pennsylvania Press, 1992.

Teare, Richard. *Managing Projects in Hospitality Organizations.* New York: Cassell, 1992.

Tourism U.S.A. *Guidelines for Tourism Development*, Columbia, Mo.: Department of Recreation and Park Administration, University Extension, University of Missouri.

Williams, Alan M., and Gareth Shaw. *Tourism and Economic Development: Western European Experiences.* London: Belhaven Press, 1988.

Woodside, Arch G., and Jeffrey A Carr. "Consumer Decision Making and Competitive

Marketing Strategies: Applications for Tourism Planning." *Journal of Travel Research,* Vol. 26, No. 3 (Winter 1988), pp. 2–7.

World Tourism Organization. *Presentation and Financing of Tourist Development Projects.* Madrid: WTO.

Yesawich, Peter C. "Planning: The Second Step in Market Development." *Cornell Hotel and Restaurant Administration Quarterly,* Vol. 28, No. 4 (February 1988), pp. 71–81.

Yu, Lawrence. "Hotel Development and Structures in China." *International Journal of Hospitality Management,* Vol. 11, No. 2 (May 1992), pp. 99–110.

Tourism and the Environment

LEARNING OBJECTIVES

- Recognize the worldwide importance of natural resource conservation and sustainable tourism development.
- Learn how ecotourism can benefit local people.
- Understand the dangers and limitations of ecotourism.
- Understand tourist codes of ethics and guidelines.
- Learn current environmental practices of tourism organizations and suppliers.
- Learn how to maintain natural destinations.

INTRODUCTION

As tourism moves into the twenty-first century, the enterprise will have to make the environment a priority. Because tourism is now the world's largest industry, the environment is taking center stage in tourism development. Tourism is not only a powerful economic force but a factor in the physical environment as well. Because more attention will be paid to the environment in the future, projects that are economically feasible but not environmentally desirable will remain unbuilt. The environment is the core of the tourism product. Profitability in tourism depends on maintaining the attractiveness of the destination people want to see and experience.

Tourism has the power to enhance the environment, to provide funds for conservation, to preserve culture and history, to set sustainable use limits, and to protect natural attractions. It also has the power to destroy. If tourism is not properly planned and implemented, it can destroy vegetation, create overcrowding, litter trekking areas, pollute beaches, result in overbuilding, eliminate open space, create sewage problems, cause housing problems, and ignore the needs and structure of the host community.

It is being recognized that tourism must preserve and protect the environment and natural attractions so that people will continue to travel and to set use limits so that sites will be truly sustainable. The problem is how to do this. Concepts such as ecotourism, nature tourism, sustainable development, carrying capacity, and alternative tourism have been proposed and are examined in this chapter. Also, we look at the industry's efforts to be environmentally responsible.

Unspoiled tropical rainforests are of great interest to ecotourists such as this one in southeast Asia. (Photo courtesy of International Expeditions, Inc. by William Boehm)

COMMON TERMS USED

Ecotourism, nature tourism, green tourism, low-impact tourism, adventure travel, alternative tourism, environmental preservation, symbiotic development, responsible tourism, soft tourism, appropriate tourism, quality tourism, new tourism, sustainable development, sustainable tourism—all are monikers for similar types of tourist activities and developments. Of all the terms, *ecotourism* and *sustainability* are most frequently used. The principle of both is to sustain or even enhance the quality and attractiveness of the natural environment.

Definitions of ecotourism abound. A workable one is simply: "responsible travel to natural areas that conserves the environment and sustains the well-being of local people." A more expansive definition given by International Expeditions is: "purposeful travel to natural habitats to create an understanding of the cultural and natural history pertaining to that environment, emphasizing care not to alter the integrity of the ecosystem, while producing economic benefits to local people and governments that encourage the preservation of the inherent resources of the environments there and elsewhere." Dianne Brouse[1] defines ecotourism as responsible travel in which the visitor is aware of and takes into account the effects of his or her actions on both the host culture and the environment.

Other definitions reported in the Travel Industry Association of America's study, *Tourism and the Environment*, are as follows:

- Ecotourism is environmentally friendly travel that emphasizes seeing and saving natural habitats and archeological treasures
- Ecotourism is a tool for conservation
- Ecotourism is ecologically responsible tourism
- The World Wildlife Fund, which issued a study on ecotourism in 1990, defines it in

[1]Dianne Brouse, "Socially Responsible Travel," *Transitions Abroad* (January/February 1992), p. 23.

Seeing koalas in their native Australian habitat is a rewarding experience for ecotourists. (Photo courtesy of International Expeditions, Inc. by Richard Ryel)

general terms: "tourism to protect natural areas, as a means of economic gain through natural resource preservation . . . any kind of tourism that involves nature. . . ."

- The Ecotourism Society defines ecotourism as "purposeful travel to natural areas to understand the culture and natural history of the environment, taking care not to alter the integrity of the ecosystem, while producing economic opportunities that make the conservation of natural resources beneficial to local people."
- Broadly defined, ecotourism involves more than conservation. It is a form of travel that responds to a region's ecological, social, and economic needs. It also provides an alternative to mass tourism. It encompasses all aspects of travel—from airlines to hotels to ground transportation to tour operators. That is, each component of the ecotourism product is environmentally sensitive.
- As a form of travel, ecotourism nurtures understanding of the environment's culture and natural history, fosters the ecosystem's integrity, and produces economic opportunities *and* conservation gains.

If the definitions above sound like a case of the best of all possible worlds for the traveler, the destination, and the locals, to a degree it is. The problem is living up to the promises of the definitions and making ecotourism a reality. Otherwise, ecotourism becomes an oxymoron bringing visitors to fragile environments and ruining them rather than preserving them. In fact, many people quarrel with the word "ecotourism." If you consider the two parts of the word *ecotourism*—"ecology" and "tourism"—the inconsistencies are apparent. *Ecology* is defined as the science of the relationships between organisms and environment. When *tourism* is connected to it, a foreign entity is introduced and nature's relationships are changed. Thus the term *ecotourism* is really an oxymoron (an epigrammatic combination of contradictory or incongruous terms). This is especially true when a magazine such as *Popular Mechanics* refers to ecotourism using high-clearance four-wheel-drive vehicles in the back country to view wildlife. Ecotourism does not work when ecotours are so popular that they destroy the very environment they seek to protect.

EXAMPLES OF ECOTOURISM

A recent travel trend is the increase in the number of travelers who are interested in nature, educational, adventure, and active vacations. Research by the U.S. Travel Data Center shows that over 8 million Americans took part in ecotours sponsored by over 300 tour companies in 1991. The following have been cited as examples of ecotourism: (1) adventure travel that uses the body, such as bicycle tours, white-water rafting, backpacking, sea kayaking, canoeing, and hiking; and (2) environmental or ecological travel that focuses on environmental awareness, protection, and recovery such as trail cleanup, tropical rainforest tours, trail building, National Audubon Society bird watching tours, and "save wildlife habitat" tours. The World Wildlife Fund (WWF) advertisement (see Figure 16.1) shown here is a typical example of ecotours sponsored by responsible organizations.

Ecotours are commonly sponsored by conservation organizations such as the Nature Conservancy, World Wildlife Fund, Audubon Societies, the Smithsonian, museums of natural history, and others. Their main objective is to increase members' awareness of conservation principles and programs. By visiting protected areas, they see the results of actual programs and accomplishments—implementing sound ecological principles. In many cases, these have been assisted or promoted by the organization. Ecotourism thus has the excellent potential of increasing nature conservation objectives. Such tours are also used to generate revenue. Usually, a modest part of the tour cost constitutes a contribution to the organization. These funds, in turn, support local conservation programs.

Field instruction and interpretation by a local expert is an important function of the Amazon Center for Environmental Education and Research. (Photo courtesy of International Expeditions, Inc. by Richard Mills)

TRAVEL WITH WWF

To enhance members' understanding of natural systems and conservation challenges, WWF offers trips to areas of the world rich in wildlife that highlight the organization's goals. Led by a naturalist and WWF staff, travel in the congenial company of other members who share your commitment to the conservation of wildlife and wildlands. Your participation helps WWF to advance conservation around the globe.

QUEEN CHARLOTTE ISLANDS

Aboard the 70-passenger *Sea Bird*. May 16-23, 1993. Eight days. Prices start at $2,100, not including airfare.

From Seattle, explore the waters around Puget Sound's San Juan Islands, where orcas abound and wildflowers carpet the landscape. Cruise through splendidly scenic waterways and fjords to Canada's Queen Charlotte Islands, where unique and fascinating wildlife has evolved in the temperate rain forest.

GALAPAGOS ISLANDS

Aboard the 38-passenger *Isabela II*. May 28-June 9, 1993. 13 days. Price: $5,510, including roundtrip airfare from Miami.

Wildlife in remarkable profusion will greet you everywhere in this austerely beautiful showcase of geologic history and evolution. From extraordinary proximity, observe fascinating and fearless creatures, including thousands of colorful sea birds, tiny Darwin's finches, diminutive Galapagos penguins, giant tortoises, iguanas, seals, sea lions, and more.

ROCKY MOUNTAINS

June 9-18, 1993. 10 days. Price: $2,450, not including airfare.

Grand Teton, Yellowstone and Glacier—explore these national parks in the spectacular Rocky Mountains at the optimal time of year for wildlife viewing, looking for elk, antelope, bison, moose, coyote, bear, beaver, otter, diverse birdlife, and more. Moderate hikes, float trips, and drives will take you through active geothermal areas and wildflower-filled meadows, with majestic mountains towering beyond.

BOTSWANA AND NAMIBIA

July 1-18, 1993. 18 days. Price: $7,950, including roundtrip airfare from New York.

Hauntingly beautiful, the towering dunes and vast, arid landscapes of Namibia support populations of leopard, cheetah, elephants, ostrich, zebra, and wildebeest—and offer a stunning counterpoint to Botswana's lush Okavango Delta. Explore the Delta's papyrus-lined waterways and islands on foot, by boat, and in open safari vehicles, looking for elephant, red lechwe, tsessebe, lions, hippos, the rare sitatunga, and countless birds.

THE ALASKAN ARCTIC AND RUSSIAN FAR EAST

Aboard the 138-passenger *World Discoverer*. July 21-31, 1993. 10 days. Prices start at $3,500, not including airfare.

Polar bears, walrus, whales, snow geese, and countless sea birds ...there are exceptional opportunities to view wildlife on this unique exploration of the Bering and Chukchi Seas. Cross the Bering Strait and Arctic Circle, visiting remote islands and the rugged coast of this fascinating region—much of which is slated to become an international park to protect its common natural and cultural heritage.

ALASKA'S INSIDE PASSAGE

Aboard the 70-passenger *Sea Lion*, August 4-13, 1993. 10 days. Prices start at $2,970, not including airfare.

Humpback whales, orcas, dolphins, bears, bald eagles, puffins, sea otters, harbor seals—encounter them all against an unforgettable backdrop of the fjords, spectacular glaciers, and snow-capped mountains of Alaska's Inside Passage. On shore, walk along polished-rock beaches and rushing salmon streams, and through cathedral-like spruce and hemlock forests.

Figure 16.1 World Wildlife Fund Travel Advertisement (*Source: Focus*, January/February 1993)

Paos Volcano National Park, Costa Rica, is a popular natural attraction. This park also possesses abundant wildlife and unusual vegetation. (Photo courtesy of International Expeditions, Inc. by Richard Mills)

A number of these organizations participate in debt for nature swaps, which are a rather unique method of financing new or enlarging existing natural areas. The World Wildlife Fund and Conservation International arrange to pay off a country's debt, in part, and at a discount, in exchange for protecting certain areas. These areas are usually new national parks possessing superb scenic and natural history resources or the country involved promises to enlarge existing parks, wildlife refuges, or forests. Such plans have already succeeded in Latin America and Asia. An example is an agreement between Bolivia and Conservation International. This pact provides that in return for $650,000 of Bolivia's outstanding debt purchased by Conservation International, Bolivia will provide a 3.7 million acre expansion of the Beni Biosphere Reserve in the heart of the Amazon rainforest wilderness. Over a decade or so, the cumulative effect of this kind of imaginative program in countries rich in natural resources for ecotourism will be to possess very attractive destinations for the ecotourist. Similar programs in other parts of the world are also taking place.

Benefits and Importance of Ecotourism

1. Provides jobs and income for local people
2. Makes possible funds for purchasing and improving protected or natural areas to attract more ecotourists in the future
3. Provides environmental education for visitors
4. Encourages heritage and environmental preservation and enhancement (the creation of new or enlarged national and state parks, forest preserves, biosphere reserves, recreation areas, beaches, marine and underwater trails, and attractions)

Third World countries host many ecotourists. The total for all types of tourism to Latin America, Africa, and Indonesia has been estimated at about $55 billion.[2] In Brazil, nature travel has become the country's largest new source of revenue. In south central Africa, Rwanda's ecotourism is the third largest source of foreign exchange earnings. Much of this is generated by visitors to the Mountain Gorilla Project begun in the 1970s. The success of this project has convinced the national government to preserve and protect the critical habitat of the gorilla. It has also brought about support for other parks and reserves in that country.

In Costa Rica, 60 percent of visitors are interested in seeing the national park system, which comprises 11 percent of the country's land area. If biological and private reserves are added, the protected areas total 23 percent of the nation.

Ecuador's Galápagos Islands in the eastern Pacific had about 50,000 ecotourists in 1990, about twice the number that the government deemed optimal.[3] Strict rules of conduct enforced by national park trained and educated tour guides have essentially maintained the quality of the visitor experience.

Dangers and Limitations

A low-density rural population is typically found at ecotourism destinations. Most of these people depend on the use of the natural environment for their livelihood. The usual arrangement made for such visitors is to participate in a group tour. The tour operator may or may not hire locals to perform services needed by the group. Yet if the financial benefits of tourism are not shared with them, then in effect, their use of the natural resources will tend to compete with ecotourism. To be successful as tour operators, it is imperative that locals be involved. If not, their pressing needs for survival will doubtless prevail. This is very likely to damage the very natural attractions that first lured visitors there. To prevent this from happening, the basics of sustainable tourism must be practiced.

SUSTAINABLE DEVELOPMENT

The concept of sustainable development has achieved prominence and acceptance in recent years and hopefully, it will permeate all levels of economic development and tourism development, from local to global in the future. It has become popular because it is an approach that holds out the promise of maintaining a standard of living somewhat similar to that which we possess today while recognizing that we cannot continue to exploit the global environment as we have in the past. While other sectors of the economy are undoubtedly the greatest focus of concern, tourism is increasingly being brought under the microscope regarding its role in contributing to the long-term well-being of the planet. So far, tourism has not attracted the cries of alarm that have accompanied major oil spills, the depletion of nonrenewable resources, or the destruction of the ozone layer. To date, the criticisms directed at tourism from an impact of

[2]Ruth Norris, "Can Ecotourism Save Natural Areas?" *National Parks* (January/February 1992), pp. 30–34.
[3]J. Molner, "Ecotourism—with Conscience as Our Guide," *The Seattle Times* (March 24, 1992), Sunday, Final Edition.

development standpoint have tended to focus on the deterioration of natural and cultural environments that tourism can cause. Clearly, the foregoing is a much too simplistic assessment of tourism and its impacts (both positive and negative) on our total environment. Because of its pervasive and diverse nature, tourism affects, and is affected by, many factors relating to our social and economic well-being. The use of nonrenewable petroleum is perhaps the best single example; tourism depends heavily on the fuel that is burned to transport travelers both around the block and around the world. As such, any policies that affect the use of petroleum-based fuels will affect the tourism sector.

This point, the interdependency of tourism with other sectors, is being emphasized because any effort to deal with the topic in isolation would be naive and futile. Once this is recognized, however, it is also true that tourism does have major responsibility to contribute to the debate (and the subsequent action) concerning sustainable development.

We Are All Responsible

If it is to work, sustainable development must become a normal way of thinking and acting by a majority of the global community. It cannot be the exclusive purview of the enlightened segments of a society or of an industry. It cannot be something we practice on Sunday. It cannot be only the burden of the less privileged members of the local or the world community. And it cannot be only the concern of those nations and regions whose population growth is under control. In brief, if sustainable development is to be an effective model for the future, it must be a workable approach to ensuring that we can replace what we consume and that in the process of consumption we do not create by-products that pollute or destroy the ecosystem on which future generations depend.

In discussing the responsibility for sustainable development in the field of tourism, four main areas need to be addressed:

1. The premises on which sustainable development policy in tourism should be based
2. The most critical areas of sustainable development as applied to tourism
3. How responsibility for sustainable development in tourism should be allocated
4. An agenda of suggested sustainable development actions for the tourism sector

Some Premises of Sustainable Development in Tourism

The concept of sustainable development is not new. Although the words are more modern and more widely accepted, there have always been similar causes. The concepts of conservation, preservation, and environmental protection have always had as their goal the desire to prevent the destruction of desirable natural conditions and species. What is perhaps new is the insertion into the equation a recognition that the human race seeks economic, social, and cultural development—and that any attempt to prevent such development on a strictly ideological basis is unlikely to gain widespread acceptance. In parallel, there is also the recognition that demographic, economic, social, and cultural growth that is consumptive and/or destructive cannot continue unabated without serious impacts on the natural environment on which we depend for life itself.

This said, we need to enunciate several key premises on which sustainable development policy, as it applies to tourism, should be based. These premises are simply statements that need to be kept clearly in mind as we in the tourism industry attempt to wrestle with the concept of sustainable development and how it can best be applied to tourism.

THE PREMISE OF INTERDEPENDENCY As implied above, tourism as a sector affects, and is affected by, a whole range of social and economic activities. We first need to identify the most important of these interdependencies. We then need to work with those individuals/groups/organizations that have responsibility for and a commitment to sustainable development in the sectors affected by these interdependencies.

THE PREMISE OF MULTIDISCIPLINARITY In seeking to implement initiatives to support sustainable development it will be essential to draw on the ideas and experience of a broad range of disciplines. Indeed, as we have realized for some time now, a true understanding of the phenomenon of tourism is not possible using the thinking and the tools of a single discipline. Similarly, an understanding and implementation of actions to realize sustainable development in tourism will, by necessity, involve the seeking and acceptance of concepts, methodologies, and approaches of individuals from many fields.

An arctic fox. The world's cold regions are rich in wildlife, inducing ecotours to Alaska, northern Canada, and elsewhere, including Antarctica and its nearby regions. (Photo courtesy of International Expeditions, Inc. by William Boehm)

For example, natural resource managers have developed carrying-capacity limits so that natural attractions will not be overwhelmed by visitors. Carrying capacity is defined as the maximum amount of development, use, growth, or change that a site can endure without an unacceptable alteration in the physical environment, the community's social fabric, and the local economy; and without an unacceptable decline in the quality of experience by the visitor. Thus for sustainable development one needs to call on experts in many fields: botanists, ornithologists, zoologists, and foresters, to name a few.

THE PREMISE OF PREVIOUS EXPERIENCE It is always difficult to accept that there is nothing new under the sun, or at least not much. When it comes to sustainable development, we certainly do not know everything, but we do know a lot as to what may work and what may not work. For example, there is much useful research knowledge gained from the energy crisis of the 1970s concerning how various segments of the population reacted to a range of alternative approaches to reduce consumer energy use. Undoubtedly, there are many findings from other fields that would also be helpful. While they, of course, need to be screened and assessed for their continued relevance and significance, they should not be ignored.

THE PREMISE THAT NATURE IS BETTER Perhaps one of the most important premises of the sustainable development movement is that the natural state is generally preferred to the developed state. This is, of course, one of the areas that provides the greatest room for both apparent agreement and mutual deception on the part of individuals and groups that have substantially different views. This important problem aside, it would seem that adherents to the sustainable development lifestyle generally believe that the natural ecosystem is preferable to artificially built environments or settlements. The compelling argument—that the balance of nature is sounder than the imbalance of civilization—has considerable merit. At the same time, the educated world is only too well aware of certain of the excesses and cruelties of nature, as well as the continuous changes that occur in nature over long periods of time. As a result, there is still room for a legitimate questioning of this premise and its universality.

THE PREMISE OF POLITICS AND POWER This premise has been left until the last because it is both the easiest and the most difficult to deal with. As the world has evolved over the past several centuries, we have seen the growing disparity that has developed between the have and have-not nations. Today, we find ourselves in a situation where a relatively few advanced nations having small populations possess most of the world's wealth and consume most of its resources. At the other end of the spectrum we find the poorer countries with rapidly growing populations. By any logic, a long-term projection of this situation and associated trends would lead to the conclusion that the present equilibrium is far from being sustainable. So in our discussions of sustainable development for tourism, we need to keep in mind constantly the question: Sustainable for whom?

Sustainable Development and Tourism: The Critical Areas

Now that at least some of the critical premises underlying sustainable development have been identified explicitly, it may be useful to define those areas in tourism that merit our consideration. Four such areas are presented for discussion.

DEFINING THE RELEVANT POPULATION/COMMUNITY   This issue takes off directly from the last premise discussed above and focuses on the question of sustainable development for whom? As professionals in the field, we need to know if we are to take a global, macro perspective in our discussions of tourism and sustainable development, or whether we should restrict our thinking to a more local focus. While recognizing that there is a need for global thinking, we also need to recognize that we may need to restrict the allocation of our energies to those jurisdictions where we have the power to act and to make a difference.

In any event, the principle being enunciated here is that, as professionals, we need to define our sphere of interest and action. If we are acting as part of the World Tourism Organization, we will have a very global sphere of concern. If we are responsible for tourism in Prince Edward Island, we will have a different sphere of responsibility. In each of these cases, the impacts and populations of relevance may be quite different, and consequently, so may our likely actions.

DEFINING THE TIME HORIZON   While sustainable developments as a concept implies *forever,* this may be impractical to deal with and can even lead to a feeling of helplessness. There is some merit in seeking to develop programs that are sustainable in perpetuity, but such programs may require huge amounts of resources and considerable time for their implementation. It may be wiser and more effective to undertake a less demanding series of phased programs that initiate movement in desired directions rather than delaying action until longer-term programs can be put in place.

DEFINING THE DIMENSIONS OF SUSTAINABILITY   The concept of sustainability is relevant in practical terms only when we define what is to be sustained. From a tourism perspective, discussions on sustainability may pertain to the environment, cultural identity, economic well-being, or social stability. Individuals responsible for, or interested in, each of these areas taken separately may very legitimately focus on their area of concern and attempt to achieve sustainability in relation to some acceptable ongoing carrying capacity of the destination.

However, from an overall destination management perspective, the task becomes much more complex. Here the challenge becomes one of attempting to balance the sustainability of economic, cultural, social, and environmental systems. While one hopes for compatibility in the pursuit of sustainability within and across these systems, such is not always possible. Often, the reason for such incompatibility is a divergence of the values from which the goal of sustainability is being pursued.

DEFINING THE VALUES THAT UNDERLIE SUSTAINABLE DEVELOPMENT   In any democratic society, at any given point in time, there is bound to be a range of values as to what is really important in life. Through time, these values become reflected in the political process and the decisions that flow from elected leaders. Unfortunately, this is a somewhat traditional view of the political process and one that is being called into question by today's movements for direct involvement of the people with regard to decisions that affect their lives. Tourism will not, indeed should not, escape this emerging but powerful trend.

Regardless of the way in which the values of a society are determined, they will ultimately determine the policies that emerge with regard to sustainable development. Whether these policies are the result of compromise or consensus is the concern of the political entity involved. In the end, however, the political process and the power of different political units will determine the level and form that sustainability will take. Those of us in the tourism sector have traditionally ignored this reality, and we are weaker for it.

Allocating Responsibility

It should be apparent from the nature of the foregoing discussion that the allocation of responsibility for tourism-related sustainability issues and decisions will not be a neat and tidy exercise. The highly interdependent, multidisciplinary, multisector, and political nature of the decisions does not allow for simplistic answers. However, as long as this caveat is taken seriously, it may be possible to provide some guidelines as to how the process might be conducted and how the prime agents might be assigned to different areas of responsibility.

The Concept of Shared Responsibility

Society is no longer (if it ever was) contained in neat boxes. Rather, at best, it may be viewed as consisting of very ill-defined clusters that change shape constantly as they interface with one another. To complicate matters, a particular citizen may belong to more than one cluster (indeed, probably does) and may change his or her perspective as he or she assumes different roles in society. For example, as a wage earner, we may have one perspective, as a parent another, and as a member of a particular religious group, yet another. In the end, however, each person must reach a weighted position with respect to any given issue.

From the standpoint of the tourism sector, the reality is that all questions related to the nature and extent of tourism development must be supported by the community at large. This means that whatever direction tourism development takes in a community, region, or country, it must have the support of the majority of citizens who are affected by it. This means very simply that the perceived benefits from tourism must be seen to outweigh the total costs (economic, environmental, cultural, social) associated with it.

All this said, it then becomes necessary to propose an operational allocation of responsibility that remains true to the democratic model and the concept of resident-responsive tourism. See Table 16.1 for a proposed allocation of responsibilities.

An Agenda for Action

Once a framework for the allocation of responsibility has been agreed upon, it becomes imperative to establish an agenda and a process for implementation. While the total community bears the ultimate responsibility for this agenda, it is suggested that in practice the destination management organization should assume a leadership role in developing the action agenda and should serve as a catalyst for generating the process that brings about its implementation. Examples of the kind of activities involved in this process include:

- Coordinating the development of a tourism philosophy and vision for the community/region
- Specifying the major goals of the community/region with respect to tourism

Table 16.1   Sustainable Development (SD) in Tourism: A Possible Allocation of Responsibility

Level/Organization	Responsibilities
Host community/region	Defining the tourism philosophy and vision for the community/region
	Establishing social, physical, and cultural carrying capacity for the host community/region
Destination management/community organization	Coordination of implementation of community SD plan for tourism
	Monitoring of levels and impact of tourism in the community/region
Individual tourism firms and operators	Fair contribution to implementation of SD plan for tourism
	Observance of regulations, guidelines, and practices for SD
Host community/region	Encouragement/acceptance of tourism within parameters of SD plan
Visitors/tourists	Acceptance of responsibility for minimal self-education with respect to values of host region
	Acceptance and observance of terms and conditions of host community SD plan for tourism

- Obtaining consensus concerning the social, physical, and cultural carrying capacity of the community/region in question
- Identifying the specific action initiatives necessary to meet the tourism development objectives while respecting the destination's carrying capacities
- Gaining agreement on the measures to be used in monitoring the impacts of tourism in the community/region
- Gathering and disseminating information concerning the impacts of tourism on the community/region

Based on these findings, it is suggested that an action agenda to support a sustainable development program for tourism might include the following elements:

- Maximum total visitation levels to a community/region
- An obligatory tax to support tourism infrastructure planning, development, and maintenance
- Community-supported legislation to protect and preserve unique resources and heritage sites
- Community and industry consensus concerning architectural and signage standards
- Support for standards and certification programs that encourage staff development and the delivery of high-quality service

Tourism has long been touted as a "renewable industry" that is to be greatly preferred over the traditional "smokestack industries" of the manufacturing age. However, we have learned that tourism can engender its own forms of degradation to the environment and to a society unless it is carefully planned and managed.

The concept of sustainable development is an approach by which efforts are made to balance the benefits or outputs of an industry with the investments and restrictions required to ensure that the industry can continue to exist without depleting or destroying the resource base on which it depends. In the tourism sector, this implies caring for the natural and built environments in a way that will ensure their continuing viability and well-being. Although we in the tourism sector are starting to understand what this implies, there is much that remains to be learned. The industry needs to identify an action agenda and allocate responsibility for its implementation so that we can move toward the goal of a truly sustainable tourism system.

CURRENT TOURISM INDUSTRY PRACTICES

It is fortunate that a concern for the environment has become a major trend that is still gathering momentum. Environmentalism is now a major international and national force with the development of the green movement and other concerned groups. Protection of the environment has been embraced by the tourism industry. Recognition is a start and progress is under way.

Individual Tourists' Responsibilities

If ecologically sustainable tourism is to become a reality, it will require efforts by all the players in the tourism arena, starting with the tourists themselves. Tourists have responsibilities and must be educated as to their obligations and responsibilities to contribute to socially and environmentally responsible tourism. Tourists must first be brought into the process as clients (guests) for the tourist destination and second as persons coresponsible for maintaining the destination.

Several "codes of ethics," guidelines, and ten commandments for tourist behavior have been developed. Again, they are a start in the process of educating the tourist. Two examples are presented here. The first, and one of the most publicized, was produced by the American Society of Travel Agents (ASTA).

ASTA's Ten Commandments on Ecotourism

Whether on business or leisure travel:

1. *Respect the frailty of the earth.* Realize that unless all are willing to help in its preservation, unique and beautiful destinations may not be here for future generations to enjoy.
2. *Leave only footprints.* Take only photographs. Leave no graffiti. Do not litter. Do not take away "souvenirs" from historic sites and natural areas.
3. To make your travels more meaningful, *educate yourself about the geography, customs, manners, and cultures of the region you visit.* Take time to listen to the people. Encourage local conservation efforts.
4. *Respect the privacy and dignity of others.* Inquire before photographing people.
5. *Do not buy products made from endangered plants or animals, such as ivory, tortoise*

shell, animal skins, and feathers. Read "Know Before You Go," the U.S. Customs list of products that cannot be imported.

6. *Always follow designated trails.* Do not disturb animals, plants, or their natural habitats.
7. Learn about and *support conservation-oriented programs and organizations* working to preserve the environment.
8. Whenever possible, *walk or utilize environmentally sound methods of transportation.* Encourage drivers of public vehicles to stop engines when parked.
9. *Patronize those* (hotels, airlines, resorts, cruise lines, tour operators, and suppliers) *who advance energy and environmental conservation;* water and air quality, recycling; safe management of waste and toxic materials; noise abatement; community involvement; and which provide experienced, well-trained staff *dedicated to strong principles of conservation.*
10. Ask your ASTA travel agent to *identify those organizations that subscribe to the ASTA Environmental Guidelines* for air, land, and sea travel. ASTA has recommended that these organizations adopt their own environmental codes to cover special sites and ecosystems.

The second code is that developed by the Tourism Industry Association of Canada and the National Round Table on the Environment and the Economy of Canada.

Code of Ethics for Tourists

A high-quality tourism experience depends on the conservation of our natural resources, the protection of our environment, and the preservation of our cultural heritage. The Canadian Tourism Industry has developed and adopted a Code of Ethics and Practices to achieve these objectives. You can help us in our continuing efforts to provide a high-quality tourism experience for you and future guests by giving consideration to the following guidelines.

1. Enjoy our diverse natural and cultural heritage and help us to protect and preserve it.
2. Assist us in our conservation efforts through the efficient use of resources, including energy and water.
3. Experience the friendliness of our people and the welcoming spirit of our communities. Help us to preserve these attributes by respecting our traditions, customs, and local regulations.
4. Avoid activities which threaten wildlife or plant populations, or which may be potentially damaging to our natural environment.
5. Select tourism products and services which demonstrate social, cultural, and environmental sensitivity.

These codes address the conduct of individual travelers and provide guidelines for responsible behavior while traveling. They emphasize travel behavior associated with natural resources, languages, host populations, cultural heritage, shopping, and social interaction. Although the codes above are illustrative of the work being done, it should be recognized that other organizations are also active. The National Audubon Society has been a leader, publishing their "Travel Ethic for Environmentally Responsible

Ecotourists discover a dramatically different perspective of the world of nature when they proceed along the rainforest canopy walkway at the Amazon Center for Environmental Education and Research. (Photo courtesy of International Expeditions, Inc. by Richard Mills)

Tourism" in 1989. Save Our Planet published "Guidelines for Low-Impact Vacations" in 1990. The Center for Responsible Tourism in San Anselmo, California, has also developed a "Tourist Code of Ethics."

Codes and guidelines are fine, but the next step is making tourists aware of the codes and educating them to follow the important guidelines so they will become responsible travelers.

Travel Organizations Efforts

Efforts to increase environmental protection are being made by major tourism organizations such as the World Tourism Organization (WTO), World Travel and Tourism Council (WTTC), Pacific Asia Travel Association (PATA), Travel Industry Association of Canada (TIAC), and the Travel Industry Association of America (TIA).

As evidenced by their 1982 statement, WTO has been an advocate of protecting the environment for years: "The satisfaction of tourism requirements must not be prejudicial to the social and economic interests of the population in the tourist areas, to the environment, or above all, to natural resources which are fundamental attractions of tourism." Today, WTO has an Environmental Committee because they have recognized the need to understand and manage the link between tourism and the environment. The WTO Environmental Committee is developing a set of internationally acceptable indicators. A set of indicators will help tourism planners and managers prevent problems and protect the resource base.

Environmental concerns led the WTTC to establish the World Travel and Tourism Research Center (WTTERC) in September 1991 in cooperation with the Oxford Centre for Tourism and Leisure Studies. The center is a key component in WTTC's comprehensive program to achieve lasting environmental improvement. The center's aims are (1) to collect information about current corporate practice in the field of tourism and the environment, from which to establish ways that the center can contribute to practical environmental management; (2) to provide an international database designed to define and promote environmentally compatible growth in the tourism industry which enhances the experience of visitors and host communities; (3) the development of contacts with other international organizations dealing with the environment; (4) the preparation of objective analyses, evaluations, and summaries of principles of "good practice" for growth in environmentally compatible tourism, with particular reference to environmental impact assessments and audits to be carried out at the company level; (5) the identification of projects around the world relevant to enhancing and sustaining the environment through tourism; and (6) the communication to the tourism industry of current developments and practices in the field of the environment. In addition to its environmental center, the WTTC has also published a set of environmental guidelines that are based on principles established by the International Chamber of Commerce (ICC) Business Charter for Sustainable Development. These guidelines are given in Reading 16.2 at the end of the chapter.

Regional organizations such as the Pacific Asia Travel Association (PATA) have also developed codes for environmentally responsible tourism. The PATA code lists 18 guidelines that their 2100-member organizations are to follow with respect to tourism's environmental relationships.

The Pacific Asia Travel Association Code urges association and chapter members and their industry partners to:

- Adopt the necessary practices to conserve the environment, including the use of renewable resources in a sustainable manner and the conservation of nonrenewable resources
- Contribute to the conservation of any habitat of flora and fauna, and of any site, whether natural or cultural, which may be affected by tourism
- Encourage relevant authorities to identify areas worthy of conservation and to determine the level of development, if any, which would ensure that those areas are conserved
- Ensure that community attitudes, cultural values, and concerns, including local customs and beliefs, are taken into account in the planning of all tourism-related projects
- Ensure that environmental assessment becomes an integral step in the consideration of any site for a tourism project

- Ensure that assessment procedures recognize the cumulative as well as the individual effects of all developments on the environment
- Comply with all international conventions in relation to the environment
- Comply with all national, state, and local laws in relation to the environment
- Encourage those involved in tourism to comply with local, regional, and national planning policies and to participate in the planning process
- Provide the opportunity for the wider community to take part in discussions and consultations on tourism planning issues insofar as they affect the tourism industry and the community
- Acknowledge responsibility for the environmental impacts of all tourism-related projects and activities and undertake all necessary responsible remedial and corrective actions
- Encourage regular environmental audits of practices throughout the tourism industry and encourage necessary changes to those practices
- Foster environmentally responsible practices, including waste management, recycling, and energy use
- Foster in both management and staff an awareness of environmental and conservation principles in all tourism-related projects and activities
- Support the inclusion of professional conservation principles in tourism education, training, and planning
- Encourage an understanding by all those involved in tourism of each community's customs, cultural values, beliefs, and traditions, and how they relate to the environment
- Enhance the appreciation and understanding by tourists of the environment through the provision of accurate information and appropriate interpretation
- Establish detailed environmental policies and/or guidelines for the various sectors of the tourism industry

National organization codes have also been developed, with the Travel Industry Association of Canada (TIAC) leading the way. TIAC has created not just one code, but a series of ethical codes for the tourism industry as a whole, for tourists, and for specific sectors of its membership, such as accommodation, food services, tour operators, and government bodies. A particularly distinguishing feature of the TIAC codes is that they extend beyond just protection of the environment guidelines and incorporate the philosophy of sustainable development, which includes all facets of development—social, cultural, and economic. For those seeking more information or a copy of TIAC's Code of Ethics for Tourists, Code of Ethics for the Industry, or Guidelines of Tourist Industry Associations, contact the Tourism Industry Association of Canada, 1016-130 Albert Street, Ottawa, Ontario, Canada K1P 5G4.

Individual Firm Efforts

A third set of environmental codes focuses on individual companies. These codes tend to be quite technical and operations oriented, covering the day-to-day management practices of businesses such as airlines, accommodations, cruise lines, theme parks, tour operators, and others. What distinguishes these codes from those discussed previously is their effort to integrate the best business practices with sound environmental management. Companies such as Canadian Pacific Hotels and Resorts, ITT Sheraton, Ramada International Hotels and Resorts, Marriott International, British Airways, American Airlines, United Airlines, USAir, Avis Rent a Car/System, Busch Entertainment Corporation, Anheuser-Busch, Universal Studios, Walt Disney Company, and American Express have focused on recycling, reuse, energy conservation, water conservation, community involvement, and community environmental obligations to employees and guests.[4]

Some case descriptions illustrate the activities of some firms environmental responsibility. Since actions speak louder than words, these cases represent enlightened current practice.

Inter-Continental Hotels has produced and distributed a 300-page manual for its properties worldwide with guidelines on waste management, product purchasing, air quality, energy conservation, noise pollution, fuel storage, asbestos, pesticides, herbicides, and water.[5]

Ramada International Hotels and Resorts has made a company-wide commitment to environmental integrity. Many of the Ramada hotels in North America have expanded or initiated solid waste recycling programs for items such as tin, aluminum, paper, glass, broken china, and plastics (including dry cleaning bags and empty amenity bottles in guest rooms).

The WAT&G-designed Ramada in Cairns, North Queensland, Australia, was designed and built without disrupting one tree. It has been used in full-page ads to promote Ramada's commitment to the environment.[6]

As evidence that recycling has taken on an important role at the Four Seasons, the heads of design and engineering, Chris Wallace and J. Peter Buyze, are working to develop design standards for future hotels, which incorporate the increased space and power required for bailers, crushers, and containers. Looking beyond recycling, the Four Seasons will not use halon at new properties and is modifying specifications for all new hotels to eliminate CFC (chlorofluorocarbon) usage in refrigeration.[7]

Hyatt Hotels and Resorts has implemented an international recycling program that saves the organization more than $3 million annually. Hyatt's commitment is not only to recycle, but to close the recycling loop by establishing a market for recycled products. This is important when you consider that a typical Hyatt guest room generates 383 pounds of garbage annually, according to the consulting firm International Recycleco.

Under Hyatt's new plan, the same guest room will generate an average of only 37 pounds of nonrecyclable garbage annually, saving the company $2 million in annual waste-hauling costs. Under design is a trash container for guest rooms to encourage separation of paper, plastics, and aluminum.

With the help of their recycling consultant, the Chicago Hyatt Regency is now operating its own miniature materials recovery facility. The MRF processes nine different items, including leftover soap, and cuts the annual disposal costs in half. The

[4]Suzanne Hawkes and Peter Williams, *The Greening of Tourism* (Burnaby, B.C.: Centre for Tourism Policy and Research, Simon Fraser University, 1993); and U.S. Travel Data Center, *Tourism and the Environment* (Washington, D.C.: Travel Industry Association of America, 1992).
[5]Wimberly Allison Tong and Goo, *Do Not Disturb* (Newport Beach, Calif.: WAT&G, n.d.).
[6]Ibid.
[7]Ibid.

program has saved the hotel money by retrieving hotel items discarded by mistake, including linens, silverware, and coffee pots.

In addition, all new Hyatt hotels in the United States will be designed with recycling centers. Hotels outside the United States will implement programs in accordance with local guidelines and availability of environmentally friendly products.[8]

A recent report by Disney to cast members on company-wide environmental activities includes these recycling statistics: Lumber: Disney has recycled enough lumber to give everyone in the United States a popsicle stick—768,000 pounds of lumber. Paper: The amount of office paper recycled by the entire company to date is equivalent to the weight of a 747—2,000,000 pounds of paper. Cardboard: In 1990, the company recycled enough cardboard to cover Epcot, The Magic Kingdom, and Gatorland—2,300,000 pounds of cardboard. Aluminum cans: Disney has recycled enough aluminum cans to produce a cola can more than 100 miles high—26,000 pounds of aluminum.[9]

According to Ritz-Carlton President Horst Schulze, an employee asked him why the company wasn't doing more in the area of recycling. Thanks to that employee, Blake Edwards, an engineer with the Ritz-Carlton, Buckhead in Atlanta, a part-time recycling effort has blossomed into a full-time environmental management program and Edwards has been named environmental recycling systems manager. Prior to initiating the recycling program, Ritz-Carlton's disposal costs in the Atlanta property were increasing 50 to 62 percent annually. By decreasing the volume and weight of waste material, costs have been reduced by 50 percent. Food that is prepared but unused is donated to organizations for the homeless. At the Ritz-Carlton, Laguna Niguel, 13,000 pounds of cardboard, 5000 pounds of computer paper, and 6000 pounds of glass are being collected on a monthly basis.[10]

ITT Sheraton has several programs. They select products such as cleaning solvents and containers for their conservation and recyclability. Their "Going Green" program invites guests at Sheraton hotels in Africa and the Indian Ocean region to add a dollar to their final bill. Sheraton then matches this amount in local currency and contributes the money to local conservation projects that the World Society for the Protection of Animals has identified.[11]

United Airlines recycles aluminum aboard its aircraft and food containers up to 30 or 40 times. It has also reduced the amount of water carried on board and is replacing its fleet with quieter, more fuel-efficient aircraft.[12]

Busch Entertainment Corporation works for an improved environment through recycling, community involvement, corporate environmental planning, and conservation education to solve critical environmental problems.[13]

Sea World of Florida operates a beached animal rescue and rehabilitation program which aids sick, injured, or orphaned manatees, dolphins, whales, otters, sea turtles, and birds.[14]

[8]Ibid.
[9]Ibid.
[10]Ibid.
[11]U.S. Travel Data Center, *Tourism and the Environment.*
[12]Ibid.
[13]Ibid.
[14]Ibid.

A CLOSING NOTE

This chapter concludes with a statement by Ken Brown, Chairman of Mauna Lani Resorts, Inc., in Hawaii. It epitomizes the attitude that developers need to have to be sensitive to the environment. Having orchestrated one of the most highly acclaimed destination resorts in the world, his views bear careful study. Brown states: "Developers must not act like elephants at a picnic." He reminds us: "We should not only be sensitive to the environment, we should also add something to the life of the people—something aesthetic, physically beautiful, socially and economically enriching. We need to examine our actions and ask, 'Is this really benefiting the community?'"

Public response and numerous awards attest to Mauna Lani's success as an environmentally conscious achievement in tourism development. Among other honors, the resort has received a prestigious historic preservation award for the restoration and maintenance of ancient fish ponds, creation of a 27-acre historical park, and contributions to preserve petroglyphs (ancient rock carvings) along the Hawaiian Islands' Kohala coast.

Brown's convictions about environmental responsibility run deep. "I am absolutely convinced that environmental concerns are ethical and moral issues." Acknowledging the high economic cost of environmentally responsive development, Brown expresses confidence in its long-range profitability. In that he has been inspired by the late Noboru Gotoh—Japanese industrialist, Tokyu Group chairman, and Mauna Lani developer—whose motto, "For the Betterment of Mankind," set exacting standards for Mauna Lani.[15]

SUMMARY

The main concept of ecotourism is responsible travel to natural areas that conserves the environment and sustains the well-being of local people. From the tourists' viewpoint, ecotourism is typically the gratification provided by a unique experience in an undisturbed natural environment viewing flora, fauna, birds, animals, land forms, scenery, and natural beauty.

Benefits of ecotourism include providing jobs, helping preserve more areas, educating, and encouraging heritage and environmental enhancement. Benefits to the local people are maximized by hiring as many locals as possible and obtaining supplies and services locally.

Carrying capacity for visitors must be determined. It is defined as the maximum number of daily visitors that the area can receive without damaging its attractive features. Enforcement of this limit, as well as good management and maintenance, are essential.

Sustainable tourism development is development that has been carefully planned and managed. It is the antithesis of tourism that has developed for short-term gains. Because of the expected continuing growth of tourism, sustainable development is the approach that will be needed. Because of the pressure on the world's resources, it is the only sensible approach.

[15]Wimberly Allison Tong & Goo, *Do Not Disturb*.

No business sector has greater reason to promote and enforce environmental and business ethics codes than tourism. The environment is the resource base for tourism, and without protection, the natural attraction that brought the tourist in the first place will be lost. As a result, a number of codes for tourists, the tourism industry, and the environment have emerged. If the codes developed by the American Society of Travel Agents, World Travel and Tourism Council, Pacific Asia Travel Association, the Travel Industry Association of Canada, and other organizations are followed, the possibility of truly sustainable tourism can be a reality.

About the Readings

Reading 16.1 is "Ecotourism: Nature's Ally," by Richard Ryel of International Expeditions, Inc., of Birmingham, Alabama. International Expeditions has been identified as one of the leading responsible ecotour companies. Mr. Ryel addresses ecotourism and ends with a challenge for everyone.

The World Travel and Tourism Council (WTTC) is a global coalition of Chief Executive Officers from all sectors of the industry working to promote environmentally compatible tourism growth. They have developed a set of environmental guidelines that are reproduced in Reading 16.2

Reading 16.3 discusses tourism as a way to preserve the natural environment and emphasizes that if wildlife conservation efforts are to succeed, local people must share in the economic benefits of ecotourism.

Reading 16.1

Ecotourism: Nature's Ally

BY RICHARD RYEL
International Expeditions, Inc.

There is a growing global concern over the rapidly deteriorating ecological state of the Earth. As we gobble up more and more of our natural resources, it becomes alarmingly obvious how finite they are. Clean waters, pristine forests, untilled moorland and unfilled swamps are becoming very rare indeed. Still, the most ecologically aware of us are hard pressed to come up with even an insignificant part of our daily lives that we would be willing to give up in order to alleviate the problem. Starving, cold and desperate folk eking out a living from eroded land don't have the luxury of even making a choice.

It is into this miserable scenario a glimmer of hope shines. The populations of richer nations seem to be more concerned than ever with conservation matters. People are traveling more, and by doing so come to realize for themselves the actuality of the world's ecological problems. Acid rain legislation, controlled timber cutting, and protection of habitats are finally coming about—and more is being done.

Ecotourism (culturally and ecologically sensitive travel) has evolved as a result of two basic facts of modern life—the struggle of poor nations to catch up by exploiting their splendid natural resources, and the concern of rich nations for the Earth's preservation. Ecotourism operators are discovering that if governments can be persuaded to preserve their unspoiled natural habitats, the result will be a great boost to their national economies from tourism dollars. This has been demonstrated in Rwanda where the Mountain Gorillas, once poached to near extinction, are slowly making a comeback as a result of carefully controlled tourism.

Obviously, tourism to such delicate and endangered habitats can have its hazards. Extreme caution cannot be overemphasized. It is easy to see the effect of trash on a forest walkway, but what of the effects we cannot see—the effect of flashbulbs on nesting patterns of birds or the unaccustomed noise of people on animal populations and habits. It all takes a vigilance that before now was not considered vital, and therefore not encountered in the travel industry. Naturalists, biologists, anthropologists and others of similar background are needed to make these expeditions work both for the enlightenment and enjoyment of the travelers and, most importantly, for the preservation of the dwindling wild places of our Earth.

With this awareness of the state of world resources, what element or elements of your lifestyle would you be willing to give up for the sake of conservation? We welcome your comments.

READING 16.2

The World Travel & Tourism Council Environmental Guidelines

Travel & Tourism is the world's largest industry. A clean, healthy environment is essential to further growth.

The World Travel & Tourism Council is working with governments and international organizations to promote environmentally compatible growth, improve industry practices through education and information and track Travel and Tourism environment implementation programs.

The WTTC commends these guidelines to companies throughout the Travel & Tourism industry and to governments to take them into account in policy formulation.

Travel & Tourism companies should state their commitment to environmentally compatible growth

The WTTC recommends a pro-active approach for Travel & Tourism companies. This includes conducting Environmental Impact Assessments for all new projects and conducting annual Environmental Audits for all ongoing activities, leading to the development of environmental improvement programs.

Targets for improvements should be established and monitored

Wherever possible, specific goals should be developed and communicated for environmental improvement programs, including cost/benefit assessments. Results should be reviewed and assessed regularly by senior management.

The environment commitment should be company wide

The environmental improvement programs should carry the full support of the Board of Directors, should be an integral part of management practices, and should be communicated to all personnel, who should be encouraged to participate in the process. Such programs should also be communicated to the public.

Environment improvement programs should be systematic and comprehensive

They should aim to:

1. Identify and minimise product and operational environmental problems, paying particular attention to new projects;
2. Pay due regard to environmental concerns in design, planning, construction and implementation;
3. Be sensitive to conservation of environmentally protected or threatened areas, species and scenic aesthetics, achieving landscape enhancement where possible;
4. Practise energy conservation;
5. Reduce and recycle waste;
6. Practise fresh-water management and control sewage disposal;
7. Control and diminish air emissions and pollutants;

8. Monitor, control and reduce noise levels;
9. Control, reduce and eliminate environmentally unfriendly products, such as asbestos, CFC's, pesticides and toxic, corrosive, infectious, explosive or flammable materials;
10. Respect and support historic or religious objects and sites;
11. Exercise due regard for the interests of local populations, including their history, traditions and culture and future development;
12. Consider environmental issues as a key factor in the overall development of Travel and Tourism destinations.

Education and research into improved environmental programs should be encouraged

Company training and research programmes should incorporate environmental issues.

Travel and Tourism companies should seek to implement sound environment principles through self-regulation, recognising that national and international regulation may be inevitable and that preparation is vital

Travel & Tourism companies should translate the conclusions of Environmental Impact Assessments and Audits into management policies. They should co-operate with other companies and the public sector in the advancement of environmental improvement.

These Guidelines have been prepared taking into account the International Chamber of Commerce (ICC) Business Charter for Sustainable Development.

READING 16.3

Tourism as an Alternative to Natural Resource Destruction in Developing Countries

MAGNITUDE OF THE PROBLEM

Today in many parts of the world, particularly in the tropics and in warm-weather developing countries, forests, other vegetation, and wildlife are being destroyed at an alarming pace. The Nature Conservancy recently estimated that tropical rain forests are being devastated at an annual rate about the size of the state of Nevada (110,000 square miles or 28,490,800 hectares).[1] Destruction of this magnitude should disturb even the most dispassionate. In Africa, throughout the 1980s, 2,000 elephants a week were killed. In Kenya which began the 1980s with over 55,000 elephants, by decade's close had but 16,000.[2] In many countries in Africa and elsewhere, the killing of wildlife has been on a scale much beyond natural rates of reproduction.

Poor people living in rural or in forested areas have few options for making a living. In most African countries, the most common way is subsistence farming supplemented by killing wildlife. The larger animals such as buffalo, lion, and elephant are most often seen as threats to their livelihood. In fact, in Zimbabwe at the start of the planting season, fields are guarded 24 hours a day to prevent destruction of crops by buffalo and elephant. In some instances, farmers have been killed by angry elephants attempting to reach crops when ready for harvest. The farmer has but one thought—kill that elephant if he can find it.

The establishment of national parks and game areas have created additional problems. Large, legally protected animals often leave the park boundaries and cause damage to nearby farms. But park rangers and game wardens inform farmers that such animals are protected and should not be shot. Understandably, such situations create alienations from wildlife. What is needed is to create conditions such that local people will perceive undisturbed forests and wildlife as important contributors to their economic well being. When this is accomplished, they will conserve their natural resources.

Economic Arguments Against Destruction

An established principle of tourism development states that if properly planned, developed, and coordinated, this industry has the potential to provide local people with sustained economic benefits at minimal cost. By contrast, destruction of forests and other vegetation with the subsequent soil erosion and loss of wildlife habitat creates dreadful situations. The ecosystem takes many years (if ever) to regain its former productivity.

Alternative Land Use Diversification (To Forest Destruction)

Tourism, if properly managed, can sustain the ecosystem and ecobalance for a long time. Various combinations of agriculture and tourism as well as direct or indirect employment serving the tourist can be achieved. Income to local people can equal or exceed that derived

[1]John Sawhill, "Using Debt to Save the Rainforest," *Nature Conservancy* (January/February 1991), p. 3.
[2]Paul Winfield, "Can the Elephant Be Saved," *WGBH-TV Journal Graphics*, NOVA Show No. 1717, 1990, pp. 2–3.

from slash and burn deforestation, hunting, or (too often) illegal poaching. Here are some examples:

1. In Kenya, cattle ranchers have been encouraged to have their domestic cattle coexist along side wildlife. These ranchers can lease tourist camping sites. Such an experience provides a thrilling nearness to the African natural landscape. Imagine relaxing near your tent in the evening and hearing lions roaring in the distance. Such leases, of course, provide a supplemental income for the rancher. Some ranches have been successful in obtaining permits to crop surplus wildlife (mainly antelopes) for their meat. This is sold to special wild game restaurants such as the world-famous Carnivore Restaurant in Nairobi.

2. Small scale farms grow vegetables, pigs, rabbits, chickens, and other small animals. Such enterprises can provide a living for an average family of five persons. Sometimes some of the pigs can be sold as can eggs, dressed rabbits, and similar products. A few head of cattle can also be kept if feasible. The livestock can be penned at all times to established "zero grazing." This avoids misuse of grazing land from trampling or overuse. A family might also raise maize, beans, potatoes, and cassava. The livestock produces manure which can be applied to the soil to improve fertility and friability.

3. In tropical South America indigenous people living in the rain forest practice extractive industries which do no harm to the trees nor other components of the natural environment. They collect latex, chicle, and nuts. Some also raise poultry, iguanas, and do fish farming.

4. A small but significant industry is that of producing herbal medicines. In Kenya this small industry has existed for millennia. In recent years the practitioners have formed a national association to protect their interests. This action has gained recognition for them. Producing plants for use as herbal medicines has been termed "agroforestry." These agricultural pursuits are not directly related to tourism. However, products of such farms and forests do find their way into restaurants on occasion and thus help supply tourists' needs.

TOURISM—THE BEST ALTERNATIVE

Wildlife Management

In Zimbabwe the national government has allowed the people of Nyaminyami (in the northwestern part of the country) the right to manage and utilize the wildlife on their land. Local wildlife management districts are established as part of the National Parks "Campfire Program." Any district can participate, within sustainable limits, to use wildlife to meet community needs. Problem animals are shot and the meat distributed among the local villages. If parts of the animal are saleable, they are sold and the profits shared by the villages. The present ban on ivory exports has diminished this market.

But the most important revenue is from big game safaris. Many hunters sincerely believe that their sport is consistent with good wildlife conservation. There is, of course, a cost to having large animals shot. But if this taking is carefully controlled from an adequate stock, thinning their numbers can actually benefit the herd. It allows a more adequate food supply for the remaining animals. However, this principle remains highly controversial.

Financially, a safari to take one bull elephant can earn at least $20,000 for a district. A large proportion of that can be returned directly to the villages in the district in which the elephant was hunted. Each household sharing this profit could double their annual income. A typical community in rural areas of Zimbabwe represents households whose annual income may be only 200 or 300 Zimbabwe dollars. Thus a doubling of this is indeed significant.

Looking at wildlife in this way, the families will say, "we want those elephants and we want them healthy and plentiful." No poaching nor indiscriminate killing would be allowed!

Wildlife revenues can be used in various beneficial ways which might include compensation to those who have had crop damage, invested in social infrastructure such as schools, roads, and medical clinics. Also, they can be distributed to individual households for family use. One village last year received $16,000 as its share of the district's wildlife utilization earnings. Some of the money was used to buy solar-powered electric fences to protect crop fields and homes. Another bought a grinding mill, saving women countless hours of pounding grain by hand.[3]

Private land owners can control wildlife under the same law that made it possible on communal land districts. Some ranchers who have had great difficulty raising cattle due to depradation by lions, leopards, wild dogs, and hyenas now realized that they could do much better by "raising" wildlife. By creating favorable environments for various kinds of wild animals, the ranchers are far exceeding profits made from cattle. For example, a steer which took 3 or 4 years to raise was marketed for about $80. A beautifully tanned zebra skin can be sold to tourists for around $800.[4] Other sources of revenue include selling photographic opportunities, animals to zoos and game parks, and strictly controlled hunting safaris seeking trophy animals. Thus ranching game has proved to be far more rewarding than trying to ranch cattle in this area. In Zimbabwe there are now over 500 commercial farms where wildlife is the major enterprise.

If wildlife conservation efforts are to succeed, rural Africans must be provided with economic benefits. National parks generate revenue from tourists. The photo safari has continued to be a major tourism export for several African countries. It is necessary to provide the landowners with a share of this revenue when wildebeest, zebra, antelope, and elephant move across their land. Revenue obtained from the national parks must be shared, somehow, with people peripheral to the park.

Photo Safaris

In Kenya, tourism in the form of photo safaris is the number one generator of international hard currency. However, in order to achieve a rewarding international tourist industry, a country must have political stability, reasonably adequate tourism infrastructure, and properly educated and trained personnel. Investment in tourist game lodges, hotels, and national parks is hard to justify when there is urgent need for better schools, clinics, hospitals, and roads. Also, the micro-habitat must be suitable. Thick brush and forest obscures tourist viewing of most wildlife.

Employment

Most of the game lodges in Kenya are managed by well educated personnel. But below them it is usually the local people of the area (Maasai, Samburu, etc.) who supply the manual labor and other semiskilled and skilled positions such as cooks, waiters, housekeepers, drivers, maintenance and others. After a number of years, these workers gain experience and are readily promoted to positions such as bartenders, food and beverage captains, and head waiters, head gardeners, chefs, and head housekeepers. Other employment is as hunting guides.

---

[3]Ibid.
[4]Buck DeFries, "Can the Elephant Be Saved," *WGBH-TV Journal Graphics,* NOVA Show No. 1717, 1990, p. 8.

A photo safari in a Kenya national park. Staying inside their minibus, ecotourists approach wildlife at close range for exciting pictures. The driver and guide are local tour company employees. (Photo courtesy of International Expeditions, Inc. by Richard Ryel)

Another dimension in tourism employment is self employed artists who make wood carvings, gemstone jewelry and artifacts. This is a thriving industry in Kenya and supports a sizeable population, especially at or near tourist centers. These artists are self-taught or learn their craft from parents or friends as they become more skillful over the years.

Conclusions and Recommendations

The international market for nature (eco) tourism to little-visited places is growing. There is an appeal to visit somewhat remote destinations with the natural environment the principal allure. Many such places are in undeveloped countries. Tourists' expenditures in such areas can have a very positive effect on the social and economic well-being of local people. Tourism has become one of the world's largest industries employing 56 million people and accounting for 25 percent of all international trade services. Tourism receipts internationally are expected to reach $3 trillion in 1996.[5] Thus, there appears rather favorable prospects for tourism to become of increasing importance in the lives of poor (moneywise) rural people.

Improvement in an existing tourism plant or planning for additional facilities and services is best undertaken using the following steps in the order given:

1. *Review of likely demand.* Understanding the expected visitor is fundamental and of the highest priority—likes, dislikes, interests, prices and willingness to pay, susceptibility to marketing programs, location and identification of markets, and description of target markets.
2. *Provision of supply components.* These can then be predicated upon the findings of the market research described above. What is supplied now and what will future markets desire?
3. *Assessment of accessibility.* Can the tourist conveniently reach the destination? How adequate are the various forms of transportation?

[5]Jean-Michel Cousteau, "Tred Lightly Ecotourists," *Calypso Log* (July 1991), p. 3.

4. *Securing of technical know-how.* Specialists knowledgeable in the needs of visitors must be available. Examples are planners, engineers, land use and natural resource experts, wildlife technicians, transportation specialists, economists, financiers, educators, hotel managers, and others.
5. *Development of financing plan.* This makes or breaks the proposals and plans. Financing must be adequate. Shortages and short cuts are usually causes of failure.
6. *Establishment of time schedules.* Such schedules are vital. What is to be done and when it is to be done are integral parts of successful planning for tourism.
7. *Determination of optimum capacities.* A proper capacity plan prevents overuse, deterioration, and destruction. The planning must be done from a long-range viewpoint. Steps must be taken to protect wildlife and human cultures from excesses. Local tourism authorities should create a "Credo of the Nature-Loving Tourist." This would describe the desired behavior while visiting that particular destination, warn of offending or destructive acts and advise on how best to preserve natural attractions. Special credos for hunters could be used, also.

Key Concepts

ASTA's ten commandments	land-use planning
benefits of ecotourism	local populations and benefits
"campfire program"	management of natural areas
carrying capacity	national parks
code of ethics	natural resources and attractions
conservation organizations	PATA Code for Environmentally
debt for nature swap	Responsible Tourism
ecotourism	sustainable development
ecotourism development	sustainable tourism
environmental destruction	wildlife management
environmental preservation	WTTC
importance of education	WTTC Research Centre

For Review and Discussion

1. What exactly is ecotourism? Why are there so many different terms for this idea?
2. Why has this concept become so popular?
3. Give some examples of the resources necessary for an ecotourism destination.
4. Are resources other than natural ones involved? Are these meaningful? Explain.
5. Describe the role of local people.
6. Why are preservation planning principles so important?
7. What should be the goals of ecotourism for a tour company; the ecotourist; the local population; the local government; a conservation organization.
8. Differentiate ecotourism policy in developing and developed countries.
9. Identify the principal limitations to ecotourism.
10. Referring to question 9, state some ways that these limitations might be ameliorated.
11. Why is capacity so important?

12. As a travel agency counselor, how would you proceed to sell a nature tour to your best friend?
13. Is a bull elephant worth $20,000?
14. Define a debt-for-nature swap. Identify the principles involved. Give some examples. What benefits accrue? To whom?
15. Evaluate the importance of education and training for local staff in a destination area.
16. Is ecotourism education important for the public at large? Why?
17. Explain why ASTA should be so supportive of ecotourism.
18. Similarly, discuss WTTC's establishment of their Environment Research Centre at Oxford Polytechnic, Oxford, England.

Case Problems

1. Bonnie S., CTC, is an agency travel counselor. She has decided that her agency's market area has a good potential to sell more ecotours. How should Bonnie proceed to identify prospective buyers of such tours?
2. As director of Ecuador's national park system, Ernesto B. has become increasingly concerned about the overuse of Galápagos National Park. He worries that the current popularity of the park—about 50,000 tourists each year—may actually be sowing the seeds of destruction. This situation may be inducing a disastrous future drop in visitor numbers. Outline some steps that he might take to:
    a. Ascertain the present quality of the visitor experience.
    b. Remedy some aspects of overuse of the park, to assure future success.
3. Nathan M. is the local managing director of a tour company specializing in ecotourism. His company operates big game/bird photo safaris in Tanzania. He has decided that his firm would be more socially responsible if his tours (by minibus) would obtain practically all needs from local sources. Give some examples of how he might do this and describe the benefits that would accrue locally. (When discussing, include both economic and social benefits.)
4. Upon graduation, you have secured a job as tourism specialist with the World Wildlife Fund. Your first assignment is to be a team member charged with helping to formulate plans for some kind of wildlife protection area in Zambia. This country is located in south central Africa. Their government is considering a new national park and has requested expert assistance from the fund. Kathryn Fuller, president of the fund, has made it very clear to the team that such plans must also aim to improve living standards for the local population. These standards, at present, are grievously low. Most local people are subsistence farmers. They occasionally shoot big game animals that damage their crops, and also for meat.

    After extensive field study, a particularly attractive area has been found in which the scenery is spectacular, climate very pleasant, the natural history resources outstanding, and the local people friendly and hospitable. Thus the proposed park seems to have an excellent potential for attracting substantial numbers of ecotourists. Propose some conceptual ideas as to how this challenge can be met successfully.
5. A very vocal environmental group has recently voiced harsh criticism of the state's tourism business. They claim that the industry rapidly consumes valuable natural resources, provides mostly low-paying unskilled employment, and degrades the

culture of the main tourist centers. As the state's tourism director, how would you answer these charges?

6. Referring to case 5, the same environmental group has succeeded in convincing the state's attorney general that all roadside billboards be eliminated. The various state hotel, motel, restaurant, attractions, and tourist promotion organizations vehemently oppose such legislation. Can you think of some kind of compromising plan that might satisfy both of these opposing groups?

Selected References

Bell, Charles A. "Bali's Example: Fragile Resort Areas and How to Maintain Them." *Cornell Hotel and Restaurant Administration Quarterly*, Vol. 33, No. 5 (October 1992), pp. 28–31.

Boo, Elizabeth. *Ecotourism: The Potentials and Pitfalls* (2 vols.). Washington, D.C.: World Wildlife Fund, 1990.

Boo, Elizabeth. "Tourism and the Environment: Pitfalls and Liabilities of Ecotourism Development," *WTO News*, Vol. 9 (October 1992), pp. 2–4.

Braithwaite, Richard. "Ecotourism in the Monsoonal Tropics," *Issues*, Vol. 23 (May 1993), pp. 29–35.

Bramwell, Bill. "Green Tourism in the Countryside." *Tourism Management*, Vol. 11, No. 4 (December 1990), pp. 358–360.

Cooper, C. P., and I. Ozdil. "From Mass to "Responsible" Tourism: The Turkish Experience." *Tourism Management*, Vol. 13, No. 4 (December 1991), pp. 377–386.

Cousteau, Jean-Michel. "Tred Lightly Ecotourists," *Calypso Log*, Vol. 18, No. 3 (1991), p. 3.

D'Amore, Louis J. "A Code of Ethics and Guidelines for Socially and Environmentally Responsible Tourism." *Journal of Travel Research*, Vol. 31, No. 3 (Winter 1993), pp. 64–66.

DeFries, Buck, and Paul Winfield. "Can the Elephant Be Saved," *WGBH TV Journal Graphics*, NOVA Show No. 1717 (1990), pp. 2–3 and 8.

Downs, Bob. "Study: Environment Big Issue with Travelers," *Travel Trade*, Vol. 58, No. 27 (1992), p. 7.

Eagles, Paul F. "The Travel Motivations of Canadian Ecotourists." *Journal of Travel Research*, Vol. 31, No. 2 (Fall 1992), pp. 3–7.

Farrell, Bryan H., and Dean Runyan. "Ecology and Tourism." *Annals of Tourism Research*, Vol. 18, No. 1 (1991), pp. 26–40.

Fennel, David A., and Paul F. Eagles. "Ecotourism in Costa Rica: A Conceptual Framework." *Journal of Park and Recreation Administration*, Vol. 8, No. 1 (Spring 1990), pp. 23–24.

Fuller, Kathryn S. "Balancing Tourism and Conservation," *Focus*, World Wildlife Fund (September/October 1993), p. 2.

Fuller, Kathryn S. "Local People Play Critical Role in Protecting World's Forest Resources," *Focus*, World Wildlife Fund (March/April 1993), p. 2.

Griffin, George. "Ecotourism: The Good and the Bad of It," *Florida Living* (April 1992), pp. 30–31.

Gunn, Clare A. "Rerefining the Tourism Product, the Environmental Experience," *WTO News*, Vol. 3 (March 1992), pp. 2–3.

Hawkes, S., and Peter Williams. *The Greening of Tourism: From Principles to Practice*. Burnaby, British Columbia, Canada: Center for Tourism Policy and Research, Simon Fraser University, 1993.

"Local Conservation Efforts Prompt Environmental Award," *Focus*, World Wildlife Fund (July/August 1993), p. 4.

May, Vincent. "Tourism, Environment and Development Values, Sustainability and Stewardship." *Tourism Management*, Vol. 12, No. 2 (June 1991), pp. 112–118.

McKercher, B. "The Unrecognized Threat to Tourism: Can Tourism Survive Sustainability?" *Tourism Management*, Vol. 14, No. 2 (1993), pp. 131–136.

Millman, Roger. "Pleasure Seeking vs. the 'Greening' of World Tourism." *Tourism Management*, Vol. 10, No. 4 (December 1989), pp. 275–278.

Nelson, J. G., R. Butler, and G. Wells. *Tourism and Sustainable Development: Monitoring, Planning, Managing.* Waterloo, Ontario: University of Waterloo, 1993.

Ruschmann, Doris M. "Ecological Tourism in Brazil." *Tourism Management,* Vol. 13, No. 1 (March 1992), pp. 125–128.

Sawhill, John. "Using Debt to Save the Rainforest," *Nature Conservancy,* Vol. 41, No. 1 (1991), p. 3.

Singh, Tej Vir. "The Development of Tourism in the Mountain Environment: The Problem of Sustainability." *Tourism Recreation Research,* Vol. 16, No. 2 (1991), pp. 3–12.

Sofield, Trevor. "Sustainable Ethnic Tourism in the South Pacific: Some Principles." *Journal of Tourism Studies,* Vol. 2, No. 1 (1991), pp. 56–72.

Stankovic, Stevan. "The Protection of Life Environment and Modern Tourism." *Tourist Review,* No. 2 (April/June 1991), pp. 2–4.

Travel & Tourism Environment and Development. Brussels: World Travel and Tourism Council, 1992.

U.S. Travel Data Center. *Tourism and the Environment.* Washington, D.C.: Travel Industry Association of America, 1992.

Vasanthakaalam, Hilda. "Environmental Concern for Tourism Planning in India." *Indian Journal of Tourism and Management,* Vol. 1, No. 1 (January/March 1992), pp. 1–9.

Wheatcroft, Stephen. "Airlines, Tourism and the Environment." *Tourism Management,* Vol. 12, No. 2 (June 1991), pp. 119–124.

Whelan, Tensie. *Nature Tourism.* Washington, D.C.: Island Press, 1991.

Wight, Pamela. "Ecotourism: Ethics or Eco-sell?" *Journal of Travel Research,* Vol. 31, No. 3 (Winter 1993), pp. 3–9.

Witt, Stephen F., and Susan Gammon. "Sustainable Tourism Development in Wales." *The Tourist Review,* No. 4 (1991), pp. 32–36.

PART FIVE

ESSENTIALS OF TOURISM RESEARCH AND MARKETING

CHAPTER 17

Travel and Tourism Research

LEARNING OBJECTIVES

- Recognize the role and scope of travel research.
- Learn the travel research process.
- Study secondary data and how it can be used.
- Understand the methods of collecting primary data.
- Know who does travel research.

Information is the basis for decision making, and it is the task of travel research to gather and analyze data to help travel managers make decisions. Travel research is the systematic, impartial designing and conducting of investigations to solve travel problems. Examples of travel research are:

1. Delta Airlines investigating consumer attitudes and behaviors to enable the airline to better serve the flying public
2. Marriott Hotels and Resorts studying the leisure travel market
3. The Aspen Skiing Company conducting a market profile study to understand its customers
4. The U.S. Travel Data Center measuring the economic impact of travel in the United States

Although travel research does not *make* decisions, it does help travel decision makers operate more effectively. Managers can plan, operate, and control more efficiently when they have the facts. Thus research, which reduces the risk in decision making, can have a great impact on the success or failure of a tourism enterprise.

ILLUSTRATIVE USES OF TRAVEL RESEARCH

Some of the uses or functions of travel research are:

1. *To delineate significant problems.* The constant pressure of day-to-day business operations leaves the travel executive with little time to focus on problem areas that handicap operations. The isolation of causes and problems that are creating inefficiency is often one of the most important single contributions that travel research makes to management.
2. *To keep an organization or a business in touch with its markets.* Travel research identifies trends, interprets markets, and tracks changes in markets so that policies can be developed that are aimed in the right direction and are based on facts rather than on

hunches or opinions. Research reduces the risk of unanticipated changes in markets. In a way, research is insurance against these changes to make sure that a business does not stick with a product until it becomes obsolete.

3. *To reduce waste.* Research has always been effective in measuring methods of operation to eliminate those methods that are inefficient and to concentrate on those that are the most effective. Automation of travel makes this use even more important. The energy crisis led to research that has produced dramatic savings in aircraft fuel requirements.

4. *To develop new resources of profit.* Research can lead to the discovery of new markets, new products, and new uses for established products. Research can show the lodging industry the types of rooms and the type of lodging facilities that should be offered to meet customers' needs.

5. *To aid in sales promotion.* Many times the results of research are interesting not only to the firm but also to the public and can be used in advertising and promotion. This is particularly true of consumer attitude research and research where consumers are asked to rank products and services.

6. *To create goodwill.* Consumers react favorably to travel research; they feel that the company that is involved in research really cares about them and is trying to create a product or service that will meet their needs.

THE STATE OF THE ART

Travel research today runs from the primitive to the sophisticated—from simple fact gathering to complex, mathematical models. For those who really wish to dig into the subject, there are several references worth noting. The most important is *Travel, Tourism and Hospitality Research: A Handbook for Managers and Researchers,* published by John Wiley & Sons in 1994; a second is *Tourism Analysis,* published by Longman in 1989; a third is an article that appeared in the *Journal of Travel Research* entitled "Some Critical Aspects of Measurement Theory and Practice in Travel Research"; a fourth and one of the most useful documents is "Identifying Traveler Markets, Research Methodologies," published by the U.S. Travel Service in 1978; and a fifth is a six-part series on marketing research by Robert C. Lewis, University of Massachusetts, which appeared in *The Cornell Hotel and Restaurant Administration Quarterly* in 1984 and 1985.

Measurement is a critical element in research activity, and the lack of standard or precise definitions has hampered the development of travel research. Without definitions, measurement cannot be taken and data cannot be generated and compared from study to study. Economic projections or analytical findings made by sophisticated models or pure intuition must be based on some kind of data. Without a quantitative record of past experiences, only individual, isolated studies making a limited contribution to the state of the art are possible. That is basically where we stand in the area of travel research at the present time. Giant strides are being made, improving travel research by adopting techniques developed by other disciplines and utilizing new and more sophisticated techniques; however, the existing body of literature largely consists of individual isolated studies utilizing different definitions that were set up only to solve the immediate problem at hand.

THE TRAVEL RESEARCH PROCESS

The key to good travel research is to define the problem and work through it in a systematic procedural manner to a final solution. The purpose of this section is to describe briefly the basic procedures that will produce a good research result.

1. *Identify the problem.* First, the problem must be defined or identified. Then you are in a position to proceed in a systematic manner.
2. *Conduct a situation analysis.* In this step you gather and digest all the information available and pertinent to the problem. The purpose is to become familiar with all the available information to make sure that you are not repeating someone else's work or that you have not overlooked information that will provide a ready solution to the problem. The situation analysis is an exhaustive search of all the data pertinent to the company, the product, the industry, the market, the competition, advertising, customers, suppliers, technology, the economy, the political climate, and similar matters. Knowledge of this background information will help you to sort out the likely causes of the problem and will lead to more efficient productive research. The organization will get the most from the research result when you understand the organization's internal environment and its goals, strategies, desires, resources, and constraints.
3. *Conduct an informal investigation.* After having gotten background information from available sources, you will talk informally with consumers, distributors, and key people in the industry to get an even better feel for the problem. During both the situation analysis and informal investigation, you should be developing hypotheses

One of the first steps in researching a tourism problem is to discuss it with the firm's representative. (Photo courtesy of the Travel and Tourism Research Association)

that can be tested. The establishment of hypotheses is one of the foundations of conducting research and is a valuable step in the problem-solving process. An hypothesis is a supposition, a tentative proposal, a possible solution to a problem. In some ways it could be likened to a diagnosis. If your automobile quit running on the interstate, you might hypothesize that (1) you were out of gas or (2) the fuel pump had failed or (3) you had filter problems. An investigation would enable you to accept or reject these hypotheses.

4. *Develop a formal research design.* Once adequate background information has been developed and the problem has been defined against this background, it is time to develop the specific procedure or design for carrying out the total investigation or research project. This step is the heart of the research process. Here you have to develop the hypotheses that will be tested and determine the types and sources of data that are to be obtained. Are secondary sources available, or will it be necessary to conduct primary research? If primary research has to be conducted, then it is necessary to develop the sample, the questionnaires, or other data collection forms and any instruction sheets and coding methods and tabulation forms. Finally, it is necessary to conduct a pilot study to test all of the foregoing elements. The results are then written up in a detailed plan that serves as a guide that any knowledgeable researcher should be able to follow and conduct the research satisfactorily.

5. *Collect the data.* If the data are available from secondary sources, then collecting the data becomes primarily desk research. However, if primary data are collected, this step involves actual fieldwork in conducting survey research, observational research, or experimental research. The success of data gathering depends on the quality of field supervision, the caliber of the interviewers or field investigators, and the training of investigators.

6. *Tabulate and analyze.* Once the data have been collected, they must be coded, tabulated, and analyzed. Both this step and the previous one must be done with great care; it is possible for a multitude of errors to creep into the research process if collection, tabulation, and analysis are not done properly. For example, if one is going to use the survey method, then interviewers must be properly selected, trained, and supervised. Obviously, if instead of following the carefully laid out sample the interviewers simply fill out questionnaires themselves, the data will not be useful.

In today's environment, it is likely that tabulation will take place on the computer. A number of excellent packages are available for this purpose. One of the most used is SPSS, the Statistical Package for the Social Sciences.

7. *Interpret.* Tabulation results in stacks of computer printout, with a series of statistical conclusions. These data must now be interpreted in terms of the best action or policy for the firm or organization to follow—a series of specific recommendations of action. This reduction of the interpretation to recommendations is one of the most difficult tasks in the research process.

8. *Write the report.* Presentation of the results of the research is extremely important. Unless the data are written up in a manner that will encourage management to read them and act upon them, all of the labor in the research process is lost. Consequently, emphasis should be put on this step in the research process to produce a report that will be clearly understood with recommendations that will be accepted.

9. *Follow up.* Follow up means precisely that. A study sitting on the shelf gathering dust

accomplishes nothing. While many people will consider the researcher's task to be done once the final report or presentation has been made, the work is *not* completed until the results of the survey are put into action. Research is an investment, and an ultimate test of the value of any research is the extent to which its recommendations are actually implemented and results achieved. It is the task of the researcher to follow up to make the previous investment of time and money worthwhile.

SOURCES OF INFORMATION

Primary data, secondary data, or both may be used in a research investigation. Primary data are original data gathered for the specific purpose of solving the travel research problem that confronts you. In contrast, secondary data have already been collected for some other purpose and are available for use by simply visiting the library or other such repositories of secondary data. When researchers conduct a survey of cruise passengers to determine their attitudes and opinions, they are collecting primary data. When they get information from the Bureau of Census on travel agents, they are using a secondary source.

The situation analysis step of the travel research process is emphasized as it focuses

A library is a good source of secondary data for a situation analysis. Gin Hayden, Project Director, Travel Reference Center, University of Colorado, is in charge of maintaining the largest collection of travel research studies in North America. She can conduct literature searches of the collection by 973 descriptions. (Photo courtesy of Business Research Division, University of Colorado)

on the use of secondary sources; however, their use is not confined to this step. One of the biggest mistakes in travel research is to rush out and collect primary data without exhausting secondary source information. Only later do you discover you have duplicated previous research when existing sources could have provided information to solve your problem for a fraction of the cost. Only after exhausting secondary sources and finding you still lack sufficient data to solve your problem should you turn to primary sources.

Secondary Data

In the last 10 years there has been a virtual explosion of information related to tourism, travel, recreation, and leisure. A competent researcher must be well acquainted with these sources and how to find them. Appendix B contains a concise list of major secondary sources of travel information.

If you are fortunate enough to find secondary sources of information, you can save yourself a great deal of time and money. Low cost is clearly the greatest advantage of secondary data. When secondary data sources are available, it is not necessary to construct and print questionnaires, hire interviewers, pay transportation costs, pay coders, pay keypunchers, and pay programmers; it is easy to see the cost advantage of utilizing secondary data. Secondary data can also be collected much more quickly than can primary data. With an original research project, it typically takes a minimum of 60 to 90 days or more to collect data; secondary data could be collected in a library within a few days.

Secondary data are not without disadvantages; for example, many times information does not fit the problem for which you need information. Another problem is timeliness—many secondary sources become outdated. For example, the Census of Population and Housing is conducted every 10 years; as we get to the end of that time period, the data are not very useful.

Evaluating Secondary Data

While it is not expected that everyone will be a research expert, everyone should be able to evaluate or appraise secondary data. Any study, no matter how interesting, must be subjected to evaluation: "Is it a valid study? Can I use the results to make decisions?" On such occasions the researcher must evaluate the secondary data and determine whether they are usable.

The following criteria may be used to appraise the value of information obtained from secondary sources:

1. *The organizations supplying the data.* What amount of time went into the study? Who conducted the study? What experience did the personnel have? What was the financial capacity of the company? What was the cost of the study? An experienced research firm will put the proper time and effort into a study to yield results whereas a novice or inexperienced organization may not.
2. *The authority under which the data are gathered.* For example, data collected by the IRS are likely to be much better than data collected by a business firm. Data that are

required by law, such as census data, are much more dependable than is information from other sources.

3. *Freedom from bias.* One should always look at the nature of the organization furnishing the data. Would you expect a study sponsored by airlines to praise the bus industry for providing the lowest-cost transportation on a per mile basis in the United States?

4. *The extent to which the rules of sampling have been rigidly upheld.* What is the adequacy of the sample? Adequacy is frequently difficult to evaluate because deficiencies in the sampling process can be hidden. One indication of adequacy is the sponsor's willingness to talk about the sample. Will the sponsor release sampling details? Are the procedures well-known, acceptable methods?

5. *The nature of the unit in which the data are expressed.* Here even simple concepts are difficult to define. In defining the term "house," how do you handle such things as duplexes, triplexes, mobile homes, and apartment houses? Make sure that good operational definitions have been used throughout the research so there will be no problems in understanding it. Research results that are full of terms such as "occasionally" and "frequently" are not likely to be useful; these terms have different meanings to different people.

6. *The accuracy of the data.* The need here is to examine the data carefully for any inconsistencies and inquire into the way in which the data were acquired, edited, and tabulated. If at all possible, check the data against known data from other sources that are accurate. For example, check the demographics in a study against known census data.

7. *Pertinency to the problem.* You must be concerned with fit. You may have a very good study, but if it does not pertain to the problem at hand, it is not worth anything to you. The relevance of secondary data pertaining to the problem must stand up; otherwise, the study cannot be used.

8. *Careful work.* Throughout your evaluation always look for evidence of careful work. Are tables constructed properly? Do all totals add up to the right figures or 100 percent? Are conclusions supported by the data? Is there any evidence of conflicting data? Is the information presented in a well-organized, systematic manner?

Primary Data

When it is not possible to get the information you need from secondary sources, it is necessary to turn to primary sources—original, firsthand sources of information. If you need information on travelers' attitudes, you would then go to that population and sample it. As stated earlier, you should turn to collecting primary data only after exhausting all reasonable secondary sources of information.

Once you have determined that you are going to collect primary data, then you must choose what method of gathering primary data you are going to use. The most widely used means of collecting primary information is the survey method. Other methods are the observational method and the experimental method. It is not uncommon to find one or more of these methods used in gathering data. These basic methods are discussed in the next section.

BASIC RESEARCH METHODS

The Survey Method

If we look at the methods of collecting travel research data, we will find that the survey method is the most frequently used. The survey method, also frequently referred to as the questionnaire technique, gathers information by asking questions. The survey method includes factual surveys, opinion surveys, or interpretative surveys, all of which can be conducted by personal interviews, mail, or telephone techniques.

FACTUAL SURVEYS   A quick look at the types of surveys will reveal that factual surveys are by far the most beneficial. "In what recreational activities did you participate last week?" is a question for which the respondent should be able to give accurate information. While excellent results are usually achieved with factual surveys, all findings are still subject to certain errors, such as errors of memory and ability to generalize or the desire to make a good impression. Nonetheless, factual surveys tend to produce excellent results.

OPINION SURVEYS   In these surveys, the respondent is asked to express an opinion or make an evaluation or appraisal. For example, a respondent could be asked whether tour package A or B was the most attractive or which travel ad is the best. This kind of opinion information can be invaluable. In studies of a ski resort conducted by the University of Colorado, vacationer respondents were asked to rate the resort's employees' performance as excellent, good, average, or needs improvement. The ratings

An experienced tourism research firm can fulfill the processes of surveys, observations, or experiments to accomplish the goals of the research project. (Photo courtesy of the Travel and Tourism Research Association)

allowed resort management to take action where necessary. Opinion surveys tend to produce excellent results if they are properly constructed.

INTERPRETIVE SURVEYS   On interpretive studies the respondent acts as an interpreter as well as a reporter. Subjects are asked why they chose a certain course of action—why they participated in a particular recreation activity the previous week (as well as what activity), why they flew on a particular airline, why they chose a particular vacation destination, why they chose a particular lodging establishment.

While respondents can reply accurately to "what" questions, they often have difficulty replying to "why" questions. Therefore, while interpretive research may give you a feel for consumer behavior, the results tend to be limited. It is much better to utilize motivational and psychological research techniques, which are better suited for obtaining this information.

In summary, try to get factual or opinion data via the survey method and utilize in-depth interviewing or psychological research techniques to get "reason why" data.

It was mentioned earlier that surveys can be conducted by personal interviews, telephone, or mail. The purpose of a survey is to gather data by interviewing a limited number of people (sample) that represents a larger group. Reviewing the basic survey methods, one finds the following advantages and disadvantages.

PERSONAL INTERVIEWS   These are much more flexible than either mail or telephone surveys because the interviewer can adapt to the situation and the respondent. The interviewer can alter questions to make sure that the respondent understands them or probe if the respondent does not respond with a satisfactory answer. Typically one can obtain much more information by personal interview than by telephone or mail surveys, which by necessity must be relatively short. Personal interviewers can observe

Group discussion of ideas enhances the process of deciding on the research methods to be used. (Photo courtesy of the Travel and Tourism Research Association)

the situation as well as ask questions. For example, an interviewer in a home can record data on the person's socioeconomic status, which would not be possible without this observation. The personal interview method permits the best sample control of all the survey techniques.

A major limitation of the personal interview method is its relatively high cost. It tends to be the most expensive of the three survey methods. It also takes a considerable amount of time to conduct, and there is always the possibility of personal interviewer bias.

TELEPHONE SURVEYS   Respondents are interviewed over the telephone with this approach. Telephone surveys are usually conducted much more rapidly and at less cost than are personal interviews. The shortcomings of telephone surveys are that they are less flexible than personal interviews, and of necessity they are brief. While a further limitation of phone surveys is that not everyone has a telephone, those with telephones tend to have the market potential to travel or buy tourism products. Consequently, this limitation is not very serious for travel research. Speed and low cost tend to be the primary advantages of telephone interviews.

MAIL SURVEYS   Mail surveys have the potential of being the lowest-cost method of research. As would be expected, mail surveys involve mailing the questionnaire to carefully selected sample respondents and requesting them to return the completed questionnaires. This survey approach has a great advantage when large geographical areas must be covered and when it would be difficult to reach respondents. Other advantages of this approach are that personal interview bias is absent and the respondent can fill out the questionnaire at his or her convenience.

The greatest problem in conducting a mail survey is having a good list and getting

CAREY AMERICAN LIMOUSINE Colorado Springs Shuttle Service

Please take a moment to respond to the following questions. This information will be used to evaluate areas of service to afford you qu for your next trip. Thank you.

1. Was the vehicle on time? Yes _____ No _____ (Delay time: _____ Reason given
2. What was the condition of the equipment? Clean _____ Average _____ Unkempt _____
3. Was your driver courteous? Yes _____ No _____
4. How was your service: Excellent _____ Fair _____ Poor _____ (Why?
5. Was it easy to make your reservation? Yes _____ No _____ (Why:
6. Where did you find out about our company? Travel agent _____ Advertisement _____ Referred by:
7. Was the scheduled time convenient for you? Very _____ Acceptable _____ Inconvenient _____
8. Were you traveling on Business _____ Pleasure _____
9. Will you recommend our service to others? Yes _____ (Name & Address   ) N
Comments:

Name:
Address:
City: _____ State: _____ Zip: _____
COLORADO TRANSPORTATION GROUP

If you represent a company or travel agency, please inclu
information:

Telephone (   )

Self-administered questionnaires are an excellent way to receive feedback from customers. This short questionnaire is illustrative of how Carey American Limousine evaluates its service.

an adequate response. If a large percentage of the target population fails to respond, you will have to question whether those who did not respond are different from those who have replied and whether this introduces bias. Length is another consideration in mail questionnaires. While they can be longer than telephone surveys, they still must be reasonably short. Another limitation of mail surveys is that questions must be worded carefully and simply so that respondents will not be confused. While questions may be very clear to the person who wrote them, they can be very unclear to the respondent.

ELECTRONIC DEVICES   A relatively new way of conducting survey research is the use of computer-type electronic devices to ask the consumer questions and immediately record and tabulate the results. This equipment can be placed in a hotel lobby, mall, or other high-traffic location and attract consumers to record responses to questions. Use of these machines is a low-cost method of getting consumer information because the questions are self-administered, saving the cost of interviewers, and the results are tabulated automatically. A disadvantage is that children, who like to play with such machines, may distort the results. However, it is predicted that such devices will become increasingly popular in the future.

Another technological innovation is computer-assisted telephone interviewing. This involves a survey questionnaire entered into computer memory. The interviewer reads the questions from the computer screen and records the respondent's answers into computer memory by using a keyboard and simply touching a sensitive screen. Since the data are recorded immediately, these systems tend to be faster and less expensive than traditional methods.

Observational Method

The observational method relies upon the direct observation of physical phenomena in the gathering of data. Observing some action of the respondent is obviously much more objective and accurate than is utilizing the survey method. Under the observational method, information can be gathered by either personal or mechanical observation. Mechanical recorders on highways count the number of cars that pass and the time that they pass. Automatic counters at attractions observe and count the number of visitors.

Advantages of the observational method are that it tends to be accurate and it can record consumer behavior. It also reduces interviewer bias. Disadvantages are that it is much more costly than the survey method and it is not possible to employ in many cases. Finally, the observational method shows what people are doing but does not tell you why they are doing it. It cannot delve into motives, attitudes, or opinions. If the "why" is important, this would not be a good method to use.

Experimental Method

This method of gathering primary data involves setting up a test, a model, or an experiment to simulate the real world. The essentials of the experimental method are the measurement of variations within one or more activities while all other conditions and variables are being controlled. The experimental method is very hard to use in tourism research because of the difficulty of holding variables constant. There is no physical laboratory in which tourism researchers can work. However, it is possible for resort areas to run advertising experiments or pricing experiments or to develop simulation models to aid in decision making. Such test marketing is being conducted successfully, and as time passes, we will see the experimental method being used more and more.

WHO DOES TRAVEL RESEARCH?

Many organizations are involved in the use and conduct of travel research. The types of firms and organizations that engage in travel research include government, educational institutions, consultants, trade associations, advertising agencies, media, hotels and motels, airlines and other carriers, attractions, and food service organizations.

Government

The federal government has been a major producer of travel research over the years. Appendix B indicates the role of the government in travel research, citing work by several government agencies. The U.S. Travel and Tourism Administration conducts studies on international visitors, focusing on both marketing information and economic impact. State and local governments also employ travel research to assist in making marketing and public policy decisions. Examples are studies of highway users, the value of fishing and hunting, the economic impact of tourism in various geographic areas, inventories of tourism facilities and services, tourism planning procedures, and visitor characteristics studies. In other countries, research inaugurated by the official tourism organization of a state or country often has very significant ramifications for tourism development and promotion. Research done in Mexico, England, Spain, France, Poland, and Croatia has been outstanding.

Educational Institutions

Universities conduct many travel research studies. The chief advantage is that the studies are usually conducted without bias by trained professionals. Many of the studies have contributed greatly to the improvement of travel research methods. Institutions of higher learning, particularly universities with departments of hotel and restaurant management, hospitality management, and tourism, have a vital need for such information. Such educational organizations are concerned with the teaching of tourism or related subjects and need the most current available research findings to do an effective teaching job. Research is also needed by such academic departments as geography, fisheries and wildlife, resource development, park and recreation resources, and forestry. All these departments have an interest in the effect on the environment because of the use of the natural landscape for recreation and tourism.

Many departments of universities are qualified to accomplish pure research or applied research in tourism. Bureaus of business and economic research are often active in this field. An example is the research accomplished by the Business Research Division of the University of Colorado at Boulder. This organization has published many tourism research findings, including a bibliography of tourism and travel research studies,

Creating a successful tourism product depends upon accurately assessing its best markets by identifying demographics and lifestyles. These can be accomplished by a research firm proficient in making such determinations. (Photo courtesy of the Travel and Tourism Research Association)

reports, and articles. Departments of universities that can be helpful include psychology, sociology, economics, engineering, landscape architecture and urban planning, management, hotel and restaurant administration, theater, home economics, human ecology, forestry, botany, zoology, history, geography, and anthropology.

Consultants

Numerous organizations specialize in conducting travel research on a fee basis for airlines, hotels, restaurants, ski areas, travel agents, resorts, and others. Consultants offer the service of giving advice in the planning, design, interpretation, and application of travel research. They will also provide the service of conducting all or a part of a field investigation for their clients.

The primary advantage of consultants or consulting firms is that they are well trained, experienced specialists who have gained their experience by making studies for many different clients. They also provide an objective outsider's point of view, and they have adequate facilities to undertake almost any job. The disadvantage of consultants is that of any outsider—the lack of intimate knowledge of the internal problems of the client's business; however, management can provide this ingredient. Many travel firms with their own research departments find it advantageous to use consultants or a combination of their own internal staff and consultants.

There are many well-known firms specializing in travel research. A few of these are Opinion Research Corporation, Davidson-Peterson Associates, Economic Research Associates, the Gallup organization, Arthur D. Little, Midwest Research Institute, Plog Research, Robinson, Yesawich & Pepperdine, SDR, Inc., Angus Reid Group, Arthur

Davidson-Peterson Associates, Inc., is illustrative of the many firms available to conduct travel and tourism research studies. (Photo courtesy of Davidson-Peterson Associates, Inc.)

Andersen, Coopers & Lybrand, D. K. Shifflet & Associates, Longwoods International, Menlo Consulting Group, National Demographics & Lifestyles, Somerset R. Waters, and Simmons Market Research Bureau.

An example of a syndicated service is one offered by the Menlo Consulting Group in Palo Alto, California called TravelStyles, which provides research on the U.S. market for international travel. It is a source of information on travel trends, market segments, and the changing preferences of Americans who travel outside the country.

Trade Associations

Extensive travel research is conducted by trade associations. Appendix B also indicates the role of trade associations as a source of travel information. The trade association often provides facilities for carrying on a continuous research service for its members, particularly in the area of industry statistics.

Advertising Agencies

Today advertising agencies typically maintain extensive research departments for both their own and their clients' needs. The agency must have basic facts if it is to develop an effective advertising campaign for its travel client in today's rapidly changing world. Advertising agencies that have been leaders in travel research are Ogilvy and Mather Worldwide; J. Walter Thompson; BBDO Worldwide; Foote, Cone and Belding; Leo Burnett; and DDB Needham Worldwide.

Media

Trade journals often conduct outstanding tourism research. Experts in various disciplines are brought together in symposia to discover relationships and applications of their disciplines to problems and opportunities in tourism. Travel Weekly's comprehensive study of the travel agency market is a classic example of good media research. The 1993 edition represents the publication's twelfth in-depth probe of the travel agency industry. Consumer magazines have also been active producers of travel research. *Time, U.S. News and World Report, Newsweek, Better Homes and Gardens, National Geographic, New Yorker, Sunset, Southern Living, Sports Illustrated,* and *Travel/Holiday* are all known for their travel research.

Hotels and Motels

Hotels and motels constantly use current research findings concerning their markets, trends in transportation, new construction materials, management methods, use of electronic data processing, human relations techniques, employee management, advertising, food and beverage supplies and services, and myriad other related information.

Airlines and Other Carriers

This group offers services designed for the business and vacation traveler. Because of their needs and the importance of research to their operations, airlines and other carriers will usually have their own market research departments to conduct ongoing studies of their customers and the market. They are also frequent employers of outside consultants.

Attractions

The most ambitious private attractions in the country are the major theme parks, and research has played a major role in the success of these enterprises. That research has run the gamut from feasibility studies to management research. Walt Disney's thinking still dominates the industry. The Disney formula of immaculate grounds, clean and attractive personnel, high-quality shops, tidy rest rooms, and clean restaurants are the consumers' preferences today. Research shows that if attractions are not clean, they are not likely to be successful.

Food Service

Much of the pioneering work in the use of research by restaurants has been done by franchises and chains because what will work in one location will typically work in others, resulting in a large payoff from funds invested in research. All travel firms, whether they are restaurants, airlines, hotels, or other hospitality enterprises, need to be in touch with their markets and find new and better ways of marketing to sell seats, increase load factors, and achieve favorable occupancy ratios.

THE U.S. TRAVEL DATA CENTER AND THE TRAVEL AND TOURISM RESEARCH ASSOCIATION

Two unique organizations serve the travel research area: the U.S. Travel Data Center (USTDC) and the Travel and Tourism Research Association (TTRA). Following is a brief description of the operations of these organizations.

The U.S. Travel Data Center is a nonprofit, privately supported agency that devotes its resources to measuring the economic impact of travel and monitoring changes in travel markets. The Data Center has become a recognized source for current data used by business and government to develop tourism policies and marketing strategy. Market and economic research provided by the Data Center is utilized by all major sectors of the travel industry. Its members represent lodging; food service; transportation, entertainment; attractions; federal, state, county, and city promotion agencies; travel-related media; marketing organizations; universities; and tourism associations.

The objectives of the Data Center are to (1) develop and encourage standard, sound travel research terminology and techniques; (2) develop and encourage consistent estimates of travel activity over time and geographic areas; (3) monitor trends in travel activity and the travel industry over time; (4) measure the economic impact of travel over time and on geographic areas; (5) evaluate the impact of major government programs affecting travel and the travel industry; (6) monitor, evaluate, and help develop techniques to forecast travel supply and demand; and (7) develop techniques to measure the cost and the benefits of travel in the United States.

The Data Center holds an annual outlook for travel and tourism each fall and carries

The U.S. Travel Data Center is one of the nation's most important tourism research organizations. It is a nonprofit, privately supported group that provides essential data on tourism's economic impacts and reports on significant changes in travel markets. (Photo courtesy of the Travel and Tourism Research Association)

on an active research and publications program. The majority of its publications are available for purchase by writing its office. The Data Center also conducts a *National Travel Survey* on a monthly basis, performs custom research, has developed the Travel Economic Impact Model, and maintains the U.S. Travel Data Bank. The U.S. Travel Data Center is located at 1100 New York Avenue N.W., Washington, D.C. 20005.

The Travel and Tourism Research Association is an international organization of travel research and marketing professionals devoted to improving the quality, value, scope, and acceptability of travel research and marketing information. The association is the world's largest travel research organization, and its members represent all aspects of the travel industry, including airlines, hotels, attractions, transportation companies, media, advertising agencies, government, travel agencies, consulting firms, universities, students, and so on.

TTRA's mission is to be the global leader in advocating standards and promoting the application of high-quality travel and tourism research, planning, management, and marketing information, with the following specific objectives:

- To serve as an international forum for the exchange of ideas and information among travel and tourism researchers, marketers, planners, and managers.
- To encourage the professional development of travel and tourism researchers, marketers, planners, and managers.
- To facilitate global cooperation between producers and users of travel and tourism research.
- To promote and disseminate high-quality, credible, and effective research to the travel and tourism industry.
- To foster the development of travel and tourism research and related curricula in institutes of higher education.
- To advocate the effective use of research in the decision-making process of professionals in the travel and tourism industry.

TTRA has chapters in Canada, the Central States, Florida, Texas, Arizona, New York, the Mountain States, the Southeast, Southern California, Northern California, Hawaii, the South Central States, and Washington, D.C. TTRA contributes to the publication of the *Journal of Travel Research,* the TTRA newsletter, annual conference proceedings, and other special publications. TTRA has an extensive awards program that recognizes excellence and encourages professional development of researchers, marketers, planners, and students involved in the travel and tourism industry. The organization helped establish the Travel Reference Center located at the Business Research Division, University of Colorado, Boulder, Colorado 80309. This service was established to assist the travel industry in finding information sources and solving business problems. Those wishing further information on TTRA should write to Francine Butler, TTRA Executive Director, 10200 W. 44th Ave., Suite 304, Wheat Ridge, CO 80033.

SUMMARY

Travel research provides the information base for effective decision making by tourism managers. Availability of adequate facts allows managers to plan, operate, and control more efficiently and decreases risk in the decision-making process.

Useful travel research depends on precise identification of the problem; a thorough situation analysis supplemented by an informal investigation of the problem, careful research design; and meticulous collection, tabulation, and analysis of the data. The researcher must also present a readable written report with appropriate recommendations for action and then follow up to ensure that the recommendations are actually implemented so that results can be achieved.

The research itself may use secondary (preexisting) data or require collection of primary data (original research). Primary data may be gathered by survey—personal interview, mail, or telephone surveys—or by the observational and experimental methods. Numerous organizations and agencies use and conduct travel research. Two professional organizations serve the field: the U.S. Travel Data Center and the Travel and Tourism Research Association.

About the Readings

Knowing how travel research is accomplished and actually doing it are very different. The reading provides an example of how a major lodging firm used consumer-product oriented research to determine what travelers wanted in accommodations. The research findings then became the basis for continuing changes and improvements in the lodging facilities. This firm's growth and success are testimonials to the value of research.

READING 17.1

Researching Travel the Procter and Gamble Way
BY RUSSELL A. BELL, Past President
Travel and Tourism Research Association

Reprinted from *Innovation and Creativity in Travel Research and Marketing, 12th Annual Conference Proceedings,* Travel and Tourism Research Association.

Unquestionably, research has grown in importance across America over the last decade, proving very emphatically that the businesses that prosper are those that utilize research to chart the course of action.

At Holiday Inns we have expanded our horizons considerably over the past several years, primarily because of research. When we began our hotel chain in 1952, the major criterion for highly satisfactory accommodations was a clean, comfortable room. Then, as lifestyles improved appreciably over the years, expectations of the hotel guest skyrocketed. The increasingly sophisticated traveler demanded accommodations equal to or even better than what he left at home.

Consequently, the old philosophy of merely providing a serviceable room suddenly became obsolete. We were faced with the necessity for drastic improvements of our entire operation if we were to successfully compete in the market place. So, we began to develop an overall strategy that would position us much more aggressively in the hotel market. Intense consumer-products research proved to be the catalyst that was needed to accomplish this.

I will tell you about the methodology and findings of two of our research projects a little later on which will illustrate this new strategy, but first I would like to give you an overview of our Research Department and the businesses that we support. We have a staff of 21 people who handle the research function, a function that costs close to $2 million a year to operate. That figure gives you an idea of the importance which management places on our area. We are organized into four research groups—two for lodging, one for gaming and one for restaurants.

The lodging groups are responsible for all research that involves the more than 1,700 Holiday Inn hotels in 59 countries. One lodging group tracks the chain's performance in the marketplace, including traveler mix, size of market share and product quality. The other lodging group handles the advertising, promotional, and room development activities.

The restaurant group handles research for our hotel restaurants as well as the entire Perkins Cake & Steak chain, acquired by Holiday Inns in 1979, today the fourth largest full-service family restaurant in the U.S.

And finally, our gaming group is devoted to research for Harrah's Casino which Holiday Inns required a year and a half ago, and which along with our interest in a Las Vegas casino now comprises the largest gaming operation in the country, in terms of square footage.

So you can see that we have wide areas of interest and responsibilities. Our research staff represents a good cross-section of the country and most have advanced degrees in marketing, marketing research or related fields. A number of our people have had previous research experience within the consumer products industry.

Here's how our staff usually functions: First, we define the basic problem and then design a research project to match the criteria that have been set down. Next, we contract with a research supplier who handles the interviewing and computer processing necessary for the project. Our department then does the analysis and writes reports.

Now, let me talk in more detail about the research strategy I mentioned earlier. When we decided it was imperative to market more aggressively, we directed our attention specifically to large-scale consumer products market analysis. Obviously, we had to modify our methods to the specific needs of the lodging industry, but, overall, we believe we have achieved the type of research knowledge about our customer that exists throughout the consumer products industry. And we have learned to utilize this information to build effective and aggressive promotions. For example, just as Procter & Gamble markets soap with coupons, we have turned to promotions such as the $5 guest check certificate, good for $5 off the price of the next Holiday Inn room. This was a promotion we had on the shelf, waiting for a lull in business, and which we were able to implement quickly when last summer's slump in travel occurred.

To me, one of the most unusual facets of our Holiday Inn research department is its total integration into the management decision process. This is one of the major reasons why we operate as a completely self-funded department. This fact give us substantial leeway in deciding what projects we wish to work on and the priorities involved since we are not working from someone else's budget. And, at the same time, we are challenged by management to justify each project and the methods which we employ.

Also, because of the way management perceives the research function, we actively participate in the effective utilization of research information. For example, the research function is organized into the Product Management division and we are jointly charged with the implementation of research findings. As a result, research has become an integral part of the planning, development and execution stages of systemwide operations.

This attitude gives us a refreshing break from the all too frequent "thanks for the report, good job" comments we sometimes receive in the research industry while at the same time, never hearing another word about the report which we have labored on so painstakingly. In contrast, Holiday Inn officials often ask for advice about implementation of a new product, a new promotion, or advertising theme, based on what we have learned through extensive research.

A study on various room configurations illustrates what I mean about effective research follow through. We wanted to develop a room concept which in general was conceived as a "home away from home." We started with secondary research on various items in the home that had the most dramatic appeal, such as bedding quality, mattress size, or the type of showerheads that were most popular.

Then we created room prototypes. We took photographs of these prototypes and asked people what they found most appealing about the various room components. Shopping malls and hotel lobby intercepts among travelers were utilized to obtain this information. From there, we installed rooms in hotels specifically for research purposes. We recruited guests in the hotels and walked them through the rooms. We showed them the new rooms along with the traditional double/double configurations. We asked them what they liked or did not like about the rooms.

From that, we developed two room concepts . . . King Leisure, which includes a king-size bed and enlarged work/leisure area with a table and two upholstered chairs; and King Sofa, which includes all the amenities of King Leisure with the addition of a sofa bed, so four people can be accommodated.

The final stage involved the installation of enough rooms in geographically dispersed hotels in order to obtain live-in research information. Then we called guests after they had spent at least one night in the new rooms, and from these findings, developed standards for the rooms. These rooms are now well into the process of installation in our hotels and are guided by the guest mix at each property.

Our research shows that King Leisure rooms enjoy a high guest preference over the conventional double/double room and that guests are more willing to pay a few dollars more for these improved accommodations. As a result of the popularity of King Leisure amenities, we have introduced several systemwide standards such as thicker towels, glass tumblers rather than plastic, larger bars of soap and massaging showerheads.

Another study which we call the Anatomy of the Lodging Experience is a good example of consumer products-oriented research approach. The purpose of this study was to find out in great detail how guests used the hotel facilities . . . where they put their suitcase, what electrical outlets they used, and so on.

The study was made during two different seasons, summer and winter. We intercepted people in the lobbies after check-in and conducted short interviews, concentrating on details such as method of travel, size of party, purpose of the trip and length of stay.

We gave the guests questionnaires, along with complimentary gifts, and asked them to fill out the questionnaires after checkout and then mail them to us. Forty-five percent responded which provided us with an excellent base. The surveys worked well, I believe, because we carefully explained to guests that we wanted to improve the quality of their lodging experience, and then we gave them a gift in advance to make them feel a little guilty if they didn't return the questionnaires.

I would like to point out that we took a very broad sample from a number of Holiday Inns and then did a complete folio audit on everyone who stayed at the hotels involved. This gave us necessary in-depth information that helped us adjust our research findings accordingly. For instance, we found that we had greatly under-represented the single night lodgers in our sample and used that information to weight the results.

You might be interested in some of the things we learned about how people use our hotels, so let me mention some of the findings. First, the people—they came to our properties mostly by car; 58 percent in their own, 23 percent in a rental car, and 17 percent arrived by plane.

Most are men, but a growing percentage of our guests are women—some 24 percent. The vast majority, 81 percent—have reservations. Seventy-three percent of our guests are traveling alone or with their spouses which makes you wonder why the hotel industry usually puts two double beds in the room.

Sixty-seven percent have only one or two pieces of luggage aside from their briefcase and 80 percent don't want the bellhop to give them help. Thirty-six percent put their luggage on top of the dresser; 23 percent on the bed (the one they have no other use for) and 8 percent put it somewhere else. Ninety-four percent hang something in the closet.

Once they get their luggage all settled:

46 percent use a vending machine
30 percent use the pool area
50 percent make a local phone call
61 percent make a long distance phone call
and 67 percent use our ice machines and ice buckets.

You might be interested to know that use of the ice buckets is highest among people traveling with children—74 percent—which is clear statistical evidence that kids really can drive you to drink!

The average guest spends two hours in the room when he or she is not asleep. Ninety-two percent of all travelers watch TV an average of one hour each night. Business travelers work in their rooms about 50 minutes each night. You'd think some hotel company would give them a comfortable place to work, wouldn't you?

Twenty percent of our guests take baths—mostly in the evening. You may find it interesting that only 5 percent of salesmen take baths. After a good night's sleep, 40 percent of our guests are greeted by a wake-up call. But it is worth noting that another 37 percent of our guests bring their own alarm clock.

Once out of bed, 95 percent take a shower, in case you ever wondered at 7:15 what happened to the hot water.

I could go on and on with these tidbits. To what point have I told you this? Specifically, I want to illustrate how Holiday Inns has set about achieving product supremacy in its segment with this well-researched lodging knowledge. We are now designing, constructing, and furnishing our properties in accordance with the way people use them today, and that is, in many ways, vastly different from the way they used them just ten years ago.

This is a very significant difference. It was, in retrospect, product superiority that spurred Holiday Inn growth during the decade of the 60s. And it is, we believe, the re-establishment of this superiority which will spur very impressive growth in the new decade we have entered. Undoubtedly, research will continue to play a very important role in making this happen.

Key Concepts

advertising agencies
airlines and other carriers
analytical findings
attractions
basic research methods
collection and analysis of data
consultants
consumer attitude studies
consumer-products research
data
decision making
definitions
economic impact study
economic projections
educational institutions
experimental method
facts
feasibility studies
follow-up
food service firms
government
hotel and motel firms
identification of the problem

information
intuition
investigations
measurement
media
methodology
observational method
primary data
recommendations for action
report
research design
risk
secondary data
situation analysis
sources of information
surveys
systematic
trade associations
travel research process
Travel and Tourism Research Association
uses of travel research
U.S. Travel Data Center

For Review and Discussion

1. What does a situation analysis cover?
2. What problems can travel research solve?
3. When should you use primary data? Secondary data?
4. What are the basic research methods?
5. Why are research findings so important to intelligent decision making?
6. If you were director of a major city's convention and visitors bureau, how would you use travel research?

7. As a consultant, you are researching the feasibility of a new resort hotel project. What procedures would you use, step by step?

8. How would a resort developer use a consultant's report when the report is completed? Once the resort is built, does the manager need further research?

9. What methods could be used by a state tourist office to survey out-of-state visitors?

10. Should a state tourist office conduct its own research or hire an outside supplier? Why?

11. Why would your office consider being a supporter of the U.S. Travel Data Center?

12. Would you join TTRA? Explain your answer.

Selected References

Barnett, Lynn A. *Research About Leisure: Past, Present, and Future.* Champaign, Ill.: Sagamore Publishing, 1988.

Baron, Raymond. *Travel and Tourism Data.* London: Euromonitor, 1989.

Barsky, Jonathan D. "Customer Satisfaction in the Hotel Industry: Meaning and Measurement." *Hospitality Research Journal,* Vol. 16, No. 1 (1992), pp. 51–74.

Camacho, Frank E, and D. Matthew Knain. "Listening to Customers: The Market Research Function at Marriott Corporation." *Market Research: A Magazine of Management and Applications,* Vol. 1, No. 1 (March 1989), pp. 5–14.

Dann, Graham, Dennison Nash, and Philip Pearce. "Methodology in Tourism Research." *Annals of Tourism Research,* Vol. 15, No. 1 (1988), pp. 1–28.

Gitelson, Richard, and Deborah Kerstetter. "The Focus Group Interview: An Untapped Resource." *Visions in Leisure and Business,* Vol. 6, No. 3 (1987), pp. 60–67.

Green, Howard, Colin Hunter, and Bruno Moore. "Application of the Delphi Technique in Tourism." *Annals of Tourism Research,* Vol. 17, No. 2 (1990), pp. 270–279.

Hartmann, Rudi. "Combining Field Methods in Tourism Research." *Annals of Tourism Research,* Vol. 15, No. 1 (1988), pp. 88–105.

Pacific Asia Travel Association. *PATA Annual Statistical Report: 1992.* San Francisco: PATA, 1993.

Pearce, Douglas G., and Richard Butler. *Tourism Research: Critiques and Challenges.* New York: Routledge, 1993.

Reuland, Ruud, Janet Choudry, and Ans Fagel. "Research in the Field of Hospitality." *International Journal of Hospitality Management,* Vol. 4 (1985), pp. 141–146.

Ritchie, J. R. Brent, and Charles R. Goeldner, eds. *Travel, Tourism and Hospitality Research: A Handbook for Managers and Researchers.* New York: Wiley, 1994.

Rogers, Judy. "A Non-technical Perspective on Data Collection Methodologies for Travel Surveys: A Discussion Paper." *Journal of Travel Research,* Vol. 29, No. 3 (Winter 1991), pp. 43–46.

Sheldon, Pauline J., Juanita C. Liu, and Chuck Y. Gee. "The Status of Research in the Lodging Industry." *International Journal of Hospitality Management,* Vol. 6, No. 1 (1987), pp. 89–96.

Smith, Stephen L. J. *Tourism Analysis.* Harlow, Essex, England: Longman, 1989.

Theuns, H. Leo. *Third World Tourism Research: 1950–1984.* Frankfurt: Peter Lang, 1991.

Toy, Daniel, Robin Rager, and Frank Guadagnolo. "Strategic Marketing for Recreational Facilities: A Hybrid Conjoint Analysis Approach." *Journal of Leisure Research,* Vol. 21, No. 4 (1989), pp. 276–296.

World Tourism Organization. *World Directory of Documentation Resource and Systems for the Travel and Tourism Sector.* Madrid: WTO, 1992.

CHAPTER 18

Tourism Marketing

LEARNING OBJECTIVES

- Recognize the extreme importance of a well-planned, vigorous marketing program to the success of any tourist business and how this must be based on research.

- Become familiar with the marketing mix and be able to formulate the best mix for a particular travel product.

- Appreciate the importance of the relationship between the marketing concept and product planning and development.

- Understand the vital relationship between pricing and marketing.

- Know about distribution systems and how this marketing principle can best be applied to a variety of travel products.

- Be able to do market segmentation to plan a marketing program for the business you are the most interested in.

NATURE AND SCOPE

Tourism marketing is:

- The State of New York creating a tourism promotion fund, developing a marketing plan, and creating an advertising campaign around the theme "I Love New York."
- Marriott International's segmenting its lodging product into four brands: Marriott Hotels, Resorts and Suites, the company's full-service lodging division; Courtyard, the moderate-priced lodging product; Residence Inns, the extended-stay product; and Fairfield Inn, the economy lodging offering.
- United Airlines offering different classes of service, supersaver fares, Mileage Plus, advertising the "friendly skies," developing a logo, adding new routes and schedules, using their own reservation system and travel agents, and working with tour groups.

Marketing includes all of the above and much more. Marketing has been defined in a variety of ways. The American Marketing Association defines marketing as "the performance of business activities that direct the flow of goods and services from the producer to the consumer or user." Others have stated that marketing is the delivery of the standard of living to society. You are no doubt acquainted with the old adage, "nothing happens until somebody sells something."

Most people have little idea what marketing is all about and would probably say that it has something to do with selling or advertising. However, marketing is a very broad concept, of which advertising and selling are only two facets. Marketing is goal-oriented, strategic, and directed. It both precedes and follows selling and advertising activities. Marketing is the total picture in getting goods and services from the producer to the user.

Unfortunately, "marketing" often conjures up unfavorable images of used car salespeople, TV furniture advertisers, high-pressure selling, and gimmicks, leading to the perception of marketing in terms of stereotypes. In fact, marketing plays a critical role in all organizations whether they are nonprofit educational institutions, tourist resorts, or manufacturers. The role of marketing is to match the right product or service with the right market or audience.

Marketing is an inevitable aspect of tourism management. Marketing can be done effectively and well, with sophistication, or it can be done poorly in a loud, crass, intrusive manner. It is the goal of this chapter to discuss the basic elements of marketing so that it can be done effectively, with style, and with a favorable economic impact.

MARKETING CONCEPT

The heart of good marketing management today is the marketing concept, or a consumer orientation. Tourism organizations which practice the marketing concept find out what the consumer wants and then produce a product that will satisfy those wants at a profit. The marketing concept requires that management thinking be directed toward profits rather than sales volume.

Assume that you are going to develop a new major resort area. This is a difficult exercise in planning that requires that the designs that are developed be based on how consumers view the product. One of the first steps is to employ the marketing concept and do research to understand the consumer's (the market's) needs, desires, and wants. Designers of products and consumers of products often perceive them differently. Architects, for example, may see a hotel in terms of such things as space utilization, engineering problems, and design lines or as a monument; consumers may see the hotel as a bundle of benefits—as being attractive, as offering full service and outstanding food, as having recreational facilities, and so on. Once consumer views are determined, the task is to formulate strategic marketing plans that match the resort and its market. In today's competitive environment where consumers have choices, firms need to employ the marketing concept.

THE MARKETING MIX

The marketing program combines a number of elements into a workable whole—a viable, strategic plan. The tourism marketing manager must constantly search for the right marketing mix—the right combination of elements that will produce a profit. The marketing mix is composed of every factor that influences the marketing effort:

1. *Timing*. Holidays, high season, low season, upward trend in the business cycle, and so on must all be considered.
2. *Brands*. The consumer needs help in remembering your product. Names, trademarks, labels, logos, and other identification marks all assist the consumer in identifying and recalling information about your product.
3. *Packaging*. Although tourism services do not require a physical package,

Good marketing requires expert handling of guests from the beginning to the end of their experience. Cypress Gardens has gracious Southern belles who greet visitors and welcome them to the Central Florida theme park. (Photo by David Woods, courtesy of Cypress Gardens)

packaging is still an important factor. For example, transportation, lodging, amenities, and recreation activities can be packaged and sold together or separately. Family plans or single plans are other forms of packaging.

4. *Pricing.* Pricing affects not only sales volume but also the image of the product. A multitude of pricing options exist, ranging from discount prices to premium prices.
5. *Channels of distribution.* The product must be accessible to the consumer. Direct selling, retail travel agents, wholesale tour operators, or a combination of these methods all comprise distribution channels that must be developed.
6. *Product.* The physical attributes of the product help to determine its position against the competition and provide guidelines on how to best compete.
7. *Image.* The consumer's perception of the product depends to a great extent on the important factors of reputation and quality.
8. *Advertising.* Paid promotion is critical, and the questions of when, where, and how to promote must be carefully considered.
9. *Selling.* Internal and external selling are essential components for success, and various sales techniques must be incorporated in the marketing plan.

A good marketing plan attracts visitors, filling hotels, restaurants, and other enterprises with tourists. (Photo courtesy of Division of Travel and Tourism, State of New Jersey)

10. *Public relations.* Even the most carefully drawn marketing plan will fail without good relations with the visitors, the community, suppliers, and employees.

The preceding list makes it obvious that the marketing manager's job is a complex one. Using knowledge of the consumer market and the competition, the marketing manager must come up with the proper marketing mix for the resort, attraction, or other organization. The marketing manager's job begins with planning to allow direction and control of the foregoing factors.

The many elements in the marketing mix have been defined most frequently as "the four Ps," a term popularized by E. Jerome McCarthy, author of *Basic Marketing* and *Essentials of Marketing.*[1] While the four Ps are an oversimplification, they do provide a neat, simple framework in which to look at marketing and put together a marketing program. The four Ps are product, place, promotion, and price. The product includes not only actual physical attributes of the product but also product planning, product development, breadth of the line, branding, and packaging. Planning the product should consider all these aspects in order to come up with the "right" product.

Place is really concerned with distribution. What agencies, channels, and institutions can be linked together most effectively to give the consumer easy access to the purchase of your product? Where is the "right" place to market your product?

Promotion communicates the benefits of the product to the potential customers and includes not only advertising but sales promotion, public relations, and personal selling. The "right" promotional mix will use each of these promotional techniques as needed for effective communication.

Price is a critical variable in the marketing mix. The "right" price must both satisfy customers and meet your profit objectives.

[1]E. Jerome McCarthy and William D. Perreault, *Essentials of Marketing* (Homewood, Ill.: Richard D. Irwin, 1994).

Product Planning and Development

The objective of most firms is to develop a profitable and continuing business. To achieve this objective, companies must provide products and services that satisfy consumer needs, thereby assuring themselves of repeat business. Product planning is an essential component in developing a profitable, continuing business and has frequently been referred to as the "five rights"—planning to have the right product, at the right place, at the right time, at the right price, in the right quantities.

A product is much more than a combination of raw materials. It is actually a bundle of satisfactions and benefits for the consumer. Product planning must therefore be approached from the consumer's point of view. Creating the right service or product is not easy; consumer needs, wants, and desires are constantly changing, and competitive forces typically carry products through a life cycle, so that a product that is successful at one point declines and "dies" at a later time.

Figure 18.1 shows the phases that a new product goes through from inception to decline: (1) introduction, (2) growth, (3) maturity, (4) saturation, and (5) decline. Because of the rapidly changing consumer lifestyles and technological changes, the life cycle for products and services has become shorter, but the product life cycle remains a useful concept for strategic planning. Each stage of the product life cycle has certain marketing requirements.

INTRODUCTION   The introductory phase of the product's life cycle requires high promotional expenditures and visibility. (The most productive time to advertise a

Logos identify products and companies, assisting the consumer in identifying and purchasing products and services.

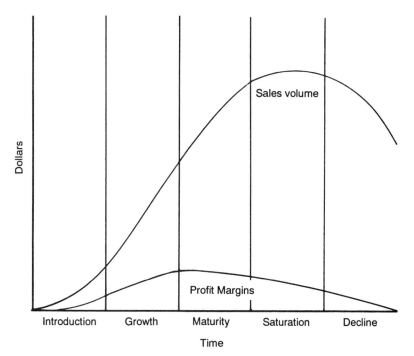

Figure 18.1 Product Life Cycle

High quality and good service are important elements of the product mix.
(Photo courtesy of Cunard Lines)

product or service is when it is new.) Operations in this period are characterized by high cost, relatively low sales volume, and an advertising program aimed at stimulating primary demand; in this stage of the life cycle, there will be a high percentage of failures.

GROWTH   In the growth period, the product or service is being accepted by consumers. Market acceptance means that both sales and profits rise at a rapid rate, frequently making the market attractive to competitors. Promotional expenditures remain high, but the promotional emphasis is on selective buying motives by trade name rather than on primary motives to try the product. During the growth stage, the number of outlets handling the product or service usually increases. More competitors enter the marketplace, but economies of scale are realized and prices may decline some.

MATURITY   The mature product is well established in the marketplace. Sales may still be increasing but at a much slower rate; they are leveling off. At this stage of the product's life cycle, many outlets are selling the product or service, and they are very competitive, especially with respect to price, and firms are trying to determine ways to hold on to their share of the market. The ski resort is an excellent example of a mature product. After years of spectacular growth, sales are now leveling off, and the resorts are looking for ways to hold market share and diversify.

SATURATION   In the saturation stage, sales volume reaches its peak; the product or service has penetrated the marketplace to the greatest degree possible. Mass production and new technology have lowered the price to make it available to almost everyone.

DECLINE   Many products stay at the saturation stage for years. However, for most products, obsolescence sets in, and new products are introduced to replace old ones. In the decline stage, demand obviously drops, advertising expenditures are lower, and there is usually a smaller number of competitors. While it is possible for a product to do very well in this stage of the product life cycle, there is not a great deal of comfort in getting a larger share of a declining market. Hot springs resorts are a good example of a tourist product in the decline stage. These facilities, at their peak in the 1920s, are no longer the consumer's idea of an "in" place to go.

Pricing

One of the most important marketing decisions is the pricing decision. Price determines how consumers perceive the product and strongly affects other elements of the marketing mix.

Firms have a choice of three strategies in pricing their products. First, they may decide to sell their product at the market price, which is the same price that everyone else charges. They then compete on nonprice terms. Selling at a price equal to competitors' tends to prevent price cutting and protect margins, and customers are not driven away by price. However, because there is no price individuality, there can be no price demand stimulation.

Second, firms may decide to price below the current market price. Firms that adopt such a discount policy are trying to create the reputation of having the lowest prices and underselling all competitors. To be successful, such firms must make sure that demand is elastic; otherwise, they will gain only at the expense of their competitors and start a price war. This pricing strategy is more successful when it is based on the elimination of services. Motel 6, Inc., for example, took its name from its original $6-a-night charge and built its network on a no-frills philosophy. Today it is one of the top budget chains in the United States.

The third approach is to charge above-market prices. Premium pricing strategy must be coupled with the best service in the industry and other features and amenities to make this higher price attractive. Such an approach emphasizes quality, which many consumers think is a function of price; provides higher margins; generates more revenue for promotion; and makes better service possible. However, premium pricing reduces volume, raises overhead costs, and encourages substitution. Nevertheless, numerous tourism firms successfully use this approach, including the Ritz-Carlton (winner of the U.S. Malcolm Baldrige National Quality Award in 1992), Fairmont, Hyatt, Marriott, and Westin hotels.

Some firms choose to employ two or three pricing strategies and develop a product to appeal to consumers in each market segment. The lodging industry has moved to employing this strategy in the last decade. Ramada, Choice, Marriott, Holiday Inn Worldwide, and others have developed products to appeal to a broad range of market segments.

The tourism marketing manager must consider the following factors that influence price policies:

1. *Product quality.* The quality of the product really determines the price-value relationship. It is common sense that a product that offers greater utility and fills more consumer needs than a competitive product can command a higher price.
2. *Product distinctiveness.* A staple or standard product with no distinctive features offers little or no opportunity for price control. However, a novel and different product may be able to command higher prices. The Hyatt Corporation, for example, features lobby atriums; this attractive novelty combined with excellent service and facilities makes it possible for the Hyatt Hotels to command higher prices.
3. *Extent of the competition.* A product that is comparable to competitors' products must be priced with the competitors' prices in mind. The product's price to some extent determines its position in the market.
4. *Method of distribution.* The price of the product must include adequate margins for tour operators, travel agents, or the company's own sales force.
5. *Character of the market.* It is necessary to consider the type and number of possible consumers. If there is a small number of consumers, then the price must be high enough to compensate for a limited market. However, one must also consider the ability of consumers to buy and their buying habits.
6. *Cost of the product and service.* It should be obvious that price must exceed cost over the long run or else the business will not survive. Both cost and market conditions should serve as guides to pricing.
7. *Cost of distribution.* Distribution costs must also be included in the pricing equation. Unfortunately, in many cases they are much more difficult to estimate than other costs.
8. *Margin of profit desired.* The profit margin built into the price of the product must be more than returns realized on more conventional investments in order to compensate for the risk involved in the enterprise.

9. *Seasonality.* Most tourism products are affected by seasonality because of school year patterns and vacation habits; consequently, the seasonal aspects must be considered in developing prices.

10. *Special promotional prices.* Many times it is good strategy to offer introductory prices and special one-time price offers to acquaint consumers with your product. However, these must be carefully planned so that they fill the proper intent and do not become a regular discount price.

11. *Psychological considerations.* Throughout our economy we see psychological pricing employed, usually using prices that are set in odd amounts such as 19¢, 99¢, $19.95, or $29.99. Consumers respond well to odd pricing, and there seems to be something particularly magical about prices that end in nine.

PRICE SKIMMING   In the pricing of a new product or service, the two pricing philosophies that prevail are called price skimming and penetration pricing. A price-skimming strategy sets the price as high as possible. No attempt is made to appeal to the entire market, but only to the top of the market; consequently, this approach is frequently called skimming the cream. The strategy is to sell the product to as many consumers as possible at this price level; then, as either buyer resistance or direct competition develops, the seller will lower prices step by step. This approach typically results in higher profits and more rapid repayment of development and promotion costs. It also tends to invite competition. Skimming is appropriate when the product or service has the following characteristics: (1) price inelasticity, (2) no close substitutes, (3) high promotion elasticity, and (4) distinct market segments based on price.

PENETRATION PRICING   The opposite approach to price skimming is market penetration, in which the seller attempts to establish the price of the product as low as possible to penetrate the market as completely as possible. A low price makes the product available to as many income levels as possible, and the sellers are likely to establish a large market share quickly. When penetration pricing is used, this introductory price tends to become the permanent price of the product. It results in a slower recovery of fixed costs and requires a greater volume to break even. The factors that would recommend a penetration pricing approach would be (1) high price elasticity, (2) large savings from high-volume production (economies of scale), and (3) an easy fit of the product into consumer purchasing patterns.

Place (Distribution)

Another difficult decision for the marketing manager concerns what distribution channel or channels will be used. The distribution decisions affect the other elements of the marketing mix, and in the best marketing mix all aspects will be compatible with each other. Chapter 7 contains a description of the travel distribution system.

Channels of distribution are selected by (1) analyzing the product, (2) determining the nature and extent of the market, (3) analyzing the channels by sales, costs, and profits, (4) determining the cooperation you can expect from the channel, (5) determining the assistance you will have to give to the channel, and (6) determining the number of outlets to be used. For example, if you want intensive distribution, exposing your product to maximum sale, you will use many travel agents. In contrast, with an exclusive distribution policy, you would sell your product through one or a few agents, who would have the sole right to sell your product or service in a given area.

Promotion

The aim of promotion activities is to create demand for a product or service. Promotion is a broad term that includes advertising, personal selling, public relations, publicity, and sales promotion activities such as give-aways, trade shows, point of purchase, and store displays.

To sell the product it is necessary to (1) attract attention, (2) create interest, (3) create a desire, and (4) get action. Either personal selling or advertising can carry out all of these steps in the selling process; however, the two used together tend to be much more powerful. Advertising is ideally suited to attract attention and create interest in the products and services. Personal selling is best suited to creating desire and conviction on the part of the customer and to closing the sale. Advertising and personal selling are even more effective when supplemented by publicity and sales promotion activities.

ADVERTISING   Advertising has been defined as any nonpersonal presentation of goods, ideas, or services by an identified sponsor. In travel marketing, these paid public messages are designed to describe or present a destination area in such a way as to attract consumers. This can be done through the use of the major advertising media such as newspapers, magazines, direct mail, television, outdoor, or radio. Effective advertising gains the attention of the prospective visitor, holds the attention so the message can be communicated, and makes a lasting positive impression on the prospect's mind.

Each advertising medium has advantages and disadvantages. A key decision in developing promotional strategy is to select the right medium to maximize advertising expenditure. To assist in media selection, turn to Standard Rate and Data Service, 5201 Old Orchard Road, Skokie, Ill. 60077. SRDS publications contain advertising rates and other media information required to make intelligent decisions. The advantages and disadvantages of the major media are as follows.

Newspapers   Newspapers give comprehensive coverage of a local market area, are lower in cost than other media, are published frequently, are flexible (short lead time) and timely, have a wide audience, and get a quick response. Most newspapers have travel sections. The major disadvantages are low printing quality and short life.

Direct Mail   Although mail costs have increased rapidly, direct mail is one of the most important advertising methods for tourism enterprises. It is the most personal and selective of all the media; consequently, it is the most effective medium in minimizing waste circulation. Direct mail gets the message directly to the consumers one wishes to contact. Direct mail advertising is self-testing when it asks for a response. The critical problem with direct mail is obtaining and maintaining the right mailing lists. Many types of lists are commercially available through firms specializing in this activity. (One source of such information is Standard Rate and Data Service.)

For the tourism industry, previous visitors comprise the most important mailing list sources. However, names and addresses must be correct, and the lists must be kept in ready-to-use form, such as address plates or on a computer. Other good sources of prospects are the inquiry lists.

Television   Television presents both an audio and visual message and comes as close to approximating personal selling as a mass medium can. Television requires minimal exertion on the part of listeners and is very versatile. However, television is not a flexible medium, commercials have a short life, and advertising on television is expensive relative to the costs of using other media. Nevertheless, despite television's expense, many destinations are using television and finding it is very cost effective.

Magazines   The major advantage of magazines is their print and graphic quality. Other advantages are secondary readership, long life, prestige, and favorable cost per 1000 circulation. Many special interest magazines reach specialized market segments effectively, making it possible to target markets. Regional editions allow further selectivity, with a minimum of waste circulation. Some of the unfavorable characteristics of magazines are that they require long lead times and that changes cannot be made readily. Magazines also reach the market less frequently than do newspapers, radio, and television.

Radio   Radio has the advantage of outstanding flexibility and relatively low cost. While the warmth of the human voice adds a personal touch to the selling message, radio has the disadvantage that it presents only an audio message. Tourists driving in their automobiles are typically radio listeners, and many attractions find radio an excellent medium.

Outdoor Advertising   Outdoor advertising has been used with great success by many tourism organizations. It is a flexible, low-cost medium that reaches virtually the whole population. It has made the Wall Drugstore in Wall, South Dakota, world famous. Outdoor advertising has the disadvantage that the message must be short; however, it does reach travelers. An additional problem is highway signing laws, which are making it more difficult to advertise tourism attractions.

Using an Advertising Agency   While promotion managers must know the fundamentals of marketing, advertising, personal selling, and public relations, the specialized skill and experience of an advertising agency can greatly increase business—and can do it profitably. An advertising agency will:

1. Work with ideas in copy and layout. "Copy" is the term used to describe written messages; "layout" refers to the arrangement of copy, art, and pictures.
2. Advise on the choice of media to convey advertising messages, devising an organized and carefully worked-out plan using newspapers, magazines, radio, TV, guide books, posters, direct mail, postcards, folders, or other advertising media.
3. Conduct market analysis and research so that advertising efforts can be directed to the best prospects.
4. Assist in planning and carrying out a public relations program.

The advertising program must be planned objectively by setting forth specific, achievable goals. The advertising agency can help to establish such goals. When seeking the services of an advertising agency, look at the agency's experience in promoting tourism, and check the agency's past advertising campaigns and clients to determine the campaign's effectiveness.

The Advertising Budget   No magic formula exists for setting the advertising budget. How much to spend is always a perplexing question. Commonly used methods include a percentage of last year's sales, a percentage of potential sales, or the industry percentage. These methods are all flawed because advertising should create sales and cause things to happen, not react to what has happened in the past or in other companies. Consequently, the best method of setting advertising budgets is to determine the objectives to be performed and allocate the proper amount to reach these objectives.

Promoting a new tourist destination area will require more money than will promoting one with an established clientele. The specific amount to budget for advertising and sales promotion will depend on each situation. However, as a rule of thumb most resorts spend about 3 percent of sales on media advertising and about 3 percent on other sales promotion activities.

No matter what expenditures are, efforts should be made to coordinate the promotion program so it is consistent with the product offered and consumer expectations will be met. Word of mouth is the least expensive, most convincing form of personal advertising. A friendly and capable host encourages this type of communication. Visitors who are treated as very important persons will not only come back, they will recommend the area to their friends. All facilities, services, hospitality, and pricing policies must be directed to this one goal—a happy, satisfied visitor.

RESEARCH   Successful tourism marketing depends in large part on research. Tourism promotion efforts undirected by research are largely wasted effort. Unless the following characteristics are known, advertising expenditures cannot be productive:

1. Who are the present visitors, and where do they live?
2. What do you know about their likes and dislikes?
3. Who are your potential customers, and where do they live?
4. What are their travel and vacation preferences and interests?
5. What are your visitors' travel destination preferences?
6. What are your visitors' preferences for shopping and entertainment?
7. What is your competitive situation?
8. What are the trends in competition?
9. What are the likely future trends in your share of the market?
10. What are the prospects for increasing demand for your area?
11. What kind(s) of marketing program(s) appears to be needed?
12. How will these programs be implemented?

Carefully review questions of this kind; adequate answers to them are obtained only through research.

In determining the market, research can be classified into three main categories: geographic market orientation (where present and potential visitors reside), demographic market orientation (age, sex, levels of education, income, population distribution, family status, and similar data), and psychographic market orientation (motivations, interest, hobbies, responsiveness to advertising, and propensity to travel). Guidance of the subsequent marketing program will rest largely on the results of such research and the success of the marketing upon the adequacy of the research. See Chapter 17 for methods of conducting tourism research.

PERSONAL SELLING   Personal selling is the most used and oldest method of creating demand. Because it is adaptable to the prospect, it is the most compelling and effective type of selling. In contrast to advertising, which is the impersonal component in the promotional mix, personal selling consists of individual, personal communication. The U.S. economy depends on salespeople; there are over 13 million compared to about 500,000 working in advertising. In many companies, personal selling is the largest operating expense item, ranging from about 8 to 15 percent of sales. Expenditures for salespersons' compensation, expenses, training, and supervision and the cost of operating sales offices make management of the sales force an important task.

Personal selling is so widely used because it offers maximum flexibility. Sales representatives tailor their presentation to each individual customer. They can tell which approaches are working and which are not and adjust accordingly. Prospects can be identified so target market customers are approached and efforts are not wasted.

Counterbalancing these advantages is the fact that personal selling is the most expensive means of making contact with prospects, and productivity gains are unlikely. Another limitation is that it is not always possible to hire the caliber of person needed for the sales job.

Because of the importance of personal selling, all staff should be sales-minded. All salespeople must be trained to offer sales suggestions to prospects when opportunities present themselves. This includes expert selling on the telephone as well as the telephone receptionist, who can create a favorable image for a resort. Inquiries can often be the opening for a polite and skillful sales effort. Obviously, an unfriendly manner can discourage customers and sales.

PUBLIC RELATIONS   Public relations may be defined as an attitude—a "social conscience" that places first priority on the public interest when making any decisions. Public relations permeates an entire organization, covering relations with many publics: visitors, the community, employees, and suppliers.

Acceptance of any tourist destination by the public is of utmost importance. No business is more concerned with human relations than is tourism, and all public interests

Cheerful, friendly employees are an important part of the selling process. (Photo courtesy of Delta Airlines)

Pictures and press releases are an integral part of public relations. This photo distributed by the South Dakota Department of Tourism features Mount Rushmore, site of the world's most famous mountain carving.

must be served. Serving one group at the expense of another is not sound public relations. Furthermore, each individual business manager and the group he or she represents must be respected and have the confidence of the community. There is no difference between a personal reputation and a business reputation.

Favorable public relations within the firm emphasize respect for people. Employees must have reasonable security in their jobs and be treated with consideration. Externally, tourism employees have a powerful influence on the public as they represent the owners in the public's eye. Employees should be trained to be courteous, respectful, and helpful to guests. Little things make a big difference, and the attitude of employees can make or break a public relations effort.

Considerations for the public relations effort include being aware of public attitudes toward present policies—ask some of the visitors for feedback. Communication is the lifeblood of good relations. In publicizing the firm, first do good things and then tell the public about them. Above all, give the public factual information about your area. False information is detrimental; you must describe conditions as they exist.

MARKET SEGMENTATION

The strategy of market segmentation recognizes that few vacation destination areas are universally acceptable and desired. Therefore, rather than dissipate promotion resources by trying to please all travelers, you should aim the promotional efforts specifically to the wants and needs of likely prospects. One of the early steps in

The handicapped comprise a market segment that has special needs and numbers 47 million. A number of travel agencies have identified this segment as a target market they wish to serve and specialize in meeting its needs. (Photo by Fred Marvel, courtesy of Oklahoma Tourism Department)

marketing tourism, then, is to divide the present and potential market on the basis of meaningful characteristics and concentrate promotion, product, and pricing efforts on serving the most prominent portions of the market—the target markets.

An effective market strategy will determine exactly what the target markets will be and attempt to reach only those markets. The target market is that segment of a total potential market to which the tourism attraction would be most salable. Target markets are defined geographically, demographically (age, income, education, race, nationality, family size, family life cycle, gender, religion, occupation), or psychographically (values, motivations, interests, attitudes, desires) (see Figure 18.2).

Once target markets have been determined, appropriate media are chosen to reach these markets. For example, if tennis players are a target market, advertising in tennis magazines would give comprehensive coverage of this market. This would be using a "rifle approach" to zero in exactly on the market in which you are interested. In contrast, a "shotgun approach" would be to advertise in *Time* magazine, which would reach only a small number of your target market and result in large waste circulation.

Market segmentation must be employed in the marketing programs if a shotgun approach is to be avoided. Every tourism attraction can appeal to a multitude of market segments, and market segments can overlap a great deal. The marketing manager must look at market segments and determine which ones offer the most promising potential for his or her services. An excellent example of target marketing to a particular segment is provided by the LaQuinta Motor Inns, headquartered in San Antonio and now the world's twenty-first largest hotel chain and still expanding. The product was designed to appeal to the business traveler with a moderate price and an attractive room. La Quinta has been very successful in attracting this market segment.

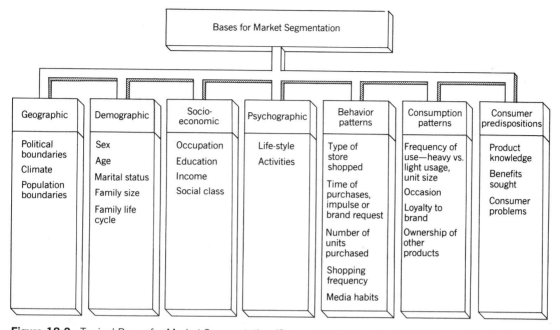

Figure 18.2 Typical Bases for Market Segmentation (Source: W. Zikmund and M. D'Amico, *Marketing*, 3rd ed., copyright © 1984, John Wiley & Sons, Inc., New York; adapted by permission of Prentice-Hall, Inc., Englewood Cliffs, N.J., from Philip Kotler, *Principles of Marketing*, copyright © 1980, p. 297)

Tourist resorts typically segment in a variety of ways. One of the most common is geographic. Here the segments tend to be destination visitors (those visitors traveling long distances to vacation at the resort), regional visitors (those who live within the region of the resort and can arrive within four hours' driving time), and local residents.

Proximity of the destination area to the market is an important factor. Generally, the nearer the tourist destination is to its major market, the more likely it is to attract large numbers of visitors. For example, Boblo Island is just a few miles from Detroit and may be reached by excursion boat. As might be expected, this vacation destination receives many times the number of visitors from the greater Detroit area than does Bermuda or the Bahamas.

It follows then that the prime target area for promotion of any given tourist destination area will be that area of greatest population density nearest the vacation area. In the United States, the best concentration of markets for tourism promotion are the metropolitan statistical areas (MSAs), formerly called standard metropolitan statistical areas (SMSAs). These are defined by the U.S. Bureau of Census as a county or group of contiguous counties containing at least one city of 50,000 inhabitants or more. An authoritative source of market data concerning these areas is found in *Survey of Buying Power* published by Sales and Marketing Management, 355 Park Avenue South, New York, N.Y. 10010.

Demographics also provide good segmentation variables. Demographics are the social statistics of our society. Age groups are an excellent example.

Psychographic Market Segmentation

Several models have been developed to classify people according to psychographic types. One such model was developed by Stanley C. Plog, who classified the U.S. population along a psychographic continuum—ranging from the psychocentric at one extreme to the allocentric at the other.[2]

The term *psychocentric* is derived from *psyche* or *self*-centered, meaning the centering of one's thought or concerns on the small problem areas of one's life. Such a person tends to be self-inhibited and nonadventuresome. Allocentric, on the other hand, derives from the root word *allo*, meaning "varied in form." An allocentric person is thus one whose interest patterns are focused on varied activities. Such a person is outgoing and self-confident and is characterized by a considerable degree of adventure and a willingness to reach out and experiment with life. Travel becomes a way for the allocentric to express inquisitiveness and satisfy curiosity. Table 18.1 shows personality and travel characteristics of allocentrics and psychocentrics.

Plog found that the U.S. population was normally distributed along a continuum between these two extreme types. This is illustrated in Figure 18.3. Other groups have been identified between the allocentrics and psychocentrics. Most people fall in the midcentric classification.

A new dimension was added with the establishment of an energy vs. lethargy scale. It was determined that this dimension was not correlated, making it possible to place individuals into four quadrants based on how they scored on the two scales. The four quadrants were high-energy allocentrics, low-energy allocentrics, high-energy psychocentrics, and low-energy psychocentrics. High-energy allocentrics have an insatiable desire to be active on trips, exploring and learning what is new and exciting of a destination. Low-energy allocentrics would travel at a more leisurely pace, be more intellectual, and delve into culture, history, and local customs. At the other end of the continuum, the low-energy psychocentrics were most likely to stay at home.

Through further research, Plog identified the travel preferences of psychocentrics and allocentrics. These are summarized in Figure 18.4. In studying the population on the basis of income level, Plog discovered another interesting relationship. At the lower end of the income spectrum, he discovered a heavy loading of psychocentrics. People at the upper end of the income levels were found to be predominantly allocentric. However, for the broad spectrum in between—for most of America—interrelations are only slightly positive. This finding has several implications.

It is evident that at extremely low levels of family income, travel patterns may be determined largely by the income constraints. Regardless of the psychographic type, a person at the low end of the income spectrum may be compelled to take what Plog considers to be psychocentric-type vacations. College students are a good example of this. They may be allocentric by nature but cannot afford an allocentric-type vacation since such vacations are generally very expensive (a trip to Antartica or a mountain climbing expedition in Nepal). They travel, instead, to nearby destinations, spend less money, and participate in familiar activities. Therefore, it may be erroneous to conclude

---

[2]Stanley C. Plog, "Why Destination Areas Rise and Fall in Popularity," *The Cornell Hotel and Restaurant Administration Quarterly*, Vol. 14, No. 4 (February 1974), pp. 55–58; and Stanley C. Plog, *Leisure Travel: Making It a Growth Market . . . Again!* (New York: Wiley, 1991).

Table 18.1   Personality and Travel-Related Characteristics of Allocentrics and Psychocentrics

Psychocentrics	Allocentrics
Intellectually restricted	Intellectually curious
Low risk taking	Moderate risk taking
Withhold income	Use disposable income
Use well-known brands	Try new products
Territory bound	Exploring/searching
Sense of powerlessness	Feel in control
Free-floating anxiety/nervousness	Relatively anxiety free
Nonactive lifestyle	Interested/involved
Nonadventurous	Adventurous
Lacking in confidence	Self-confident
Prefer the familiar in travel destinations	Prefer non-touristy areas
Like commonplace activities at travel destinations	Enjoy sense of discovery and delight in new experiences, before others have visited the area
Prefer sun'n'fun spots, including considerable relaxation	Prefer novel and different destinations
Low activity level	High activity level
Prefer destinations they can drive to	Prefer flying to destinations
Prefer heavy tourist development (lots of hotels, family-type restaurants, tourist shops, etc.)	Tour accommodations should include adequate-to-good hotels and food, not necessarily modern or chain-type hotels, and few "tourist-type" attractions
Prefer familiar atmosphere (hamburger stands, familiar-type entertainment, absence of foreign atmosphere)	Enjoy meeting and dealing with people from a strange or foreign culture
Complete tour packaging appropriate, with heavy scheduling of activities	Tour arrangements should include basics (transportation and hotels) and allow considerable freedom and flexibility
Travel less	Travel more frequently
Spend more of income on material goods and impulse buys	Spend more of income on travel
Little interest in events or activities in other countries	Inquisitive, curious about the world and its peoples
Naive, nondemanding, passive traveler	Demanding, sophisticated, active traveler
Wants structured, routinized travel	Wants much spontaneity in trips
Expects foreigners to speak in English	Will learn languages or foreign phrases before and during travels
Wants standard accommodations and conventional (American) meals	Seeks off-the-beaten-path, little known local hotels, restaurants
Buys souvenirs, trinkets, common items	Buys native arts/crafts
Prefers returning to same and familiar places	Wants different destination for each trip
Enjoys crowds	Prefers small numbers of people

Source: Stanley C. Plog, *Leisure Travel: Making it a Growth Market . . . Again!* (New York: Wiley, 1991).

that a person with a low income is likely to be psychocentric. The severe income constraint may distort the person's classification in terms of psychographics.

Having defined types of destinations and types of tourists, one is tempted to link these two classifications directly, as Plog has done. Plog superimposed a list of destinations on the population distribution curve, suggesting that allocentrics would travel to such destinations as Africa or the Orient. Psychocentrics, on the other hand, would

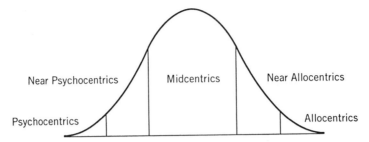

Figure 18.3 U.S. Population Distribution by Psychographic Type (*Source:* Stanley C. Plog, "Why Destination Areas Rise and Fall in Popularity," *Cornell Hotel and Restaurant Administration Quarterly*, Vol. 14, No. 4 (February 1974), pp. 55–58; and Stanley C. Plog, *Leisure Travel: Making It a Growth Market . . . Again!* John Wiley & Sons, New York, 1991)

vacation in nearby destinations (such as Cedar Point, Ohio, theme park for a psychocentric from Toledo). The intervening psychocentric types are similarly identified with particular destinations (refer to Figure 18.4).

Plog determined it is possible to define the psychological character of the destinations in terms of the types of people they appeal to based on the psychographic curve presented in Figure 18.3. Figure 18.4 indicates where some world spots appeared when the concept was first presented. Figure 18.5 shows the view for the early 1990s and verifies Plog's contention that over time there is a steady movement of most destinations toward more psychocentric characteristics. What starts out as a grand exotic place loses favor and image as more tourists discover it and come.

Such a direct linkage between the classification of tourists and of destinations does not consider the important fact that people travel with different motivations on different occasions. A wealthy allocentric may indeed travel to Africa on an annual vacation, but may also take weekend trips to a typically psychocentric destination during other times of the year. Similarly, though probably not as likely, psychocentrics could conceivably vacation in essentially allocentric destinations (with the exception of people with

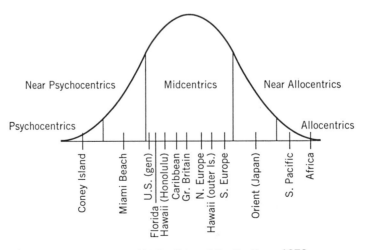

Figure 18.4 Psychographic Positions of Destinations, 1972

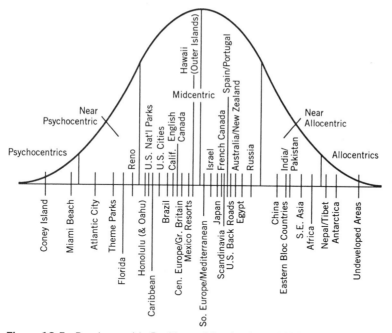

Figure 18.5 Psychographic Positions of Destinations, 1991. (*Source:* Plog Research, Inc.)

extremely low incomes). For instance, a psychocentric may travel to a remote area under the security provided by traveling with a group of similar tourists, which, being escorted at all times, may persuade a psychocentric to travel, say, to Asia. Is Asia, then, a psychocentric or an allocentric destination? Clearly, a direct relationship between psychographic types and destinations is tenuous at best.

What, then, is the link between the types of tourists and the types of destinations? To develop such a linkage, which will provide a method for predicting travel patterns, two things must be realized. First, as already pointed out, a tourist may travel for different reasons from one trip to the next. Second, a given destination can provide a variety of travel experiences, suitable to a wide range of tourists, depending on the manner in which the trip is planned. The only way in which a systematic linkage can be developed between the types of destinations and the types of tourists is to consider each trip in isolation and examine the motivations that have prompted the trip.

Figure 18.6 illustrates the relationship between types of tourists, travel motivations, and types of destinations. As indicated in the figure, travel motivations link types of tourists and types of destinations in two ways:

1. The primary link is the tourist flow and client satisfaction that will result when a customer is directed to the appropriate type of destination. Such a choice is most likely to maximize satisfactions and produce the kind of travel experience that he or she seeks. A clear understanding is needed of the client's psychological and demographic profile and hence his or her travel motivations for that particular trip. Knowing this enables the purveyor of tourism services (such as a travel counselor) to recommend the types of tour packages (escorted or unescorted, fully planned or

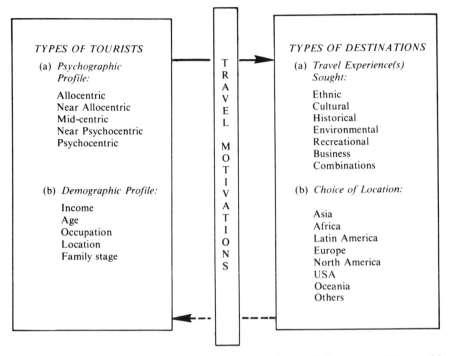

Figure 18.6   Relationships Among Types of Tourists, Travel Motivations, and Types of Destinations.

flexible), the types of destinations, and the types of travel experiences that will best suit the client or customer's needs. Travel experiences planned in this manner will yield the highest level of client satisfaction.

2. The secondary link relates to the promotion, development, and marketing of destinations to appropriate target markets. Understanding the types of tourists in the target market and the travel motivations of this market will provide a sound basis for deciding the types of environments and services that should be provided at the destination. These understandings will also govern the message content of a promotion campaign.

The following list shows many travel motivations. It should be clear from this list that some motivations are shared by a wide variety of tourists (from allocentric to psychocentric), while other motivations relate to a more narrow spectrum of psychographic types.

ALLOCENTRIC MOTIVATIONS

1. Education and cultural motives—learning and increased ability for appreciation, scientific or purposeful; trips with expert leaders or lecturers
2. Study of genealogy
3. Search for the exotic—Hawaii, Polynesia, Japan, Thailand, East Africa, India
4. Satisfactions and sense of power and freedom—anonymity, flying, control, sea travel, fast trains

5. Gambling—Las Vegas, Atlantic City, Monte Carlo, Bahamas, Puerto Rico
6. Development of new friendships in foreign places
7. Sharpening perspectives—awaken senses, heighten awareness
8. Political campaigns, supporting candidates, government hearings
9. Vacation or second homes and condominiums

NEAR-ALLOCENTRIC MOTIVATIONS

10. Religious pilgrimages or inspiration
11. Participation in sports events and sports activities
12. Travel as a challenge, sometimes a test of endurance such as exploring, mountain climbing, hiking, diving
13. Business travel, conferences, meetings, conventions
14. Theater tours, special entertainment
15. A chance to try a new lifestyle

MIDCENTRIC MOTIVATIONS

16. Relaxation and pleasure—just plain fun and enjoyment
17. Satisfying personal contacts with friends and relatives
18. Health—change in climate, sunshine, spas, medical treatment
19. The need for a change for a period of time
20. An opportunity to escape from life's problems
21. The real or imagined glamour of the destination
22. Appreciation of beauty—national and state parks, forests, lakes, wilderness areas, canoe trips, ocean shores
23. Sensual indulgence—food, comforts, luxuries for the body, romance, sexual enjoyment, rest, relaxation
24. Shopping—souvenirs, gifts, expensive possessions like cameras, jewels, furs, cars, antiques, art
25. Joys of transportation—cruise ships, gourmet meals, buffets, comfortable trains, buses, airplanes, autos
26. Pleasure of pre- and post travel—planning the trip, anticipation, learning, dreaming; then showing pictures and describing the trip after completion
27. Family or personal matters

NEAR-PSYCHOCENTRIC AND PSYCHOCENTRIC MOTIVATIONS

28. Ego enhancement, quest for status
29. Travel for acceptance, to be comfortable socially
30. Travel as a cultural norm—paid vacations required by law
31. Visit to places seen or read about in the news
32. Visit to amusement parks

Plog first developed his model in 1972, some 23 years ago, and it has been widely cited in tourism literature since that time. It was one of the first attempts to provide a framework within which to analyze tourist behavior. The world has changed considerably since Plog introduced his model. For example, today there are fewer countries that are considered exotic. Also, there are now other ways to look at tourists, such as through lifestyle analysis or benefit segmentation. Plog's pioneering efforts, however, should not be overlooked. His model still provides a way to examine travel and think about developments using current market conditions.

Michigan Vacation Classification

In an effort to improve the economic impact of tourism, the Michigan Travel Bureau performed a market segmentation study on the state's tourism industry. A consumer survey conducted in Michigan, five adjacent states, and Ontario, Canada, produced new attitudinal and behavioral data. From this data six vacation activities preference types were developed on the basis of factor analysis.

These were noninclusive groups; that is, an individual could belong to more than one of the types. For communication purposes, they were given names descriptive of the kinds of activities they liked to do on vacation. The types are illustrated in Figure 18.7 with the activities which ranked highest on the factors that described them: young sports, outdoorsman/hunter, winter/water, resort, sightseer, and nightlife activities.

The market segmentation study pointed out the segments not being reached and demonstrated where advertising should be increased or introduced. Strategies were developed and implemented, resulting in a 12 percent growth in the state's tourist industry.

VALS

A popular segmentation system used today is VALS, which stands for "Values, Attitudes, and Lifestyles" and was developed by SRI International. Its use as a tool for tourism market research in Pennsylvania has been reported by David Shih of the Pennsylvania Department of Commerce.[3]

The basis of the Value and Lifestyle Program is the VALS typology. It divides Americans into nine lifestyles or types, which are grouped in four categories based on their self-images, their aspirations, their values and beliefs, and the products they use. The four categories and nine lifestyles are the following:

- Need-driven groups
    Survivor lifestyle
    Sustainer lifestyle
- Outer-directed groups
    Belongers lifestyle
    Emulator lifestyle
    Achiever lifestyle
- Inner-directed groups
    I-am-me lifestyle
    Experiential lifestyle
    Societally conscious lifestyle
- Combined outer- and inner-directed group
    Integrated lifestyle

---

[3]David Shih, "VALS as a Tool of Tourism Market Research: The Pennsylvania Experience," *Journal of Travel Research*, Vol. 24, No. 4 (Spring 1986), pp. 2–11.

YOUNG SPORTS TYPE

Bicycling
Canoeing
Camping
Hiking
Horseback Riding
Swimming
Tennis

OUTDOORSMAN HUNTER

Power boating
Fishing
Hunting
Ice fishing
Snowmobiling

WINTER/WATER TYPE

Sailing
Canoeing
Snow skiing
Snowmobiling
Tennis
Water skiing

RESORT TYPE

Golf
Tennis
Casino gambling

SIGHTSEER TYPE

Seeing natural resources
Seeing historical sites
Culture-concerts/plays
   art shows
Man-made attractions
Museums
Special festivals

NIGHTLIFE ACTIVITIES

Professional sports
Major amusement parks
Man-made attractions
Nightclubs & restaurants
Casino gambling

Figure 18.7 Vacation Activity Preference Types

The VALS program can be a useful tool for tourism marketing. Lifestyle variables reveal something beyond demographics and are real, meaningful, and relevant. The key VALS segments—belongers, achievers, and the societally conscious—provide valuable information about market segmentation, advertising copy appeals, and media selection.

VALS research conducted in Pennsylvania substantiates the "friendly people" theme as an effective message for the state. Overall, no radical change is indicated in the Pennsylvania tourism campaign's creative approach. However, an objective should be to strengthen the "belonger" base traveling to Pennsylvania, while at the same time to attract more achievers and societally conscious persons. Also, in-state TV advertising

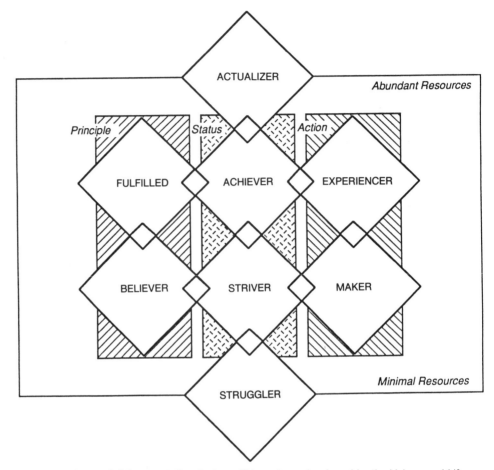

Figure 18.8 VALS 2 Segmentation System. This system, developed by the Values and Life-styles Program at SRI International, is a new psychographic system for segmenting consumers and predicting consumer behavior. (Source: SRI International)

should be continued, and additional print advertising in appropriate publications is warranted to attract the achievers and the societally conscious.

One thing that can be counted on in marketing is change; consequently, SRI International has come up with a new VALS 2 (Figure 18.8). The nine original VALS psychographic segments have been replaced by eight new psychographic groups. The eight VALS 2 groups and some of their characteristics are

- *Actualizers:* have highest incomes, high self-esteem, abundant resources. Consumer choices are directed toward "the finer things in life."
- *Fulfilleds:* mature, responsible, well-educated professionals, open to new ideas. High-income, practical, value-oriented consumers.
- *Achievers:* successful, work-oriented, receive satisfaction from jobs and family. Favor established products.

- *Experiencers:* youngest of segments, median age of 25. Seek variety and excitement. Avid consumers spending on clothing, fast food, music, and other youthful favorites.
- *Believers:* lives centered on family, church, community, and nation. Conservative and predictable consumers who favor American products and established brands.
- *Strivers:* have values of achievers but few resources. Style is important as they strive to emulate the people they wish they were.
- *Makers:* practical people who value self-sufficiency. They focus on the familiar.
- *Strugglers:* have lowest incomes. Lives are constricted. Within means tend to be brand-loyal consumers.

JOINT MARKETING EFFORTS

In the majority of cases, a tourism organization will want to market its product and services individually; however, in other cases, joint cooperative efforts will be the most profitable. Typically these efforts are launched through associations or government agencies. Colorado Ski Country, USA and the Utah Ski Association are groups that jointly promote the services of their members, many of whom are in competition with each other. Publishing posters and directories, answering inquiries, and providing snow reports promote the industry in the most cost-effective way. In addition to these joint marketing efforts, the areas have their own individual marketing programs. They may also work with other private firms such as airlines, rental car companies, and credit card firms to stretch their marketing dollars.

Experience to date has shown that tourism promotion on a country or state basis is best accomplished by a cooperative effort of private industry and government. Joint promotion by private interests and official government tourist organizations is an effective and efficient procedure. One of the examples of the pooling of private and government funds is the Hawaii Visitors Bureau, an independent nonprofit organization that conducts tourism promotion under contract with the State Department of Planning and Economic Development. Approximately 10 percent of the funding comes from private sources and 90 percent from state sources.

In some states, specific "matching funds" are provided by a government tourism agency for tourist promotion, such as the provision of a portion of advertising costs of a private regional tourist promotion association. Various combinations of "matched" funds are possible, depending on the amount of funds available and the provisions of the legislation that authorizes such expenditures of public funds. The Pennsylvania Bureau of Travel Development operates the largest matching grants fund program in the United States.

SUMMARY

Marketing can be defined as the performance of business activities that direct the flow of goods and services from the producer to the consumer or user. Such activities are vital to tourist businesses. The finest, most satisfying tourist facility would be unprofitable without marketing. People have to be informed about a travel destination and become interested in going there before a market can be created.

Basic to the marketing effort are the marketing concept, the marketing mix, product planning and development, pricing, distribution channels, promotion, market research, personal selling, public relations, and market segmentation.

Joint marketing efforts among official tourism organizations, public carriers, and providers of accommodations or even with nearby competing destination areas are strategically sound and typically successful.

About the Readings

The first reading presents a short case example of the use of tourist promotion by a small city. Traverse City, Michigan, has grown to national prominence through good tourism planning and successful promotion. This reading covers the highlights of that effort.

The second reading deals with promotion and describes how to develop a promotional plan to achieve a marketing objective.

The third reading discusses how to market a new resort development in terms of trends of resort features and the tourist market. The points made are relevant to every resort project but are especially relevant to Mexico.

Successful Tourism Promotion— The Case of Traverse City, Michigan

In 1984 Traverse City was designated as an "All-America City" by the National Municipal League—one of only nine so honored in the United States. Also, with its population of 15,516, it was the smallest city so honored. The five-county area surrounding the city has a population of about 58,000.

What is the allure of this area? What marketing methods are used to attract an average of about 100,000 visitors each day during the summer season and a substantial number during other seasons of the year?

First the community of Traverse City appeals to its residents. One resident stated, "Traverse City has a spiritual pull of some kind. Its beauty entrances you and makes you want to stay. To me, it's a fantastic town. It's a real 'can do' place. There's a positive attitude, the quality of life is great, and the people are tremendous. The physical beauty can't be beat. Everything looks good and crisp and clean. It's a great place to live."

Second, several miles of the main highway skirt both Grand Traverse Bays (of Lake Michigan), so that passing motorists can't help but see and admire the community's natural setting. Finally, Traverse City is a center for medical and hospital services, oil production, food processing (mainly cherry and bakery products), boating, golf, cultural events, and winter sports. There are numerous government offices, and retirees often choose the community as a place to live.

TOURISM PROMOTION PROBLEMS IDENTIFIED— PARTIALLY SOLVED

The evolution of good tourism promotion since the 1950s has brought about a solution to a major problem—myopia in individual business promotion. Now, businesses do not promote just their own interests; they also consistently advertise their geographical area as an attractive destination. This philosophy is thus a broad-based one, reflecting conviction that the destination *must* be marketed along with the individual business. An example of this is the cooperative marketing program of the five-area ski resorts. Although they are competitors under different ownership, their sales reps attend travel shows as a group. Each resort is individually promoted, of course, but skiing in the entire area is also publicized. The resorts also market a "ski free" midweek program for children during the holidays and a gold and silver ski pass honored at any of the resorts. The passes are marketed through the Chamber of Commerce and receipts are kept by the chamber to be used for ski promotion.

A problem that so far has been only partially solved is that of local people who are overly optimistic about the community's tourism success. Many feel that visitors will come regardless of the amount of effort expanded to attract them, and such a philosophy is hard to change. This philosophy, when coupled with a fairly widespread feeling that their area should be kept secret and the sense of protectiveness that prevails, makes all-out tourism promotion difficult. A major strategy to overcome this resistance to promotion has been the creation of the Traverse City Area Convention and Visitors Bureau, which markets the area to any type of visitor, including families, groups, conventions, or tours. The bureau is financed by a small levy on local commercial lodging receipts.

DEVELOPMENT OF SUPPLY COMPONENTS

The most urgent continuing problem is to increase publicly owned recreational land. Most desirable is that of beaches along the two bays. Removing unsuitable structures from the waterfront areas and creating elongated parks have been major accomplishments in the past decade, and today miles of beautiful parkways attract motorists who stop to enjoy the views and are often inclined to return for a vacation.

A new boardwalk along the downtown riverside is a recent example of improving the infrastructure; this feature is enjoyed by locals as well as visitors. New resorts of the "world class" have also been built near the city. Such developments include convention facilities and adjacent condominium construction as well as golf courses and sports resources.

Increasing demand for transportation has brought about more adequate air travel services with one major airline and two regionals providing about 18 flights per day. For motorists, only two-lane highways service the area. This situation is viewed as a major limiting factor for increasing tourism.

HOW TARGET MARKETS ARE DECIDED UPON

Geographic Considerations: The East North Central states comprise the primary market, with emphasis on Michigan, Illinois, and Indiana.

Psychographic Considerations: Focus is on outdoor sports, cultural activities, and agriculture. Special promotion is devoted to the National Cherry Festival, one of the 10 top festivals in the nation. Other promotions feature cherry blossoms in the spring, fishing and boating, golf, tennis, racquetball, canoeing, public beaches, rainy day activities, colored-leaf tours in fall, and winter sports. Cultural assets include an opera house, Interlochen Center for the Arts, antique shops, and indigenous arts and crafts.

Demographic Considerations: Efforts are made to attract all age categories and a wide range of income groups. Public parks with campgrounds as well as deluxe accommodations are featured.

The mode of transportation to be used by those who respond to marketing efforts is consistently included in advertisements. For example, air travel is emphasized in convention promotion, motorcoach in promoting group tours, and the auto for family vacations.

A GOAL-SETTING PROCESS

Two major objectives have been stated as slogans: "fill every guest room every night" and "make ski resorts year-round vacation places." To accomplish these goals, all-season community promotion is undertaken. At ski resorts, all-year operation is made possible by providing golf courses, indoor-outdoor swimming pools, and other athletic facilities; expanding numbers of guest rooms; adding more restaurants; and developing real estate such as condominiums and sale of building sites.

Along with these goals, however, is the less exciting but meaningful objective of maintaining and improving the livability of the area. The promotion people sincerely believe that this is indeed accomplished by effective tourism marketing and by increasing the amount and quality of the infrastructure and superstructure. These activities benefit not only the community's visitors, but the local inhabitants as well. Increased employment and raised standards of living are brought about by visitor spending. An added benefit is the economic impact of the construction and maintenance of these facilities, which results in increased direct or indirect incomes for all of the area's residents.

HOW THE PROMOTION PROGRAM IS ORGANIZED

Staff members of the Traverse City Area Convention and Visitors Bureau prepare an annual marketing plan. This includes a situational analysis, goals, target markets, potential markets, programs to reach these markets, budgets, and a system of evaluation of results.

This plan is reviewed by the marketing committee with final reconsideration and approval by the board of directors.

There are three main thrusts:

1. Creating a vigorous demand for holding meetings, seminars, and conventions in their area
2. Marketing the area as a destination or stopover for motor coach tours
3. Expanding the visitor industry of family vacations, sports, festivals, cultural events, and similar activities

These programs are under the direction of two account executives who specialize in (1) group marketing and (2) vacation travel promotion.

Elements of the various programs include media selection, publicity materials, a meetings planner booklet, newspaper supplements, editorial solicitation, coordination of promotions with the Michigan Travel Bureau (official), distribution of promotional literature, and direct personal sales, including those at travel and sports shows.

Something unique is their community volunteer program in which qualified volunteers help at convention registration desks and also serve as guides for local tours.

A guiding philosophy of the bureau is that, for the most part, the Chamber of Commerce helps to create and enhance the tourism product and the bureau sells the product in the area's travel markets. The bureau is thus a strictly promotional-sales-marketing organization for tourism.

MEASURING MARKETING EFFECTIVENESS

Immediately after Labor Day, the Chamber of Commerce, in cooperation with the bureau, surveys 200 area firms to ascertain what percentage change in business was experienced in the past season compared with the previous year. These surveys have been conducted each year since 1979. The same firms are surveyed each year, which assures good continuity and comparability. Lodging places (in representative groupings) are asked to compare occupancy percentages; all other businesses compare dollar volume. Businesses are selected by category: lodging, restaurants, wholesale beverage distributors, major department stores, other retailers, campgrounds, attractions, farm markets, travel agencies, gift shops, wineries, tourist inquiries received by the chamber, and even visits to the emergency rooms of area hospitals! Results of the survey are reported to all members in the October issue of the chamber's business publication.

FUTURE CHALLENGES

A primary effort must be made to better identify potential markets. When pinpointed, how are these markets to be reached? What amounts of supply components will be needed to successfully accommodate these? Should these primary efforts be successful, how will the necessary investments in infrastructure and superstructure be attracted to the area?

The feasibility of such investments rests upon the effectiveness of tourism promotion. Thus, intelligent development and productive marketing are inseparably interchanged. They must be if satisfactory contributions to the area's economy and ways of life are to be achieved.

READING 18.2

Developing the Promotional Plan

> Reprinted from *Tourism U.S.A.,* Volume III, *Marketing Tourism,* U.S. Department of Commerce.

. . . The basic procedure in the development of a promotional plan is summarized below:

- Forecast expected revenues considering the planned budget expenditures for the forecasted period.
- Clearly define the specific market target(s) to be cultivated.
- Determine the motivational factors possessed by the target market(s) which will attract them to the tourism site.
- Develop specific promotional goals.
- Develop the overall campaign theme, the "big idea" or creative strategy which will allow an integration of all the foregoing points in its implementation.
- Develop a media strategy.
- Compose and create the specific advertisements in the campaign.
- Test the effectiveness of the individual ads and the campaign itself.

The paragraphs which follow will provide a brief discussion and application of the planning procedure shown above.

FORECAST EXPECTED REVENUES

In the absence of the sophisticated forecasting methods, even a crude estimate of the expected tourism demand will be useful. In most instances the starting point will be the history of demand for previous years. The average growth rate then can be projected into the next year.

It must be remembered, however, that the projection into the future assumes a continuation of past marketing effectiveness. By the same token any improvement in effectiveness will raise the original forecasted estimate. Most importantly, the promotional budget for the upcoming period may cause the estimate to be changed significantly. If, for example, last year's 10% increase in budget provided a 20% increase in revenues, we might assume a doubling of last year's 10% budget increase to 20% this year, might cause revenues to go up by 40% if your effectiveness remains the same. A reverse condition could also be true, however, if the budget is contracted. The important point to remember is that a simple mathematical projection of an estimate must be modified to consider the new investment you are willing to commit to a marketing or promotional plan for the forthcoming period. The modified forecast in effect, then, becomes the tourist site's overall goal.

SPECIFY MARKET TARGETS

One certain way to fail is to try to please everyone. Everyone is not an equally avid tourist and therefore, everyone is not equally important as a potential tourism visitor. Markets can be defined in a number of ways. *Geographic segmentation,* for example, might allow the tourism promoter to focus on a particular city or group of cities or, perhaps, only on locations within a specified distance of the site. Similarly, the *age of tourists,* or, perhaps, the *stage in family life cycle* may provide a very good basis for market segmentation. By examining past research you might find, for example, a heavy incidence of travelers at a particular site are families with children in the 6- to 15-year-old category. Similarly, you may find that few young unmarrieds or visitors under age 25 visit that particular site.

Other segmenting bases are available which may be even superior. The major precaution must be the necessity of locating good market descriptors so that a few specific markets can be actively cultivated while others may be entirely passed over. Seldom are budgetary resources so abundant that promotion can use a shotgun approach to market development. Moreover, it is virtually impossible to write advertising copy which will motivate everyone. It is much more effective to study intensively your major market segments or a specific potential target which has a good probability of being developed.

DETERMINE TOURIST MOTIVATIONS

Once the target market(s) has been defined, the segment(s) must be studied to discover why they travel and why they would choose to travel to your specific site. Again, it is best not to use a shotgun approach with too many appeals directed at a specific targeted segment. People who choose to visit historical attractions or communities of restored older buildings are not motivated in the same way as those who travel to man-made attractions which offer athletic activities, gambling casinos or musical shows.

The objective is to sell, for example, the mystique which is created by a site's historical importance, or the mystique of witnessing a past era. The main reason people travel is to experience a new or different environment. Modern hotel facilities may be appreciated and even play a vital part in any tourism site; however, it is not the magnet which attracts the visitor. The impetus for travel must remain focused on the benefits offered by the core attractions which provide the new or different experiences which will be enjoyed by the traveler.

DEVELOP SPECIFIC PROMOTIONAL GOALS

Goals play an important part in developing promotional strategies. A well thought out goal should, if possible, be expressed quantitatively and should be measurable. Goals should also be expressed in terms of a given time period during which the goal should be accomplished. Goals should be written and be as specific as possible. Finally, it is generally agreed that promotional goals which are stated in terms of their communicative purposes are more realistic than expressing them in more general terms, such as expected sales or revenues.

The following, to illustrate, could be developed as communications goals:

- To create and measure the *awareness* of a particular tourism attraction in a specific market.
- To communicate a specific tourism appeal in your promotion to a specific market and then determine how many people can recall it.
- To communicate a basic campaign theme to a specific market and then determine how many people can restate the premise without aided recall.
- To communicate a particular image or try to create a particular attitude about a tourism site and then determine if the message registered in the potential prospect's mind creates the correct image.

- To promote and measure the usage of a coupon in the advertisement as a means for locating interested prospects and mailing out information.

The above are only illustrative and should be stated quantitatively and more fully. To be of value there should be a "before" and "after" measurement to determine the effectiveness of the promotion, a measurement of how effectively it produced.

DEVELOP THE CAMPAIGN THEME

One of your promotional goals could be to increase awareness of the tourism site to targeted residents in a neighboring state which research data shows produces many travelers for you. An overall theme may be developed which will encompass this stated goal. The campaign theme is primarily an exercise in creativity and often performed by specialists at an advertising agency. To illustrate, Illinois Tourism is currently using a theme aimed at tourists in Missouri. Expressed in a musical jingle is a theme which states, "Right at your own back door is a state called Illinois." This theme in all advertisements provide a thread of continuity to the individual ads and pulls them together in a series. Using this theme the Illinois Department of Tourism points out a number of special tourism attractions in Illinois which can be reached conveniently by Missouri travelers. Each advertisement, moreover, is well planned to convey the special mystique of the individual site. It is clearly evident to most observers of these ads that each is part of an overall theme relating to Illinois tourism.

DEVELOP A MEDIA STRATEGY

Because the market has been carefully segmented, it becomes much easier to locate effective media to channel the message. Radio stations and magazines, for example, are highly selective means of reaching specific market segments. Geographic segmentation can often be accomplished through newspapers and regional editions of magazines. Mailing lists are highly specialized in reaching particular tourist groups such as campers, historical societies, educators, and the like.

Cost efficiency will play a large part in the particular vehicle which is finally chosen. It is best expressed in terms which measure cost per target market reached.

Timing is also an important element of media strategy. Generally it is difficult to interest people in traveling when they are not inclined to do so. While the tourism season might be extended somewhat by advertising earlier in the season and/or later in the season, it would be difficult to encourage tourism in the off-season. The largest part of the budget should be placed to anticipate by a few weeks the best tourism periods.

As a concluding comment, it is recognized that certain media may be more effective than others in their special ways of presenting ads. No doubt television, because of its ability to visualize and demonstrate, is very effective in a communicative sense. On the other hand, the cost is very often prohibitive. Radio, however, cannot show a beautiful scene even though the driver and family may be traveling or vacationing at the very time a radio commercial is heard. Newspapers may offer the inducement of a travel section which helps to segment the tourism market for the newspaper and newspaper-reading tourist. On the other hand outdoor advertising, while it is not especially effective in transmitting information or major benefits, may attract attention very well and direct a traveler in the immediate area to your particular tourism site.

COMPOSITION OF SPECIFIC ADVERTISING COPY

Following the procedure shown above, the task of good and effective copy writing should be much easier. It is easier to write copy when you know to whom (market target) you are writing, what motivates the target market, the goals which are intended to be accomplished, the basic theme which is to be used, and the advantages and disadvantages of using specific mediums to convey the copy writer's message. All of the above influences should clearly direct the copy writer into producing more effective messages. At the copy writing stage it is again the creativity of the individual writer which dominates. The foregoing procedure will allow the copy writer to channel his/her energy and talents into producing more relevant and effective commercials.

TEST ADVERTISING EFFECTIVENESS

It should be obvious that if a goal-oriented approach to promotion is to be used, there must be some way to measure the degree to which those goals have been accomplished. How are you to judge your effectiveness if there are no "before" and "after" benchmarks to evaluate performance?

Promotional research is necessary in four basic areas:

- It is necessary to use research to determine the motivations, attitudes, and opinions of your potential customers.
- Once advertising copy is created it should be tested *before* it is placed in the media to determine whether there is reason to believe you have empathized with the target market, whether he understands your message as intended, and whether he draws conclusions from it which allow your goals to be accomplished.
- In most instances, it is worthwhile to investigate the demographic characteristics of the promotional vehicle being considered. It is also often worthwhile to judge the effectiveness of competing media available to you through their ability to produce inquiries, coupons for tourism brochures, and the like. The coupons or "departments written to" can be coded to help judge the effectiveness of the vehicle and the advertisement itself.
- The overall effectiveness of the campaign should be researched in order to determine the degree of accomplishment you have attained in reaching the specific communication goals spelled out early in the planning procedure.

Paradise Planned: New Horizons for the 1990's and Beyond

By Michael M. S. Chun, AIA
Wimberly Allison Tong & Goo

The 1990's should be an optimum period for new resort development. Simply put, there are more potential travelers today than ever before, and this wide and varied market has larger amounts of disposable income and more leisure time than in any other period in the past. Travelers today are better educated, more sophisticated in their attitudes about tourist destinations and therefore more likely to venture off into new places. They are supported in their enthusiasm by the world of mass marketing and communications, the international tourist industry and its rapid expansion of charter and package services, and by improved and less expensive transportation. The stress of modern life, which has made rejuvenation and relaxation as much a necessity as a luxury, acts as an inducement for taking a holiday and made employers more likely to encourage, or even finance, vacations for their employees.

Affluent singles of all ages are off in search of adventure and entertainment. More young married couples with disposable income are traveling, many of them with their children; more retirees are seeing the world; more and more business is conducted on an international scale, and many business executives are taking their families along for the trip. From every aspect, the resort market in the decades ahead will be a viable force.

The time is right for new resort development and successful development is inevitable as long as insight, experienced planning, and skillful follow-through are exercised. In this paper I will discuss what I see as past, current and future trends and what I feel are the most important considerations affecting the success of a destination resort. But before discussing trends of resort features and the tourist market, I want to emphasize one point that is, I believe, relevant to every resort project and especially relevant to Mexico and Mexico's future in the tourist industry.

In the forty-five years of experience gleaned at Wimberly Allison Tong & Goo, a basic philosophy has emerged, a philosophy shared by each of the firm's members. This is the strong belief that a resort project must be integrated appropriately with its cultural and physical environment. We call this important ingredient for economic, functional and aesthetic success a SENSE OF PLACE. Without this sense of place, the resulting project may lose its potential vibrancy and individual character to become a sterile copy of some other design, some other place.

This does not mean that resort projects in other locales should not be studied and evaluated. Aspects of other projects may be of immense value as patterns to be reshaped and recreated with a fresh, innovative approach. But whatever element or idea is incorporated from a distant model should be considered with great scrutiny and adapted with consummate skill to harmonize with every part of the local environment; its people, their characteristic way of life, and the history, culture, climate, resources, social and economic significance of the immediate area.

The variety and excitement of Mexico fit extremely well into the picture of an expanding tourist industry. Mexico's climate, topography, her rich heritage and abundant opportunities for recreation and adventure make the country a natural attraction for tourists from around the world. I believe that Mexico, this land that offers so much, will gain in popularity as a destination resort in proportion to its emphasis on the particular characteristics and personality that belong to Mexico alone.

Looking at the overall resort industry, there are some trends in facilities well worth considering when planning any new resort development. A large segment of the travel market today is highly discriminating in judging and choosing a resort. These experienced travelers seek out and expect quality of design and atmosphere in the total setting, from an exterior and an interior standpoint.

Views, for instance, are more important than ever before. Whereas, twenty years ago, a small ocean view might have seemed a luxury, today's traveler anticipates pleasant vistas from every corner and aspect of a resort. This expectation calls for careful site planning, particularly in regard to placement of guest facilities. Landscape plans must address the creation of open space and the separation of restful from active areas.

The quality factor is also sought out in inside facilities where larger, more luxurious bathrooms, more spacious sleeping and lounging accommodations are expected. There is a noticeable direction toward incorporating an important arrival experience into the resort complex. This may involve a secluded private drive leading to the hotel entrance or porte cochere, a fountained courtyard or some additional sense of drama to make the specialness of the upcoming experience evident for the guest. With the trend toward more opulence and touches of elegance, there is also a trend toward architecture that is scaled to people. Today's guests are more sensitive to the total environment and seek a high level of comfort and humanness in their surroundings.

A worldwide awakening to the values of physical fitness has led to a major trend in the tourism industry. On-site health spa facilities that provide exercise equipment, fitness instructors, steam rooms, and specialized workout areas have become highly desirable. Jogging and walking paths, bike trails, par courses, and other fitness amenities fit into this category.

In the area of recreational activities, golf has become of prominent importance, especially for larger resorts. Tennis facilities, racquetball and paddleball courts, and equestrian trails continue to be important amenities for many destination hotels.

Pools, once considered merely sideline attractions for a quick dip, have become focal points in many resorts. A pool often serves as a social gathering spot for hotel guests and may be an activity and entertainment center—a featured attraction—in its own right. The pool designed by WAT&G for the Hyatt Regency Maui, for example, is a spectacular affair with swim-through waterfalls and rock mountains, grotto bar, water slide and a rope bridge, all set within tropical gardens.

In addition to trends in the features and facilities provided by resorts, there are specific market directions affecting the type of resort that is being built. Each new segment of the traveling public brings its own set of new expectations, and there is a concurrent trend towards market segmentation and the tailoring of resort projects to these specific categories of tourists.

The mega-resort of over a 1,000 or more rooms, which has been a major attraction for many years, continues in its appeal. This grand-scale resort, however, is currently under-going a change in style and approach from the single project "strip development" along ocean fronts and city entry corridors. Today's mega-resort tends towards the integrated, master-planned development in which visitor accommodations merge with a broad range of activities and amenities.

The huge convention facility, so popular in the 60's and 70's for large incentive travel groups and charters, remains popular in limited, well-located areas. Today it tends to a grand scale of a thousand or more rooms and often incorporates the theme of fantasy and requires a massive support system.

The market for this convention oriented resort is made up primarily of two major portions, the incentive traveler (the salesperson, for example, rewarded by his employer with a paid vacation) and the large-scale convention traveler. This is a relatively inexperienced, less sophisticated market seeking a source of pleasure and total escape from daily routine.

The public's desire for fantasy and nostalgia is manifest among families, honeymooners and retirees as well as convention participants and incentive travelers. The Grand Floridian Beach Resort, which WAT&G recently designed for Disney World near Orlando, Florida, is a prime example of a resort built to meet this prevailing taste for escape into another world. This 900-room hotel, a thoroughly integrated development with five lodge buildings and one main building of five stories, is carefully massed for a village effect. In a semi-tropical setting, WAT&G has recreated the magic of the Victorian era beach-front hotels of Florida, circa 1900. The result is appropriate to the locale and does not feel contrived. This sort of project, the creation of a world from the past, could be applied in historic context in Mexico.

It is in the category of the mid-sized, world-class hotel that the newly-rich traveler seeking glamour and exposure often merges with the upscale traveler who exudes glamour and is accustomed to luxury. Premier resorts in this size range can offer varied amenities, personal service and an atmosphere conducive to the pampered exclusivity this clientele is seeking. As an example, the Ritz-Carlton Laguna Niguel is this type of resort which meets these requirements in a concept readily adaptable to Mexican coastal sites. The hotel was designed by WAT&G in classic Spanish Mediterranean style to complement its location on the bluffs of the Pacific in Southern California. From the aspect of the visitor, the hotel is reminiscent of a monumental old world villa; from the beach it appears to be a village which has evolved slowly along the promontory.

The vertical elevator tower of the planned Acapulco Marriott symbolizes the drawing power of a luxurious, sophisticated environment that offers a sense of sociability and pleasure. The boldness of the hotel's exterior, the four-story lobby with its sculpted fountain, every aspect of the hotel's elegant design suits the international reputation of Acapulco as a jet setters' paradise and the natural beauty of the city's location.

The Sands of Monterey in Monterey, California is a worldclass 375-room hotel and residential resort designed for the discriminating guest who is looking for a distinctive setting and a high level of service. This hotel, with its beamed-ceiling lobby and gabled, hip-roof exterior construction reflects the rugged, environmentally sensitive, site.

A new idea in mid-sized hotels today is the urban retreat designed primarily for the business executive. In both the Four Seasons Newport Beach and the Shangri-La Hotel Garden Wing, Singapore, as well as the planned Four Seasons Mexico City, the architectural design by WAT&G serves to bring the outdoors inside, creating an oasis in the midst of a thriving commercial center. The Four Seasons Mexico City will be located in the heart of the business district, but its concept of all rooms directed toward the inside courtyard and fountain gives it a secluded, retreat atmosphere. The Four Seasons Newport features an airy lobby with floor to ceiling windows, meeting rooms opening onto landscaped terraces, individual balconies and panoramic ocean view from 100% of guest rooms.

In the design and construction of resort hotels today, there is a growing counter-trend to large-scale resorts which is epitomized by the small getaway hotels such as the well-established Hotel Bora Bora in Tahiti and the Tanjong Jara Beach Hotel/Rantau Abang Visitors Center and Museum resort complex on the Malaysian Peninsula. Both resorts were designed by WAT&G to characterize, rather than contrast with, their particular locations and to suit a growing market of travelers who seek experience-oriented holidays.

The Hotel Bora Bora is designed in the style of the ancient Tahitian house and consists of sixty-five beach and fifteen overwater bungalows located at the reef's edge. These units offer modern conveniences amid South Seas authenticity.

The getaway resort can be several kinds designed to appeal to one of many different divisions of this particular tourist market. Travelers seeking adventure may look to this type of resort as a form of base-camp with minimum amenities but optimum opportunity to enjoy an exciting experience like scuba diving or sportfishing. Another kind of getaway traveler may be looking for a quieter, education-oriented experience such as the study or photography of native animal and plant life. As with the adventurer, amenities will be less important for this individual than the chance to participate in the desired activity. A third division in this category is the very upscale tourist who seeks a true hideaway from crowds and from modern life. This is the experienced traveler who expects excellence in dining and service but is not interested in surface glitz or a large amenity base.

The getaway/hideaway resort is a facility particularly adaptable to smaller sites in Mexico that are noted for one special attraction or feature such as fishing, parasailing, windsurfing, archaeological exploration, photographic opportunities and folk festivals.

In designing any resort in Mexico, whether in the context of a small and intimate resort for the adventurous few or in a resort of grand proportions designed for the many, it is essential to remember that there is no other place on earth that IS Acapulco or Guadalajara, no other beaches exactly like the beaches of Cancun, nothing anywhere in the world that matches the rich array of archaeological sites throughout the Yucatan Peninsula.

These and hundreds of other locales are the treasures that make Mexico a unique and enticing place. It is in the retention, enhancement and preservation of Mexico's particular PLACES that Mexico will become a leader in the world resort field that it deserves to become.

Key Concepts

advertising	marketing mix
advertising agency	packaging
channels of distribution	place
consumer orientation	pricing
definition of marketing	product
demographics	product life cycle
four Ps	product planning and development
image	promotion
individual business-destination	psychographics
marketing	public relations
joint marketing efforts	selling
market research	*Survey of Buying Power*
market segmentation	target market
marketing concept	timing

For Review and Discussion

1. What is the marketing concept?
2. Do you regard the concept of consumer-oriented marketing as a step forward? Why or why not?
3. What are the stages in the product life cycle? What are the marketing implications of each stage?
4. What are the key factors a tourism marketing manager must consider in setting price?
5. Discuss the conditions when penetration pricing should be used. Price skimming?

6. Discuss how a tourism firm's pricing strategy may influence the promotional program.
7. How are channels of distribution selected? Using an example, explain.
8. As the manager of a tourism enterprise, what can you do when customers complain that the price of your product is too high?
9. What are the advantages and disadvantages of the various advertising media?
10. What can an advertising agency do?
11. What is the objective of advertising?
12. The cost of running an ad on the back cover of *Time* magazine is more expensive than is hiring a salesperson for a year. As the marketing manager for a leading hotel chain, you have just been told by the president of the company to eliminate ads and hire more salespersons. You feel that this would be a serious mistake. What would you do to change the president's mind?
13. What are some examples of realistic objectives of a tourism marketing program? Use a resort hotel, a motorcoach, and a tour company.
14. Explain the statement "tourism promotion efforts undirected by research are largely a waste of effort." Do you agree?
15. What are the advantages of marketing vacation packages?
16. Give an example of a vacation package that might be marketed in your area. How would you market it? To whom?
17. What value do you see in market segmentation? Give an example.
18. If you were a hotel manager in a resort community, how would you use the marketing concept? Give details.
19. You are the assistant vice-president for marketing of a regional airline. Your current target market is youth. Give the marketing mix you would propose to your boss.
20. As the planner of a new wing on your resort hotel, how does product planning and development in a marketing context apply?
21. You are a restaurant manager in a popular year-round resort area. How do you decide on the price levels of your meals?
22. As a tour operator you are trying to improve the distribution system for marketing your tours. How might this be done?
23. What kind of advertising program is best for a cruise company?
24. As president of your local convention and visitors bureau, propose a joint marketing scheme that would have surefire results.
25. As a resort hotel manager, would you *always* advertise your destination area along with your individual resort property? Explain why or why not.

Case Problem

A Midwest lakeshore community is economically depressed. By 1989 industrial employment had fallen to 50 percent of its 1970 level. Tourism seems to be a logical industry to expand. The county has 25 miles of beautiful Lake Michigan sandy beaches and is adjacent to a 1.5 million-acre national forest. The forest has many fine rivers and inland lakes, offering bountiful year-round recreation. This area is only about a five hours' drive from Chicago or Detroit and has thrice-daily air service from Chicago.

The chamber of commerce has virtually no budget for tourism promotion. State law authorizes an added 2 percent local tourism promotion tax to the 4 percent state rooms tax. However, enacting the added tax must be approved by local lodging establishments. Vote is apportioned by number of rooms owned. Managers of the two larger motels are in favor of the tax, but they suspect that the smaller motel owners will not collect all or part of the tax, lowering their room rates proportionally and creating a price advantage over the honest larger motels. Added tourism is greatly needed to stimulate the local economy. How can this impasse be resolved?

Selected References

Abbey, James R. *Hospitality Sales and Advertising,* 2nd edition. East Lansing, Mich.: Educational Institute of the American Hotel and Motel Association, 1993.

Ananth, Mangala, et. al. "Marketplace Lodging Needs of Mature Travelers." *Cornell Hotel and Restaurant Administration Quarterly,* Vol. 33, No. 4 (August 1992), pp. 12–24.

Barsky, Jonathan D., and Richard Labagh. "A Strategy for Customer Satisfaction." *Cornell Hotel and Restaurant Administration Quarterly,* Vol. 33, No. 5 (October 1992), pp. 32–40.

Burke, James F. "Computerized Management of Tourism Marketing Information." *Tourism Management,* Vol. 7, No. 4 (December 1986), pp. 279–289.

Burke, James E., and Barry P. Resnick. *Marketing and Selling the Travel Product.* Cincinnati, Ohio: South-Western Publishing Company, 1991.

Chon, Kye-Sung, and William P. Whelihan III. "Changing Guest Preferences and Marketing Challenges in the Resort Industry." *FIU Hospitality Review,* Vol. 10, No. 2 (Fall 1992) pp. 9–16.

Crompton, John L., and Charles W. Lamb. *Marketing Government and Social Services.* New York: Wiley, 1986.

Davidoff, Philip G., and Doris S. Davidoff. *Sales and Marketing for Travel and Tourism.* Englewood Cliffs, N.J.: Prentice Hall, 1994.

Dev, Chekitan S. "Marketing Practices of Hotel Chains." *Cornell Hotel and Restaurant Administration Quarterly,* Vol. 31, No. 3 (November 1990), pp. 54–63.

Etzel, Michael, J., and Russell G. Wahlers. "The Use of Requested Promotional Material by Pleasure Travelers." *Journal of Travel Research,* Vol. 23, No. 4 (Spring 1985), pp. 2–6.

Faulkner, Bill, and Robin Shaw. *Evaluation of Tourism Marketing.* Canberra, Australia: Bureau of Tourism Research, no date.

Fick, Gavin R., and J. R. Brent Ritchie. "Measuring Service Quality in the Travel and Tourism Industry." *Journal of Travel Research,* Vol. 30, No. 2 (Fall 1991), pp. 2–9.

Fodness, Dale. "The Impact of Family Life Cycle on the Vacation Decision-Making Process." *Journal of Travel Research,* Vol. 31, No. 2 (Fall 1992), pp. 8–13.

Gartner, William, and John D. Hunt. "A Method to Collect Detailed Tourist Flow Information." *Annals of Tourism Research,* Vol. 15, No. 1 (1988), pp. 159–165.

Gartrell, Richard B. *Destination Marketing for Convention and Visitor Bureaus.* Dubuque, Iowa: Kendall/Hunt, 1988.

Goodrich, Jonathan N. "An American Study of Tourism Marketing: Impact of the Persian Gulf War." *Journal of Travel Research,* Vol. 30, No. 2 (Fall 1992), pp. 37–40.

Health, Ernie, and Geoffrey Wall. *Marketing Tourism Destinations: A Strategic Approach.* New York: Wiley, 1992.

Javalgi, Rajshekhar, Edward G. Thomas, and S. R. Rao. "Consumer Behavior in the U.S. Pleasure Travel Marketplace: An Analysis of Senior and Nonsenior Travelers." *Journal of Travel Research,* Vol. 31, No. 2 (Fall 1992), pp. 14–19.

Journal of Travel Research, Special Marketing Issue, Vol. 20, No. 4 (Spring 1982), 9 articles, Business Research Division, University of Colorado, Boulder, Colorado.

Laws, Eric. *Tourism Marketing: Service and Quality a Management Perspective.* Leckhampton, England: Stanley Thornes, 1991.

Lewis, Robert C. *Cases in Hospitality Marketing and Management.* New York: Wiley, 1989.

Lewis, Robert C., and Richard E. Chambers. *Marketing Leadership in Hospitality: Foundations and Practices.* New York: Van Nostrand Reinhold, 1989.

Lickorish, Leonard, and Alan Jefferson. *Marketing Tourism: A Practical Guide.* Harlow, Essex, England: Longman, 1991.

Mancini, Marc. *Selling Destinations: Geography for the Travel Professional.* Cincinnati, Ohio: South-Western Publishing Company, 1992.

McCarthy, E. Jerome. *Essentials of Marketing.* Homewood, Ill.: Richard D. Irwin, 1994.

McCleary, Ken W. "A Framework for National Tourism Marketing." *International Journal of Hospitality Management,* Vol. 6, No. 3 (1987), pp. 169–175.

Messmer, Donald J., and Robert R. Johnson. "Inquiry Conversion and Travel Advertising Effectiveness." *Journal of Travel Research,* Vol. 31, No. 4 (Spring 1993), pp. 14–21.

Metelka, Charles J. "Tourism Advertising: A Window to the World, a Reflection of Ourselves?" *Hospitality Education and Research Journal,* Vol. 11, No. 3 (1987), pp. 77–81.

Middleton, Victor T. C. *Marketing in Travel and Tourism.* Oxford, England: Heinemann, 1988.

Morrison, Alastair M. *Hospitality and Travel Marketing.* Albany, N.Y.: Delmar, 1989.

National Technical Information Service. *Psychographic Marketing.* Springfield, Va.: NTIS, 1989.

Plog, Stanley C. *Leisure Travel: Making It a Growth Market . . . Again!* New York: Wiley, 1991.

Ramzy, Ashraf. *How to Advertise Your Hotel for Success: The Marketing Guide to Hotel Advertising.* Orlando, Fla.: Townhouse Publishing, 1991.

Reid, Robert D. *Hospitality Marketing Management.* New York: Van Nostrand Reinhold, 1989.

Ryan, Chris. "Tourism and Marketing: A Symbiotic Relationship?" *Tourism Management,* Vol. 12, No. 2 (June 1991), pp. 101–111.

Shaw, Margaret. "Positioning and Price: Merging Theory, Strategy and Tactics." *Hospitality Research Journal,* Vol. 15, No. 2 (1992), pp. 21–30.

Stevens, Blair. "Price Value Perceptions of Travelers." *Journal of Travel Research,* Vol. 31, No. 2 (Fall 1992), pp. 44–48.

Stewart, Elizabeth, and Suzanne Cook. *The Mature Market.* Washington, D.C.: Travel Industry Association of America, 1990.

Sullivan, Jim, and Phil Roberts. *Service That Sells!* Denver, Colo.: Pencom, 1991.

Tunstall, Ruth. "Catering for the Female Business Traveler." *Travel and Tourism Analyst,* No. 5 (1989), pp. 26–40.

Waldrop, Judith, and Marcia Mogelonsky. *The Seasons of Business: A Marketer's Guide to Consumer Behavior.* Ithaca, N.Y.: American Demographic Books, 1992.

Woodside, Arch G. "Measuring Advertising Effectiveness in Destination Marketing Strategies." *Journal of Travel Research,* Vol. 29, No. 2 (Fall 1990), pp. 3–8.

TOURISM PROSPECTS

CHAPTER 19

Tourism's Future

LEARNING OBJECTIVES

- Examine forecasts concerning the growth of international tourism.
- Identify the major global forces that are shaping the tourism of to-morrow.
- Understand the impacts, both positive and negative, which these forces are likely to have on tourism markets and on the ability of destinations to respond to the demands of these markets.
- Highlight the powerful and positive impact that the environmental movement has had, and will increasingly have, on tourism development.
- Evaluate the contributions that international tourism can make toward world peace.

TOURISM IN THE THIRD MILLENNIUM

The purpose of this book has been to provide the student with a basic understanding of the principles, practices, and philosophies of tourism as they relate to the industry of today. To understand the present, it has, of course, been necessary to review the evolution and historical development of the field. Clearly, the tourism industry of today is the product of many forces that have shaped both its structure and the manner in which it functions. As has been pointed out on several occasions, the growth and development of tourism has been particularly rapid over the past half century. As noted by the World Tourism Organization:[1]

- Since 1950, when international travel started to become accessible to the general public, tourist activity has risen each year at an average rate of 7.2 percent, from 25 million to 476 million arrivals in 1992, and by 12.5 percent based on international tourism receipts (at current prices and excluding spending on international transport) from U.S.$2.1 billion to U.S.$279 billion.
- International tourism receipts grew faster than world trade in the 1980s and now constitute a higher proportion of the value of world exports than all sectors other than crude petroleum/petroleum products, and motor vehicles/parts/accessories.

The result is that tourism in the mid-1990s is a very large and dynamic sector of the economy. Because of the rapid growth and change of the past, one might be inclined to

[1]World Tourism Organization, *Global Tourism Forecasts to the Year 2000 and Beyond* (Madrid: WTO, 1993).

believe that tourism has now reached a mature phase of its development in which the rate of change and expansion will decrease.

On the other hand, a realistic assessment of the probable future suggests that tourism is likely to continue to grow and develop much more rapidly and more dynamically than many other sectors for many years to come. Although the impact of the global economic recession has slowed the rate of tourist expansion, this appears to be only temporary. In consequence, a marked differential in growth rate between the two halves of the decade seems probable. Overall, a growth rate of 3 to 3.5 percent is forecast for 1990–1995, and 4 to 5 percent for the second half of the 1990s. More specifically, international tourist arrivals are forecast to rise to 534 million in 1995 and to 661 million in 2000 (see Table 19.1). For the first decade of the twenty-first century, a growth rate close to 3.5 percent is anticipated, leading to a figure of 937 million arrivals by 2010. The level of international tourist arrivals will thus have doubled between 1990 and 2010.

With respect to regional market share, it is anticipated (see Table 19.2) that in overall terms, Europe and the Americas will lose market share (as a percentage of world international tourist arrivals). Although Europe will remain the leading destination region, it will lose market share to the other five regions—principally to East Asia and the Pacific. In addition, the Caribbean subregion of the Americas and the South Asia region also hold above-average prospects for attracting inbound tourism in the 1990s. The regions that will achieve the fastest growth in outbound tourism are the Central and South American subregions, and all parts of Asia, Africa, and the Middle East (see Table 19.3).

THE PROJECTED IMPACTS OF TOURISM

Based on such forecasts of growing domestic and international travel, the World Travel and Tourism Council (WTTC) has projected that by 1994, travel and tourism will generate $3.4 trillion in gross output, and that by the year 2005, this figure will reach $7.9 trillion. Similarly (as indicated in Figure 19.1), the WTTC estimates that in 1994, travel and tourism will:

Table 19.1   Forecasts of International Tourist Arrivals (millions) Worldwide and by Region, 1990–2010

Region	Base Year 1990	Forecasts 1995	2000	2010	Average Growth Rate p.a. (%) 1990–1995	1995–2000	1990–2000	2000–2010
Africa	15	19	24	36	4.5	5.5	5.0	4.0
Americas	94	114	147	207	4.1	5.0	4.6	3.5
East Asia/Pacific	52	70	101	190	6.1	7.5	6.8	6.5
Europe	284	317	372	476	2.2	3.2	2.7	2.5
Middle East	7	9	11	18	3.4	4.6	4.0	5.0
South Asia	3	4	6	10	5.1	7.15	6.1	6.0
World	456	534	661	937	3.2	4.4	3.8	3.55

Note: Totals may not add up due to rounding.
Source: WTO.

Table 19.2   Trends in Regional Market Share (1970–2010)
(Percent of World International Tourist Arrivals)

Region	1970	2010	Change (Percentage Points)
Europe	68.1	50.8	–17.3
Americas	25.3	22.1	–3.2
East Asia/Pacific	3.0	20.3	17.3
Africa	1.2	3.8	2.6
Middle East	1.2	1.9	0.7
South Asia	0.6	1.1	0.5

Source: WTO.

- Create employment for 204 million people, or one in every nine workers
- Produce 10.1 percent of world GDP
- Invest $693 billion in new facilities and equipment
- Contribute more than $654 million in tax revenue

Figure 19.1 further indicates how the impacts of travel and tourism are expected to grow by the year 2005.

THE NATURE OF FUTURE GROWTH

As we have seen, tourism is expected to continue to grow. However, the nature of this growth and development will in many ways be quite different from that of the previous

Table 19.3   Tourist Directional Flow Growth Prospects, by Origin/Destination Region,
1990–2000

Region Outbound	Region Inbound						
	Europe	Americas	East Asia/The Pacific	South Asia	Middle East	Africa	Overall
Europe	✈	✈✈✈	✈✈✈	✈✈✈	✈✈	✈✈	✈
Americas	✈	✈	✈✈	✈✈	✈✈	✈✈✈	✈✈
East Asia/The Pacific	✈✈	✈✈✈	✈✈✈	✈✈✈	✈✈	✈✈✈	✈✈✈
South Asia	✈✈	✈✈	✈✈✈	✈✈✈	✈✈✈	✈✈	✈✈✈
Middle East	✈	✈✈✈	✈✈✈	✈✈✈	✈✈✈	✈✈✈	✈✈
Africa	✈✈	✈✈	✈✈✈	✈✈✈	✈✈	✈✈✈	✈✈✈
Overall	✈	✈✈	✈✈✈	✈✈✈	✈✈	✈✈	✈✈

Key: ✈ below average   ✈✈ average   ✈✈✈ above average

Source: Based on WTO presentation at Seminar on *Tourism Trends to the Year 2000 and Beyond,* Seville, September 1992, and amended in the light of WTO analysis undertaken between October 1992 and July 1993.

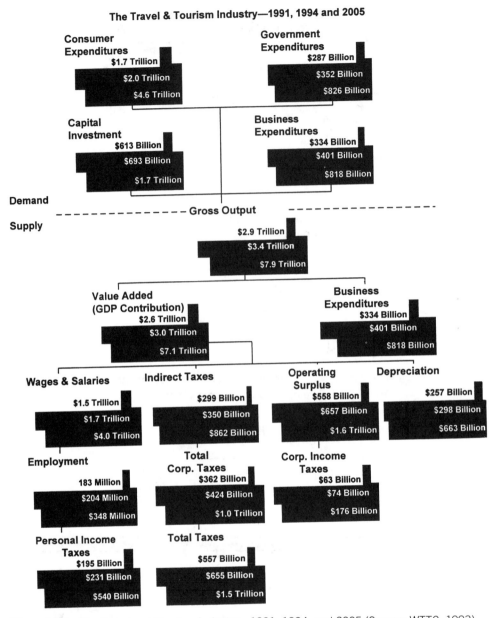

Figure 19.1   The Travel and Tourism Industry—1991, 1994, and 2005 (Source: WTTC, 1993)

five decades. As has become abundantly clear over the past several years, the period of the 1990s is proving itself to be dramatically different from that of the previous three decades. As a global community we are living through widespread changes whose scope and significance are barely perceptible at this point in time. Yet somehow, we know that what has come to be known as the "New World Order" of the post–cold war era is evolving in some very fundamental ways as we rush toward the magical year 2000 and the third millennium of Western history.

Some of the dimensions of this evolution are already recognizable, and indeed, some are even predictable. Others are but as yet stirrings of anxiety or discontent. These stirrings are possibly the most disconcerting for the mature adults of the so-called "developed" nations, whose well-being and prosperity has improved constantly over their lifetime. For perhaps the first time, the fundamental changes occurring around them threaten to leap out of control and to undermine the foundations of their secure and attractive lifestyles. Others, in less fortunate circumstances, see these same changes as possibly the only glimmer of hope for what they view as a more equitable distribution of all the opportunities that life has to offer. Ironically, they may see these same changes as irrevocably condemning themselves to a life of endless poverty.

LEISURE, TOURISM, AND SOCIETY IN THE THIRD MILLENNIUM

A significant component of the high-quality lifestyle that has characterized the last half of the twentieth century has been access to, and the use of increasing amounts of leisure time. Although the extent of this increase in leisure time has been questioned for decades,[2] there is little doubt that in aggregate terms, the populations of the developed Western nations have had greater and more broadly based access to recreation and travel opportunities than has any previous society. As a result, tourism has grown to the point where it can now claim to be the "world's largest industry."[3] While traditionally those in the tourism sector have lamented the lack of recognition received by the industry from both governments and the public, this situation is changing dramatically—in many cases, to the chagrin of the tourism establishment. Suddenly, tourism is being blamed for the destruction of cultures, degradation of the environment, and homogenization of lifestyles. In brief, because of its growing economic and social importance, tourism has suddenly found itself thrust into the mainstream of societal concerns—this at a time when all aspects of society are being questioned as to their value, their continued relevance, and perhaps above all, their sustainability over the long term.

It is against this background of global societal change that several leading organizations and individuals having a strong interest in the future of tourism have attempted to understand the important forces of change in the world and their likely implications for the future of tourism. A review and analysis of the conclusions of these efforts indicates that the tourism of tomorrow will face a number of constraints and limitations that cannot be ignored. These "new realities" will force tourism policymakers and the tourism industry to alter dramatically the way it both develops and operates. They will also require that tourists themselves alter their demands and their behaviors. These changes which are now imposing themselves are, however, by no means entirely negative. Many can be viewed as corrections to the bad judgments and excesses of the past. Others represent opportunities for innovative and exciting new products and

[2]Juliet B. Schor, *The Overworked American: The Unexpected Decline of Leisure* (New York: Basic Books, 1991).
[3]World Travel and Tourism Council, *Travel and Tourism: A New Economic Perspective* (Brussels: WTTC, 1993).

experiences. These "new horizons" in tourism may well prove more rewarding, and certainly more sustainable, than those of the past.

THE FUTURE SHAPE OF TOURISM

Three reviews of the future shape of tourism are those carried out by the World Tourism Organization,[4] by the firm Economic Research Associates,[5] and by the International Tourism Policy Forum (ITPF).[6] While there are a number of other valuable sources of information in this regard (see the Selected References at the end of this chapter), the WTO, ERA, and ITPF reports provide the most comprehensive and perhaps most insightful assessments of the forces that are affecting tourism and their probable implications for its future.

The WTO study involved a review and analysis of an extensive range and volume of existing research reports, papers, and articles produced by various authoritative institutions, tourism operators, and experts. In contrast, the ERA perspective reflects the collective experience of the members of a leading consulting firm in the field of tourism. Finally, the ITPF analysis used as its initial input the views of over 90 industry experts from 21 countries that were brought together for three days under the direction of the International Tourism Institute at the George Washington University. These experts were given the task of identifying those global forces which it was felt will most highly shape the entire spectrum of human activities in the coming years and to examine how these forces are likely to affect tourism in the 1990s and beyond.

WTO: Tourism to the Year 2000

The World Tourism Organization study was undertaken to provide an overview of the factors affecting the long-term development of tourism worldwide. The intent of the project was to provide policymakers in the travel and tourism sector with a series of probable scenarios contemplating future development patterns and alternative strategies to cope with them. A particular emphasis of the WTO strongly was to identify and understand the qualitative aspects or factors which combine to "shape" the way in which tourism will grow.

ERA: The New Tourism and Leisure Environment

A second approach to examining the future shape of tourism is the thinking of the firm Economics Research Associates (see Reading 19.1). The author of this paper, Clive Jones, examines a number of dimensions along which tourism and leisure behavior patterns appear to be changing. His analysis then proceeds to identify some of the specific shifts which he believes are likely to occur along each of these dimensions.

[4]World Tourism Organization, *Global Tourism Forecasts to the Year 2000 and Beyond* (Madrid: WTO, 1993).

[5]Clive B. Jones, *The New Tourism and Leisure Environment* (San Francisco: Economic Research Associates, 1993).

[6]J. R. Brent Ritchie, "Global Tourism Policy Issues: An Agenda for the 1990s," *World Travel and Tourism Review*, Vol. 1 (Wallingford, England: C.A.B. International, 1991).

ITPF: The Global Forces of Change

The International Tourism Policy Forum identified some 19 major forces that it felt should be the focus of leaders and decision makers in the field in the coming decade (Ritchie, 1991):

- The physical environment is taking 'center stage' in tourism development and management.
- There is a recognition that there are finite limitations to tourism development, in terms of both physical and social carrying capacity of destinations.
- Residents responsive tourism is the watchword for tomorrow: community demands for active participation in the setting of the tourism agenda and its priorities for tourism development and management cannot be ignored.
- Tourism must strive to develop as a socially responsible industry; more specifically, it must move proactively rather than simply responding to various pressures as they arise.
- Cultural diversity should be recognized within the context of a global society.
- Demographic shifts are occurring which will dramatically influence the level and nature of tourism.
- The human resource problem: there is a continuing and growing need to increase the supply of personnel and to enhance their professionalism.
- Patterns of tourism are being transformed by increasingly diverse lifestyles.
- The political shift to market-driven economies is bringing about a global restructuring in which market forces rather than ideology are used to guide decisions and develop policy.
- The trend to market economies and shrinking government budgets is creating strong pressures for privatization and deregulation of tourism facilities and services.
- Regional, political, and economic integration/cooperation will predominate.
- The growing demands of the high cost of capital for development of the tourism infrastructure and rising taxation/fees will maintain and increase financial pressures on the tourism industry.
- The rise in influence of the global transnational firm will accelerate.
- The widening gap between the north/south (developed/developing) nations continues to cause frictions and to be a constant source of concern for harmonious tourism development.
- Continued regional conflicts and terrorist activities are impediments to the development and prosperity of tourism.
- Health and security concerns could become a major deterrent to tourism travel.
- Technological advances are giving rise to both opportunities and pressures for improved productivity, human resource development, and restructuring of the tourism industry.
- Despite recent progress, recognition by governments of the tourism industry and its importance to social and economic development and well-being of regions is still far from satisfactory: one part of the reason is a lack of credibility of tourism data.
- Growing dissatisfaction with governing systems and processes may lead to a new framework (paradigm) for tourism.

There is little doubt that these forces and the associated policy issues do represent very significant and very powerful pressures that will reshape the tourism of tomorrow.

However, two important questions that beg to be asked when reviewing such conclusions are (1) whether or not the forces represent strong but merely temporary winds of change or whether they represent a more fundamental, more powerful metamorphosis of our society which is likely to harden with time, and (2) whether or not the list, which has been generated in a tourism context, has truly identified all the societal forces that are likely to alter the shape of tourism, even if in a more indirect manner.

With respect to the first question, a reexamination of the 19 forces leads one to conclude that they do in fact reflect some very real and very fundamental forces for lasting societal change. Such a reexamination also reveals the possibility of reducing this set of forces to a more limited set of major themes. Seven such themes are proposed:

ENVIRONMENTALISM   As noted by the Tourism Policy Forum, concern for the environment has now taken "center stage" in tourism. This tourism reality is, however, a reflection of a much broader societal realization that it is now time that the world's population—all of it—must now get serious about the health of our planet. At this stage, it is abundantly clear that spaceship earth has a limited capacity to sustain life as we know it.

As the Tourism Policy Forum noted explicitly: "Development must, in the future, be compatible with the environment." The Forum also pointed out, however," . . . that tourism is among the better alternatives for land use." While such compatibility is laudable, it must also be stressed that there are other areas where compatibility between tourism and the environment is perhaps not so obvious. It was noted by the Forum that the use of fossil fuels for transportation and their polluting effect cannot be denied.[7] As a consequence, the sustainability of tourism in the long term is in doubt unless alternative nonpolluting energy sources become available.

THE SPREAD OF DEMOCRACY   Historians will long debate exactly why the period 1989–1991 was the specific point in time that saw such a dramatic spread of the democratic movement. The record will show that very few individuals (experts or ordinary people) foresaw the very rapid transformations of the political systems that occurred in Eastern and Central Europe during this period. Of course, all is not as simple as it seems. Many other forces were at work which allowed this rather focused eruption of democracy to occur. Indeed, as will be argued later, this very visible political shift was only symptomatic of a much more fundamental and underlying desire by people all over the world to participate more directly in the governing processes that affect their lives. From a tourism perspective, these forces have led to the very powerful concept of *resident responsive tourism.* No longer can it be assumed that the residents of a tourism destination/region will automatically accept all (or any) forms of tourism development that the industry proposes or attempts to impose. Tourism development in the third millennium will actively have to seek the support of the communities it affects most directly. To do this, those responsible for tourism will have to seek to involve destination region residents on an ongoing basis in the assessments of the costs and benefits associated with all forms of proposed (and even existing) facilities and activities. Unless a consensus is reached that the net benefits to the community are positive, it is questionable that tourism development in the year 2000 will have the support necessary to proceed.

[7]Ibid.

DEMOGRAPHIC SHIFTS   Although very little in the social sciences is truly predictable, there is one notable exception—the demographics of the world's present population. In this regard, the forces of change that will drive and shape the face of the next generation are already evident. The populations of the developed Western world are aging and will decline in relative size. At the same time, the populations of the developing world continue to explode. While, in the short term, such changes may present opportunities for the tourism industry, they also raise some very fundamental long-term questions. These questions concern not only the distribution of the income and wealth on which travel depends, but also upon the geographic distribution of the world's population.

THE ECONOMIC IMPERATIVE   While history may very well prove us wrong in the longer term, the foreseeable future indicates that economic forces will continue to triumph over ideologies. Over the past decade, throughout the world, we have seen the emergence of what appear to be overpowering pressures to adopt the model of the market economy. As part of this model, we have seen movements to deregulation, to privatization, to regional economic integration, and to a greater role for the transnational corporation. Whether or not these movements represent winds of change or a lasting restructuring of our economic system remains to be seen. However, for the moment, the direction of the tide is unquestionable.

DIVERSITY WITHIN A HOMOGENEOUS WORLD   One of the more insightful observations of the Tourism Policy Forum was that despite the trend to "sameness" around the world, there are strong counterpressures to maintain individual and cultural distinctiveness. A visit to any major city in the world demonstrates how information, economic pressures, and the tendency to imitate has left the world "less different" than it was a century, even decades, ago. It seems, however, that the human entity, while recognizing the pragmatic value of sameness, is determined at the same time to make every effort to preserve and enhance his or her unique identity. Whether or not the culture that spawned the Bolshoi Ballet is threatened by the arrival of McDonald's restaurants remains to be seen. However, if the determination of those who are facing this issue is any indication, the existence of cultural diversity within a global society is a reality whose time has come.

THE TECHNOLOGY–HUMAN RESOURCE DILEMMA   While tourism has traditionally been characterized as a "people industry," it is now coming face to face with the realities of the massive advances in technology that have occurred over the past several decades. During this period, industries which are less dependent on the human interactions that characterize the tourism sector have adapted laborsaving technology with a vengeance. As a consequence, these industries have been able to improve wage levels and enhance career opportunities for employees while keeping costs under control.

On the other hand, the travel industry (or should we call it the "hospitality industry" in this context?) has generally preferred to keep wages low, thus avoiding the need for technological innovation, particularly in the actual delivery of its services. Although technology has been used extensively in a supporting role to enhance performance and effectiveness (e.g., computer reservation system, air control technology), there has been a great reluctance to replace human service providers with technologically driven alternatives (such as the banks did when replacing human tellers with automatic teller

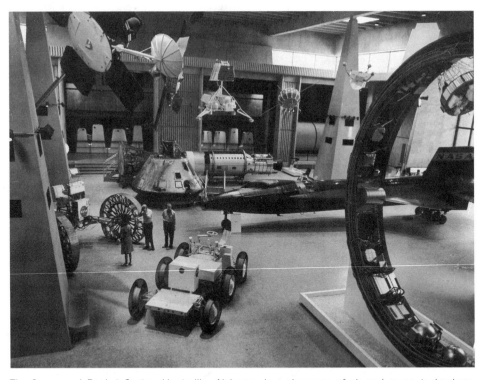

The Space and Rocket Center, Huntsville, Alabama, is a showcase of air and space technology, supersonic transportation, space travel, and possible interplanetary travel. (Photo courtesy of the Alabama Bureau of Tourism and Travel)

machines). Similarly, aside from fast-food restaurants, there has been relatively little focused effort to undertake a major rethinking or redesign of travel-related facilities and support systems so as to substantially reduce personnel requirements or to enhance the productivity of employees. While some "tinkering" has occurred in selected areas and sectors, we have not yet seen the benefits from technology that are possible. Until technology is adapted more widely, it will be difficult for the travel industry to make new travel experiences available to a mass audience and to do so at prices that are affordable by much of the population.

On the other side of the coin—and this is the dilemma—the introduction of technology is viewed as a "job killer." Indeed, the conclusion of the Policy Forum was that both skilled and not-so-skilled personnel in the labor force could be replaced by various forms of technology. While some argue that the increased use of capital and technology will require highly skilled labor, others argue that technology (particularly computer technology) may, in fact, increase the demand for a less skilled labor force.

ADDRESSING THE "NORTH-SOUTH GAP"   Despite the recognition that economic and social disparities are a destabilizing influence on global affairs, and despite efforts to reduce such disparities, the problem grows worse instead of better. As the summary report of the Tourism Policy Forum stated: "While . . . this issue needs to be addressed on a very broad scale by all sectors of the economy, tourism must also do its part. In this regard . . . there is a growing demand for specialized tourism research facilities particularly focused on developing countries . . . a need for . . . greater assistance to third world tourism enterprises. In particular, they must be given the benefits of appropriate technology and human resource development programs to enhance their international competitiveness. In addition, they must be supported by policies that minimize the leakage from tourism development so as to ensure a fair and equitable return from tourism development to the host nations." Little else needs to be said.

Other Forces of Change

In addition to the foregoing, there are several other less evident yet equally powerful forces at work which will less directly but no less significantly shape the global society of tomorrow. Some are logical consequences of the forces described above, while others are much less obvious. Some are already evident and their impact fairly predictable; others are only emerging. As such, their potential for change, and the nature of the changes they may bring about, are still very uncertain.

SHIFTING VALUE SYSTEMS   Consistent with the increasing concern for the environment (which runs somewhat counter to the movement to a market economy model) is the emergence of what appears to be a shift in the value system which drives human behavior. Although difficult to characterize, it would seem to reflect a certain rejection of hedonism and materialism and a return to simpler human values. In certain societies, this shift contains strong elements of religious fundamentalism. In others, it reflects a tendency to turn inward to family and friends—in more popular terminology, a "cocooning" behavior.[8] One must take care not to imply that the human race is suddenly and dramatically about to change the way it lives from day to day. However, there would seem to be some discomfort—a certain malaise—concerning the pace of life and the level of consumption of resources necessary to feed that pace of life. Taken to the extreme, this malaise and the accompanying shift of values could position tourism as "socially undesirable," due to its heavy use of nonrenewable resources. This view of tourism could lead to a widespread movement to limit all "nonessential" travel. While the parallel is by no means perfect, the similarity with the impact that the animal protection movement has had on the sale and consumption of fur products should not be ignored.

THE QUEST FOR STABILITY AND SECURITY   Although it should perhaps be obvious, the cocooning phenomenon referred to above is but one example of the efforts of many members of Western society to deny or escape from what has suddenly become a somewhat frightening world. After literally decades of economic growth and relative stability, many highly successful and valued persons are suddenly facing the prospect of decreasing economic well-being—and in many cases, even unemployment. This was not how it was suppose to turn out. In response to this threat, we have seen a strong reluctance to spend, even by those who have the resources. Although the resulting increase in saving rates may provide the investments necessary for modernization and long-term economic growth, the more immediate impacts on leisure and tourism spending are already being felt.

In the area of physical (as opposed to economic) security, we have known for some time that risk of physical danger is certain to diminish the prospects of a given tourism destination or travel-related firm. War in the Middle East has affected tourism both

[8]Faith Popcorn, *The Popcorn Report* (New York: Doubleday, 1991).

locally and worldwide. Terrorism aimed at U.S. air carriers has diverted traffic to competitors. Concern for health is of increasing importance, particularly for older travelers. In a different, yet related vein, the growing threat of AIDS has added yet another dimension of concern—only this time for younger segments of the population. Without exaggeration, the wise tourist visiting certain regions of the world now seeks a traveling companion having a compatible blood type in case a blood transfusion is required. Such concern and attention to detail with respect to health care while traveling should not be dismissed as an aberration of the few.

EMERGENCE OF THE KNOWLEDGE-BASED SOCIETY   Certain of the developed nations have already entered the era where one of their greatest competitive advantages is the information or knowledge they possess rather than their ownership of natural resources or their access to cheap labor. Assuming that such a trend continues and expands to other countries, it behooves the tourism industry to examine how the travel behavior of people in a knowledge-based society might differ from that of people in a manufacturing or more traditional service-based setting.

If the world's leading economies are any indication of trends in this regard, we can expect travelers from knowledge-based economies to be more experienced, more discerning, and more demanding. In particular, we can expect that they will be seeking more individualized experiences, often characterized as *special-interest travel.* Such travelers " . . . are more interested in enriching their lives with experience rather than hands-off entertainment. They seek interactive, highly involved, quality travel experiences, focusing on in-depth coverage of the special interest topic or destination at hand."[9]

Pushing the limits even further, certain individuals and groups are now espousing the potential of *virtual reality* as a replacement for travel.[10] This technology represents perhaps the outer limits of the knowledge-based industries in that it purports to provide simulated experiences which conceptually are equivalent to the real thing. By merely strapping on the necessary technology, it is asserted that some day (supposedly not too far away), people will be able to "experience" a destination without actually visiting it. While it is easy for the traveler of today to dismiss such an idea as sheer fantasy, it does seem logical that such an approach would (if truly feasible) find ready acceptance among members of a knowledge-based society. It goes without saying that (if successful), "virtual reality tourism" would have profound impacts on the travel industry as we know it.

A DECLINE IN THE MEGANATION—THE RISE OF THE CITY-STATE   Participants in the International Tourism Policy Forum very appropriately noted the increasing importance of regional trading blocs. The new "borderless Europe" is almost a reality. The North American Free Trade Agreement has created another bloc. In response to these two initiatives, the Asian nations are starting to reflect on the need for an equivalent arrangement.

Although it is too early yet to reach firm conclusions regarding the changes that free movement of labor will bring to the social fabric of Europe, it does seem reasonable

---

[9]Robert J. Forbes and Maree S. Forbes, "Special Interest Travel," *World Travel and Tourism Review,* Vol. 2 (Wallingford, England: C.A.B. International, 1992).
[10]Travel and Tourism Research Association, "Examining the Dynamics of New Partnerships, Strategies and Products," *Newsletter,* (Wheat Ridge, Colo.: TTRA, 1992).

to anticipate that the importance of each existing nation state will decline. Indeed, one of the major goals of European integration is to arrive at common standards, a common currency, and a more common political system. At first glance, one might argue that the creation of the new Europe will result in another meganation. In strictly pragmatic terms, this may be the case. Certainly, the effective elimination of borders will greatly facilitate travel flows. At the same time, it will, over time, greatly reduce national distinctiveness and thus the appeal of a particular country as a unique travel destination.

Although speculative at this point, there is some evidence that as a reaction to the decline of national identities, there will be a reactive rise in the importance of major metropolitan centers—or *city-states*. These city-states, it is argued, may become the focal point for both economic development and for individual identity. Of direct relevance to tourism is the possibility that the new city-states may also become the primary basis for destination development and promotion.

PRESSURES FOR MASS MIGRATION   As fading borders increasingly facilitate population movements within trading blocs, there will be those who will first request, and then demand, the right for such freedom of movement to be extended. The day is not far off when freedom of movement of all peoples of the world may be termed a "basic human right." Although this certainly does not mean that this right will be granted, it will undoubtedly be asserted. Indeed, such demands are already emanating from such groups as the Vietnamese and Haitian "boat people" and mass refugee movements throughout Asia. Clearly, the implications of this still weak but emerging pressure go far beyond the concerns of those in the leisure and tourism field. This said, however, it is very clear that should such pressures succeed in even a modest way, the entire landscape of leisure and tourism planning and development will change dramatically.

New Realities, New Horizons

It is an interesting exercise to identify the global forces that are likely to affect societal behavior and well-being in the coming millennium, but the exercise does not serve much purpose unless it can provide some insight into the possible implications of these forces. As indicated at the beginning, an important goal of this essay is to assist in providing these insights. Toward this end, Table 19.4 attempts to provide an assessment of some of the most significant realities that must be addressed by the tourism sector in relation to each of the global forces discussed above. The table seeks, as well, to identify some important initial insights into the realities that must be faced by the tourism sector as we proceed toward the year 2000 and beyond. Finally, they furnish some ideas concerning the opportunities that are likely to emerge as evolving global forces shape the nature of leisure and tourism in the third millennium.

TOURISM AND PEACE

Although the foregoing discussion paints a fairly optimistic future for tourism, we must constantly keep in mind that tourism can prosper only in a peaceful environment. As pointed out in Chapter 11, fear (concern for safety) is a powerful deterrent to travel. To ensure the continued growth of the industry, travelers need to be confident that they

Table 19.4   Tourism in the Third Millennium: New Realities and New Horizons Resulting from Emerging Global Forces

New Horizons	New Realities
Environment on Center Stage	
◆ Virtually all future tourism development will be constrained by the need for environmental sensitivity.	◆ Conservation, preservation, and restoration present new themes for the design of tourism experiences. Regions that are presently undeveloped or in a natural state have a unique opportunity to provide an attractive experience to visitors.
◆ The noneconomic costs of tourism will need to be factored into development decisions. The costs of development, using nontraditional accounting frameworks, will increase, thus forcing higher prices on the travel experience.	◆ Emphasis on the quality of the tourism experience will reduce growth in the number of travelers but enhance net financial and nonfinancial impacts on tourism destinations.
The Spread of Democracy	
◆ The tourism planning and development process will be increasingly constrained and slowed by the need for meaningful public involvement and input.	◆ Implementation of approved development plans will be easier as "surprises" will be minimized and as broader agreement results from public involvement.
◆ It will be more difficult for individual operators to proceed with nonconforming developments— sometimes at the risk of inhibiting innovation.	◆ The formulation of "resident responsive visions" of local/regional tourism will provide more commitment to tourism and greater coherency in the tourism product/experience provided by a destination.
Demographic Shifts	
◆ The aging of travelers from traditional tourism-generating countries will cause demands for new experiences and new facilities. As a consequence, existing tourism plant may become economically obsolete.	◆ For the next 20 years, residents of developed nations in the 45–65 age category will increase substantially. These individuals will have the time, the discretionary income, and the desire to travel.
◆ Increasingly diverse lifestyles will make market segmentation increasingly important. However, the tailoring of "designer vacations" will make it harder to standardize the tourism product, and thus to control costs.	◆ Firms that can read, anticipate, and respond to the specific needs/desires of high quality niche or "special interest" markets in innovative ways will have great opportunities for success.
Shifts to The Market Economy	
◆ Many high-quality public facilities and attractions which have traditionally been supported and/or subsidized by governments will come under serious funding pressures.	◆ Market competition will prove a powerful force in keeping the costs of travel under control, thus keep tourism accessible to a large percentage of the population.
◆ It will become more difficult to justify and to publicly finance large-scale "megaprojects" or "megamonuments," some of which have become major, symbolic tourism attractions. As well, supporting infrastructure, such as roads and airports, will be more difficult to finance.	◆ There will be new opportunities for innovative financing approaches for megaprojects and megadevelopments that enjoy the support of the residents of a destination (e.g., community bonds).
Cultural Diversity in a Homogeneous World	
◆ The power and success of global brand names and franchises will increasingly put pressure on small, independent travel and tourism operators.	◆ Traditional cultural events and activities that no longer are economically feasible may be preserved through tourism.
◆ The integrity of truly unique and interesting cultural events and attractions will be threatened as they attempt to respond to visitor demands reaccess and frequency.	◆ Increasing acceptance of the value of other cultures will greater broaden the range of facilities, events, and attractions which are of potential interest to tourists.
The Technology–Human Resource Dilemma	
◆ The human resource base of the tourism industry is ill-equipped and thus ill-disposed toward the widespread adoption of technology. At least passive resistance can be expected at all levels.	◆ Because of the present low level of penetration of technology on tourism, there is much potential for significant gains on performance and productivity both in terms of facility design and service delivery.

Table 19.4 Continued

New Horizons	New Realities
♦ Introducing technology without losing the warmth of the human experience will be difficult. Choosing the appropriate balance of high-tech/high-touch will require insight and good judgment.	♦ Education and training levels will have to increase if managers and staff are to select and implement technology-based improvements in an effective manner (EIESP, 1991).

Addressing the "North–South Gap"

♦ The tourism infrastructure in developing countries (in both quantitative and qualitative terms) is in many cases totally inadequate at the present time.	♦ Many developing countries have extremely rich cultures and histories which have not been experienced by many segments of the traditional tourism markets.
♦ The disparity in the wealth and well-being that exists between developing world residents and developed-world tourists frequently creates unhealthy tensions between hosts and guests as well as distortions of local lifestyles.	♦ The relatively low level of visitation to many developing countries provides an alternative to take the pressure off heavily visited sites in traditional tourism destinations.

Shifting Value Systems

♦ Leisure/vacation travel could be viewed as frivolous, wasteful, and harmful in a world where economies are stagnant, renewable resources are declining, and toxic emissions threaten the health of the planet.	♦ An increased emphasis on special interest tourism—such as cultural, educational, and professional development travel—may greatly strengthen and enrich the meaning of the travel experience.
♦ The developing mood to "look inward" may lead to greater economic protectionism (at the macro level) and more home/family oriented uses of leisure time (at the micro level). Both would reduce the demand for travel.	♦ An increased emphasis on "human relationships" may encourage new forms of tourism in which contact between hosts and guests is less superficial, leading to more intensive and enduring relationships.

Quest for Stability and Security

♦ Increasing levels of crime in tourist destinations is a major deterrent to both leisure and conference travel.	♦ Organized travel and/or receptive visitor services that shelter and protect the traveler from crime will be welcomed; destinations that eliminate or control crime will be preferred.
♦ Aging populations, underfunded medical systems, and the growth of AIDS have heightened concerns about the cost, availability, and safety of health care services when traveling.	♦ Firms that offer specialized products and services that protect the health of the traveler and/or facilitate access to reliable and reassuring medical services while in foreign environments will have a strong competitive edge.

The Knowledge-Based Society

♦ Modem technology is increasingly attempting to provide alternatives to physical travel. Teleconferencing is finally gaining wider acceptance; virtual interface technology purports to provide the travel experience without travel.	♦ Travelers will increasingly want to truly experience and understand a destination. As a result, they will be interested in spending more time in a region and interfacing with residents in more meaningful ways.
♦ Knowledge-based employees tend to work in sanitized, controlled environments. As such, they may shun travel experiences which are physically challenging, moderately uncomfortable, or culturally threatening.	♦ Travelers of the future will be increasingly receptive to technologies and services which facilitate travel while reducing costs and minimizing the need for menial and/or demeaning labor.

Rise of the City State

♦ Large countries will find it less desirable and less productive to undertake general awareness-type promotion; budgets for such promotions will decline.	♦ Those highly focused destinations that have high visibility, good access, an attractive product, and which can develop a distinctive image will dominate the market.
♦ Smaller destinations having no particularly unique characteristics will find it even more difficult to compete with higher-profile centers.	♦ Strategic alliances and reciprocal agreements between city-states that complement one another will grow in importance.

Table 19.4 Continued

New Horizons	New Realities
Pressures for Population Migration	
◆ Nations/economic communities may become much more demanding in terms of visitor entry requirements as they perceive that "tourists" risk transforming themselves into refugees or defacto immigrants.	◆ Diverse, multicultural societies brought about through immigration will create increased demand for travel as people exchange visits with families and friends.
◆ Destination residents may become increasingly less tolerant of "visibly" or "linguistically" different visitors whom they see as posing a threat as a potential immigrant.	◆ Ethnic groups in tourism generating countries will have the opportunity to develop, educational/ cultural travel experiences for their compatriots. Such experiences could involve both pretravel and travel experiences.

can move about in safety. In this section we explore some contributions that tourism can make to peace and the vital relationship between peace and tourism.

Tourism: A Vital Force for Peace

In October 1988, the first global conference on the theme "Tourism: A Vital Force for Peace" was held in Vancouver, B.C., Canada. Some 500 delegates from 65 countries

The International Peace Garden spans the border along the longest unfortified boundary in the world. It is a symbol of peace between Canada and the United States. (Photo courtesy of North Dakota Tourism Promotion)

attended. The purpose of the conference was to explore ways in which the world's hundreds of millions of international travelers could, by increasing interests, improving attitudes, and engaging in various social and other activities, contribute to better mutual understanding and appreciation—an important contribution toward world peace.

The conference provided a forum to examine tourism and its many dimensions as a force for peace. It brought recognition that tourism has the potential to be the largest peacetime movement in the history of humankind because tourism involves people: their culture, economy, traditions, heritage, and religion. Tourism provides the contacts that make understanding possible among peoples and cultures. The conference clearly demonstrated that tourism has the potential to make the world a better place in which to live.

One of the outcomes of the conference was distribution of the following:

CREDO OF THE PEACEFUL TRAVELER

Grateful for the opportunity to travel and to experience the world, and because peace begins with the individual, I affirm my personal responsibility and commitment to:

- Journey with an open mind and gentle heart
- Accept with grace and gratitude the diversity I encounter
- Revere and protect the natural environment which sustains all life
- Appreciate all cultures I discover
- Respect and thank my hosts for their welcome
- Offer my hand in friendship to everyone I meet
- Support travel services that share these views and act upon them and, by my spirit, words and actions,
- Encourage others to travel the world in peace.

A Philosophy of Tourism and Peace

Great leaders in many fields have extolled the social benefits to humanity that result from travel. Travel is one of the noblest human occupations. The famous Greek statesman, Solon, in 550 B.C. recommended that we travel "in order to see." To see is to increase understanding and appreciation of other peoples, other cultures, and other lands. Jason, leader of the Argonauts—those incessant sailors in Greek mythology who were searching for the Golden Fleece—said, "The essential thing is not to live, the essential thing is to navigate."

Marco Polo became a prince of merchants, papal envoy, governor of a Chinese city, favorite of Kublai Khan, master of exotic languages, war correspondent, and the first travel writer. His book describing his adventures, written in A.D. 1296, established the first bond between East and West. Polo was wonderstruck at splendors that he saw and of which he heard. During the Renaissance, his book was the chief and almost the sole Western source of information on the East.

This brief dip into history and mythology has but one purpose—to emphasize that travel—and often written accounts of it in later years have done more to create bonds and mutual understanding between various peoples of the world than any other single force throughout civilization's long existence.

There's no better way in which to gain a panoramic view of civilization than making a trip around the world. Being a guest for dinner is probably the best way to sense the

Meeting people from other parts of the world can be one of the most rewarding aspects of travel. (Photo courtesy of the Boeing Company)

unity that exists among peoples throughout the world. Here, people joined by blood or friendly spirit gather to break bread under the same roof. A few examples might include a dinner with a Japanese family, marveling at the swift movement of chopsticks gracefully picking rice from small snow-white porcelain bowls. Or a meal with Thais in the floating markets of Bangkok where sampans loaded with pyramids of tropical fruits, vegetables, and fish ply the klongs in search of buyers. With Arabs in Tunisia, it may be having a delicious lunch in the shade of a tent out on the Sahara desert—in a landscape of stark, wild beauty, enriched by the lively warm hospitality of these friendly people.

Whatever happens in any home—be it

- a modest wooden house furnished with straw mats and rice paper windows in Kyoto
- a solemn British mansion on Victoria Hill
- a mud hut on the banks of the Nile

One of the best ways to meet people in other lands is to sign up for a "people-to-people" program. (Photo courtesy of the Boeing Company)

- a Cape Cod bungalow
- a Rio de Janeiro apartment

being born, living, eating, drinking, resting, and dying are the same the world over. These similarities reflect the basic unity of people. This unity is really well understood by people but, alas, too often forgotten by nations and their rulers and leaders.

There are many ways in which a traveling family can meet and become acquainted with families in other lands. One of the best known of these plans is the "people-to-people" program. Arrangements can be made by a travel agent through a local contractor, say, in Copenhagen, to provide a program of social contacts and other activities to enrich the visitor's acquaintanceship and understanding of the Danish people. Arrangements can be made to stay in a private home or to attend a seminar or similar program. Such opportunities can be and are operating in hundreds of places, in many parts of the world. A greater awareness of such possibilities and more widespread use of this type of program would increase understanding, friendship, and appreciation of other people.

A tourist standing on the balcony of a $100 to $200 per-day hotel room looking at the passersby below obtains little real knowledge of the people in the country being visited. However, if opportunities are readily available for social contacts with locals of that country, increased understanding and appreciation for the people of that area will take place.

Can tourism contribute to peace? If understanding and increased appreciation for other people's way of life, mores, culture, and language make us more a part of a world community, then the answer must be "yes." This is especially so if at least casual acquaintance can be made with residents of the host country. Tourism provides a vehicle whereby people from one area become acquainted with people of another. Efforts to build that acquaintance will contribute to understanding. And understanding is at least the first step in creating and maintaining friendly national relationships.

Countries whose leaders understand and encourage tourism (at least in-tourism) are making an effort to improve the personal relationship between their citizens and those of other countries. Although economic considerations may be uppermost, the importance of social contacts is also recognized.

Tourism flourishes in a climate of peace and prosperity. Political unrest, wars, depressions, recessions, and civil strife discourage tourism.

Tourism, if properly planned, organized, and managed can bring understanding, appreciation, prosperity, and a better life to all who are involved. Let it grow and its positive effects increase. Tourism, if not a passport to peace, is at least a worthy effort toward building peace. Wherever and whenever visitor and host meet and greet each other with mutual appreciation, respect, and friendship, a movement toward peace has been made.

The Holiday Inn *Passport*, which lists and describes worldwide properties associated with this company, contains this statement:

> In today's shrinking world, neighbors are across the ocean, down the continent, and in every corner of the world. Time is different. So is dress, language, even food. But for all to live as neighbors, mankind must understand each other.
>
> Understanding is impossible without communication. That which is unknown often seems forbidding, even wrong. People must learn other ways of life besides their own.
>
> Only travel and communication closes this gap of knowledge. By world tourism it is possible to discover distant neighbors, how they live and think as human beings.
>
> World tourism and understanding go hand in hand. For travel is the way to knowledge. So let everyone do his part, traveling about the earth, keeping his mind and heart open. And the world will become a better place for all.

FINAL THOUGHTS

The world is a great book, of which they who never stir from home read only a page.

St. Augustine of Hippo (A.D. 354–430)
Christian theologian and philosopher

Of journeying the benefits are many: the freshness it brings to the heart, the seeing and hearing of marvelous things, the delight of beholding new cities, the meeting of unknown friends, the learning of high manners.

Saadi (A.D. 1184–1291)
Persian poet

Voyage, travel, and change of place impart new vigor to the mind.

Lucius Annaeus Seneca (4 B.C.–A.D. 65)
Roman statesman and philosopher

SUMMARY

Social and economic trends in developed countries seem to favor long-term growth in both domestic and international travel demand. More long-term leisure, increased disposable income, higher levels of education, and more awareness of other countries and peoples are significant factors influencing a growing market for travel.

Technological trends are also favorable. Transportation equipment is now more efficient and more comfortable; hotel and motel accommodations have become more complete, attractive, convenient, and comfortable; and new developments have given much more attention to environmental considerations.

Tourism is believed to have a positive effect on world peace. As people travel from place to place with a sincere desire to learn more about their global neighbors, knowledge and understanding grow. Then at least a start has been made in improving world communication, which seems so important in building bridges of mutual appreciation, respect, and friendship.

We trust that you are now ready to contribute your part toward making this world a bit more prosperous and peaceful through tourism.

About the Readings

The first reading takes yet another look at how major shifts in the leisure and tourism environment will change not only tourist behavior and travel patterns, but indeed the very nature of tourism itself. The implications for the way we travel and the way in which the industry must adapt both its products and its marketing efforts are profound.

Along with its obvious international economic pact, tourism transcends governmental boundaries by bringing peoples of the world closer together through the understanding of different cultures, environments, and heritage. It is potentially one of the most important vehicles for promoting understanding, trust, and goodwill among peoples of the world. The second reading explores these opportunities to achieving peace through tourism.

READING 19.1

The New Tourism and Leisure Environment

BY CLIVE B. JONES, Senior Vice President
Economics Research Associates (ERA)

The tourism and recreation industry is increasingly recognized as an important economic, environmental and social force which can bring both benefit and adversity. The financial community (and governments) also know that the industry has had spectacular successes and colossal failures. We have found that a key element of successful development is the ability to recognize and deal with change across a wide range of behavioral and technological factors and the way they interact. In ERA, we annually discuss the fundamental changes in our industry. For the Nineties, we see major shifts in the leisure and tourism environment reflecting changing consumer values, political forces, and the explosive growth of information technology. No aspect of the industry will remain untouched.

Means Turning Away From	And Turning Towards
Old Travel Patterns ———→	*New Travel Patterns*
• East–West flows	• North–South flows
• Atlantic dominance	• Asia-Pacific dominance
• Long trips	• Short breaks
• Travel barriers	• Free trade

New travel patterns reflect changes in consumer behavior, economic strength of source markets, new destinations, and political realignments. Shifts to North–South flow are occurring in Asia (towards Australia and Pacific Islands), in North America (towards Mexico, Central and South America) and in Europe (towards North and South Africa). Along with the growth in North–South travel is the shift in travel to within the Asia-Pacific region. This region represented 25% of worldwide air travel in 1985 and is forecast to represent 40% by 2000.

The shift from long trips to short breaks will increase the demands for leisure facilities close to source markets. This has been reflected in the success of the close-in Centerparc type resorts in Europe (95% ± occupancy) while long haul resort products are failing. These close-in "artificial environments experiences will spread to North America and Asia." Disney is reportedly developing a similar product.

Artificial barriers to travel will continue to come down with the deregulation of international air travel and the decline in use of bilateral agreements. Political realignments in the EC and North America free trade zone will encourage travel to and within each region. Reduction in differential on branded goods as well as duties and tariffs will encourage many forms of travel but reduce the importance of shopping as a trip generator. (As the price differential for branded goods in Japan drops below 20%, both shopping trips and expenditures will decline).

Countering this trend are destructive efforts to increase direct and indirect industry taxes (through departure fees; air fuel surcharges and tourist business taxes).

Means Turning Away From	And Turning Towards
Established Destinations ——→	*Emerging Destinations*
	• Indo/China
	• Eastern Europe
	• North and South Africa
	• Latin/South America

New destinations will provide the traveler with greater choice and lower cost alternatives to established destinations. Principal new destinations include Indochina (Vietnam is the newest member of the Pacific Asia Travel Association), Eastern Europe (the EC is funding massive tourism infrastructure and development programs), North Africa (primarily financed by World Bank and UNDP) and Latin America.

There are also emerging markets, including the new economic powerhouses of Asia (Korea, Taiwan, Hong Kong, Singapore) and the increasing number of potential travelers in large population countries (India, China, Indonesia, Brazil, Argentina, Mexico and, to some extent, the Eastern European countries). Existing markets, however, will continue to dominate leisure development.

Means Turning Away From	And Turning Towards
Old Products ——————→	*New Products*
• Sensitive environments	• Artificial environments
• Separate activities	• Integrated experiences
• Single activity focus	• Multiple activity product
• Seasonal visitation	• All weather tourism

New leisure products will move away from environmentally and culturally sensitive environments and use new technology to create artificial environments close to origin markets. The Centerparcs "Tropical Paradise" waterparks represent a first stage of this but other environments will follow. Simulation and virtual reality experience being developed in California and elsewhere will revolutionize the design of resorts, attractions, retail and education/interpretive facilities. Virtual reality body suits will be able to simulate any human experience.

Multi dimensional development will move further to the true integration of shopping and recreation, entertainment and education, and culture and meetings/business center development. Leisure destinations will also have to provide a greater menu of activities to accommodate the increasingly wide range of activities and interests of the individual consumer and the family. Destinations and products will also seek to become both weather independent (through artificial environments) as well as attractive to markets that are less weather dependent (conventions; specialty markets—ecotourism, culture/heritage, education and training).

Means Turning Away From	And Turning Towards
Fragmented Tourism Industry ——→	*Economic Development Tool!*
• Number of visitors	• Economic and social benefit per visitor
• Regional competition	• Intelligent cooperation
• Product dominance	• Customer orientation

Governments are slowly realizing that tourism is not fun and games, but serious business with far reaching community consequences. In ERA's recent study of the impact of the L.A. riots, we found a 25% drop in tourism accounting for a loss of thousands of jobs in the most affected areas and a fiscal hit of over $10 million in lost transient occupancy and sales taxes.

Destinations will increasingly measure leisure and tourism success not by number of visitors but by total benefit and, particularly, net benefit per visitor. The old 'numbers game' inevitably means greater mass marketing and eventually into giving away product for no net benefit. The emphasis on net benefit will mean targeted marketing to consumers who spend more and interact well with social and environmental resources.

Means Turning Away From	And Turning Towards
Developer Control ⟶	*Community Control*
• Political lobbying	• Approvals via referendum
• Economic impact	• Jobs and small business
• Environmental protection	• Environmental improvement
• Cultural intrusion	• Heritage protection

This greater realization of the business of tourism will lead to more intelligent cooperation among destinations and regions in marketing, promotion, and product development.

The host community is becoming increasingly sophisticated and demanding in terms of leisure development. Entitlements are increasingly difficult to obtain and maintain if the developer cannot demonstrate a range of economic, social, and environmental benefits.

Community interest and tourism must work together for any chance of long term success. The most rewarding forms of tourism are those that involve both residents and tourists. "Rewarding" means both in terms of the visitor and resident experiences and the economic viability to the developer. In ERA's experience, the reasonably safe range of participation must be a balance between 30% and 70% for either resident or tourist attendance. Being outside this range generally leads to alienation and an inefficient operating environment.

Small business development opportunities, not just jobs, will be an increasingly important element of the community benefit package (ERA recently conducted a national policy study in this area for the U.S. Congress).

Means Turning Away From	And Turning Towards
Financial Illusion ⟶	*Financial Reality*
• Mega attractions	• Franchise opportunities
• Meeting everyone's needs	• Needs of the investors
• Exit scenarios	• Operating Discipline
• Ego architecture	• Economic simulation
• New investment	• Revenue enhancement
• Price inflation	• Price resistance

The last four years have not been kind to the schemes and dreams of many recreation promoters and investors. The sad state of the hotel industry is well known (some new mega resorts are reportedly losing up to $3 million per month) and major theme parks have had to reduce effective prices to maintain attendance. Economic reality brings a renewed discipline to the planning, development and financial community to first improve the performance of existing assets; and second, acquire strategic undervalued assets before considering major new investments. Experienced market analysis and economic simulation models will guide future development.

Major leisure operators are also looking to capitalize on their brand equity by franchising smaller scale, specialty recreation opportunities.

Means Turning Away From	And Turning Towards
Mass Markets ────────▶	*Specialty Markets*
• Mega attractions	• Ecotourism
• Meeting everyone's needs	• Adventure tourism
• Exit scenarios	• MICE
• Ego architecture	• Any specialty you can think of

At first segmenting markets seems a more difficult task and a more expensive way to reach consumers. In reality it is a great opportunity—since each of the markets usually has a sophisticated information system and network distribution to reach its members. These are often represented by reasonably accessible databases for direct customer communication. Examples include:

- 140 ecotourism and adventure tourism operators in USA that control market factors and set standards/expectations for product delivery.
- 6,000 meeting planners control the vast majority of meeting business—about 10,000 room nights each and total visitor expenditures of around $12 billion.

Targeted communication to specialty markets is extremely cost effective given this type of leverage.

Means Turning Away From	And Turning Towards
Passive Consumers ────────▶	*Involved Participants*
• Inexperienced tourist	• Value conscious traveler
• Self-destruction	• Self improvement
• Fully packed tours	• Menu of optional experience
• Theme parks	• Individual experience centers

Leisure participants, like anyone else, need to be treated as individuals and feel an interaction with their environment. As travelers become more experienced, they are no longer satisfied to be processed through an impersonal, non-interactive system. It is the "old tourism" to see rows and rows of deck chairs surrounding some Californian's idea of a rockwork/waterfall tropical paradise. This style reflects an attitude of "processing the numbers" rather than providing a rewarding customer experience. The new consumers want to be involved—to learn new experiences, to interact with the community, and to learn about and appreciate the destination at more than a superficial level.

Means Turning Away From	And Turning Towards
Mass Marketing ──────────▶	*Direct Customer Communication*
• Socio-economic groups	• Customer databases
• Media placement	• Telemarketing/targeted messages
• One-way communication	• Building customer relationships

Possibly the most powerful tool in marketing, customer databases are poorly utilized by visitor industry associations and the public sector. Database marketing programs of certain airlines and hotels are renowned for their effectiveness. However, National Tourism Organizations, local Visitors Bureaus and many recreation operators are reluctant to apply this technology. They prefer to place expensive (and generally ineffective) media rather than pursue direct customer contact. Exceptions include the Hi-Line booking and reservation system (Scotland), ATLAS (Queensland), and the Club France frequent visitor program. At least six U.S. states are looking at developing such systems and the USTTA is considering the nationwide implications.

The conventional ways of looking at consumer behavior—especially in tourism and leisure—have become outdated. No longer (if they ever were) are the purchasing habits of the leisure customer predictable by labeling a group as a segment of the market and describing it with average characteristics. More and more, marketers are turning to tailored and targeted marketing to individuals. This is now possible through new technology with sophisticated database management systems and immense amounts of historical and purchased information (lists) on individual preferences and consumption patterns. This trend is particularly appropriate for tourism marketing since there is a world of paradoxes in leisure behavior. Sameness and diversity and security and risk taking seem side by side. Some accountants sky dive; people eat at McDonalds for lunch and a four-star restaurant for dinner; take luxury BMW's to the self service petrol pump; trade a large investment portfolio through a discount broker; visit Hawaii and never go in the ocean. Leisure lifestyles, in particular, are inconsistent and contradictory.

This multi-profile customer is difficult to motivate by traditional institutional means. The 1990s and beyond belong to the individual. Destination marketing and leisure product development must adjust to this new environment.

READING 19.2

Tourism: The World's Peace Industry
BY LOUIS D'AMORE
L. J. D'Amore and Associates

Reprinted from the *Journal of Travel Research,* Vol. 27, No. 1, Summer 1988.

THE ECONOMIC SIGNIFICANCE OF TOURISM

Tourism has been one of the world's most consistent growth industries of the past 30 years. Prospects for the continued growth of world tourism appear to be most promising. Societal trends are favorable to the continued growth of demand and low-cost air travel is becoming increasingly available. As well, the governments of many nations are playing a stronger role in encouraging the growth of both domestic and international tourism as a means of job creation, economic diversification, and source of foreign exchange.

Current forecasts suggest that international travel will double by the year 2000 and will account for fully 10% of international trade.

Beyond its economic significance, there is a growing realization of the role of international travel in promoting understanding and trust among people of different cultures. This is not only a precondition for additional trade in goods and services, particularly with newly emerging trading partners, but also a foundation on which to build improved relationships towards the goal of world peace and prosperity.

WHAT IS PEACE?

Peace is commonly viewed as "the absence of war." Negatively defined as such, our efforts as a society are on national defense through the building of armaments and armies, and the formation of military coalitions with other nations who have common interests.

For nearly half a century now, there has been a military confrontation among the world's major powers. From this perspective, most of the world has been at peace (negatively defined as above). Yet, in 1986, the United Nations "Year of Peace," some 3–5 million people died in 36 wars and armed conflicts around the world. Beyond the 41 nations directly engaged, other countries are involved in providing weapons and support—particularly the United States and Soviet Union who support opposing factions in virtually every conflict. In the continuing Persian Gulf War between Iran and Iraq, some 53 countries have sold arms to one side or the other since the war started in 1980.[1]

Beyond these situations of actual armed conflict, the threat of nuclear war and the havoc it would bring us profoundly affected the people of the world, particularly the young. (Recent developments toward the reduction of nuclear weapons in the arsenals of the United States and Soviet Union, as this is being written, offer some hope for optimism in this area.)

More recently, peace researchers have suggested that the opposite of peace is not war, but violence. At some point during the summer of 1987, world population reached 5 billion people. Nearly one third of its population is living in absolute poverty (a number equal to the total world population at the start of the century); nearly one half does not have access to basic health services; more than half a billion are seriously undernourished.

In just the last three years, the drought-triggered crisis in Africa resulted in the death of about a million persons and put 35 million at risk; an estimated 60 million people (mostly children) died of diseases related to unsafe drinking water and malnutrition; and the world witnessed the technological tragedies of Bhopal and Chernobyl.

It is difficult to conclude that we are living in a peaceful world, given this second definition of peace as "the absence of violence."

There have been successes nonetheless, and the signs of hope are many. Infant mortality is falling; human life expectancy is increasing; the literacy rate is climbing; the proportion of children starting school is rising; and global food production has increased more rapidly than population. But clearly, we have a large agenda to complete before we can claim that world peace is a reality for most of the world's population, if our criterion for peace is "the absence of violence."

Beyond violence to humanity, we have experienced an escalating rate of violence to our environment, which in turn is threatening the survival of a wide range of species and the lives of humans as well. More than 11 million hectares of forests are destroyed yearly. Over three decades this would equal an area approximately the size of India. The world's deserts are expanding at a rate of 6 million hectares a year.

In developed countries, acid precipitation is killing forests and lakes and is damaging the artistic and architectural heritage of nations. Toxic wastes and chemicals are penetrating our water systems and the food chain.

Environmental threats might indeed be the most serious threats to global security in the 21st century. A United Nations study group recently concluded that, "there can no longer be the slightest doubt that resource scarcities and ecological stresses constitute real and imminent threats to the future well-being of all peoples and nations."[2]

Within this global context, more than $1 trillion U.S. was spent on weapons and warfare in 1987. To this amount we are now adding billions more in the "war on terrorism" and for "security" against terrorists. This is more than $200 for every man, woman and child in the world—the per capita income of most nations. It is the aggregate GNP of some 130 nations.

One-tenth that amount could feed all the people of the world. Another one-tenth could educate all school aged children. One-tenth could provide new towns and communities with housing for the displaced persons of the world. Less than one-tenth would provide clean water, sanitation and basic health services to the one-third of the world's population who lack these services.

The philosophy and ethic of "industrial man" originating with Descartes, Bacon and other philosopher/scientists who ushered in the industrial era, was one of domination and control over nature. The environmental "alerts" of the late 1960s and current issues including acid rain and toxic waste, have caused a re-evaluation of our relationship with nature. We are now recognizing that sustainable development requires a custodial relationship with our environment and living in harmony with nature.

Similarly, international terrorism. Third World debt and nuclear arms proliferation are the "alert signals" of the 1980s which call for a re-conceptualization of man's relationship to man in the global village of an information age.

Long term global security in relationships with our neighbors in the global village will not come from a growing proliferation of weapons, wars, and swift retaliatory strikes to acts of terrorism. Former Canadian Prime Minister Lester B. Pearson warned us a quarter century ago that "no planet can survive half slave, half free; half engulfed in misery, half careening along toward the joys of an almost unlimited consumption . . . neither ecology nor our morality could survive such contrasts."

TOWARD A POSITIVE DEFINITION OF PEACE

Perhaps the most powerful and symbolic photographs ever taken were the photographs of planet earth as the first U.S. astronauts began their probe into space. Edgar Mitchell described what he saw from space as "a beautiful, harmonious, peaceful looking planet, blue with white clouds, and one that gave you a deep sense . . . of home, of being, of identity."

The photographs brought back from space generate similar reactions of awe, connectedness, and mutual dependency among people on earth, a heightened awareness of the relationship between humanity and the planet, and the need to live in harmony with one another and our environment.

Historians may well conclude that this vision of planet earth will have a greater impact on the future direction of human thinking than the Copernican Revolution of the 16th century which revealed that the earth was not the center of the universe. From space, we view the world as one living organism where the health of the total organism is necessary for the health of each component part, and the health of each component part, in turn, contributes to the health of the total organism.

Once we accept the perspective of an organic and interconnected world as described above, we can begin to think in terms of a *positive* definition of peace. In this context the Russian word for peace and its various meanings are illuminating. The word is "mir" which means:

    the universe
    plant earth
    the human race
    peace and tranquility
    concord in relations between people and states
    freedom from war

The Russian definition of peace is both multidimensional and positive. It implies peace and tranquility within ourselves; peace with our fellow humans and between nations; peace with nature and our spaceship earth; peace within the universe (and perhaps we can add—with our God).

To achieve such a positive concept of peace, we must first have a vision of what peace in positive terms can be. The vision of a world at peace so defined. Once we have created that vision, we have already set the forces in motion to bring about the actualization of that vision. We must be armed with new insights rather than new weapons. Insights which harness the resources of nature and the intelligence of humans for the common good of all. New visions will be required from fields other than politics—from fields such as anthropology, psychology, sociology, and geography; from the scientific community with visions for the constructive use of science and technology; from the environmental and ecological sciences with visions of ecological harmony; from the cultural community and the full range of creative art forms for a spirit of celebration in cultural diversity; and from the business community for a vision of the benefits from international trade and the free flow of goods, people, and ideas.

Most importantly, we must as individuals and ordinary people work towards and contribute to a positive vision of our common destiny, new visions of how to relate and ways of relating. President Dwight D. Eisenhower said in 1959, "I like to believe that people in the long run are going to do more to promote peace than are governments. Indeed, I think that people want peace so much that one of these days, governments had better get out of their way and let them have it."

IMAGES OF THE "ENEMY"—THE "OTHER"

Throughout human history, our "mental map" of the rest of the world and the people of that world, has been constructed from behind borders—behind city walls; political borders; or the mental borders of political ideology and ethnocultural differences.

World history provides many examples of how closed societies are prone to suspicion, hostility, and armed conflict. It is the separateness from other nations and cultures that creates the psychological distance and mind-set conducive to nurturing fears and suspicions and contributes subsequently to the potential for destructive conflict. "The unleashed powers of the atom has changed everything, save our modes of thinking," wrote Albert Einstein in 1946, "and thus we drift toward unparalleled disaster."

Some forty years after this warning, scientists and scholars from the Soviet Union and the United States came together to explore a new "mode of thinking" appropriate to an interdependent world with jet planes, computer technology, global communications, and a proliferation of nuclear weapons.

The focus of two of the scientists, Dr. Jerome Frank, Professor of Psychiatry at Johns Hopkins University and Dr. Andrei Melville, of the Moscow Institute on U.S.A. and Canadian Studies, was on "perception of the enemy." They concluded that "the mutual image of the enemy is always similar, no matter who the enemies are, and they mirror each other. That is, each side attributes the same virtues to itself and the same vices to the enemy. 'We' are trustworthy, peace loving, honorable and humanitarian; 'They' are treacherous, warlike and cruel . . . because of the belief that what is bad for the enemy is good for us, any efforts toward peace are seen as weak or naive on 'Our' part, and cunning and treacherous on 'Theirs'."

Images of the enemy are sustained by a disposition to accept as truth only those facts or assertions that meet our preconceived beliefs. Thus we tend to believe only the worst of our enemies and the best of ourselves.

Survey research tends to support these conclusions. A 1983 Gallup Poll found that only 9% of the U.S. public had favorable views toward the Soviet Union. In a separate poll taken by Daniel Yankelovich, most Americans expressed their belief that the Soviet Union would attack the U.S. or its allies if the U.S. were weak (65%); that the Soviets saw U.S. friendly gestures as weaknesses (73%); that force was the only language understood by the Soviets (62%); and that the U.S. should weaken the Soviets at every opportunity "because anything that weakens our enemies makes us more secure."[3]

The survey also found, however, that these sentiments were mainly directed at the leaders of the Soviet Government. Nearly 90% of the American public agreed that "the Russian people are not nearly as hostile to the U.S. as their leaders are and, in fact the Russians could be our friends if their leaders have a different attitude." This is confirmed by the many travelers to the Soviet Union who are impressed by the high regard most Soviets have for the American people.

TRACK TWO DIPLOMACY

In a seminal article on citizen diplomacy, written in the Winter 1981–82 issue of *Foreign Policy*, William D. Davidson and Joseph V. Montville defined the official channel of governmental relations as "track one diplomacy" and the unofficial channel of people-to-people relations as "track two diplomacy." Their article suggests that the two tracks run parallel. Track two diplomacy is "supplement to the understandable shortcomings of official relations." To defend their nation's interests, track one diplomats must make worst case assumptions about an adversary's intentions, but these very assumptions can set in motion a chain reaction of mutual distrust, threats, and hostilities that can culminate in war. Track two diplomats, they argued, create an alternative set of relationships that can prevent such a chain reaction.

"Track two diplomacy is unofficial, non-structured interaction. It is always open-minded, often altruistic, and . . . strategically optimistic, based on the best case analysis. Its underlying assumption is that the actual or potential conflict can be resolved or eased by appealing to common human capabilities of reason and goodwill." They concluded that "both tracks are necessary for psychological reasons and both need one another."

Tourism operates at the most basic level of "track two" diplomacy by spreading information about the personalities, beliefs, aspirations, perspectives, culture and politics of the citizens of one country to the citizens of another.

THE ROLE OF TOURISM IN BUILDING BRIDGES OF REALITY
AND UNDERSTANDING

To develop a world view that is realistic—that conforms to the reality of the world and our role in it—we must constantly revise and extend our understanding to include new knowledge of the larger world. Louis Brandeis, one of America's great jurists and thinkers, once said that there could be no true community "save that built upon the personal acquaintance of each with each."

Travel and tourism provide such an opportunity; the opportunity for individuals to gain first-hand knowledge of the larger world.

Some thirty years ago, the European Economic Community was established with the objective of reconciling the enemies of two world wars. The EEC was based on the premise that if the peoples of these countries got to know each other better, there would be less likelihood of war. One of the main cornerstones of EEC policy is freedom to travel and minimizing frontier controls.

The People's Republic of China, a nuclear-armed country widely regarded as a "yellow menace" in the 1960s, has in the past fifteen years become a friend. The key to a changed political relationship between the United States and the People's Republic of China has been an opening to travel and the web of relationships that have developed through cultural exchanges, conferences, sports, twinning of cities, trade, and a growing set of common interests.

The People's Republic of China opened its doors to the outside world in 1978 following visits from Canadian Prime Minister Pierre Trudeau and U.S. President Richard Nixon. Visitor arrivals have grown annually by 20–30% since 1978. More than 2.0 million foreign visitors will travel to China in 1988. By the year 2000, foreign visitors are expected to number 7–8 million.

It is interesting to note that over the past two years, the People's Republic of China has been reducing the size of its army by a million soldiers.

U.S.–SOVIET RELATIONS

In the Soviet Union, the leadership of Mikhail Gorbachev, with his policies of "glasnost," "perestroika," and "demokratizatsiya," is signalling a new era in relationships with Western nations. The new generation of Soviet leadership is recognizing that it cannot continue to expend 13% of its GNP on the military establishment and at the same time meet the requirements of its domestic economy. The annual demand for consumer goods exceeds supply by more than $30 billion. The task of acquiring needed supplies for a family of four alone requires some 20 hours a week of effort.

Gorbachev's policy of "perestroika," or economic restructuring, calls for a doubling in economic output by the year 2000. To achieve this goal, requires a relaxation of international tensions and the focus of energy and resources on domestic reform. It will also require constructive economic relations with the West to which the Soviets already are turning to learn about motivation and modern principles of management. The U.S.S.R. will also have a need for the technological tools of Western nations. Therefore the potential exists for the Soviet Union to become a major trading partner with the West and eventually to become integrated with the world economy.

It is becoming increasingly clear that the United States as well, is losing its economic capacity to sustain a large military establishment and ever-growing expenditures for a sophisticated nuclear arsenal. Paul Kennedy, in a recent article "The (Relative) Decline of America," points out that in 1945, the U.S. commanded a 40% share of the world economy. Today that share is 20%. Yet military commitments have grown dramatically.[4] Along with a diminished share in the world's economy has come a weakening of the U.S. financial position in terms of staggering deficits in international trade and the Federal budget. The U.S. Federal debt by the end of 1988 will be approximately $2.5 trillion or almost three times greater than the $0.9 trillion debt at the start of the decade in 1980. The trade deficit persists in a range of $140–150 billion a year.

These deficits are supported by importing ever larger amounts of capital. In the space of a few short years, the U.S. international position has shifted from being the world's leading creditor nation, to the position of being the world's leading debtor nation. At the end of 1987, U.S. liabilities were approximately $400 billion. (Brazil, the Third World's largest debtor nation, has a debt of $104 billion.)

The net foreign assets of Japan, on the other hand, have soared and approached some $300 billion by the end of 1987.

Kennedy states that, "while the U.S. devotes 7% of its GNP to the Defense budget and the military establishment utilizes the majority of the country's ablest scientists and engineers, Japanese and West Germans concentrate their financial and human resources on the design of commercial products." He goes on to suggest that a heavy investment in armaments "while bringing greater security in the short term, may so erode the commercial competitiveness of the American economy that the nation will be less secure in the long term."

Clearly, the easing of tensions between the U.S. and the Soviet Union would also help to restore balance between U.S. military commitments and the economic capacity to sustain those commitments.

The Geneva Summit, in November 1986, sent forward a clear signal to the world that the relaxation of tensions was possible, and had begun. Recognizing the benefits of travel in achieving better relationships among the two countries, Secretary Gorbachev and President Reagan declared in their joint statement following the Summit: "There should be greater understanding among our peoples and to this end we will encourage greater travel."

A few days before President Reagan met with Secretary Gorbachev, he gave what has since been called his "People to People" speech:

"Imagine how much good we could accomplish, how the cause of peace would be served, if more individuals and families from our respective countries could come to know each other in a personal way. . . .

"I feel the time is ripe for us to take bold new steps to open the way for our peoples to participate in an unprecedented way in the building of peace . . .

"Such exchanges can build in our societies thousands of coalitions for cooperation and peace. Governments can only do so much; once they get the ball rolling, they should step out of the way and let people get together to share, enjoy, help, listen, and learn from each other. . . .

"It is not an impossible dream that our children and grandchildren can someday travel freely back and forth between America and the Soviet Union; visit each other's homes; work and study together; enjoy and discuss plays, music, and television; and root for teams when they compete."

Some 120,000 Americans will visit the Soviet Union in 1988, making approximately 1 million visitors overall. What is also significant is the types of visitors traveling to the Soviet Union. They include environmentalists, developers, economists, movie producers, political leaders, professors and others who are meeting with their professional counterparts in the exchange of ideas and exploration of joint projects.

Various conferences have included an International Peace Forum in February 1987, and the Seventh Annual Convention of Physicians for the Prevention of Nuclear War. Other events have included a Walk for Peace, a Moscow Marathon for Peace, a Bering Strait Swim for Peace, a Conference of High School Students for Peace, and an Ice Cream Exchange for Peace.

TOURISM—THE WORLD'S PEACE INDUSTRY

As we travel and communicate in ever-increasing numbers, we are discovering that most people, regardless of their political or religious orientation, race, or socioeconomic status, want a peaceful world in which all are fed, sheltered, productive, and fulfilled.

The story is told about a Senator approaching Abraham Lincoln amidst the passions of the Civil War and saying, "Mr. President, I believe that enemies should be destroyed." Lincoln replied, "I agree with you sir, and the best way to destroy an enemy is to make him a friend."

Through travel, people are finding friends in every corner of the earth: finding common bonds with the rest of humanity and spreading messages of hope for a peaceful world.

Tourism properly designed and developed, has the potential to help bridge the psychological and cultural distances that separate people of diverse races, colors, religions and stages of social and economic development. Through tourism we can come rather to an appreciation of the rich human, cultural, and ecological diversity that our world mosaic offers; to evolve a mutual trust and respect for one another and the dignity of all life on earth.

The tourism industry, combined with our world parks systems, can make a contribution to living in harmony with our environment as well. The tourism industry makes possible the setting aside and preservation of vast tracts of land as national parks and wilderness areas. More than 3,000 protected areas in 120 countries and covering more than 4 million square miles are now preserved in their natural state. Visitors to these areas experience the beauty and majesty of the world's finest natural features and come away with a heightened appreciation of environmental values. In national parks townsites such as Banff and Jasper, we have the opportunity for "Man" to be co-creators with nature, bringing the best of human design in juxtaposition with the best of nature.

Transfrontier parks, or border parks, provide a special category of national parks. These are protected areas located along the boundaries of countries and are increasingly recognized as "Peace Parks." Border parks, on each side of a frontier, offer the benefits of larger, contiguous protected areas, increased cooperation between nations, and improved international understanding.

Tourism contributes to both preservation and development of the world's cultural heritage. It provides governments with the rationale for the preservation of historical sites and monuments and the motivation for indigenous groups to preserve unique dimensions of heritage in the form of dance, music, and artifacts. Tourism also provides both the audience and the economic engine for museums, the performing and visual arts, and the restoration of historical areas.

Severe poverty, stemming from under-development, is not only an active cause of conflict, but is inherently a form of violence. Pope Paul VI once said that "development is the new name for peace." The tourism industry is a human resource-intensive industry. It has the capacity to generate foreign exchange and a high ratio of government revenues as a proportion of total expenditures. As well, it has a capacity for both forward and backward linkages with other sectors of the economy. Properly designed, it can contribute to social and cultural enrichment as well as economic development. For these reasons, it is increasingly attractive as an industry among developing nations.

The 5,000 international conferences held each year increasingly draw on people of all nations to share their concerns; propose solutions to problems; exchange ideas; and create "opportunity networks." The growth in student exchanges, cultural exchanges, twinning of cities, and international sporting events not only give us an appreciation of our differences, but also show us the commonality of our goals and aspirations as a human family. The collective outcomes of these travel and tourism experiences help all humankind to appreciate the full meaning of the "Global Village" and the bonds that people everywhere have with one another.

Approximately 400 million persons will travel to another country in 1988. This number is growing by 5–7% each year. Millions more will act as "hosts" to these travelers as part of their daily job and/or as interested residents of the host country.

These millions of daily person-to-person encounters are potentially a powerful force for improved relations among the people and nations of the world; relations which emphasize a sharing and appreciation of cultures rather than the lack of trust bred by isolation.

CONCLUSION

The countdown to the 21st century has begun. Less than 15 years remain before the dawning of a new millenium, a period in which the late Buckminster Fuller believed humankind would be taking its "final exam."

Humankind will pass its "final exam" when we recognize the need to live in harmony with our fellow human beings, as well as with nature—when we recognize that we are our brother's keeper. We will have passed our "final exam" when the one-half of the world's scientists who are currently conducting research into weaponry and destruction have shifted their focus to human and social development and a sustainable environment. We will have passed our "final exam" when the U.S. and the Soviet Union join together, with other nations, in a program of de-militarization and the re-allocation of vital resources to achieve sustained global development for the benefit of all humankind.

For the first time in human history, all the problems which the world faces are man-made problems. And so too, humankind has the capacity to solve them. Ninety per cent of the scientists who ever lived are alive today, and our scientific knowledge base continues to expand exponentially.

The key to solving global issues is the human, institutional, corporate, and political will to do so.

In the 1960s, President John F. Kennedy had a vision of putting a man on the moon within that decade. The articulation of this vision brought about the marshalling of human, scientific, and fiscal resources to make that vision a reality.

So too, the year 2000 offers an occasion for visionary thinking. There are roughly 40–50 million persons engaged in the tourism industry around the world. The value of the global tourism plant is in the trillions of dollars.

Just as John Kennedy's vision put a man on the moon within a decade, the vision of tourism leaders around the world can marshall immense human and physical resources to help achieve global peace in this century.

The tourism industry has achieved its goal of becoming the world's largest industry. It now has the promise of becoming the world's first "Peace Industry;" an industry which recognizes, promotes and supports the belief that every traveler is potentially an "Ambassador for Peace," an industry which will be a model for other industries to follow.

READING ENDNOTES

1. Findings of the Stockholm International Peace Research Institute as reported in the *Montreal Gazette,* June 18, 1987.
2. World Commission on Environment and Development (1987), *Our Common Future,* U.S.A.: Oxford University Press. p. 300.
3. Don Carlson and Craig Comstock (ed.) (1986), *Citizen Summitry-Keeping The Peace When It Matters Too Much To Be Left To Politicians,* U.S.A.: Jeremy P. Tarcher, Inc., p. 11.
4. The Atlantic Monthly, August 1987.

Key Concepts

city-state	medical services for tourists
concern for safety	need for stability
cultural diversity	"north–south gap"
decline of planned economics	population migration
demographic changes	public-sector decline
education and training for tourism	quality of tourism experience
environmental sensitivity	resident responsive tourism
futures	special-interest tourism
global forces of change	spread of democracy
high-tech/high-touch interface	strategic alliance technological trends
knowledge-based society	tourism and peace
lifestyle diversity	value-system changes
market economy	virtual reality
market evaluation	

For Review and Discussion

1. As a travel counselor, what questions might you ask of a prospective tourist to determine his or her interest in a life-seeing or local hosting program?
2. What might be an obstacle to the optimistic projections of increased international tourism forecast in this chapter?
3. Intelligent, creative, sensitive tourism developments can actually improve the environment and heighten the appeal of an area. Give examples of how this might happen.
4. Can tourism enhance and improve a destination area's cultural and hospitality resources? Provide actual or hypothetical examples.

5. What is the expected trend in health-oriented accommodations and programs? Food services?

6. Can tourism really contribute to a narrowing of the "north-south gap"? What specific initiatives or programs do you think would help to make this happen?

7. What are the realistic prospects for a four-day workweek?

8. Does early retirement appeal to most workers?

9. How can tourism interests obtain a growing share of leisure market expenditures?

10. Specifically, in what way can world peace be enhanced by tourism?

Selected References

Archdale, G. "Computer Reservation Systems and Public Tourist Office." *Tourism Management*, Vol. 14, No. 1 (1993), pp. 3–14.

Ashford, D. M. "Prospects for Space Tourism." *Tourism Management*, Vol. 11, No. 2 (June 1990), pp. 99–104.

Chervenak, Larry. "Hotel Technology at the Start of the New Millennium." *Hospitality Research Journal* (The Futures Issue), Vol. 17, No. 1 (1993), pp. 113–120.

Christensen, Julia. "The Diversity Dynamic: Implications for Organizations in 2005." *Hospitality Research Journal* (The Futures Issue), Vol. 17, No. 1 (1993), pp. 69–86.

Collins, Galen R. *Hospitality Information Technology: Learning How to Use It*. Dubuque, Iowa: Kendall/Hunt, 1992.

D'Amore, L. J., and Jafar Jafari. *Tourism: A Vital Force for Peace*. Montreal: First Global Conference, 1988.

Durocher, Joseph F., and Neil B. Niman. "Information Technology: Management Effectiveness and Guest Services." *Hospitality Research Journal* (The Futures Issue), Vol. 17, No. 1 (1993), pp. 113–120.

Edgell, David L. *World Tourism at the Millennium*. Washington, D.C.: U.S. Travel and Tourism Administration, 1993.

Edgell, David L., and Ginger Smith. "Tourism Milestones for the Millennium: Projections and Implications of International Tourism for the United States Through the Year 2000." *Journal of Travel Research*, Vol. 32, No. 1 (Summer 1993), pp. 42–46.

Enz, Cathy A. "Organizational Architectures for the 21st Century: The Redesign of Hospitality Firms." *Hospitality Research Journal* (The Futures Issue) Vol. 17, No. 1 (1993), pp. 103–112.

Forbes, Robert J., and Maree S. Forbes. "Special Interest Travel," in *World Travel and Tourism Review*, Vol. 2, J. R. Brent Ritchie and Donald E. Hawkins, eds. Wallingford, Oxon, England: C.A.B. International, 1992, pp. 141–144.

Go, F. "The Role of Computerized Reservation Systems in the Hospitality Industry." *Tourism Management*, Vol. 14, No. 1 (1992), pp. 15–21.

Godbey, Geoffrey. "Time, Work, and Leisure: Trends That Will Shape the Hospitality Industry." *Hospitality Research Journal* (The Futures Issues), Vol. 17, No. 1 (1993), pp. 49–58.

Goeldner, Charles R. "Trends in North American Tourism." *American Behavioral Scientist*, Vol. 36, No. 2 (November 1992), pp. 144–154.

Haywood, K. M. "A Strategic Approach to Managing Technology." *Cornell Hotel and Restaurant Administration Quarterly*, Vol. 30, No. 1 (1990), pp. 39–45.

Hitchins, Fred. "The Influence of Technology on U.K. Travel Agents." *Travel and Tourism Analyst*, No. 3 (1991), pp. 88–105.

Hobson, Perry, and Muzaffer Uysal. "Infrastructure: The Silent Crisis Facing the Future of Tourism." *Hospitality Research Journal* (The Futures Issues), Vol. 17, No. 1 (1993), pp. 209–218.

Lago, Dan, and James Poffley. "The Aging Population and the Hospitality Industry in 2010: Important Trends and Probable Services." *Hospitality Research Journal* (The Futures Issue), Vol. 17, No. 1 (1993), pp. 29–48.

Mieczkowski, Zbigniew. *World Trends in Tourism and Recreation.* Frankfurt: Peter Lang, 1990.

Mills, Susan F., and Hudson Riehle. "Food Service Manager 2000." *Hospitality Research Journal* (The Futures Issue), Vol. 17, No. 1 (1993), pp. 147–160.

Moore, Richard, and Scott Wilkinson. "Communications Technology." *Hospitality Research Journal* (The Futures Issue), Vol. 17, No. 1 (1993), pp. 133–146.

Mowlana, H., and G. Smith. "Tourism, Telecommunications, and Transnational Banking." *Tourism Management,* Vol. 11, No. 4 (1990), pp. 315–324.

Parsa, H. G., and Mahmood A. Khan. "Quick Service Restaurants of the 21st Century: An Analytical Review of Macro Factors." *Hospitality Research Journal* (The Futures Issue), Vol. 17, No. 1 (1993), pp. 161–174.

Poon, A. "Tourism and Information Technologies." *Annals of Tourism Research,* Vol. 13, No. 4 (1988), pp. 531–549.

Poon, A. *Tourism, Technology and Competitive Strategies.* Wallingford, Oxon, England: C.A.B. International, 1993.

Popcorn, Faith. *The Popcorn Report.* New York: Doubleday, 1991.

Powers, Thomas F. "The Standard World of 2005: A Surprise-Free Scenario." *Hospitality Research Journal,* Vol. 16, No. 1 (1992), pp. 1–19.

Reid, R. Dan, and Melvin Sandler. "The Use of Technology to Improve Service Quality." *Cornell Hotel and Restaurant Administration Quarterly,* Vol. 33, No. 3 (June 1992), pp. 68–73.

Ritchie, J. R. Brent. "Global Tourism Policy Issues: An Agenda for the 1990's." *World Travel and Tourism Review,* Vol. 1. Wallingford, Oxon, England: C.A.B. International, 1991.

Schor, Juliet B. *The Overworked American: The Unexpected Decline of Leisure.* New York: Basic Books, 1991.

Shafer, E. L. "Future Encounters with Science and Technology." *Journal of Travel Research,* Vol. 27, No. 4 (Spring 1989), pp. 2–7.

Shanklin, Carol W. "Ecology Age: Implications for the Hospitality and Tourism Industry." *Hospitality Research Journal* (The Futures Issue), Vol. 17, No. 1 (1993), pp. 219–230.

Stipanuk, D. M. "Tourism and Technology: Interactions and Implications." *Tourism Management,* Vol. 14, No. 4 (1993), pp. 267–278.

Travel and Tourism Research Association. "Examining the Dynamics of New Partnerships, Strategies and Products." *Newsletter.* Salt Lake City, Utah: TTRA, 1992.

U.S. Travel Data Center. *Weekend Travel: American Growth Trend.* Washington, D.C.: USTDC, 1990.

Wallace, Jane Y. "Gateway to the Millennium." *Hospitality Research Journal* (The Futures Issue), Vol. 17, No. 1 (1993), pp. 59–68.

World Tourism Organization. *Global Tourism Forecasts to the Year 2000 and Beyond.* Madrid: WTO, 1993.

World Tourism Organization. *Tourism to the Year 2000: Qualitative Aspect Affecting Global Growth.* Madrid: WTO, 1991.

World Travel and Tourism Council. *Travel and Tourism: A New Economic Perspective.* Brussels: WTTC, 1993.

Key Travel Industry Contacts

ASSOCIATIONS AND ORGANIZATIONS

Adventure Travel Society
Suite 160
6551 S. Revere Parkway
Englewood, Colorado 80111

Air Transport Association of America
1301 Pennsylvania Avenue N.W.
Suite 1100
Washington, D.C. 20004

American Association of Retired Persons
601 E Street N. W.
Washington, D.C. 20049

American Automobile Association
1000 AAA Drive
Heathrow, Florida 32746

American Bus Association
1100 New York Avenue
Suite 1050
Washington, D.C. 20005

American Car Rental Association
927 15th Street N.W.
Suite 1000
Washington, D.C. 20005

American Hotel and Motel Association
1201 New York Avenue N.W.
Washington, D.C. 20005

American Recreation Coalition
1331 Pennsylvania Avenue N.W.
Suite 726
Washington, D.C. 20004

American Resort and Residential
  Development Association
1220 L Street N.W.
Suite 510
Washington, D.C. 20005

American Sightseeing International
211 East 43rd Street
New York, New York 10017

American Society of Travel Agents
1101 King Street
Alexandria, Virginia 22314

American Youth Hostels
P.O. Box 37613
Washington, D.C. 20013

Association of Retail Travel Agents
1745 Jefferson Davis Highway
Suite 300
Arlington, Virginia 22202

Association of Travel Marketing
  Executives
808 17th St. N.W., No. 200
Washington, D.C. 20006

Bureau of Economic Analysis
U.S. Department of Commerce
Washington, D.C. 20230

Bureau of the Census
Demographic Surveys Division
U.S. Department of Commerce
Washington, D.C. 20233

Caribbean Tourism Association
20 East 46th Street
New York, New York 10017

Cruise Lines International Association
500 Fifth Avenue
Suite 1407
New York, New York 10110

European Travel Commission
630 Fifth Avenue
New York, New York 10111

Federal Aviation Administration
800 Independence Avenue S.W.
Washington, D.C. 20591

Gray Line Sight-Seeing Association
13760 Noel Road
Suite 1000
Dallas, Texas 75240

Highway Users Federation
1776 Massachusetts Avenue N.W.
Washington, D.C. 20036

Hospitality Sales and Marketing
   Association International
1300 L Street N.W.
Suite 800
Washington, D.C. 20005

Institute of Certified Travel Agents
148 Linden Street
Wellesley, Massachusetts 02181

International Academy for the Study
   of Tourism
WTO Building
Capitan Haya, 42
28020 Madrid, Spain

International Airline Passengers
   Association
P.O. Box 870188
Dallas, Texas 75287

International Air Transport Association
   (IATA)
IATA Building
2000 Peel Street
Montreal, Quebec
Canada H3A 2R4

International Association of Amusement
   Parks and Attractions
1448 Duke Street
Alexandria, Virginia 22314

International Association of Convention
   and Visitors Bureaus
2000 L Street N.W.
Suite 702
Washington, D.C. 20036

International Association of Scientific
   Experts in Tourism (AIEST)
Varnbuelstrasse 19
CH-9000 St. Gallen
Switzerland

International Bureau of Social Tourism
   (BITS)
63, rue de la Loi
B-1040 Brussels, Belgium

International Civil Aviation Organization
   (ICAO)
International Aviation Square
1000 Sherbrooke Street West
Montreal, Quebec
Canada H3A 2R2

International Touring Alliance (AIT)
179 Louise Avenue
B-1050 Brussels, Belgium

National Air Carrier Association
1730 M Street N.W.
Suite 806
Washington, D.C. 20036

National Association of RV Parks &
   Campgrounds
8605 Westwood Center Drive
Suite 201
Vienna, Virginia 22182

National Caves Association
Route 9, P.O. Box 106
McMinnville, Tennessee 37110

National Park Hospitality Association
P.O. Box 29041
Phoenix, Arizona 85038

National Park Service
Socio-Economic Studies Division
P.O. Box 25287
Denver, Colorado 80225

National Recreation and Park Association
2775 S. Quincy Street
Suite 300
Arlington, Virginia 22206

National Restaurant Association
1200 Seventeenth Street N.W.
Washington, D.C. 20036

National Ski Areas Association
133 S. Van Gordon Street
Lakewood, Colorado 80228

National Tour Association
546 East Main Street
P.O. Box 3071
Lexington, Kentucky 40596

National Trust for Historic Preservation
1785 Massachusetts Avenue N.W.
Washington, D.C. 20036

Pacific Asia Travel Association (PATA)
One Montgomery Street
West Tower, No. 1750
San Francisco, California 94104

Recreation Vehicle Industry Association
P.O. Box 2999
1896 Preston White Drive
Reston, Virginia 22090

Society of American Travel Writers
1155 Connecticut Ave N.W.
Suite 500
Washington, D.C. 20036

Society of Incentive Travel Executives, Inc.
21 W 38th Street
10th Floor
New York, New York 10018

Tourism Canada
235 Queen Street
Ottawa, Ontario
Canada K1A 0H6

Tourism Industry Association of Canada
130 Albert Street
Ottawa, Ontario
Canada K1P 5G4

Travel and Tourism Government Affairs
  Council
1100 New York Avenue, N.W.
Washington, D.C. 20005

Travel and Tourism Research Association
10200 W. 44th Ave.
Suite 304
Wheat Ridge, Colorado 80033

Travel Industry Association of America
1100 New York Avenue, N.W.
Washington, D.C. 20005

United Bus Owners of America
1300 L Street N.W.
Suite 1050
Washington, D.C. 20005

United States Tour Operators Association
211 East 51st Street
New York, New York 10022

U.S. Travel and Tourism Administration
U.S. Department of Commerce
Washington, D.C. 20230

United States Travel Data Center
1100 New York Avenue, N.W.
Washington, D.C. 20005

Universal Federation of Travel Agents'
  Associations (UFTAA)
17, rue Grimaldi
Monaco, Monaco MC-98000

World Tourism Organization
Calle Capitan Haya 42
Madrid, Spain E-28020

World Travel & Tourism Council
Chausée de La Hulpe, 181
1170 Brussels, Belgium

STATE CONTACTS

Alabama
Alabama Bureau of Tourism and Travel
401 Adams Avenue
Montgomery, Alabama 36103

Alaska
Alaska State Division of Tourism
P.O. Box 11081
Juneau, Alaska 99811

Arizona
Arizona Office of Tourism
1100 West Washington Street
Phoenix, Arizona 85007

Arkansas
Arkansas Department of Parks and
  Tourism
1 Capital Mall
Little Rock, Arkansas 72201

California
California Office of Tourism
801 K Street, Suite 1600
Sacramento, California 95814

Colorado
Denver Metro Convention and Visitors
  Bureau
1555 California
Suite 300
Denver, Colorado 80202

Connecticut
Connecticut Department of Economic
  Development
865 Brook Street
Rocky Hill, Connecticut 06067

Delaware
Delaware Tourism Office
99 Kings Highway
P.O. Box 1401
Dover, Delaware 19903

District of Columbia
Washington Convention and Visitors
  Association
1212 New York Avenue N.W.
Suite 600
Washington, D.C. 20005

Florida
Florida Division of Tourism
Department of Commerce
126 Van Buren Street
Tallahassee, Florida 32399

Georgia
Georgia Tourist Division
Department of Industry & Trade
P.O. Box 1776
Atlanta, Georgia 30301

Hawaii
Hawaii Visitors Bureau
2270 Kalakaua Avenue
Suite 801
Honolulu, Hawaii 96815

Idaho
Division of Travel Development
700 West State Street
Boise, Idaho 83720

Illinois
Illinois Office of Tourism
State of Illinois Center
100 W. Randolph, Suite 3-400
Chicago, Illinois 60601

Indiana
Indiana Tourism Development Division
Department of Commerce
One North Capitol, No. 700
Indianapolis, Indiana 46204

Iowa
Iowa Division of Tourism
Department of Economic Development
200 East Grand Avenue
Des Moines, Iowa 50309

Kansas
Kansas Travel and Tourism Division
700 SW Harrison Street
Suite 1300
Topeka, Kansas 66603-1300

Kentucky
Kentucky Department of Travel
  Development
Capital Plaza Tower, 22nd Floor
Frankfort, Kentucky 40601

Louisiana
Louisiana Office of Tourism
P.O. Box 94291
Capitol Station
Baton Rouge, Louisiana 70804-9291

Maine
Office of Tourism
Department of Economic and Community
  Development
189 State Street
Augusta, Maine 04333

Maryland
Maryland Office of Tourist Development
217 E. Redwood Street
9th Floor
Baltimore, Maryland 21202

Massachusetts
Massachusetts Office of Travel and
  Tourism
100 Cambridge Street
Boston, Massachusetts 02202

Michigan
Travel Bureau
Michigan Department of Commerce
P.O. Box 30226
Lansing, Michigan 48909

Minnesota
Minnesota Office of Tourism
375 Jackson Walkway
250 Skyway Level
St. Paul, Minnesota 55101

Mississippi
Division of Tourism
Mississippi Department of Economic
  Development
P.O. Box 849
Jackson, Mississippi 39205

Missouri
Missouri Division of Tourism
P.O. Box 1055
Jefferson City, Missouri 65102

Montana
Montana Travel Promotion Division
Department of Commerce
1424 Ninth Avenue
Helena, Montana 59620

Nebraska
Nebraska Travel and Tourism Division
Department of Economic Development
P.O. Box 94666
Lincoln, Nebraska 68509

Nevada
Nevada Commission on Tourism
5151 Carson Street
Carson City, Nevada 89710

New Hampshire
New Hampshire Office of Vacation Travel
P.O. Box 856
Concord, New Hampshire 03302

New Jersey
New Jersey Division of Travel and Tourism
Department of Commerce and Economic
  Development
CN 826
Trenton, New Jersey 08625

New Mexico
New Mexico Tourism and Travel Division
Economic Development and Tourism
  Department
1100 St. Francis Drive
Santa Fe, New Mexico 87503

New York
New York Division of Tourism
State Department of Economic Development
1515 Broadway
New York, New York 10036

North Carolina
Division of Travel and Tourism
North Carolina Department of Commerce
430 North Salisbury Street
Raleigh, North Carolina 27611

North Dakota
North Dakota Tourism Promotion
Liberty Memorial Building
State Capitol Grounds
Bismarck, North Dakota 58505

Ohio
Ohio Division of Travel and Tourism
Department of Development
P.O. Box 1001
Columbus, Ohio 43266-0101

Oklahoma
Oklahoma Tourism and Recreation
  Department
500 Will Rogers Building
Oklahoma City, Oklahoma 73105

Oregon
Oregon Economic Development Department
Tourism Division
775 Summer Street N.E.
Salem, Oregon 97310

Pennsylvania
Pennsylvania Bureau of Travel
  Development
Department of Commerce
Room 453 Forum Building
Harrisburg, Pennsylvania 17120

Rhode Island
Tourist Promotion Division
Rhode Island Department of Economic
  Development
7 Jackson Walkway
Providence, Rhode Island 02903

South Carolina
South Carolina Department of Parks, Rec-
  reation and Tourism
Edgar A. Brown Building, Suite 106
1205 Pendleton Street
Columbia, South Carolina 29201

South Dakota
South Dakota Tourism
711 E. Wells Avenue
Pierre, South Dakota 57501

Tennessee
Tennessee Department of Tourist
  Development
320 Sixth Avenue, North
Nashville, Tennessee 37202

Texas
Texas Tourism Division
Department of Commerce
P.O. Box 12008, Capital Station
Austin, Texas 78711-2008

Utah
Utah Travel Council
Capitol Hill
300 North State
Salt Lake City, Utah 84114

Vermont
Vermont Department of Travel and
  Tourism
Agency of Development and Community
  Affairs
134 State Street
Montpelier, Vermont 05602

Virginia
Virginia Division of Tourism
1021 East Cary Street
14th Floor
Richmond, Virginia 23219

Washington
Tourism Development Division
Department of Trade and Economic
  Development
P.O. Box 42513
Olympia, Washington 98504

West Virginia
West Virginia Division of Tourism and
  Parks
Capitol Complex Building 17
Charleston, West Virginia 25305

Wisconsin
Wisconsin Division of Tourism
123 West Washington Avenue
P.O. Box 7970
Madison, Wisconsin 53707

Wyoming
Wyoming Division of Tourism
Frank Norris Junior Travel Center
I-25 and College Drive
Cheyenne, Wyoming 82002-0660

PROVINCE CONTACTS

Alberta
Alberta Department of Tourism
18th Floor, Imperial Oil
  Building
10025 Jasper Avenue
Edmonton, Alberta
Canada T5J 3Z3

British Columbia
Tourism British Columbia
Ministry of Tourism
865 Hornby Street
Suite 802
Vancouver, British Columbia
Canada V6Z 2G5

Manitoba
Travel Manitoba
155 Carlton Street, 7th Floor
Winnipeg, Manitoba
Canada R3C 3H8

New Brunswick
Department of Tourism, Recreation and
    Heritage
Marysville Place
P.O. Box 12345
Fredericton, New Brunswick
Canada E3B 5C3

Newfoundland
Newfoundland Department of
    Development and Tourism
4th Floor, Confederation Building Complex
P.O. Box 8700
St. John's, Newfoundland
Canada A1C 5T7

Northwest Territories
Division of Tourism and Parks
Northwest Territories Department of
    Economic Development and Tourism
Northern United Place, Box 1320
Yellowknife, Northwest Territories
Canada X1A 2L9

Nova Scotia
Nova Scotia Department of Tourism and
    Culture
P.O. Box 456
5151 Terminal Road
Halifax, Nova Scotia
Canada B3J 2R5

Ontario
Ontario Ministry of Tourism and
    Recreation
77 Bloor Street West
Toronto, Ontario
Canada M7A 2R9

Prince Edward Island
Prince Edward Island Department of
    Tourism and Parks
Shaw Building, 3rd Floor
105 Rochford Street
P.O. Box 2000
Charlottetown, Prince Edward Island
Canada C1A 7N8

Quebec
Ministere du Tourisme
Boite Postale 125
Montreal, Quebec
Canada H4Z 1C3

Saskatchewan
Saskatchewan Tourism and Small Business
5th Floor, 1919 Saskatchewan Drive
Regina, Saskatchewan
Canada S4P 3V7

Yukon
Tourism Planning and Development
    Branch
Heritage and Cultural Resources
Government of Yukon
P.O. Box 2703
Whitehorse, Yukon
Canada Y1A 2C6

Data Sources for Travel and Tourism Research

The sources of secondary information available on tourism, travel, and recreation continue to grow. In the rapidly expanding, dynamic world of tourism, practitioners must know what is available and where to find it. Information gathering requires a great deal of tourism executives' time; yet little exists to guide them to the best sources of data for their particular concerns. Thus, this appendix provides a comprehensive list of numerous sources along with a summary of the type of information available in each.

This appendix is organized into eight main categories: (1) Indexing Services, (2) Bibliographies and Finding Guides, (3) Periodicals, (4) Trade and Professional Associations, (5) Government, (6) Yearbooks, Annuals, Handbooks, Etc., (7) Databases, and (8) Some Final Suggestions. The sources are arranged alphabetically within each heading.

There has been considerable effort to make the list up-to-date and give enough information to enable users who cannot find the information in their own libraries or the public library to send requests to the sources indicated. Readers should be aware that names, addresses, and prices change frequently.

One of the biggest mistakes in travel and tourism research is to rush out and collect primary data without exhausting secondary source information. Only later do researchers discover they have duplicated previous research. Existing sources can often provide information to solve the problem for a fraction of the cost. Therefore, users should exhaust secondary sources before turning to primary research for additional data.

In selecting sources of information, efforts have been made to (1) emphasize prime data, (2) list sources that can be used to locate more detailed data, and (3) keep the list brief enough to be actually read and used rather than just filed. Effective utilization can save money, hours of time, and provide useful information that might otherwise be missed.

1. INDEXING SERVICES

Unfortunately, there is no one convenient heading where you can look and automatically find travel research information listed. Travel research studies may be found under many headings. The most important subject heading in the indexes is tourism or tourist trade. Examples of other headings that contain useful information are travel,

travel agents, vacations, transportation, tourist camps, motels, hotels, recreation, and national parks.

Business Periodicals Index (New York: H.W. Wilson, monthly, except August). A cumulative subject index covering periodicals in the fields of accounting, marketing, finance, advertising, banking, and so on.

The Hospitality Index: An Index for the Hotel, Food Service and Travel Industries (Washington, D.C.: American Hotel and Motel Association, quarterly and annual). $99.00. This comprehensive database comprising citations of articles, reports, and research from more than 40 different journals and periodicals has been published by the Consortium of Hospitality Research Information Services (CHRIS), a joint effort of Cornell University's School of Hotel Administration, the University of Wisconsin–Stout, and the Information Center of the American Hotel and Motel Association. Information contained in the published index is organized under more than 1500 subject headings.

Lodging and Restaurant Index (West Lafayette, Indiana: Purdue University, annual). A periodical index of over 40 major journals of the hospitality industry.

Predicasts F & S Index Europe (Cleveland, Ohio: Predicasts, Inc., monthly). Devoted exclusively to Europe. Covers the European community, Scandinavia, other West European countries, the former Soviet Union, and other East European countries.

Predicasts F & S Index of Corporations and Industries (Cleveland, Ohio: Predicasts, Inc., weekly, quarterly, and annual cumulations). Indexes U.S. company, product, and industry information from articles in financial publications, business newspapers, trade magazines, and special reports. Includes foreign company operations in the United States. Presented in two sections: (I) *Industries and Products,* arranged by S.I.C. code, and (II) *Companies,* arranged alphabetically.

Predicasts F & S Index International (Cleveland, Ohio: Predicasts, Inc., monthly). Indexes articles from foreign publications. Information arranged by (1) industry and product, (2) country, and (3) company. Covers Canada, Latin America, Africa, Middle East, Oceania, and other Asian countries.

Predicasts F & S Index United States (Cleveland, Ohio: Predicasts, Inc., weekly). Indexes articles from the United States and from foreign sources that may affect U.S. business.

Reader's Guide to Periodical Literature (New York: H. W. Wilson, semimonthly). An index of the contents of the nation's general magazines.

The Travel and Tourism Index (Laie, Hawaii: Brigham Young University Hawaii Campus, quarterly). This quarterly index covers 47 travel and tourism publications. Annual subscription fee $40.00.

2. BIBLIOGRAPHIES AND FINDING GUIDES

Baretje, R. *Tourist Analysis Review.* (Aix-en-Provence, France: Centre des Hautes Études Touristiques, Immeuble Euroffice, 38, Av. de l'Europe, 13090). Published every three months, this review printed on 40 heavy-duty pages gives complete references of studies and a short synopsis of their contents. Each issue analyzes 160 books or articles dealing with tourism.

Engass, Peter. *Tourism and the Travel Industry: An Information Sourcebook* (Phoenix, Arizona:

Oryx Press, 1988), 152 pp. This bibliography lists and describes almost 900 books, journals, government publications and proceedings dealing with domestic and international tourism.

Goeldner, C. R., and Karen Dicke. *Bibliography of Tourism and Travel Research Studies, Reports and Articles* (Boulder, Colorado: Business Research Division, College of Business, University of Colorado, 1980), 9 vols., 762 pp., complete set $60. This nine-volume bibliography is a research resource on travel, recreation, and tourism. Volume I, *Information Sources,* covers bibliographies, classics, books, directories, proceedings, list of travel and tourism trade and professional publications, list of U.S. travel and tourism associations, list of universities involved in travel and tourism research, list of U.S. travel contacts, selected list of Canadian travel contacts, and list of world travel contacts. Volume II, *Economics,* covers general, analysis, balance of payments, development, employment, expenditures, feasibility studies, impact, indicators and barometers, international, and multipliers. Volume III, *International Tourism,* covers general; Africa; Asia and the Pacific; Canada; Central, Latin, and South America; Europe (excluding the United Kingdom); Middle East; and the United Kingdom. Volume IV, *Lodging,* covers general, financial aspects, innovations, management, marketing and market research, statistics, and second-home development. Volume V, *Recreation,* covers general, boating, camping, carrying capacity, demand, economics, forecasts, forests, hiking, hunting and fishing, land development, management, parks, planning, public input, research and research methodology, rural, skiing, snowmobiling, sports, statistics, urban, user studies, and water. Volume VI, *Transportation,* includes transportation—general and forecasts; air—general, costs, commuters, deregulation, economics, fares, forecasts, international, passengers, planning, and statistics; highways and roads—bus, auto, and recreational vehicles; rail; water; and other. Volume VII, *Advertising–Planning,* covers advertising and promotion, attitudes, business travel, clubs, conferences and conventions, education, energy, environmental impact, food service, forecasts, gambling, handicapped traveler, hospitality, leisure, management, and planning. Volume VIII, *Statistics–Visitors,* includes statistics, tourism research, travel agents, travel research methodology, vacations, and visitors. Volume IX, *Index,* includes several indices to the material in Volumes I–VIII.

Herron, Nancy. *The Leisure Literature* (Englewood, Colorado: Libraries Unlimited, Inc., 1992), 181 pp., $28.50. This book endeavors to identify, describe, and organize into a usable format 283 reference sources that support research related to leisure. Contains an excellent section on travel and tourism.

The Hospitality Bibliography (Mineola, New York: Hospitality Valuation Services, 1991), 80 pp. Publication is a compilation of titles pertaining to the financial and real estate aspects of the hotel and restaurant industries. It is annotated.

Jafari, Jafar. "Tourism and the Social Sciences: A Bibliography." *Annals of Tourism Research* (Elmsford, New York: Pergamon Press), Vol. 6, No. 2 (1979), pp. 149–194. The purpose of this bibliography is to bring together a selection of publications dealing with the study of tourism. This list of bibliographies is from 1970 to 1978.

Jafari, Jafar, and Dean Aaser. "Tourism as the Subject of Doctoral Dissertations." *Annals of Tourism Research* (Elmsford, New York: Pergamon Press), Vol. 15, No. 3 (1988), pp. 407–429. This article discusses tourism as a field of study and presents the results of a computer search of doctoral dissertations on tourism. The search resulted in 157 titles with a touristic focus written between 1951 and 1987. Titles, authors, and schools are given.

Jafari, Jafar, Philip Sawin, Christopher Gustafson, and Joseph Harrington. *Bibliographies on Tourism and Related Subjects: An Annotated Sourcebook* (Boulder, Colorado: Business Research Division, College of Business, University of Colorado, 1988), 81 pp., $25. A bibliography of bibliographies dealing with tourism and associated fields. There are 271 annotated entries, and information is arranged in three ways: (1) alphabetical listing, (2) author index, and (3) subject index. Also included is a listing of the tourism bibliographies available from the Centre des Hautes Etudes Touristiques in Aix-en-Provence, France.

Leisure, Recreation and Tourism Abstracts (formerly *Rural Recreation and Tourism Abstracts*). (Wallingford, Oxon, England: C.A.B. International, quarterly). Annual subscription rate is $171. The abstracts, arranged by subject, provide short informative summaries of publications with full bibliographical details and often a symbol for locating the original documents.

Nixon, Judith. *Hotel and Restaurant Industries: An Information Sourcebook* (Phoenix, Arizona: Oryx Press, 1988), 240 pp. This bibliography is based primarily on the Consumer and Family Sciences Library at Purdue University, which has been specializing in hotel and restaurant materials for many years.

Pisarski, Alan. *An Inventory of Federal Travel and Tourism Related Information Sources* (Boulder, Colorado: Business Research Division, College of Business, University of Colorado, 1985), 107 pp., $25. This inventory of existing federal data programs relevant to travel and tourism provides a comprehensive listing and description of pertinent government sources.

Pizam, A., and Z. Gu. *Journal of Travel Research Index and Abstracts, Volumes 6–24* (Boulder, Colorado: Business Research Division, College of Business, University of Colorado, 1988), 182 pp., $48. Comprehensive index and abstracts of the articles that have been published in the *Journal of Travel Research* and its predecessor, the *Travel Research Bulletin*. Covers articles through Volume 24. Articles indexed by author, title, subject, and destination outside the United States. *Journal of Travel Research Index and Abstracts,* Volumes 25 and 26, 1989, 39 pp; $18.

Recent Acquisitions (Ottawa, Ontario, Canada: Tourism Research and Data Centre, Tourism Canada, 235 Queen Street, K1A 0H6, monthly). This is a listing of publications received by the Tourism Reference and Documentation Centre of Tourism Canada.

Tourism and Vacation Travel: State and Local Government Planning (Springfield, Virginia: National Technical Information Service, U.S. Department of Commerce, May 1988), 50 pp., $40. Economic and socioeconomic aspects of vacation travel and tourism in various localities of the United States are documented. Most of these studies deal with the use of tourism for the economic development of local communities. Special attention is given to wilderness, coastal zone, lake, waterway, and Indian reservation areas. This updated bibliography covers the period 1970 to May 1988 and provides 175 citations.

Tourism: A Guide to Sources of Information (Edinburgh, Scotland: Capital Planning Information Ltd., 6 Castle Street, Edinburgh E112 3AT, Scotland, 1981), 73 pp. This publication gives a selected and evaluative listing of tourism literature primarily about the United Kingdom; however, it also includes some international sources.

"The Travel Research Bookshelf," *Journal of Travel Research* (Boulder, Colorado: Business Research Division, College of Business, University of Colorado). A regular feature of the quarterly *Journal of Travel Research.* "The Travel Research Bookshelf" is an annotated bibliography of current travel research materials. Sources and availability of materials are shown for each entry.

Whitlock, W. and R. Becker. *Nature-based Tourism: An Annotated Bibliography* (Clemson, South Carolina: Clemson University, 1991), $40. Containing over 300 citations this bibliography includes author, geographical, and subject indices. Approximately 150 subjects are referenced.

3. DATABASES AND DOCUMENTATION CENTERS

Several databases containing travel and tourism information are available now. One of the quickest ways of finding information is to conduct a computer search of these databases. Some databases available are listed below. For a comprehensive list of databases and documentation centers, check the final entry in this section.

ABI/INFORM, 620 South Third Street, Louisville, Kentucky, 40202; (800) 626-2823. A computerized database of business information for the most current five years. It consists of abstracts and indexes to business articles contained in more than 800 different journals.

AVIATION LINK, BACK Information Services, 65 High Ridge Road, Suite 346, Stamford, Connecticut 06905; (800) 446-2225. Computerized information service on almost all facets of the airline industry. Database includes information from the International Air Transport Association, U.S. Department of Transportation, Association of European Airlines, Official Airlines Guide, and other sources.

CENTRE DES HAUTES ÉTUDES TOURISTIQUES, Immeuble Euroffice, 38, Avenue De L'Europe, 13090, Aix-en-Provence, France. This center maintains a comprehensive collection of the world literature on tourism, which has now been computerized. The center has been publishing since 1964 in the collection *Études et Memoires*, "Bibliographie Touristique" which is a reference book of studies in tourism. The 160 volumes issued to date have recorded over 240,000 documents. The center also publishes *Touristic Analysis Review* every quarter. Rene Baretje heads the center and requests that everyone send him complimentary copies of their tourism studies.

DIALOG, Information Services, Inc., 3460 Hillview Avenue, Palo Alto, California 94304; (415)-858-2700. Included in Dialog are the C.A.B. Abstracts, a comprehensive file of the 26 journals published by Commonwealth Agricultural Bureaux in England. C.A.B. Abstracts includes a subfile entitled "Leisure, Recreation and Tourism Abstracts." Subject areas covered in LRTA are leisure, recreation, and tourism; natural resources; tourism; recreation activities and facilities; culture and entertainment; and home and neighborhood activities.

INFORMATION CENTER, American Hotel and Motel Association, 1201 New York Avenue, Washington, D.C. 20005; (202) 289-3100. Contains information on more than 1300 subjects related to hotel/motel operation. Divided into two divisions, the five-year files (information printed in the last five years) and "historical" files, information is provided on 30 major subject categories. There is a charge for services.

INFOTRAC, Information Access, Inc., Foster City, California (monthly laser disk). A self-contained periodical reference system. Indexes over 900 business-related journals and regional publications. Covers current three years on laser disc.

PAIS on CD-ROM, Public Affairs Information Service, PAIS Inc., New York. This database indexes journal articles, books, and government publications pertaining to business, economics, political science, law, public administration, and other social sciences.

PERIODICAL ABSTRACTS ONDISC, University of Michigan, Ann Arbor, Michigan. This is an index to articles in over 300 general-interest periodicals, covering such topics as current events, health, business, science, arts, and entertainment. It began in January 1988 and is updated quarterly.

SIRLS, Faculty of Human Kinetics and Leisure Studies, University of Waterloo, Waterloo, Ontario, Canada N2L 3G1; (519) 885-1211, Ext. 2560. A computerized, bibliographical database and documentation center in the areas of leisure, sport, recreation, play, games, and dance. More than 12,000 citations are listed at the present time and the system is accessible from external institutions.

TOURISM RESEARCH AND DOCUMENTATION CENTRE (TRDC), Third Floor West, 235 Queen Street, Ottawa, Ontario K1A 0H6, Canada; (613) 954-3943. The center maintains the most comprehensive collection of tourism-related information in Canada. The holdings of more than 5000 books and documents include research papers, statistics, surveys, analyses, journals, conference proceedings, speeches, proposals, feasibility studies, legislation, guidebooks, bibliographies, and more. Information on this material is held in a data bank that can be accessed by TRDC staff or by the users of remote terminals in other parts of the country.

The computer system at TRDC is a bilingual bibliographic information storage and retrieval system that allows users to search the holdings using 1500 key words or "descriptors." Information is classified into eight major sectors: transportation, accommodation, conventions, hospitality services, events and attractions, recreational activities and facilities, education, and tourist-related enterprises. The descriptors can be used singly or in combination to produce the information required. Searches can be undertaken, for instance, by subject, author, sponsor, date, document type, geography, or various combinations of these. The information has been compiled to assist the industry and officers of Tourism Canada; however, it is also available to the general public.

TRAVEL REFERENCE CENTER, Business Research Division, Campus Box 420, University of Colorado, Boulder, Colorado 80309; (303) 492-5056. The reference center was established in 1969 to assist the travel industry in finding information sources and provide a facility to house a comprehensive collection of travel studies. The center now comprises the largest collection of travel, tourism, and recreation research studies available at any one place in the United States. The present collection numbers over 10,000 documents and is growing daily. The collection was computerized in 1985, and the center can do literature searches using more than 900 descriptors. Ths cost for a literature search is $50.

THE WORLD DIRECTORY OF DOCUMENTATION RESOURCES AND SYSTEMS FOR THE TRAVEL AND TOURISM SECTOR, World Tourism Organization, Madrid. 1991, 200 pp., $30. Contains information on more than 100 national and international tourism information centers. Included are libraries, documentation centers, and computerized documentation databases. Published in English, French, and Spanish.

---

4. PERIODICALS

The following are periodicals that contain travel research information.

Annals of Tourism Research (Elmsford, New York: Pergamon Press, quarterly), $270 per year.

ASTA Agency Management Magazine (Greensboro, North Carolina: Pace Communications Inc.), United States and Canada, subscription fee: free for members; $36 a year for nonmembers in the United States; $55 elsewhere.

The Cornell Hotel and Restaurant Administration Quarterly (Ithaca, New York: School of Hotel Administration, Cornell University, six issues per year), $65 for individuals; $130 for institutions.

Courier (Lexington, Kentucky: National Tour Association, monthly), $36 a year.

Hospitality and Tourism Educator (Washington, D.C.: Council on Hotel, Restaurant and Institutional Education, quarterly), $50 a year in the United States; $60 international.

Hospitality Directions: Forecasts and Analyses for the Hospitality Industry (New York: Coopers and Lybrand, quarterly), $295 a year.

Hospitality Research Journal (Washington, D.C.: Council on Hotel Restaurant, and Institutional Education, three times a year), $50 a year in the United States.

Hotel and Motel Management (Duluth, Minnesota: Edgell Communications, 18 times per year), $35 a year in the United States, $60 in Canada, $110 elsewhere; single copies $3 in the United States, $5 in Canada, $10 elsewhere.

Hotels: The International Magazine of the Hotel and Restaurant Industry (Des Plaines, Illinois: Cahners, 12 times a year). $64.95 a year in the United States, $96.25 in Canada, $89.95 in Mexico, elsewhere $119.95 surface mail or $189.95 air mail; single copy $10.

The Hotel Valuation Journal (Mineola, New York: Hospitality Valuation Services, Inc.), $125 annual subscription.

International Journal of Hospitality Management (Elmsford, New York: Pergamon Press, quarterly), $245.

International Visitor (New York: International Visitor Publishing, Inc., 10 issues a year), $78.50 a year.

International Tourism Reports (London: The Economist Intelligence Unit, quarterly), $470 a year.

Journal of Hospitality and Leisure Marketing (Binghamton, New York: Haworth Press, Inc., quarterly), $28 individuals, $36 institutions, and $48 libraries.

Journal of Travel and Tourism Marketing (Binghamton, New York: Haworth Press Inc., quarterly), $28 individuals, $32 institutions, and $36 libraries.

Journal of Leisure Research (Alexandria, Virginia: National Recreation and Park Association, quarterly), United States, member U.S. $25; foreign $28 a year; foreign, nonmember, $40 per year, foreign $43. Single copies are $10 domestic and $12 foreign.

Journal of Sustainable Tourism (Clevedon, Avon, England: Channel View Publications), $73.

Journal of Travel Research (Boulder, Colorado: Business Research Division, College Business, University of Colorado, quarterly), free to members of the Travel and Tourism Research Association; nonmembers $90 a year in the United States, $95 in Canada and Mexico, $105 elsewhere.

Journal of Tourism Studies (Townsville, Queensland, Australia: James Cook University of North Queensland), $35 a year.

Leisure Sciences (Washington, D.C.: Taylor & Francis, quarterly), $99 a year institutions; $55 personal.

Lodging (New York: American Hotel Association Directory Corporation, monthly except August), $35 a year nonmember, $23 a year member.

Lodging Hospitality (Cleveland, Ohio: Penton Publishing Inc., monthly), $60 a year in the United States, $85 in Canada, $90 in Mexico, $100 elsewhere.

Meetings and Conventions (Secaucus, New Jersey: Reed Travel Group, monthly), $65 a year in the United States, $110 elsewhere; single copies $20 in the United States, $25 elsewhere.

Revue de Tourism—The Tourist Review—Zeitschrift für Fremdenverkehr (St. Gallen, Switzerland: AIEST, Varnbuelstrasse 19, CH-9000 St. Gallen, quarterly), 52 Sfr.

Tour and Travel News (Manhasset, New York: CMP Publications Inc., weekly), $75 a year in the United States and Canada, $125 in Mexico and Central America, $135 in Europe, $135 in South America, and $150 in Asia and Africa.

Tourism Management (Oxford, England: Butterworth-Heinemann Ltd., six issues per year), £220 a year in the United States, single copies £44.

Tourism Recreation Research (Indira Nagar, Lucknow, India: Centre for Tourism Research, semiannually), $75 a year.

The Travel Agent (New York: Universal Media Inc., weekly), $250.

Travel Industry Indicators (Miami, Florida: James V. Cammisa, monthly), $95 a year U.S., $105 elsewhere.

Travel & Tourism Analyst (London: The Economist Intelligence Unit, six times a year), $910 a year in North America.

Travel-log (Ottawa, Ontario, Canada: Statistics Canada, quarterly), annual subscription fee: $42 in Canada, U.S. $50 in the United States, and U.S. $59 in other countries.

Travel Printout (Washington, D.C.: U.S. Travel Data Center, monthly), $75 in the United States and $85 in other countries.

Travel Trade (New York: Travel Trade Publications, weekly), $10 per year in the United States, $13 in Canada, and $25 elsewhere.

Travel Weekly (Secaucus, New Jersey: Reed Travel Group, twice weekly), $26 a year in the United States and Canada; single copies $.50.

Visions in Leisure and Business (Bowling Green, Ohio: Appalachian Associates, quarterly), $25 a year individual, $45 institutional in the United States, $40 and $80 in other countries.

There are also many other periodicals and journals dealing with the travel field. The sources for locating these are:

Business Publications Rates and Data, comes in 3 vols. (Wilmette, Illinois: Standard Rate and Data Service, monthly). A list of more than 5244 U.S. and 170 international business, trade, and technical publications.

1992–1993 Travel Media Directory (Washington, D.C.: Travel Industry Association of America, annual). A list of some 1200 key editorial and advertising contacts at travel trade and consumer publications in more than 40 countries.

Ulrich's International Periodicals Directory, comes in 3 vols. (New York: R. R. Bowker, annual). Includes entries for more than 108,590 in-print periodicals published throughout the world.

---

5. TRADE AND PROFESSIONAL ASSOCIATIONS

Many trade and professional associations publish valuable data on the travel industry. Examples are:

Association International d'Experts Scientifiques du Tourisme (AIEST), Varnbuelstrasse 19, CH-9000, St. Gallen, Switzerland. AIEST is composed primarily of academicians interested in tourism research and teaching. It publishes the *Tourist Review* and annual proceedings of its meetings.

Pacific Asia Travel Association (PATA), Telesis Tower, Suite 1750, 1 Montgomery Street, San Francisco, California 94104, publishes the *PATA Annual Statistical Report* and other publications and holds research seminars.

Travel and Tourism Research Association (TTRA), 10200 West 44th Avenue, Suite 304, Wheat Ridge, Colorado 80033, helps sponsor the *Journal of Travel Research* and publishes proceedings.

Travel Industry Association of America, 1100 New York Avenue N.W., Washington, D.C. 20005, has a publication program that includes special reports and newsletters.

The World Tourism Organization (WTO), Capitan Haya, 42, E-28020 Madrid, Spain. One of the main tasks of the WTO is to give members continuing information on tourism and its influence on the social, economic, and cultural life of nations. It offers a number of publications and educational programs. A publications list can be received by writing the organization.

Some other associations are the Tourism Industry Association of Canada, 130 Albert Street, Suite 1016, Ottawa, Ontario, Canada; Air Transport Association of America, 1301 Pennsylvania Avenue, N.W., Washington, D.C. 20006; International Air Transport Association, IATA Building, 2000 Peel Street, Montreal, Quebec, Canada H3A 2R4; American Hotel and Motel Association, 1201 New York Avenue N.W., Washington, D.C., 20005; International Association of Amusement Parks and Attractions, 1448 Duke Street, Alexandria, Virginia 22302; International Association of Convention and Visitors Bureaus, 200 C Street N.W., Suite 702, Washington, D.C. 20036; Association of Travel Marketing Executives, P.O. Box 43563, Washington, D.C. 20010; American Society of Travel Agents, 1101 King Street, Alexandria, Virginia 22314; National Tour Association, P.O. Box 3071, 546 East Main Street, Lexington, Kentucky 40596; Institute of Certified Travel Agents, 148 Linden Street, P.O. Box 82-56, Wellesley, Massachusetts 02181; National Recreation and Park Association, 2775 South Quincy Street, Suite 300, Arlington, Virginia 22206

If you are in doubt about trade associations in the field, you can check:

Encyclopedia of Associations: 1994, 28th ed. (Detroit, Michigan: Gale Research, 1993), Volume I, *National Organizations of the United States*, 3482 pp; Volume 2, *Geographic and Executive Indexes*, 961 pp; *International Organizations*, Parts I and II, 1994, 2918 pp. A guide to over 35,000 national and international organizations.

6. GOVERNMENT

Probably no group collects more information on the tourism industry than government agencies. The government agencies vary according to the objectives of the particular country and in most cases to the degree of importance of the tourism sector. Generally, the following public agencies are involved in tourism and travel research activities: (1) ministries of tourism; (2) undersecretarial or underministerial tourism organizations; (3) specific government organizations for tourism and travel; (4) statistical agencies for collection, analysis, and publication of data related to tourism and travel, such as Statistics Canada and U.S. Census Bureau; and (5) state or provincial tourism organizations.

Most government travel organizations are members of the World Tourism Organization (WTO), Capitan Haya, 42, E-Madrid, 20/Spain. Researchers can write for a list of members and associate members.

The major U.S. government tourism development organization is the U.S. Travel and Tourism Administration, Department of Commerce, Washington, D.C. 20230. An inventory of federal agencies by Pisarski is listed in Section 2: Bibliographies and Finding Guides.

Selected examples of useful government publications in the travel field include:

Canadian Travel Survey (Ottawa, Ontario, Canada; Statistics Canada, Travel, Tourism and Recreation Section, quarterly). This report provides statistics on travel by Canadians on trips of 80 kilometers or more with destinations in Canada. Information is provided on who the travelers are, why they traveled, when they traveled, how they traveled, where they stayed, how much they spent, and what they did. A general summary of the travel situation in Canada is given and the importance of domestic travel is demonstrated.

1993 Annual Abstract National Park Service (Denver, Colorado: National Park Service) 1994, 37 pp. Provides visit data to national parks.

A Strategic Look at the Travel and Tourism Industry (Washington, D.C.: U.S. Department of Commerce, U.S. Travel and Tourism Administration, 1989). The report discusses the following topics concerning the tourist trade: planning assumptions; the external environment; U.S. competitive position in the world tourism market; tourism market opportunities for the United States; constraints confronting the U.S. tourism industry; and barriers to international trade in tourism.

In-Flight Survey of International Air Travelers (Washington, D.C.: U.S. Department of Commerce, United States Travel and Tourism Administration, annual), $400. The in-flight survey provides a comprehensive consumer marketing data base on international travel to and from the United States, including travelers' residence, purpose of trip, port of entry, multiple destinations visited, duration of stay, type of lodging, information sources used, means of booking, use of package trips, domestic transportation, demographics and expenditure categories. Two reports are available: (1) Overseas Visitors to the United States and (2) United States Travelers to Overseas Countries. Reports can be purchased separately for $200 each. Quarterly reports are available on a special request basis.

National Tourism Policy Study—Final Report (Washington, D.C.: Committee on Commerce, Science and Transportation, U.S. Senate, 1979), 361 pp. This report by Arthur D. Little, Inc. presents the findings of the final phase of the *National Tourism Policy Study*. It was designed to develop a proposed national tourism policy for the United States; to define appropriate roles for the federal government, the states, cities, private industry, and consumers in carrying out, supporting, and contributing to the national tourism policy; and to recommend organizational programmatic, and legislative strategies for implementing the proposed national tourism policy.

United States Congress, House Committee on Small Business, Subcommittee on Procurement, Tourism, and Rural Development. *The Impact of the Threat of Terrorism and the Recession on the Travel and Tourism Industry.* This is the hearing before the Subcommittee on Procurement, Tourism, and Rural Development of the Committee on Small Business, House of Representatives, One Hundred Second Congress, first session, Washington, D.C., March 7, 1991.

United States Congress, Senate Committee on Commerce, Science, and Transportation, Subcommittee on Foreign Commerce and Tourism. *Importance of Scenic Byways to Travel and Tourism.* This is a hearing before the subcommittee on Foreign Commerce and Tourism of the Committee on Commerce, Science, and Transportation, United States Senate, One Hundred First Congress, first session, April 14, 1989.

User Friendly Facts: A Resource Book 1992 (Washington, D.C.: U.S. Travel and Tourism Administration, 1992), 135 pp., $50. Provides a bibliography of USTTA publications and a quick reference on international data available from USTTA.

7. YEARBOOKS, ANNUALS, HANDBOOKS, AND OTHER SOURCES

Air Transport (Washington, D.C.: Air Transport Association of America, annual). The official annual report to the U.S. scheduled airline industry containing historical and current statistical data on the industry.

The Annual Review of Travel 1992 (New York: American Express Related Service Company, annual), 98 pp., $25. This book contains the seven winning essays of the 1992 American Express Review of Travel International Essay Competition. 1993 and 1994 publications are also available.

Discover America 2000 (Washington, D.C.: U.S. Travel Data Center, 1989), 80 pp. Gives the implications of America's changing demographics and attitudes on the U.S. travel industry.

The 1992–93 Economic Review of Travel in America (Washington, D.C.: U.S. Travel Data Center, annual), $70. This annual report on the role of travel and tourism in the American economy reviews the economic contributions of travel away from home, developments in the travel industry, and the effects of economic changes on travel and tourism.

1994 Outlook for Travel and Tourism (Washington, D.C.: U.S. Travel Data Center), approximately 150 pp., annual, $125. Proceedings of the 19th annual Travel Outlook Forum.

1994 Travel Agency Survey (Secaucus, New Jersey: Reed Travel Group, 1994), 126 pp. This 1994 Louis Harris Survey presents the findings of the 12th comprehensive study of the travel agency business. It updates information obtained in previous studies on the dimensions and scope of the travel agency market and on the sources and components of agency business. Like previous studies, this study also describes the importance of various criteria influencing travel agents' choices of air carriers, hotels, cruise ships, car rental agencies, and package tours for their clients. The August 18, 1994, issue of *Travel Weekly* (Vol. 53, No. 65) is the Louis Harris study issue.

Travel Market Close-up: National Travel Survey Tabulations (Washington, D.C.: U.S. Travel Data Center, quarterly and annual). In March 1979, the U.S. Travel Data Center began conducting a monthly *National Travel Survey*. Since that time, quarterly and annual summaries of the results have been published to provide researchers with timely, consistent, and relevant data on major trends in U.S. travel activity.

The Meeting Market 1992 (Secaucus, New Jersey: Reed Travel Group, 1992), 138 pp., $250. Report gives dimensions, expenditures, and characteristics of the off premise meetings market. The size of the total meetings market is estimated at $38.7 billion.

PATA Annual Statistical Report (San Francisco: Pacific Asia Travel Association), $70.00 to members, $100 to nonmembers. This report presents the visitor arrival statistics and other relevant data reported by PATA member governments. The report gives visitors arrival data for the individual countries by nationality of residence and mode of travel. Selected market sources of visitors to the Pacific area are given, along with data on accommodations, length of stay, visitor expenditures, and national tourist organization budgets.

Compendium of Tourism Statistics, 11th Ed. (Madrid: World Tourism Organization, 1991), 230 pp., $25. Annual digest of basic tourism statistics. First part: Country-tables (170 countries and territories) containing the following categories of data: Movements; Transport; Motivations; Accommodation; Tourism and the Economy. Data cover the period 1985–1989. Second part; background information on international tourist arrivals and receipts at world and regional levels based and tourism series 1985–1990. Available in English, French, and Spanish.

Tourism Policy and International Tourism in OECD Member Countries (Paris: The Organization for Economic Co-operation and Development, annual). This is an annual report on tourism statistics in Australia, Austria, Beligum, Canada, Denmark, Finland, France, Germany, Greece, Iceland, Ireland, Italy, Japan, Luxembourg, the Netherlands, New Zealand, Norway, Portugal, Spain, Sweden, Switzerland, Turkey, the United Kingdom, and the United States.

Tourism to the Year 2000: Qualitative Aspects Affecting Global Growth (Madrid: World Tourism Organization, 1991), 42 pp., $15. The executive summary of a major WTO study. Includes an inventory of variables likely to affect tourism development over the next decade. Available in English, French, and Spanish.

Tourism Works for America (Washington, D.C.: National Travel and Tourism Awareness Council, 1994), $10. Reports magnitude of travel and tourism industry in the United States; $361.8 billion in 1992.

Travel Industry World Yearbook: The Big Picture—1994 (Rye, New York: Child and Waters, annual), $79 in the United States, $88 foreign airmail. This annual issue presents a compact up-to-date review of the latest happenings in the world of tourism.

Travel Trends in the United States and Canada (Boulder, Colorado: Business Research Division, College of Business, University of Colorado, 1984), 262 pp., $45. This document provides statistics on visits to recreation areas, number of tourists, tourist expenditures, length of stay and size of party, economic impact of tourism, tourism-related employment, mode of transportation used, tourism advertising, passport statistics, international travel, foreign visitor arrivals, travel costs, and highlights from national travel surveys. Data have been compiled from 260 sources.

Trends in Travel and Tourism Advertising Expenditures in United States Measured Media (New York: Ogilvy and Mather, 1993), various paging, $115. Annual volume that reports on advertising spending in U.S. media by U.S. or foreign flag airlines, states or other domestic destinations, foreign countries and destinations, and by cruise lines.

World Air Transport Statistics (Montreal, Quebec, Canada: International Air Transport Association, annual). This is an annual compilation of facts and figures illustrated with numerous graphs and charts, representing the most up-to-date and complete source of data on the air transport industry.

World Travel and Tourism Review: Indicators, Trends, and Issues, Volume 3, 1993 (Wallingford, Oxon, England: C.A.B. International, annual), 314 pp., $170. Part I provides a comprehensive overview of the most pertinent indicators of travel and tourism activity, Part II contains market and industry trends, and Part III contains a special report featuring island tourism.

Yearbook of Tourism Statistics (Madrid: World Tourism Organization, 1991), approximately 1000 pp., $60. Two volume set of global tourism statistics. Volume I (1990) covers world and regional totals for arrivals, overnight stays, receipts and expenditures, accommodation capacity, and domestic tourism. Volume II (1990) provides statistics for 150 countries. Published in English, French, and Spanish.

8. SOME FINAL SUGGESTIONS

This section provides information on the U.S. Travel Data Center and identifies some well-known books and reports on travel research.

U.S. Travel Data Center, 1100 New York Avenue, N.W., Washington, D.C. 20005, was organized early in 1973 as a nonprofit corporation dedicated to serving the travel research needs of the industry and nation. Today, the center is the focal point of a multitude of efforts to measure and understand the travel activities of Americans and of foreign visitors to this country. In some instances, the center gathers, analyzes, and disseminates statistical data published by other recognized research organizations. In other cases, the center collects original data for analysis and publication. Selected programs of the center are (1) National Travel Survey, (2) Impact of Travel on State Economies, (3) Survey of State Travel Offices, (4) Travel Price Index, and (5) Annual Travel Outlook Forum. A catalog of its publications is available and can be obtained by writing to the center.

American Outdoors: The Legacy, The Challenge (Washington, D.C.: Island Press, 1987), 426 pp. This volume is the final report of the President's Commission on Americans Outdoors. The report makes an important contribution to our understanding of the nation's outdoor recreation needs and resources.

Edgell, David. *International Tourism Policy* (New York: Van Nostrand Reinhold, 1990), 204 pp., $45.95. Book examines global tourism policy issues, discusses economic considerations, and covers emerging cultural developments.

Fridgen, Joseph. *Dimensions of Tourism* (East Lansing, Michigan: Educational Institute of the American Hotel and Motel Association, 1991), 361 pp. Book discusses the historical, psychological, social and cultural, international, economic, environmental, and managerial dimensions of tourism.

Gartrell, Richard. *Destination Marketing for Convention and Visitor Bureaus* (Dubuque, Iowa: Kendall/Hunt, 1988), 336 pp., $29.95. Text provides theoretical and practical guidelines to marketing a destination, management of a convention bureau, and developing convention and visitor marketing programs.

Gee, Chuck Y. *Resort Development and Management, 2nd Ed.* (East Lansing, Michigan: The Educational Institute of the American Hotel and Motel Association, 1988). Updates information about such important topics as the master planning of resort destinations, writing environment impact statements, designing recreational and sports facilities, managing the resort investment, and technological changes influencing the future of the resort industry.

Gee, Chuck Y., Dexter J. L. Choy, and James C. Makens. *The Travel Industry* (New York: Van Nostrand Reinhold, 1989), 352 pp., $34.95. The emphasis in this text is on introducing concepts about travel as an industry. It provides a basic understanding of travel and tourism and provides insights into the development and operations of the various components of the travel industry.

Getz, Donald. *Festivals, Special Events and Tourism* (New York: Van Nostrand Reinhold, 1991), 374 pp., $39.95. Book covers systematic planning, development, and marketing strategies for promoting special events as tourism attractions and as image builders for destination areas.

Gunn, Clare A. *Tourism Planning* (New York: Taylor & Francis, 1994), 460 pp. This book takes a human ecology approach and describes opportunities, on the state and regional scale, for greater expansion of tourism without damage to our delicate natural resources. The book provides a unique framework for understanding and regrouping the complicated elements that make up tourism. By relating to tourism, constructive guides for the future are offered.

Gunn, Clare A. *Vacationscope: Designing Tourist Regions* (New York: Van Nostrand Reinhold, 1988), 208 pp. This volume is a sourcebook of theory, new ideas, and real-world examples for designers, tourism developers, promoters, and students.

Howell, David W. *Passport: An Introduction to the Travel and Tourism Industry* (Cincinnati, Ohio: South-Western Publishing Co., 1993), 436 pp. The book is designed to help readers understand the roles played by various components of the travel and tourism industry and to help them decide which of the many different careers would best suit them.

Khan, Mahmood, Michael Olsen, and Turgut Var. *VNR's Encyclopedia of Hospitality and Tourism* (New York: Van Nostrand Reinhold, 1993), 1008 pp.

Krippendorf, Jost. *The Holiday Makers* (London: William Heinemann Ltd., 1987), 160 pp. This book analyzes the different forms of tourism, examines the effects on various countries and their people, and outlines positive steps to reconcile people's holiday requirements with the world's economic and social structures.

Mill, Robert C., and Alastair M. Morrison. *The Tourism System* (Englewood Cliffs, New Jersey: Prentice Hall, 1992), 506 pp. A book presenting a comprehensive systems view of tourism, stressing the interrelationships and interdependencies of its various elements. The authors cover all aspects from a marketing point of view and describe how tourism works.

Pearce, Douglas. *Tourist Development* (New York: Wiley, 1989), 341 pp. The general focus of this book is the way tourism develops and the economic and social effects of that development on the community, local economy, region, or country.

Plog, Stanley. *Leisure Travel* (New York: Wiley, 1991), 244 pp. Book presents an overview of the leisure travel market and follows with a psychologically based allocentrism-psychocentrism framework for understanding why people do or do not travel, the different types of vacations they take, their expectations, and sources of dissatisfaction.

Powers, Thomas F. *Introduction to Management in the Hospitality Industry* (New York: Wiley, 1992), 634 pp. This book covers the hospitality industry. It discusses the management problems of institutions that offer shelter or food or both to people away from their homes.

Shriver, Stephen J. *Managing Quality Services* (East Lansing, Michigan: The Educational Institute of the American Hotel and Motel Association, 1988). This book defines quality assurance as a management system that ensures the consistent delivery of products and services. Quality assurance enables managers, supervisors, and employees to increase the profitability and productivity operation by solving problems and developing performance standards.

Smith, Valene. *Hosts and Guests, The Anthropology of Tourism* (Philadelphia: University of

Pennsylvania Press, 1989), 341 pp. This second edition is a unique collection of essays on the profound cultural impact of tourism in societies ranging from the American Southwest to Tonga to Alaska to Iran.

Tourism's Top Twenty (Boulder, Colorado: Business Research Division, College of Business, University of Colorado, 1992), approximately 118 pp., $50. This book, compiled in cooperation with the U.S. Travel Data Center, Washington, D.C., provides facts and figures on travel, tourism recreation, and leisure. Information is presented primarily for the United States; however, there is some coverage of world tourism. It provides fast facts on a wide array of tourism-related subjects, including advertising, airlines, attractions, expenditures, hotels and resorts, recreation, world travel, and travel statistics. Sources are given for each table and complete addresses for the sources are provided in an appendix. A subject index is also included for ease in locating information. Available from the U.S. Travel Data Center, 1100 New York Avenue N.W., Washington, D.C. 20005.

Witt, Stephen, and Luiz Moutinho. *Tourism Marketing and Management Handbook* (Hemel Hempstead, Hertfordshire, England: Prentice Hall International, 1994), 617 pp. This handbook provides a comprehensive business and academic reference source related to the most crucial issues in tourism marketing and management. Over 100 tourism topic entries are included.

The WTTC Report, Travel and Tourism: The World's Largest Industry (New York: World Travel and Tourism Council, 1993), approximately 80 pp., $200 or $95 per disk. Report examines the economic contribution of the travel and tourism industry to the world and national economies.

Glossary

Affinity group A group bound together by a common interest or affinity. Where charters are concerned, this common bond makes them eligible for charter flights. Persons must have been members of the group for six months or longer. Where a group configuration on a flight is concerned, the minimum number of persons to which the term would apply may be any number determined by a carrier rule-making body. They must travel together, on the departure and return flight, but they can travel independently where ground arrangements are concerned.

Agreement, bilateral An agreement regulating commercial air services between two countries.

Agreement, multilateral An agreement regulating commercial air services between three or more countries.

Airline Reporting Corporation (ARC) A corporation set up by the domestic airlines that is concerned with travel agent appointments and operations.

Air Transport Association of America (ATA or ATAA) The authoritative trade association maintained by domestic airlines.

American plan A room rate that includes breakfast, lunch, and dinner.

Balance of payments or trade Practical definition of an economic concept. Each nation is assumed to be one tremendous business doing business with other big businesses. When a business (country) sells (exports) more than it buys (imports), there is a positive balance of payments. When a country buys (imports) more than it sells (exports), there is a negative balance of trade. Tourism is a part of balance of trade classified under Services.

Cabotage The ability of an air carrier to carry passengers exclusively between two points in a foreign country.

Capacity The number of flights multiplied by the number of aircraft seats flown.

Carrier A public transportation company, such as air or steamship line, railroad, truck, bus, monorail, and so on.

Carrier—participating Means a carrier over whose routes one or more sections of carriage under the air waybill or ticket is undertaken or performed.

Charter The bulk purchase of any carrier's equipment (or part thereof) for passengers or freight. Legally, charter transportation is arranged for time, voyage, or mileage.

Charter flight A flight booked exclusively for the use of a specific group of people who generally belong to the same organization or who are being "treated" to the flight by a single host. Charter flights are generally much cheaper than regularly scheduled line services. They may be carried out by scheduled or supplemental carriers.

Clients Those persons who patronize travel agencies.

Code sharing An agreement between two airlines which allows the first carrier to use the airline designation code on a flight operated by the second carrier.

Concierge This is a wonderful European invention. Depending on the hotel, the concierge is a superintendent of service, source of information, and link between the guest and city or area.

Conservation Management of human use of the environment to yield the greatest sustainable benefit to present generations while maintaining its potential to meet the needs and aspirations of future generations.

Consolidator A travel firm that makes available airplane tickets, cruise tickets, and sometimes other travel products at discount prices. These are usually sold to retail travel agencies but are also sometimes sold directly to the public.

Consortium A privately owned firm (not owned by its members as is a cooperative) that maintains a list of preferred suppliers. This list is made available to members, resulting in superior commissions earned.

Continental breakfast A beverage, roll, and jam. Sometimes a fruit juice is added. In Spain, Holland, and Norway, cheese, meat, or fish is sometimes included.

Continental plan A hotel rate that includes continental breakfast.

Cooperative A membership group of retail travel agencies that offers advantages to each agency member, such as lower prices on wholesale tour offerings, educational opportunities, problem solving, and other aids.

Coupon flight The portion of the passenger ticket and baggage check or excess baggage ticket that indicates particular places between which the coupon is good for carriage.

Destination The ultimate stopping place according to the contract of carriage. Can also be defined as a place offering at least 1500 rooms to tourists.

Development Modification of the environment to whatever degree and the application of human, financial, living and nonliving resources to satisfy human needs and improve the quality of human life.

Domestic independent travel (DIT) A tour constructed to meet the specific desire of a client within a single country.

Environment All aspects of the surroundings of human beings both cultural, natural, and man-made, whether affecting human beings as individuals or in social groupings.

Eurailpass A special pass sold overseas for unlimited first-class rail travel in 15 European countries. Youth and children's passes are also available. They are sold for varying numbers of days.

European plan A hotel rate that includes only lodging, no food.

Excursionist A traveler who spends less than 24 hours at a destination.

Familiarization tour A free or reduced rate arrangement for travel agents or public carrier employees that is intended to stimulate them to sell travel or tours as experienced on the "fam" tour.

Federal Aviation Administration (U.S.) A governmental regulatory agency concerned with airport operation, air safety, licensing of flight personnel, and other aviation matters.

Flag carrier An international airline often owned and/or operated by the government of its home country.

Flight, connecting A flight that requires a change of aircraft and flight number en route to a destination.

Flight, direct A flight that may make intermediary stops en route to a destination.

Flight, nonstop A flight that travels to a destination without any intermediary stops.

Foreign independent travel (FIT) An international prepaid tour for an individual or family planned for them by a travel agent or tour operator. It is individually designed.

Freedoms of the Air: Principles defined by representatives of 52 nations at the 1944 Chicago Convention:

- First—the right of an air carrier from one nation to fly over another nation.
- Second—the right of an air carrier from one nation to make a technical or fueling stop in another nation.
- Third—the right of an air carrier to transport passengers from its home nation into another nation.
- Fourth—the right of an air carrier to transport passengers from another nation into its home country.
- Fifth—the right of an air carrier to transport passengers between two foreign nations on a route beginning or ending in its home country.
- Sixth—the right of an air carrier to transport passengers between two foreign nations, via its home country.
- Seventh—the right of an air carrier to transport passengers between two foreign nations without stopping in its home nation.

Ground arrangements All those services provided by a tour operator after reaching the first destination. Also referred to as land arrangements.

Group inclusive tour (GIT) A tour that includes group air and ground arrangements for a minimum of 15 persons. They may or may not stay together as a group for both the land and air portions of the trip.

Hub and spoke A system which feeds connecting passengers into major gateway airports from short-haul or point-to-point downline routes.

Incentive tour A tour arranged especially for employees or agents of a company as a reward for achievement, usually sales. Spouses are typically included on the trip.

Inclusive tour A travel plan for which prearranged transportation, wholly by air or partly by air and partly by surface, together with ground facilities (such as meals, hotels, etc.) are sold for a total price.

International Air Transport Association (IATA) The authoritative trade association maintained by international and overseas airlines.

Modified American plan   A room rate that includes a full American breakfast and lunch or dinner, usually dinner.

Open jaw   A pairing of two or more nearby destinations which allows a passenger to arrive at one airport and depart from a second.

Open skies   An agreement between two or more nations which allows its air carriers to fly unrestricted within each others' borders; the United States and the Netherlands recently signed an open skies pact.

Package   A prepaid tour that includes transportation, lodging, and other ingredients, usually meals, transfers, sightseeing, or car rentals. May be varied, but typically includes at least three ingredients sold at a fixed price.

Passport   Issued by national governments to their own citizens as verification of their citizenship. It is also a permit to leave one's own country and return.

Pension   A French word widely used throughout Europe meaning guest house or boarding house.

Reception agency   A tour operator or travel agency specializing in foreign visitors. American Adventure Tours is such a company.

Retail travel agency   Mostly in the United States. Travel agents sell carriers' tickets and wholesalers' or operators' tours. In perspective, retail agents are commissioned or subagents. Usually, all or most of the gross revenue is from commissions.

Revalidation   The authorized stamping or writing on the passenger ticket showing it has been officially altered by the carrier.

Run-of-the-house   A hotel term to guarantee a firm price that applies to any room in the house. Often a hotel will provide a superior room, if available, in an effort to please the guest and the tour operator.

Spa   A hotel or resort providing hot springs or baths and other health-enhancing facilities and services.

Supplier   An industry term meaning any form of transportation, accommodations, and other travel services used by a travel agency or tour operator to fulfill the needs of travelers.

Tariffs   The published fares, rates, charges, and/or related conditions of carriage of a carrier.

Tour-basing fare   A reduced, round-trip fare available on specified dates, and between specified times, only to passengers who purchase preplanned, prepaid tour arrangements prior to their departure to specified areas.

Tourism   (1) The entire world industry of travel, hotels, transportation, and all other components, including promotion, that serves the needs and wants of travelers. Tourism today has been given new meaning and is primarily a term of economics referring to an industry. (2) Within a nation (political subdivision or transportation-centered economic area of contiguous nations), the sum total of tourist expenditures within their borders is referred to as the nation's tourism or tourist industry and is thus ranked with other national industries. More important than just the total monetary product value of tourism is its role in the balance of trade. Here tourism earning from foreigners truly represents an export industry. Tourism is an "invisible" export.

Tourist   A person who travels from place to place for nonwork reasons. By U.N. definition, a tourist is someone who stays for more than one night and less than a year. Business and convention travel is included. This thinking is dominated by balance-of-trade concepts. Military personnel, diplomats, immigrants, and resident students are not tourists.

Tour operator A company that specializes in the planning and operation of prepaid, preplanned vacations and makes these available to the public, usually through travel agents.

Tour organizer An individual, usually not professionally connected with the travel industry, who organizes tours for special groups of people, such as teachers, church leaders, farmers, and the like.

Tour package A travel plan that includes several elements of a vacation, such as transportation, accommodations, and sightseeing.

Tour wholesaler A company that plans, markets, and (usually) operates tours. Marketing is always through intermediaries such as retail travel agents, an association, club, or tour organizer—never directly to the public as is sometimes done by tour operators. The wholesaler would not operate the tour if, for example, it was functioning as a wholesaler in the United States for tours operated by a foreign firm. In industry jargon tour operator and tour wholesaler are synonymous.

Travel (*see* Tourism) Often interchangeable with tourism. Actually, this term should represent all direct elements of travel. Included in the term travel are transportation, vacations, resorts, and any other direct passenger elements, including but not limited to national parks, attractions and auto use for any of the above purposes. To make a journey from one place to another.

Visa Document issued by a foreign government permitting nationals of another country to visit or travel. The visa is usually stamped on pages provided in one's passport but may also be a document fastened to the passport.

Yield management The use of pricing and inventory controls, based upon historical data, to maximize profits by offering varying fares over time for the same product.

SELECTED TOURISM ABBREVIATIONS

AAA	American Automobile Association	**ATME**	Association of Travel Marketing Executives
AAR	Association of American Railroads	**Amtrak**	National Railroad Passenger Corporation
ABA	American Bus Association		
ABC	Advanced Booking Charter	**ANTA**	Australian National Travel Association
ACTO	Association of Caribbean Tour Operators	**AP**	American Plan
AHMA	American Hotel and Motel Association	**APEX**	Advance Purchase Excursion Fare
AIEST	International Association of Scientific Experts in Tourism	**ARC**	Airlines Reporting Corporation
AIT	Academie Internationale du Tourisme	**ARRDA**	American Resort and Residential Development Association

ARTA	Association of Retail Travel Agents
ASTA	American Society of Travel Agents
ATA	Air Transport Association of America
ATC	Air Transport Committee (Canada)
BIT	Bulk Inclusive Tour
BTA	British Tourist Authority
CEDOK	Czechoslovakia Travel Bureau
CHRIE	Council on Hotel, Restaurant and Institutional Education
CITC	Canadian Institute of Travel Counselors
CLIA	Cruise Lines International Association
CNTA	China National Tourism Administration
COTAL	Conference of Tourist Organizations of Latin America
CRS	Computerized Reservations System
CTA	Caribbean Travel Association
CTC	Certified Travel Counselor
CTO	Caribbean Tourism Organization
DC	Diner's Club
DIT	Domestic Independent Tours
DOT	U.S. Government Department of Transportation
ECOSOC	Economic and Social Council of the United Nations
EP	European Plan
ETC	European Travel Commission
FAA (U.S.)	Federal Aviation Administration
FHA	Federal Highway Administration
FIT	Foreign Independent Tour
GIT	Group Inclusive Tour
HSMAI	Hotel Sales Management Association International
IAAPA	International Association of Amusement Parks and Attractions
IACVB	International Association of Convention and Visitors Bureaus
IAF	International Automobile Federation
IAST	International Academy for the Study of Tourism
IATA	International Air Transport Association
IATAN	International Airlines Travel Agent Network
ICAO	International Civil Aviation Organization
ICC	Interstate Commerce Commission
ICCL	International Council of Cruise Lines
ICSC	International Council of Shopping Centers
ICTA	Institute of Certified Travel Agents
IFWTO	International Federation of Women's Travel Organizations
IHA	International Hotel Association
IIPT	International Institute for Peace Through Tourism
IIT	Inclusive Independent Tour
ILO	International Labor Organization
IT	Inclusive Tour
ITC	Inclusive Tour Charter

IYHF	International Youth Hostel Federation	**SITE**	Society of Incentive Travel Executives
MAP	Modified American Plan	**S&R**	Sell and Report
MCO	Miscellaneous Charges Order	**SST**	Supersonic Transport
NACOA	National Association of Cruise Only Agents	**STTE**	Society of Travel and Tourism Educators
NAPVO	National Association of Passenger Vessel Owners	**TC**	Tourism Canada
NARVPC	National Association of RV Parks and Campgrounds	**TIA**	Travel Industry Association of America
NCTA	National Council of Travel Attractions	**TIAC**	Tourism Industry Association of Canada
NCUTO	National Council of Urban Tourism Organizations	**TTRA**	Travel and Tourism Research Association
NRA	National Restaurant Association	**UFTAA**	Universal Federation of Travel Agents Associations
NRPA	National Recreation Parks Association	**UNESCO**	United Nations Educational, Scientific and Cultural Organization
NTA	National Tour Association	**USTDC**	United States Travel Data Center
NTTAC	National Travel and Tourism Awareness Council	**USTOA**	United States Tour Operators Association
OAG	Official Airline Guide	**USTTA**	United States Travel and Tourism Administration
OAS	Organization of American States	**WATA**	World Association of Travel Agents
OECD	Organization for Economic Cooperation and Development	**WEXITA**	Women Executives in Tourism Administration
PAI	Professional Association of Innkeepers	**WHO**	World Health Organization
PATA	Pacific Asia Travel Association	**WTAO**	World Touring and Automobile Organization
RAA	Regional Airline Association	**WTO**	World Tourism Organization
RPM	Revenue Passenger Miles	**WTTC**	World Travel and Tourism Council
RTF	Rural Tourism Foundation	**XO**	Exchange Order
RVIA	Recreational Vehicle Industry Association		
SATW	Society of American Travel Writers		

INDEX